THE ROUTLEDGE HANDBOOK OF SHAKESPEARE AND ANIMALS

Shakespeare's plays have a long and varied performance history. The relevance of his plays in literary studies cannot be understated, but only recently have scholars been looking into the presence and significance of animals within the canon. Readers will quickly find—without having to do extensive research—that the plays are teeming with animals! In this Handbook, Karen Raber and Holly Dugan delve deep into Shakespeare's world to illuminate and understand the use of animals in his span of work. This volume supplies a valuable resource, offering a broad and thorough grounding in the many ways animal references and the appearance of actual animals in the plays can be interpreted. It provides a thorough overview; demonstrates rigorous, original research; and charts new frontiers in the field through a broad variety of contributions from an international group of well-known and respected scholars.

Karen Raber is a Distinguished Professor of English at the University of Mississippi. She is the author of *Shakespeare and Posthumanist Theory* (2018) and *Animal Bodies, Renaissance Culture* (2013), and editor with Monica Mattfeld of *Performing Animals: History, Agency, Theater* (2017).

Holly Dugan is an Associate Professor of English at The George Washington University. She is the author of *The Ephemeral History of Perfume: Scent and Sense in Early Modern England* (2011).

ROUTLEDGE LITERATURE HANDBOOKS

Also available in this series:

THE ROUTLEDGE HANDBOOK OF LITERATURE AND SPACE
Edited by Robert T. Tally

THE ROUTLEDGE HANDBOOK OF CONTEMPORARY JEWISH CULTURES
Edited by Laurence Roth and Nadia Valman

THE ROUTLEDGE HANDBOOK OF SHAKESPEARE AND MEMORY
Edited by Andrew Hiscock and Lina Perkins Wilder

THE ROUTLEDGE HANDBOOK TO THE GHOST STORY
Edited by Scott Brewster and Luke Thurston

THE ROUTLEDGE HANDBOOK OF INTERNATIONAL BEAT LITERATURE
Edited by A. Robert Lee

THE ROUTLEDGE HANDBOOK OF SHAKESPEARE AND GLOBAL APPROPRIATION
Edited by Christy Desmet, Sujata Iyengar and Miriam Jacobson

THE ROUTLEDGE HANDBOOK OF SHAKESPEARE AND ANIMALS
Edited by Karen Raber and Holly Dugan

For more information about this series, please visit: https://www.routledge.com/Routledge-Literature-Handbooks/book-series/RLHB

THE ROUTLEDGE HANDBOOK OF SHAKESPEARE AND ANIMALS

Edited by Karen Raber and Holly Dugan

NEW YORK AND LONDON

First published 2021
by Routledge
52 Vanderbilt Avenue, New York, NY 10017

and by Routledge
2 Park Square, Milton Park, Abingdon, Oxon, OX14 4RN

Routledge is an imprint of the Taylor & Francis Group, an informa business

© 2021 Taylor & Francis

The right of Karen Raber and Holly Dugan to be identified as the authors of the editorial material, and of the authors for their individual chapters, has been asserted in accordance with sections 77 and 78 of the Copyright, Designs and Patents Act 1988.

All rights reserved. No part of this book may be reprinted or reproduced or utilised in any form or by any electronic, mechanical, or other means, now known or hereafter invented, including photocopying and recording, or in any information storage or retrieval system, without permission in writing from the publishers.

Trademark notice: Product or corporate names may be trademarks or registered trademarks, and are used only for identification and explanation without intent to infringe.

Library of Congress Cataloging-in-Publication Data
A catalog record for this title has been requested

ISBN: 978-1-138-71016-0 (hbk)
ISBN: 978-1-003-05719-2 (ebk)

Typeset in Bembo
by codeMantra

CONTENTS

List of Figures	*viii*
Introduction	1

PART 1
Animal Metaphors: History, Theory, Representation 11

1 Avian Shakespeare 13
Rebecca Ann Bach

2 Shakespeare's Fishponds: Matter, Metaphor, and Market 21
Dan Brayton

3 "I Am the Dog": Canine Abjection, Species Reversal, and
Misanthropic Satire in *The Two Gentlemen of Verona* 34
Bryan Alkemeyer

4 Learning from Crab: Primitive Accumulation, Migration, Species Being 45
Crystal Bartolovich

5 Beasts, Animals, and Animal Metaphor, in Shakespeare and His
Fellow Dramatists 61
Karl Steel

Contents

PART 2
Scales of Meaning — **75**

6 Cow-Cross Lane and Curriers Row: Animal Networks in Early
Modern England — 77
Ian F. MacInnes

7 "Everything Exists by Strife": War and Creaturely Violence in
Shakespeare's Late Tragedies — 90
Benjamin Bertram

8 Zoonotic Shakespeare: Animals, Plagues, and the
Medical Posthumanities — 104
Lucinda Cole

9 Flock, Herd, Swarm: A Shakespearean Lexicon of
Creaturely Collectivity — 116
Joseph Campana

PART 3
Animal Worlds/Animal Language — **127**

10 Swarm Life: Shakespeare's School of Insects — 129
Keith Botelho

11 Bernardian Ecology and Topsell's Redemptive Bee in *The Tempest* — 138
Nicole A. Jacobs

12 What Does the Wolf Say? Animal Language and Political Noise in
Coriolanus — 150
Liza Blake and Kathryn Vomero Santos

13 Shrewd Shakespeare — 163
Bruce Boehrer

PART 4
Training, Performance, and Living with Animals — **175**

14 The Training Relationship: Horses, Hawks, Dogs, Bears, and Humans — 177
Elspeth Graham

15 Performing *The Winter's Tale* in the "Open": Bear Plays, Skinners'
Pageants, and the Early Modern Fur Trade — 190
Todd A. Borlik

Contents

16	Counting Shakespeare's Sheep with *The Second Shepherd's Play* *Julian Yates*	204
17	Silly Creatures: *King Lear* (with Sheep) *Laurie Shannon*	219

PART 5
Animal Boundaries and Identities   **229**

18	The Lion King: Shakespeare's Beastly Sovereigns *Nicole Mennell*	231
19	"Wearing the Horn": Class and Community in the Shakespearean Hunt *Jennifer Allport Reid*	242
20	On Eating, the Animal that Therefore I Am: Race and Animal Rites in *Titus Andronicus* *Steven Swarbrick*	256
21	"What's This? What's This?": Fish and Sexuality in *Measure for Measure* *Robert Wakeman*	270
22	My Palfrey, Myself: Toward a Queer Phenomenology of the Horse- Human Bond in *Henry V* and Beyond *Karen Raber*	282
23	"Forgiveness, Horse": The Barbaric World of *Richard II* *Erica Fudge*	292

Appendix	*307*
Notes on Contributors	*313*
Bibliography	*319*
Index	*345*

FIGURES

4.1	Frontispiece, Thomas Harman's *Caveat or Warning for Common Cursiters* (1567)	46
4.2	Cover, *Daily Mirror*, Saturday August 1, 2015	55
4.3	Swarm/illegal/human poster, Photo courtesy of David Wallace	56
6.1	Archers, laundry, and cows—Agas map detail	79
6.2	Animals on the Agas map	80
6.3	Kennels—Agas map detail	80
6.4	Animal-named roads around Smithfield—Agas map detail	82
6.5	Claes Visscher, *panorama of London* detail. 1616	82
6.6	Livery halls in the animal trade—from MoEML	85
7.1	Hans Weiditz, "War, the Father of All Things," from Von der Artzney bayder Glück, des guten und widerwertigen, 1532. Courtesy of the Augsburg Stadtbibliothek	91
12.1	John Ogilby, *The Fables of Aesop* (London, 1651), sig. I3r. Call #: 168-220q. Photograph by Liza Blake, from the collections of the Folger Shakespeare Library	154
15.1	W.B. Morris. Portrait of Edward Alleyn (c. 1900). DPG 551. Dulwich Portrait Gallery	192
15.2	Queen Elizabeth (c. 1600). The Coronation Portrait. © National Portrait Gallery, London	194
15.3	The Skinners' Arms, London. Photo by Author	200
16.1	"June." Manuscript illustration from Thomas Fella's *Booke of Divers Devises* (Folger Shakespeare Library, V. a. 311), showing the labors of the season. By permission of the Folger Shakespeare Library, Washington, DC	215
17.1	*King Lear with Sheep*, image courtesy of Heather Williams	225

INTRODUCTION

I Wild Shakespeare

To commemorate the 400th anniversary of Shakespeare's death, *National Geographic* published "Shakespeare Gone Wild: Meet the Animals in the Bard's Plays." Pairing up Shakespeare's animal references with photographs from Joel Sartore's *Photo Ark* project (a visual record of some of the world's most endangered species), the magazine clearly intended to bring Shakespeare to bear on our current devastating problem of species extinction. Viewed in tandem, Shakespeare's language and Sartore's portraits juxtapose the highest and lowest levels of human achievement, connecting one of the world's best known playwrights and his innovative use of literary language with the plight of animals in a new era of mass extinction. The effect is striking: what do the metaphorical resonances of a poet dead for over 400 years have to do with the plight of today's animals and the climate crisis they face? And what can animal studies teach us about Shakespeare? How might Shakespeare's plays, as they depict an early modern world in which both wild and domesticated animals were prolific and intimately familiar to most—even if in many cases, that familiarity was with myth and legend as much as actual experience—have created the intellectual, political, economic conditions for the way we think about and treat animals now? These have been some of the overarching questions for animal studies scholars who work on Shakespeare and early modern literature. Many if not most of the animals Sartore photographed will soon be extinct, but some few, the photographer hopes, will survive because his portraits have inspired interest and concern. Scholars who write about the animals in Shakespeare's plays are motivated by a similar hope, that by excavating the many dimensions of our historical encounters and understandings of animals we might rescue some of our planet's creatures, whether from cruelty, suffering, or death—and in so doing, rescue ourselves, the planet's most ingenious, and sadly most destructive inhabitants.

Described by his contemporaries as both an upstart crow and a poet-ape, Shakespeare, we might say, has always been wild, ungovernable, irreducibly uncontained. Yet his works have also been used to discipline other creatures, functioning as a dividing line between the human—civilized, cultured, and English—and the rest of the earth's living creatures. Wild is a capacious term, describing human and nonhuman creatures as well as spaces, environments, and forces of nature. The forests of Arden are wild, as Jacques reminds us in

As You Like It, but so are the lovers of Charmian in *Antony and Cleopatra*, while Adriana in *The Comedy of Errors* describes the man she thinks is her husband as a "too-unruly deer" who escapes his fenced enclosure (2.1.99). All uncultivated plants are wild, Imogen reminds us in *Cymbeline*, a point that Horatio uses to describe Hamlet's language and mood, evinced by his "wild and whirling words." It is a term that signals a need for human dominance over the animal world, as when the Earl of Worcester describes Hotspur as "wild as young bulls," and over human licentiousness, as when Hotspur describes Hal as a "wild … libertine." Its boundaries are imagined as the limits of the nation, excluding those who are not a part of what the English consider "civil" society: Glendower is wild, but so too are the forests of Kent (*I Henry IV*) and the "high wild hills" of Gloucestershire (*Richard II*) as is the ocean that disrupts, terrifies, destroys, and sometimes renews. We might, with the Earl of Northumberland, conclude, "The times are wild."

Sartore's *Photo Ark* is a response to rapidly changing climates: deforestation, industrialization, and population increases have radically changed the earth's habitats, provoking some to question whether we are entering into a sixth extinction period. Human domestication of animal bodies has led to disproportionate populations of domesticated vs. wild species: estimates from five years ago posited that there were then over 22 billion chickens and over a billion and half cattle on earth, but just over a hundred thousand gorillas and 50,000 orangutans.[1] Things become dire if we focus more narrowly on particular breeds. There are under 100 Armur leopards in the world and fewer than 900 mountain gorillas. Sartore's project is linked to the devastating danger of extinction: an ark that seeks to preserve the world's creatures from an impending climate disaster, his simple portraits are an attempt photograph the 12,000 species of animals currently in human care, documenting them "before they disappear—and to get people to care while there is still time."[2]

In his recent overview of the field, Paul Waldau argues for four comprehensive ways in which animal studies as a field offers a methodological challenge to think differently about the past; the present; and, most importantly, the future. First and foremost, animal studies calls for a creative reimagining of the ways in which we think about nonhuman living beings in order to put them at the center of our focus. Such a leap is difficult (indeed some might say almost impossible), but the attempt is still worthwhile: placing animals at the heart of our narratives changes the knowledge we derive from them. It is, as Waldau argues, an expansive and creative act, one that seeks "to tell an entire story of our past with other living beings," both the ones that we love, train, mimic, or identify with and those that remain elusive, repulsive, or terrifying.[3] That range puts pressure on the very title of the field: defining the animal in animal studies has also been a critical part of its development, sharpening its contributions (both historically and politically) by narrowing its objectives to include living beings rather than the ways in which animals have been harvested for food, sport, or profit.

The third and fourth prongs, as Waldau identifies them, focus on the epistemological limits of this methodology so that we might better attune to the work that can be achieved, politically and ethically. For Waldau, animal studies as a field is rooted in our human perspectives, even as we seek to take up questions that move us "beyond the species" line, redefining our communities to include nonhuman beings and, importantly, engaging and reanimating questions of ethics to include "others" in our midst.

As the essayists in this volume note, however, "species" is not a stable and salient historical category of difference; early modern approaches to community—whether human or animal—focused (as Hamlet quips) on both kin and kind. The methodological divides that structure animal studies center upon this question of history. As a field, ecocriticism has developed two primary modes of inquiry. The first focuses on the present moment by

Introduction

making an important ethical contribution: connecting the politics of representation with the data of scientific inquiry, this model of scholarship argues for political action. Yet this has, at times, occluded historical models that defined ecocriticism more broadly. The emergence of "species" as a term of meaning in historical periods after the Renaissance has shaped how we interpret animals in earlier sources. Would we be better served, for example, in registering the complexity of ecosystems by taking up an early modern approach to the wealth of animal types by considering animal populations in terms of the bestiary, a compendious genre that rejects compartmentalization, rather than sorting them by species?

Likewise, a historical approach helps us with the fourth task, perhaps the most salient and politically pressing for all of animal studies: grappling with the fact that the world was not made for us, that there are limits to what we can know and experience of another creature's joy or pain, and that we lack the language to even describe that experience. These are humbling truths, but ones that make space for new and different engagements with the world around us.[4] Animal studies, as a field, resonates with the political work of critical race studies, postcolonial studies, gender studies, and studies of class, but it expands these foci to include nonhuman creatures as well; likewise, one of the most beneficial payoffs from paying critical attention to animals is that it allows us to practice decentering our privileged positions. It allows us not only to interrogate the deep connection with nonhuman creatures that we often feel but also to recognize that such an affinity is just that a feeling, one rooted in the dynamics of exchange and the temporality of such encounters. Those feelings dictate animal history: how we attend to other animals, the ones we don't recognize as linked to human modes of meaning, often reveals the extent of our species' brutality, and extends to violence towards fellow humans positioned in similar categories. And the history of how we've treated the animals that we do care for often reveals forms of unrecognized proximate violence rooted in our intimacies. In the delta between the past and the present, between how we've treated animals and how we've imagined them, lies a more nuanced understanding of both Shakespeare and the animals referenced in his plays.

Shakespeare's animals dwelt in the wilderness of literary criticism for centuries, banished to the wilds of obscurity by the apparent triviality of such study. Erica Fudge points out that it was not so long ago that the whole concept of a history of animals in Shakespeare's day was simply a joke; the proper subject of history, or any of the humanities, was humanity and only humanity (hence the name for those disciplines.[5] Even if the work were not treated as farcical, the obstacles to writing about animals were and are legion—creatures who are so completely overwritten with symbolism and metaphor, that cannot in the traditional textual way "speak" for themselves, and whose entire being is often elided in preference for human representations of them are not easy to write about.

Initially the field belonged mainly to enthusiasts. For example, James Harting's well-known 1841 *The Birds of Shakespeare* tries to prove that the poet was a budding ornithologist, with its extensive catalog of all the birds that appear in the plays and poems. Harting's is a paradigm that persists until well into the 1970s. Claims about Shakespeare's attachment to—or disdain for—particular animals (like dogs) often guide these inquiries, activating some of Shakespeare's metaphors for modern audiences more so than others. In the last several decades, however, an increasing volume of substantial and serious studies of Shakespeare's animals has appeared—the poet's menagerie has crept out from behind the bars of humanist disciplinarity and begun to repopulate both wild and domestic spaces. This sea-change in scholarship responded to large-scale shifts in literary theory and philosophy, changing how we read Shakespeare's works to include groups of living beings previously thought to be absent or discounted within them. Feminist, critical race, postcolonial, and working-class perspectives have changed how we interpret and understand Shakespeare's literary history. This widening of approach also includes animals. It is no longer possible to think about social justice from human perspectives alone; nor is it possible to change these systems of oppression without grappling with the ways in which animals, as markers and inscribers of categories, have defined the human in exclusionary ways.

These are political issues, but they also point towards a need to understand historical frames of reference. What did Shakespeare and his audiences know about animals? Which animals did they care about and why? And how did this knowledge shape human–animal interactions? Historicist approaches to Shakespeare and animal studies have their roots in early work such as Keith Thomas's *Man and the Natural World*, which raised questions about the historical, political, and cultural significance of animals. Historians like Joan Thirsk, writing on early modern European agrarian conditions; environmental historians like William Cronon studying American ecology; or Alfred Crosby, who brought science and medicine to bear on geography and history in his work on the intersection of early modern imperialism and global species exchanges established the central importance of animals in studies of history and geography. These broader analyses, while not specifically focused on Shakespeare, laid the groundwork for the field to emerge in coherent ways.

Attention to the place and function of animals in literary works of art helped to define the subfield as it emerged. Critics debated what, if anything, Shakespeare's art could offer to animal studies, and what, if anything, animal studies offered Shakespeare criticism. Erica Fudge's *Perceiving Animals* (2002) and the contributors to her edited collection *Renaissance Beasts* (2004) outlined the central paradox that would shape the field: animals were key to almost every aspect of early modern culture, yet every source about them in the period is shaped by human perspectives. Tracing early modern philosophies about human–animal relationships, the essays in this collection aimed to analyze anthropocentrism as a historically defined category, one that occludes animal lives. Fudge's *Brutal Reasoning* (2006) explored speciesism as a historical category, examining what early modern people (including Shakespeare) thought about animal-capacities for reasoning, connecting humanist philosophy to its effects upon animal lives. Bruce Boehrer's *Shakespeare Among the Animals* (2002) took a different approach: Shakespeare's works, he argued, reveal a tremendous amount of knowledge about the material reality of animals. Taking up Shakespeare's animal metaphors, Boehrer traced how these tropes sometimes recognized, but at other times evacuated knowledge about animal lives. These authors collectively provided the groundwork for a next generation of scholars by detailing the literary and historical evidence of broader cultural shifts in human–animal relationships.

Questions about literature, philosophy, and human assumptions about dominion over animals have animated more recent work, including questions about the performative, material, and political aspects of human–animal relationships. Andreas Höfele's *Stage, Stake, and Scaffold* (2011), for instance, focuses specifically on performance history, examining how theater networks drew upon these beliefs, staging the paradoxes of the human/animal divide for audiences in Southwark. Höefele's work showed how traces of animal subjugation are embedded in almost all of Shakespeare's most memorable human performances of suffering. Karen Raber's *Animal Bodies, Renaissance Culture* (2013) argues that the choreography of human and animal bodies in cultural and textual artifacts of the past challenges what we now think of as human exceptionalism, extending the boundaries of the human body to include shared experiences of embodiment with animal flesh. In her influential monograph *The Accommodated Animal* (2013), Laurie Shannon asks whether the "animal" in "animal" studies is even a useful term to define and describe the creatures that surrounded Shakespeare and his audiences. "Animal," she finds, is a thoroughly reductive term for all the cornucopia of creatures Shakespeare's contemporaries imagined: "There were creatures. There were brutes, and there were beasts. There were fish and fowl. There were living things. There were humans" (10). What Shakespeare's works reveal, Shannon argues, is a more comprehensive lexicon, mapping the ways in which human political discourse positioned animals within systems of subjugation.

Critics have begun to explore this new, more diversely populated terrain. Rebecca Ann Bach's *Birds and Other Creatures in Renaissance Literature: Shakespeare, Descartes, and Animal Studies* (2017) introduces readers to avian species in a completely different manner than did Harting in the nineteenth century, establishing the critical importance of a much more expansive understanding of Renaissance hierarchical systems of nature. Benjamin Bertram's work on Shakespeare's beastly ecologies extends animal studies to include humanist theories of warfare, while Joseph Campana and Keith Botelho's *Lesser Living Creatures: Insect Life in the Renaissance* (forthcoming) asks why insects are so consistently overlooked in scholarship on the period, and what might change in our understanding of the early modern world if they are made visible again. These works and more demonstrate that Shakespeare and animal studies is now a thriving field, with new research emerging in almost every aspect of early modern studies.

II Beastly Shakespeare

Shakespeare's plays are teeming with animals. Some steal the spotlight, like Crab, the mischievous dog in *Two Gentlemen of Verona* or the bear of *The Winter's Tale*; others, like the nightingales and larks of *Romeo and Juliet*, lurk in the background, just out of view. Some must be imagined by the audience, like the horses of the history plays, and some are staged (badly) by humans, like Snug's performance of a lion in *A Midsummer Night's Dream*. Others function as metaphors, adding imagery and texture to Shakespeare's poetry: Ariel flies on "a bat's back," Quince reads his lines like "a rough colt," while old Hamlet boasts of tales that will make one's hair stand on end "like quills upon the fretful porcupine." Love is "a chameleon" that can "feed on air," the troops that Henry V famously rallies outside of Harfleur are encouraged to "imitate the action of the tiger," while others are rendered brute by such references. Dromio of Syracuse is called a "slug" and a "snail" by his mistress's sister; Shylock is denounced as a "cur" by the Christians on the rialto; Katherine, a "wasp," by Petruchio; and both Desdemona and Cleopatra are described as being like "crocodiles."

Archives about Shakespeare's work are also teeming with animals: the manuscripts, leather-bound books, quills, and ink with which he wrote; the hooves that lined the floor of early stages like the Curtain; the blood spilled on them that brought his characters and plays to life; and the prepared food that fed his audiences during the performance all were made from animals. Whereas these are often thought of as commodities, their biohistory is important; scholars are beginning to partner with scientists in order to excavate the biological aspects of historical records: research in premodern animal studies now includes biocodicology of collagen in medieval manuscripts and early printed books, GIS-mapping of food pathways, and data visualization of animal populations. Such tools link macroanalyses of how animals moved (and were moved) through early modern landscapes and cityscapes. Yet as discrete creatures—unique, individuated living beings—these creatures remain almost unknowable. Like Shakespeare himself, there is much that we don't know—and will never know—about them as bio-specimens.

5

Introduction

As we've noted, accounts of Shakespeare's animals from the nineteenth to the early twentieth century followed a collectors' approach. Apart from addressing editing concerns, nineteenth-century scholars were often devoted to categorizing and providing narrative supplements to the plays. From the sections on animals in Caroline Spurgeon's *Shakespeare's Imagery and What It Tells Us* (1935) to Alan Dent's *World of Shakespeare: Animals and Monsters* (1973) animals are a focus because they provide an entrée into the plays' or poems' complex webs of signification. Historical treatments of early modern animals were likewise aimed at recapturing the texture of early modern thought on animals: Anthony Dent's *Horses in Shakespeare's England* (1987), for example, offers sets of ideas and attitudes to supplement the plays by fleshing out the world from which they came. And like George Boas in his 1933 *The Happy Beast*, or Thomas's discussions of animals in *Man and the Natural World*, historians have been concerned with providing the prehistory of a contemporary position—in Boas's case, theriophily, in Thomas's the relationship between humans and nature.

The animal turn in humanities scholarship has made new methods available for investigating Shakespeare's animals: readers may now reasonably investigate not merely animals' metaphoric or symbolic function, but their material existence, even at times their own possible capacities, perspectives, and agencies. Such an interpretive framework aligns critical animal studies with other kinds of historical inquiry, including feminist and ecofeminist interventions, as well as critical race theory, queer theory, disability studies, and postcolonial scholarship. Whether because of an activist interest in nonhuman rights and welfare, or because of theoretical concerns about the status of "the human," scholarship on Shakespeare's animals embraces a more copious understanding of nonhuman life and its often-resistant autonomy in the plays and their world. Shakespeare's works sit uneasily amid all of these approaches, both constitutive of troubling paradigms, yet also integral to work that decenters them. The role of Shakespeare's plays within colonial systems of power, for example, is well documented, but so too are the ways in which these histories are connected to and transformed by postcolonial critique; the metaphors of race embedded in Shakespeare's plays have been instrumental to ideological defenses of enslavement, but they were also appropriated and transformed by black arts and black liberation movements.[6] Concerns about Shakespeare's equivocal history and multiplicitous uses guide our inquiry and that of many of the essays in the collection. Shakespeare's beastly metaphors, we recognize, are linked to our current ecological crises because they have been the fodder for violent shifts of power, exploitation, and industrialization, even if they might also provide the tools of change.

New materialist or posthumanist theory invites practices that challenge a constructionist and therefore anthropocentric focus on discourse, turning instead to questions of ontology and material phenomena. Early modern scholars working with such a methodology, rather than simply accounting for the ubiquity of animal uses and possible metaphorizations in literary artifacts, might investigate the various ways animal-made-objects in both cultural and literary texts resist or undo human assertions of dominion. Craig Dionne's *Posthuman Lear* (2016), for instance, argues that *King Lear's* animal references establish the tragedy of the play as revolving around whether Lear can accept the flat ontology of "his relational dependence as one forked animal among others in his environment"(148).[7] Likewise, where some scholars might note the presence of animal speech in philosophical debates about animal reason, those influenced by the field of zoosemiotics, which considers semiosis, or the making of meaning through "language," as a trans-species activity, might instead ask how some literary instances of prosopopoeia demonstrate the ways in which the structures of human poetry are indebted to animal vocalizations.[8] In both cases, the emphasis shifts away from the self-referential elaboration of "the human" in literary texts, towards a more enmeshed, entangled, interdependent view of the world those texts describe.

Although these posthumanist approaches often explicitly cast themselves as correctives to a generation of culturally- and socially-oriented criticism, including old materialisms (from Marx to Althusser), post-structuralism, or new historicism, they share techniques of reading and researching an expanded archive and an orientation towards inclusivity—in the case of animals, adding species status to categories like gender, class, race, sexual orientation, disability, and other socially constructed categories. That is not to say, however, that there are no complicating factors in this shift in theoretical methods: many forms of new materialism, to take one example, are committed to the flat ontology we see Dionne referencing, but such an approach has the potential to obscure the particularity of animals, especially of animal suffering. Nevertheless, the consequence has been to expand the scope and nature of work on Shakespeare and animals. Thus we find Fudge investigating the dance of attachment in the early modern farmyard as it is represented in wills, or Julian Yates asking what it is like to be a sheep, or Michael Clody thinking about animal voices in *King Lear*.[9]

Since the late twentieth century, scholars have also approached with increasing skepticism the proposition that Shakespeare is a prime anchor for the ideological claims of humanism— that human beings are the apex of creation, that "the human" is a unique and morally weighty category, indeed that something called the human might actually exist at all as more than merely another species among the throng. In addition to their important presence in new materialist and posthumanist criticism, animals increasingly figure in feminist Shakespeare criticism, as well as in queer studies, cultural studies, postcolonial and critical race studies. All these perspectives on Shakespeare's work inform the essays we have collected here in order to connect animals to both the current directions in literary criticism, and with histories of identity and meaning. Shakespeare studies, by its nature, requires an interdisciplinary approach, and so the various essays in this volume come at the topic of Shakespeare's animals from many perspectives and using a variety of tools. What is unique, however, are the pathways they chart through the changing contours of that field, and the fact that many of the essays we include seek to go beyond an exclusively human perspective.

III Cat Tracks

There are a number of pathways through the essays we've assembled here. We've sought to organize and categorize them in order to facilitate a clear grasp on the state of the field for those just starting out. For this reason, we've grouped the essays into clusters that allow you to explore questions about methodologies (Part 1), materialities (Part 2), habitats (Part 3), skills (Part 4), and identities (Part 5). But we also encourage you to find different routes through the material, including surveying Shakespeare's plays from "a birds' eye"—or worm's light-sensing skin's—view, randomly sampling the panorama of offerings, or settling into the deep soil of a specific topic or animal. The collection as a whole is best understood as a conversation about the intersections of "Shakespeare" with critical animal studies, rather than a comprehensive overview of either field.

Through the organization of the volume's sections, we provide the bird's eye view, an overview of the field. Each of the segments we have created is designed to foster a more robust engagement among writers on these areas of thought; the introductory headnotes provide a useful overview to the segment as well as a short description of each author's argument. Our divisions, however, are provisional and in some cases necessarily obscure other kinds of connections as we address below. Thus, we have provided an appendix that offers other tracks through the collection, some based on plays covered, others based on topics or theoretical methodologies. The appendix may foster a deeper engagement of the field beyond the connections we've drawn in each headnote by providing possible reading lists for an advanced student seeking a coherent plan to work towards an examination or for those wishing to engage in a more focused way related to their own research. Whichever pathway you follow, we encourage you to think of the collection not so much as a static object that reflects the state of the field, but rather the start of a dialogue about what it means to take animals seriously by showcasing cutting-edge scholarship that does so.

The collection begins by exploring how the claim that animals were a constitutive part of everyday life in the past reshapes our understanding of early modern history. Our scholarly notions of historical periods define change through human-oriented societal shifts that one might assume do not apply to nonhuman populations. Yet these shifts are not wholly irrelevant to the history of animals. Some authors in this section argue that such historical differences are acute; others show instead how animal studies must expand beyond human-inflected modes of meaning. Yet for all of them, Shakespeare's long (and varied) history of reception allows us to explore when and how historical context matters: essays about Shakespeare's birds, fish, and dogs open up a range of questions about human–animal relationships, both real and imagined, in the past and more recently.

Part 2, "Scales of Meaning," connects these questions of material history to questions of representation. As the essays in this section make clear, Shakespeare's animal metaphors signal the omnipresence of animal life in early modern London; but such proximity did not necessarily lead to humans treating animals in ethical ways. Shakespeare's London was a central hub in a vast economic and agricultural network, one designed to transform living creatures into commodities. The authors in this section grapple with this reality, theorizing the sheer scale of animal numbers. Starting with macroanalyses of animal life in early modern London and moving towards more localized micro histories, these essays provide a language to process animal life within sliding scales of meaning.

With this grounding of history and materiality in place, we then move towards representation. Part 3, "Animal Language/Animal Worlds," foregrounds Shakespeare's metaphors of animality in order to move beyond human-oriented epistemologies, reaching towards animal domains. Here Shakespeare's animals convey meaning in a variety of ways, redefining how we experience language, temporality, and sensory environments. Drawing from a range of methods—including editorial practices, narrative theory, and sensory history—the essays in this section examine what it might mean to use Shakespeare, that most canonical of sources, to open up nonhuman world-making. Shakespeare's language is, at various times, both a tool and an obstacle to understanding these larger realms.

Part 4 "Animal Relationships: Training & Performance" explores how different human–animal relationships formed, creating distinct and sometimes unexpected zones of communication, empathy, and shared conditions of labor. The experiences of training—whether of horses, soldiers, or bears—are explored in depth here. Because Shakespeare's stage plays such an important role in conveying or challenging ideas about what an animal is and why that matters, this segment explores theater's use of animals, and the questions that arise from that use. Their capacity to perform, to deceive, to entertain, or to appeal to audiences all connect to broader questions about the theater's place in early modern culture and thought.

Whereas the previous section analyzed shared iterations of human/animal skill, our last segment, "Categories, Boundaries, and Identities," examines how the early modern understanding of animality influenced human social identities, positioning a wide array of creatures within hierarchies of power. These essays analyze Shakespeare's animals in order

Introduction

to understand their impact on human lives: they uncover how and why Shakespeare used animal metaphors to dehumanize certain characters and position them as subordinate to others. Connecting animal studies with political theories of sovereignty, critical race theory, queer theory, and feminist analyses of gender, these essays model an intersectional approach, one that attends to the shared material conditions of oppression and literary racism by interrogating how natural history positioned humans and animals within violent structures of subjugation.

The essays in this handbook demonstrate the range and vitality in critical methods for animal studies approaches to Shakespeare. Many revisit the questions posed in previous scholarly debates, modeling new ways of answering them. And though we've limited our overview of the field to early modern and Shakespeare studies, the handbook also provides an oblique introduction to broader theoretical approaches that drive literary studies. You'll see a range of theorists invoked in these essays: authors asking questions about metaphor, translation, and representation engage with Jacques Derrida; about sovereignty, with Giorgio Agamben; about history, with Karl Marx and Michel Foucault; and about ethics, posthumanism, and embodiment, with Donna Haraway. Though this is not a comprehensive list of all the theory literary scholars employ, it may allow you to (at least temporarily) orient yourself among larger debates and disparate approaches. As you'll see, the authors in this collection often do not agree. At times, they seem to draw contradictory conclusions, each making compelling arguments for their position. These are not small disagreements: debates about political agency, the role of ethics, theories of biopower and capital run through these essays, as do debates about history, evidence, and editing practices. Authors grapple with method as well as with theory: should we focus on micro- or macro-level analyses? Should we include "animal-made-objects" within the domain of animal studies, and if so, how? Are literary metaphors useful evidence for historicizing the lives of animals in the past? And what about the histories of humans denigrated by such metaphors? Does attention to animals mitigate those harms? Finally, as Shannon has asked, what use is "animal" as a category at all? At other times, important and striking concordances emerge. It is perhaps not surprising, given the editors own work and the direction of the field in recent years, that a number of essays focus on material history. The sound and smell of animals, as well as their taste and touch, affect their histories. And while we are, as we noted above, cautious about discounting realities of exploitation and abuse, many essays here demonstrate how humans found engaging ways to work with animals towards mutual goals.

Notes

1 A recent report by the Intergovernmental Science-Policy Platform on Biodiversity and Ecosystem Services (IPBES) of the United Nation predicted that approximately a million species of plants and animals are likely to become extinct in the coming decades, a rate of extinction that this is unprecedented in human history. www.un.org/sustainabledevelopment/blog/2019/05/nature-decline-unprecedented-report/.

2 Joel Sartore, *Photo Ark*, www.joelsartorecom/photo-ark/.

3 Paul Waldau, *Animal Studies: An Introduction* (Oxford: Oxford University Press, 2013), 305.

4 Ibid., 86. See also Donna Haraway's, *When Species Meet* (Minneapolis: University of Minnesota Press, 2008), 21–23.

5 Erica Fudge, "A Left-Handed Blow: Writing the History of Animals," in *Representing Animals*, ed. Nigel Rothfeld (Bloomington: Indiana University Press, 2002), 3–18.

6 Ania Loomba, *Shakespeare, Race, and Colonialism* (New York: Oxford University Press, 2002); Ania Loomba and Jonathan Burton, *Race in Early Modern England: A Documentary Companion* (New York: Palgrave Macmillan, 2007); Jyotsna Singh, *A Companion to the Global Renaissance: English*

Introduction

Literature and Culture in the Era of Expansion (Oxford: Wiley Blackwell, 2009); Ayanna Thompson, *Passing Strange: Shakespeare, Race, and Contemporary America* (New York: Oxford University Press, 2011); Peter Erickson and Kim F. Hall, "'A New Scholarly Song': Rereading Early Modern Race," *Shakespeare Quarterly* 67, no. 1 (2016): 1–13; Rebecca LaRoche and Jennifer Munroe, *Shakespeare and Ecofeminist Theory* (London: Bloomsbury, 2017); Goran Stanivukovic, ed., *Queer Shakespeare: Desire and Sexuality* (London: Arden, 2018).

7 Craig Dionne, *Posthuman Lear: Reading Shakespeare in the Anthropocene* (New York: Punctum, 2016); See also Bruno Latour, *We Have Never Been Modern*, trans. Catherine Porter (Cambridge, MA: Harvard University Press, 1993) and Jane Bennett, *Vibrant Matter: A Political Ecology of Things* (Durham, NC: Duke University Press, 2010).

8 See Michael Clody, "The Mirror and the Feather: Tragedy and Animal Voice in *King Lear*," *ELH* 80, no. 3 (2013): 661–80; Aaron Moe, *Zoopoetics: Animals and the Making of Poetry* (Lanham, MD: Lexington Books, 2014); Tobias Menely, *The Animal Claim: Sensibility and the Creaturely Voice* (Chicago, IL: University of Chicago Press, 2016).

9 Erica Fudge, "Farmyard Choreographies in Early Modern England," in *Renaissance Posthumanism*, eds. Joseph Campana and Scott Maisano (New York: Fordham University Press, 2016), 145–66; Julian Yates, "Oves et Singulatim: A Multispecies Impression," in *Renaissance Posthumanism*, eds. Joseph Campana and Scott Maisano (New York: Fordham University Press, 2016), 167–95, and Clody, "The Mirror and the Feather."

PART 1

Animal Metaphors

History, Theory, Representation

Shakespeare's animal metaphors often raise more questions than answers. Was there an actual bear involved in early productions of *A Winter's Tale*, and if so how did they care for it and mitigate the risks it may have posed? What do Beatrice and Katherine mean when they claim they're doomed to "lead apes in hell"? To whom is Hamlet referring when he tells Gertrude to be "like the famous ape"? Other animal metaphors in Shakespeare's works remain frighteningly familiar, such as Iago's racist description of Othello as a Barbary horse or Demetrius description of Lavinia as "a dainty doe" just before he rapes her. In these instances, Shakespeare's animal metaphors attach to characters differently, connecting animal bodies with human ones in powerful ways through allusions to nature and its structures of power.

We begin with Rebecca Bach's "Avian Shakespeare," which argues for the importance of attending to historical differences in our approach to animals by looking closely at Shakespeare's avian metaphors. Bach reminds us that early modern men and women lived intimately with birds; their flight patterns, mating calls, and colorful shapes provided a rich web of associations for articulating human emotion and meaning. Shakespeare's avian metaphors are not unique, but rather trace a differently oriented animal world than the one that we are used to inhabiting. Drawing on Bruno Latour's theory of "nature culture," Bach investigates the many bird metaphors that appear in Shakespeare's plays and finds that Shakespeare's avian metaphors create a world in which nature *is* culture. Although, as Latour argues, we have never been modern, Bach reminds us that we have always been avian.

Next, Daniel Brayton wades into "Shakespeare's Fishponds," exploring the reality of the pisciculture that surrounded early modern London's theater district. Brayton argues that Southwark's fishponds shaped metaphors about other industries in that realm, including plays, animal-baiting, and sex work. The "stews" of Southwark contributed a catch-all term for describing sordid behaviors; fish metaphors provided important codes for navigating this realm, both for those who lived and worked nearby and for those visiting the neighborhood, hoping to see a play, while snacking on oysters, or to participate in other activities.

Perhaps Shakespeare's best-known (and most controversial) animal metaphors are his canine ones. In "I am the dog," Brian Alkemeyer argues that Shakespeare's canine references index historical shifts in pet cultures: rather than debating whether Shakespeare did or did not love dogs, as have generations of critics, Alkemeyer instead argues that the grounds for this debate invite us to account instead for the profound historical shift in human animal relationships that occurred in the early modern period. Alkemeyer explores how canine fidelity migrated from a quality with negative associations that marked dogs as pitiful and pathetic towards a positive one that defined them as "man's best friend." As Alkemeyer shows, for such a trait to be valued, dogs had to be "reinvented as exemplary beings," providing a new shaping paradigm for the relations between servants and masters.

Crystal Bartolovich shares Alkemeyer's focus on dogs and continues to interrogate the animal's position of privilege within contemporary human–animal relationships. In "Learning from Crab," Bartolovich takes up the case of Shakespeare's most famous animal actor in order to explore the limits of Donna Haraway's theory of instrumentality. Humans' ethical use of animals—the structures we create to care for and bond with animals in our care—can obscure a more global analysis of oppression. Bartolovich reframes questions about pet culture through an analysis of the social structures of capitalism, exploring the limits of posthumanist thinking within critical animal studies. Her argument, like Alkemeyer's, reminds us there may be nothing "natural" about loving dogs; furthermore, she argues that such affective bonds may limit our ability to move beyond "local" or micro-historical instances of human–animal interaction and towards a more planetary model of thinking.

Finally, Karl Steel broadens the grounds of analysis yet more forcefully, returning us to the questions with which we began this segment: how might we use Shakespeare's animal metaphors to understand the larger issues of history, representation, and theory that shape the field? Shakespeare, Steel argues, may not be the best author to do so. Because they were made to generate human-inflected meanings, Shakespeare's animal metaphors, Steel provocatively argues, seem predictable, especially when compared to the wide array of fabulous creatures in premodern literature. Steel queries whether we value Shakespeare's animal metaphors for their similarity to ours, rather than their alterity. Whereas Shakespeare's animals may seem boring, Shakespeare's beastly metaphors are "terrifying" for the way they attach to humans who embrace difference in order to attack conventions of sociality and community. In concert with Bartolovich, Steel's essay contends that critical animal studies must include an analysis of systems of oppression that constrain both humans and nonhumans. For Steel, the term "beast" does this best in Shakespeare's works, whereas his "animal" remains an indistinguishable plural.

1

AVIAN SHAKESPEARE

Rebecca Ann Bach

Looking for birds in Shakespeare leads one to discover the many ways Renaissance humans lived intimately with birds. They lived so intimately with the avian world that they saw the humans around them in terms of and in relation to birds, a bit like the way that some of today's American humans may see humans in terms of and in relation to dogs and cats. Actual birds also occupied human imaginations and human language in ways that are unfamiliar to many of us, even those of us who imagine, speak, tweet, and instagram in terms of and in relation to dogs and cats. We do not, after all, write using dog body parts in the way that all Renaissance writers used feathers to express themselves. Readers and playgoers in the twenty-first century may skip over many Shakespearean references to birds easily, either because we do not understand them or because they lack significance for us. In this chapter, I hope to show that understanding the avian references in Shakespeare's plays explains aspects of his human culture, and what Bruno Latour would call his "nature-culture," that we otherwise might miss. Elsewhere, I have argued extensively for the pervasiveness and significance of birds in the Renaissance world of creaturely bodies, a world where all bodies were subject to God and were seen as similar in their mortality.[1] This nature-culture, in which humans as a whole were not categorically different than other mortals, is the world Shakespeare inhabited. Thus, his avian references are triply significant at least: they show us what the avian world looked like to humans; they show us the lives of birds inside Renaissance "nature-culture"; and they also show us the many ways that human life was conceived of and negotiated in relation to bird life.

Just as Renaissance humans understood that human life was essentially hierarchical, they read avian life as hierarchical.[2] The bird hierarchy reflected and encoded hierarchies in human life—in texts, commoners were called geese, and noblemen called themselves eagles. But the bird hierarchy was material in ways that human hierarchies were not. In a world that believed in and valued God's all-seeing eye and angels with anatomical bird wings, the way that birds like eagles and falcons tower over others and most birds fly could manifest their superiority physically[3]; and this informed how birds were understood and valued. Renaissance humans knew what different birds ate: some hunted and ate other birds, some ate only dead flesh, and some were eaten by humans and other birds. Humans, who ate pigeons, chickens, geese, and ducks and who hunted some birds with the cooperation of hawks, easily thought about their own human hierarchies in avian terms, and their references are alive with the material interactions of humans and birds.

This kind of knowledge and thought about avian hierarchy appears in Richard III when Lord Hastings comments to Richard on the jailing of Richard's brother Clarence: "More pity that the eagle should be mewed / While kites and buzzards prey at liberty" (1.1.132–33). Hastings is responding to Richard's suggestion that the Queen's brothers are responsible for Clarence's arrest. Hastings calls Clarence "the eagle," who will be caged, "mewed," like an elite person might cage a hunting falcon. Clarence is going to be jailed by his brother, the King, while the Queen's brothers, characterized by Hastings as lesser carrion birds, "kites and buzzards," hunt freely. Hastings's metaphorical avian world, in which some birds fly freely while some are caged by humans, nods to a host of Renaissance human hierarchies. In Hastings's speech, Clarence's caging marks him as more significant than the Queen's brothers, not just because Hastings calls him an eagle, the highest ranging of birds, but also because only high-ranking birds like elite falcons were mewed, and, therefore, only high-ranking humans are characterized as mewed. "Kites" also hunt, like the more elite falcons that elite humans mewed and hunted with, but they were seen as virtually untrainable by humans, and thus, they were characterized by humans as hurtful predators, akin in Clarence's speech to a buzzard, who eats only dead creatures. The OED tells us that, from the Medieval period on, "buzzard" signified "a worthless, stupid, or ignorant person," and a kite signified, figuratively, "a person who preys upon others, a rapacious person."[4] Indeed, Shakespeare uses "kite" this way when Lear snaps back at Goneril, "Detested kite, thou liest!" (King Lear 1.4.229). In the Renaissance, falcons were to kites as nobles were to commoners and other people who might be despised. Reducing Goneril to a "kite" is a status insult as well as a moral one.

The OED characterizes the usage of kite for a rapacious person as figurative, but Shakespeare also often refers to birds actually feasting on human bodies. In Shakespeare's plays, kites kill other birds, and they also eat corpses. For example, Macbeth complains bitterly that, if Banquo can rise from the dead, "monuments"—graves and vaults that hold human bodies—will become "the maws of kites" (3.4.72–74). The OED explains that "maw" used to signify generally as "the stomach of an animal or of a person." Macbeth worries about kites feeding on people, and he was created as a character in a world where people's bodies were believed to have stomachs like kites'. In a similar reference to kites eating men, Coriolanus mocks Aufidius's men by claiming, when they ask where he lives, that he lives "I'th'city of kites and crows" (4.5.41). He means that he lives on a battlefield full of dead human bodies. Macbeth is afraid that the plots of earth that contain human bodies will become the feeding grounds for kites just as Coriolanus knows that open ground with dead humans on it supplies those birds with food. Perhaps in later usages of "kite" to mean "a rapacious person," the actuality of kites eating human bodies is out of mind, but I am arguing that in Shakespeare's time, the interactions of avian and human bodies were at the forefront of human minds. When Hastings characterizes the Queen's relatives as kites and buzzards, he is calling them lesser-ranked, thieving men, and this also has the resonance of men who prey on other men financially.

For elite characters in Shakespeare plays, the proper order of the avian hierarchy could signify the proper order of the world. In addition, when references to the avian hierarchy are read closely, they reveal how Shakespeare takes for granted the mutual and interactive mortality of birds and people and also gives birds agency. The elites in Richard III, like Hastings, deeply resent how Edward's Queen has elevated her relatives who lack noble blood. Thus, Hastings depicts her relatives as the kites of the avian and human world, upsetting the hierarchy in which the eagles of the avian and human world should rule. Likewise, in other Shakespeare plays, the "world turned upside down" is shown when avian hierarchies are reversed. In Julius Caesar, Cassius explains that when his soldiers were victorious, "Two mighty eagles" fed from their hands, but he foresees his army's defeat because, now that his army is at Philippi, the eagles have "fled" and been replaced by "ravens, crows, and kites," who "fly" over his and his soldiers' "heads" and "look down at them" as if they "were sickly prey" (5.1.82–88). Cassius tells a reversal story in which the birds and humans interact in ways that suggest their intimacy as well as their similar mortal bodies. As a sign of Cassius's army's success at Sardis, eagles, the most successful, dominant birds, land on his banner, "perch" there, and eat from his men's hands; these eagles on men's hands evoke Shakespeare's world in which hunting hawks were trained very commonly on and by the hands of the elite or those who served the elite. These eagles also have agency: they are significant in themselves—"mighty"—and also, by deigning to eat from the hands of the men, the eagles show the mutual comfort among men and birds. The eagles retain their dominance even when they are signs of human success; they choose their perches, alight where they please. In contrast, in the upside-down world Cassius is facing in his defeat, he and his men are subordinate to carrion birds who see all of these men's mortal bodies as food. As a sign of Cassius's coming failure, he and his soldiers have become equalized as food for the lowly of the avian world, carrion birds, whose abilities to fly and see them from above diminish these men utterly.

Macbeth also features a less species-interactive story about birds that signifies hierarchical reversal in the human world. After Duncan's murder, an old man tells Ross that "On Tuesday last, /A falcon, tow'ring in her pride of place, / Was by a mousing owl hawked at and killed" (2.4.11–13). In both this and the *Julius Caesar* scenario, the birds are alive in the plays, as alive as the humans.[5] The *Macbeth* story depicts the birds interacting by themselves, without human involvement, but their interaction signifies the disorder in the human world. The old man and Ross know that the world is turned upside down when owls hunt their superior birds. The owl is supposed to be hunting for mice, but it acts like a hawk and kills an actual hawk. The owl is both flying above her place and killing her superior. The point of the story is to create terror at the disorder in the world caused by the murder of Duncan, the rightful king. The owl mirrors Macbeth and Lady Macbeth's actions; it has flown above its place and hunted its superior. The old man's story is, thus, more anthropocentric than the *Julius Caesar* story; but even in this story, the falcon has grammatical personhood—she is in "her pride of place." Her world is also, and in concert, reversed, in that an owl, another flying bird, but one who hunts mainly for grounded creatures like mice, has killed her.

Just as Duncan has a rightful place in the play's kingdom, falcons, who tower over other birds and over men, have a rightful place high in the sky, a place that Renaissance humans could never physically reach. Humans were grounded creatures, and they were aware that God had placed them on the ground.[6] Even if some of their souls might reach Heaven and live with winged angels, their bodily kinship was with other grounded creatures. *Macbeth*'s towering falcon and "mousing owl" may live in a world reversed by the reversed human world, but they also live in a "nature-culture" in which they both fly above all humans, and the falcon naturally towers above all humans and most birds. Here and elsewhere, Shakespeare points to the superior heights that birds can reach. Sometimes these references are wholly figurative such as in Flavius's comment after putting down Caesar's supporters: "these growing feathers plucked from Caesar's wing / Will make him fly an ordinary pitch, / Who else would soar above the view of men" (*Julius Caesar* 1.1.71–73). This comment, though figurative and about a person, demonstrates how hierarchy and height were signified through feathers and flight. In a less figurative usage of birds, Edgar in *King Lear* refers to varied lower-flying birds to persuade his blind father that they have walked to a mighty cliff. He tells Gloucester that they have reached a point from which "the crows and choughs that wing the midway air / Show scarce so gross as beetles" (4.6.14–15). Then, when he is persuading Gloucester that he has fallen from the cliff, Edgar says, "Look up a-height, the shrill-gorged lark so far / Cannot be seen or heard" (4.6.60–61). In this scene, the inability of humans to see or hear a high-flying lark works two ways, one to mark where humans have climbed and the other to mark how low humans are. Even crows and choughs, small crows (also called (jack)daws and chewets), can "wing" the air and never fall; when humans are not on immense cliffs, larks fly far above them.

As the "shrill-gorged lark" might suggest, the "nature-culture" Shakespeare lived and wrote in also thought about voice and breath in terms of birds. It valued greatly the beauty of some avian voices, recognized avian voices as inherently different from one another, and characterized songbird voices as articulate.[7] Humans lived closely with many kinds of birds, not just the hawks they hunted with. Many elite humans kept songbirds in their houses, and those singing birds in cages leave their traces in Shakespeare's plays. In *The Taming of the Shrew*, the Lord offers Christopher Sly, the tinker, the "music" of "twenty caged nightingales" (Induction 2, 33, 34). This is a fantasy of elite life—probably no one was caging 20 nightingales—although these caged singing birds are offered to the tinker along with perfectly plausible hunting hawks. Lear's famous personal dream that he and Cordelia might live "alone" singing "like birds i'th'cage" shows us that keeping songbirds this way was customary (*King Lear* 5.3.8–9). Likewise, a reference to the practice appears in *Much Ado about Nothing*. Don John explains his devotion to villainy and his complaint at being hampered by his brother by saying, "I have decreed not to sing in my cage" (1.3.28).[8] One particularly eloquent reference appears in *Cymbeline* when Arviragus complains to Belarius that he and his brother cannot freely roam and experience the world: "our cage / We make a quire, as doth the prisoned bird. / And sing our bondage freely" (3.3.42–44). Arviragus's word "quire" may indicate another aspect of how humans used to understand avian voice. "Quire" was a common spelling for two meanings that we would now see as entirely differentiated: a group of human singers and a gathering of eight leaves of paper. In sonnet 73, Shakespeare's speaker characterizes his "time of year" as a tree in winter with "Bare ruined quiers, where late the sweet birds sang" (line 4; editors customarily silently "correct" the word to "choirs").[9] In both of these instances, Shakespeare may be pointing us to one Renaissance human usage of bird feathers—this was the only way they could write, except perhaps on waxed slates.[10] Both Arviragus and the sonnet speaker point to the sweet songs of birds and to their desire to express themselves, or in the speaker's case, his waning abilities. Voice and beautiful expression were intimately related to birds in Shakespeare's world.[11] Humans kept singing birds in their houses to experience their voices, expressed themselves by means of feathers, and attended to bird song in the world generally.

Many humans also taught birds to speak like humans. Most of these kinds of relations with birds are still practiced in our world, but they are practiced in subcultures, groups of people with particular expertise whose interests are seen as specialized. This was not the case in Shakespeare's world. The offhandedness and pervasiveness of references testifies to how ordinary teaching birds to speak human words might have been. In *The Tempest*, Antonio insults Gonzalo as part of his temptation of Sebastian. He tells Sebastian that in Naples, there are "lords that can prate / As amply and unnecessarily as this Gonzalo." He goes on to say, "I myself could make / A chough of as deep chat" (2.1.256–59). Modern editions of *The Tempest* all explain that Antonio is saying that he could teach a chough to speak as wisely as Gonzalo, whom he considers an idiot; however, Shakespeare's audiences did not need footnotes to understand this reference to training small crows to talk, nor the similar references to jackdaw's "language" in *All's Well that Ends Well* (4.1.19), in *Hamlet*, and in *1 Henry IV*.[12] In another direct reference to training a bird to speak like a human, Benedict in *Much Ado* calls Beatrice "a rare parrot teacher" (1.1.113).

That parrots can be taught to speak words is a more familiar notion to us than that small crows can, but parrots are only one type of birds who speak human language in the Renaissance.[13] It is debatable, but likely, that Macbeth is referring to many talking birds when he says, "Augurs and understood relations have / By maggot pies and choughs and rooks brought forth / The secret'st man of blood" (3.4.126–28).[14] Along with being speaking birds, Magpies, choughs, and rooks are all types of intelligent crows whose names were used in the Renaissance for people who talked excessively. All of those meanings are now obsolete probably because of the increasing scale and technological advances in England and America.[15] There is obviously a metaphorical aspect to all this talk of talking birds, but there is also material fact here. These birds have voices: some which sound like human voices, and some of them can be trained to speak like humans. In the twentieth century, the fact that jackdaws could imitate human speech was news to most people, but the imitative capacities of all of these birds was common knowledge in the Renaissance. These very evident and present facts of human life with birds in Shakespeare's time caused people to think of people's voices in terms of avian voices.

Shakespeare's plays refer to keeping singing birds and training talking birds, and the plays also are alive with all sorts of avian voices, individual to their various species. In the plays, owls sing, hoot, shriek, scream, and cry; jackdaws caw as well as speak words; wrens chirp; lapwings cry; ravens croak and chide; larks chant, sing, and sound shrill; geese cackle and hiss; and, of course, cocks crow. Characters easily understand the difference in bird voices, as we can see when Lafeu in *Alls Well That Ends Well* tells Bertram about Parolles, "I took this lark for a bunting" (2.5.5–6). Larks sing and buntings do not, at least according to human ears. Shakespeare knows that his audience would be well aware of this difference, attuned to specific avian voices. The upside-down world in *Macbeth* is not only legible in the upside-down hunting within the avian world, it is also audible in terms of birds. Before the old man tells his story about the owl killing the falcon, even before Duncan's murder is revealed, Lennox tells Macbeth that "the obscure bird / Clamoured the livelong night" (2.3.58–59). "The obscure bird" is an owl; owls were called "obscure" because they moved in darkness (*OED*). Here, an owl's very audible voice is used to signify trouble ahead. Owls' nocturnal life lets an owl be used to signify in advance *Julius Caesar's* upside-down world as well. The conspiracy against Caesar manifests in what Casca reports: "And yesterday the bird of night did sit / Even at noonday upon the marketplace, / Hooting and shrieking" (1.3.26–28). Again, the owl's voice signifies, here along with its untimely presence in the daytime and in the midst of people.

Owls' voices are mentioned often in Shakespeare, and people who speak frightening words are called owls; owls were evidently so familiar that their presence and behavior were commonly acknowledged. Richard III cries out against the bad news brought by his messengers: "Out on you, owls! Nothing but songs of death?" (4.4.421). Likewise, the French general in *1Henry VI* calls Talbot, "Thou ominous and fearful owl of death" (4.2.15). Oddly, the *OED* does not have a definition that covers these usages. In that dictionary's evidence of usage, owls can be used as figures for people active at night—the familiar term "night–owl"—and proverbially for drunken people. Shakespeare's history play usages, in contrast, call men owls because they are using their voices to advertently or inadvertently threaten the listener—their voices signify death, alluding to owls as massively successful predators. These play usages attest to the presence of avian voices, including owl voices, in Renaissance daily life.

It may be that the proverbial usages of the drunken owl that the dictionary records have to do with the lessening of audible avian presence as writers began to live in more and more urbanized settings.[16] Owls were unlikely to be seen as drunken or silly in a world in which their voices and hunting abilities were prominent, but their large eyes and odd bodies could imply drunkenness to those who did not see them as predators. Those particular prover-bial usages appear from the dictionary's evidence to be widespread from the middle of the eighteenth century on. Tellingly, under the definition that contains those usages, the only evidence from before 1764 is a reference to people being as "malicious" as owls, not to people being drunken. The actual behavior of owls would lead them to be characterized as mali-cious rather than drunken. In *Macbeth*, Lady Macduff complains to Ross about her husband having left his family. She says, "He wants the natural touch, for the poor wren / The most diminutive of birds will fight, / Her young ones in her nest, against the owl" (4.2.9–11). That owls, along with hunting mice, attacked nests and killed smaller birds, like wrens, was common knowledge in the Renaissance, and owls were apparently commonly heard.

Along with the commonness of avian voice, the belief in the beauty of bird song, the specificity of bird voices, and the ubiquitous usages of bird voices to characterize people's voices, people in Shakespeare's plays, from kings to lovers to fairies to clowns, tell time in relation to bird voice. Famously, the lark and nightingale signify dreaded daylight and beloved night in *Romeo and Juliet*—the nightingale is still a perennially figurative reference for the beauty of night song. Other references to time-related avian voices are perhaps more indicative of the actual ways people used bird voice to tell time in the Renaissance and be-fore. The lark's voice may have been functional as well as figurative. In *A Midsummer Night's Dream*, Robin alerts Oberon to the day's progress by saying, "Fairy King, attend and mark. / I do hear the morning lark" (4.1.90–91). The multiple references to cocks crowing in the plays seem clearly to refer to the place of time-marking birds in mortal circles. An offhanded reference in *Richard III* seems telling. Ratcliffe informs the king that his nobles have walked around his army "cheering" his troops "much about cock-shut time" (5.5.23). This way of referring to twilight—as cock-shut time—is now obsolete, but may have been in wide usage in the Renaissance. In the same scene, Richard asks Norfolk to "stir with the lark tomor-row," and Ratcliffe later informs Richard that "The early village cock / Hath twice done salutation to the morn" (5.5.10, 163–64). Shakespeare's characters also use the terms "first cock" and "second cock" to denote midnight and very early morning.[17]

Telling time by means of birds is only one way that birds were integral to human daily life in the Renaissance. People slept on goose feathers as well as wrote with them. Some people could afford to keep birds in the house for music; but many people, maybe most, kept birds in the yard for eggs, food, and feathers. Thus, people were quite familiar with defenseless birds living daily among them. Birds and avian-related activities were figures for familial love perhaps because of their presence so close to homes and also because nests are such natural signifiers for closeness and family care. Macduff's anguished cry, "Oh hell-kite! All? / What, all my pretty chickens and their dam / At one fell swoop?", is an indication of how thor-oughly various birds could signify in human relations (4.3.217–19). Macduff calls Macbeth a kite from hell, a carrion bird who has swooped in to hunt defenseless people. The hell-kite's prey, Macduff's defenseless children and wife, are figured as chickens. This anguished cry is related to Prospero's calling Ariel "chick" as he lovingly also calls him "My Ariel" and bids him farewell (*The Tempest* 5.1.318). Macduff's cry is also related to Petruchio's desire that Kate will consent to be his "hen" (*Taming* 2.1.225) and Volumnia's calling herself a "poor hen" who has "clucked" her son Coriolanus to the wars and back (5.3.163–64). These are very different characters with their own disparate agendas. We may understand Petruchio as attempting to dominate rather than love, and Volumnia as manipulative rather than loving, but Shakespeare gives all of these characters chicken-language to denote familial relations. Chickens figured intimate familial relations because they were in intimate familial relations with people. They were a way for people to think about intimacy.

Other small prey birds also signified vulnerability, lovers, and the hunt for love. Trapping small prey birds by means of nets and lime, a sticky paste, seems to have been a common practice. We see lime referenced often in Shakespeare. This realm of reference is visible in a series of avian references from *Much Ado About Nothing*. In that play, Claudio, in love and jealous, is called a "poor hurt fowl" (2.1.181). When he and the other men want to trap Benedick into admitting his love for Beatrice they, likewise, picture him as a prey bird. "Stalk on, stalk on," Claudio says to the men about trapping Benedick, "the fowl sits" (*Much Ado about Nothing* 2.3.84). In a similar figuration, when Hero and Ursula have succeeded in trapping Beatrice, Ursula tells Hero, "She's limed, I warrant you. We have caught her, madam" (3.1.103–4). Beatrice, here, is vulnerable prey bird in a sticky trap. Fooling her, however, involves figuring her as a bird who preys rather than one who is preyed upon. Aiming to be overheard, Hero calls her an untrainable "wild" hawk (3.1.35–36). Beatrice overhears that comment while being, unknowingly, trapped like a prey bird. She responds, after the others have left the stage, by vowing to "tame" her "wild heart" to Benedick's "loving hand" (3.1.112). Beatrice would like to see herself as a falcon, the intimate companion of an elite hunting man (or woman), but as the object of their schemes, she is more like a small preyed-upon bird caught by lime or a net.[18] One poignant invocation of a beloved as a small hunted bird comes from an unlikely source: Pandarus, in *Troilus and Cressida*. He says of Cressida, "she fetches her breath so short as a new-ta[k]en sparrow" (3.2.31–32). Although Pandarus is, as his name suggests, a crass man, Shakespeare gives him words that evoke the breathlessness of anticipatory lovers and, in concert, what must have been familiar—the panic of a small trapped bird.

One thing I hope that this chapter has made clear is how utterly differentiated the avian world in Shakespeare is. It seems almost silly to be writing one chapter about avian Shakespeare for a collection which has separate chapters on horses, dogs, and bears. In the Renaissance, bird was a category like beast, consisting of many differentiated beings such as horses, dogs, and bears; bird was not a category like horse or bear, which were categories more like songbirds, seabirds, or carrion birds. Bird signified creatures that the Renaissance world saw as deeply separate from one another, more separate than kinds of dogs were from one another. The Renaissance differentiated dogs of course. A hound was not like a spaniel or a cur. However, birds were widely understood as a much larger category than dogs, who were types of beasts. After all, some dogs do not customarily eat other dogs, the way hawks customarily eat smaller kinds of birds. Some birds were, therefore, incommensurably different from one another. In the second scene of *Macbeth*, Duncan asks the captain reporting on the battle between his thanes, Banquo and Macbeth, and the Norwegians whether the former were afraid of the latter. The Captain replies, "Yes, as sparrows eagles or the hare the lion" (1.2.35). The Captain is using two very different birds and two very different beasts to talk about how little the Norwegian assault confounded Duncan's thanes. Sparrows don't scare eagles, and rabbits don't scare lions. The reverse is also true for both pairs: sparrows are afraid of eagles, and rabbits would be afraid of lions. Treating birds as a category like dogs is perhaps accurate in terms of our world's divisions where we may attend very carefully to differences between dogs and may not know or think as much about differences between birds, but it does not reflect the Shakespeare's nature-culture.

In that nature-culture, some birds, like falcons, were allied with people, some made more beautiful music than others (and most people); some birds were terrifying, some ate human bodies, some were food for people and enabled people to sleep in comfort. They were not one kind of being. When Petruchio rhetorically asks Kate in *The Taming of the Shrew*, "What, is the jay more precious than the lark / Because his feathers are more beautiful?" Shakespeare knows that his audience knows what jays and larks look like and what both kinds of birds sound like. This is much less common knowledge today. But Shakespeare was not an ornithologist or a bird watcher. He was an ordinary human who lived like the humans around him, in a world co-created with many different birds. The obsolescence of so many words and terms that connected people to birds shows how much the world has changed, but it should not lead us to think that only specific humans in the Renaissance lived in the shared creaturely world Shakespeare lived in, a world that valued, noticed, and thought through birds.

Notes

1 See Rebecca Ann Bach, *Birds and Other Creatures in Renaissance Literature: Shakespeare, Descartes, and Animal Studies* (New York: Routledge, 2018). For "nature-culture" see 62.
2 I use the word "understood" here deliberately. Donna Haraway suggests that "any relationship of seriousness including parenting, loving, political work, labour, would have to involve having to face these issues of unequal skill and unequal power and unequal everything" (Donna Haraway, "Conversations with Donna Haraway," in *Donna Haraway: Live Theory*, ed. Joseph Schneider [London: Continuum, 2005], 114–56, 152). Haraway has to say this in our world precisely because the inequality and hierarchy in everyday life is so easily denied in our context. Shakespeare's Renaissance world was structured in a way that made that kind of denial impossible.
3 See Bach, *Birds and Other Creatures in Renaissance Literature*, 14.
4 See "buzzard, n.2," OED Online, March 2019. Oxford University Press. www.oed.com/view/Entry/25500?rskey=ROrz53&result=1&isAdvanced=false (accessed April 04, 2019) and "kite, n.2," OED Online, March 2019. Oxford University Press. www.oed.com/view/Entry/103752?rskey=-3gIz8f&result=1&isAdvanced=false (accessed April 04, 2019).
5 It is easy to forget this because birds do not have human language, and we customarily do not attend to creatures in plays that do not speak as humans speak. For one fascinating approach to this issue, see Bruce Thomas Boehrer, *Animal Characters: Nonhuman Beings in Early Modern Literature* (Philadelphia: University of Pennsylvania Press, 2010).
6 Laurie Shannon, *The Accomodated Animal: Cosmopolity in Shakespearean Locales* (Chicago: University of Chicago Press, 2013), especially Chapter 2.
7 See Bach, *Birds and Other Creatures in Renaissance Literature*, 80.
8 See also the horrifying simile in *Titus Andronicus* where Marcus compares Lavinia's excised tongue to "a sweet melodious bird," singing "sweet varied notes," that has been "torn" form her mouth, which he figures as a "pretty hollow cage" (3.1.85–87).
9 William Shakespeare, *Shakes-Speares Sonnets* (London, 1609), E4.
10 See Bach, *Birds and Other Creatures in Renaissance Literature*, 43–50. See also Erica Fudge, "Renaissance Animal Things," *New Formations* 76 (2012): 86–100.
11 For much more detail on feathers and voice, see Bach, *Birds and Other Creatures in Renaissance Literature*, 43–50.
12 See Bach, *Birds and Other Creatures in Renaissance Literature*, 124 and 139–40n. 21.
13 For one rich Shakespearean treatment of parrot language, see *Much Ado about Nothing* 1.1.113–14. See also Bruce Thomas Boehrer, *Parrot Culture* (Philadelphia: University of Pennsylvania Press, 2004).
14 See William Shakespeare, *Macbeth*, ed. Kenneth Muir (London: Methuen, 1984), 97.
15 See Bruno Latour, *Pandora's Hope: Essays on the Reality of Science Studies* (Cambridge, MA: Harvard University Press, 1999), 197.
16 The *OED* has an obsolete term "owl-flight" that seems to have the same implication. The terms meant "twilight (this being the time when owls can be seen flying)." The dictionary cites three usages, the last by Skelton in 1529.
17 The first is Edgar in *King Lear* (3.4.105); the second is the Porter in *Macbeth* (2.3.20). See also Bach, *Birds and Other Creatures in Renaissance Literature*, 12.
18 See also the conversation between Lady Macduff and her son: 4.2.31–36. That conversation about how small birds are trapped begins with her son referring to Matthew 6.26. On the spiritual significance of birds in Renaissance literature, see Bach, *Birds and Other Creatures in Renaissance Literature*, 56–65.

2
SHAKESPEARE'S FISHPONDS
Matter, Metaphor, and Market

Dan Brayton

Early modern Britons inhabited an archipelago abundant with freshwater and saltwater organisms. In every part of an island where no inhabitant lived more than 70 miles from the coast (a mere 45 from a tidal estuary), human lives were sustained by aquatic life.[1] English palates, accustomed for millennia to eating salmon, trout, and eel caught in rivers, streams, ponds, and marches, fueled an international market in saltwater species preserved by brining, salting, and smoking (or any combination thereof), which abounded at fairs, street corners, markets, and places of entertainment. Highly developed fisheries and fish markets created a cultural intimacy with diverse aquatic species; by Shakespeare's lifetime, table fish were common food items rich with cultural associations.[2] In an epistemic culture given to comparing the characteristics of humans with those of beasts and creatures of all kinds, fish held unique symbolic significance as well as betokening a particular set of material effects.[3] As in classical Greece and Rome, the larger, more expensive species of fish (tuna, sturgeon, turbot) were only available to the wealthy, while smaller, cheaper species (herring, sardines) were associated with commoners, but also with the excessive appetites of what the Greeks had termed the *opsophagos*—fish eaters—throughout the class hierarchy. In what follows I offer a brief tour of the cultural zone that lay between theater and the early modern fish market, with a particular focus on the Shakespeare corpus. My excavation of the entangled cultural and environmental history of Shakespeare's fishy metaphors connects the affective dimensions—humor, anxiety, abjection—of the Elizabethan cultural intimacy between human and aquatic lives to a terraqueous environmental history linking the Stews of Southwark to fish markets old and new.[4] By examining fishy tropes through an ecocritical lens we can begin to excavate the rich field of meaning associated with fish, fish markets, and fishponds that defined early modern London's theater districts.

I Serving the Big Fish

The religious symbology of fish ran deep in early modern European culture, so much so that consuming fish was not so much a culinary choice as an act of devotion. A religious tradition associating Christ and the Apostles with fishing and the mortification of the flesh with eating fish drove the enormous growth of medieval European fisheries. As early as the third-century CE the Roman Tertullian wrote, in his treatise on baptism, *De Baptismo*, "[w]e being little fishes, as Jesus Christ is our great fish, begin our life in the water and only when we abide in the water are we safe and sound," establishing a durable figurative link.[5] Even those who could not afford to eat large species of fish, which were rarer and more expensive than smaller ones, could partake of The Big Fish and, during periods of prescribed "fasting," of the preserved flesh of actual aquatic life forms brought to table by fishers from many European nations. The Christian calendar set aside more than half the days of the year for fasting, during which times warm flesh (red meat and poultry) was proscribed but cold flesh (marine life, including marine animals caught in the water) was not. Medieval monasteries had generated a market of hungry monks for whom cold flesh was daily fare. As these institutions grew in size and number the demand for fish did as well, and the religious proscription on consuming warm flesh on Fridays, Lent, and other periods of fasting spurred the development of an international fish trade.[6] This commerce made a variety of fish species available to growing urban populations. By the fifteenth century, a diversified international fish industry had been growing for at least five centuries as fishing fleets pushed ever farther into the North Sea and the Atlantic in order to feed a growing London population. The Henrician dissolution of the monasteries did little to impede growth of fish markets, and with the pioneering of new technologies of preservation and transatlantic fishing grounds the fish market became a truly international industry.[7]

The most important seafood product in early modern Europe was herring. Herring preserved via a multitude of cures, salted, smoked, pickled in brine, or some combination of the three (occasionally even sweetened) became a staple food throughout northern and northwestern Europe by the late Middle Ages; by the early modern period it was a staple food for Britons of all stripes, familiar by odor as well as appearance.[8] In the north, the great fair at Scarborough had grown from a seasonal herring market to a semi-permanent fixture stocked with sundry wares, while southeastward the booming fishing ports of East Anglia, especially Great Yarmouth and Lowestoft, landed massive quantities of herring, much of it then transshipped to London. To the south packhorses from Rye, on the south coast of England, transported a continual supply of fish to Canterbury and London.[9] To the southwest, in Dorset, Devon, and Cornwall, an expanding fishery provided pilchards (*Sardina pilchardus*) to local tables as well as to expanding markets in France and the Mediterranean, while gleaners and rakers gathered mollusks, such as cockles and oysters, in the Thames Estuary for the London fishmongers.[10] Throughout the sixteenth century a massive Dutch fishing fleet competed with English fishers supplying herring from the North Sea offshore fishing grounds to vendors throughout England (and in the case of the Dutch throughout Europe). As fishing technology, from drift nets and trawls to ever-larger vessels for catching and carrying, developed apace, so too did methods of distribution. Sixteenth-century London was a commercial fishing epicenter, packed with English doggers, Dutch herring busses and *schuyts* (some carrying live eels in wet storage wells), and Hanse cogs unlading their scaly cargoes on the north bank of the Thames. Shakespeare's London was, thus, a city steeped in the aroma of fish emanating from the estuarine commercial conduit of the Thames, along the various maritime commercial enterprises located along its banks, and in the streets, public houses, and theaters.

From the herring hawked at holiday fairs to the stockfish and Poor John landed at Billingsgate, aquatic life forms were an omnipresent feature of everyday life throughout the City of London. By the early sixteenth century, notes Julie Sanders,

> [n]ot only was the river a focal point in terms of activity—trade and transportation were hugely dependent on it—and a major sight on anyone's journey through London, but the sonic, olfactory, and haptic, as well as optic, experience of it would have struck the imagination forcefully.[11]

A glance at any Elizabethan London cityscape, whether by John Norden, Franz Hogenberg, Claes Visscher, or Wenceslaus Hollar, reveals the diversity of international and domestic shipping traffic on the Thames, much of it associated with fisheries.[12] Upstream of London Bridge hay barges made way for royal barges, livery boats, and the wherries (water taxis) of the London watermen; downstream, cargo and fishing craft, abounded, many of them connected, in one way or another, with the herring trade. Anyone crossing London Bridge to see a play would have recognized the trappings of the fish market by the smell and taste of its products to the visual signs of its commercial preeminence. By Shakespeare's day The Worshipful Company of Fishmongers was one of the most powerful guilds in London, older and more influential than the Worshipful Company of Stationers, boasting a coat of arms that featured an escutcheon with three crowned dolphins on a blue field flanked by two sets of crossed herrings (also wearing crowns). Surmounting all were three sets of crossed keys—the keys to the City of London.[13]

The Lenten appetites of medieval and early modern Britons could not be sated by saltwater fish species alone. The English also fed lustily upon freshwater species, particularly the European eel (*Anguilla anguilla*), Atlantic salmon (*Salmo salar*), and the Brown trout (*Salmo trutta*) for millennia before the development of offshore fishing, and continued to do so as saltwater fisheries grew.[14] These species provided protein to many and inspiration to some, from poets penning piscatory eclogues to angling aficionados, such as Dame Juliana Berners and Isaac Walton, whose treatises bear witness to the recreational value of fishing as well as to its spiritual and nutritional aspects. Anadromous species, such as salmon and trout, begin life in freshwater tributaries, often far inland, then spend the majority of their lives at sea, eventually spawning and dying in the streams where they hatched, were an ancient food source throughout Western Europe.[15] Inversely, catadromous species, such as eels, originate and eventually spawn in the open sea, yet they inhabit freshwater streams, creeks, rivers, and swamps for the majority of their lives.[16] Because of their ready availability for local fishers with limited access to capital (and hence to the abundant offshore fishing grounds), these migratory species remained important food staples for early moderns, becoming emblematic of the human traits of those who consumed them. Inevitably, these species took on a different symbolic valence than did the massively abundant saltwater species, herring and cod.

II Theater of Fish

In the context of Renaissance culture the significance of fishes took on new dimensions as artists, from Pieter Bruegel the Elder to Giuseppe Arcimboldo, depicted human and marine life in allegorical parallelism, the proverbial predation of fishes metonymically and metaphorically linked to the Eucharist.[17] Painters, particularly those belonging to nations with the highest fish consumption per capita (Dutch, Flemish, and Spanish), frequently depicted Christ the Fisher King at the Last Supper and the Miracle of the Loaves and Fishes surrounded by baskets and plates of baitfish such as herring, sardines, and anchovies. Writers of emblem literature peddled *sententiae* linking human traits with various qualities associated with fish (such as universal predation). Because of its cultural ubiquity and sensory familiarity, fish became prime fodder, by the end of the sixteenth century, for comedy as well as spiritual allegory. Indeed, so familiar was the imperfectly preserved flesh of the Atlantic Herring (*Clupea harengus*) and related *clupeidae* (baitfish to fishermen, forage fish to ecologists) to European theatergoers that it spawned a stock comedic character, a buffoon known in German as *Pickelhering* (*Pekelharing* in Dutch), whose took the stage, in various guises, on both sides of the North Sea.[18] But herring was not the only funny kind of fish. The flesh of the Atlantic Cod (*Gadus morhua*) was also the stuff of comedy. Shakespeare's audiences also laughed at the antics of a comedic actor who gave himself the nickname "Stockfish," the waterman John Taylor, who ferried customers across the Thames in his wherry, rowed a paper boat with stockfish oar blades tied to shafts of cane.[19] "Stockfish" (Dutch *stikvis*) was the term for the air-dried flesh of the Atlantic Cod (*G. morhua*), a method of preservation developed by the Vikings and later adopted by Dutch and then English fishers at a time when cod products competed for market dominance with pickled herring. Both species were commodities of everyday life in the Elizabethan world, as attested by the abundance of recipes for popular dishes based on both fishes in English (and western European) cuisine.[20]

At the London playing houses, the flesh of sundry sea creatures, like human flesh, was both a figurative and a material presence up for sale. Scholars at the Museum of London Archaeology have uncovered substantial evidence of seafood consumption at the open-air theaters; thus, "Tudor theatergoers snacked on seafood while enjoying plays by Shakespeare and Christopher Marlowe, according to new evidence unearthed at two theaters in London." Bivalves and crustaceans formed the bulk of concessions at the playing houses. As archaeologist Julian Bowsher observes, "food remains and seeds indicate that the preferred snacks were oysters, crabs, mussels, periwinkles and cockles."[21] This research sheds lights on the sociology of early modern snacking at places of entertainment, for

> remains found underneath the gallery seating suggested that the wealthier classes munched on crabs and sturgeon, as well as peaches and dried figs. Meanwhile, oyster shells were found scattered all over the yard area, where commoners stood. . . .[22]

So was pickled herring, general eaten in a cure that turned the flesh a bright shade of red. Players delivered their lines above the aromas of aquatic species in various states of corruption. Some of these seafood products, especially pickled herring, were associated with Dutch or Flemish hawkers, particularly in Southwark, where immigrants from the Netherlands were also frequently associated with houses of ill repute. This was also the case in Great Yarmouth, England's premier fishing port at the time, where fisherfolk of Netherlandish extraction worked in high numbers in both kinds of flesh market. Thomas Nashe exploits this nexus of market and cultural associations to full advantage in *Lenten Stuffe*.[23]

For Shakespeare and his audiences, fish were an uncanny ontological mirror of the human, and the language of fish as food, commodity often animates dialogue characterized by misogyny, vulgarity, and dark humor, nowhere more so than in passages that employ fish markets and fishponds as metaphors for the corruption of the flesh. Shakespeare exploits the cultural connection between pickled herring and comedy at several points in *Twelfth Night*, a play whose title gestures to a holiday season of feasting, fasting, and other entertainments, including theater, that were anathema to Puritans. Early in the play the gluttonous knight Sir Toby Belch, "half-drunk," curses "A plague o'this pickle-herring" after emitting a belch (1.5.112, 117). An *opsophagos*—which is to say gluttonous and lecherous—reveler of gentle status given to overindulging himself Sir Toby is marked as a comedic personification of theater itself. In a later act the clever Maria calls the unpopular Puritan Malvolio a trout: "Lie thou there," she instructs her co-conspirators Sir Toby, Sir Andrew, and Fabian, "for here comes the trout that must be caught with tickling" (2.5.19). This comparison is no accident, for trout are native to cold, clear, well-oxygenated waters; it is no stretch to connect the species need for clean water with a human desire for purity. Although Malvolio is Sir Toby's antithesis, there is something fishy about the former as well. Malvolio's aloofness and inflated sense of self-regard render him unwary and gullible, like a trout idling near a riverbank, and vulnerable to a form of capture requiring stealth and subterfuge. Given Shakespeare's attentiveness to the political ecology of aquatic organisms, it is no accident that he likens the Puritan Malvolio to a species of fish that only thrives in cold, clean aquatic habitats, while Sir Toby is linked to pickled herring, which was commonly associated with the alehouse and street culture as well as with theater (indeed, Sir Toby is a version of *Pickelhering*). So, too, with his sidekick Maria. Bold, brash, and native to the taphouse, Maria resembles a fishwife throughout the play. Inevitably, she is in league with Sir Toby, whose appetites and favorite haunts link him to cheaper, more commonplace (and more suspect) species of fish. With the assistance of Feste, another metatheatrical character who tropes on fish, Maria concocts the play-within-a-play that eventually catches and fillets Malvolio by revealing his corruption and hypocrisy.

Later in *Twelfth Night*, when Lady Olivia's fool Feste tells the disguised Viola (herself lately landed from a sea voyage), "fools are as like husbands as pilchards are to herrings: the husband's the bigger," he plays with a symbolically complex set of material, metaphorical, and symbolic associations between human and piscatory life (3.1.27–31). Any Bankside audience would have been familiar with both species, herring and pilchard, which school in immense numbers in the waters surrounding the British Isles; by Shakespeare's day both had become ubiquitous staple foods in England. What is more, the playwright could safely expect his audiences to know that these two species of *clupeiformes* are nearly indistinguishable; the herring is a close cousin to the pilchard (known on the European continent as the sardine) and, once cured, resembled it even more.[24] A mature herring ranges in length from approximately a foot to 18 inches, a grown pilchard approximately 6; both shrunk considerably from the desiccating effects of salting during preservation. Torpedo-shaped, "fusiform" animals, stiff from being dried, with small heads and mouths, both herring and pilchard had a distinctively phallic appearance in their food form. The near twinning of the two species gives Feste's banter a mordant tone, as well as a distinct sexual undertone. When he goes on to claim, "I am not the lady's fool, but her corrupter of words," Feste develops his metaphor in an olfactory direction, suggesting that he can turn words as rapidly as fish goes off on a warm day. No amount salting, smoking, or pickling, which merely slowed the rate of decay, could not stop the herring's oily flesh from turning. Because nothing could cloak their smell effectively for long, both species were associated with nourishment and rankness alike and experienced in terms of a mixture of abjection and desire.[25]

Like all flesh, but more quickly than most, fish turns rank no matter what efforts are made to preserve it. Few smells can equal the power of not-entirely-fresh fish to attract and to repel. The aroma has a polarizing effect on human noses: if it smells fishy, most of us won't eat it, yet open a can of tuna and within seconds the cat comes begging. Even a week-old tuna sandwich is a choice morsel for today's domestic pets, yet not for us. In another era—a time of relative protein scarcity—as it would have been. Our nasal delicacy is a luxury derived from modern methods of preservation—refrigeration, flash freezing, and next-day-air shipping—yet in a world where high-protein food staples were hard to come by, especially for the poor, few early modern English consumers could afford to turn up the nose at cheap protein, no matter how rank. If the olfactory sense is the most intimate of the five, then references to fish in Tudor and Stuart drama gesture to an intimate history. The olfactory volatility of fishy flesh offered early modern English writers a host of metaphorical possibilities having to do with mortality, appetite, sexuality, and the transience of all flesh.

In Feste's comparison of human males to phallic baitfish we encounter a somewhat rank version of what Holly Dugan has called "an olfactory performance of self," a performance, which, Dugan argues, the playing companies exploited by connecting theaters, such as The

Rose, with specific olfactory experiences mapped onto the stage.[26] Shakespeare's fish tropes are an olfactory performance of the self's transient materiality. "Smell," argues Dugan, "can provide fascinating insights into the relationship between material objects, the body, and embodiment." For Shakespeare, the smell of fish evoked connections between these objects that held equal power to fascinate and repel. For Feste the self is a mixture of rank flesh and dissimulating artifice, and human bodies are forever subject to physical comeuppances that remind one of our own proximity to the nonhuman. Shakespeare frequently exploits this notion of the constitutional corruption of words and flesh. We can locate a figurative nexus of rank matter in the strikingly intimate references to the smell of fish in various parts of the Shakespeare corpus, tokens of the early modern cultural preoccupation with what Jane Bennet has termed "the political ecology of things."[27] As Bennett argues, human lives are coextensive with nonhuman lives to an extent that has been largely repressed in Western epistemology, yet in Shakespeare's fishy tropes we discover a sustained rhetorical exploration of a fishy interspecies thingishness that has been lying under readers' noses all along—and would have been a feature of the London theater for all audiences.

Strong smells, no matter how transitory, have an immediacy that evades our best defenses, evoking memory immediately than sights or sounds; some can even destabilize our sense of ourselves as rational beings. The current boom in object-oriented ontology opens new possibilities for thinking about the cultural poetics and environmental history of smell. As Erika Fudge has recently argued,

> stable identity is shattered by odor . . . . 'I think, therefore I am,' it seems, is challenged by 'I smell, therefore I must be something else. . . In these instances. . . the self can undo itself. . . the will is recalcitrant. . . human beings themselves are things.[28]

These are powerful claims and, in my view, a sharp salvo in the ongoing siege on the citadel of the humanist subject and its castellated wall, the *cogito*, to which animal studies has so brilliantly contributed in recent years. Fudge argues that the appropriation of animal scents to mask, cover, or disguise the aromas of the human animal betrays us as beasts that continually prey on other beasts and yet persist in denying our own beastliness. The embodied human is, thus, constituted as a physically hybrid entity, never entirely at one with itself. *Twelfth Night* is a comedy marked by mourning and a melancholia born of anxieties about the duplicability of selves in a world of disguise, misrepresentation, sexuality, and death. Shakespeare exploits and explores the heteronomy of selves in his fishy tropes, particularly those that invoke fishponds, often in distinctly metatheatrical fashion. Maria and Feste are not his only characters who associate the turning of words with fish and corrupting flesh in order to interrogate the fixity of social identity and the body. Elsewhere in the Shakespeare corpus, the odoriferous decay associated with the partially preserved flesh of edible fish species serves as a tangled memento of the impermanence and corruptibility of the body, emblematic of sexuality, reproduction, aging, and death.

III Staging the Stews

A rather spectacular instance human fishiness occurs near the end of *All's Well That Ends Well*, when Lavatch and Paroles argue about the materiality of metaphor in an exchange that tropes on Paroles' having fallen into "Fortune's displeasure." "Prithee allow the wind," Lavatch entreats Paroles, implying that the latter stinks, with the added suggestion that he is also a corrupter of words. Paroles protests, "Nay, you need not to stop your nose, sire. I spake but by a metaphor." Can a metaphor stink? Lavatch persists, asserting, "if your metaphor stink I will stop my nose" (5.2.6–11) and proceeds to trope on a chain of physical associations based on smell that builds into a crescendo of insults based on Parole's decayed condition. The theatrical wit here lies in the metatheatrical reminder of the characters' embodiment; Paroles' words may not actually reek, yet he cannot cloak himself entirely behind them. Lavatch reminds us that Paroles, notwithstanding his name, is an embodied presence on the stage, constituted by transient flesh. Like Malvolio, he is somewhat fishy character, but his particular brand of fishiness associates him with a different species and a different set of cultural practices. Whereas actual trout (as opposed to deluded puritans) thrive in cold, clean, moving water, Lavatch associates Paroles with freshwater species that thrive in slow-moving, silty waters—tench, pike, loach, dace, and above all carp—and fishponds. In doing so Lavatch gestures to a significant yet now obscure environmental history—the history of European pisciculture, which had an enormous impact on continental Europe as well as London and its environs; it is a history that lies beneath Shakespeare's humorous, yet biting, references to a handful of fish species associated with fishponds.

A contextually specific set of cultural associations linking fishponds to the impermanence and corruptibility of fish and flesh attaches to Act Five, scene two of *All's Well*. When Lafeu enters Lavatch carries on insulting Paroles by connecting the latter to fishponds and their proverbial association with stench.

> Here is a purr of Fortune's, sir, or of Fortune's cat—but not a musk-cat—that has fallen into the unclean fish-pond of her displeasure and, as he says, is muddied withal. Pray you, sir, *use the carp as you may*, for he looks like a poor, decayed, ingenious foolish, rascally knave. I do pity his distress in my similes of comfort, and leave him to your lordship.
>
> *(5.2.16–21; my italics)*

Here Lavatch calls Paroles a piece of shit ("pur" or purr denoted a piece of cat's dung), then a carp, likening him to the product of a proverbially filthy form of food production and the inevitable reek of eutrophication in artificially managed aquatic habitats.[29] For an inveterate punster such as Shakespeare the polysemy of the word "carp" offered great opportunity for scatological as well as sexual double-entendre. Derived from the Vulgar Latin *carpa*, from *carpere*, "to slander, revile, or find fault with (literally to pluck)," the term "carp" signified a form of speech as well as an actual species of fish.[30] Lavatch piles his metaphors high, some of which are obscure to the modern readers but would not have been to contemporary audiences. The scene provokes laughter by exposing the social pretensions of dissimulators such as Paroles by pointing to the (somewhat abject) material basis for theatrical selves (this is particularly evident in the civet-cat reference). By associating Monsieur Words with fishponds and their quintessential product, the carp (*Cyprinus carpio*), Lavatch reminds theater-goers of the odors of excrement-laden ponds and the flesh they produced.[31]

The humor in this scene derives in part from Lavatch's metatheatrical gesture to the surrounding landscape of Southwark, a suburb infamous for its stews, which denoted three distinct kinds of structure, along with a host of cultural practices. The first of these were fishponds kept as commercial ventures on the south bank of the Thames by entrepreneurs since at least the fourteenth century; the stews also referred to the bathhouses located in the same neighborhood; finally, the stews referred to the bordellos, which were also a long-standing feature of the human geography of Southwark. All three kinds of space were closely linked, in the popular imagination, through a metonymic slide connecting water, flesh, bodily appetites, the marketplace, and the entertainments available in the Liberty of Southwark. As Steven Mullaney established decades ago in his seminal study of Southwark's pungent reputation as a locale of questionable morality, this history made theater and prostitution closely linked institutions in the minds of Londoners, so much so that Puritans railed equally at both.[32] Social historian Ruth Mazo Karras notes,

> The suburb of London most connected with houses of prostitution was Southwark. There the bathhouses were so notorious that by the middle of the fourteenth century a whole neighborhood in the liberty of the bishop of Winchester came to be called 'Les Stuwes.'[33]

London municipal leaders periodically clamped down on prostitution, attempting (unsuccessfully) to contain it in Cock's Lane and Southwark, and, Karras notes, "in 1546 Henry VIII ordered all the bathhouses in Southwark, officially recognized or not, closed."[34] The rise of the open-air theaters shortly thereafter is suggestive; at the very least Southwark retained its cultural association with prostitution and the marketing of various kinds of flesh.

To invoke the stews, then, either directly, as Shakespeare does in *Troilus and Cressida*, or obliquely, as he does in *All's Well That Ends Well*, was to traffic in lascivious contextual innuendo. What has gone unremarked in literary scholarship, however, is the degree to which the market in spectacle, located within a stone's throw of the various wharves, markets, and fish storage facilities that lined the banks of the Thames, was redolent of fish. In a culture given to comparing people with fish, the close proximity of baths to fishponds offered myriad imaginative possibilities.[35]

Shakespeare consistently links aquaculture and the freshwater fish species grown in fishponds with sexuality, reproduction, death, and decay. This contextual network of associations derived from a linked cultural and environmental history even older than the Stews of Southwark, connecting Bankside entertainments with monasteries, abbeys, and brothels. For the rapid growth of monasteries in the medieval period caused a boom in pisciculture that transformed the physical geography and aquatic ecosystems of central and Europe parts of southern England, including London and its suburbs. As water-driven mills became increasingly numerous during the late Middle Ages, swift-flowing streams of all kinds were physically slowed by mill-races and other structures, such as dams and weirs, expanding habitat for fish species that thrive in relatively warm, slow-moving waters. Some species, such as tench and dace, throve in the increasingly hypoxic and turgid waters of southern England, where mills and dams abounded, outperforming other species, such as salmon and trout, that languish in oxygen-poor conditions. By the late medieval period, Fagan argues, "natural ecosystems could no longer provide enough fish to satisfy escalating demands. The only way to provide more fresh fish was to grow it, a type of farming made possible by the technology used to build water mills."[36] Beginning in the eighth century abbeys and monasteries relied upon aquaculture to feed their inmates, providing carp and a handful of other species for the tables of those with sufficient land and labor to maintain the great houses of the Second Estate.[37] As the demand for fish rose, fueled by religious culture, the practice of keeping fishponds became widespread, particularly in the Holy Roman Empire, where whole regions were dug up and ditched for carp production. By the fifteenth century fishponds were a major feature of the rural landscape in "a huge swath of Europe from the Loire to Poitou to central Poland" that "devoted itself to aquaculture." The scale of this enterprise "was staggering," Fagan notes, pointing out "there were 25,000 ponds in Bohemia and 40,000 hectares under ponds in central France. The greatest concentration of medieval aquaculture lay inland of the 150-kilometer distance that horses, carts, or boats could carry fresh sea fish."[38] By the late medieval period "natural ecosystems could no longer provide enough fish to satisfy escalating demands. The only way to provide more fresh fish was to grow it, a type of farming made possible by the technology used to build water mills."[39] The preeminent species of fish raised in private and monastic fishponds was the European carp, a subspecies of the common carp described as "a heavy-bodied form of minnow with barbells [whiskers] on either side of the upper jaw" native to the lower Danube.

The rich white flesh of the carp was highly valued for table food, rather than as a saleable commodity, at the abbeys and monasteries. In the *Boke of St. Albans* (1486), attributed to Dame Juliana Berners, the author notes that "the carpe is a deyntous fysshe: but there ben but fewe in Englonde and therefore I wryte the lasse of hym."[40] Following the Henrician dissolution of the monasteries just a few decades later, fishponds became associated with the houses of the nobility—houses often built by converting old monastic structures on former church lands to private estates. Indeed, fishponds remained a widespread feature of private estates a century later, as the Elizabethan chorographer William Harrison took pains to note. "There is almost no house," claimed Harrison,

> even of the meanest bowers, which have not one or mo ponds or holes, made for reservation of water, unstored with some of them, as with tench, carp, bream, roach, dace, eels, or suchlike as will live and breed together.[41]

The freshwater species Harrison lists as the products of aquiculture are all native to the slow-moving, turgid waters associated with the environmental transformation wrought in southern England. Fishponds could not compete, in terms of volume or profitability, with the immense herring and cod fisheries, yet they remained an important means of supplementing what the market supplied. English pisciculture left a noteworthy history in imaginative literature and in the form of Elizabethan husbandry tracts, such as those by John Taverner and the irrepressible Gervase Markham, who offered landowners detailed descriptions of how to build their own aquaculture works.[42]

These aquaculture husbandry manuals evince some anxiety about the stigma of Roman decadence attaching to fishponds, as a look at Taverner's pamphlet "Certaine experiments concerning fish and fruite" (1600) attests. "First it is requisite to speake of ponds," writes Taverner in the first chapter of his treatise on pisciculture:

> I meane such as be necessarie, profitable, and convenient to be used with us here in England, not such in which the prodigall Romans used to spend their superfluous wealth and treasure, rather for vaine ostentation, then any honest recreation of mind, or profite unto themselves, or the common wealth. . .[43]

Taverner's anxiety about Roman decadence notwithstanding, he considers fishponds a great source of provender. By the time Shakespeare, Taverner, and Markham were writing, freshwater fish were increasingly outcompeted by oceanic species, yet we find abundant references to fishponds and their products in plays and poems from the Tudor-Stuart period.

Ben Jonson mentions both carp and pike as emblems of nutritional abundance in his country-house panegyric, which constructs a vision of abundance by erasing the social antagonisms of Tudor property ownership and replacing them with a nostalgic vision of *copia* mapped onto the landscape. "And if the high-swollen Medway fail thy dish," the speaker asserts in "To Penshurst,

> Thou hast thy ponds, that pay thee tribute fish, / Fat aged carps that run into thy net, / And pikes, now weary their own kind to eat, / As loath the second draught or cast to stay, / Officiously at first themselves betray.

> *(ll.31–36)*

While poetic images of these iconic freshwater fish sacrificing themselves for the elite mask the social tensions produced by land enclosure and intensive food production, Jonson reminds us that farmed fish supplemented the supply of wild stocks at many a table long after the carp bubble burst. The mention of these two species is an oblique gesture to the monastic past of Penshurst and the late-medieval fishpond craze associated with the monasteries. English pisciculture peaked during the late fourteenth century, when the word "carp," in its noun and verb forms, entered the English language. Long before the publication of *The Forrest* England's waterways and estuaries were depleted enough to provide only a fraction of the food fish consumed in the kingdom. If it is true, as marine environmental historian Callum Roberts observes, that "an emerging crisis in freshwater fish supply is evident from the written record of the medieval period," then Jonson's descriptive strategy of idealization and erasure offers a nostalgic inversion of monastic privation as the very stuff of aristocratic *copia*.[44]

Whereas Jonson's self-betraying carp and pike are emblems of abundance, Shakespeare tropes on fish to interrogate the human. In part because of the rank smell of fishponds, and in part because pisciculture could be understood as a charnel-house mode of food production, causing anxiety about the many forms of corruption flesh is heir to. *The Winter's Tale*, for example, employs the language of pisciculture when the tyrant Leontes reacts violently to the ungrounded suspicion of having been cuckolded by his boyhood friend Polyxenes:

> LEONTES There have been,
> Or I am much deceived, cuckolds ere now;
> And many a man there is, even at this present,
> Now, while I speak this, holds his wife by the arm,
> That little thinks she has been sluiced in's absence
> And his pond fish'd by his next neighbour, by
> Sir Smile, his neighbour: nay, there's comfort in't
> Whiles other men have gates and those gates open'd,
> As mine, against their will.

> *(1.2.191–99)*

Here the specifics of fishpond construction and maintenance become the vehicle for a horrifying conceit: Hermione's body as Leontes' private lands and her genitals as his private fishpond. Leontes associates fishponds with corruption, stench, and the equivocal nature of owning bodies (human or piscatory) as property. Unlike the fishpond metaphor in *All's Well That Ends Well*, where "corruption" lies in the association between stagnant water and rankness, here the relationship between the body, private property, and sexuality forms the basis for the social abjection of a female character. Suspicion about the possibility of dissimulation drives Leontes to perceive the gap between the performance of self and the materiality of social roles in terms of universal corruption, an alterity he glimpses but cannot control. Whereas in *All's Well* Lavatch's carping divides Paroles the dissimulator from Paroles the embodied performer, in *The Winter's Tale* we watch as Leontes undergoes a tragic self-alienation caused by the onset of a sudden paranoia linking his own status as a husband to husbandry in ways he cannot fathom or police. A paranoia mediated by a metonymic series of associations with aquaculture leads Leontes' imagination into the gutter—or, more accurately, the stews. Carp, more than carping, is Leontes' undoing. Leontes suffers from a metatheatrical affliction, the moral and olfactory taint of the fish market that attached to the London playing houses.

Literary gestures to fish and fishponds and their products belong to a complex set of early modern cultural and material associations connecting food, the marketplace, land ownership, social identity, sexuality, and theater. Fish are never, for Shakespeare, merely food, and only rarely are they described in terms of ethology, as animals living in their native ecosystems. Rather, fish in Shakespeare are rhetorical figures for the political ecology of the marketplace in a world where human life and aquatic life forms were symbolically, economically, and nutritionally linked in a complex network of cultural associations. It is no wonder that Feste, Maria, and Lavatch, characters who trod the London stage in a period when fish markets, food products, metaphors, and the odors of turning fish saturated the socio-cultural fabric that made their symbolic meaning legible, employ fish metaphors that seem cryptic today. The witticisms of these comedic characters reveal a rich socio-cultural history of the fish market, which was itself closely linked to geographically proximate markets in plays and prostitution. At some level these characters, too, were the product of a generalized marketplace that spawned new forms of embodiment and expression in the entertainments consumed by a populace fed on the flesh of imperfectly preserved aquatic life forms.

Notes

1 Richard Haywood, "Notes and Queries: Which British Town Is Furthest from the Sea?" *The Guardian*, April 25, 2012.
2 Recent studies by archeologists Brian Fagan and Barry Cunliffe convey a sense of the vast scope of maritime culture in the British Isles. See Fagan, *Fish on Friday: Feasting, Fasting, and the Discovery of the New World* (New York: Basic Books, 2006), *Fishing: How the Sea Fed Civilization* (New Haven, CT: Yale University Press, 2017); and Cunliffe, *Europe between the Oceans: 9000 BC–AD 1000* (New Haven, CT: Yale University Press, 2011), and *Facing the Ocean: The Atlantic and Its Peoples, 1000 BC–AD 1500* (Oxford: Oxford University Press, 2001).
3 See James Davidson, *Courtesans and Fishcakes: The Consuming Passions of Classical Athens* (New York: St. Martin's Press, 1997).
4 Essential recent studies of fisheries history include W. Jeffrey Bolster, *The Mortal Sea* (Cambridge, MA: Harvard University Press, 2012); Callum Roberts, *The Unnatural History of the Sea* (Washington, DC: Island Press, 2007); Mike Smylie, *The Perilous Catch: A History of Commercial Fishing* (Stroud: History Press, 2015); and Mark Kurlansky's *Cod: A Biography of the Fish that Changed the World* (New York: Penguin, 1997).
5 Quoted in Fagan, *Fish on Friday*, 3. Tertullian goes on to develop the metaphor: "The kingdom of heaven is like unto a net, that cast into the sea, and gathered of every kind: Which when it was full, they drew to shore and gathered the good into vessels, but cast the bad away." Ibid., 4.
6 Dutch, Basque, English, Icelandic, and Hanseatic states all competed to supply growing European markets.
7 See Fagan's excellent discussion of the religious origins of trans-national European fisheries, in *Fish on Friday* (2006).
8 De Vries and van der Voude attribute the geographic and market expansion of the herring market to the development of the herring buss, "a veritable factory ship on which the herring were not only caught but processed on board," in the fifteenth century, along with innovations in preservation. Jan de Vries and Ad van der Voude, *The First Modern Economy: Success, Failure, and Perseverance of the Dutch Economy, 1500–1800* (New York: Cambridge University Press, 1997), 243.

9 Fagan, *Fish on Friday*, 143.

10 See my *Shakespeare's Ocean: An Ecocritical Exploration* (Charlottesville: University of Virginia Press, 2012), 140–41; see also Fagan, *Fish on Friday*, 197.

11 Julie Sanders, *The Cultural Geography of Early Modern Drama, 1620–1650* (New York: Cambridge University Press, 2011).

12 The names and identities of some of these artists bespeak a maritime history closely linked to the fish trade. Visscher, for example, was a native of Amsterdam, a city built, according to legend, on fishbones, and never set in London.

13 Fagan, *Fish on Friday*, 114.

14 Atlantic salmon has fed western European populations for tens of millennia, as Fagan discusses in his recent study, *Fishing: How the Sea Fed Civilization* (New Haven, CT: Yale University Press, 2017). Neanderthals fished for salmon in the rivers of southwestern France; Irish saints' legends attest to the importance of the species as food; even today, when wild Atlantic salmon stocks are vastly depleted, huge quantities are raised in pens along the coasts of Scotland, the Faeroes, Canada, and Maine.

15 Unlike the various species of Pacific Salmon (Sockeye, King, Coho, Pink) familiar to US consumers, Atlantic salmon are iteroparous: they do not always die after spawning and thus can spawn more than once.

16 Tom Fort, *The Book of Eels: On the Trail of the Thin-Heads* (London: Harper Collins, 2003).

17 See Brayton, *Shakespeare's Ocean*, especially Chapter 6, 136–65.

18 Debates over the cultural provenance of such characters is immaterial to my discussion; rather, what interests me here is the widespread currency of the type. See Willem Schrikx, "Pickle-herring and English Actors in Germany," *Shakespeare Survey* 36 (1983): 135–48.

19 Peter Ackroyd, *Thames: The Biography* (London: Chatto and Windus, 2007), 156.

20 Many of these, from diverse national traditions, can be found in Kurlansky, *Cod*.

21 Rosella Lorenzi, "Oysters and Crabs, the Popcorn of Shakespearean Theatergoers," *London Times*, 2010.

22 Julian Bowsher and Pat Miller, *The Rose and the Globe: Playhouses of Shakespeare's Bankside, Southwark: Excavations 1988–1991* (Museum of London Archeology, 2009).

23 "Foreigners," notes Karras,

> particularly from the Low Countries, were often accused of keeping brothels, perhaps in part because foreigners were generally distrusted, perhaps because foreign women had few other opportunities available to them, perhaps because there would have been a large foreign clientele for brothels as many foreign merchants in port towns would not have their families with them.

See Ruth Karras, "Regulation of Brothels in Later Medieval England," *Signs* 14, no. 2 (1989): 399–433, 415.

24 As I have argued in the monograph cited above, this experience often played in terms of gender and sexuality.

25 As Brian Fagan notes in his historical study of medieval and early modern European fisheries, *Fish on Friday: Feasting, Fasting, and the Discovery of the New World* (New York: Perseus, 2007).

26 Holly Dugan, *The Ephemeral History of Perfume: Scent and Sense in Early Modern England* (Baltimore, MD: the Johns Hopkins University Press, 2011).

27 See Jane Bennett, *Vibrant Matter: A Political Economy of Things* (Durham, NC and London: Duke University Press, 2010). While Bennett's focus is not on early modern notions of matter, recent studies have explored this topic with excellent results. See Karen Raber, *Animal Bodies, Renaissance Culture* (Philadelphia: University of Pennsylvania Press, 2013). For an excellent discussion of the early modern English culture of the commodity, see Henry Turner, "Nashe's Red Herring: Epistemologies of the Commodity in Lenten Stuffe (1599)," *ELH* 68, no. 3 (2001): 529–61.

28 Lee Landes and Youngquist, eds., *Gorgeous Beasts: Animal Bodies in Historical Perspective* (University Park: Pennsylvania State University Press, 2012), 52.

29 I.e. one that is over-fertilized. Eutrophication results from accumulation of nitrates and phosphates in a body of water, usually from run-off laden with manure or other kinds of fertilizer. Because they were laden with the excrement of fish and tended to be slow-moving, stagnant, and notoriously difficult to keep clean, fishponds are textbook instances of this phenomenon.

30 Complicating this derivation is the fact that in Old Norse and Gothic *karpa*—with a "k"—meant "to brag" (OED). Whatever its derivation, "to carp," in early modern English, meant to talk, censure, or cavil. See "carp, v.1," OED Online, March 2019. Oxford University Press. www.oed.com/view/Entry/28162?rskey=NcBJFL&result=3&isAdvanced=false (accessed April 09, 2019).

31 Pisciculture mortality rates are inevitably high, even today, when fish pens are managed with massive amounts of antibiotics, and their inhabitants especially vulnerable to disease in poorly drained waters.

32 Stephen Mullaney, *The Place of the Stage: License, Play, and Power in Elizabethan London* (Chicago, IL: University of Chicago Press, 1994). See also Joseph Lenz, "Base Trade: Theater as Prostitution," *ELH* 60, no. 4 (Winter, 1993): 833–55.

33 Karras, "The Regulation of Brothels."

34 This was not the first time the Southwark stews were shut down. In 1506 18 brothels were briefly closed; only 12 were reopened. Karras, "Regulation of Brothels," 410–11.

35 Christopher K. Currie notes that fishponds in Southwark developed as commercial ventures in towards the end of the fourteenth century. "This was formerly held to be an area inhabited by prostitutes," Currie points out, "but it would seem that the real origin of the name derives from the fishponds there in the 1360s, and possibly much earlier. "The Early History of Carp and Its Economic Significance in England," *The Agricultural History Review* 39, no. 2 (1991): 97–107.

36 Fagan, ibid., 130.

37 See Fagan, *Fishing*, 172–83. Although instructions for building and maintaining fishponds in Tudor-Stuart husbandry manuals suggest a growing interest in pisciculture their heyday in England had passed by the late fifteenth century. Also see Fagan, *Writing Archaeology*, 129–41.

38 Fagan, *Writing Archeology*, 139.

39 Ibid., 130.

40 Juliana Berners, *A Treatyse of Fysshynge Wyth an Angle* (1496), 27, quoted in Emma Phipson, *The Animal Lore of Shakespeare's Time Including Quadrupeds, Birds, Reptiles, Fish and Insects* (London, 1883), 59.

41 William Harrison, *The Description of England* (Ithaca, NY: Cornell University Press, 1968; Folger/Dover reprint 1994), 319.

42 Writings on aquaculture were popular with Elizabethan readers. Another such treatise, printed in 1599 by William White in an English translation, was *A New Booke of good Husbandry, very pleasant, and of great profite both for Gentlemen and Yomen: Conteining, The Order and maner of making of Fish-pondes, with the breeding, preserving, and multiplying of the Carpe, Tench, Pike, and Troute, and diverse kindes of other Fresh-fish.* This account was originally written in Latin by Bishop Janus Dubravius and published in Breslau in 1547. See Cora E. Lutz, "Bishop Dubravius on Fishponds," *The Yale University Library Gazette* 48, no. 1 (July, 1973): 12–16.

43 John Taverner, *Certaine Experiments Concerning Fish and Fruite: Practiced by John Teverner Gentleman, and by Him Published for the Benefit of Others* (London, 1600). STC (2nd ed.) / 23708. Henry E. Huntington Library and Art Gallery. Early English Books Online. STC/ 359:04. See also Gervase Markham, *Cheape and Good Husbandry. . . .* (London, 1634).

44 Rogers, *The Unnatural History of the Sea*, 24.

3

"I AM THE DOG"

Canine Abjection, Species Reversal, and Misanthropic Satire in *The Two Gentlemen of Verona**

Bryan Alkemeyer

Contemporary English considers the dog "man's best friend" yet retains a fourteenth-century usage of *dog* to disparage "a worthless or contemptible person."[1] The paradox was familiar to Sigmund Freud but not William Shakespeare. In *Civilization and Its Discontents* (1930), Freud noted that the dog is humanity's "most faithful friend in the animal world" while *dog* nevertheless serves "as a term of abuse." This otherwise "incomprehensible" contradiction arises because humans abhor certain animal characteristics undeniable in dogs but repressed "with man's adoption of an erect posture": unlike humans after "civilization," Freud explains, dogs show neither excremental disgust nor sexual shame.[2]

The universalizing psychoanalytic account folds under literary-historical scrutiny, for views of dogs changed dramatically between Shakespeare and Freud. As Keith Thomas argues, a medieval and early modern consensus held that dogs were "filthy scavengers," but they underwent "a steady rehabilitation" over the sixteenth through eighteenth centuries.[3] A decisive factor was "[t]he spread of pet-keeping among the urban middle classes."[4] Concurring, Laura Brown writes that pet-keeping motivated a "new conception of animal character, including an array of strongly positive assumptions about the intelligence, loyalty, affection, gratitude, and courage of the canine being that was rapidly becoming understood as 'man's best friend.'"[5]

That charismatic and signally loyal animal—still beyond the horizon for Shakespeare's contemporaries—supplanted an earlier being derided as sycophantic and abject.[6] As Shakespeare deploys the negative and not quite superseded construction, his numerous dog references are misconstrued without historical contextualization. Such contextualization is crucial for *The Two Gentlemen of Verona* (c. 1594–98), which features a dog onstage.[7] Indeed, a historicist and incipiently posthumanist reading of Lance's inverse human–dog relationship with Crab makes this much maligned play start to look less like a failed comedy (the common assessment) than a pointedly misanthropic satire.

Pursuing this reevaluation, I first analyze widespread English contempt for dogs as exemplified in John Caius's *Of Englishe Dogges* (1570) and Edward Topsell's *Historie of Foure-Footed*

---

* For comments and suggestions, I thank Katharine Mershon, Anne Duggan, Maria Teresa Micaela Prendergast, John Barnard, and the editors.

Beastes (1607). After treating their authoritative accounts of canine nature, I turn to Shakespeare. Many of his works use human–dog comparisons to disparage incommensurable categories of people: non-Christians, flatterers, desperate lovers. Paradoxically, Shakespeare also uses dogs to launch a universal attack on human dignity in works like *Timon of Athens* and *The Two Gentlemen of Verona*, which satirically swaps human and canine natures. While *The Two Gentlemen of Verona*'s Proteus concludes that human nature lacks only constancy, it is rather doglike fawning on indifferent or worse masters that most compromises human perfection. Showing how this play's characters become cynomorphic to varying degrees, I contribute to a growing consensus that finds Shakespeare profoundly skeptical about human exceptionalism and self-sufficiency. More broadly, the case of *The Two Gentlemen of Verona* illustrates how historicizing animals both proves indispensable for interpreting early literature and serves a posthumanism to which it is by no means opposed, even if it does not offer an obvious or easily executed program for future discoveries.

I Early Modern Dogs

Current in the sixteenth and seventeenth centuries, the proverb "love me, love my dog" has been cited as evidence that early moderns admire canine fidelity.[8] According to *The Oxford Dictionary of English Idioms*, the saying means, rather, "if you love someone, you must accept everything about them, even their faults."[9] A 1666 source corroborates *dog*'s negative valence: "To respect a dog for the Masters sake; the English say, love me, and love my dog."[10] An underlying assumption seems to be that it is difficult to like a dog—particularly someone else's. This contemptuous attitude finds corroboration in both Caius's encyclopedic treatise of dog breeds, published in Latin in 1570 and translated into English in 1576, and Topsell's natural history of quadrupeds, published in 1607. After treating them in turn, I account for some contrary evidence of admired canines, most notably Odysseus's Argus, who perhaps furnishes a prototype for the loyal dog. Readers should beware of misrecognizing certain early modern dogs as too exactly proleptic of later dog heroes, like the "quasi-angelic agents" of Victorian melodramas, who display "inexplicable but very real knowledge of the cosmic moral order."[11] For dogs to serve such roles, they first had to be reinvented as exemplary beings.

In *Of Englishe Dogges*, Caius finds contemptible behavior across varieties. A vivid anecdote recounts how a greyhound defected from Richard II to the future Henry IV: "The Dogge forsaking his former Lord & master came to Duke Henry, fawned upon him with such resemblaunces of goodwyll and conceaved affection, as he favoured King Richarde before: he followed the Duke, and utterly left the King." Caius relays the tale as evidence of canine "foreknowledge & understanding"—not loyalty, which Richard's dog spectacularly lacks.[12] Later, Caius explains that the "tumbler" captures its prey through "deceit and guile . . . , which pernicious properties supply the places of more commendable qualities."[13] As a final example, the treatise scorns spaniels as creatures

> sought for to satisfie the delicatenesse of daintie dames, and wanton womens wills, instrumentes of folly for them to play and dally withall, to tryfle away the treasure of time, to withdraw their mindes from more commendable exercises, and to content their corrupted concupiscences with vaine disport.[14]

Although anti-canine invective here gives way to misogyny, Caius's view that playing with dogs is a worthless activity starkly contrasts later periods' esteem.[15]

Widespread contempt for dogs is documented most comprehensively by Topsell. He refers readers to two biblical passages in which dogs represent the vile, unworthy, or reprobate: "Give not that which is holy unto the dogs, neither cast ye your pearles before swine: lest they trample them under their feete, and turne againe and rent you" (Matt. 7:6); "The dog is turned to his own vomit againe, and the sowe that was washed, to her wallowing in the mire" (2 Pet. 2:22).[16] On the biblical basis, Topsell declares dogs "emblems of vile, cursed, rayling, and filthy men."[17] He also seconds claims from Caius's dog treatise by reproducing Abraham Fleming's translation in its entirety.[18]

In Topsell's most definitive pronouncement on dogs, he writes,

> There is not any creature without reason, more loving to his Maister, nor more serviceable (as shall appear afterward) then is a Dogge, induring many stripes patiently at the hands of his maister, and using no other meanes to pacifie his displeasure, then humiliation, prostration, assentation, and after beating, turneth a revenge into a more fervent and whot love.[19]

Although the sentence's opening might seem to depict the affectionate and loyal dog, it takes a disturbing turn. Topsell marvels less at the dog's fidelity than at its absolute self-abasement—even in response to violent punishment. The assessment appears in an introductory section on

> the nature of Dogges in generall, wherein they agree, and their common properties of nature, such as are not destroyed in the destinction of kindes, but remaine like infallible and invariable truths in every kinde and country of the world.[20]

For Topsell as for many of his contemporaries, servile abjection defines canine nature.

Of course, the nature and meaning of dogs are not entirely uncontested in Topsell's culture. As early "exemplars of canine fidelity," Thomas acknowledges the heroic twelfth-century greyhound who became known as Saint Guinefort and the Elizabethan mastiff who rescued Sir Henry Lee.[21] Something quite like later admiration of dogs emerges when Caius praises the watchdog, who "forsaketh not his master, no not when he is starcke deade."[22] After various supporting anecdotes, Caius asks, "what servant to his master more loving? what companion more trustie?"[23] Topsell, too, rehearses some laudatory anecdotes but then observes, "All this notwitstanding [sic], many learned and wise men in al ages have rekconed [sic] a Dogge but a base and an impudent creature."[24] Though arresting, occasional passages praising dogs represent anomalies in a paradigm of canine denigration.

The most important literary canine to consider as a counterexample is Odysseus's long-suffering dog Argus, who represents an at least partial exception to the association of dogs with sycophants. A puppy when Odysseus departs for Troy, Argus waits 20 years for Odysseus's return—to die upon their reunion.[25] Recognizing Odysseus, Argus pricks up his ears, wags his tail, and—in George Chapman's translation—"fawn[s]" on his master.[26] Although this word proves to be one of Shakespeare's favorites for contemptuous self-abasement, Argus contrasts what Odysseus calls "those trencher-Beagles, tending Kings; / Whom for their pleasures, or their glories sake, / Or fashion; they into their favours take."[27] Praise for Argus distinguishes him not only from other dogs but also, metaphorically, from sycophantic and self-serving courtiers. The ironic, deflating effect achieved by elevating dog over human recurs frequently in Shakespeare, but it depends upon the dog's low reputation. Argus seems quite plausibly—even movingly—admirable and faithful, but as an exception, he confirms the point that dogs were generally reviled. In Alexander Pope's edition, Argus becomes not only a "faithful dog" but also *The Odyssey*'s "noblest figure."[28] This eighteenth-century assessment, however, would have baffled Chapman and his contemporaries.

II Shakespeare's Dog Invective

Shakespeare's works participate in the general pattern. Indeed, even a glance at the entry for *dog* in Marvin Spevack's *Concordance* reveals that Shakespeare frequently uses the word as an insult.[29] Marjorie Garber has suggested that Shakespeare's portraits of dogs vary considerably with breed or role.[30] More extensively, Ian MacInnes has shown that early modern England associated two characteristic breeds, mastiffs and spaniels, with masculinizing valor and feminizing obeisance, respectively.[31] While acknowledging the advantages of more finely grained analyses, I find that Shakespeare, like Caius and Topsell, denigrates dogs rather uniformly across types. An overview of Shakespeare's dog invective shows how it targets non-Christians, sycophants, overly persistent lovers, and human beings in general. An account of the broadly misanthropic use of dogs in *Timon of Athens* prepares the next section's reading of *The Two Gentlemen of Verona*.

Often, Shakespeare's dog comparisons express ethnic—especially religious—denigration. Of *Titus Andronicus*'s four instances of *dog*, all refer to Aaron, the so-called "barbarous Moor."[32] Aaron ultimately likens himself to the proverbial "black dog," unable to blush with shame (5.1.122). Similarly, all but one of *Merchant of Venice*'s instances of *dog* refer to Shylock, who rebukes Antonio, "Thou called'st me dog before thou hadst a cause, / But since I am a dog, beware my fangs" (3.3.6–7). *Othello* employs *dog* in more varied contexts; but a key instance occurs in Othello's final speech, when he recalls killing "a turbaned Turk" for crimes against Venice (5.2.363). Reenacting the execution upon himself, Othello no less than his erstwhile adversary becomes "the circumcisèd dog" (5.2.365). As Julia Reinhard Lupton argues, circumcision signifies a Muslim or Jewish religious difference that early modern Christian Europeans find more threatening and insurmountable than racial otherness.[33] Othello figures his alienation from the Venetians whom he has served with a metaphor of ineradicably vile species difference. Aaron, Shylock, and Othello's self-comparisons to dogs complexly refract Eurocentric xenophobia; self-loathing; defiance; and, as Colin Dayan's work helps to elucidate, a subaltern's vexed relationship to law.[34]

Another common use of *dog* disparages self-serving flatterers, about whom political or military leaders complain in Shakespeare's histories and tragedies. When King Richard II believes key allies have defected to Bolingbroke, he curses them: "Dogs easily won to fawn on any man!" (3.2.130). (Sadly, the canine defector commemorated by Caius remains unmentioned.) In the sequel, *The First Part of King Henry the Fourth*, Hotspur recalls being in favor with Bolingbroke, now Henry IV: "This fawning greyhound then did proffer me!" (1.3.250). Reversing that king–subject relationship, *Julius Caesar*'s untrustworthy flatterers are not ungrateful rulers but treacherous citizens. When Metellus sues for his brother's pardon, Caesar accuses him of "base spaniel fawning" (3.1.44). After Caesar's death, Antony decries Senators Brutus and Cassius as "flatterers" (5.1.45) who duplicitously "fawned like hounds" on Caesar (5.1.42). In *Lear*, those who inflated the unfortunate king's self-importance "flattered / me like a dog" (4.6.96–97)—that is, an editorial note explains, "as a dog fawns."[35] Finally, just as Caesar threatens to "spurn thee [Metellus] like a cur" (3.1.47), *Coriolanus*'s protagonist holds flattery ignoble when comparing a conquered city to "a fawning greyhound in the leash" (1.6.38).

37

Dogs can also represent supplicant partners in personal relationships. The outstanding instance occurs when Helena professes love to Demetrius in *A Midsummer Night's Dream*:

> I am your spaniel; and, Demetrius,
> The more you beat me I will fawn on you.
> Use me but as your spaniel, spurn me, strike me,
> Neglect me, lose me; only give me leave,
> Unworthy as I am, to follow you.
> What worser place can I beg in your love—
> And yet a place of high respect with me—
> Than to be usèd as you use your dog?

(2.1.203–10)

For Melissa E. Sanchez, the passage provides key evidence that heterosexual desires can challenge early modern patriarchy in ways overlooked even by feminist and queer criticism.[36] While taking the point, I would situate Helena among the play's many characters whose foolishness in love vitiates claims to rationality. As Puck exclaims, "Lord, what fools these mortals be!" (3.2.115). Illustrating how irrational passions compromise human dignity, Helena's canine abjection resembles broadly misanthropic usages of dogs in other works.

Dog invective serves a crucial function in *Timon of Athens*, Shakespeare's most overtly misanthropic play. As Clifford Davidson shows, the dog is ungrateful flattery's "most important emblem": particularly Actaeon's dogs, who eat him, furnish a subtext for Timon's guests "[a]s they symbolically devour the lord who has kept and fed and pampered them."[37] After Timon converts from reckless magnanimity to disappointed misanthropy, he declares to Alcibiades, "I am Misanthropos and hate mankind. / For thy part, I do wish thou wert a dog, / That I might love thee something" (4.3.54–56). Timon detests dogs less than human sycophants because the latter fawn strategically, cynically—for gain and convenience. Analyzing Thomas Shadwell's 1678 *Timon* adaptation, Lucinda Cole writes, "Dogs embody the (absent) virtues that ostensibly define humankind's better nature."[38] This formulation captures the species inversion, but at least for Shakespeare, I would say instead that his misanthropic satire proceeds by demoting the human below even the vile dog.

III Cynomorphic Satire

The Two Gentlemen of Verona likewise deploys human/dog reversals to expose human nature to ridicule or scorn. Thomas remarks, "Chaucer has nothing good to say about the dog and neither has Shakespeare."[39] I would add that when Shakespeare has nothing good to say about human beings, he frequently uses dogs to say it. Further supporting this assertion, I propose to read *The Two Gentlemen of Verona* as cynomorphic satire. Lance's inverse human–dog relationship with Crab constitutes the paradigmatic and ironic instance of abject devotion to an averse or hostile master, friend, or beloved. Proteus, Valentine, and Julia also prove more doglike than Crab. As *The Two Gentlemen of Verona* makes fawning appear more definitively human than canine, it attacks the "self-congratulation" that Thomas finds so characteristic of the early modern period.[40]

My interpretation offers another avenue to concur with Kiernan Ryan in seeing *The Two Gentleman of Verona* as "an accomplished comedy" with an "agenda."[41] A long tradition has deemed the play—and particularly its ending—formally defective, as when Michael Mangan calls it "an apprentice piece."[42] The Lance/Crab duo has been such a major example of incoherence that even essays about them might maintain that they "were almost certainly not part of the original scheme of the play" or seem to "have wandered in from another world."[43] Against this trend, recent readings have been recuperative or, rather, explanatory, most effectively *via* historical contextualization. Without denying the play's misogyny, Jeffrey Masten and Stephen Guy-Bray show that many complaints against it reflect resistance to how early modern England prioritizes male homosocial friendship over heterosexual marriage.[44] While Masten and Guy-Bray briefly consider how Crab destabilizes friendship and courtship traditions, fully synthetic accounts of the onstage dog as the play's crux have appeared only since the development of animal studies.[45] Bruce Boehrer claims that Lance's scenes with Crab open a "theatrical black hole," making them "central failures in a play about the failures of playing."[46] Meanwhile, Erica Fudge interprets Crab as "a representation of nature as the uncivilized that stands against the rational civility that is understood to be truly human."[47] Sharing the view that the nonhuman Crab is the play's key figure, I argue that this undoglike dog functions as the fulcrum by which Shakespeare dislodges conventional understandings of the human.

The penultimate time that Proteus speaks, he seems simultaneously to declare the play's moral and concept of human nature: "Were man / But constant, he were perfect" (5.4.110–11). Proteus has betrayed both Julia and Valentine by pursuing Silvia; furthermore, Proteus's rape attempt exemplifies inconstancy because he has tried to "love you [Silvia] 'gainst the nature of love" (5.4.58). Whether Proteus's moralizing lines recommend greater constancy or lament its impossibility, they fail spectacularly to generalize about human nature, as manifested throughout the play. Despite what Proteus professes to have learned, the play furnishes more examples of excessive than deficient constancy. It is a fault shared by most characters—but improbably, not Crab.

Exchanging places in the human–dog relationship as imagined in most early modern texts, Lance displays extraordinary devotion to Crab while Crab remains comically unmoved by Lance's kindness. Crab's indifference has reached Lance's notice: while his grandmother, parents, sister, maid, other servants, and cat bewail his departure from Verona, Crab "has no more pity in him than / a dog" (2.3.10–11). Crab's subsequent offenses include stealing food from Silvia's plate (4.4.7–9) and peeing both under the Duke's table (4.4.16–19) and on Sylvia's dress (4.4.33–38). Since Lance has rescued Crab from drowning with his litter (4.4.1–6), the humiliation that Crab regularly inflicts on Lance seems particularly ungrateful. Although Crab's misbehavior, ingratitude, and marked lack of "pity" might seem typical of early modern canines, Lance and Crab swap species roles in a more decisive way.

Their first scene (2.3) introduces the human/dog inversion confirmed and concretized in a later scene, when Lance reports having suffered in Crab's place (4.4). As Lance uses various beings and props to reenact departing from his family, he imagines, "I am the dog. No, the dog is himself, and I am the dog—Oh, the dog is me, and I am myself" (2.3.21–22). After Crab urinates under the Duke's dinner table, Lance decides "to take a fault upon me that he did" (4.4.13–14), sparing Crab from being whipped—or hanged, the punishment recommended by the Duke (4.4.21–22). Instead, a servant "whips me [Lance] out of the chamber" (4.4.28). Lance regularly claims responsibility for Crab's misdeeds: "I have sat / in the stocks for puddings he hath stolen, otherwise / he had been executed. I have stood on the pillory for / geese he hath killed, otherwise he had suffered for't" (4.4.29–32). Neither humiliation nor punishment deters Lance's affection, which is precisely what Topsell reports of dogs.

Lance's abject, doglike comportment towards the indifferent and thus patently undoglike Crab provides a satirical paradigm for the play's human relationships, most expressly for Proteus's pursuit of Silvia. As Proteus prepares to woo Silvia at her window, he reflects on how she has already berated him for betraying Valentine and Julia: "spaniel-like, the more she [Silvia] spurns my love, / The more it grows and fawneth on her still" (4.2.14–15).

The spaniel simile makes Proteus's infatuation with Sylvia manifestly like Lance's devotion to Crab. Unlike his own devotees, though, Proteus overcomes doglike obsession by the play's end.

Less overtly but more permanently, Valentine and Julia occupy the role of dog because none of Proteus's outrages diminishes their love for him. So that Proteus can pursue Valentine's beloved Sylvia, Proteus engineers Valentine's exile from Milan (3.1). Later, Valentine catches Proteus first wooing and then attempting to rape Sylvia (5.4). Confronting and preventing Proteus, Valentine vehemently but only momentarily denounces him: "I am sorry I must never trust thee more, / . . . / Oh, time most accurst, / 'Mongst all foes that a friend should be the worst!" (5.4.69–72). Proteus's apology of four-and-one-half lines receives the daft response "once again I do receive thee honest" (5.4.78). Forgiving Proteus with ludicrous alacrity, Valentine furnishes but one example of abject and misplaced devotion.

Julia's case is at least as bad. In great distress, she watches Proteus professing love to Silvia (4.2). Nevertheless, Julia disguises herself as Sebastian, seeks employment as Proteus's page, carries the ring she once gave to Proteus as his love token to Silvia, and agrees to convey Silvia's portrait back to Proteus (4.4). Before undertaking these errands, Julia (as Sebastian) makes an incisive point: "She [Julia] dreams on him [Proteus] that has forgot her love; / You [Proteus] dote on her [Silvia] that cares not for your love. / 'Tis pity love should be so contrary" (4.4.80–82). This play, Shakespeare's other works, and contemporaneous writings code that "contrary" love as canine. Suffering further abjection, Julia witnesses Proteus's rape attempt and Valentine's forgiveness of it, whereupon she faints at the prospect of marriage between Proteus and Silvia (5.4). Once revived, Julia accepts Proteus's apology and proposal, and the pair eagerly anticipate a shared future (5.4.119–20). Because their contentment seems so improbable, the reconciliation perpetuates Julia's abasement.

This reading in terms of species reversal entails an ultimately surprising ranking of the play's characters according to degrees of self-abasement. The inveterate fawners Lance, Valentine, and Julia occupy the ladder's lowest rungs. Of the three, Julia most closely resembles Helena, who begs an erstwhile lover to abuse her like a dog before joyfully marrying him. Favorably contrasting these characters, Thurio renounces Sylvia instead of dueling Valentine. Although Sylvia's father upbraids Thurio for changing course so easily (5.4.136–38), Thurio seems judicious compared with characters who persist in unappreciated devotion, especially when it entails repeated risks or harms. As Thurio says, "I hold him but a fool that will endanger / His body for a girl that loves him not" (5.4.133–34). Proteus, too, furnishes a model for overcoming misplaced affection because he stops pursuing Silvia when it proves unproductive and dangerous. Helping to explain why the play trivializes Proteus's rape attempt, this construction accords with Natale Conti's account of Proteus's namesake: the shape-shifting sea god does not exemplify impulsive mutability but rather epitomizes the "prudent man," able "to make the most of every opportunity and change of circumstance," particularly in "friendship and public administration."[48] Finally, the ladder's top rungs bring about the unexpected but significant rapprochement of two characters who initially seem very different: the refined lady Sylvia and the uncouth dog Crab. Despite their social disparity, dramatized most vividly when Lance recounts that Crab has peed on Sylvia's dress (4.4.36–37), they are alike in never fawning on friends, masters, or lovers who do not deserve or, at least, reciprocate affection. Indeed, Crab surpasses Silvia in this regard: uncompromised by any affections, he is the play's best though ironic exemplar of autonomous self-sufficiency.

The Two Gentlemen of Verona thus corroborates claims by animal studies scholars attending to Shakespeare's more famous works. Against Harold Bloom's view that Shakespeare "invented the human as we continue to know it," Boehrer dubs Shakespeare "the poet of humanity in crisis."[49] Through readings of *King Lear*, *A Midsummer Night's Dream*, and *The Merchant of Venice*, Laurie Shannon shows that "early modern culture is less provincially human than ours"—a surprising discovery about "the period so often said to be incubating a model of sovereign man for the future."[50] As a final example, Karen Raber argues that *Hamlet*'s pervasive images of parasitism undermine fantasies that a human being can have "a discrete, interior self."[51] In a similar vein, *The Two Gentlemen of Verona* attacks the notion of humanity's near perfection, given voice by the adaptable but unreliable Proteus.

IV Dogged Posthumanism

As I add my voice to those of early modernists, I would conclude by submitting my essay as a demonstration that historicist scholarship has posthumanist potential, though not in a straightforward, predictable way. While *posthumanism*'s meanings have been contested, I accept Cary Wolfe's account that one "sense of posthumanism derives directly from ideals of human perfectibility, rationality, and agency inherited from Renaissance humanism and the Enlightenment."[52] With Wolfe, I prefer to call that strain *transhumanism*, since it indulges in "fantasies of disembodiment and autonomy, inherited from humanism itself," and to reserve *posthumanism* for critiques of those deeply rooted aspirations.[53] Arguing that posthumanism does not inevitably side with theory against history, Wolfe categorizes scholarship according to whether it treats humanist vs. posthumanist topics and whether it uses humanist vs. posthumanist methodologies.[54] My reading may contribute to posthumanist endeavors to the extent that it exposes what Wolfe calls the human's "constitutive dependency and finitude," which Shakespeare figures (ironically) as doggishness.[55]

Historicist scholarship shows that posthumanism has conflicted or otherwise surprising legacies from early modernity and the eighteenth century. As Cole explains, early modernists including Boehrer, Fudge, Raber, Shannon (and, I would add, Cole herself) have argued that René Descartes's "human–animal divide is often projected, ahistorically, back on to early modern texts."[56] Similarly, Joseph Campana and Scott Maisano, editors of *Renaissance Posthumanism*, propose that closer attention to pre-Cartesian phenomena reveals that "critical posthumanism has ideological allies and philosophical resources in Renaissance humanism itself."[57] Provocatively, they recommend reinvesting in "Renaissance humanism *qua* the skeptical, critical, and irreverent close readings of ancient texts and cultures."[58] A similar thesis governs the volume's contribution by Kenneth Gouwens:

> renewed attention to Renaissance Humanism can enrich current efforts to move decisively beyond the domination of the academy by Enlightenment rationalism, now doing so not only with the vigor of Foucault but with the rigor of systematic scholarly inquiry and documentation.[59]

While writing this essay, such methods have indeed seemed decisive for reevaluating early modern dogs and *The Two Gentlemen of Verona*.

I would emphasize, though, that sustained, open-ended inquiry holds more promise than easily articulated methods or principles. In this regard, the Enlightenment as well as Renaissance humanism has contributions to make. Refusing either to endorse or to repudiate the Enlightenment, Foucault maintains that it commits its successors to a "permanent critique of ourselves."[60] This Enlightenment legacy, which Foucault describes as an "attitude" rather than a "theory," has posthumanist affinities, resonating particularly with Wolfe's point that (trans)humanist aspirations towards final, comprehensive knowledge are undermined by "our subjection to the radically ahuman technicity of language."[61] Discovering a similar open-endedness in Renaissance thinking, Victoria Kahn advocates expanding definitions of *theory* to include humanism's efforts "to educate the judgment" in discerning "what is appropriate at a given moment and in a given historical context."[62] For Kahn, the name *theory* ought to belong not only to "a comprehensive system of axioms and principles of deductive reasoning" or to "a Kantian epistemological critique of the conditions of the possibility of knowledge."[63] It should also belong to the humanist "practice of examples or of an exemplary practice."[64]

Exemplarity is what I have tried to offer here. Campana and Maisano disavow the intention for their collection to "fight anthropocentrism one close reading at a time."[65] Raber, however, hails precisely that approach as "slow posthumanism."[66] While I cannot recommend an abstract theory for future scholars to apply, I hope my essay can model a historicist and nascently posthumanist literary criticism as it proceeds skeptically, carefully, and tenaciously—that is, doggedly.

Notes

1. John Ayto, ed., *From the Horse's Mouth: Oxford Dictionary of English Idioms*, 3rd ed. (2009), s.v. "man." *The Oxford English Dictionary*, 3rd ed. (2010), s.v. "dog, *n.1*," II.5.a.
2. Sigmund Freud, *Civilization and Its Discontents*, trans. and ed. James Strachey (New York: Norton, 1961), 46–47n. See also 46–47.
3. Keith Thomas, *Man and the Natural World: Changing Attitudes in England, 1500–1800* (New York: Oxford University Press, 1996), 105.
4. Thomas, *Man and the Natural World*, 119; see 101–9.
5. Laura Brown, *Homeless Dogs and Melancholy Apes: Humans and Other Animals in the Modern Literary Imagination* (Ithaca, NY: Cornell University Press, 2010), 69.
6. I am not using *abject* in the psychoanalytic sense of Julia Kristeva, *Powers of Horror: An Essay on Abjection*, trans. Leon S. Roudiez (New York: Columbia University Press, 1982).
7. For the play's date, I follow William C. Carroll, introduction to *The Two Gentlemen of Verona*, by William Shakespeare, ed. William C. Carroll (London: Bloomsbury, 2004), 116–30, especially 130.
8. For the proverb's early modern instances, see Morris Palmer Tilley, *A Dictionary of the Proverbs in England in the Sixteenth and Seventeenth Centuries* (Ann Arbor: University of Michigan Press, 1950), 166. For a dubious construal, see Erica Fudge, "'The Dog Is Himself': Humans, Animals, and Self-Control in *The Two Gentlemen of Verona*," in *How to Do Things with Shakespeare: New Approaches, New Essays*, ed. Laurie Maguire (Malden, MA: Blackwell, 2008), 199, 207n10.
9. Ayto, *English Idioms*, s.v. "love."
10. Qtd. in Tilley, *Proverbs*, 166.
11. John MacNeill Miller, "When Drama Went to the Dogs; or, Staging Otherness in the Animal Melodrama," *PMLA* 132, no. 3 (2017): 531.
12. John Caius, *Of Englishe Dogges*, trans. Abraham Fleming (London, 1576), 10.
13. Caius, *Of Englishe Dogges*, 12. A tumbler is "[a] dog like a small greyhound, formerly used to catch rabbits." *The Oxford English Dictionary*, 2nd ed. (1989), s.v. "tumbler, *n*," 2.a.
14. Caius, *Of Englishe Dogges*, 20–21.
15. On vitriol targeting woman–dog relationships, see Brown's chapter "Immoderate Love: The Lady and the Lapdog," *Homeless Dogs and Melancholy Apes*, 65–89, especially 70–81.
16. Edward Topsell, *The Historie of Foure-Footed Beastes* (London, 1607), 143. I have supplied the verses, which Topsell quotes telegraphically, from the subsequently published Authorized Version (London, 1611).
17. Topsell, *Foure-Footed Beastes*, 143.
18. Ibid., 164–81.
19. Ibid., 141.
20. Ibid., 137.
21. Thomas, *Man and the Natural World*, 105–6; quotation on 106.

22 Caius, *Of Englishe Dogges*, 30.

23 Ibid., 33.

24 Topsell, *Foure-Footed Beastes*, 141–43; quotation on 143.

25 George Chapman, trans., *Homer's Odysses* (London, n.d.), 265–66; bk. 17.

26 Chapman, *Odysses*, 265.

27 Ibid., 266.

28 Alexander Pope, trans. and ed., *The Odyssey of Homer*, 5 vols (London, 1725–26), 4:128n, 4:126n.

29 Marvin Spevack, *A Complete and Systematic Concordance to the Works of Shakespeare*, 9 vols (Hildesheim: Georg Olms, 1968–80), 4:850.

30 Marjorie Garber, *Dog Love* (New York: Simon & Schuster, 1996), 230.

31 Ian MacInnes, "Mastiffs and Spaniels: Gender and Nation in the English Dog," *Textual Practice* 17, no. 1 (2003): 21–40.

32 William Shakespeare, *Titus Andronicus*, in *The Complete Works of Shakespeare*, ed. David Bevington, 7th ed. (Boston, MA: Pearson, 2014), act 5, scene 3, line 4. Subsequent citations of Shakespeare's plays refer to this edition and appear in text by act, scene, and line numbers.

33 Julia Reinhard Lupton, "Othello Circumcised: Shakespeare and the Pauline Discourse of Nations," *Representations* 57 (1997): 73–89. See especially discussion of "a universalism minus the circumcised" on 78, 84.

34 On dogs' liminal and thus revelatory status in the history of legal personhood, see Colin Dayan, *The Law Is a White Dog: How Legal Rituals Make and Unmake Persons* (Princeton, NJ: Princeton University Press, 2011), 209–52.

35 Bevington, ed., *The Complete Works*, 1244n97.

36 Melissa E. Sanchez, "'Use Me but as Your Spaniel': Feminism, Queer Theory, and Early Modern Sexualities," *PMLA* 127, no. 3 (2012): 493–511, especially 504–6.

37 Clifford Davidson, "*Timon of Athens*: The Iconography of False Friendship," *Huntington Library Quarterly* 43, no. 3 (1980): 189. See 189–90.

38 Lucinda Cole, *Imperfect Creatures: Vermin, Literature, and the Sciences of Life, 1600–1740* (Ann Arbor: University of Michigan Press, 2016), 119.

39 Thomas, *Man and the Natural World*, 105.

40 Ibid., 31.

41 Kiernan Ryan, *Shakespeare's Comedies* (New York: Palgrave Macmillan, 2009), 43.

42 Michael Mangan, *A Preface to Shakespeare's Comedies: 1594–1603* (London: Longman, 1996), 129. See Arthur Quiller-Couch, introduction to *The Two Gentlemen of Verona*, by William Shakespeare, eds. Arthur Quiller-Couch and John Dover Wilson (Cambridge: Cambridge University Press, 1921), vii–xix; S. Asa Small, "The Ending of *The Two Gentlemen of Verona*," *PMLA* 48, no. 3 (1933): 767–76; Stanley Wells, "The Failure of *The Two Gentlemen of Verona*," *Shakespeare Jahrbuch* 99 (1963): 161–73; Clifford Leech, introduction to *The Two Gentlemen of Verona*, by William Shakespeare, ed. Clifford Leech (London: Methuen, 1969), xiii–lxxv; and Charles A. Hallett, "'Metamorphosing' Proteus: Reversal Strategies in *The Two Gentlemen of Verona*," in *"Two Gentlemen of Verona": Critical Essays*, ed. June Schlueter (New York: Garland, 1996), 153–77.

43 Richard Beadle, "Crab's Pedigree," in *English Comedy*, eds. Michael Cordner, Peter Holland, and John Kerrigan (Cambridge: Cambridge University Press, 1994), 14. Kathleen Campbell, "Shakespeare's Actors as Collaborators: Will Kempe and *The Two Gentlemen of Verona*," in Schlueter, *"Two Gentlemen of Verona,"* 180.

44 Jeffrey Masten, *Textual Intercourse: Collaboration, Authorship, and Sexualities in Renaissance Drama* (Cambridge: Cambridge University Press, 1997), 37–48; and "*Two Gentlemen of Verona*," in *A Companion to Shakespeare's Works*, eds. Richard Dutton and Jean E. Howard, vol. 3, *The Comedies* (Malden, MA: Blackwell, 2003), 266–88. Stephen Guy-Bray, "Shakespeare and the Invention of the Heterosexual," *Early Modern Literary Studies* 13, no. 2 (2007): 28 paragraphs.

45 Masten, "*Two Gentlemen of Verona*," 275–76. Guy-Bray, "Invention of the Heterosexual," para. 17–18. Others noting parallels between Lance/Crab and human pairs include Harold F. Brooks, "Two Clowns in a Comedy (to Say Nothing of the Dog): Speed, Launce (and Crab) in *The Two Gentlemen of Verona*," *Essays and Studies* 16 (1963): 96–99; Leech, introduction to *Two Gentlemen*, lv–lvi, lxi, lxvi; Carroll, introduction to *Two Gentlemen*, 68, 73–75.

46 Bruce Boehrer, *Shakespeare among the Animals: Nature and Society in the Drama of Early Modern England* (New York: Palgrave, 2002), 160; see 156–68. For similar accounts assuming that animals cannot perform roles as human actors do, see Michael Dobson, "A Dog at All Things: The

Transformation of the Onstage Canine, 1550–1850," *Performance Research* 5, no. 2 (2000): 119; and Robert Weimann, *Author's Pen and Actor's Voice: Playing and Writing in Shakespeare's Theatre* (Cambridge: Cambridge University Press, 2000), 193, quoted approvingly in Andreas Höfele, *Stage, Stake, and Scaffold: Humans and Animals in Shakespeare's Theatre* (Oxford: Oxford University Press, 2011), 49.

47 Fudge, "'The Dog Is Himself,'" 194.

48 Natale Conti, *Mythologiae*, trans. and eds. John Mulryan and Steven Brown, 2 vols (Tempe: Arizona Center for Medieval and Renaissance Studies, 2006), 2:729; bk. 8, chapter 8.

49 Harold Bloom, *Shakespeare: The Invention of the Human* (New York: Riverhead Books, 1998), xviii. Bruce Boehrer, *Animal Characters: Nonhuman Beings in Early Modern Literature* (Philadelphia: University of Pennsylvania Press, 2010), 10.

50 Laurie Shannon, *The Accommodated Animal: Cosmopolity in Shakespearean Locales* (Chicago: University of Chicago Press, 2013), 8, 175.

51 Karen Raber, *Animal Bodies, Renaissance Culture* (Philadelphia: University of Pennsylvania Press, 2013), 111. See also analysis of *Romeo and Juliet* on 144–50.

52 Cary Wolfe, *What Is Posthumanism?* (Minneapolis: University of Minnesota Press, 2010), xiii.

53 Wolfe, *What Is Posthumanism?*, xv.

54 Ibid., 99–126.

55 Ibid., xxvi.

56 Cole, *Imperfect Creatures*, 84.

57 Joseph Campana and Scott Maisano, introduction to *Renaissance Posthumanism*, eds. Joseph Campana and Scott Maisano (New York: Fordham University Press, 2016), 5.

58 Campana and Maisano, introduction to *Renaissance Posthumanism*, 3.

59 Kenneth Gouwens, "What Posthumanism Isn't: On Humanism and Human Exceptionalism in the Renaissance," in *Renaissance Posthumanism*, eds. Joseph Campana and Scott Maisano (New York: Fordham University Press, 2016), 40.

60 Michel Foucault, "What Is Enlightenment?," trans. Catherine Porter, in *The Foucault Reader*, ed. Paul Rabinow (New York: Pantheon, 1984), 43.

61 Foucault, "What Is Enlightenment?," 50. Wolfe, *What Is Posthumanism?*, 119.

62 Victoria Kahn, "Humanism and the Resistance to Theory," in *Rhetoric and Hermeneutics in Our Time: A Reader*, eds. Walter Jost and Michael J. Hyde (New Haven, CT: Yale University Press, 1997), 165.

63 Kahn, "Humanism," 149.

64 Ibid., 153.

65 Campana and Maisano, introduction to *Renaissance Posthumanism*, 33.

66 Karen Raber, *Shakespeare and Posthumanist Theory* (London: Bloomsbury, 2018), 160.

4

LEARNING FROM CRAB

Primitive Accumulation, Migration, Species Being*

Crystal Bartolovich

> I was moved in college by Shakespeare's punning between kin and kind—the kindest were not necessarily kin as family; making kin and making kind . . . stretch imagination and can change the story.
>
> —*Donna Haraway*[1]

> We are treated worse than dogs.
>
> —*Mangash, Refugee in Calais*[2]

The frontispiece for Thomas Harman's *Caveat or Warning for Common Cursiters* (1567), an influential compendium of early modern elite English fantasies of threats to social order posed by the supposedly wily and undeserving poor, underscores the book's cautionary theme. An officer with a whip upraised threatens two barebacked men hitched to a cart pulled by a harnessed horse. Another officer with a whip—for use on the horse, the human prisoners, or both—stands to the side. A dog trots in the foreground. Ties of leather, hemp, law, and office bind, unequally, cart, horse, putative vagrants, and officers, the latter signified by livery and whips. Collectively, they warn viewers of the wages of cony-catching. But what of the dog?

Has s/he wandered into the scene indifferently, or does s/he have a stake in the event? If the latter, is s/he allied with one of the officers? One of the ostensible cony-catchers? The horse? *Caveat* provides no legend for the frontispiece, but Harman variously likens vagrants to dogs, assigns dogs the role of property protectors against vagrants, and identifies dogs as companions to vagrants.[3] The frontispiece's dog seems to exceed these options. Unliveried and unleashed, s/he appears to be freer than the other participants depicted, whatever the intentions of the woodcut's carver, or whomever selected it to front Harman's book. To pursue this intimation of freedom, though, we need to understand more about the conditions out of

---

* This paper emerged out of an MLA session organized by Sharon Achinstein for the 2017 MLA convention. I am grateful for Sharon's invitation to participate, as well as for the subsequent invitation of Karen Raber and Holly Dugan to expand that paper for this volume.

Figure 4.1 Frontispiece, Thomas Harman's *Caveat or Warning for Common Cursiters* (1567)

which the book emerged. Historians have challenged Harman's account of organized troops of deceitful poor menacing sixteenth-century England, but in general they affirm that treatment of the poor—and much else, including relations of humans to nonhumans—changed in early modernity.[4]

Marx called these changes "Primitive Accumulation," the establishing of conditions in which Capitalism can thrive: "freeing" the majority of the human population from land to force their submission to wage relations, along with the massive dispossession of native peoples and transfers of key resources from around the globe to Europe through colonialism and the expansion of trade.[5] David Harvey argues that these processes repeat whenever Capital expands to capture new, or re-exploits previously abandoned, areas, through "new enclosures."[6] And Jason Moore has rethought Primitive Accumulation in ecological terms, defining it as the "restructuring of relations of production—human and extra-human alike—so as to allow the renewed and expanded flow of cheap labor, food, energy and raw materials into the commodity system."[7] In all iterations, Primitive Accumulation explains how Capitalism became, and continues to operate as, a globally dominant systemic force.

Donna Haraway's *When Species Meet*, though influenced by this tradition, ultimately privileges "face to face" embodied relations, to which she attributes "encounter value," over systemic forces.[8] She argues that ethically assessing the interactions of humans and nonhumans requires paying attention to particular ties, the "making kin(d)" of epigraph 1.[9] She wonders whether "labor" or "rights" might be more useful for understanding relations among species, favoring labor over rights, but in the end rejects both in favor of her own "encounter" model, musing: "the posthumanist whispering in my ear reminds me that animals work . . . not under conditions of their own design, and that Marxist humanism is no more help for thinking about this for either people or other animals."[10] While more attention to nonhumans from all theoretical perspectives might be desirable, Haraway's objection here seems askew, not only because Marx relentlessly exposed capitalist relations to be generally unfree, but also because the aspiration to what he called Species Being requires the closing of the false separation of humans from "Nature" imposed by Capitalism.[11] In the *Economic and Philosophical Manuscripts*, he defines Communism as "the genuine resolution of the conflict between man and nature, and between man and man . . . freedom and necessity . . . individual and species."[12] Until such conditions are attained, so-called humans lack "Species Being." Marx agrees with Haraway, then, that "we have never been human," but he proposes that human Species Being would be desirable for nonhumans as well as prospective humans since it demands the transformation of global conditions that currently underwrite the destructively "instrumental" relations of capitalism.[13]

In part because her target is "animal rights" activists who forbid all human "use" of animals categorically, Haraway defends pet ownership and lab experimentation involving nonhuman animals by focusing on the quality of immediate relations rather than systemic conditions. She argues that "instrumentality" is irreducible and that "to be in a relation of use to each other is not the definition of unfreedom and violation."[14] Defending instrumentality in this way, though, raises problems: first, what of the numerous nonhumans and humans, like Mangash (epigraph 2), who are, in effect, declared useless by global capitalism? Second, by defining instrumentality as a "relation of use to each other" rather than as oppressive relations, Haraway cleanses it (by definition, not actuality) from the aspect that made it objectionable to Marx: that Capitalist *historical conditions* reduce all participants to instruments (including of rejection and ignoring), depriviling most. Just as Racism exceeds "face to face" attitudes, wreaking its effects through structures that privilege some over others, Capitalism coerces unequal "usefulness" of some to others, and justifies the rejection of whatever cannot be made useful to it.[15] Haraway's "encounter" ethics are best understood, then, as a moment of dialectic, necessary but insufficient, rather than as its displacement. Human workers get their wages from Capitalists, an arrangement that dominant ideology views as mutually beneficial use, but Marx pointed out that this does not make the relation any less one of exploitation and oppression, however much it might be reformed (which does not mean that those hard-won reforms are unimportant). He thus insists that the capitalist system in its totality must be transformed into an "association in which the free development of each is the condition for the free development of all," as the *Manifesto* puts it, a collective, mutually enhancing effort, the antithesis of liberal society's cultivation of blind and selfish "individual" freedoms.[16]

So why does Haraway, right about so much so often, get this wrong? On the one hand, Haraway admits that her "dogs and cats live in the style in which my whole post-Lassie generation and I have become indoctrinated" (a nod to an oppressive structuring totality), while on the other, her ethics demands a focus on immediate relations, leading her to express willingness to forego her own Lipitor for the "needs" of her dogs and cats, and to claim that "no one can convince" her that chiropractic adjustments for her dog are "bourgeois decadence at the expense of my other obligations."[17] She defends these positions as the "ethical obligation of the human who lives with a companion animal in affluent, so-called first-world circumstances" to "help them achieve their full canine [or other creaturely] potential."[18] The problem here is not Haraway's individual (un)willingness to change per se. Transforming the planet[19] ecologically and justly will require numerous modifications of privileged lifestyles as well as enhanced advocacy for the deprivileged, nonhuman and human. This transformation, however, cannot be undertaken, or even assessed adequately, at the immediate level alone in a context in which "needs," as Haraway recognizes, are "historically situated," and most humans and nonhumans do not share her privileged access to healthcare and other resources.[20] By suggesting that it is possible to locate ethics in the "face-to-face" relation of humans to pets and other nonhumans, Haraway enables the bracketing of the sufferings of the countless human and nonhuman animals who support the way of life to which people and pets in the global North have been "indoctrinated."[21] Loving one's own dogs under unjust global conditions of existence cannot ensure ethical rectitude.[22] In a wrong world, as Adorno put it, there is no living rightly.[23] Capitalist property relations implicate humans and nonhumans unequally, by no means privileging all humans, and instrumentalize humans and nonhumans alike. These conditions, historically created, can be transformed—but only collectively, totally. Ethics remain undecidable at a face-to-face level; a dialectical approach, one that situates specificities in a historical totality to which they are nonetheless irreducible, is necessary.[24]

I Primitive Accumulation and the Production of the Local

It is important to understand that Primitive Accumulation does not give rise to a "seamless whole," as Manuel DeLanda tendentiously describes "totality," but instead to a dynamic historical terrain ruptured by contradiction and struggle, an effect of elite attempts to impose oppressive relations, which never succeed fully, though they become increasingly more entrenched and taken for granted as Capitalism expands its reach, intensively and extensively, in a relentless imperative to growth.[25] An early modern jest that stages an encounter between a "poor man" and a "mastiff" illustrates this struggle at an early stage, its perspective clashing profoundly with *Caveat*'s:

> A Poor man having a Pike-staff on his shoulder, and travailing through a Country Village, a great Mastiff Cur ran mainly at him, so that hardly he could defend him from himself. At the length it was his chance to kill the Dog: for which the owner immediately apprehending him and bringing him before a Justice, alleged that he had slain his Servant, which defended his life, house and goods, and therefore challenged satisfaction. The Justice leaning more in favor to the Plaintiff, as being his Friend, Neighbor and familiar, then to the justice of the cause, reproved the poor fellow very sharply, and peremptorily commanded him to make satisfaction, or else he would commit him to prison. "That were injustice," replied the poor man, "because I killed him in defense of my own life, which deserveth much better respect then a Million of such Curs." "Sirrah, sirrah," said the Justice, "then you should have turned the other end of your Staff, and not the Pike; so the Dog's life had been saved, and your own in no danger." "True, Sir" (quoth the fellow) "if the Dog would have turn'd his tail and bit with that, and not his teeth, then we both had parted quietly."[26]

Like many other items in jest books, this tale appears in multiple locations, many probably now lost; I have traced it back so far to 1620, when it was already identified as borrowed and also as a moral exemplum "in imitation of witty Aesop," a slave who, according to Herodotus, won freedom with his wit.[27] The "wit" of the jest's poor man, too—even more directly than the dog on *Caveat*'s frontispiece—intimates an aspiration to freedom.

"A *poor man*, having a pike-staff on his shoulder . . ." is "travailing *through*" a village. The tale depends upon the man's propertyless, outsider status: neither the dog, nor the dog's "owner," nor the Justice, recognize him. At a time in which a growing landless population intensified internal migration, such encounters became more common.[28] Furthermore, the poor man is not using the "pikestaff" as a walking stick, but carrying it on his shoulder, as a soldier would. A.L. Beier has argued that demobilized soldiers were especially feared among "vagrants" because they often had weapons and knew how to use them.[29] Linda Woodbridge more recently pointed out, however, that, while the law regarded all "vagrants" as suspect (as did Harman, as we have seen), stage plays were less harsh to unsettled soldiers.[30] Like the early modern drama Woodbridge examines, the jest, too, takes pains to cast the "poor man" in a positive light. First, he does not instigate the attack of the mastiff. Second, the jest explicitly attributes the dog's death to "chance," only after a fight at "length," not to the poor man's desire. Third, mastiffs, with males ranging from 150 to over 300 pounds, were associated in the period with violent threat.

John Caius's *Of English Dogs* (1576) describes mastiffs as "huge, stubborn, ugly . . . and frightful to behold."[31] Because of their fierceness, they are "appointed to watch . . . when there is any fear conceived of thieves," and "are [also] serviceable against the fox and the badger, [or] to drive wild and tame swine out of . . . places planted." Caius emphasizes that humans enlist mastiffs to these purposes by "art, use, and custom," including owners "teach[ing] . . . dogs to bait the bear, . . . the bull and other such like cruel and bloody beasts." We might question whether the humans who organize and watch such events or the "beasts" forced to participate more deserve characterization as "cruel and bloody,"[32] but what is not debatable, according to Caius, is that "the force which is in them [mastiffs] surmounts all belief." The mastiff in the jest, then, would likely be understood in the period not only as a formidable antagonist, but one that, by "use" and "custom" keeps in place a divide between owners and other humans and nonhumans targeted for attack. He runs "mainly" at the poor man—that is, "with force vigor or violence" according to *OED*—such that the latter "hardly" could, in an intriguing twist, defend the dog ("him") from "himself." If emergent proto-Enlightenment Man is supposed to glory in mastering "nature" in all its forms, this "poor man" is not a very good example.

The depiction of the "poor man" also deviates from the representation of itinerants in "rogue" literature, such as *Caveat*, that purports to expose the

> abominable, wicked and detestable behavior of all these rowsey ["disorderly," *OED*], ragged rabblement of rakehells, that under the pretense of . . . innumerable calamities which they fain . . . gain great alms in all places where they wily wander.[33]

Of English Dogs shares these views and, in the case of its Englished version, even Harman's alliterative style:

> thieves rove up & down in every corner, no place is free from them . . . . practic[ing] pilfering, picking, open robbing, and privy stealing . . . not fearing the shameful and horrible death of hanging. The cause of which inconvenience doth not only issue from ripping need & wringing want, for all that steal are not pinched with poverty, but some steal to maintain their . . . lewdness of life, their haughtiness of heart, their wantonness of manners, their willful idleness.[34]

Caius spends nearly as much time denouncing thieves along these lines as describing dogs, since the principle service of dogs to humans turns out to be property protection.

Rather than depicting the mastiff as an admirable instrument to protect property from "willful idleness," however, the jest emphasizes that the mastiff dies participating in an *unjust* cross-species alliance. When the dog is killed, his irate "owner" (not "master") drags the "poor man" before the local Justice "immediately," complaining that the poor man "had slain his *Servant*," identifying the dog as not only a worker, but also as belonging to his household and, therefore, as being a recognized member of the local community, a position affirmed by Caius's *Of English Dogs*, that also refers to the domestic dog as a "household servant."[35] The prompt arrest of the poor man raises the question of why the owner, who must have been near, hadn't called the dog away. The "Justice" does not ask this question. To the contrary, the jest informs us that not only is the Justice a "friend, neighbor and familiar" of the plaintiff, but also, therefore, inclined to overlook the "justice of the cause."

Belonging to no local household, the poor man is *not* bound up (like the dog) instrumentally with the villagers. He is superfluous, useless, by local determinations of kind. Thus, with hyperbolic flourish, the poor man appeals to a universal against local enclosures, insisting that his life should be considered worth "a [m]illion of such curs." Although this assertion seems to fuel the fire of human exceptionalism, I think that pro-canine outrage in this case would be a mistake, even for the sakes of the millions of dogs (and other nonhuman creatures) in the world. The mastiff would not have been involved in this particular battle, after all, if not pressed into service as an instrument of property protection; in addition, given the jest's emphasis on the poor man's extreme reluctance to kill the dog, the struggle of the "poor man" for "life" must be understood in the broadest sense—as it could be for all species—against property and the privileges and exclusions it sustains, the instrumentalism it universalizes. The poor man is not anti-dog, but anti-enclosure. "Such curs," in context, means dogs that have been enlisted to the protection of local property relations against excluded humans and nonhumans. "Nuisance dogs" and other "trash animals" were, too, treated with violence by cross-species alliances of kind, whose elites made and policed the categories.[36] The jest, allying itself with the tradition of mistrust of law as stacked in favor of the privileged, asserts that cross-species kind relations give rise to *injustice* under conditions of structural inequality.[37] Only on a planet in which cross-species alliances are not predicated on property and its instrumentalizing, enclosing logics, a systemic condition, would all species be able to learn to live together in an "association in which the free development of each is the condition for the free development of all."[38]

Caius instead defends incipiently capitalist enclosures, propertarian and nationalistic. Not only is he preoccupied with property protection, but his admiration for dogs does not extend to "curs . . . that keep not their kind," who he dismisses as "unprofitable implements."[39] "Unprofitable" does not mean incapable of performing tasks useful to humans or enabling financial gain, since he acknowledges that some "mongrels" of the "coarsest kind" are employed in "kitchen service excellent" (turning the spit), and that entertainer mongrels earn their "vagabundicall masters" a "little lucre." He simply doesn't consider such dogs to be properly English, just as elites more generally did not consider unpropertied humans to be properly English on the grounds that they had no "permanent interest" in the Kingdom.[40]

From this perspective, lacking property or "service" to it renders one excludable, the view held by the jest's Justice. He does not expect the dog to value the poor man's life as fully as he expects the poor man to value the dog's life because the dog is "familiar" and the "poor man" is not. Thus, when the poor man turns tables on the Justice by extending the Justice's demand on him to the dog, we might see the jest as asserting a demand for common freedom against propertarian and localizing enclosures, for humans and nonhumans alike: Species Being.

The jest's aspiration to mutual freedom for humans and nonhumans from the enforced inequality produced by uneven control over property remains symbolic, however, an intimation of possibilities in the process of being foreclosed by Primitive Accumulation. The jest can be "merry" only because we are not told what happens next, which, in early modern England, might well involve such unmerry effects as branding, imprisonment, or whipping out of the village for actual "vagrants" who come up against the power of the propertied, including their cross-species allies. This brings us back to the frontispiece of Harman's book, which depicts the likely denouement to this tale in the real world, doubtful as the contents of the book may be. I began by suggesting that the dog in the woodcut might offer an intimation of freedom, but now ask, with an eye to the jest's mastiff: how free can a dog be under proto-Capitalist conditions that strive to limit the possible relations among *all* creatures?

II "All the Kind of the Launces"

In a scene that has attracted a disproportionate share of *The Two Gentlemen of Verona's* critical attention,[41] Launce, a (human) servant, distinguishes "all the kind[42] of the Launces" from Crab, his dog:

> Nay, 'twill be this hour ere I have done weeping; all the kind of the Launces have this very fault. . . . [M]y mother weeping, my father wailing, my sister crying, our maid howling, our cat wringing her hands, and all our house in a great perplexity, yet did not this cruel-hearted cur shed one tear. He is a stone, a very pebblestone, and has no more pity in him than a dog. A Jew would have wept to have seen our parting. Why, my grandam, having no eyes, look you, wept herself blind at my parting . . . .
>
> *(2.3.1–13)*

The inclusion in Launcekind of the maid, both genders, the cat, and, even, potentially, Jews, indicates that neither blood, nor social hierarchy, nor humanity, or even religion, determine Launcekind. The dog is excluded for a specifically *affective* failure.

While the seeming fluidity and flexibility of affective kind may appear to be preferable to modern biological species designations, both can be problematical when deployed under hierarchical and exclusionary conditions of existence, as we have seen in the discussion of the jest. *Two Gentlemen,* for its part, draws attention to structuring context by heavy-handedly referencing wage relations.[43] Early on, a "Master," Proteus (who is also Launce's employer) and a "servant," Speed, engage in an extended quibble in which Speed tries to distinguish himself from a sheep by noting that "[t]he shepherd seeks the sheep, and not the sheep the shepherd; but I seek my master, and my master seeks not me...[t]herefore I am no sheep." Proteus, however, counters: "The sheep for fodder follow the shepherd, the shepherd for food follows not the sheep; thou *for wages* followest thy master, thy master for wages follows not thee. Therefore thou art a sheep" (1.1.84–90). Speed concedes with a "baa," which ends the debate. Enforced dependency predicated on unequal property determines servant-kind, not species. Furthermore, though the master depends on the labor of servants, the "proof" implies that wages make only the servant dependent, given the stakes of losing a place.[44] As Panthino reminds Launce, urging him get to the ship that will take him away from Launce-kind before the tide goes out: "in losing thy voyage, [you] lose thy master, and in losing thy master, lose thy service," which would thrust Launce into the vulnerable contingent of serviceless persons demonized in the cony-catching pamphlets and vagrancy laws of the period (2.3.40–42). Wrenching as he finds leaving his preferred kind, then, Launce complies with his master's demand, an indication of the unfreedom imposed by the instrumentalized relations he inhabits, as his melancholy response to Panthino underscores: "Lose the tide, and the voyage, and the master, and the service, and the tied [Crab]? Why, man, if the river were dry, I am able to fill it with my tears." Crab might be "tied" with a rope, but Launce is "tied" by the historical conditions he inhabits, however disconsolately.

Instructively, however, Crab, though "tied" to Launce, refuses assimilation to a world ruled by the "gentleman-like." When the hangman's boys steal the lapdog Proteus chose as a gift for Silvia and Launce substitutes Crab, the latter steals Silvia's dinner before retreating under the table and relieving himself malodorously (4.4.17). To protect Crab, Launce tells the dog-whipper that he is the culprit and takes the dog's punishment, which, we learn, he has done many times:

> How many masters would do this for his servant? . . . I have sat in the stocks for puddings he hath stolen, otherwise he had been executed. I have stood upon the pillory for geese he hath killed, otherwise he had suffered for't.
>
> *(4.4.28–32)*

These substitutions are, crucially, non-mimetic.[45] Launce doesn't become *like* the dog, but takes punishment *for* the dog's nonconformity to "gentleman-like" behavior. "Did not I bid thee still mark me and do as I do" (4.4.34–35), complains Launce to Crab, exasperated that the dog cannot "keep himself in all companies," in compliance with the existing social relations as he does (4.4.10).

Launce's substitution of himself for Crab operates quite differently from Speed's equation with a sheep, which is imposed from above by Proteus. Instead, Launce, like Jesus, sacrifices *himself* for the crimes of another ("Greater love hath no man than this, that a man lay down his life for his friends"). Launce's devotion to Crab blasphemously parodies the "love" in John 15, that dissolves hierarchy by rendering all "friends" ("henceforth I call you not servants").[46] Unlike Jesus, though, Launce acts not to redeem all of creation (that is, total conditions of existence), but his own dog only. And, yet, Crab and Launce are potential agents of transformation in a secularized sense. What if, rather than trying to assimilate Crab to elite demands, Launce allied with Crab in his affront to the "gentleman-like"?

The seeds are there: Launce is astonished when his master expresses outrage that he presented Crab to Silvia, since, he protests, Crab "is a dog as big as 10 of yours, and therefore the gift the *greater*" (4.4.55–56). Launce's lower valuation of lapdogs must be carefully distinguished from a related view in *Of English Dogs*, where lapdogs are decried as foreign. Like other corrupting imports, such dogs, Caius sneers, serve principally "to satisfy . . . wanton women's wills, instruments of folly for them to play and dally withal."[47] Rather than being useful servants, like the proper "English" dogs Caius admires, the imported lapdog is an "instrument" of "folly," a symptom of the effeminate corruption of aristocrats:

> These puppies the smaller they be, the more pleasure they provoke, as more meet play fellows for mincing mistresses . . . to lay in their laps, and lick their lips as they ride in their wagons . . . for coarseness with fineness hath no fellowship.

To Caius's particular disgust, "these *kind* of people . . . delight more in dogs that are deprived of all possibility of reason, then they do in children that be capable of wisdom and judgement." Caius's assessment of lapdogs depends on anthropocentric, utilitarian, and nationalistic logics of emergent capitalism, which is unsettling the definition of elite "kind."

Crab's insurgency and Launce's response differ markedly from Cauis's rising middle-class disdain for aristocracy. As Robert Weimann has observed, Launce belongs to an earthier, dissident lower-class humor, shared with a significant segment of the theater audience and the mass of the actual population.[48] We might wonder, then, what it means that Launce finds it difficult to exclude Crab from Launcekind after all: "I am the dog. No, the dog is himself, and I am the dog. O, the dog is me, and I am myself. Ay, so, so" (2.3.20–22). Bruce Boerher has suggested that in both *Two Gentleman* and *Merchant of Venice* passages such as this distinguish between an emergent notion of dogs as economically superfluous "pets" and dogs as "useful."[49] "Pet" seems to be an emergent category, as Boehrer argues, but dogs remain workers, as well, and uselessness can be a category of exclusion as well as inclusion. I am more interested, though, in the historical conditions of Primitive Accumulation that underwrite such determinations, and the significance of Crab's failure to act as a "gentleman-like dog" in this context. The gap between being viewed as useless and refusing to be useful is wide. Because of Crab's noncompliance, "kind" turns out to be a conceptual site through which *Two Gentlemen* worries the politics of exclusion at a moment in which seemingly "settled" social relations are challenged by forced dislocation, not only Launce's rush towards the tide/tied at his master's bidding, but larger forces of dislocation at work in Primitive Accumulation underway when the play was first performed.

Crucially, situating Crab dialectically in this way underscores his singularity. Crab is not just any dog (even if any—or at least many—dogs might play him).[50] Among dogs, as among people, Crab remains distinct: "I think Crab my dog be the sourest natured dog that lives," laments Launce, the superlative underscoring the dog's specificity. Similarly, when John Madden's costume drama *Shakespeare in Love* imagines a performance of *Two Gentlemen* at Elizabeth I's Court, it depicts Crab as tugging on a garter of his "master" who struggles, ultimately unsuccessfully, to remain upright while he attempts to speak. *Two Gentlemen* does not call for it explicitly, but such extemporizing with dogs was commonplace in the period, especially in street performance, whence it possibly migrated to the professional stage.[51] In any case, whether Crab or Launce is "master" is far less decidable than with Launce and Proteus, not only because Launce confuses their roles, but also because both Crab and Launce are unpropertied.

This structurally unequal condition, though, is not inevitable. Like the dog on the frontispiece to *Caveat*, and the "poor man" in the jest, Crab gestures towards a planet in which different conditions than those imposed by the "gentleman-like" might pertain, but this possibility is undermined by the play's conclusion, when everyone and everything is (ostensibly) knit up in "one feast, one house, one mutual happiness." Unsettlingly, though, this "happiness" conspicuously includes a would-be rapist, to the horror of many critics, and excludes both Launce and Crab, Launce having been dismissed in Act IV to seek out the stolen lapdog and instructed not to return to his master's household without it.[52] Ultimately, Launce, like Crab, fails to live up to the expectations of "gentleman-like" kind and is banished. "Gentleman-like dogs" have a more secure place in the social order than either Crab or Launce. This is the usual story. What would it mean to truly "*change* the story," then, as Haraway asks? Only a massive alliance of oppressed humans and nonhumans—a formation we might call Crabkind—in collective struggle against the conditions that uphold the rule of the "gentleman-like" (human and nonhuman) can truly bring about a planet organized for the "mutual happiness" of all.

III Species Being, Dialectic, and Border Control in the Capitalocene

Considering the various positions of her friends—a group that includes fervent vegans as well as avid hunters—on the ethics of animal eating, Haraway muses: "Dialectics is a powerful tool for addressing contradictions, but [my friends] do not embody contradictions. Rather, they embody finite, demanding, affective, and cognitive claims . . . which require action and respect without resolution."[53] The "knotty" problem of eating animals, though, is never only immediate. Contradictions under capitalist conditions don't depend on personal attitudes alone, but on the totality of relations in which those attitudes, conscious and unconscious, as well as actions predicated on them, unfold. That is why Haraway's "knots" can only be moments—necessary but insufficient—of dialectic, not an alternative to it.

Take, for example, "Mangash," a particular human, face to face with a particular dog, "English" and beloved, at Calais. When interviewed, Mangash does not suggest that he should be treated better than any such dog. He would be thrilled to move freely across the border as he sees countless English dogs doing: "dogs are allowed in cars here, but refugees are not."[54] EU citizens regularly secure "Pet Passports" to facilitate the movement of their nonhuman companions across Schengen borders. Meanwhile, Mangash and thousands of other human migrants sleep in the rough (under conditions worsened since the demolition of the Jungle encampment) while trying to enter the UK.[55] How can such a situation be assessed ethically? We have already seen in the discussion of the jest that a localizing approach is insufficient to "face" migrants justly, since it enables blindness to undesirable effects of local kind relations on the excluded, a privilege-protecting strategy Gayatri Spivak calls "sanctioned ignorance."[56]

A dialectical approach demands instead that the beneficiaries of what Haraway calls "affluent, so-called first-world circumstances" cannot isolate themselves from Mangash and other refugees—as well as those who remain behind in conflict zones, sites of extreme economic deprivation or ecological devastation—that is, from global totality, when assessing ethics of their immediate face-to-face relations. In the current context, a privileged family adding a dog to their middle-class existence helps perpetuate privilege while increasing ecological devastation.[57] Since privilege rarely divests itself without a fight, refugees like Mangash, declared superfluous, must struggle against it, though uncollectivized their efforts are unlikely to prevail. It's not that "knotty" ecological and social justice problems have no answers; the privileged just don't like them.

Haraway argues that the best alternative to the current impasse between unrepentant anthropocentrists ("greater human good trumps animal pain") and animal advocates ("sentient animals are always ends in themselves") is her "face-to-face" ethics, practiced in particular labs or farms or households, where humans and nonhumans "learn to pay attention to each other in a way that changes who and what they become together."[58] This, though, is an incomplete index of alternatives. Michael Pollan, who, like Haraway, does not view the domestication of animals as necessarily a disaster, still insists on attention to the total context in which domestication now occurs: the capitalist pressures that encourage the ravaging of the planet. This is so because unless we transform these conditions "everything eventually morphs into the way the world is," as one of Pollan's interviewees, a former hippie back-to-the-lander who now presides over an "organic" industrial empire, disturbingly puts it.[59]

Thus, dialectic, in contrast to Haraway's attempt to clear her meat-eating and vegan friends of the charge of "contradiction," insists that we all *live* contradictions because the conditions of our existence are contradictory: wrong life cannot be lived rightly. Adorno's observation warns against settling for ostensibly caring "face-to-face" relations because transforming capitalism seems too hard. Less than 5% of the global population, Americans use 25% of the

Primitive Accumulation, Migration, Species Being

Figure 4.2 Cover, *Daily Mirror*, Saturday August 1, 2015

world's oil.[60] Our "global footprint" is many times that of Haitians or Somalis.[61] There is no way to assess the ethics of the American way of life, including the eco-impact of animal companions, or to pursue ecologically reparative planetary relations, without taking this global inequality into account.

Haraway's interviewees produce many thoughtful descriptions of their attempts to improve relations with their lab animals, just as Caius's *Of English Dogs* includes many moving examples of canine acts of devotion to human companions, but in a world where all the labs and all the households must march to the beat of a capitalist drummer to continue to exist as they now do, the very best lab practices or pet love willy-nilly helps reproduce an uneven world. One must struggle collectively against capitalism *at the same time* as one struggles for better face-to-face human/nonhuman co-subjectivity, because the current global conditions in which these latter struggles unfold make only so much "good" possible and co-incidentally produce much global "bad."

Reese Jones thus observes that "the violence of borders today is emblematic of a broader system that seeks to preserve privilege and opportunity for some by restricting access to resources and movement for others," a state of affairs he situates in the long history of Primitive Accumulation's enclosures.[62] Whether at the U.S./Mexico border, the West Bank, or the EU, borders attempt to preserve global privilege for some (not all) nonhumans as well as humans. Jones discusses the devastating ecological effects of border walls on various nonhuman species whose migration patterns are disrupted by them, as well as the plight of human migrants, but he does not take up the contribution of pets on the wealthier side of the walls to reinforcing privilege. Gregory Okin, however, has calculated that American cats and dogs are the fifth largest factory-farmed meat consumers in the world (after the humans of Russia, Brazil, the U.S., and China), with all the negative environmental impact that such consumption wreaks—and that is only a part of the disproportionate cost to the planet of American pets.[63]

So I will close by gesturing towards the *system* of food production. Despite the contention of Latourians that "knowledge claims are a terrible basis for politics," it is crucial to realize that we already know a great deal about how to transform the global food production system to make it reparative instead devastating to the planet.[64] It is also important to recognize that Cargill and Bayer (which just bought Monsanto) and other agri-conglomerates—entities embraced by Latour's Parliament of Things—as well as the whole way of life of the privileged, through and by which these conglomerates continue to thrive, *resist* such transformation.[65] Reparative agriculture would mean the end of industrial farming from which agri-business profits, as well as much less meat eating, and, therefore, much less pet keeping as now practiced in the currently richer countries. Such changes are possible, but resisted by stakeholders who benefit from the current arrangements, ravaging as they are to others, human and nonhuman. Thus, only an alliance of humans and nonhumans in struggle to bring about Species Being, a planet of mutual thriving rather than one organized for the thriving of global capitalism above all, can "change the story." I have suggested that *Caveat*'s frontispiece dog, the "poor man" in the jest, Crab, and Mangash, all point us in this direction, dialectically, against past and current cross-species alliances of property, with their whips of ideology and repression, that strive to keep current exclusions and inequalities in place.

Figure 4.3 Swarm/illegal/human poster, Photo courtesy of David Wallace

Notes

1 Haraway, Donna, "Anthropocene, Capitalocene, Plantationocene, Chthulucene: Making Kin," *Envinronmental Humanities* 6 (2015): 161.

2 Emily Goddard, "Calais: 'Dogs Are Allowed in Cars Here, but Refugees Are Not'," *Independent*, May 26, 2017. www.independent.co.uk/news/long_reads/calais-refugees-france-uk-pakistan-a7742136.html.

3 Thomas Harman, *Caveat or Warning for Common Cursiters* (London, 1567), Sigs. BIIIv, CIIIr, E1v.

4 See Craig Dionne and Steve Mentz, eds., *Rogues and Early Modern English Culture* (Ann Arbor: University of Michigan press, 2004) and the special issue on "Poverty and Mobility in England, 1600–1800," *Rural History* 24, no. 1 (2013). Christopher Dyer, in "Poverty and Its Relief in Late Medieval England," *Past and Present* 216 (2012): 41–78, takes a longer view, though I dispute that this makes his account less "linear," or casts doubt that quantitative accumulation of changes eventually result in qualitative systemic historical difference.

5 Karl Marx, *Capital*, trans. Ben Fowkes, vol. 1 (New York: Penguin, 1990), 873–940.

6 David Harvey, *The New Imperialism* (Oxford: Oxford University Press, 2003), Chapter 5.

7 Jason Moore, *Capitalism in the Web of Life* (New York: Verso, 2015), 98.

8 Donna Haraway, *When Species Meet* (Minneapolis: University of Minnesota Press, 2008), 46.

9 Haraway, *When Species Meet*, 42.

10 Ibid., 73.

11 Rather than the division of Science from Politics, as Bruno Latour argues, *We Have Never Been Modern*, trans. Catherine Porter (Cambridge, MA: Harvard University Press, 1993). Recent work on Species Being includes Elizabeth Johnson, "At the Limits of Species Being," *South Atlantic Quarterly* 116, no. 2 (2017): 275–92; Gerda Roelvink, "Rethinking Species-Being for the Anthropocene," *Rethinking Marxism* 25, no. 1 (2013): 52–69; Ben Dibley, "Nature Is Us: The Anthropocene and Species-Being," *Transformations* 21 (2012): 1–22.

12 Karl Marx, *Early Writings*, trans. Rodney Livingstone (New York: Vintage Books, 1975), 348.

13 Haraway, *When Species Meet*, 1; Marx outlines a materialist predication of "instrumentality" in *Capital*, vol. 1, and cites Edmund Burke, who illustrates its effects when he describes the worker as an "instrument" alongside others enacting the purposes of a "farmer" (or any other capitalist):

> Of all the instruments of the farmers' trade, the labour of man … is that on which he is most to rely for the repayment of his capital. The … the working stock of the cattle and … carts … and so forth, without a given portion of the first, are nothing at all.

14 Haraway, *When Species Meet*, 72, 74.

15 With a similar "micro," Latour-inflected, emphasis, Heather Love also goes astray, collapsing attentiveness to "microaggression" in the work of Claudia Rankine with *remaining at the "micro" level* in social analysis, even though (unacknowledged by Love) Rankine herself views Racism as *systemic*: Heather Love, "Small Change: Realism, Immanence, and the Politics of the Micro," *Modern Language Quarterly* 77, no. 3 (2016): 419–45. See also Kate Kellaway, "Claudia Rankine: 'Blackness in White Imagination Has Nothing to Do with Black People," *Guardian*, December 2015. www.theguardian.com/books/2015/dec/27/claudia-rankine-poet-citizen-american-lyric-feature.

16 Friedrich Engels and Karl Marx, *The Communist Manifesto*, trans. Samuel Moore (New York: Penguin Classics, 2015), 244.

17 Haraway, *When Species Meet*, 49, 51.

18 Ibid., 61.

19 I use "planet" to mark an aspirational formation against capitalist globality with a nod to Gayatri Spivak's "planeterity," *Death of a Discipline* (New York: Columbia University Press, 2003). The emergence of the early modern imaginary of world and globe is detailed in Ayesha Ramachandran's *The Worldmakers* (Chicago, IL: University of Chicago Press, 2015).

20 Haraway, *When Species Meet*, 49. Rita Felski makes the opposite case to mine, collapsing two quite different issues: the balefulness of privileging the context in which a literary text was first written alone (I agree), and the impossibility of totalizing (I disagree). The *effects* of the capitalist context stink, not, as Felski (via Latour) argues, the concept. See "Context Stinks!" *New Literary History* 42, no. 4 (2011): 573–91.

21 In an email to Haraway, Thom van Dooren also calls attention to

global human relationships in which we are all very definitely implicated in the suffering of countless humans (e.g. in the way our lifestyles are made possible by theirs), and also in factory farming . . . . [and] much of this suffering seems completely unjustified and preventable.

(Haraway, *When Species Meet*, 351, n. 5)

Haraway *acknowledges* historical context, but then seems to detach immediate participants from it as they work out their "co-subjectivity," which, for me, as van Dooren, renders her approach problematical because it brackets questions like: is it ethical for an Americans to have pets at all?

22 Gregory Okin, "Environmental Impacts of Food Consumption by Dogs and Cats," *PLoS One* 12, no. 8 (2017). On other negative effects of human cross-species alliances with dogs, see Robert Tindol, "The Best Friend of the Murderers: Guard Dogs and the Nazi Holocaust," in *Animals and War*, ed. Ryan Hediger (Leiden: Brill, 2012); Tyler Wall, "'For the Very Existence of Civilization': Police Dogs and Racial Terror," *American Quarterly* 68, no. 4 (2016): 861–82. Haraway admits such possibilities, without explaining how her "encounter" ethics addresses them.

23 Theodor Adorno, *Mimima Moralia: Reflections from Damaged Life*, trans. E.F.N. Jephcott (New York: Verso, 1978), 39.

24 Adorno calls this irreducibility the "preponderance of the object," but also insists that no object can be understood in isolation from totality. *Negative Dialectics*, trans. E.B. Ashton (London: Continuum, 1973).

25 Manuel DeLanda, *New Philosophy of Society* (London: Continuum, 2006). On the incompatibility of capitalism with ecological justice, see Andreas Malm, *The Progress of This Storm* (New York: Verso, 2018).

26 *Poor Robin's Jests*, 1667, 28. On early modern jests, see Linda Woodbridge, "Jestbooks, the Literature of Roguery and the Vagrant Poor," *English Literary Renaissance* 33, no. 2 (2003): 201–10; Pamela Allen Brown, *Better a Shrew than a Sheep* (Ithaca, NY: Cornell University Press, 2003).

27 It appears in a dedication to an anonymous translation of *Decameron*, sigs. A2v-A3r, suggesting that the translator, as the "poor man," hopes that the dedicatee will protect him from mastiff-like critics. On early modern understandings of Aesop, see Annabel Patterson, *Fables of Power* (Durham, NC: Duke University Press, 1991).

28 Patricia Fumerton, *Unsettled* (Chicago, IL: University of Chicago Press, 2006).

29 A.L. Beier, *Masterless Men* (York: Methuen, 1985).

30 Linda Woodbridge, "The Neglected Soldier as Vagrant, Revenger, Tyrant Slayer," in *Cast Out: Vagrancy and Homelessness in Global and Historical Perspective*, eds. A.L. Beier and Paul Ocobock (Columbus: Ohio University Press, 2008).

31 John Caius, *Of English Dogs*, trans. Abraham Fleming (London, 1576), 25–28. This book first appeared in Latin in 1570. All quotations from this source have been modernized.

32 Rebecca Bach, "Bearbaiting, Dominion and Colonialism," in *Race, Ethnicity and Power in the Renaissance*, ed. Joyce MacDonald (Madison, NJ: Fairleigh Dickenson University Press, 1997).

33 Harman, *Caveat*, 3.

34 Caius, *English Dogs*, 26–27.

35 Ibid., 16.

36 Kelsi Nagy and Phillip David Johnson II, eds., *Trash Animals* (Minneapolis: University of Minnesota Press, 2013). "Trash" corresponds in part to Haraway's "killable." I am equally concerned with the "ignorable" (who, too, are vulnerable). On the early modern "trash" dog, see Emily Cockayne, "Who Did Let the Dogs Out?—Nuisance Dogs in Late Medieval and Early Modern England," in *Our Dogs, Ourselves*, ed. Laura Gelfand (Leiden: Brill, 2016).

37 "Custom" was sometimes wielded from below against legal codes and anti-commoner manipulations of them, but this practice can be romanticized, since migrants and the poorest of the poor were typically disadvantaged in relation to both. Andy Wood, *The Memory of the People* (Cambridge: Cambridge University Press, 2013).

38 The *Manifesto* implies "all" means "humans," but "Species Being," as I argued earlier, suggests that the "human" can only emerge as an effect of relations of mutual thriving of "all" the planet.

39 Caius, *English Dogs*, 34.

40 Property valued at 40 shillings ostensibly determined permanent interest, but political participation often was even narrower, Robert Bucholz and Newton Key, *Early Modern England*, 2nd ed. (Hoboken, NJ: Wiley-Blackwell, 2009), 50. In the "Putney Debates," collected in *Puritanism and Liberty*, ed. A.S.P. Woodhouse (Chicago, IL: University of Chicago Press, 1951), 52–76, Henry

Ireton averred that only men who had a "permanent fixed interest" in the Kingdom should make laws, and compared native born unpropertied man to "foreigners," 54–55, in terms of political rights. For two contrasting recent takes on early modern "foreigners," see Jacob Selwood, *Diversity and Difference in Early Modern London* (New York: Routledge, 2010) and Scott Oldenburg, *Alien Albion* (Toronto: University of Toronto Press, 2014).

41 Harold Brooks, "Two Clowns in a Comedy (to Say Nothing of a Dog)," in *Two Gentlemen of Verona: Critical Essays*, ed. J. Schlueter (Shrewsbury: Garland, 1996); Bruce Boehrer, *Shakespeare among the Animals* (Basingstoke: Palgrave, 2002); Marge Garber, *Shakespeare after All* (New York: Pantheon, 2004); Erica Fudge, "The Dog Is Himself," in *How to Do Things with Shakespeare*, ed. Laurie McGuire (Hoboken, NJ: Wiley-Blackwell, 2007); Lesley Kordecki, "True Love and the Nonhuman," *Social Alternatives* 32, no. 4 (2013): 28–33. Karen Raber, *Shakespeare and Posthumanist Theory* (London: Arden, 2018); Laurie Shannon, "Poor Things, Vile Things: Shakespeare's Comedy of Kinds," in *Oxford Handbook of Shakespearean Comedy*, ed. Heather Hirschfield (New York: Oxford University Press, 2018), 358–73. All quotations are from William Shakespeare, *Two Gentlemen of Verona*, ed. Will C. Carroll (London: Arden, 2004).

42 Linda Pollock, "The Practice of Kindness in Early Modern Elite Society," *Past and Present* 211 (2011): 121–58, argues that historians have paid insufficient attention to "kindness," even though it turns up "conspicuously frequently throughout the domestic correspondence of the propertied" (122), as a term for a special favor in excess of ordinary obligation. While "charity" was due to all, she argues, "kindness" was understood to be particular and exclusive, an observation that intersects intriguingly with my argument about propertied "kind" exclusive here, even though she is dismissive of "coercive" social forces (151). In Shakespeare studies, consideration of "kind" has been considerable, but only Shannon, *op cit*, discusses *Two Gentlemen* and kind at any length, though differently than I do here. Two other recent explorations of "kind" and Shakespeare: Urvashi Chakravarty, "More than Kin, Less than Kind: Similitude, Strangeness, and Early Modern English Homonationalisms," *Shakespeare Quarterly* 67, no. 1 (2016): 125–35; Peggy Kamuf, "'This Were Kindness': Economies of Difference in the Merchant of Venice," *Oxford Literary Review* 34, no. 1 (2012): 71–87.

43 Wages also come up when Launce considers whether to marry the milkmaid, 3.1.267.

44 Elizabeth Rivlin provides a useful overview of the (voluminous) recent work on servants more generally, especially in Shakespeare Studies, in "Service and Servants in Early Modern English Culture to 1660," *Journal of Early Modern Studies* 4 (2015): 17–41.

45 Contrast Elizabeth Rivlin's reading in "Mimetic Service in *Two Gentlemen of Verona*," *ELH* 72, no. 1 (2005): 105–28.

46 "Friendship" (especially "queer" readings) is also an influential recent approach to the play. See Jeffrey Masten, *Textual Intercourse* (New York: Cambridge University Press, 1997); Stephen Guy-Bray, "Shakespeare and the Invention of the Heterosexual," *EMLS* 16 (2007): 12.1–28, http://purl.oclc.org/emls/si-16/brayshks.htm; David Orvis, "'Which Is the Worthiest Love'," in *Queer Shakespeare: Desire and Sexuality*, ed. Goran Stanivukovic (London: Bloomsbury, 2017), 33–49.

47 Caius, *English Dogs*, 20.

48 Annabel Patterson, *Shakespeare and Popular Culture* (Baltimore, MD: John Hopkins University Press, 1978), especially 253–60. On the use of the category of "class" to discuss historical relations before the nineteenth century see Raymond Williams's discussion of "structure of feeling." The lived experience of any historical moment is always contradictory and largely unconscious, such that later reflection and terminology can elucidate that which was obscure to immediate participants. *Marxism and Literature* (Oxford: Oxford University Press, 1977).

49 Bruce Boehrer, "Shylock and the Rise of the Household Pet," *Shakespeare Quarterly* 50, no. 2 (1999): 156.

50 Indeed, reviews and playbills now often give the actor-dog billing: see Alfred Hickling, "Two Gentlemen of Verona Review—Shakespeare on a Gap-Year Adventure," *Guardian*, August 14, 2016. www.theguardian.com/stage/2016/aug/04/two-gentlemen-of-verona-review-shakespeare-grosvenor-park-theatre-chester.

51 In "A Dog at All Things: The Transformation of the Onstage Caninie, 1550–1850," *Performance Research* 5, no. 2 (2000): 116–24, Michael Dobson argues that the "performing" Crab of *Shakespeare in Love* is anachronistic because onstage dogs are akin to "props" until the eighteenth century, whereas Richard Beadle, "Crab's Pedigree," in *English Comedy*, eds. Michael Cordner et al. (Cambridge: Cambridge University Press, 1994), citing the popularity of animal street performers, proposes that these off-stage antics might have influenced the professional stage.

52 Along similar lines, I discuss the significance of the exclusion of the Nurse from the conclusion of *Romeo and Juliet*, "'First as Tragedy, Then as …': Gender, Genre, History and Romeo and Juliet," in *Rethinking Feminism in Early Modern Studies*, eds. Ania Loomba and Melissa Sanchez (New York: Routledge, 2016), 75–91.

53 Haraway, *When Species Meet*, 300.

54 See Goddard, "Calais."

55 Ibid.

56 See Gayatri Spivak, *A Critique of Postcolonial Reason* (Cambridge, MA: Harvard University Press, 1999), 2.

57 See Caroline Mortimer, "Having Children Is One of the Most Destructive Things You Can Do to the Environment, Says Researchers," *Independent*, July 12, 2017. www.independent.co.uk/environment/children-carbon-footprint-climate-change-damage-having-kids-research-a7837961. html.

58 Haraway, *When Species Meet*, 89, 208.

59 Michael Pollan, *Omnivore's Dilemma* (New York: Bloomsbury, 2007), 152. Chapter 10 of *When Species Meet* comes closest to this view, but Haraway's dispute with animal activists over meat eating leads her to sidestep questions of what food system might result in planetary justice for humans and nonhumans beyond the "affluent, so-called first world," and what the implications would be for the affluent of such transformations (including for pet keeping).

60 British Petroleum Statistical Review of World Energy, 67th edition, June 2018. www.bp.com/content/dam/bp/en/corporate/pdf/energy-economics/statistical-review/bp-stats-review-2018-full-report.pdf.

61 Ecological Footprint, *Data Footprint Network*, www.footprintnetwork.org/.

62 Reece Jones, *Violent Borders: Regugees and the Right to Move* (New York: Verso, 2016).

63 See Okin, "Environmental Impacts."

64 In *Bruno Latour: Assembling the Political* (London: Pluto, 2014), Graham Harman describes some of the ongoing sticking points between Marxists and Latourians frankly, including the possibility that Latour's approach allows "insufficient room for sub-revolutionary change that would still be significant" (119–20). Overall, he defends Latour, however, including his characterization of "knowledge" as a weak basis for politics. In contrast, I view practical knowledge concerning regenerative agriculture (among other things) as abundant and crucial to political action: in addition to Pollan, *op cit.*, Philip Lymberry, *Farmageddon* (London: Bloomsbury, 2014); Raj Patel, *Stuffed and Starved* (New York: Melville House, 2012); Wangari Maathai, *The Green Belt Movement* (Seattle: Lantern Books, 2003); La via Campesina: https://viacampesina.org/en/.

65 In *We Have Never Been Modern* (*op cit.*), Latour imagines a Parliament of Things: "let one of the representatives talk . . . about the ozone hole, another represent the Monsanto chemical industry, a third the workers of the same chemical industry, another the voters of New Hampshire, a fifth the meteorology of the polar regions, let still another speak in the name of the state" (144).

5

BEASTS, ANIMALS, AND ANIMAL METAPHOR, IN SHAKESPEARE AND HIS FELLOW DRAMATISTS

Karl Steel

I The Last Honest Beast

In a wilderness, having abjured the false company of humankind, *Timon of Athens* once more endures the society of the only person who lives down to his expectations, the philosophical churl Apemantus. As he gnaws on roots, disdains a trove of accidentally unburied gold, and competes in misanthropic insults, Timon demands to know what Apemantus would do with the world had he absolute power: "Give it to the beasts, to be rid of the men" (IV.iii.366).[1]

Speaking at least in a strictly quantitative sense, none of the plays ascribed to Shakespeare is as beast-ridden as *Timon of Athens*.[2] The word and its variants appear in it 20 times, easily eclipsing the mere eight uses of its closest rival, *Hamlet* (the other plays average at slightly more than three apiece).[3] In Shakespeare's hands, "beast" can sometimes be a slightly insulting description, as with the phrase "strange beasts," used twice, when Trinculo tries to classify the sleeping Caliban (*Tempest* II.ii.31), and when Jacques mocks two rustic clowns (*As You Like It* V.iv.38). That is about as good as it gets for beasts, because otherwise, a beast is life in its wretchedness. A human possessing no more than its natural needs would be as "cheap as beast's" (*King Lear* II.iv.307). "Beast" is also a contemptuous pejorative: "O, you beast! / O faithless coward, O dishonest wretch" (*Measure for Measure* III.i.153–54). Finally, *Richard III*'s "not to relent is beastly, savage, devilish" (I.iv.273) illustrates the word's most potent meaning, that of being an enemy to all society, order, and peace ("contumelious, beastly, mad-brained war" (*Timon* V.i.200)), or of being nothing except as a certain force of "fury" (*Timon* III.v.74) and "wicked[ness]" (*Timon* III.ii.46). The beast thus matches Timon's "I am Misanthropos and hate mankind" (IV.iii.59), for a beast is life at its most antisocial, wanting no less than destruction for everyone and everything.

Saying that "beasts" are furious and terrifying may seem otiose, because everyone already knows beasts are bad. But one method of critical animal studies, and indeed any other form of cultural critique, is simply to redescribe the things that "go without saying," as if these familiar things were strange or somehow new to us. Deliberately naive redescription, not a view from nowhere, but, as it were, a "view from Mars," estranges us from the familiar and loosens long-sedimented ideas. Here I follow the call in Derrida's groundbreaking *The Animal that Therefore I am* for a "limitrophic" attention to distinctions between humans and that heterogeneous mass of living things that humans homogeneously classify as "animals."

61

As Derrida insists, the point is not to erase the difference between humans and animals, but to examine that limit anew by attending to the cultural work that nourishes the limit (as limitrophy derives in part from the Greek verb *trophein*); it recognizes human/animal differences as "foliated," not a single line, but a shifting set of culturally variable borders.[4]

Redescription helps us understand that there is not just one form of animalization. The following pages will explore three limitrophic problems of animalization's varieties: humans metaphorized as beasts are antisocial, a class of unclassifiable things, but, as I'll observe, antisocial only to a certain point. Those humans described as a particular kind of animal—a wolf or a fox or a sheep—are likened to something with qualities (unlike a beast), but usually just one, predictable quality: here "animalization" is a temporary simplification of human character into a single, familiar trait; but, as my final section will explore, humans metaphorized as particular kinds of animals might also explode the settled expectations of the familiar, because early modern natural science still preserved some of the wonder of classical and medieval natural science. To be a sheep is one known thing, but to be a bear's embryo, or a hyena or panther, quite another—here, in Shakespeare and his contemporaries, an animalized human might be understood not as insulted, nor as constrained, but rather liberated through animal metaphor.

In Shakespeare's works, being a beast is something quite different than being an animal. The word "animal" never appears in *Timon*, and only rarely elsewhere in Shakespeare; and as Laurie Shannon in particular has observed, the use of "animal" to mean nonhuman, nonplant living things was not yet common in English during Shakespeare's life.[5] "Animal" in Shakespeare generally refers to living things in their helplessness or limitations, the "wretched" or "bare forked" animals, or a character scorned as "only an animal, only sensible in the duller parts" (*Love's Labor's Lost* IV.ii.29). Hamlet's "paragon of animals" attests to human animality, since we are also living things (as "animal" derives from the Latin *anima*, soul, the immaterial extra quality that gives life to a body). A human called an "animal" might be animalized not by being misrecognized as lacking its supposedly unique rational and linguistic capacities, but rather by being recognized as participating in the common lot of dependent and mortal living things; to be "animalized," then, can be a kind of mercy. Such sympathetic attention to the shared vulnerability of humans and nonhumans would be alien to a play as bilious as *Timon*. A human called a "beast," on the other hand, is animalized in a radically different way. Apemantus's reference to "beastly ambition" (IV iii.368) marks how the adjective "beastly" need not have anything to do with animals at all, for what ambition could an animal possibly suffer from? Instead, "beast" here just marks an *excess*. Timon becomes a beast, crucially not an animal, because he makes himself so unfit for and such an enemy to everything. Abandoning his hangers-on and his debts,[6] he sloughs off all communal ties and all obligations, ultimately becoming less a kind of thing than a mad, unclassifiable force that refuses the domestication of any certain order.

When Timon echoes Apemantus, by himself wishing that "beasts" would have "the world in empire" (IV.iii.438), his wish is for an impossibility, because an "empire" implies a collective. Particular kinds of animals might be gregarious, but not beasts: so says a key source for Timon, William Painter's widely read *Palace of Pleasure*, an English-language compendium of Italian stories that includes, for example, a chapter on Romeo and Juliet, and another that provided material for *As You Like It*. Its chapter on Timon observes "how like a beast (in deede) [Timon] was: for he could not abide any other men, beinge not able to suffer the company of him, which was of like nature."[7] Painter's Timon persists even past his death in his commitment to this "beastly and churlish life" and its refusal of all community, as he demands that his corpse be thrown into the ocean, refusing any ritual, and thus any collective recognition, that would transform his carcass into a corpse. (Shakespeare's Timon, on the other hand, just dies offstage, leaving behind nothing but a tomb inscribed with an epitaph addressed to "some beast" (V.iii.4), addressed, that is, to nothing that could read it or care.) Wanting nothing but destruction for and escape from everyone, dwelling in a wilderness whose nature is to refuse everyone and everything a home, Timon and Apemantus at least pretend to want only that the false world be returned to chaos.

Yet at the center of that chaos remain these two beastly truth-tellers, having abandoned everything except their confidence in their rightness. Aristotle's *Politics* observes that "he that cannot abide to live in company, or through sufficiency hath need of nothing, is not esteemed a part of member of a city, but is either a beast or a god,"[8] or, we might say, both at once, or a philosopher, even in or because of his antisocial, righteous fury. The divine, judgmental beastliness of Timon and Apemantus makes them associates of what David Hershinow calls a "Diogenical" outsider, an early modern character type whose cynical railing against flatterers, contempt for all merely cultural comforts, and certainty that they alone know the truth grants them a "sovereign autonomy," mastery, that is, without any responsibility towards any subjects.[9] Timon the beast condemns Athens as a "forest of beasts" (IV.iii.391) and wants it because he believes that he alone is indifferent to the appetites that unthinkingly motivate others.[10] His becoming a beast, in other words, makes him believe that everyone else is but a beast in relation to his singularly rational self. And finally, in his sovereignty answerable only to this own perfected, antisocial reason, Timon has much in common with Giorgio Agamben's analysis of the animal paradox of sovereignty. Agamben's *Homo Sacer* observed that the wolf is, of course, an outlaw, but so too is the sovereign, because a sovereign relies on nothing but its own self to justify its decisions.[11] Just as the sovereign is kin to the wolf in its refusal to be constrained by the law, and a god kin to the beast in its refusal to be constrained by dependency to others, so too the hyper-rational philosopher, alien to all desire and all mere worldly ambition, is at its heart a beast, that supposed enemy of reason.

We should be wary, however, of the allure paradox holds for theoretically inflected literary criticism. It delights in the pretense of any pure concept collapsing into its opposite: the host becomes the enemy[12]; our own body becomes indistinguishable from an intruder[13]; and beastly rage and philosophical detachment, unrestrained by custom or social obligation, are, in their lawless contempt for social constraints, ultimately indistinguishable. But the difference in social power between beast and sovereign must be remembered. Whatever the intellectual neatness of the paradox that collapses beast into sovereign, the sovereign still holds the singular position of being the one whose decisions have the force of law, and thus of possessing social recognition and the power to enforce that recognition with legalized violence, whereas the beast is always the outsider. The difference between the two might be marked this way: the beast is alone, while the sovereign is *singular*. Similarly, however much Timon paradoxically takes on the condition of beastliness by becoming the ultimate philosopher, he still maintains his position of possessing normative judgment, both because he believes himself to be among the only truly rational humans, and especially because he clings to his position as a rational *man*.

Those few Athenians who escape Timon's scorn—Flavius, his loyal steward; Alcibiades, betrayed by Athens, and for that begrudgingly admired; and especially Apemantus, whose philosophy and demeanor Timon imitates—all have in common their maleness. The play's few women are spared nothing, however, suggesting the entanglement of the pose of antisocial rational contempt and misogyny. Though the bestial philosopher acts as if he has removed himself from all social rules, he still maintains this one foundation to the social order. The Amazons of Timon's first, lavish banquet, costumed dancers, are scorned by Apemantus as a "sweep of vanity" (I.ii.136), and Alcibiades' two concubines, the prostitutes Phrynia and Timandra, receive from Timon both gold and unrelenting scorn. And when Timon urges

Alcibiades to destroy Athens, his hopes for merciless slaughter concentrate especially on women. His list of targets begins with an old man, then continues like so:

> Strike me the counterfeit matron;
> It is her habit only that is honest,
> Herself's a bawd. Let not the virgin's cheek,
> Make soft they trenchant sword, for those milk paps,
> That through the window-bars bore at men's eyes,
> Are not within the leaf of pity writ,
> But set them down horrible traitors.
>
> (IV.iii.124–33)

And Phrynia and Timandra, indistinguishably delivering their lines mostly together, are brought on stage just to be seen through: Timon is certain that Phrynia's "cherubin look" (IV.iii.70) only masks the disease he is certain she carries, and he heaps her and Timandra with gold to help their beauty disfigure all Athens with syphilis. When they depart with Alcibiades, Timon next turns his scorn on the earth itself, that "common mother" (III iii.203), so echoing his earlier scorn for his unburied gold as "damnèd earth, / thou common whore of mankind" (III.iii.46–47). In women, whether virgins, mothers, prostitutes, or old matrons—this list being his full taxonomy—Timon turns up the material form itself of "prostituted humanity" and thus the form of the irredeemably false social order his beastly philosophy aims to undo.[14] These women, all women, are for Timon Athens as it really is.

We are all familiar with the cliché of the lonely man, the enemy of all fraud, and all too familiar with their habitual targeting of women. Timon is no exception: who gives a prostitute gold but a client? Yet Timon believes himself beyond all that. The man who transforms himself into a beast is generally a misogynist, because the commitments of independent, solitary, contemptuous, and smugly hypocritical men, at any rate, typically scorn desire and comforts, usually coded as "female"; still more misogynist is scorn for the fundamental dependency that obligates all of us to each other. Beware the man who believes he is beyond all common desire or responsibility.

Animalization strips away humanity, but not in any one way, because there is no one way for a human to be an animal. By bestializing himself, Timon also bestializes the rest of the world, because he believes he knows what irredeemably drives them, and therefore why they must be destroyed. He shuts himself away in solitude, away from all dependence, in a lonely, arrogant hyper-rational hyper-masculinity. Late in the play, Timon misidentifies Flavius, because of his weeping, as a woman (IV.iii.541), and then proclaims him the "one honest man" (IV.iv.557): his last brief willingness to receive compassion—with its hint of a collapse of gender difference, and its willingness to acknowledge the good in others—might have been Timon's escape from cynic philosophy, and a redemption for himself, for others, and for other life. It might have been his return to a new humanization, founded not on the supposed supremacy of reason, but on entanglement of humans and nonhumans in mutual need, without any disdain for dependency. But at last he drives Flavius away, so driving from himself, again, all common delights, all obligation. In feeling himself only scorned, Timon becomes a beast, and for that, everything else must suffer his truth.

II Ethology's Limits

To be just, William Painter's *The Palace of Pleasure* is of at least two minds about beasts. Despite repeating the old idea of beastly solitude ("how like a beast (in deede) he was"), the first

Beasts, Animals, and Animal Metaphor

sentence of Painter's Timon chapter imagines beasts as typically social: "all the beastes of the worlde do applye themselves to other beasts of theyre kind, Timon of Athens only excepted." And while Shakespeare is generally hostile to beasts, he likewise observes that "nature teaches beasts to know their friends" (*Coriolanus* II.i.6). Beasts are furious, raging, destructive, except when they cluster into their own particular kinds. The fantasy of beastly self-sorting attests both to a belief in a naturally communal quality to all life—not a "red in tooth and claw" war of all against all, but a massive set of what we might call homogeneous animal republics[15]— and to a taxonomic imagination that atomized the homogenized mass of beasts into species, each having their own individual characteristics. Being a beast might just be awful, but what it means to be a particular kind of beast, and to be *compared* to a particular kind of beast, depends on the beast. Because a sheep is not a wolf is not a fox, there is no one form of animalization.

But the metaphorical use of animals might be said not to have all that much to do with animals themselves. In response to Apemantus' "beastly ambition" (IV.iii.368) for a world denuded of humans, Timon imagines Apemantus becoming various animals:

> if thou wert the lion, the fox would beguile thee. If thou wert the lamb, the fox would eat thee. If thou wert the fox, the lion would suspect thee when peradventure thou wert accused by the ass. If thou wert the ass, thy dullness would torment thee, and still thou lived'st but as a breakfast to the wolf,
>
> *(IV.iii.370–75)*

and so on. Timon of course is not the only one in Shakespeare's work to make such a speech. *King Lear's* Edgar, during his feigned madness, bemoans a woman "false of heart, light of ear, bloody of hand; hog in sloth, fox in stealth, wolf in greediness, dog in madness, lion in prey" (III.iv.98–101). Comparisons like these do not actually imagine their human targets transformed into animals; instead, the rich and varying lifeworld of an animal disappears into the one trait each is made to embody. The metaphorical lion is less a big hairy feline carnivore than just something "valiant" (*Henry IV, Part 1* II.iv.286), "proud" (*Macbeth* IV.1.103), and possessed of a terrible roar (*Henry VI, Part 2* III.1.19; *King John* II.1.306). Being compared to a fox implies nothing about furriness or pointed tails; instead, it is just that the fox, always "subtle" (*Cymbeline* III.iii.44), aptly illustrates treachery:

> For treason is but trusted like the fox,
> Who, never so tame, so cherished and locked up,
> Will have a wild trick of his ancestors.
>
> *(Henry IV Part 1 V.ii.11–13)*

And likewise with lambs and wolves and pigs. Each metaphorization distills the animal into a single, predictable unitary trait expressing specific actions and moods: the fox is nothing but a beguiler, the lamb nothing but meek prey, the donkey nothing but a dullard, and the wolf nothing but a despoiler of other people's property. Because the animal metaphor sloughs off nearly the whole of the animal life, affixing an adjective to an animal—a ravenous wolf, for example—is otiose, because in metaphor, the wolf is nothing but its appetite.

The animal provides a distinct kind of natural metaphor, of course, different from a rock or a river, for example. Animals have faces, they move on their own, they want things, and they can die. But the metaphorical refinement of animal behavior to a singular trait—in what we might call a tradition of poetic ethology—makes animals have desires, motion, and vulnerabilities only in highly constrained, predictable ways, without any choice to be anything other than what they do. When metaphor applies animal singularity to humans, it briefly freezes human multiplicity into one neat quality. The animal metaphor does not achieve its effects from the yoking together of unlikeliness. Only the human is unlikely, because a human might be anything at any given moment, in any given circumstance; but the animal side almost never varies. If human emotional expression has a history—if we expect men to faint and cry in twelfth-century French warrior tales, and to keep themselves stoic in the sixteenth and seventeenth, as with "Dispute it like a man" (*Macbeth* IV.iii.259)—the character of animals in metaphor functions as a transhistoric emotional resource, predictable stages on which the variations of human comportment might play. Metaphorical animals thus work in a state of suspended animation, without any surprises, for the animal rendered into metaphor is less the gradual spilling out of a life than a GIF, an off-the-rack flipbook of satisfyingly looping action.

Critical animal theorists are fond of quoting Walter Benjamin's comments on the animals in Kafka[16] that they are "repositories of the forgotten," like Kafka's tubercular cough, which he called "the animal," and which Benjamin glossed as "the last outpost of the great herd."[17] There is a similar fondness for John Berger's "if the first metaphor was animal, it was because the essential relation between man and animal was metaphoric."[18] Derrida finds philosophy wanting, for "thinking concerns the animal … derives from poetry," and poetry "is what philosophy, essential, had to deprive itself of" to present itself as making sense.[19] The "animetaphor," as Akira Mizuta Lippit writes, "supplements the dream, language, and world systems, providing an external source of energy that changes the machine."[20] For these writers, for the "becoming animal" of Deleuze and Guattari too, the animal is something not quite captured by human limitations; it is a source of energy, surprise, of a lurking surplus in our pretensions of order; it is what gets free and disarranges. Nicole Shukin's *Animal Capital* demonstrates the failures of such fantasies: the animal as outsider or natural foundation requires an undialectical, ahistorical, even nostalgic faith in an uncorrupted outside, a faith that sometimes supports a politics of liberation and resistance, but not inevitably.[21] Even without needing to appeal to Shukin's critique, we can simply mark the utter predictability of so many of Shakespeare's animal metaphors: if the "animetaphor" is a "fabulous machine," Shakespeare's animal metaphors are often just the half of that, mechanical. There is no "cough" in them, nothing to unsettle their smooth operation. Certain and straightforward, they set nothing free, but instead, briefly bind the human to an already bound animal.

His metaphors work so reliably because he typically draws them from how animals function for humans.[22] Foxes are sneaky, because they slyly steal our things; wolves are ravenous, because they eat our animals, and they frighten us; sheep are meek and helpless and edible, because we have bred them to be just that. His animal metaphors therefore tend to be not quite so much animal metaphors as to be animals-for-us metaphors, already trapped in a human orbit even before the obviously anthropocentric work of his metaphor. Foxes and wolves and lions might do other things, out of our sensing, but we are unlikely to hear about them from Shakespeare; and if his dogs and horses have a more unpredictable liveliness, this is because dogs and horses serve more functions for humans. More likely than foxes and wolves and even sheep to be familiar to urban poets, they cannot be so easily smelted into one pure quality. His metaphorical dogs might be mad (*Anthony and Cleopatra* IV.xv.93) or beaten (*Coriolanus* IV.v.56) but, like actual dogs, they might also be our intimates (*Henry IV Part 2* II.ii.105). And his horses tend to be just that, horses, not metaphors.

Critical animal theory encourages literary scholars to read textual animals as something other than just symbols, as witnesses, in other words, to other-than-human life. We would be expected to salvage Shakespeare's animals by proposing, for example, that his animal metaphors nevertheless infect the human with animality, as no human can escape the touch of a metaphor unscathed. We could "blur the boundary" between human and animal by demonstrating how much of our emotional lives, for example, our rage and hunger and loyalty is really animal, at least to the poets; the belief that category mobility is equivalent to liberation would encourage us to such an interpretation.

Such interpretations are possible, even welcome, but we might hold off on these interpretations until we have more fully recognized Shakespeare's limitations. It may be that Shakespeare strikes so many as a modern because his animals are often so familiar to us: they are constrained in ways we expect them to be constrained, anticipating how the fabulous qualities of animals of classical and medieval natural history would give way to the anthropocentric prejudices of certain strains of modern science. For animal metaphors better suited for shaking what Jeffrey Jerome Cohen calls the "specious boundaries of the human,"[23] we should expand our attention to read Shakespeare along with the poetic ethology of other early modern dramatists, to get a wider sense of the strange potentials of animal metaphor.

III Other Natures

Shakespeare can feel contemporary to us because we are unlikely to find his animals surprising. Shakespeare's panthers are hunted (*Titus Andronicus* 1.i.502), spotty (*The Tempest* IV.1.284), and dangerous to deer (*Troilus and Cressida* III.iii.196), but they lure no prey to their dens with their sweet breath. His hyenas laugh (*As You like It* IV.1.163), but never draw humans to their doom by counterfeiting their voices. His beavers are just parts of armor, not animals at all, and certainly not animals that castrate themselves to escape their hunters. His eagles are the steeds of Jupiter (*Cymbeline* V.iv.95), the insignia of Rome (*Cymbeline* V.v.566), far-sighted (*Love's Labor's Lost* IV.iii.240 and *Richard II* III.iii.70), and noble, disdainful master predators (*King John* V.ii.128); one may be long-lived (*Timon* IV.iii.247), and another stare directly into the sun (*Love's Labor's Lost* IV.iii.246–48 and *3 Henry VI* II.i.92–93), but his never renew their youth by soaring far into the sky. It has been said, sometimes laughingly, that Shakespeare invented the human[24]; but we might say instead, just as seriously, that, to the degree that Shakespeare is understood, or misunderstood, as "modern," he might well be blamed for inventing the boring animal.[25] To combat that misunderstanding, and to consider one last form of animalization, this section foregrounds some of the animal surprises we can find by looking at what Shakespeare, and especially his contemporaries do, with animal metaphor rooted on what is now outmoded knowledge.

Drawn from classical writers like Pliny and Solinus, repeated and refined by the great Latin medieval natural history compendia of Albert the Great (*On Animals*, and *Questions Concerning Aristotle's 'On Animals'*), Thomas of Cantimpré (*On the Nature of Things*), Vincent of Beauvais *(The Mirror of Nature)*, and Bartholomew the Englishman *(On the Properties of Things)*, or even from the Bible itself—Psalms 103:5 praises God renewing our youth, "like the eagle's"—the old strains of animal lore would be repeated well into the seventeenth century, preserved, sometimes skeptically, in texts like Stephen Batman's slightly updated version of John Trevisa's late fourteenth-century English translation of the Bartholomew (1584), or in Edward Topsell's widely reprinted *Historie of Foure-Footed Beastes* (1607).

Some old facts might be met with doubt: Topsell repudiates, for example, the notion that bear cubs are born shapeless:

> And whereas it hath been believed and received, that the whelps of Bears at their first littering are without all form and fashion, and nothing but a little congealed blood like a lump of flesh, which afterwards the old one frameth with her tongue to her own

likeness, as Pliny, Solinus, Aelianus, Orus, Oppianus, and Ovid have reported, yet is the truth most evidently otherwise, as by the eye-witness of Joachimus Rhetious, and other, is disproved: only it is littered blind without eyes, naked without hair, and the hinder legs not perfect, the fore-feet folded up like a fist, and other members deformed by reason of the immoderate humor or moystness in them.[26]

He is just as certain, however, about the sweet breath of panthers. Some natural historians argued that panthers hunt by hiding in trees and changing the color of their spots, so camouflaging themselves into murderous invisibility. Topsell counters with a perhaps uncharacteristic conservativism, "there is no cause to draw the Beasts unto him, but the attractive power of his sweet savour." Batman on beavers approvingly repeats the old belief about castration ("they geld themselues when they be ware of the hunter"[27]); for his part, Topsell thinks this "most false," akin to the "poyson [that] hath also crept into and corrupted the whole body of Religion."[28] Topsell nonetheless endorses the belief—found, for example, in Gerald of Wales' twelfth-century *History and Topography of Ireland*[29]—about how aged beavers, their teeth too worn to gnaw through trees, remain useful to their fellows:

> upon his belly lade [the fellow beavers] all their timber, which they so ingeniously work and fasten into the compasse of his legs that it may not fall, and so the residue by the tail, draw him to the water side, where these buildings are to be framed: and this the rather seemeth to be true, because there have been some such taken, that had no hair on their backs, but were pilled; which being espied by the hunters, in pity of their slavery, or bondage, they have let them go away free.[30]

That pity for these living sleds is a striking moment of cross-species sympathy. Just as striking is the dynamic of doubt and credulousness, in which written authority wavers before eyewitness testimony, even if just second-hand. Topsell relies on hunters for parts of his beaver knowledge. One of his chief sources, the mid sixteenth-century *Historiae animalium* of Conrad Gessner, proudly relays a story from the astronomer Georg Joachim Rheticus about Polish hunters who had taken a bear with a tiny bear-shaped fetus still in its uterus.[31] Old knowledge might be on its way out, but could be preserved at least so long as someone could be provided to believe in it.

That is, belief can be a more complicated matter than a simple determination of truth or falsity. Sometimes simply knowing *about* something can be a record of a kind of belief. Scholars have broken themselves for centuries on the question of whether Shakespeare read Batman,[32] but even if he never did, Shakespeare, like his fellow dramatists, would have certainly known something of traditional animal lore even without reading him or writers like him, because others outside the natural history compendia still repeated the old knowledge. Michael Drayton's preface to a reprinting of his tragic poems on Robert of Normandy, Queen Matilda, and Piers Gaveston (1596) complains that sections had been released "contrary to my will," full of mistakes, "left unformed and undigested, like a Bear whelpe before it is licke by the Dam"[33]; after William Bullein's *Bulkwarke of Defense against Sickness* (1562) praises bear fat for soothing the pains of footmen, it pauses to disprove "the common fable among the people, that …. Beare hath a disformed Whelp in the time of deliverance, without Members"[34]: as a poet and as a physician, Drayton and Bullein each has his own, differing standards of truth. But even by disproving common knowledge, Bullein attested to its continued currency, even if just as a target to let him present himself, a physician, as an authority. We can safely assume that Shakespeare, as well-read as he was, and as social as he

Beasts, Animals, and Animal Metaphor

was by profession, had at least a passing familiarity with the common wisdom of his era.[35] And familiarity is enough for a poet to make an effective allusion.

We should therefore avoid two great mistakes of dealing with early modern natural history. We should not assume that classical and medieval writers were more credulous than the early moderns, nor that Shakespeare was *less* credulous when his animals behave in ways more familiar to us. Although the thirteenth-century Dominican Albert the Great, for example, is well-known for arguing that barnacle geese hatch not from shellfish, but from eggs, William Turner's *Avium praecipuarum, quarum apud Plinium et Aristotelem mentio est* [1544; *The Principle Birds mentioned by Pliny and Aristotle*] repeats the old belief: he doubts his main source, Gerald of Wales' *Topography*,[36] but then offers the testimony of an Irish theologian of his own era, who swore on the Gospels that he had seen and touched the barely formed chicks.[37] The third volume of Conrad Gessner's natural history, on birds, repeats a similar story from "not very truthworthy" men he met in Normandy about geese hatched from rotting wood.[38] And John Gerard's *Herball* (1597) concludes

> with one of the marvels of this land (we may say of the world) … certaine trees, whereon doe growe certaine shell fishes, of a white colour tending to russet; wherein are conteined little living creatures: which shels in time of maturitie doe open, and out of them grow those little living things; which falling into the water, doe become foules, whom we call Barnakles.[39]

Nor should we assume that the use of odd ethology for metaphor necessarily required that either the writer or their audience straightforwardly believed in the fact being metaphorized. The new science of the seventeenth century slowly relegated the old ethology to only antiquarian knowledge,[40] but it did not erase the knowledge altogether. Responding to or recognizing a metaphor requires a kind of belief in it, albeit of a different form than scientific knowledge: we skeptical moderns still know what it means to talk about ostriches putting their heads in the sand. Likewise, for the sake of making a metaphor, John Marston need not have *scientifically* believed anything about the "Scotch barnacle, now a block, instantly a worm, and presently a great goose."[41] It was enough that he knew, and that he expected his audience, to know about it. The subtlety of Shakespeare's one barnacle reference attests to his faith in general knowledge of this fact: Caliban warns Stephano and Trinculo to leave off their looting, for otherwise "We shall lose our time / And all be turned to barnacles or to apes / With foreheads villainous low" (*Tempest* IV.i.274–76), which is to say, he fears their being made, or treated as, fools, like an ape, or like a barnacle, that is, like a *goose*.

Much of the old natural history lent itself readily to dramatic metaphor. Even seemingly inapposite material could be used, like barnacles and bear cubs and beavers and long-lived eagles. *The Rebellion*, a tragedy by the engraver Thomas Rawlins, performed in 1629–30, has its "Count Machvile" scheme like so:

> Plot, plot, tumultious thoughts, incorporate;
> Beget a lump how e're deformed, that may at length
> Like to a Cub licked by the careful Dam,
> Become like to my wishes perfect vengeance.[42]
>
> (I.i.91–95)

Shakespeare's *3 Henry VI* has Richard III compare his body to "a chaos, or an unlicked bear-whelp, / That carries no impression like the dam" (164–65). William Strode's *The Floating Island, a statescraft allegory* performed in 1636 has its Iratus, an angry lord, speak of extracting himself

69

from a plot with "Thus when the Beaver smells the Hunters aime, / He throwes away the price of his escape" (I.vii).[43] Though the eagle's keen sight was, expectedly, a frequent source for metaphor, even its youth-restoring powers could be put to use: Ben Jonson's *Alchemist* has Sir Epicure Mammon believe in an elixir that can "Restore his years, renew him, like an eagle, / To the fifth age" (II.i.55–56),[44] while William Davenant's *The Just Italian* (1629) has its crafty suitor Florello imagining that "The gentle Turtle shall direct us how / T'augment our loves; the Eagle to renew / Our youth."[45] The deadly deceits of panthers and hyenas unsurprisingly proved more popular, because of their obvious utility for dramatic metaphors about speech, deception, and murder. John Lyly's comedy *Midas* (1589) speaks of "the craftines of the fox, the cruelty of the tiger, the ravening of the woolfe, [and] the dissembling of Hyena" (IV.ii.31)[46]; John Marston resorts to hyena metaphors at least twice, in *Eastward Ho* (1605; "I am deaf still, I say. I will neither yield to the song of the siren nor the voice of the hyena")[47] and *What You Will* (1601; "He Is a Hyena, and with Ciuitt scent / Of perfumed words, draws to make a prey / For laughter of thy credit"), although in the later allusion, he confuses the hyena with the panther.[48] Ben Johnson also slips, by mistaking the panther ("whose unnatural eyes / will strike thee dead," *The Poetaster* IV.vi.11–12) for the basilisk.[49] Shakespeare's pelicans, to be sure, still do what they had done since the classical writers; in *Hamlet* (IV.v.167), *Richard II* (III.iv.76), and *King Lear* (II.1.131), they pierce their breasts and feed their young with their own blood.

Shakespeare's beasts are the enemy of all familiarity, a mode of life that existed only for itself. His animals are mostly familiar, because they are for us. Constrained, they reflect our own prejudices about our emotional lives and our own vulnerabilities. They are there to be obediently eaten, to be pestiferous or dangerous or angry or noble, but generally do not challenge us to think of how the other ways we might live. They live as we do, but in a narrower way. For a richer world, one that better represents both the treasure of prescientific animal lore, one that anticipates the new treasures of modern ethology and biology, and one that allows animals to live for themselves, utterly indifferent to us, we need to give up on any embarrassment over the "vulgar errors" about early modern "unscientific" animals, and find in these lost facts, lost metaphors, and other possibilities for what might happen to humans when they entangle with animals.[50]

For the animals of early modern English writers can do strange things: not strange, of course, to the traditional animal lore—they would have been familiar from storytelling, despite the tendency of the panther to be blurred with hyenas and basilisks—but strange to how we imagine life to operate. They might live at different scales than us: occupying the sky, beyond our sight; possessed of senses and capacities that we could never imagine ourselves having; the bear mother is a female who provides form, challenging the Aristotelian model of conception in which only the male can shape matter into coherence[51]; and trees might become birds. Modern ethology can sometimes still leave old prejudices unsloughed: Vinciane Despret's *What Would Animals Say If We Asked the Right Questions* complains of the continued prevalence of a certainly that animals are motivated only by a "quasi-autonomous plumbing system" of thoughtless natural selection.[52] And many cultural conservatives profess believe in a natural two-gender model, despite the rarity of sexual reproduction among living things, and despite the 36,000 genders of some fungi.[53] Colin Dickey's review of Marah J. Hardt's *Sex in the Sea* speaks of an undersea world "sovereign and strange," whose world is not parallel and instructive to our own, but rather one that informs us "how alien our own behavior is to the vast range of life that we share the Earth with."[54] Such wonderful and various ways to be alive give us a nature that teaches us that nothing is normative except life's ceaseless creativity. If a bear can lick a baby into shape, what foolishness it is to think there is only one way to be!

Notes

1 All quotations from Shakespeare are from the Folger Digital Editions, consulted in August 2018 and January 2019.

2 For a recent treatment of the collaborative writing of *Timon*, Eilidh Kane, "Shakespeare and Middleton's Co-Authorship of Timon of Athens," *Journal of Early Modern Studies* 5 (2016): 217–35. The passages I discuss were, for the most part, probably written by Shakespeare. Any study of Shakespeare and animals would do well to begin with Karen Raber, "Shakespeare and Animal Studies," *Literature Compass* 12, no. 6 (2015): 286–98.

3 Spevack Marvin, *The Harvard Concordance to Shakespeare* (Cambridge, MA: Harvard University Press), 1973.

4 Jacques Derrida, *The Animal that Therefore I Am*, ed. Marie-Louise Mallet, trans. David Wills (New York: Fordham University Press, 2008), 29–31.

5 Laurie Shannon, *The Accommodated Animal: Cosmopolity in Shakespearean Locales* (Chicago, IL: University of Chicago Press, 2013).

6 For treatments of debt as a central theme of *Timon*, Amanda Bailey, *Of Bondage: Debt, Property, and Personhood in Early Modern England* (Philadelphia: University of Pennsylvania Press, 2013); Laura Kolb, "Debt's Poetry in Timon of Athens," *Studies in English Literature 1500–1900* 58, no. 2 (2018): 399–419.

7 William Painter, *The Palace of Pleasure*, ed. Joseph Jacobs, vol. 1 (London: D. Nutt, 1890), 112–13.

8 1598 English translation, quoted from the introductory material to William Shakespeare and Thomas Middleton, *Timon of Athens*, ed. John Jowett, The Oxford Shakespeare (New York: Oxford University Press, 2009), 29–30.

9 David Hershinow, "Diogenes the Cynic and Shakespeare's Bitter Fool: The Politics and Aesthetics of Free Speech," *Criticism* 56 (2015): 815. For another reading of *Timon* in the context of the history of cynicism, David Mazella, *The Making of Modern Cynicism* (Charlottesville: University of Virginia Press, 2007), 71–80. For wilderness fantasies of absolute sovereignty, see especially the first several seminars of Jacques Derrida, *The Beast and the Sovereign*, eds. Marie-Louise Mallet, Ginette Michaud, and Michel Lisse, trans. Geoffrey Bennington, 2 vols (Chicago, IL: University of Chicago Press, 2009), vol. 2.

10 For an allied, but alternate reading of *Timon*, see Ranier Emig, "Renaissance Self-Unfashioning: Shakespeare's Late Plays as Exercises in Unravelling the Human," in *Posthumanist Shakespeare*, eds. Stefan Herbrechter and Ivan Callus (New York: Palgrave MacMillan, 2012), 133–59.

11 Giorgio Agamben, *Homo Sacer: Sovereign Power and Bare Life*, trans. Daniel Heller-Roazen (Stanford, CA: Stanford University Press, 1998), 104–11.

12 Jacques Derrida, "Hostipitality," in *Acts of Religion*, ed. and trans. Gil Andijar (New York: Routledge, 2002), 356–420.

13 Jean-Luc Nancy, "L'Intrus," trans. Susan Hanson, *CR: The New Centennial Review* 2, no. 3 (2002): 1–14.

14 Kay Stanton, *Shakespeare's 'Whores': Erotics, Politics, and Poetics* (New York: Palgrave MacMillan, 2014), 55; for more on *Timon* and women, Coppélia Kahn, "'Magic of Bounty': *Timon of Athens*, Jacobean Patronage, and Maternal Power," *Shakespeare Quarterly* 38 (1987): 34–57, and Janet Adelman, *Suffocating Mothers: Fantasies of Maternal Origin in Shakespeare's Plays, Hamlet to the Tempest* (New York: Routledge, 2012).

15 Shannon, *The Accommodated Animal* is a key resource for such thinking.

16 For example, Kári Driscoll and Eva Hoffmann, "Introduction," in *What Is Zoopoetics?: Texts, Bodies, Entanglement*, eds. Kári Driscoll and Eva Hoffmann (Cham: Springer, 2018), 2.

17 "Franz Kafka, On the Tenth Anniversary of His Death," in Walter Benjamin, *Illuminations*, ed. Hannah Arendt, trans. Harry Zohn (New York: Schocken Books, 1968), 132.

18 John Berger, *Why Look at Animals?* (New York: Penguin, 2009), 7.

19 Derrida, *Animal that Therefore*, 7.

20 Akira Mizuta Lippit, "… From Wild Technology to Electric Animals," in *Representing Animals*, ed. Nigel Rothfels (Bloomington: Indiana University Press, 2002), 130.

21 Nicole Shukin, *Animal Capital: Rendering Life in Biopolitical Times* (Minneapolis: University of Minnesota Press, 2009).

22 For a contrasting emphasis, see Bruce Boehrer's *Animal Characters: Nonhuman Beings in Early Modern Literature* (Philadelphia: University of Pennsylvania Press, 2010). Boehrer describes a "model of literary character" rooted in Aristotle and Theophrastus founded, in part, on behavioral types

ascribed to animals; Boehrer focuses, however, on the "interactivity" (17) of animal metaphors, which, through the historical and cultural pressures of the late medieval and early modern periods, alters understandings of both animals and humans, while I focus on the one-way traffic that uses fixed animal types to temporarily limit more variable human types.

23 Jeffrey Jerome Cohen, "Inventing with Animals in the Middle Ages," in *Engaging with Nature: Essays on the Natural World in Medieval and Early Modern Europe*, eds. Barbara A. Hanawalt and Lisa J. Kiser (Notre Dame, IN: University of Notre Dame, 2008), 55.

24 Harold Bloom, *Shakespeare: Invention of the Human* (New York: Penguin, 1998).

25 Fully treating ethology and natural history in English drama from the sixteenth through the mid-seventeenth century—that is, up to point when the gravity of the scientific revolution began to generally deform and break apart the old beliefs—would be beyond the scope of my chapter. A sample suffices for identifying patterns. I used the https://corpus.byu.edu/eebo/, the TCP-EEBO corpus, with semantic markings carried out by the UCREL team at Leeds University; Visualizing English Print's Early Modern Drama Collection, https://graphics.cs.wisc.edu/WP/vep/vep-early-modern-drama-collection/, which I searched with DocFetcher, http://docfetcher.sourceforge.net/en/index.html. Where possible, I have checked quotations against modern editions. I also used Robert William Dent, *Proverbial Language in English Drama Exclusive of Shakespeare, 1495–1616: An Index* (Berkeley: University of California Press, 1984). I make no claims that the prevalence of terms or ideas in a corpus necessary indicates anything about their prevalence or influence in a larger culture. I heed the hesitations of Katherine Bode, "The Equivalence of 'Close' and 'Distant' Reading; or, toward a New Object for Data-Rich Literary History," *Modern Language Quarterly* 78, no. 1 (2017): 87–89, about "distant reading": the frequency or paucity of any given term, phrase, or idea in a given corpus by no means reflects which texts were read or reread or neglected, how they were ignored or loved, or, for that matter, where they were read.

26 Edward Topsell, *The History of Four-Footed Beasts* (Ann Arbor, MI: Text Creation Partnership, 2008), 30.

27 Stephan Batman, *Batman vppon Bartholome his Booke De proprietatibus rerum* (Ann Arbor, MI: Text Creation Partnership, 2003), 356.

28 Topsell, *Four-Footed Beasts*, 37.

29 Gerald of Wales, *The History and Topography of Ireland*, trans. John Joseph O'Meara, Revised (London: Penguin, 1982), 48–49.

30 Topsell, *Four-Footed Beasts*, 36.

31 Conrad Gessner, *Historiae animalium: de quadrupedibus viviparis*, 2nd ed. (Frankfurt: Bibliopolio Cambieriano, 1602), 944. Thank you to Karl Galle for directing me to the Gessner.

32 Elizabeth Keen, *The Journey of a Book: Bartholomew the Englishman and the Properties of Things* (Canberra: Australian National University E Press, 2007), 150–53.

33 Michael Drayton, *The Tragicall Legend of Robert, Duke of Normandy, Surnamed Short-Thigh, Eldest Sonne to William Conqueror* (Ann Arbor, MI: Text Creation Partnership, 2003), no page number.

34 William Bullein, *Bulleins Bulwarke of Defense against All Sicknesse* (Ann Arbor, MI: Text Creation Partnership, 2004), no page number.

35 For a similar observation, David Greetham, "On Cultural Translation," reprinted in *Textual Transgressions: Essays toward the Construction of a Biobibliography* (New York: Routledge, 1998), 500.

36 Gerald of Wales, *The History and Topography of Ireland*, 41–42.

37 William Turner, *Avium Praecipuarum, Quarum apud Plinium et Aristotelem Mentio Est, Brevis et Succincta Historia* (Cologne: Johannes Gymnicus, 1544), n.p., s.v., "ansere."

38 Conrad Gessner, *Historiae Animalium: Liber III, de Avium Natura* (Frankfurt: Roberti Cambieri, 1635), 162, "Audisse me nuper ex hominibus non indignis fide in Normannia putrescentibus lignis ad mare aviculas quasdam gigni."

39 John Gerard, *The Herball* (London: John Norton, 1597), 1391. For further discussion, see F. David Hoeniger and J.F.M. Hoeniger, *The Development of Natural History in Tudor England* (Boston, MA: MIT Press, 1979), 40–42, and John G.T. Anderson, *Deep Things Out of Darkness: A History of Natural History* (Berkeley: University of California Press, 2013), 44–46.

40 Greetham, "On Cultural Translation," 496–512.

41 John Marston, *The Malcontent*, ed. George K. Hunter (Manchester: Manchester University Press, 2001), 73.

42 Thomas Rawlins, *The Rebellion* (Ann Arbor, MI: Text Creation Partnership, 2004), no page numbers.

43 William Strode, *The Floating Island* (Ann Arbor, MI: Text Creation Partnership, 2008).

44 Ben Jonson, *Four Plays*, ed. Robert N. Watson (London: Methuen, 2014).

45 William d'Avenant, *Dramatic Works*, eds. James Maidment and W.H. Logan, 5 vols (Edinburgh: William Patterson, 1872), vol. 1, 279.

46 John Lyly, *Galatea; Midas*, ed. G.K. Hunter (Manchester: Manchester University Press, 2000).

47 John Marston, *Works*, ed. A.H. Bullen, 3 vols (London: J.C. Nimmo, 1887), vol. 3, 115.

48 Marston, *Works*, vol. 2, 347.

49 Ben Jonson, *The Devil Is an Ass and Other Plays*, ed. Margaret Jane Kidnie (New York: Oxford University Press, 2000).

50 "Vulgar error" comes from the treatment of barnacles in the notes to *The Dramatick Writings of William Shakspere*, vol. III (London: John Bell, 1788?), 84, whose annoyed tone is repeated, and information expanded, in *The Plays and Poems of William Shakespeare* (London: R. C. and J. Rivington, etc., 1821), vol. XV, 155–56.

51 Robert Mayhew, *The Female in Aristotle's Biology: Reason or Rationalization* (Chicago, IL: University of Chicago Press, 2010), 43, for a quick treatment; for a similar point about bears and their cubs, Jenny Mann, "Pygmalion's Wax: 'Fruitful Knowledge' in Bacon and Montaigne," *Journal of Medieval and Early Modern Studies* 45 (2015): 384.

52 Vinciane Despret, *What Would Animals Say If We Asked the Right Questions?* trans. Brett Buchanan (Minneapolis: University of Minnesota Press, 2016), 38.

53 Charles Arthur, "Scientists Discover Why Fungi Have 36,000 Sexes," *The Independent*, September 15, 1999. www.independent.co.uk/news/scientists-discover-why-fungi-have-36000-sexes-1119181.html.

54 Colin Dickey, "The Sex Lives of Sea Creatures," *The New Republic*, February 11, 2016. https://newrepublic.com/article/129669/sex-lives-sea-creatures.

PART 2

Scales of Meaning

While Shakespeare's animal metaphors open up questions of history, theory, and representation, the size, location, and human exploitation of animal populations can be used to interrogate scales of environmental thinking. Renaissance creatures were imagined in relationship with one another, connecting microcosmic animal worlds with macrocosmic, planetary forces. The essays in this part explore questions of the animal in precisely these ways, tracking not only how Renaissance scientific frameworks provided new ways of surveying the natural world at a miniscule level but also how understanding of scale affected narratives about human populations.

Early modern London's rapid population growth at the end of the sixteenth century transformed both the city's urban environments and the surrounding agricultural networks that fed its hungry inhabitants. In the first essay of this segment, Ian MacInnes examines the impact of this growth on animals via an unlikely archival trace: London's street names. Using a familiar source, *Civitas Londinum* (1561), now known as the Agas map of London, MacInnes emphasizes the imprint of animal movement left on the city's infrastructure. MacInnes turns to the digital *Map of Early Modern London* to make his case: this resource offers its audience the ability to zoom in and out on areas of the map, providing audiences with both a bird's eye and a worm's eye view of the city. The map's data provides MacInnes a starting point for mapping animal migrations through early modern economic industries.

The material and economic networks MacInnes investigates impacted both human and animal populations in other ways. In "Zoonotic Shakespeare: Animals, Plagues, and the Medical Posthumanities," Lucinda Cole revisits accounts of plague in order to show that the spread of diseases was exacerbated by the growing trade in animals and animal byproducts. In doing so, she argues for a zoonotic Shakespeare: "[t]o read Shakespeare from the perspective of a medical posthumanities, then, is to take seriously species-jumping viruses and epidemics whose effects were exacerbated by the trade in animals and animal products in an increasingly global ecology and economy." Cole's image of a Europe under siege from rinderpest and anthrax, which turned large swaths of it into a "putrefying and potentially corruptive animal graveyard," reminds us of what it was like to experience such an outbreak. A zoonotic Shakespeare, Cole argues, shows us how disease reformed "anatomical, neurocognitive, physiological, moral, and affective distinctions between the human and the animal."

Just as disease reshapes categories through microcosmic shifts, warfare changed human animal bonds in both subtle and overt ways. Animal technologies were a key part of early modern warfare, choreographing human and animal bodies into a weaponized force. In "War and Creaturely Violence in Shakespeare's Late Tragedies," Benjamin Bertram analyzes this history, using Shakespeare's depictions of creaturely violence, violence that exceeds species boundaries. As Bertram shows, conflict was constitutive to early modern understandings of nature; early modern accounts of warfare conceptualized both the causes and effects of brutality in broader than just political terms. Humans were merely one species of actants in Shakespeare's theater of war. Shakespeare's depictions thus decenter "human exceptionalism, singularity, and superiority." Such depictions, including Shakespeare's vision of an all-encompassing definition of strife, force "humans to confront their deep ontological bond with non-human animals," returning us to earlier questions about human/animal affinities and the need for varied scales of analysis in order to grapple with the global effects of warfare.

Read together, these three essays raise important questions about the roles of animals in shaping early modern demography. Each demonstrates how analysis of the changing uses and mobility of animal populations provides insights into changing conditions for all, human and nonhuman alike. In the final essay of this part, Joseph Campana addresses early modern demographic shifts directly by analyzing Shakespeare's language of scale. In "Flock, Herd, Swarm: Shakespearean Lexicon of Creaturely Collectivity," Campana offers a "brief tour" through Shakespeare's "lexicon of creaturely collectivity." Shakespeare's three key terms—flock, herd, and swarm—register Shakespeare's "population thinking." Order and disorder both intensify with changes in population: "populous and prodigious" creatures explode that cornerstone of Renaissance humanism, the individual. While terrifying to humans, aggregates also offer "creaturely articulations of civic order, as when birds or bees hold their own parliaments." Shakespeare's flocks, herds, and swarms allow us to see an early form of "population management" that "cuts across" species divides and intersects with political theory.

6

COW-CROSS LANE AND CURRIERS ROW

Animal Networks in Early Modern England

Ian F. MacInnes

Of the enormous number of animals that entered London in the last half of the sixteenth century, few ever left the city alive. This process captures what Erica Fudge has called the creation of "animal-made-objects," and by its logic the city itself can be considered a vast tool for turning animals into objects, from food to clothing. But Fudge also coined her term to conjure up its reversed meaning: not animals objectified but "objects constructed from animals."[1] If we extend both meanings of the term more widely, we might say that while early modern England made animals into objects, it was also a country made out of animals: it was itself an animal-made-object.

In the past 15 years, early modern animal studies has explored animal bodies largely through individual details and a close attention to living animals. But the large numbers of living domestic animals in England were part of a system, a vast assemblage of creatures and things. This phenomenon can be addressed by what anthropologists have called "multispecies ethnography," an approach that takes "the human as a kind of corporeality that comes into being relative to multispecies assemblages, rather than as a biocultural given."[2] In the case of early modern England, animal networks came to shape the country and particularly its capital city, not only economically and materially but imaginatively as well. This process can be demonstrated by combining the work of historians with layers of geographical content such as those created by Janelle Jenstad and others in the Map of Early Modern London project (MoEML). These multiple layers make it possible to demonstrate the interrelationship between different stages in animal-encounters throughout the country, from generation through transportation, processing, and consumption. From this perspective, the country itself was an assemblage whose procedures made complex persuasive arguments about animal bodies, arguments that bound the major cities, especially London, to distant parts of the kingdom. In particular, the networks of early modern England constantly drew its human inhabitants into multiple and historically persistent forms of identification with animal material, shaping their behavior, their language, and their sense of communal identity. It has traditionally been argued that urbanization alienated the natural world and made animals "marginal to the processes of production."[3] But early modern England's developing animal network suggests that its people were bound far more tightly to animals and to animal-made-objects than was true in the Middle Ages or indeed in most other premodern societies. The value of approaching early modern animal networks as a coherent persuasive system is that doing so allows us to see how its logic both underlies and causes the kind of persistently animal-centered textual discourse that has become so familiar to us in Shakespeare and others.

The story of the animal (or pastoral) economy of the British Isles in the sixteenth and seventeenth century is to a large degree the story of London, the sensational growth of which overturned the traditional system of medieval markets and created a national agrarian economy. Historians have long recognized the existence of a feedback loop. As Yeomans puts it, "London's growth partially led to economic changes but ... external stimuli were responsible for the dramatic growth of London."[4] The greatest changes finally occurred in the industrial revolution, but it was the agrarian economy that altered first, during the sixteenth and seventeenth centuries, and it was the animal economy that led the way. London's population quadrupled during the course of the sixteenth century; by 1600 it represented 5% of the entire country. And because Londoners consumed roughly twice as much as their countrymen, their influence upon agriculture was immense. The shires closest to the city saw the greatest influence. Mark Overton estimates that by the end of the sixteenth century London consumed up to 15% of all food produced within 60 miles.[5] But its influence was much wider when it came to animals, which could be walked to London. Sheep were brought from Gloucestershire and Northampton, and cattle were imported from Wales, Ireland, and the northwest.[6] Eggs and poultry came from Bedfordshire and Northamptonshire.[7] Animals were thus the first element of English agriculture to become part of a national system, and that system was focused upon London.

London was the grisly heart of the animal economy. Live animals converged upon the city in a vast systolic movement and were either consumed on the spot or distributed back outward in another vast diastolic movement of objects made from animals. A cow born and raised in Wales could end up, through the agency of London, simultaneously as salt beef in a cask bound for the East Indies and as a leather whip bound for colonial plantations. Animal products themselves also began to converge upon London, transforming smaller cities into processing centers. For example, during the sixteenth century, over 20% of the population of cities like Northampton and Chester worked in the leather trade.[8] These processes were not neutral; they acted powerfully and persuasively upon people's imagination. Each different stage in animal encounters, from generation through transportation, processing, and consumption, acted as a slightly differently form of persuasion.

The persuasive procedures of the network began with the way animals were raised and/or transported specifically for the London market and the profound social changes wrought by this developing rural part of the animal economy. Historian F.J. Fisher points out that a national trade could not have developed by sizing up the medieval market system in which farmers brought their wares to market and sold them directly to consumers: "London had long passed and was rapidly leaving behind the stage when its needs could be even approximately satisfied in any such way."[9] In part, increased demand in London simply increased the number of animals and the extent of animal ownership outside of London. In the countryside, Joan Thirsk says, "there were few men who did not have an animal of some kind, usually a cow, sometimes a couple of sheep, and sometimes a horse."[10] One study shows overall livestock density in England doubling in the first half of the sixteenth century.[11] On the other hand, market pressures required increasing specialization in the raising and delivery of animals. Some regions, like the fens, for example, became devoted entirely to fattening where "everie man to his abilitie, layd out what money hee could spare uppon Heiffors, and such other young ware, emptying their purses of Crownes to cram the Fens with Cattell."[12] In the vicinity of the city, specific provisioning trades (drover, grazier, warrener, poulter, factor, etc.) grew and flexed their power, sometimes treading upon one another's territory. The changes required by an animal-centered London also profoundly altered the countryside itself because the demand for livestock created a parallel demand for fodder that put pressure on traditional methods. As Overton explains it,

> In the early sixteenth century pastures and meadows were in a natural biological state, but by the end of the seventeenth century many were systematically cultivated, fertilized, and sown with seeds imported onto the farm.[13]

Fodder and pasture contributed enormously to the way animals were valued. In Shakespeare's *Henry V*, the king exhorts his troops to "show us here / The mettle of your pasture; let us swear / That you are worth your breeding; which I doubt not."[14] That his somewhat unusual metaphor can be implied rather than stated suggests the degree to which the regional origin of domestic animals was already a highly visible part of a persuasive system.

The 1561 Agas map bears witness to the origin of London's animals in the many depictions of cattle and other animals in small fields and enclosures on the outskirts of the city. In fact, there are nearly as many animals as people (94 vs. 145). For several reasons we know these are not simply map decorations, like mermaids or dragons in early atlases. First, the distribution of animals is not random. Many large spaces have no animals at all, while some very small enclosures have several. Cattle and sheep are also present in some regions and absent in others. Elsewhere, the map depicts activities we know from other documents are historically accurate, as in the figures of archers practicing in Finsbury field.

Only mature animals are depicted, something that accords with the work of historians who point out that cattle and sheep were rarely bred and raised near London. They were brought in as adults. Some stopped in farther suburban areas such as Islington (Woodward 43),[16] but many were brought closer in to the city for fattening, particularly those bought alive by London's butchers. In 1624 a bill was presented to Parliament restricting the butchers' grazing rights. In a broadside that year, the butchers argued among other things that having live animals close by would help

Figure 6.1 Archers, laundry, and cows—Agas map detail[15]

the city in the event that weather or other events prevented graziers from bringing them to the city from a distance.[17] It is no coincidence that roughly half of all the animals on the Agas map are cattle. These are, of course, the largest and most visible of the animals consumed for food. On the simplest level, we can say that even the most completely urban members of the English population would have been familiar with the sight, smell, sound, and even the daily habits of their living diet as well as with other animals. But the presence in the city of so many live animals, many destined for slaughter (though not yet engaged on their final gruesome journey), also acts as a persuasive network. It connects the bodies of the humans with the bodies of the nonhuman animals they made use of.

The presence of so many dogs on the Agas map suggests that although farm animals were important through sheer numbers, other animals also participated in the network of generation, transportation, and consumption. Most of the dogs on the map, for example, are the ones depicted in the kennels associated with the bear-baiting and bull-baiting arenas in Southwark.

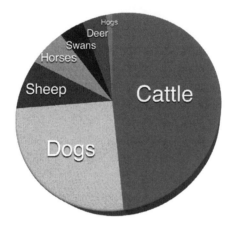

Figure 6.2 Animals on the Agas map

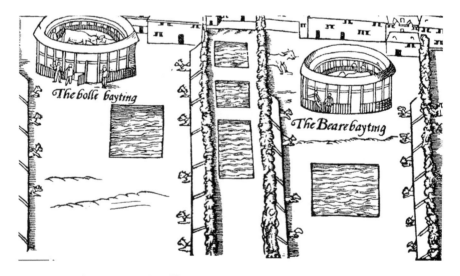

Figure 6.3 Kennels—Agas map detail[18]

Bull baiting itself was not a stand-alone practice but deeply implicated in the larger cattle economy, as we can see from fifteenth-century statutes that require the baiting of bulls before their slaughter.[19] Dogs, essential to baiting, were often obtained from far outside London, as we know from evidence of breeding centers like the Legh family of Lyme, whose mastiffs were in demand in London.[20] People were also welcome to bring in and bet on their own dogs.[21] Dogs sometimes perished in the arena, necessitating a constant supply. And archaeological evidence suggests they may have also served as food in times of famine.[22] More exotic animals followed a similar pattern. Since bears were extinct in England, all of the bears in Southwark arenas were imported from the continent. But there is evidence in the names of the 19 named bears in Taylor's *Bull, Beare & Horse* that these animals came into the country not directly to London but through the North Sea ports (like Ipswich) and were brought to London circuitously, along the same roads as cattle and sheep, with the opportunity for performances in various towns and fairs along the way. Only apes bypassed this systolic movement through the English countryside, being imported to London directly from North Africa.[23] But we have at least some evidence that apes may have regularly participated in the diastolic movement of animals outside of London. In 1636, for example, the Member of Parliament and royalist soldier Edmund Verney wrote to his son in the country that a merchant who had asked for "2 or 3 apes" from his factor in North Africa forgot the "r" and got 203 by mistake. Verney says, "if yorself or frends will buy any to breede on, you could never have had such a chance as now."[24] Clearly the idea of obtaining (and breeding) exotic captive animals was beginning to take hold. Other aristocrats such as Frances Legh and Lady Brereton obtained, bred, and sold smaller primates, some of which could go for as much as 60 pounds.[25] The market for exotic animals was eventually fueled by trade and exploration; numbers of these animals were on the rise in the seventeenth century.

The presence of living animals in the city was made visible to its inhabitants not only in the cows, sheep, pigs, and others who were fattened in enclosures close by but in the more or less constant stream of animals being transported, a stream which was far more visible than the movement of goods in a later industrial setting. The transport of animals is yet another part of a persuasive system. Most of the animals on the street in London were being driven to slaughter. There were a number of shambles in London, mostly placed at the entrances to the city (Temple Bar, for example), but the single dominant market for all agricultural products was of course Smithfield. Its economic centrality is betrayed by its placement (close to the center of early maps), the way the surrounding roads converge upon it in a star pattern, and the fact that it is one of the few functional open spaces in the growing urbanization of the city. The surrounding roads themselves tell a story about the transportation of animals. The most significant animal-named streets are those that converge upon Smithfield: Cow Lane, Chick Lane, Duck Lane, Goose Lane, Cow Cross Lane, etc. The names of public houses add to the list: The Ram, The Black Bull, etc.

Given the needs of the city, animals must have been a daily presence on these streets, although seasonal variations would have meant that there were times when certain animals predominated (as was the case during St. Bartholomew's fair, when "Bartelmas Beef" was the special product).[27]

Since Smithfield is north of the river and close by the old walls of the city, one might think that animals were brought there without traversing the rest of the city, but the evidence suggests otherwise. First, some sheep and cattle originated south of the city, and one of the logical crossing points was London Bridge, avoiding a potentially dangerous and inconvenient river crossing (Woodward cites a log of a droving journey to London in which money was paid to chase down cows who panicked upon boarding the ferry across the Humber). Did cows travel across London Bridge? Claes Visscher's 1616 panorama of London appears to think so, showing two cows being driven to the bridge from the south.

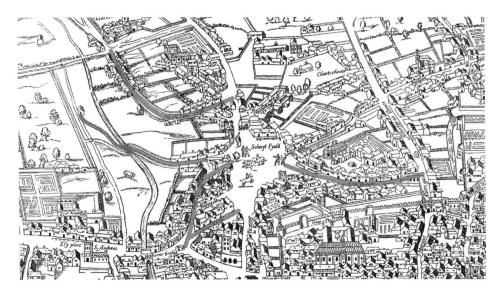

Figure 6.4   Animal-named roads around Smithfield—Agas map detail[26]

Figure 6.5   Claes Visscher, *panorama of London* detail. 1616[28]

From the north end of the bridge, these animals could have taken any number of paths to Smithfield, their likely destination. What this evidence suggests is that animals other than the horses and mules of the ubiquitous carriers or sumpters could probably be found individually or in groups, being driven along the streets and alleys throughout the city.

Their presence means that with some caveats we might approach street names across the city as a record of the presence of real animals. And on the whole, early modern London was astonishingly animal-centered in its naming patterns. The 1768 *London and Westminster Guide* lists 7,900 distinct street names: nearly 10% of these refer to actual animals (not counting animal products or related industries).[29] The 1561 Agas map lists far fewer street names, but the conservation of both urban geography and listed street names between the Agas map and eighteenth-century London maps suggests that many of these smaller streets had existed for many years and that the large proportion of animal names had begun in earlier times.

Of course, some animal street names reflect a medieval heraldic heritage or family names: lions were a bit thin on the ground outside of the Tower, for example! But the predilection for animal names appears to reflect archaeological truth as well as a cultural phenomenon. The city was not simply a place in which its human inhabitants would frequently encounter the animals that it operated upon. It became a place whose geography, traditions, and habitual paths were mediated and channeled by its evolved function as a system to make objects from animals. It would have been impossible to traverse the city without setting foot on streets named for the animals, who also used those same streets. The direction of streets themselves would inevitably guide people into following the same paths to the same destinations, although they were sent to buy where the animals were sent to die. To be an early modern human on the streets of London was to see oneself in some ways as the mirrored companion of the animals out of which one very likely made one's living. The fact that street names persisted, many into the present day, shows not only how culturally powerful geography can be but also how persistent are forms of animal identification.

The systematic and deeply persistent aspects of animal transportation can help us explain the development of certain well-recognized animal metaphors in the period. In *Henry VI pt. 2*, for example, the king compares his sense of powerlessness to help Gloucester with a cow whose calf has been taken away:

> And as the butcher takes away the calf
> And binds the wretch, and beats it when it strays,
> Bearing it to the bloody slaughter-house,
> Even so remorseless have they borne him hence;
> And as the dam runs lowing up and down,
> Looking the way her harmless young one went,
> And can do nought but wail her darling's loss,
> Even so myself bewails good Gloucester's case
> With sad unhelpful tears, and with dimm'd eyes
> Look after him and cannot do him good,
> So mighty are his vowed enemies.

(3.1)

Ordinarily we might simply say that Shakespeare had once seen such a sad drama, perhaps in his country youth, but events like this were in fact a daily part of life in the city and its environs as well as in the country. Veal was even a city-dweller's meat. The easy mixture of pathos and sympathy in the passage also suggests that the audience would have been prepared not only to authenticate the event through repeated experience, but to acknowledge that the animal stories played out on their streets were parallels to their own experience. The anthropomorphism that Boehrer and others have seen as so characteristic of the early modern period can in some ways be understood as a product of the larger persuasive procedural claims of the system itself.[30]

The point at which animals are killed or die is usually the point at which they cease to be the subject of animal studies, which for many good reasons has insisted on a close focus on real animals rather than their objectified remains or dematerialized representation. However, there are equally good reasons to understand the system which operated upon the bodies of animals after death as part of the same system that brought them, alive, to the shambles. Both were part of complementary systolic/diastolic movement to and from major cities. Animal-processing jobs demonstrated a bewildering variety of specific names, and not just expected jobs like butchers, poulterers, woolstaplers, and fishmongers. Leather alone had a bewildering variety of associated trades, from leatherdressers such as skinners, tanners, shearmen, curriers, felters, tawyers, whitawers, cordwainers, fellmongers, to their customers: glovers, girdlers, lorimers, saddlers, shoemakers, furriers, bookbinders, parchmentmakers, and haberdashers. The horn trade included horners, comb-makers, button-makers, ivory cutters, cutlers, and pinners, and the vast trade in tallow comprised soap boilers and chandlers. To some extent the multiplicity of highly specific job titles is typical of many early modern industries, but animal industries attracted notice even at the time. In his *Bull, Beare, and Horse*, John Taylor includes a long panegyric to the many products produced from cattle alone. He concludes,

> Thus from the Bull, and the Bulls Breed you see,
> A world of people still maintained be;
> He finds flesh, Bootes, Shooes, Lights, and stands in stead
> And great importance to afford us Bread.[31]

The animal trades were major activities; many were represented by a livery company, a long-standing trade association with deep economic and social roots. Nearly 30% of the city's liveries were, in fact, directly involved in the market for animal products. Some, like the Salters' guild, without whom meat products could not have been preserved were a major force in the city. When overlaid on the city's animal markets and animal thoroughfares on the Agas map, the various guild halls for these liveries demonstrate the degree to which animal processing diffused throughout the city. Guild halls were usually founded in areas dominated by a particular trade and rarely moved throughout the sixteenth and seventeenth centuries. Only the Butcher's hall was possibly near a shambles or market.[32]

Like the city streets, the trade associations provided a deeply conservative identification with past practice, even as the city evolved. Many are still active to this day, transformed, like the Skinners, into community service organizations or, like the Salters, into research foundations. These centers of industry, commerce, and society brought people into a different kind of identification with animal material: not a narrative and sympathetic identification (as with the transport of animals), but rather an identification with animal bodies as essential to their communal and economic identity.

A good picture of early modern England's repeated identification with animal material can be assembled simply by telling the most likely story of the cow and her calf behind Shakespeare's simile in *Henry VI pt. 2*. The cow would most likely have been purchased as a heifer from a northern or western location, perhaps Wales, by a grazier.[33] She would have been shod with up to two separate shoes per foot, an arduous process in which she was thrown on her back with her feet tied together.[34] From her birth pastures she would travel the long drove roads towards London, moving perhaps 15 miles a day, driven by drovers

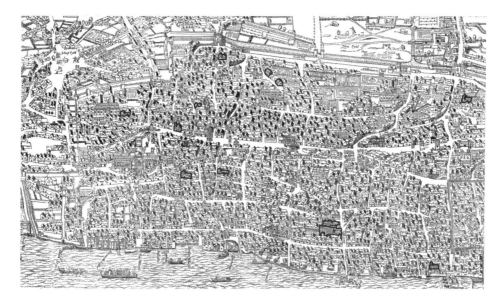

Figure 6.6 Livery halls in the animal trade—from MoEML

who would sleep at night with the cattle. She would end at a pasture where she would be fattened and bred, along with many others.[35] After the birth of her calf, the two would be driven to a city market and separated by the butcher, prompting the sad scene Shakespeare describes. Her calf's flesh would be sold as fresh veal, "the best flesshe and most nutrytyve meate that can be for mans sustenaunce,"[36] an increasingly lucrative market. The calf's skin would be sold to a tanner or whitawyer who would lime it and scrape it, and might sell it to a parchmentmaker (if the calf was young enough) to satisfy the still growing market for vellum.[37] The cow herself would remain in the city for a time as one of the thousands of dairy cows living within the city limits.[38] Eventually she herself would be slaughtered. Her flesh would most likely be salted and perhaps powdered, since fresh cow's flesh was considered less wholesome than that of bull or ox. Her fat would be sold to chandlers and soapmakers. Her horns would be sawn off and sold to horners who would remove the core and turn the covering into flat sheets of horn that would in turn be sold to buttonmakers, pinners, combers, and lanternmakers. Her skin would be tanned in a process taking up to a year, then sold to curriers who would "stuff" it with oil and sell it on to cordwainers and other leather manufacturers. Archaeological evidence shows that her bones and horn waste would be used as a substitute for brick in lining drains and industrial pits.[39]

Eventually, animal bodies moved from processing into the hands of what modern economists would call consumers and that consumption itself became another persuasive element in the system with its own procedural logic. One of the most ubiquitous forms of consumption, for example, was of fat, or tallow, derived from a variety of animals. Tallow was so valuable that during one of the period's natural disasters, a flood near Bristol in 1607, the most notably looted item was the tallow from sheep carcasses.[40] A small amount of animal fat went to soap making, but most ended up as artificial light. As Taylor says, "were there no Buls, Chandlers were beggerd quite / [n]or could they sell our darknesse any light."[41] What Taylor points out is rarely acknowledged by modern scholars: virtually all artificial light in the early modern period was an animal product,[42] as were the activities such light made possible, such as indoor theater. Chandlers were such an important part of England's animal-centered economy that the word "chandler" itself quickly became a byword for any kind of dealing or trading and eventually attached itself to distant trades such as "ship-chandler" (OED 3a & b). Tallow candles were smoky and smelly. Their reeking physicality made animal bodies unavoidable in a variety of indoor contexts and contributed ironic depth to the metaphor of the candle as human life, as in Macbeth's "Out, out, brief candle! Life's but a walking shadow" (5.5.25–26).

Of course the most obvious form of consumption was literal. Here also the networks created a highly persuasive multispecies assemblage. Diet was partly determined by the calendar and provided by specialized markets for fish, poultry, beef, etc. Most importantly, the choices made by the consumer repeatedly encourage them to identify with the animal body. In his 1612 book, *The Haven of Health*, Thomas Cogan reviews a large variety of meats. In each case he distinguishes between the age and sex of the animal as well as its condition and the method of processing. In the case of beef, for example, he mentions salt beef, smoked beef, powdered beef, and fresh beef.

> Oxe Biefe is better than Bull Biefe, except for those that would looke big. And Cowbiefe, if it be young, is better than both. But by master Eliot's judgment, Oxe biefe not exceeding the age of foure yeeres is best of all … The flesh of beasts that be gelded is better than others.[43]

What Cogan's descriptions tell us is that early modern English markets would present consumers with choices quite different from those we are familiar with (such as cut and "grade"), choices moreover that explicitly connect the body of the customer with the body of the animal, given the dominant Galenic theories of health. James Hart, for example, recommends old beef only for "strong labouring people, that in a manner can turn Iron into nourishment; especially Bull-beefe, which is the worst of all others."[44]

Consumption also underlined and confirmed the ways that the entire system made animals a logical source of larger cultural concepts. Beef is the first meat Cogan discusses because, as he says, "Biefe of all flesh is most usuall among English men":

> I neede not to shew how plentifull it is throughout this land, before all other countries, and how necessary it is both by sea and for the victualling of ships, and by land for good house-keeping, insomuch that no man of honour, or worship, can be said to have good provision for hospitality, unlesse there be good store of Biefe in readinesse. And how well it doth agree with the nature of Englishmen the common consent of all our nation doth suficiently prove.[45]

In this light, the predominance of cattle on the Agas map reflects the perceived sense that the English were partly defined by beef.[46] But other animals that were essential to the procedural logic of early modern English animal networks were also the subject of this cultural process. Dogs, particularly the mastiff, and horses were also connected with the Englishness.[47] In Shakespeare's *Henry V*, the French lord Rambures contemplates the peculiarly animal-centered nature of the English. "That island of England breeds very valiant creatures," he says, "their mastiffs are of unmatchable courage":

> and the men do sympathize with
> the mastiffs in robustious and rough coming on,
> leaving their wits with their wives. And then give
> them great meals of beef and iron and steel, they
> will eat like wolves and fight like devils.

(3.7.142–54)

When seen as part of a larger system based on animals, these arguments about diet, about the sympathy with and consumption of animal bodies, are consistent with the procedural arguments made by the system itself. Early modern England was not just a nation that turned animals into objects on a large scale; it was a nation that was produced by animals, an animal-made-object on a national scale.

Viewing the violence done to animals as part of a large system has certain dangers, since it both distances and objectifies individuals (both humans and non-human animals),[48] but it allows us to draw valuable conclusions as well. We are (by now) accustomed seeing persistent anthropomorphism and certain kinds of animal metaphor in early modern English texts. Considering the economy and geography as a vast assemblage, however, allows us to understand how the ideas expressed in imaginative literature are themselves the result of a cultural persuasion whose rhetoric was primarily procedural and systemic rather than textual. Considering animal/s-made-object/s as a persuasive assemblage also offers us some conclusions about our own industry of domestic animals. These days we are accustomed to think that our own deeply inhumane treatment of most animals might somehow be ameliorated if people were less alienated from the process: the factory farms, the cattle cars, the slaughterhouses. But early modern London constantly required its human inhabitants to identify closely with both animals and animal material. The results profoundly shaped their behavior, their urban environment, and their sense of communal identity, but they did not result in either a humane or sustainable set of relations. Ironically, the movement for humane treatment of animals could not begin until the nineteenth century when the economic transformation of the city destroyed the centuries-old system through which it made animals into objects, erasing the geography and social organization of that system.

Notes

1 Erica Fudge, "Renaissance Animal Things," in *Gorgeous Beasts: Animal Bodies in Historical Perspective*, eds. Joan B. Landes, Paula Young Lee, and Paul Youngquist (University Park: Pennsylvania State University Press, 2012), 42.

2 Laura A. Ogden, Billy Hall, and Kimiko Tanita, "Animals, Plants, People, and Things," *Environment and Society* 4, no. 1 (September 1, 2013): 5–24, https://doi.org/10.3167/ares.2013.040102. Ogden and Hall credit their basic relational concepts to scholars such as Donna Haraway, Bruno Latour, Gilles Deleuze, and Félix Guattari. This direction in Human Animal Studies emerged early in anthropology. In its lead (2012) issue, the editors of the journal *Environmental Humanities* asked a fundamental question: "How are human identities and responsibilities to be articulated when we understand ourselves to be members of multispecies communities that emerge through the entanglements of agential beings?" Matthew Chrulew et al., "Thinking through the Environment, Unsettling the Humanities," *Environmental Humanities* 1 (2012), http://environmentalhumanities.org. 3.

3 Keith Thomas, *Man and the Natural World: Changing Attitudes in England 1500–1800* (New York: Oxford University Press, 1983), 181.

4 Lisa Yeomans, "A Zooarchaeological and Historical Study of the Animal Product Based Industries Operating in London during the Post-Medieval Period" (University College London, 2006). These ideas derive from E.A. Wrigley, "A Simple Model of London's Importance in Changing English Society and Economy," *Past and Present* 37 (1967): 44–70.

5 Mark Overton, *Agricultural Revolution in England: The Transformation of the Agrarian Economy 1500–1850*, Cambridge Studies in Historical Geography 23 (Cambridge: Cambridge University Press, 1996), 138. John Taylor, *Bull, Beare, and Horse* (London, 1638), A8, claims that Londoners ate 3,000 cattle a week.

6 A. Everitt, "The Marketing of Agricultural Produce," in *The Agrarian History of England and Wales*, ed. J. Thirsk, vol. 4 (Cambridge, 1967), 466–589.

7 F.J. Fisher, "The Development of the London Food Market, 1540–1640," *The Economic History Review* a5, no. 2 (1935): 51.
8 Yeomans, "Zooarchaeological and Historical Study," 30.
9 Fisher, "Development of the London Food Market," 58.
10 Joan Thirsk, ed., *The Agrarian History of England and Wales*, General ed. H.P.R. Finberg, vol. 4 (London: Cambridge University Press, 1967), 185.
11 Overton, *Agricultural Revolution in England*, 111.
12 Anon., *A True Report of Certaine Wonderfull Ouerflowings of Waters, Now Lately in Summerset-Shire, Norfolke, and Other Places of England* (London, 1607), L2.
13 Overton, *Agricultural Revolution in England*, 111.
14 Barbara Mowat et al., eds., *Henry V* (Washington, DC: Folger Shakespeare Library, n.d.), accessed January 1, 2018. www.folgerdigitaltexts.org. Act 3, Scene 1. Lines 28-20. Future references to Shakespeare's plays are to the Folger digital texts and will be noted by act, scene, and line number in parentheses.
15 *Civitas Londinvm* (1562?) 2012. The Agas Map. *The Map of Early Modern London,* ed. Janelle Jenstad (*MoEML*, 2012), map.
16 D.M. Woodward, "Cattle Droving in the Seventeenth Century: A Yorkshire Example," in *Trade and Transport: Essays in Economic History in Honour of T. S. Willan*, eds. William Henry Chaloner and Barrie M. Ratcliffe (Manchester: Manchester University Press, 1977), 43.
17 Free Butchers of London, *Reasons Tendred by the Free Butchers of London against the Bill in Parliament to Restraine Butchers from Grazing of Cattle* (London, 1624).
18 Jenstad, *Map of Early Modern London*.
19 Oscar Brownstein, "The Popularity of Baiting in England before 1600: A Study in Social and Theatrical History," *Educational Theatre Journal* 21 (1969): 237–50. Because of its connections with the theater, bull baiting and bear baiting have been carefully studied for many years. Animal studies have focused on them beginning with Erica Fudge's two 2002 books, *Perceiving Animals* and *At the Borders of the Human*.
20 John Egerton, "Letter to Sir Peter Legh," Legh of Lyme Correspondence, 1615.
21 John Taylor, *Bull, Beare, and Horse, &c.* (London, 1638), 19.19.
22 Rebecca Gordon, "From Pests to Pets: Social and Cultural Perceptions of Animals in Post-Medieval Centres in England (AD 1500-1900)," *Papers from the Institute of Archeology,* 27.1 (2017), https://pia-journal.co.uk/articles/10.5334/pia-478/.
23 So called "Barbary Apes" are actually macaques (a species of old world monkey).
24 Lady Frances Parthenope Verney and Lady Margaret Maria Williams-Hay Verney, *Memoirs of the Verney Family during the Seventeenth Century* (Longmans: Green, 1904), 82.
25 Legh Family Letters (Manchester, n.d.), 194. It's also possible that what is referred to as monkeys could have been lemurs, tarsiers, lorises, or other popular exotics.
26 Ibid.
27 Thomas Cogan says that Bartlemas beef is so called because it is killed at that time of year —*The Haven of Health* (London, 1612), 113. However, recipe books suggest that Bartlemas beef could also be a seasonal dish, and if prepared from salt beef would not necessarily have resulted in more slaughter in the days leading up to the festival.
28 "Visscher's view of London, 1616." *Wikimedia Commons.*
29 *The London and Westminster Guide, through the Cities and Suburbs… To Which Is Added an Alphabetical List of All the Streets, Etc.* (London: W. Nicoll, 1768).
30 Bruce Boehrer, *Shakespeare among the Animals: Nature and Society in the Drama of Early Modern England* (New York: Palgrave, 2002).
31 Taylor, *Bull, Beare, and Horse*, B3.
32 One source places this next to St. Bartholomew's Hospital by Smithfield. John Kennedy Melling, *London's Guilds and Liveries* (Oxford: Osprey Publishing, 2003).
33 Fisher, "Development of the London Food Market," 51.
34 Woodward, "Cattle Droving in the Seventeenth Century," 42.
35 Anon., *A True Report*, L2.
36 Andrew Boorde, *Here Foloweth a Compendyous Regimente or Dyetary of Health Made in Mount Pyllor* (London, 1562), F2.
37 One might think the development of the paper industry would reduce the demand for vellum, but perhaps because vellum was used for legal documents, demand actually increased.

38 Rebecca Louise Gordon, "Feeding the City: Zooarchaeological Perspectives on Urban Provisioning and Consumption Behaviours in Post-Medieval England (AD1500–AD1900)" (School of Archaeology and Ancient History, 2016).
39 Yeomans, "A Zooarchaeological and Historical Study."
40 Anon., *A True Report.*
41 Taylor, *Bull, Beare, and Horse*, B2.
42 Some candles were beeswax, another animal product. Links and torches were commonly made with tallow, though a few might have used pitch.
43 Thomas Cogan, *The Haven of Health* (London, 1612), 114.
44 James Hart, *Klinikh or the Diet of the Diseased* (London, 1633), 122.
45 Cogan, *Haven of Health*, 113.
46 Robert Applebaum, "Aguecheek's Beef," *Textual Practice* 14, no. 2 (2000).
   See also Ben Rogers, *Beef and Liberty* (Vintage, 2004). Rogers begins his analysis in the early modern period.
47 Ian MacInnes, "Mastiffs and Spaniels: Gender and Nation in the English Dog," *Textual Practice* 17, no. 1 (2003): 21–40. Karen Raber, "A Horse of a Different Color; Nation and Race in Early Modern Horsemanship Treatises," in *The Culture of the Horse: Status, Discipline, and Identity in the Early Modern World* (New York: Palgrave, 2005), 225–44.
48 Helen Kopnina has recently pointed out that the abstract and highly analytical nature of multispecies ethnography has particular difficulty in dealing with violence done to animals: "Beyond Multispecies Ethnography: Engaging with Violence and Animal Rights in Anthropology," *Critique of Anthropology* 37, no. 3 (September, 2017): 333–57, https://doi.org/10.1177/0308275X17723973.

7

"EVERYTHING EXISTS BY STRIFE"

War and Creaturely Violence in Shakespeare's Late Tragedies

Benjamin Bertram

In the German edition of Petrarch's *De remediis utriusque fortunae* (Remedies for fortune fair and foul) from 1532, a series of woodcuts by Hans Weiditz illustrate the Heraclitean adage that "war is the father of all and king of all,"[1] or "everything exists by strife."[2] One of the images, remaining true to Petrarch's preface, presents the inexorable decline of a household immersed in a universal *bellum omnium in omnes*. Even as two of the home's occupants are separated by victorious Death, a potentially glorious future for arachnids is heralded by the giant web engulfing the edifice itself. Although we might wonder about the couple's story, humans are only a small part of the drama unfolding. "Is there a living creature without war?" Petrarch asks. The illustration builds on his answer: "Fish, wild beasts, fowl, snakes, men—one species harasses the other, none lives peacefully" (1). Constituting life in all its forms, strife is found in the elements as well: there are earthquakes and windstorms, shipwrecks, fires, hail, rainstorms, thunder, lightning, tempests, and surging rivers (1). The woodcut puts many of these on display, though the compendium of fortunes foul is so vast only a few can be squeezed into it: storks fight snakes and frogs, a serpent attacks an elephant, hail forcefully descends, a weary sun struggles to spread its rays, dogs surround and leap upon a stag. "What, then," Petrarch asks, "can you hope for, surrounded by hatred? There is hatred in love, war in peace, dissent in agreement" (5).

If the illustration has a didactic quality suitable to the anthropocentric Christian Stoicism of Petrarch's work as a whole, it is not readily discernible; indeed, the image, like the preface it accompanies, is so replete with the vitality of the nonhuman world that it seems distant from the human-centered philosophical themes of *De remediis*.[3] Amid this profusion of life and death, even a relatively stable human construct—the home—faces imminent destruction. If the home remains, it has a distinctly posthuman future as birds and spiders threaten to take possession of it. The woodcut forces us to see human stories as merely a small portion of the action taking place among and between countless life forms.

War, we tend to assume, is a human affair. After all, only humans worry about whether or not a war is "just," only humans fight for "holy" causes, and only humans seek immortal fame through acts of organized violence. At times, Shakespeare seems to encourage a human-centered view of war focused on such concerns. In *Henry V*, for example, the eponymous character urges his men to "imitate the actions of the tiger,"[4] yet he also believes that war involves a special kind of violence, one that separates humans from animals, the latter left

"Everything Exists by Strife"

Figure 7.1 Hans Weiditz, "War, the Father of All Things," from Von der Artzney bayder Glück, des guten und widerwertigen, 1532. Courtesy of the Augsburg Stadtbibliothek

buried and forgotten in a dunghill while the former are granted immortal fame. Fellowship in Henry's "band of brothers" not only confirms soldiers' English identity, it also grants them a higher ontological status as human, since only humans have "honor" that rises to heaven while "leaving their earthly parts" behind (4.3.99–103). The value of honor and glory in war would be diminished if the prize of immortality were to be withdrawn, and the appeal of this prize has traditionally relied upon a distinction between humans who eventually shed their mortal coils and animals that have nothing other than "earthly parts."[5]

But warfare in Shakespeare's plays is much less human centered than critics have generally acknowledged; in fact, it frequently looks like the proliferation of violence we see in the hylozoic, vibrant worlds imagined by Weiditz and Petrarch. While it often makes sense to define war as "hostile contention by means of armed forces," and especially organized violence "between nations, states, and rules" (OED 1a), in reading Shakespeare's plays we must also consider an alternative definition that includes animals, vegetables, and minerals entangled in the strife that forms the bedrock of life itself. War, in that case, is better defined as "active hostility or contention between living beings" (OED 1b). Petrarch mentions strife between brothers and between nations, two of Shakespeare's favorites, of course, but both writers also make us aware of wolves, worms, dogs, fish, and birds of all kinds, not to mention water, "the most restless of all things" (5).

These two definitions of war are not mutually exclusive; indeed, the consideration of war as "contention between living beings" radically alters our understanding of war as "contention by means of armed forces." What happens when we view organized, military violence as a manifestation of war on a much grander scale that encompasses all of nature? One ideological direction this approach has taken can be seen in the work of Shakespeare's contemporaries, Sir Walter Ralegh and Christopher Marlowe. Both connect violent, male ambition with strife in the natural world: the former sees it as an inherent part of an unstable world in which "everything either ascends or declines,"[6] and the latter (or at least his character Tamburlaine) sees it through the lens of a pre-Socratic, Empedoclean philosophy of strife as part of a lesson taught by "nature": "Nature that framed us of four elements/Warring within our breasts for regiment, /Doth teach us all to have aspiring minds" (1:2.7.12–20).[7] But there are many other directions this acknowledgment of the teeming presence of nonhuman actants can take. I will focus on *Macbeth*, *Coriolanus*, and *Othello* to argue that Shakespeare's version of war as strife not only subverts claims of human exceptionalism, singularity, and superiority, it also forces humans to confront their deep ontological bond with nonhuman animals; the ecology of war leaves them unable to see themselves as autonomous, rational agents removed from the rest of "nature."

If we were to follow what most critics have said about animal violence in *Macbeth*, we would miss the most important connection between this play and the woodcut by Weiditz: both demonstrate that war among humans is merely one scene of strife on a vast stage with innumerable clashing entities. There are too many nonhuman forms of strife in this play to list: the witches seek vengeance upon a "rump-fed ronyon" by tormenting her husband, horses break out of their stalls "as they would /Make war with mankind" (2.4.17–18), mousing owls hunt falcons, winds "fight/Against churches" and "waves/Confound and swallow navigation up" (4.1.52–53).[8] Moreover, the play hints of a world of strife that we don't actually see.[9] Macbeth surely has himself and murderers in mind, but given the "wild and violent sea" that humans "float upon," it cannot only be humans who are "night's black agents."[10] We can assume that diverse, invisible actants are in operation. Shakespeare gives us a sense of a vast world of strife that is not simply present as a reflection of human events or desires. Emphasizing three focal items—the witches' brew, the rooky wood, and Birnam wood—I wish to follow Christine Vernando's analysis of a "queer nature" in *Macbeth* by emphasizing the generativity, rather than the barrenness, of strife.[11]

One common, if now dated, reading of the play asserts that nonhuman animals and elements appear in "images" of disorder that are merely reflections of disorder in the sociopolitical life of humans.[12] Because the timeline of the old man's description is not clear, we can't assume that unruliness in nature applies only to the night of Duncan's death. As a constant of all life, unruly motion can be seen in the swelling and swarming of multiple life forms. Just as the ocean swells in anger in Petrarch's *De remediis*, here we find "shipwrecking storms and direful thunders" as "discomfort swells" (1.2.26, 28) and rebels teem like insects (1.2.11–12). To describe Macbeth and Banquo's counter to such ever-expanding forces of rebellion, the Captain compares them to eagles, lions, and "cannons over-charged with double cracks" (1.2.35–38). These two similes, one drawn from standard bird lore and the other from early modern warfare, are bundled together, the force of human art bound up with other forces of nature. Indeed, there is no human-nature dualism in the play because strife binds all together in the material workings of an ecology of war.[13]

Strife in *Macbeth* can be seen not only in the dazzling array of predatory birds, but also in the competition between day and night and the fragments of human and animal bodies in the witches' cauldron. "One time of day vies with another," Petrarch writes, "each thing against another thing, and all things against us" (1). Macbeth's murderous rise depends upon the victory of night, of course, as well as those indeterminate "black agents."

> Light thickens
> And the crow makes wing to th' rooky wood.
> Good things of day begin to droop and drowse,
> Whiles night's black agents to their preys do rouse.

> (3.2.51–54)

The thickening of light into dark resembles not only the texture of blood, but also the hell broth of the boiling cauldron with its stew of strife—a "gruel thick and slab" (4.1.32)—that includes such ingredients as the "sow's blood that hath eaten/Her nine farrow" (63–64) or the "Finger of birth-strangled babe/Ditch-delivered by a drab" (30–31). For humans and swine alike, turbulence is the norm, not the deviation from the norm. Like "the rooky wood," the cauldron is mysterious and fecund despite its associations with death and bane. The livers, blood, eyes, and noses of "strange," menacing creatures (Jews, baboons, newts, and Turks, respectively) are hardly harbingers of death. This list indexes homologous threats in which non-Christians, in this case Jews and Turks, are degraded and dehumanized. But it also contains the variegated "stuff" of conflict, the many ingredients required to generate life in a universe driven by strife. Strife, in other words, divides humans from one another while also moving them beyond the binaries of life/death, good/evil, and even host/symbiont. As Timothy Morton states, a "symbiont can become toxic or strange-seeming relationships can form, which is how evolution works."[14]

Banquo's "temple-haunting martlet" and Malcolm's trees severed from Birnam Wood may be symbols of orderly, civilized generation and regeneration, respectively, but the play suggests that the social order of humans, "natural" only in the sense that it may be, as Robert Watson argues, "more durable" for them, is immersed in an overwhelmingly unpredictable natural strife that allows for destruction *and* generation.[15] The witches are, of course, the best example of this generative strife, especially since they seem inseparable from the turbulent weather as they multiply the power of wind, look into the "seeds of time," and display voracious sexual appetite. Draining the sailor "dry as hay" (1.3.18), the witches present the possibility of generating offspring after the nocturnal visit as a succubus.

To be sure, the witches' prophecy "sets the play's tragic aspect in motion. . . by luring Macbeth away from the normal cycle of generation," (141) and yet the play allows us to think about generation as more chaotic, untethered from the political norms of linear succession. The witches continually expose the strife that cannot be removed from nature, including the sexual desire and appetite Malcolm would repress (4.3.126). Their "I'll do, I'll do, I'll do" (1.3.10) matches the kind of appetite found in the "ravined salt sea shark," whose "maw" (4.1.23–24) is placed in the cauldron, the vulture that Macduff uses to symbolize an apparently "acceptable" level of lust in a future king (4.3.74), and the "rat without a tail" (1.3.9). The world of darkness and evil, far from representing barrenness, displays a fecundity that at times outstrips that of the world of light, linear order, goodness, and purity.

Unlike the organic wholeness found in Malcolm's "regenerative," seemingly ecofriendly speech at the end of the play, the witches' cauldron provides what Morton calls the "symbiotic real," which he defines as "a weird 'implosive whole' in which entities are related in a non-total, ragged way."[16] Although the cauldron is filled with sundry poisons (from toads, snakes, hemlock, etc.), we also get a sense of the messiness and discord that is an intrinsic part of ecology. That messiness, however, is less evident with Birnam Wood, whose trees still carry the symbolic context of the idealized human and political order.[17] The apparition that introduces Banquo's line is an example of such an order, consisting of a child crowned with a tree in hand. Unlike Birnam, the witches' cauldron is both a place of death and a record of the pain and struggle amidst chaos that we know accompanied Duncan's reign. Thus, Macbeth's role is not to introduce chaos and death, but merely to shift the direction of its generative side-effects, turning them to his own profit, rather than his king's. Birnam Wood is about making the world whole again, while the witches' cauldron acknowledges the strife, fragmentation, and difference in a time out of joint, a world of Heraclitean flux and the Empedoclean war among the elements.

Yet even Birnam Wood is messier than such symbolism at first suggests. It may not have been uprooted, as Macbeth claims, but it has been impressed (4.1.94–95), forced into warfare, and what remains is less fertile in our imagination than the dark, wild beauty of the "rooky wood" with its multiplying conclave of crows. Macbeth implies that the woods have remained intact, that they've merely been transferred from one place to another. In reality, however, the trees of Birnam have become part of an assemblage of war, with the soldiers as vegetalized agents. The word "impressed" is not merely anthropomorphism; it also conveys the connection between the soldiers, the trees, and other materials that comprise the English army. Rather than the power of unspoiled ("uprooted") trees ready to re-spread their roots in Dunsinane, or the power of *homo faber*, Birnam wood represents a complex entanglement of human and nonhuman forces. This wood exists at the crossing of life and death, liveliness and immobility. The "rooky wood," on the other hand, in its unadulterated evil, is a place of pleasing, vital, nonhuman motion (the crow "makes wing"), and fecundity, with crows moving in and out of the trees as darkness begins to spread. The rooky wood, we sense, remains relatively untouched and unaltered by human hands. For all of their differences, however, both woods have in common a resistance to being cast as simply a symbol of life or death, generativity or barrenness.

As in *Macbeth*, *Coriolanus* documents an expansiveness of strife that flattens ontological distinctions, making it difficult to believe in human exceptionalism or singularity. The eponymous heroes of both plays compete to be the mightiest, even if it means losing their "humanity." But in *Coriolanus* Shakespeare disposes of the pretense that war might be fought for lofty or at least "just" causes such as the defeat of Scotland's tyrant; the very nature of war is hardly different from predators hunting prey in the rest of the animal kingdom. For example, when Aufidius joins forces with Coriolanus, he echoes his new partner's naturalistic, hierarchical language as he relishes the prospect of mass slaughter in Rome, a slaughter that would essentially be revenge for the war Martius (not yet "Coriolanus") led against Corioli when the people of the city were, in Martius' analogy, "fluttered" like doves (5.6.116): "I think he'll be to Rome/As is the osprey to the fish, who takes it/By sovereignty of nature"

(4.7.33–35).[18] The analogy is appropriate for describing someone who, as one of the citizens remarks, has not treated the plebeians "humanely" (1.1.17).

Descriptions of his god-like status notwithstanding, Coriolanus is most often positioned in the animal kingdom or amidst an elemental, universal strife that runs through all life forms, from the motion of osprey to the force of a planet, and the suffering of his victims is similarly depicted as embedded in the material world—they are like weeds "before a vessel under sail" or the earth trembling at the sound of his thunderous voice. When Coriolanus repeatedly emphasizes the herd-like behavior of the plebeians, going so far as to shun their collective, corporeal existence as the "rank-scented meinie" (3.1.68), he is not simply trying to make them appear inferior to "humans"; rather, he is trying to make them appear inferior to beasts like the osprey or the dragon that are more "singular" and even accomplish their feats alone, away from the multitude.[19] Yet in viewing himself as "alone" and singular, he ultimately rejects the very civic order that gave him human status to begin with. Banished from Rome, he lives "I'th'city of kites and crows" (4.5.43) and can never establish a genuine political identity when he forms an allegiance with the Volscians. For Coriolanus, the human/animal distinction is only relevant when it pertains to violence, and in that case humans are praised for behaving like powerful animals, for being the king of the jungle, as it were. Had the plebeians behaved more like lions or foxes (rather than hares, geese, or rats), we are led to believe, Coriolanus might have come to their defense.

While Coriolanus hardly denies the influence of his animal passions, he mistakenly sees his own courage and passion as singular when in reality his affect—especially his rage—binds him to the very plebeians he despises. Critics sometimes point the finger at the tribunes as the cause of the riot that culminates in the plebeians threatening to throw Coriolanus from the Tarpeian rock, but I prefer to think of the tribunes and the plebeians as components of what Gilles Deleuze calls an "assemblage of war" in which "bodies interpenetrate, mix together, transmit affects to one another."[20] *Coriolanus* often relies upon metaphors of a complete, self-enclosed organism (the body politic) or self-contained mechanisms (Coriolanus "stamping") but the Deleuzian machine/assemblage, with its de-territorializing, ever-changing connections with other desiring machines, offers a better conceptual frame for explaining what ultimately emerges out of political strife in the play, namely an affective contagion that spreads from one body to another. Violence appears to be inevitable, as it is the result of an affective circuitry connecting living creatures.

Individual humans might aspire for singularity within their species—as Coriolanus aspires to be the most effective warrior—but humans as a species are not ontologically distinct. Rather than a human/nature or human/animal distinction, we have creatures with distinct abilities and behaviors. Coriolanus is himself in a paradoxical position when it comes to his own "nature." To be his natural self (osprey-like, Aufidius says) he must be unnatural, that is, he must repress what he calls, referring to his potentially boyish behavior, a "gosling" instinct (or what others might see as acting like a good father, husband, and even Roman). As with Macbeth's "valued file" of dogs, some birds are mightier than others. If he were to act like an osprey, he would become another Macbeth, only he would be responsible for his own family's death, as Macbeth is responsible for the death of Macduff's "pretty chickens and their dam," taking them, as the osprey takes the fish, at "one fell swoop" (4.3.221–22).

Human identity is important to Coriolanus strictly when it comes to the species' ability to successfully wage war. Despite its multiplicity of animals representing a plurality of roles, *Coriolanus* provides an obvious example of how, as Karl Steel has argued, the "human" is established as an "oppositional identity" that relies upon the fiction of the "animal."[21] Unable to escape their own animality, humans must reinforce a human identity "by repeatedly enacting domination against animals."[22] That is precisely what Coriolanus attempts to do. The plebeians are "rats," "curs," and "geese" because they lack his courage and his thirst for "fame": "You souls of geese/That bear the shapes of men, how have you run from slaves that apes would beat!" (1.4.35–37). This means of differentiating the human animal from other, inferior—that is, weaker—animals, hardly goes un-criticized. Indeed, praise for Coriolanus' violence, especially that proffered by his mother, calls into mind negative human exceptionalism. What other creature could compete with one possessing such power to slaughter its own kind? Coriolanus is the avatar of the anthropological machine, manufacturing ad nauseam a boundary between human and beast via perpetual war.[23]

The argument that Shakespeare was a pacifist surely finds support here,[24] as we see him taking the baton from Erasmus and other humanists for whom hunting served as a metaphor—or even a literal enactment of—both war and tyranny. Macbeth and Coriolanus are both described as creating stacks of bodies that resemble the "quarries" of deer corpses commonly found after a hunt.[25] Macbeth is much beloved when he "carves a passage" through Duncan's enemies, but at the end of the play he is denounced as a "butcher." *Coriolanus* leaves us with little reason to see a distinctly human realm of war or even politics that transcends animal violence. Menenius compares the plebeians to dogs maneuvering for position in a hunt, but it is Coriolanus who is more closely bound up with the experience of both dogs and humans during the chase. He is an animal that enjoys the sport more than any other. As he says of Aufidius, "he is a lion/That I am proud to hunt," and Aufidius, the weaker of the two, places himself in the position of a hare fleeing a hunting party: "If I fly, Martius, hollo me like a hare" (1.8.7). While this "hollo" might come from a human, the sounds of the hunt—horns blowing, hounds crying, huntsmen hallowing—would blur, as would the boundary between human and non-human participants, and in this case Martius himself is in the position of both the human hallowing and the hound chasing, or rather he is representative of the hunting party as an assemblage. The bodily, sensuous experience of hunting—sights, sounds, and smells—allowed humans to, as Charles Bergman puts it, enjoy an "intoxicating rush" and the "animalistic release of passion."[26] What could better describe Coriolanus' addiction to war?

Strife in *Coriolanus* penetrates the experience of vitality and eros in a dynamic universe such that love and strife do not remain discrete entities. Over time, or even "on a dissension of a doit," the love and friendship celebrated in Shakespeare's comedies give way to "bitterest enmity." Conversely, "fellest foes," leading to love, not strife, might "by some chance" find reason to "interjoin their issues" (4.4.12–22). Such "interjoining," however, takes on new erotic possibilities as the attraction of the marriage bed, the hallmark of Erasmian cosmic love and generation, is transferred to men "unbuckling helms, fisting each other's throat" (4.5.127). Aufidius invokes a common metaphor from love poetry when he says to Coriolanus, "let me twine/Mine arms about that body" (4.5.108–9). Erasmus creates a similar image when he refers to the literal attraction, the natural *philia* of the vine for the elm (ASD 4-2: 62). For Aufidius, the partnership promises even more erotic fulfillment: they will join forces so they can sadistically "pour[. . .] war/Into the bowels of ungrateful Rome, / Like a bold flood o'erbear't" (4.5.131–33). Unlike his comparison of conquest to the solitary osprey diving for fish, this metaphor envisions the two men pleasurably "interjoined" in an excessively destructive power, an enema-like purgation of weak Romans expressed in the image of natural, elemental strife—a river overflowing its banks.[27]

Othello is not typically thought of as a "war play," yet in addition to a war between Venice and the Ottomans, Christianity and Islam, and frequent allusions to military practices, we have a protagonist who enjoys strife to an extent that might make Coriolanus and Volumnia blush. Although he, too, will become a victim of strife, Iago, thinking of his own control over the battlefield of love, sees himself sailing freely and smoothly with, rather than against, the elements: "If consequence do but approve my dream/My boat sails freely, both with wind and stream" (2.3.59–60).[28] Iago might be accurately described as having human, all too human qualities—he is a resentful, malcontented, racist soldier who happens to be good at detecting human frailty and insecurity—yet his actions become increasingly uncanny as the play progresses, and his malice is bound up with inhuman, elemental forces. Iago is the embodiment of the strife Petrarch sees penetrating all human experience, even love. As Petrarch says, "Strife does not cease. Just think what searing ardor there is in love, what discord in marriage, how many complaints, what suspicion among lovers, what sighs, what sorrow!"(5). Iago is not the creator of jealousy, the "green eyed monster"; he simply knows how to unleash this force in the minds and bodies of others. As we will see, when Iago instigates a conflict over Othello's marriage to Desdemona, he channels the energy of nonhuman forms of strife into a war between two groups of humans, allowing racial conflict to take center stage.

Iago exposes the strife deep within the psyche of soldiers like Cassio and Othello. This inner strife is the product of military discipline that relies heavily on the human/beast distinction, a fiction Iago employs for devious ends. Drunkenness, rashness, and sex, the three major temptations that create anxiety among soldiers in the play, were also forms of "bestial" behavior frequently denounced in military manuals.[29] Iago not only turns love into a kind of battlefield in which friends transform into enemies, he also turns Cypress itself into something like a military camp in which orderly behavior has been compromised. The tragic strife associated with multiple sites of war finds its way into the comic, festive atmosphere of Cypress after the defeat of the Ottomans at sea. With Iago's assistance, bestial appetite defeats reason in the soldiers' psychic struggles. Cassio's anxiety about losing the "immortal" part of himself, his "reputation," echoes Henry V's notion that fame and honor lift human souls up to heaven, leaving animals behind. Like Cassio, Othello has concerns about reputation, only in his case it is sexual appetite, or at least others' perception of it, that has the potential to damage his career (1.3.276). Of course, the general ultimately loses his reputation through other kinds of passion, namely anger and jealousy, and he becomes the opposite of the model soldier. Thus, the human/beast distinction comes back to haunt the very men who have perpetuated it. As critics have pointed out, Iago is aware of others' anxieties about the bestial and is able to use that anxiety for his own ends. Ironically, it is their fear of the beast within that, with the help of Iago, transforms them into beasts. The central conflict appears to have shifted from a fight with an external enemy—the Turk—to soldiers' struggle with "raging motions" in themselves and in others.

For all of his rational calculation, Iago is really a subverter of reason, including the kind we find in military manuals that—it was often hoped—would maintain orderly camps, battle formations, and marches. Iago has, in fact, turned military discipline against itself by poisoning the calm of peace with the strife of war. Iago appears to be reinforcing human/animal boundaries when he prompts Brabantio to imagine Othello violating them and when he invades Venetians' psyche with animal images that add to their pre-existing fears. But the strife he brings ultimately makes the human/animal distinction untenable. In his own militaristic mindset, love becomes merely animal appetite and there is no distinction between animal violence and human violence. Love is "merely a lust of the blood and a permission of the will" (1.3.330), and he makes it indistinguishable from the practices of war: "Faith, he tonight hath boarded a land Carrack" (1.2.50), he tells Cassio, speaking of Othello and Desdemona's presumed consummation of their marriage. He characterizes Desdemona's charms (eyes, voice) as "a parley to provocation" and "an alarum to love" (2.3.20, 22). More than an Ovidian trope on erotic pursuits as a kind of war, these lines are a means of fusing love and strife, peace and war. Even when Iago seems to be articulating a classic example of what Bruce Boehrer calls "absolute anthropocentrism," he winds up being more eclectic and undermines the human/animal distinction one might have expected him to follow.[30] Rather than set humans above animals for their intellect, as his extended metaphor of the "will" as a "gardener" suggests he might, he seems to really believe they are nothing but appetitive machines assisted by practical reason.

Viewing Iago as an avatar of strife who uses the human/animal distinction for disruptive ends adds a new twist to the way we think about race in *Othello*. Iago tries to turn sparks of racism into raging flames of a race war, setting the stage for what Foucault calls "perpetual war." "The war that is going on beneath order and peace," Foucault states, "the war that undermines our society and divides it in a binary mode is, basically, a race war."[31] In particular, the play telescopes the wide array of meanings for "Moor" into a racial category that allows a race war to take shape, and this puts the spotlight on one form of human strife. Although other Venetians recognize Othello's blackness, it is Iago, Brabantio, and Roderigo who bring race into play by characterizing the coupling of Othello and Desdemona as bestial. As Ania Loomba points out, "the power of this play is that it brings blackness and religious difference into simultaneous play while also making visible the tensions between them."[32] Othello's behavior fits the stereotype of the jealous and lascivious Turk, the Moslem enemy, and his physical features are used against him through a discourse on blackness that had long been part of Western racism.[33]

Iago places race at the center of war by undermining Othello's relatively peaceful integration into Venetian society. Venice, as Kim Hall points out, "had a reputation for tolerance."[34] The Venetian writer Gasparo Contarini, for example, says, "Others exceedingly admired the wonderful concourse of strange and foreign people, yea, of the farthest and remotest nations, as though the City of Venice were a common and general market onto the whole world."[35] Iago initially brings strife to Venice by making Brabantio fear that his house had become a "grange," that an "old black ram/Is tupping [his]white ewe" (1.1.90). Iago, seeing he has hit a nerve, adds more imagery by linking miscegenation to bestiality. Above all, what Iago brings is strife's disruption of love, including the generative potential of Othello and Desdemona. Having become a "stranger" once more, the man who had found an identity in Venice is unable to consummate his marriage or reproduce.

For race to develop as a category in *Othello*, there has to be an us vs. them, friend vs. foe mentality, and that unfolds as diverse forms of strife are channeled into the demonization of the Moor. As Gail Kern Paster's study of the physiology of emotion, the "embodied passions," has shown, nonhuman forms of strife exist in a material form that shapes human behavior.[36] The most dramatic form of nonhuman strife can be seen in the storm near Cypress in which "the wind ... hath ruffianed so upon the sea" (2.1.7). This storm is not merely symbolic of the imminent violence among humans in Cypress; it is also a material presence within the physiology of emotion in the man who, as a result of Iago's machinations, becomes a racialized threat to Christian Venice. By the play's end, Othello still sees himself in the role of Venice's heroic protector, only now the strife spurred on by Iago's race war takes place within himself, as he kills the "dog," the "turbaned Turk," within. Daniel Vitkus points out that "Othello is a theatrical embodiment of the dark, threatening powers at the edge of Christendom,"[37] but we have to remember that it is Iago, a figure of Strife on grand scale, who urges the Venetians to think in binaries about race. The stereotype of the violent, lustful, and cruel Turk becomes a crucial component of racial animus as Iago incorporates it into his plot to turn love into war. Indeed, the racial animus is a fabrication (though one built on long-standing hatreds of the "other" in European history); the energies of various forms of strife such as the storm, always present, are channeled into the battle between Christian vs. Turk.

The racial animus that bolsters a wartime us vs. them mentality is encouraged by the concept of the "animal" that underlies just about all of the play's anxiety about sexuality, race, and gender. Racism, it would seem, was already present without Iago's intervention. Nevertheless, his pernicious fiction of the "human," now readily seen in the light of day, makes exclusion much more likely. "This agreement concerning philosophical sense and common sense that allows one to speak blithely of the Animal in the general singular," Jacques Derrida points out, "is perhaps one of the greatest and most symptomatic *asinanities* of those who call themselves humans."[38] To be sure, there is an impressive array of different animals in this play—rams, ewes, horses, goats, monkeys, guinea hens, baboons, etc.—but just about all of these nonhuman creatures merely provide a metonymy for lust or animal passions. Ania Loomba points out that the ram/ewe metaphor makes the coupling of Othello and Desdemona "just as unnatural as the supposed lust between animals and people in Africa."[39] Iago's racial animus incorporates animal references as a means of reducing the complexity of the signifier "Moor." The multifaceted dimensions of Othello's existence are effaced in order to racialize his identity. Iago turns an insider into an outsider, using the "animal" as a way to set up even stronger conditions for war as focused organized violence between two groups, namely Christians and Moslems. This is what Erasmus, taking a pacifist stance, condemned in the racist language of Christians whose first impulse was always to go to war:

> whenever the ignorant mob hear the name 'Turk,' they immediately fly into a rage and clamour for blood, calling them dogs and enemies to the name of Christian; it does not occur to them that, in the first place, the Turks are men, and what is more, half-Christian.[40]

At the same time, the play won't allow the human/animal binary to serve as an adequate means of grasping Iago's malice. Perhaps the most tragic feature of the play is his unwillingness to explain his motive(s): "What you know, you know" (5.2.311). He has nothing to say because, as a figure of strife, there is no solid explanation for the violence he sought—he is just a force of negation or enmity. Roderigo's phrase "inhuman dog" is not, in fact, as tautological as it seems, since "dog" is hardly sufficient to describe him. Iago is not inhuman merely because he lacks "human" qualities like compassion, pity, or love, but because he is the embodiment of strife. Given this uncanny dimension of Iago's malice, the play has much in common with other tragedies, *King Lear* in particular, in which strife is not telescoped to form a human-centered, friend-versus-foe, ideology, such as the Christian versus Turk that English audience would certainly find engaging. *King Lear* has a French invasion that takes a back seat to the other forms of strife. Who worries about whether or not Edmund's order to execute Cordelia is a "normal" procedure of war? Instead, we focus on the strife in the animal kingdom as humans, competing with one another as predators and prey, try—and fail—to distinguish themselves from animals. "Why should a dog, a horse, a rat have life," Lear asks, "And thou no breath at all?" Try as he might, Lear cannot demonstrate a hierarchical, ontological separation of human and animal, nor does the play as a whole present human beings as singular or exceptional (except, as in *Coriolanus*, for the possibility of negative exceptionalism).[41] As I have argued, Iago manages to foreground racial conflict as the central form of strife; nevertheless, his silence is a reminder that strife exists well beyond the religious, political, or cultural ideologies that pit one group of humans against another.

It is hard to see war in Shakespeare's tragedies simply as organized violence controlled by specific groups of humans. Humans take on the qualities of specific "war-like" animals—eagles, tigers, lions, boars—in many plays, but the human/animal boundary, always porous, becomes especially problematic in the tragedies after 1600. In these plays, humans are positioned as one species among many others in a universe of natural strife. An encounter with the zoographic diversity of *Troilus and Cressida*, *King Lear*, and the tragedies we have discussed can also enable us to read other, more human-centered plays differently. For example, we might be inspired to take Henry V's comparison of his soldiers to tigers and greyhounds a step further, and add other, less dignified creatures such as horse-leeches to the list. After all, Pistol's comic line "Let us to France, like horse-leeches, my boys, / To suck, to suck, the very blood to suck!" (2.3.53–54) prepares us for the bathos at the play's end, when the chorus informs us about the loss of France by Henry's successor. Not long after Henry V describes his soldiers' "honor" rising to heaven, their fame outlasting their earthly, animal bodies, the chorus reminds us that Henry's successor "lost France and made England bleed" (Epilogue 11–12). The claims that the war is "just" or "holy," already questionable, now seem absurd in light of the war's short-lived political benefits, not to mention the war crimes committed by the king himself. In the late tragedies, however, warfare enables human exceptionalism, autonomy, and singularity to come under much greater scrutiny. The muddled nature of the play's genre notwithstanding, it seems appropriate to end with a quotation from *Troilus and Cressida*. Refusing any celebration of military virtue as a form of human greatness yet lacking a proper *jus contra bellum*, the play entangles all creatures great and small in a universe of strife. Such entanglement is best expressed late in the play when Thersites, himself a "dog," places the ideologies of wartime heroism and glory under the microscope:

> To be a dog, a mule, a cat, a fitchew, a toad, a lizard, an owl, a puttock, or a herring without a roe, I would not care; but to be Menelaus! I would conspire against destiny. Ask me not what I would be, if I were not Thersites, for I care not to be the louse of a lazar so I were not Menelaus.[42]

Notes

1 G.S. Kirk and J.E. Raven, eds., *The Presocratic Philosophers: A Critical History with a Selection of Texts* (Cambridge: Cambridge University Press, 1957), 193.

2 *Petrarch's Remedies for Fortune Fair and Foul*, trans. Conrad H. Rawski, vol. 3 (Bloomington: Indiana University Press, 1991), 1. All quotations of *De Remediis* will be from this edition. The German edition from 1532: Francesco Petrarcha, Peter Chalybs, and Georg Spalatin, *Von der Artzney bayder Glück, des guten und widerwertigen: Unnd weß sich ain yeder inn Gelück und Unglück halten sol* (Augspurg, 1532), www.mdz-nbn-resolving.de/urn/resolver.pl?urn=urn:nbn:de:bvb:12-bsb11200493-3.

3 Petrarch undermines his own assertion late in the preface that "Man" is "lord of the earth and ruler of all living creatures" by pointing out that while he is supposed to be "the only one who with the rudder of his reason should be able to control calmly the course of life and its swirling, turbulent seas," he in fact negates that role because he "engages in continuous strife, not only with others, but with himself" (10). With his passions ruling over his reason, man is just one of a multitude of life forms caught up in endless change and strife. The woodcut is accompanied by a German poem that expounds the same philosophy as Petrarch's preface.

4 William Shakespeare, *Henry V*, ed. T.W. Craik (New York: Bloomsbury, 2009). All quotations of the play will be from this edition.

5 For more on the way human identity is created through the concept of immortality, see Karl Steel, *How to Make a Human* (Columbus: Ohio State University Press, 2011), Chapter 3.

6 Sir Walter Ralegh, "A Discourse of War in General," in *The Works of Sir Walter Ralegh*, eds. William Oldys and Thomas Birch (New York: Burt Franklin, 1829), 293.

"Everything Exists by Strife"

7 Christopher Marlowe, *Tamburlaine Parts One and Two*, ed. Anthony B. Dawson (New York: WW Norton, 1997). For more on Empedocles and strife, see Jeffrey Cohen and Lowell Duckert, eds., *Elemental Ecocriticism: Thinking with Earth, Air, Water, and Fire* (Minneapolis: University of Minnesota Press, 2015). They point out that

> Empedocles believed human bodies to be microcosms: composed of all four "roots," with love and strife as roiled soul. Yet earth, air, water, and fire do not exist in order to become *anthropos*. Human form is simply one composition among many, not the measure of the world.
>
> (12)

8 William Shakespeare, *Macbeth*, eds. Sandra Clark and Pamela Mason (London: Bloomsbury, 2015). All quotations will be from this edition.

9 Part of what makes this and other plays "tragic" is that they do not balance Strife and Love. We might contrast this handling of strife with the more optimistic cosmology we find in his comedies or in other authors such as Erasmus or Spenser. Erasmus says in *Querela Pacis* (The complaint of peace) humans remain outsiders in a universe of cosmic harmonies, a universe in which Love and Strife are balanced and all is held together by *philia* or what is sometimes called *Concordia discors*. Celestial bodies, plants, minerals, and animals all enjoy greater peace than humans do, and humans are at their best, that is, their most peaceful, when they tap into this real cosmic force of *philia*. That occurs when they generate and raise children. Although the play allows for the hope that such philia will return once Macbeth is killed, that hope seems likely to be overwhelmed by the spread of darkness. Humans are continually at war, Erasmus argues, while there is "friendliness" ("amicitiam") in trees and plants, elements maintain mutual agreement and commerce or communication ("commercioque mutuo concordia alunt"). See *Opera Omnia Desiderii Erasmi Roterodami* (Amsterdam: Elzevier, 1969), 4–2:62.

10 On Macbeth and "nocturnal agencies," see Laurie Shannon, *The Accomodated Animal* (Chicago, IL: University of Chicago Press, 2013), Chapter 4.

11 See Christine Vernando, "Queer Nature, or the Weather in *Macbeth*," in *Queer Shakespeare: Desire and Sexuality*, ed. Goran Stanivukovic (New York: Bloomsbury, 2017), 177–95. She argues that

> the witches' spells blur any easy distinction between natural and unnatural forms of generation; they signal that this fragmented, dismembered, bubbling chaos is how nature works, by demonstrating the thorough inter-dependence of destruction and generation, and of nature and artifice.
>
> (192)

12 See, for example, Peter Daly, "Of *Macbeth*, Martlets, and Other 'Fowles of Heaven'," *Mosaic* 12, no. 1 (1978): 23–46. For a critique of readings that make animals and other forms of nonhuman nature seem "merely metaphorical," see Andreas Hofele, *Stage, Stake, and Scaffold: Humans and Animals in Shakespeare's Theatre* (Oxford: Oxford University Press, 2011), 16–30.

13 On the blurring of the nature/art boundary in *Macbeth* and other plays, see Steve Mentz, "Shakespeare's Beach House, or the Green and the Blue in *Macbeth*," *Shakespeare Studies* 39 (2011): 84–93. An alternative reading can be found in Randall Martin, *Shakespeare and Ecology* (Oxford: Oxford University Press, 2015). Martin sees the weird sisters as a "third party" that provides an "ecocritique" of war technology, especially gunpowder. I don't see such a separation of "nature" and war technology that would allow for such an ecocritique of war to appear.

14 Timothy Morton, *Humankind* (Brooklyn, NY: Verso, 2017), 2.

15 Robert Watson, *Shakespeare and the Hazards of Ambition* (Cambridge, MA: Harvard University Press, 1984), 141.

16 Morton, *Humankind*, 1.

17 On "discord" in ecology, see Daniel B. Botkin, *Discordant Harmonies* (Oxford: Oxford University Press, 1990). What critics sometimes refer to as the "ecology" of *Macbeth* is an example of, as Botkin puts it, the "conviction that undisturbed nature, or perhaps a nature with human beings playing their 'natural roles,' is good, while a changing nature is bad" (13). *Macbeth* would be an example of an ecological harmony given by "the divine" (12). Botkin challenges ecological thinking that looks for a "highly structured, ordered, and regulated, steady-state ecological system" (9). For a discussion of ideas of "harmony" and "wholeness," in the early modern period, see Karen Raber, *Shakespeare and Posthumanist Theory* (New York: Arden, 2018), Chapter 2. Raber points out that instead of "nature's organic wholeness," posthumanist ecocritics "posit. . . a Shakespearean

cosmos that takes as its norm the chaotic and unhinged mutations of the elements and of beings (gods, goddesses, fairies) that early moderns so feared" (32).

18 William Shakespeare, *Coriolanus* (New York: Bloomsbury, 2013). All quotations from this play are from this edition.

19 On Coriolanus' rejection of the crowd/rioters as it relates to urban experience in ancient Rome and London, see Holly Dugan, "*Coriolanus* and the 'Rank-Scented Meinie'," in *Masculinity and the Metropolis of Vice 1550–1650*, eds. Amanda Bailey and Roze Hentschell (London: Palgrave, 2010), 139–59.

20 Gilles Deleuze, "On the Superiority of Anglo-American Literature," in *Dialogues II*, eds. Gilles Deleuze and Claire Parnet (New York: Columbia University Press, 1977), 70.

21 Karl Steel, *How to Make a Human* (Columbus: Ohio State University Press, 2011), 19.

22 Steel, *How to Make a Human*, 19.

23 On the "anthropological machine," see Giorgio Agamben, *The Open* (Stanford, CA: Stanford University Press, 2004), 33–38.

24 On Shakespeare's pacifism, see Steven Marx, "Shakespeare's Pacifism," *Renaissance Quarterly* 45, no. 1 (Spring, 1992): 49–98. Marx, detecting an Erasmian or "pacifist" bent in Shakespeare's Jacobean plays, sees "anti-military critiques" growing more powerful around 1602 and "affirmations of peace" appearing more regularly in the late Romances. Shakespeare, in my view parted ways with humanist pacifism in one major respect: while Erasmus believed that nature created human beings as exceptional in a positive as well as negative sense, Shakespeare's plays do not ultimately endorse exceptionalism at all, positive or negative. Erasmus saw humans as the unaccommodated animal designed to find bestial violence repugnant.

25 On hunting and war, see Matt Cartmill, *A View to a Death in the Morning* (Cambridge, MA: Harvard University Press, 1993).

26 Charles Bergman, "A Spectacle of Beasts: Hunting Rituals and Animal Rights in Early Modern England," in *A Cultural History of Animals*, ed. Bruce Boehrer, vol. 3 (New York: Berg, 2007), 55.

27 See, for example, Leonardo da Vinci's description of the warlike, predatory forces of nature that defy human attempts to contain them. He personifies a river as a beast that "gnaws on the land and drags its prey—houses, trees, humans, animals—to the sea. Da Vinci, quoted in Roger D. Masters, *Fortune Is a River: Leonardo da Vinci and Niccolò Machiavelli's Dream to Change the Course of Florentine History* (New York: Free Press, 1998), 9.

28 William Shakespeare, *Othello*, ed. Kim F. Hall (Boston, MA: Bedford Books, 2007). All quotations to the play will be from this edition.

29 For more on military manuals, reason, and desire, see Benjamin Bertram, *Bestial Oblivion: War, Humanism, and Ecology in Early Modern England* (New York: Routledge, 2018), Chapters 2–3. The classic work on Renaissance human/animal distinctions based on "reason" is Erica Fudge, *Brutal Reasoning: Animals, Rationality, and Humanity in Early Modern England* (Ithaca, NY: Cornell University Press, 2006). See, in particular, her discussion of drunkenness and rage, both important to *Othello*, Chapter 3.

30 Bruce Boehrer, *Shakespeare among the Animals* (New York: Palgrave, 2004), 6–17.

31 Michel Foucault, *Society Must Be Defended: Lectures at the Collège de France 1975–1976* (New York: Picador, 1997), 60.

32 Ania Loomba, *Shakespeare, Race, and Colonialism* (New York: Oxford University Press, 2002), 107.

33 On racism in the Middle Ages, see in particular the essays in Miriam Eliav-Feldon, Benjamin Isaac, and Joseph Ziegler, eds., *The Origins of Racism in the West* (New York: Cambridge University Press, 2009).

34 Shakespeare, *Othello*, 235.

35 Quoted by Kim F. Hall, Ibid., 235.

36 Gail Paster, *Humoring the Body* (Chicago, IL: University of Chicago Press, 2004), Chapter 1. Paster argues that we "find abstraction and bodily metaphor where the early moderns found materiality and literal reference" (26).

37 Daniel Vitkus, *Turning Turk: English Theater and the Multicultural Mediterranean, 1570–1630* (New York: Palgrave, 2004), 90.

38 Jacques Derrida, *The Animal that Therefore I Am*, trans. David Wills (New York: Fordham University Press, 2008), 41.

39 Loomba, *Shakespeare, Race, and Colonialism*, 51.

40 Erasmus, "On the War against the Turks," in *The Erasmus Reader*, ed. Erika Rummel (Toronto: University of Toronto Press, 1990), 317.

41 On *King Lear* and animal violence, see Laurie Shannon, "Poor, Bare, Forked: Animal Sovereignty, Human Negative Exceptionalism, and the Natural History of *King Lear*," *Shakespeare Quarterly* 60, no. 2 (Summer, 2009): 168–96.

42 William Shakespeare, *Troilus and Cressida*, ed. Kenneth Palmer (London: Routledge, 1989), 5.1.60–65. For more on this play's references to animals and elemental strife, see the essays by Rebecca Bushnell, Steve Mentz, and Karen Raber in Dympna Callaghan and Suzanne Gossett, eds., *Shakespeare in Our Time* (New York: Bloomsbury, 2016), 327–41.

8

ZOONOTIC SHAKESPEARE
Animals, Plagues, and the Medical Posthumanities

Lucinda Cole

Between 1600 and 1900, both zoonotic and enzootic diseases became global problems, exacerbated by European colonialism and a transnational trade in animals and animal products. In contrast to the many books and articles written on early modern plague outbreaks among humans, comparatively little attention has been paid to the "great mortalities" of sheep, oxen, birds, and even cats recorded during this period. This is odd because throughout the early modern era agricultural writers returned again and again to the violence and trauma of cattle plagues in Britain and elsewhere. Edward III's reign had become a cautionary tale for how bad things could get. "It rained from Midsommer till Christmas," John Speed reports, "and so terrible a plague ranne through the world, that the earth was filled with graves, and the aire with cries; which was seconded with murren of Cattle, and dearth of all things."[1] John Fitzherbert's *Boke of Husbandry* (1540) was the first text to deal with murrains or mass animal die-offs; it was followed by Girolamo Fracastoro's comparative treatise on human and animal diseases in 1546, and Leonard Mascall's *First Booke of Cattell* in 1587.[2] By the time Shakespeare wrote his early plays, at the end of the sixteenth century, Europe had suffered at least nine major cattle plagues since 1500—roughly one a decade—and had recorded least 300 years of organized efforts to understand and manage these diseases. These records do more than simply provide a context for reading Shakespeare's references to dead, dying, or sick animals; they gesture towards the experience of living in a world rife with zoonotic diseases.

In response, focusing on revealing passages in *The Merchant of Venice, Coriolanus*, and *Troilus and Cressida*, this chapter exemplifies and advocates for what I call the medical posthumanities, a cross-disciplinary inquiry that combines concerns from both animal studies and the medical humanities. Animal studies scholars, relying heavily on husbandry manuals, have provided many valuable analyses of everyday relationships between humans and their animals, the most recent being Erica Fudge's *Quick Cattle and Dying Wishes: People and Their Animals in Early Modern England*.[3] Outside of animal studies, however, many scholars of the early modern period either ignore references to animal diseases or treat them symbolically, as though they were merely figurative registers of human emotional and biophysical susceptibilities. Such anthropocentric reading practices have all but erased the reality of enzootic and zoonotic disease recognized and described by writers in the sixteenth and seventeenth centuries, even as our own collective understanding of contemporary zoonotic disease—West Nile Virus, AIDS, avian flu, and COVID-19—has deepened. 75 percent of the million currently identified animal viruses are now considered zoonotic.[4] Although the twenty-first century may have eliminated once-common diseases like rinderpest (which gave rise to measles), the last few remaining viral samples now confined to high risk storage facilities, traces of animal disease, including great plagues, remain in our historical and literary record. To read Shakespeare from the perspective of the medical posthumanities, then, is to take seriously species-jumping viruses and epidemics whose effects, as we shall see, were exacerbated by the trade in animals and animal products in an increasingly global ecology and economy.

I Dogs, Plague, and Miasma Theory

Zoonotic diseases are technically diseases that can be transmitted from vertebrate animals to humans, even when that transfer involves a non-vertebrate disease vector. They can be transmitted by inhalation (anthrax), ingestion (salmonella, brucellosis), animal bites (rabies), exposure of skin (leptospirosis, fleas), or through arthropods (Lyme disease). Although the term "zoonotic disease" was not coined until the nineteenth century, the recognition that nonhumans could carry diseases and transmit them to humans goes back for centuries. The most telling and widely discussed evidence in the sixteenth and seventeenth centuries for cross-species contagion was rabies.

Rabies presented early modern readers and writers with the clearest evidence of how humans and animals are vulnerable to the same neurological diseases. Rabies was often described as an "an ungovernable fury," and, before 1700, no clear distinction existed between the psychological state of being furious and the medical diagnosis of rabid, bodily infection. In fact, the term "rabies" (from the Latin *rabere*, "be mad, rave") was applied primarily to humans and only secondarily to dogs.[5] The Abbess in *The Comedy of Errors*, in describing the origin of the presumed madness of Antipholus of Syracuse, voices a common assumption about rabies and madness: he has run mad because "The venom clamours of a jealous woman/ Poisons more deadly than a mad dog's tooth."[6] When Edgar in *King Lear* assumes the character of Poor Tom, a "Bedlam beggar," he "shift[s]/ Into a madman's rags, t'assume a semblance/ That very dogs disdained."[7] Underwriting the references to dogs in both of these plays is a perception of zoonotic disease: humans, infected with (or "poisoned" by) a creature of a different species, can sink from God-given rationality to a madness that turns "man" into beast.

In Act Three of *Lear*, Edgar imagines himself embedded in a pack of dogs; some of the animals seem rabid, and, in his performance as Tom o' Bedlam, he behaves like them or even threatens to outdo them:

> Avaunt, you curs!
> Be thy mouth or black or white,
> Tooth that poisons if it bite;
> Mastiff, greyhound, mongrel grim,
> Hound or spaniel, brach, or him,
> Bobtail tyke or trundle-tail,
> Tom will make them weep and wail.

(3.6.20–26)

Tom takes on potentially rabid dogs (with "tooth that poisons if it bite") even as he symptomizes, at least performatively for the benefit of his onstage audience, the fury of being rabid. He has, in the words of an eighteenth-century treatise on rabies, "taken on the canine nature" to disguise his identity.[8] Yet what makes this performance plausible for Shakespeare's audience is the belief that the psychological and biophysical symptoms of rabies can result from a cross-species infection. Rabid dogs, in this instance, may mark the limits of human knowledge about madness, but they also reveal how early modern biopolitics turned on the recognition that zoonotic diseases could blast crops, minds, and familiar species hierarchies.[9]

Although dog bites were the most dramatic instance of zoonosis, most theories of contagion during this time were based on miasmic theory or theories of "bad air." Among early modern physicians, disease vectors and pathogens were hotly debated subjects, and the literature of the period is rife with references to infections arising from putrefying wetlands. Caliban's curses Prospero in *The Tempest* by invoking miasma theory explicitly: "All the infections that the sun sucks up/ From bogs, fens, flats, on Prosper fall, and make him by inch-meal a disease."[10] At a time when the Crown and investors were launching print and financial campaigns to garner support for draining the Fens in the east of England, Caliban's lines invoke a causal mechanism familiar to seventeenth-century audiences: low-lying wetlands were breeding grounds for infectious diseases, both because they gave rise to venomous creatures—snakes, frogs, rats, and so on—and because they were perceived as sinkholes for organic matter that was rotting and giving off noxious fumes.[11] The links between disease and unhealthy environments were capacious enough during the period that, under the rubric of miasma theory, "infestation" and "infection" often were indistinguishable.[12]

Correspondingly, dogs—carriers of rabies, carrion eaters, and biowagons for fleas—were identified with more than one source contagion. Along with witches, rodents, rabbits, wolves, demons, cats, and Jews, they were often blamed for the pestilences of Shakespeare's London. A popular plague book reprinted in 1603 advocates that people "keep their houses, street, yards, and sinks, and ditches sweet and clean from all standing puddles, dunghills, and corrupt moistures" in order to prevent outbreaks; most importantly, they should not let dogs run in the house, since these "will be most apt cattle ... to carry the infection."[13] In this case, humans fear the capacity of dogs to expose them (through touch or air) to "putrefactions," "corruptions," and "effluvia"—what we call bacteria—from standing water and waste. Consequently, dogs (and sometimes cats) were subject to extermination in plague-ridden London, at least through 1665. In 1636, London exterminated 3,720 dogs, roaming animals that, according to Mark Jenner, were perceived as "visible sources of disorder, out of control and unsanitary."[14] A common complaint was that dogs ate carrion, itself a possible source of contagion, and by the early eighteenth century, city dogs (at least) had been forced into regimes of containment, hygiene, and control.[15]

Especially in texts like *The Merchant of Venice*, dogs function largely, although not exclusively, as metonymical figures bound up in this discourse of disease and contagion. As Bruce Boehrer argued almost 20 years ago, of all Shakespeare's characters, only Caliban is more consistently associated with the "brute orders of creation" than Shylock; the Jew is identified repeatedly with dogs and curs in what Boehrer calls a "strain of metaphor ... brutally overdetermined."[16] "Thou called'st me a dog before thou hadst a cause," Shylock says to his tormenters, "But since I am a dog, beware my fangs."[17] Boehrer provides in his analysis a still-shocking anti-Semitic image of a German woodcut; in it, two dogs and a Jew hang over a fire in what has been called a "reverse Crucifixion." Boehrer understandably focuses on the ethnic identities being contested in the play, and especially on Shylock's passionate claims to a common humanity. For much of the period, both dogs and Jews were scapegoated as vertebrate carriers of zoonotic disease.

Other aspects of the play, however, suggest a less ideological, more material understanding of animals as disease vectors. Zoonotic disease figures elliptically in figures of infection through ingestion. In Act One, Shylock refuses to eat dinner with Antonio because he does not want "to smell pork" (1.3.28). The Jewish taboo against eating pork is widely attributed to the scavenging habits of hogs—animals that, like dogs, were disparaged as carrion eaters and therefore considered as disease vectors. Shylock's disdain for pork, significantly, is only one of actual and figurative references to a potentially diseased meat—and meat market—in the play. Shylock uses the Old Testament story of Laban's sheep (Genesis 30:25–43), as theological cover for his cruel bargain with Antonio.[18] Collapsing differences between humans and animals, he covenants to exact a pound of flesh if Antonio is unable to meet his bond (1.3.72–88). Shylock's bond recalls the medieval anti-Semitic stereotype of the blood libel, Jews baking the blood of Christian children into matzoh, but it also points to the realm of edible animals as commodities, reminding us that Venice was a center for trade in live animals. Shylock himself makes the connection: "A pound of man's flesh taken from a man/ Is not so estimable, profitable neither/ As flesh of muttons, beeves, or goats" (1.3.161–64). Another reference to the meat market occurs on Shylock's daughter's conversion to Christianity: Lancelot jokes, "This making of Christians will raise the price of hogs. If we grow all to be pork-eaters we shall not shortly have a rasher on the coals for money" (3.5.19–21). While the languages of commerce and animality permeate this play, they are yoked by an international meat market. Ethnic differences are figured as dietary norms, where dietary norms evoked by Shylock and Lancelot drive the trade in animal flesh.

II Venice as Epicenter of Global Animal Trade

Between 1470 and 1570, a new system emerged in the marketing of livestock, partly prompted by the increased cultivation of arable land, and, by the time Shakespeare wrote, an international trade in cattle had all but eclipsed former regional marketing systems.[19] This international trade in animals had a dark and persistent underside: Venice was also an epicenter of zoonotic disease. Although Great Britain seems to have been less frequently plagued with cattle disease than Italy—in part because, until 1666, it imported most of its cattle from a comparatively isolated Ireland—its farmers and butchers were also compelled to deal with rinderpest, anthrax, foot and mouth disease, and other afflictions. The most important lines in *The Merchant of Venice*, given these concerns, are Antonio's. At the trial, as he patiently awaits the knife by which Shylock will exact his "pound of flesh," he encourages Bassiano to leave him. "I am a tainted wether of the flock," he says, "Meetest for death" (4.1.113–14). Greenblatt's edition defines "tainted" as "castrated," although the more common definition is "corrupted," "stained," or "infected"; "wether" refers to a sheep or ram; and "meetest for death" reflects the necessity for culling this diseased animal before the rest of the herd becomes afflicted. Antonio's identification with a diseased animal, in one respect, points to the moral and sacrificial economies of Christianity; in another, his identification with *infected* cattle points to the commercial, environmental, agricultural, and medical economies in which humans and animals are equally vulnerable to zoonotic disease.

Because it was a center for trade in livestock, Venice was also an epicenter for epizootic diseases and efforts to control them. In the sixteenth and seventeenth centuries, "great mortalities" or "pestilences" of cattle were reported throughout Germany, the Netherlands, Italy, and Great Britain. C.A. Spinage, in his monumental study *Cattle Plague*, discusses what probably was a zoonotic outbreak in or around 1514 in Venice and the surrounding areas. Around this time, he reports, people in Padua and Venice were "afflicted" by an "epidemic dysentery" after eating diseased cattle flesh—"flesh from cadavers"—imported from Hungary, a trade that sometimes reached as many as 7,418 head in one day (97). Spinage suggests that the cattle "had died of rinderpest" (97). Shortly thereafter, the Council of Venice temporarily "forbade the distribution" of beef, veal, and butter, milk, and cheese from any animal that had been identified as diseased and was therefore "under penalty of death" (97). Only mutton was considered safe enough to eat. A similar outbreak—this one in oxen—occurred in 1590, when the Council of Venice once again outlawed beef, cheese, butter, and milk (98). In 1598, rinderpest erupted in Germany and the next year spread to Italy where 13,000 cattle died. When human dysentery followed, the Venetian state ordered the destruction of infected animals (98). The plague nevertheless spread to France where, in 1604, the health department in Lyon commanded that any cattle intended for slaughter be inspected by "a master butcher in the presence of a commissioner of health" and that infected bodies be buried 2 meters deep and covered with quicklime (98). 1609—the year Shakespeare wrote *Troilus and Cressida*—and 1616 (the year Shakespeare died) were equally infectious for eastern and central Europe, with veal and beef once again prohibited; in Italy, beef and oxen stocks were nearly depleted through disease and extensive herd culling (98).

Shakespeare's reference to "culling" infected cattle in *The Merchant of Venice*, then, suggests more than a casual familiarity with disorders affecting livestock. In different ways, Erica Fudge, Karen Raber, Bruce Boehrer, Laurie Shannon, and Nathaniel Wolloch have explored the role of animal husbandry in Shakespeare's work, especially in relation to horses.[20] In *The Taming of the Shrew*, Biondello's description of Petruchio's "hipp'd" horse is a virtual catalog of equine afflictions:

> possessed with the glanders and like to mose in the chine, troubled with the lampas, infected with the fashions, full of windgalls, sped with spavins, rayed with the yellows, past cure of the fives, stark spoiled with the staggers, begnawn with the bots.[21]

Glanders (or farcy) is a bacterial disease, like rinderpest and anthrax, capable of wiping out entire generations of livestock. In Shakespeare such diseases provided a vocabulary for human self-diagnosis. The word "giddy," for example, which appears over 30 times in Shakespeare's plays, is associated with the most characteristic symptom of gid: its brain infested with a parasite, the animal turns in circles. When the Widow in *The Taming of the Shrew* says to Katherina, "He that is giddy thinks the world turns round" (5.2.20), she invokes centuries of everyday knowledge collected in late sixteenth-century England through early modern animal husbandry texts, primarily the works of Gervase Markham and Leonard Mascall.

Such playful references, however, do not capture the geographical and quantifiable *scale* of animal disease and its historical and etiological comparisons to human plague. During the first year of a rinderpest or anthrax outbreak, some 70% of cattle were usually lost, often tens and even hundreds of thousands, a mortality rate that outstrips those reported for human plague.[22] Both human and animal diseases were interpreted in Biblical terms as signs of God's displeasure. Quoting Scripture, one sixteenth-century divine insists that murrains cannot simply be attributed to "Witches and Sorcerers" but to God, who warned a sinful nation: "*Cursed shall be the increase of thy kine, and the flocke of thy sheepe. The beastes and the birdes are consumed for their sin, that dwel in the land.*"[23] Some husbandry texts, in contrast, attempted to balance religious explanations with etiologies that could lead to practical advice. "The cause of this Infectious disease," Michael Harward writes, "is infection of the Air":

> ... as I found once in two Towns ... where a dark stinking fogg continued three dayes together, in the middle of Summer; and within one week after many of their Cattle

were infected with this disease: I was called thither, and found the disease so predominate, that I was forc'd to go from field to field wit a Lanthorn and Candle to give medicines to sick Cattle. Also is taken by stinking caren lying unburied, or from other infected Cattle; however it makes a quick dispatch, for after it once begins, they are dead within twenty four hours, if help be not found.[24]

Harward relies mostly on theories of miasma, ecological explanations intended to counter the panic murrain could evoke. Spinage describes a fourteenth-century British epizootic during which "panic stricken" shepherds, fearing the Black Death, fled from their herds (5). A few surviving animals then roamed the countryside, spreading disease, but, because people feared the contagion, no one would chase down the creatures and contain or kill them. Other responses to outbreaks included a variety of local and often occult remedies: cutting off the head of a live two-year-old animal and hanging it up in the house with the eyes facing east (Northern Germany); hiding a skull under the ridge of a house (Northern Europe); hanging the head of a horse in a stall (Wales) (96). Together, sermons and animal husbandry record a history of mass animal die-offs that parallel and sometimes, it was thought, serve as a frightening prelude to human plague. Fields of rotting corpses, after all, were often a poorly understood prelude to widespread human illnesses.

Thomas Brooks, a popular seventeenth-century Puritan divine who stayed in London during the plague to look after his flocks, attempts to unite the religious and ecological explanations. Some physicians, he says, "ascribe it to the heat of the Air," and sometimes to "driness"; sometimes they blame it on "corruption" of the air and sometimes on "mens blood"; sometimes "Satan, and sometimes to the malignancy of the Planets."[25] He insists, however, physicians are "of no value" unless they look beyond these "second causes, to the First Cause," to "*the wheel within the wheel*":

> The Plague is a hidden thing, a secret thing; it is a sickness, a disease, that more immediately comes from God, than any other sickness or disease doth. *Behold the hand of the Lord is upon thy cattel which is in the field, upon the horses, upon the asses, upon the camels, upon the oxen, and upon the sheep, there shall be a very grievous murrain.*
>
> (7)

For Brooks, as for many others, etiological differences between humans and animal plague, murrains and plagues, collapse under the rubric of "First Causes," or divine retributions and Biblical interpretations. "The word here [in Exodus 9:3]," he continues,

> translated *murrain,* is in *chap. 5. v. 3.* termed *pestilence;* and it is one and the same disease, though when it is applied to cattel, it be usually rendred by murrain, yet when 'tis applied to men, as in the Scripture last cited, it is commonly called the pestilence.
>
> (6)

This characterization of "one and the same disease" affecting humans and animals should make us wary of reading a whole host of Shakespearean images as merely or primarily metaphoric. Zoonotic diseases crossed species boundaries; outbreaks among any livestock were associated with the same rhetoric of punishment and divine retribution that accompanied the human epidemics of the early modern period.

III Rereading "Murrain"

As a rule, ambiguities between "murrain" and more general forms of "pestilence" have led many commentators on Shakespeare's text to anthropocentric interpretations of complex references to zoonotic disease. In *Troilus and Cressida*, which Jonathan Gil Harris has called Shakespeare's most "disease-ridden" play, Ajax and Thersites insult each other in imagery rife with the language of zoonotic disease[26]: the venom-tongued Thersites invokes running boils, the "plague of Greece," horses, dogs, scabs, itches, porcupines, witches, scurvy, asses, and "draught-oxen" to characterize Ajax, a "mongrel beef-witted lord."[27] When the exasperated Ajax starts beating Thersites, the latter curses him with "A red murrain on o' thy jade's tricks" (2.1.19). Although "jade" is glossed as a "temperamental horse," the Norton edition ignores the string of references to animals and defines "murrain" as "a bloody plague." Thersites' line, "A red murrain on o' thy jade's tricks," can then be treated as a general form of swearing, comparable to Caliban's line in *The Tempest*: "The red plague rid you" (1.2.367). Yet, placed within the context I have outlined, Thersites' curse is redolent of a neglected history of zoonotic disease, and of the associations between disease and livestock that form the substratum of his insults.

Admittedly, the term "red murrain" is hard to define. Beyond a "bloody plague," it may refer to one of the four horses of Apocalypse, each of which had a different color. Famine is red.[28] In *Coriolanus*, a play, in part, about famine, Volumnia mentions a "red pestilence" that strikes all trades in "Rome/ And occupations perish" (4.1.14–15). In *Troilus and Cressida*, in contrast, if one follows on through Thersites' reference to the "plague of Greece," the "red murrain" may refer to the rash-like symptoms of an epidemic that struck Athens in 430, described by Thucydides in his *History of the Peloponnesian War*. Epidemiologists and classicists still debate whether this epidemic was measles, smallpox, typhus, anthrax, or some other zoonotic disease because, depending on how Thucydides' text is translated, a vast number of humans may (or may not) have died alongside sheep.[29] Within early modern medical literature, "red murrain" also may refer more generally to the color of the pustules or buboes that accompanied both human and animal diseases. Anthrax, which was often confused with rinderpest, starts with a reddish-brown raised spot; this spot becomes even redder until the center forms an ulcerated crater with blood-tinged drainage. And while accounts of bubonic plague frequently refer to these pustules as black, depending on the type and nature of disease, pustules could also appear as yellow, purple, or red.[30] In short, given the witches' brew of animal imagery in Thersites' speech, it seems difficult to remove "murrain" from its creaturely context, or to collapse it into a metaphor for bubonic plague. Like Brooks' "[f]irst cause," Thersites' "red murrain" invokes specific knowledge of animal disease; to interpret it as a general curse or metaphor glosses over the material entanglement of nonhumans and humans in the early modern world.

Making our collective neglect of zoonotic disease even more surprising is that Shakespeare was the son of a wool merchant and tanner, who whitened and softened animal skins by a technique called "whittawing."[31] Katherine Duncan-Jones speculates that Shakespeare, through his father's profession, had "early and familiar acquaintance with animal skins, both raw and treated," and that many of the plays "allude either to animal slaughter, or to the processing animal skins, or both."[32] As a tanner, Shakespeare's father would have been directly affected by animal pestilence and the ordinances and practices by which it was managed. He was one of thousands of artisans whose livelihood depended on the kind of knowledge that has come down to us in books of husbandry. Mascall's *First Booke of Cattell*, published in 1587 (but borrowing liberally from Joseph Blagrave's earlier text), includes remedies for cattle diseases and advice for managing murrain. He recommends flaying or skinning the beast, burying it a "deepe pitt," covering it within enough earth to disguise the smell from carrion dogs, and carrying the skin straight to the tanner rather than home. He warns, however, that many people believe the more prudent course is to bury the carcass whole.

> There haue beene some Beastes that haue dyed of the murren (as I haue beene credibly tolde) hee that fleade him died soone after, and he that went with it to the tanner, and the horse that carried it, and the tanner that tanned it, all these died soone therevppon, which was thought it was by the infection of the stinking skinne, but beeing true, it was a maruellous infection.

> *(67)*

In Mascall's description, the animal, butcher, and tanner may be mutually and fatally infected, caught up in a multi-species cycle of contagion—a phenomenon typical of anthrax, but not rinderpest. Both diseases, however, turned swaths of Europe into a putrefying and potentially corruptive animal graveyard, one sometimes stretching for miles, and remnants from which could be found in Shakespeare's boyhood home.

Given Shakespeare's apparent proximity to the flayed victims of animal plague, and given incidences of murrain during his lifetime, how, then, should one read plague curses, such as the one in *Coriolanus*? "All the contagion of the south light on you," the would-be consul Coriolanus rails, targeting the Romans who have fled the scene of battle:

> You shames of Rome! You herd of—boils and plagues
> Plaster you o'er, that you may be abhorred
> Farther than seen, and one infect another
> Against the wind a mile!

> (1.5.1–5)

This scene of shaming, I would argue, bears significant historical and biopolitical weight. The south wind was associated with the spread of disease because it presumably brought effluvia and even noxious insects from Africa.[33] Given the perceived ability of the wind to carry both odors and disease, a "herd" plagued by "boils" that "plaster" the skin would be "abhorred" before it was seen. Through his anathema, Coriolanus figuratively transforms his soldiers into afflicted cattle, wandering the countryside, shunned because they threaten other populations. He weaponizes zoonotic disease in ways that conjure up what should be acknowledged as a material history of mass animal mortalities, along with the human devastation such murrains entail.

IV Beyond Scapegoats, towards a Medical Posthumanities

Among the ancient fables collected by Jean de la Fontaine is "The Animals Ill With the Plague." It tells the story of sick and dying creatures meeting in the midst of a murrain—"a blight whose very name gives cause for fear and trembling" —in order to consider their options.[34] The lion proposes a sacrifice:

> To make amends
> And cleanse us of this scourge, the worst
> Sinner amongst us must, in sacrifice,
> Be offered to the gods. That is the price
> Their wrath demands.

> (157)

The lion confesses that he has devoured weak and blameless sheep, and even their harmless keeper. He offers himself as the "guiltiest," but the fox quickly comes to his defense; in flattering terms, the fox argues, first, it is no "sin" to eat worthless sheep and, second, that—because the shepherd shared with other "evil" humans the desire to subjugate other creatures—he deserved his fate (157). The other carnivores follow suit, minimizing their kills and declaring themselves "saintly souls" (158). Finally, an ass confesses that one day he nibbled a little fresh grass from a meadow belonging to monks. As a group, the animals turn on him; a "slightly lettered wolf" "heaping" evidence against the ass "Proved that his sin had brought the plague upon them!" (158). The ass is hanged.

La Fontaine uses this story to pass judgment on flattery at court—in this translation, "our courtiers judge us black or white: / Moral? The weak are always wrong; the strong are right" (158). For animal studies scholars, however, the fable contains a different kind of cautionary tale. Links among carnivores, scapegoats, and plagues remind us how much early modern England was imbricated in what Jacques Derrida calls the logic of "carno-phallologocentrism"—a term he coins to describe the capitalist, sexist, Abrahamic society out of which modern ideas of the full, "human" subjectivity emerge.[35] Central to such cultures are stories and practices of nonhuman animal sacrifice. A sacrificial logic unites Noah's killing of every clean animal before the Flood (Genesis 8:20), Abraham's near-sacrifice of Isaac, for whom, in the last minute, an animal is substituted (Genesis 22:2), burnt offerings in the Temple, and—according to Derrida—the contemporary factory farm, which he regards as an *"unprecedented"* and unethical site of human biopower.[36] To Derrida's philosophical condemnation of Confined Animal Feeding Operations (CAFOs) might be added a twenty-first century medical warning. CAFOs are profitable because they depend on tightly penned animals shot up with antibiotics, but, as a consequence, they are also breeding grounds for zoonotic outbreaks. At the same time, climate change and the loss of natural habitat for thousands of animal species have forced animal populations, wild and domestic, into new and often dangerous proximities, increasing the likelihood that viruses, as they evolve, will jump species, evolve again, and multiply vectors for the transmission of genetically virulent diseases. COVID-19 is the most prominent, but hardly the only, such disease in the modern world.

Within this context, the occasion for La Fontaine's fable—a murrain—reminds us that meat-eating cultures are mediated by "great mortalities" as much as by the culture of sacrifice. Although some early modern physicians rightly perceived the possibility of zoonosis as an ominous environmental danger, others, like the Paracelsian physician Robert Fludd, sought to minimize the fact of cross-species infection. "Do we not commonly see," Fludd asks, "that a like nature being altered by putrefaction, is most deadly unto its like?" (294) For Fludd, all beings may be related, but diseases cannot cross species boundaries: when a "Mans spirit is infected with the Plague, he insists, it "will multiply it in his kind chiefly," and if the "Murren doth chiefly rage in the spirits of Sheep," it "meddles not with the spirits of Men" (294).[37] If Fludd is referring to bubonic plague, his assumption is flat wrong; as we now know, unlike pneumonic plague, it involves a complicated, unpredictable, and cross-species chain of disease vectors: fleas, rodents, bacteria, warm-blooded animals, and infected humans. His statement about "Murren," which could include either rinderpest or anthrax, is also off. Closely related to the human measles virus, rinderpest jumps readily among different mammals, and anthrax, derived from *Bacillus anthracis*, was and is an ongoing threat to humans, whether transmitted through sloppy leather-rendering processes or through a bioterrorist's white powder in an unmarked envelope. In some sense, then, zoonotic diseases connect not only different species, but the past and the present.

In the twenty-first century, the American Veterinary Association (AVA) has cosponsored with the American Medical Association, the Center for Disease Control, and other medical institutions the One Health Initiative—an effort to promote work on health across disciplinary boundaries and species divisions. The AVA's 2008 executive summary emphasizes that we are facing "demanding, profound, and unprecedented challenges" associated with a rising demand for "animal protein," a loss of biodiversity, and the fact that over 75% of human infectious diseases are zoonotic.[38] In calling for a collaborative, holistic approach to human, animal, and ecological health, the One Health Initiative has an implicit historical dimension that asks us to reconsider the era in Western Europe when the anatomical, neurocognitive, physiological, moral, and affective distinctions between the human and the animal were actively in the process of being formed.[39] Located before the life sciences divided themselves into environmental, veterinary, and medical disciplines, early modern animal studies, with its messy nature-cultures, can serve as useful corrective to knowledge-making in which the world, its creatures, and its humans are thought to exist on three separate, if functionally related, existential planes. An historically informed medical posthumanities, correspondingly, can help us better understand both Shakespeare and the early modern period, and with it some of Europe's most devastating human and animal plagues.

Notes

1 John Speed, *The Theatre of the Empire of Great Britaine Presenting an Exact Geography of the Kingdomes of England, Scotland, Ireland, and the Iles Adioyning* (London, 1611–12), 110.

2 John Fitzherbert (attributed), *The Boke of Husbandry* (London, 1540); Girolamo Fracastoro, *De Contagione et Contagiosis Morbis* (Rome, 1646); Leonard Mascall, *The First Book of Cattel* (London, 1587). Hereafter cited parenthetically in the text.

3 Erica Fudge, *Quick Cattle and Dying Wishes: People and Their Animals in Early Modern England* (Ithaca, NY: Cornell University Press, 2018). Foundational studies on animals in the early modern period include Keith Thomas, *Man and the Natural World: Changing Attitudes in England, 1500–1800* (London: Allen Lane, 1983); Erica Fudge, Ruth Gilbert, and Susan Wiseman, eds., *At the Borders of the Human: Beasts, Bodies, and Natural Philosophy in the Early Modern Period* (New York: St. Martin's Press, 1999); Erica Fudge, *Perceiving Animals: Humans and Beasts in Early Modern Culture* (Urbana: University of Illinois Press, 2002); Bruce Boehrer, *Shakespeare among the Animals: Nature and Society in the Drama of Early Modern England* (New York: Palgrave, 2002); Karen Raber and Treva J. Tucker, eds., *The Culture of the Horse: Status, Discipline, and Identity in Early Modern World* (New York: Palgrave, 2005); Frank Palmierei, ed., *Humans and Other Animals in Eighteenth-Century British Culture: Representation, Hybridity, Ethics* (Burlington, VT: Ashgate, 2006); Laurie Shannon, *The Accommodated Animal: Cosmopolity in Shakespearean Locales* (Chicago, IL: University of Chicago Press, 2013); and Karen Raber, *Animal Bodies, Renaissance Culture* (Philadelphia: University of Pennsylvania Press, 2013).

4 According to Peter Daszak, President of EcoHealth Alliance. Quoted in Lynne Peeples, "Contagion Connections: How Links among Humans, Animals, and the Environment May Be Spawning Infectious Disease," *Huffington Post*, September 30, 2011, www.huffingtonpost.com/2011/09/30/contagion-infectious-disease-animals-environment-health_n_987455.html.

5 Historical accounts of rabies include John Blaisdell, "Rabies in Shakespeare's England," *Historia Medicinae Veterinariae* 16 (1991): 22–23; John Douglas Blaisdell, "A Frightful, but Not Necessarily Fatal, Madness: Rabies in Eighteenth-Century England and English North America" (1995). *Retrospective Theses and Dissertations.* Paper 11041; Neil Pemberton and Michael Warboys, *Dogs, Diseases and, and Culture, 1830–2000* (Basingstoke: Palgrave Macmillan, 2007).

6 William Shakespeare, *The Comedy of Errors*, in *The Norton Shakespeare*, eds. Stephen Greenblatt et al. (New York and London: Norton, 1997), 5.1.71–72. All subsequent Shakespeare references are to this edition and are cited parenthetically in the text.

7 William Shakespeare, *The Tragedy of King Lear*, in *The Norton Shakespeare*, eds. Stephen Greenblatt, et al. (New York and London: Norton, 1997), 5.3.181–83.

8 Daniel Layard, *An Essay on the Bite of a Mad Dog*, 2nd ed. (London, 1763).

9 See Richard A. Barney and Warren Montag, eds., *Systems of Life: Biopolitics, Economics, and Literature on the Cusp of Modernity* (New York: Fordham University Press, 2019).

10 William Shakespeare, *The Tempest*, in *The Norton Shakespeare*, eds. Stephen Greenblatt, et al. (New York and London: Norton, 1997), 2.2.1–5.

11 See Eric H. Ash, *The Draining of the Fens: Projectors, Popular Politics, and State Building in Early Modern England* (Baltimore, MD: Johns Hopkins University Press, 2017).

12 See Anita Guerrini, "The Pathological Environment," *The Eighteenth Century: Theory and Interpretation* 31 (1990): 173–79.

13 Cited in Charles F. Mullett, "Some Neglected Aspects of Plague Medicine in Sixteenth-Century England," *The Scientific Monthly* 44, no. 4 (1937): 325–37.

14 Mark Jenner, "The Great Dog Massacre," in *Fear in Early Modern Society*, eds. William G. Naphy and Penny Roberts (Manchester: St. Martin's Press, 1997), 44–61.

15 See Lucinda Cole, *Imperfect Creatures: Vermin, Literature, and the Science of Life 1600–1740* (London and Ann Arbor: University of Michigan Press, 2016), 136–38.

16 Boehrer, *Shakespeare among the Animals*, 161. See also Shannon, *The Accommodated Animal*, 218–69, on dogs, laws, and animal trials.

17 William Shakespeare, *The Comical History of the Merchant of Venice*, in *The Norton Shakespeare*, eds. Stephen Greenblatt, et al. (New York and London: Norton, 1997), 3.3.6–7.

18 In the marriage plot, Graziano's self-congratulatory remark—"We are the Jasons, we have won the fleece" (3.2.240)—echoes the references to sheep in a comic register.

19 A succinct overview of international trade routes may be found in Ian Blanchard, "The Continental European Cattle Trades," *The Economic History Review* 39 (1986): 427–60.

20 Fudge, *Quick Cattle*; Raber, *Animal Bodies*; Bruce Boehrer, *Animal Characters: Nonhuman Beings in Early Modern Literature* (Philadelphia: University of Pennsylvania Press, 2010); Shannon, *The Accommodated Animal,* and Nathaniel Wolloch, *Subjugated Animals: Animals and Anthropocentrism in Early Modern European Culture* (New York: Prometheus Books, 2006); see also Peter F. Heaney, "Petruchio's Horse: Equine and Household Management in *The Taming of the Shrew*," *Early Modern Literary Studies* 4, no. 1 (1998): 1–12. On sheep and moles, see Karen Raber, "Working Bodies: Laboring Moles and Cannibal Sheep," in *Animal Bodies, Renaissance Culture* (Philadelphia: University of Pennsylvania Press, 2013), 151–78.

21 William Shakespeare, *The Taming of the Shrew*, in *The Norton Shakespeare*, eds. Stephen Greenblatt, et al. (New York and London: Norton, 1997), 3.2.45–50.

22 The Netherlands in particular has been devastated by cattle plagues in astonishing numbers. See J.A. Faber, *Cattle Plague in the Netherlands during the Eighteenth Century* (Amsterdam: Veenman-Zonen, 1962).

23 Gervase Babington, *Comfortable Notes upon the Bookes of Exodus and Leviticus, as before upon Genesis Gathered and Laid Downe Still in This Plaine Manner* (London, 1604), 110.

24 Michael Harward, *The Herds-Man's Mate, or, a Guide for Herds-Men Teaching How to Cure All Diseases in Bulls, Oxen, Cows and Calves* (Dublin, 1673), 8.

25 Thomas Brooks, *A Heavenly Cordial for All Those Servants of the Lord that Have Had the Plague* (London, 1666), 4–5.

26 Jonathan Gil Harris, "'The Enterprise Is Sick': Pathologies of Value and Transnationality in *Troilus and Cressida*," *Renaissance Drama* 29 (1998): 3–37, 4.

27 William Shakespeare, *Troilus and Cressida*, in *The Norton Shakespeare*, eds. Stephen Greenblatt, et al. (New York and London: Norton, 1997), 2.1.1–12.

28 See Alexander More, *A Sermon Preached at the Hague, at the Funeral of the Late Prince of Orange*, trans. Daniel la Fite (London, 1694): Death "will send his pale, black and red Horse, Plague, War and Famine, that shall reap your Provinces" (5).

29 On the plague of Athens, see, J.F.D. Shrewsbury, "The Plague of Athens," *Bulletin of the History of Medicine* 24 (1950): 1–25.

30 See Samuel Collins, *A Systeme of Anatomy, Treating of the Body of Man, Beasts, Birds, Fish, Insects, and Plants* (London, 1685).

31 Samuel Schoenbaum, *William Shakespeare: A Documentary Life* (Oxford: Clarendon, 1975), 60.

32 Katherine Duncan-Jones, "Did the Boy Shakespeare Kill Calves?" *Review of English Studies*, new series 55 (2004): 189.

33 See Lucinda Cole, "Out of Africa: Locust Infestation, Universal History, and the Early Modern Theological Imaginary," in *Lesser Creatures of the Renaissance*, eds. Keith Botelho and Joseph Campana (State College, PA: Pennsylvania State University Press, forthcoming).

34 Jean de La Fontaine, *The Complete Fables of Jean de la Fontaine*, Book VII, trans. Norman Shapiro (Urbana: University of Illinois Press, 2007), 156. All references are to this edition.

35 Jacques Derrida, "'Eating Well,' or the Calculation of the Subject: An Interview with Jacque Derrida," in *Who Comes after the Subject?* eds. Eduardo Cadava, Peter Conner, and Jean-Luc Nancy (London: Routledge, 1991), 96–119. Hereafter cited in the text.

36 See Jacques Derrida, "The Animal that Therefore I Am (More to Follow)," trans. David Willis, *Critical Inquiry* 28 (2002): 369–418, 394.

37 Robert Fludd, *Mosaicall Philosophy Grounded upon the Essentiall Truth, or Eternal Sapience* (London, 1659), 294.

38 Lonnie King et al., "One Health Initiative Task Force," *JAVMA* 233, no. 2 (July 15, 2008): 259.

39 The scholarly arm of this movement is exemplified in a recent collection of essays; see Abigail Woods et al., eds., *Animals and the Shaping of Modern Medicine: One Health and Its Histories* (Basingstoke: Palgrave Macmillan, 2018).

9

FLOCK, HERD, SWARM

A Shakespearean Lexicon of Creaturely Collectivity

Joseph Campana

Giovanni Botero wondered how many people, at its height, the great city of Rome could boast. It was the heart of an empire and a city of exemplary magnitude, "for no other people," he argued, "took so much care to propagate itself."[1] He was not the first to wonder. By his own account, Botero's answer to the question—two million—was an advance over those of previous thinkers including Dionysius of Halicarnassus and other later, unnamed ones. More interesting, even, than Botero's considered calculation is that he arrived at this greatly expanded figure by accounting for unaccounted populations. Foreigners and slaves, Botero suggests, never made it into prior estimates. Counting depends, so often, on what is excluded.

Over the centuries, Botero may have languished in the shadow of his predecessor in political theory, Machiavelli, but his two most influential works, *The Reason of State* and *On the Causes of the Greatness and Magnificence of Cities*, were widely read and translated across Europe including in England multiple times and even distilled in a summary form by Sir Walter Raleigh. Botero is often described as a figure committed to reintroducing Christian virtue into the seemingly amoral reflections on politics of Machiavelli. Yet his focus on population feels unexpectedly timely. Indeed, by the time Thomas Robert Malthus became the watchword for population studies, his *Essay on the Principle of Population* had already directed attention to that subject by advancing a chilling thesis "Population, when unchecked, increases in a geometric ratio. Subsistence increases only in an arithmetical ratio."[2] That is to say, population comes into view when it appears as a problem of unsustainable growth.

Decades ago, Michel Foucault directed attention to what he termed biopolitics, a term now taken up by myriad thinkers and used to cover a wide range of issues and objects. Foucault defined the term numerous times and in varying relationships to other core principles in his work. He argues that truly modern governance emerges when "the basic biological features of the human species became the object of a political strategy" through regimes "exercised over a whole population."[3] Such governance is typified by "a power that has taken control of both the body and life or that has, if you like, taken control of life in general— with the body as one pole and the population as the other."[4] How much easier it has been to take up the many facets of the body as an object of power and discipline. Despite the seemingly overly familiar nature of the work of Foucault, population still remains a subject too easy to glance past. Moreover, how easily the *bio* of biopower or biopolitics has, until recently, referred primarily to human life.

Shakespeare's England was learning to count with renewed interest in a range of fields from mathematics to what we might now call demographics.[5] Although Foucault focuses his attention, as usual, on Enlightenment-era thought, he does point to a series of important earlier phenomena. Indeed, he describes his focus on population as being "entirely in keeping with the famous mortality tables ... England in particular had established mortality tables that made a quantification and knowledge of the causes of death possible."[6] And yet he also cautions against the failure to understand population in its positivity because of spectacular instances of desertification, which is to say the destruction of population due to famine, war, and plague, the latter particularly memorialized in England's mortality tables. Understandably, it is hard to turn away from such spectacles. Andrew Cunningham and Ole Peter Grell remind us that in the early modern period "in every year between 1494 and 1649 plague was killing its thousands and its ten thousands suddenly and horribly somewhere in Europe" but that Europeans of this era were "victims of their own *demographic* success."[7] It is no surprise, then, that negative enumeration dominates at a time of recurrent depopulating plagues, which resulted in the counting of numbered-off corpses. And yet, one might ask, where does population appear in what, following Foucault, we might call its "positivity"?

In this brief chapter, I will explore several related points. The first is that even in a field organized both around the great character of Shakespeare and dedicated, understandably, to his characters large and small, which is to say a field dedicated to *persons*, population has a defining role in the literature and theater of Shakespeare and his contemporaries. This point carries implications for a wide range of fields and phenomena, from plague to urban planning and far beyond. But more specifically, and most relevant for the project of this handbook, is my second point: a primary source of population thinking is to be found in the wide world of creatures. I will not, here, engage in a kind of historical demography with some Botero-inspired attempt to survey the populations of early modern English creatures—be they cattle, sheep, or bees—other than to say that, as in most eras, humans were, as they are now, massively outnumbered by other creatures. I will suggest that creatures allowed population to appear in its positivity as a prodigious, and sometimes terrifying, *numerousness* that can appear in tension with creaturely articulations of civic order, as when birds or bees hold their own parliaments. Such figurations indicate how central nonhuman creatures are not only to discourses of sovereignty but also to theories of political collectivity.[8] And for all their uses in the political tracts of the eras, these creatures were no mere metaphors—transparent windows through which to see the face of the human staring back. Tellingly, references to the numerousness of creatures abound across a wide range of early modern disciplines—husbandry manuals and works of natural history, to be sure, but also political treatises and works of literature and theater. As such, and this is my third point, it is more useful to designate all such thinking as an early form of population management that cuts, if not indifferently, across species designations and that intersects with a variety of ways of thinking about social groups and political hierarchies.

How, then, does Shakespeare manage populations—demographically and politically—with a series of creaturely figures familiar to us? The answer here will be necessarily simple and therefore conducted in the manner of a preliminary investigation. How do we count creaturely populations? With herds, swarms, and flocks, and, to conclude, with the many and the multitude. Certainly other terms may eventually be added, although "school" was surprisingly infrequent and "crowd" was all-too-human. What follows, were it to be named by Polonius, might be called initial observations about a Shakespearean literary-politico-lexicon of bio-creaturely power. And that lexicon depends on a kind of form that designates a collectivity capable of standing above or separate from individuals within what we now call species or a generalized description of a species. Herds, swarms and flocks, along with swarms, manies, and multiple may be composed of various creatures. That is to say, despite a cultural fondness for forms of naming that give us a murder of crows or a skulk of foxes, the core terms for populous collectivity need not associate with one species alone; many different creatures might herd, flock, or swarm. Multiple and many (or manies) are even less coded to a particular creature. Moreover, such collectivities might be heterogeneous or homogeneous. "Flock" invokes the dangers of charisma and compulsive collectivity. "Herd" indexes the precariousness of collectivity, which easily becomes subject to violence. "Swarm" (and its sibling "hive") evokes the ambivalence of collectivity while "multiples" and "manies" seem to suggest that membership in a collectivity might utterly forbid individuation and denude specificity. In tracing these terms, which arise as Shakespearean moments and as extensions of proverbial lore, a grammar for collectivity emerges, one that is "structurally innovative, but politically ambivalent," as Eugene Thacker has argued of networks, swarms, and multitudes.[9]

★ ★ ★

Flock is, among other things, a pastoral designation, as when Rosalind refers in that most pastoral of Shakespeare's plays to "the cottage, pasture and the flock," the basic furniture, one might say, of the genre (*As You Like It* 2.4.84).[10] Pastoral, being rooted in reality yet disclosed in well-nigh confectionary elaborations of fantasy, may test belief but it also remains powerfully capacious in reference. Suspended in its orbit, then, might be anything from practices of animal husbandry to depictions of rural landscapes to allegories of political rule and ecclesiastical community. Thus, is it perhaps no surprise that Henry VI, at his lowest moment, watching, helpless, as the battle for succession and the soul of the kingdom rages far from him, might deploy a familiar comparison between shepherd and king:

> So many hours I must tend my flock.
> So many hours I must take my rest
> So many hours must I contemplate
> So many hours must I sport myself
> So many days my ewes have been with young
> So many weeks ere the poor fools will ean
> So many years ere I shall shear the fleece
> So, minutes, hours, days, months and years
> Pass'd over to the end they were created,
> Would bring white hairs unto a quiet grave.

(3 Henry VI 2.5.31–41)

Flock, here, is part of the invocation of a placid and meditative world of care and mutual obligation. Henry constitutes this pastoral as a static analogy. And as someone likely to have never tended a sheep in his life, it is especially easy to praise the simple life of the shepherd tending his sheep: "Ah, what a life were this! How sweet! How lovely!" Henry's analogy is thus also politically escapist; the flock is a passive object of maintenance, not a significant collective. Similarly, passive flocks appear in *A Midsummer Night's Dream* in Titania's great catalog of political and ecological disorder: "The fold stands empty in the drowned field, / And crows are fatted with the murrion flock" (2.1.96–97).

And yet at times, flock often indexes the irresistible charisma of a political leader, the compulsion of the "many young gentlemen" who "flock" to the exiled Duke in *As You Like It* (1.1.100). Similarly, in *2 Henry IV*, the rebellious Archbishop "turn insurrection to religion" and thus is "follow'd both with body and with mind" by the many who "do flock to follow him" (1.1.D21). In *3 Henry VI*, the Earl of Warwick notes the "many giddy people" who "flock" to the invading Edward of Belgia (4.9.5). A push-pull pulsion and tension governs flock, as a collectivity is imagined to be easily drawn or driven before a charismatic figure. Falstaff jokes, and perhaps threatens, that he could replace Hal, "a king's son," the evidence for which is his capacity to "drive all thy / subjects afore thee like a flock of wild-geese" (*1 Henry IV* 2.5.114). Transferred from vigorous wild geese and even more placid sheep is a political kinetics, which is why we can see the outlines of creaturely collectivities, as when Richard III learns from a messenger of his enemies massing against him, "And every hour," he says, "more competitors / Flock to their aid, and still their power increaseth" (*Richard III* 4.4.505).

References to flocks and flocking seem ambivalently split between species, at times referring primarily to sheep and at other times to birds (often, though not always, geese). As such these varying creatures imply differing relationships to docility and ductility. Of sheep, who live sandwiched between the rhinoceros and the squirrel, in Edward Topsell's *History of Four-Footed Beasts* we learn of the superiority of "wilde sheep" over domesticated, which possess a manifest robustness, being "swifter to run, stronger to fight."[11] Sheep, wild and tame, might both flock, but it is the wild sheep, Topsell claims, that "at times fight with wild boars and kill them."[12] Given the prominence of sheep in both animal husbandry cultures and pastoral literatures, ancient and early modern, it is no surprise that Topsell's entry would conceive of sheep as creatures to be managed, unlike some of his purely wild beasts. That is, the shepherd is never too far from the sheep in this entry, which is packed full of advice from Columella but also Virgil. And yet Topsell's discussion of the sheep includes a fascinating set of qualifications with respect to their docility as creatures. In a subsection titled "the general discipline of shepherd," which indicates the shepherd is one who rather should desire to be loved that feared. The shepherd

> must rather be a guide unto them then a Lord or Master over them, and in driving them forward, or receiving them home after they have stragled, he must rather use his chiding voice, and shake his staffe at them, then cast either stone or dart at them: neither must he go far from them at any time, nor sit down but stand still, except when he driveth them, because the flock desireth direction of their Keeper, and his eye like a lofty watch-tower, that so he suffer not to be separated asunder.[13]

Thus, although the shepherd might be an analogy for the sovereign, this is not an absolute sovereign but rather one who must learn to manage the desire for direction. Although the sheep may seem to be the most docile and vulnerable of the creatures of pastoral who pass fluidly between natural history and political theory, the state of management or care witnesses a subtle reciprocal power more complex to cater to than might at first appear. A set of proverbs seem to memorialize the power of shepherd, as in "as is the shepherd such is the flock" or "the complexity of flock might suggest reversals of polarity." How many Shakespearean kings (or would-be kings) could have learned such a lesson!

As proverbs seem to affirm, the sheep is a creature of collectivity. "The lone sheep," that is, "is in danger of the wolves" (S306).[14] One sheep is in perpetual danger, but the singular sheep might also be dangerous precisely because of this creature's tendency towards collectivity. After all, "One scabbed sheep mars a flock" (S308). This penchant for group identity may also be, in the context of human–ovine comparison, the source of a slur: "They are but sheep that flock together" (S309), a saying easily juxtaposed with the sentiment that "eagles fly alone" (E7). Flocking, with respect to sheep, implies a conveniently culpable homogeneity. The desire for political docility—from sheep and men alike in the world of Shakespeare pastoral and pastoral rule—is longed for up until one's sheep (or fellow men) flock to the wrong shepherd.

"Flocking," with reference to winged creatures, shares both the aspiration to a collectivity that is easily drawn or driven and the potential for denigration in the image of insubstantial individuals gathered into a group either consumed by chaos or controlled by a leader. Although gaggles of wild geese flock in Shakespeare's corpus, birds, unlike sheep, seem to suggest a greater degree of individuation. Eagles are perhaps no surprise in this regard, but perhaps the most common flocking proverb—irrespective of species—would be "birds of a feather flock together." The sentiment offers the same intimations of an instinct or compulsion to create homogenous collectivity. That is to say, "birds of a feather" may flock together, but "birds" of different varieties gathered for conversation and debate. The texts on birds and birding in the era tend not to reflect on group formations like flocks but, rather, to continue the work of individuation, defining and differentiating particular varieties of birds from one another. Many, that is, consider questions of collectivity in the vein of Chaucer's fourteenth-century work *Parliament of Fowls*, in which the parliament is constituted as a conversation across kind based on the articulation of individuated points of view associated with birds of a feather. Similarly, the anonymous seventeenth-century ballad *The Birds Harmony* offers an avian complaint; the birds "did warble forth their griefs" but they do so in separate stanza with each kind of bird—cuckoo, blackbird, swallow, etc.—speaking for kind even as their language is relatively undifferentiated from the generic mode of complaint.[15] The similarly anonymous *Parlament of Byrdes* assembles a veritable United Nations of avian creatures so as "to keepe among them peece and rest" given the predatory behavior of the hawk, which is brought to the attention of the sovereign eagle. Stanza by stanza lays out the complaint of each individual kind of bird.[16] *The Pleasant History of Cawwood the Rook, or the Assembly of Birds* gathers its many kinds in a familiar variety of complaint against rooks by the other members of the assembly. These creatures also appeal to the sovereign eagle, and in the end the rook is banished, providing a convenient human moral: "Crafty fellows, albeit they scape a great while, yet at last are brought to ruine and disgrace."[17]

Some combination of literary precedents from at least Chaucer onward and the actual presence of so many varieties of birds, as opposed to the more limited if not negligible varieties of sheep, no doubt encouraged these constitutive gestures of inventorying and separating. John Ray's brief but capacious *A Collection of English Words* (1674) includes a separate *Catalogues of English Birds and Fishes* (not to mention *an account of the preparing and refining such metals and minerals as are gotten in England*). Ray was also the compiler of *The Ornithology of Francis Willoughby*, a devoted observer in a "Busie and inquisitive Age of the History of Animals," who did not live to publish his observations of a wide range of European birds.[18] Willoughby and, by extension, Ray's tactic is to begin with general comments about the anatomy, generation, age, and habitat of birds in general, though peppered with individuating comments, followed by sections that divide birds into categories ("rapacious diurnal birds" or "poultry kind" or "pigeon kind") and then species (raven, pheasant, etc.).

The multiplicity of the flock, then, is perhaps best understood as a multiplicity of relations to the idea of a collectivity or group. The flocking of sheep suggests a meditation on collectivity and homogeneity, while flocking birds suggest more complexly individuated groups that can be aligned, at times, in hierarchies of value often articulated in relation to one another and in some state of disputation. What, then, of herds? For many of us, herd mentality may be the first notion to arise when considering the nature of that particular

Flock, Herd, Swarm

creaturely collective. This is largely a consequence of turn of twentieth-century thought on group psychology, crowd organizational behavior. Not least of these efforts would be those of the aptly named William Trotter, an English surgeon whose *Instincts of the Herd in Peace and War* (1916) is of note in such efforts. Trotter was keen to expose—in humans and animals—a fourth core instinct, above and beyond the instincts for self-preservation, nutrition, and sex. Thus, he argues, "[f]rom the biological standpoint, the probability of gregariousness being a primitive and fundamental quality in man seems to be considerable."[19] To use Trotter's parlance, man too is a "gregarious animal" making the formations of other gregarious animals of note. "The cardinal quality of the herd," he argues,

> is homogeneity. It is clear that the great advantage of the social habit is to enlarge the numbers to act as one, whereby in the case of the hunting gregarious animal strength in pursuit and attack is at once increased to beyond that of the creatures preyed upon, and in protective socialism the sensitiveness of the new unit to alarms is greatly in excess of that of the individual member of the flock.[20]

Certainly, the herd and the flock share some similar qualities, including a tendency towards (or at least question about) homogeneity. Herd does not feature prominently in proverb lore, although the notion that "ill herds make fat wolves" certainly reinforces the defensive dynamic Trotter articulates. In Shakespearean usage, the herd is quite frequently composed of deer. Numerous references concern cuckolding—as in the "horned herd" (3.13.97) in *Antony and Cleopatra*—while others suggest that cervine collectivity is vulnerable and prone to scattering or predation. This is quite literally the case in *3 Henry VI*, when the First Keeper warns that "the noise of thy cross-bow / [w]ill scare the herd." But even in works in which literal referents rub shoulders with political allegories, like *As You Like It*, reference to a "careless herd" appears closely related to the pitying invocation of "poor deer" (2.1.47). Talbot refers to his soldiers derisively as "a little herd of England's timorous deer, / [m]azed with a yelping kennel of French curs!" (*1 Henry IV* 4.2.46–47). In sonnet 12, as Shakespeare imagines the destructive sway of time, he imagines its depredations as destructions of shelter, as in the case of "lofty trees" now "barren of leaves / [w]hich erst from heat did canopy the herd" (Sonnet 12.5–6). Although not in reference to deer, the yet-to-be Richard III describes his "valiant father" in battle as one who "in the thickest troop / [a]s doth a lion in a herd of neat," or cattle (*3 Henry VI* 2.1.14). And although Antonio refers to "a whole herd of lions" (2.1.301) in *The Tempest*, precariousness more commonly haunts a herd.

Flocks connote vulnerability to influence, while herds seem prone to scattering and violence—except, perhaps, in populous Rome. Any metaphor or figure, however rooted it may be in its original circumstance, may drift into abstraction and general usage. Such departures from solely literal usage are necessary, although some usages retain more or less a trace of original circumstances, or, to be more creaturely, some figurations are more redolent of creaturely life than others. A fascinating aspect of the "herd" in Shakespeare's Roman works is the lack of a trace of a specific creature. Multiplicity is a fascinating problem in these works, as I have argued elsewhere more primarily with reference to insect life.[21] In these works, herd is one of many terms of denigration for commoners, as when Casca refers to the "common herd" that Caesar panders to (*Julius Caesar* 1.2.256). But when Coriolanus shames and denigrates his cowering soldiers, the creaturely references cascade:

You shames of Rome. You herd of—Boils and plagues
Plaster you o'er, that you may be abhorred
Farther than seen, and one infect another

Against the wind a mile! You souls of geese
That bear the shapes of men, how have you run
From slaves, that apes would beat!

(1.5.2–7)

Nothing should surprise a reader in the fact of Coriolanus' disdain. Its terms, however, seem to indicate a transition to the generally bestial. Too-easily scattered soldiers would understandably be called "souls of geese /[t]hat bear the shapes of men." That they are less than apes, too, makes sense. But what kind of "herd" are these men? Coriolanus interrupts an insult ("You herd of—) to call down a curse ("boils and plagues") upon his men. Later, after Brutus and Sicinus sabotage his attempt to woo the people, Coriolanus exclaims:

Are these your herd?

Must these have voices that can yield them now,
And straight disclaim their tongues? What are your offices?
You being their mouths, why rule you not their teeth?
Have you not set them on?

(3.1.33–37)

What animals are they, precisely? Other than the lions of *The Tempest*, the herd is a mostly docile figuration, more prone to flight than fight. Here they have teeth—are they wolves that masquerade as sheep or some other predator with "teeth"? As the political disaster unfolds, Menenius Agrippa resents the idea of a conciliatory gesture from Coriolanus might have to "stoop to the herd" (3.2.31). While it may be too ambitious to argue for an evolutionary pattern in Shakespeare's use of the term by the time of *Coriolanus*, it does seem notable that "herd" becomes more ambiguously bestial. To call people a "herd" is to render them less than human. But the term has attained a level of generality that departs from figurations of collectivity that preserve a greater degree of creaturely specificity. And perhaps there is a more insidious power in such invocations, which do not rely on particularity for their powers of denigration. Perhaps no figuration of creaturely collectivity was more ambiguous, more mobile than swarm. Less tractable than a herd or flock, the swarm finds its obverse in the fixed solidity of the hive. At times hive seems merely a synonym for home or another place of belonging, as when Lord Talbot imagines his scattered soldiers as "bees with smoke and doves with noisome stench / [a]re from their hives and houses driven away" (*3 Henry VI* 1.7.23–24). Smoke was—and still is—a common method for either driving bees from their hives or stunning them to prevent stinging. In either case, extraction of honey often, and soon, follows smoke. Sometimes that domicile appears as a figure of vulnerability, as when Lucrece refers to herself as a "drone like bee," and her body and her home as a "weak hive" into which "a wandering wasp hath crept" (*Rape of Lucrece* 839). Whether an actual domicile or not, hive is noun and a verb of affiliation. Occasionally, hive refers to a collectivity more like a swarm, as when the Early of Warwick refers to the commons as "an angry hive of bees" (*2 Henry VI* 3.3.111). Shylock even uses hive as a verb that indicates the making or refusing of collectivity, as in "drones hive not with me" (*Merchant of Venice* 2.5.47). But generally, hive formations, whether named as such or not, designate an ideal polity and, in fact, distinguish apian references from other less sovereign insects. Frequent recourse to extended apian analogy was a mainstay of Renaissance humanism, and perhaps no passage about bees in the Shakespearean corpus more notable than the extended portrait of the commonwealth in the first act of *Henry V*, where the hierarchical organization of "the honey-bees" makes them "Creatures that by a rule in nature teach / The act of order to a peopled kingdom"

(1.2.188–89). Although the passage refers neither to a swarm nor a hive, this is clearly an articulation of the hive logic that encouraged analogies between the bee society and the structure of a commonwealth. When Shakespeare uses the specific word hive, its references indicate organizational and architectural logic.

In a moment of self-abnegation, The King of France in *All's Well That Ends Well* imagines himself a drone ejected from the apian collective: "Since I nor wax nor honey can bring home, / I quickly were dissolved from my hive, / To give some labourers room" (1.2.66). In *2 Henry IV*, hive is merely the location of apian activity. King Henry IV imagines himself an industrious bee:

> When like the bee, tolling from every flower
> Our thighs with wax, our mouths with honey packed,
> We bring it to the hive, and, like the bees,
> Are murdered for our pains.

(4.3.205–8)

Henry's point was proverbial. Ludovico Ariosto's impresa features bees fleeing a smoke-saturated hive with the simple motto, "pro bono malum" or "bad for good." Moses Rusden clarifies this well-known adage in the epistle dedicatory to his 1679 *A Further Discovery of Bees*, when he refers to "cruel and ungrateful Mankind, who hitherto, like the worst of Robbers, hath spoiled them at once of their lives and treasures."[22] Man thus rewards the bees' virtuous industry with larceny and destruction: pro bono malum. Yet what seems most compelling in these two otherwise unrelated instances of "hive" is that two sitting monarchs deploy the apian analogy but imagine themselves as lowly and lazy male drones, annually expelled from the hive by the female workers, in the case of the King of France, or a mere worker bee, in the case of King Henry, whose industry invites evil. Hive logic dictates sovereign order and functionally defined members of a commonwealth. And one wonders if the central, sovereign bee is ultimately less important than the articulated structure of the hive.

Unlike hive logic, swarm logic is not surprisingly wilder and less stable. While the spring swarming of bees was a predictable part of the reproductive cycle, swarms themselves were anything but predictable. And in fact Shakespeare's sparse uses of the term witnesses a tendency to represent a numerousness to which indistinction, generality, and abstraction attach. The Earl of Worcester reminds Henry IV of the "swarm of fair advantages" that enabled him to depose Richard II (*1 Henry IV* 5.1.55). In the case of *Macbeth's* "merciless Macdonwald," on the other hand, the same swarm delivers unbridled negativity, for "the multiplying villainies of nature / Do swarm upon him" (*Macbeth* 1.2.9–12). A swarm may have prodigious powers to wreak havoc but it is constituted by the lowly, which becomes clear when the Constable of France refers to the "our superfluous lackeys and our peasants / Who in unnecessary action swarm / About our squares of battle" (*Henry V* 4.2.26–28). In his dejected, dying monologue, Lord Clifford notes how disastrously, in support of the York cause, he and the common people swarm "like summer flies; / I and ten thousand in this luckless realm… And whither fly the gnats but to the sun?" (*3 Henry VI* 2.6.16–17; 8),[23] a sentiment echoed in its inverse by the Earl of Warwick who welcomes this phenomenon: "The common people by numbers swarm to us" (*3 Henry VI* 4.2.2). The political language of parts and multiples, including references to insect life, impacts Roman works like *Coriolanus*, works set in the shadow of Rome, which Botero understood to be the center of prodigious powers of population. But it comes to make sense proverbially as well that insects connote numerousness and that numerousness connotes in- or un-humanity. A populous phenomenon might be "as thick as bees," certainly, but multiplicity also does not require creaturely specificity. Proverbs teach that there can be "too many to be good" (M638), that "the multitude is a beast of many heads" (M1308), and that "where multitude is confusion" (M1309). And if "a crowd is not company" (C861) surely it is because numerousness defines human intimacy, which is predicated on singularity.

How almost Manichean are these swings between positive and negative evaluations of the swarm and between orderly hive logic and chaotic swarm logic. One moment, insect life provides a perfect analogy for human behavior while the next it seems utterly unhuman. But perhaps more than anything, insects connote an experience of numerousness associated with attention to the counting of population, to a sheer accumulation that, at times, defied any logic of distinction or principle of order. No doubt this partly reflects the population paradox that was early modern London, the epicenter of a decades-long upswing in population colliding with radical depopulation due to plague. One might say the haunted space that London sometimes was threw into relief the numerous press of bodies.[24] The swarm may be the image of quantity overwhelming quality, which is also perhaps why it seems so easily generalizable. And perhaps, too, this explains why swarms direct our attention to words like "many" and "multitude," words that seem to have shed creaturely referents while retaining a broad and denigrating sense of the less than human. The citizens of *Coriolanus* know exactly what to think when they are called not merely "fragments" (1.1.205) but more potently "the many headed-multitude" (2.3.12) and "the mutable rank-scented meinie" (3.1.67).[25] As commoners they do not even merit specific forms of denigration. To the noble Romans they are part of an expanse unworthy of individuation. What to think, then, of the creatures from which such denigrations were drawn? And what to think of the growing urban populations, which were clearly of concern in *Coriolanus*, a play whose titular protagonist is said to be the viper who "would depopulate the city" (3.1.263).

This brief tour through the Shakespearean lexicon of creaturely collectivity offers a portrait of an age increasingly inclined to count and increasingly anxious about the results. Human population alone was unstable, creating moments of extreme density punctuated by plague-, war-, and famine-driven desertification. The numerousness of other creatures was both more nebulous and more imposing. Perhaps it is no surprise that one response to the terrifying expanse of life beyond the human was to domesticate that multiplicity with an array of terms for animal collectivity. To peruse, for instance, *A Barrel of Monkeys: A Compendium of Collective Nouns for Animals*, one of any number of gift book dictionaries of collective nouns for creatures, is to witness, with accompanying engravings by Thomas Berwick, a series of captivating terms. We may be used to a herd of cattle or deer, a flock of birds or sheep, and a swarm (or hive) of bees, but what prepares us for a shrewdness of apes, an obstinacy of buffaloes, or a madness of marmots?[26] A murmuration of starlings or an exultation of larks? The fascination of collective animal nouns may run counter to the lexicon traced here; surprising or wondrous terms work to tame the multitude. Populous life, the sheer numerousness of creatures, inspired Shakespeare and his contemporaries to think about the nature of the polity and the consequences of collectivity not to name the cuteness of creatures but to give habitation and name to an awesome multiplicity.

Notes

1 Giovanni Botero, *On the Causes of the Greatness and Magnificence of Cities* (Toronto: University of Toronto Press, 2012), 79.
2 Thomas Robert Malthus, *An Essay on the Principle of Population* (New York: Norton, 2004), 19.
3 Michel Foucault, *Security, Territory, Population* (New York: Palgrave, 2007), 1.
4 Michel Foucault, *Society Must Be Defended* (New York: Picador, 2003), 253.

5 For recent work on mathematics see particularly David Glimp and Michelle Warren, *Arts of Calculation: Numerical Thought in Early Modern Europe* (New York: Palgrave Macmillan, 2004); Katherine Hunt and Rebecca Tomlin, "Numbers in Early Modern Writing," Special Issue, *Journal of the Northern Renaissance* 6 (2014).

6 Ibid., 67.

7 Andrew Cunningham and Ole Peter Grell, *The Four Horsemen of the Apocalypse: Religion, War, Famine and Death in Reformation Europe* (Cambridge: Cambridge University Press, 2000), 274, 300.

8 On early modern sovereignty and animality see particularly Laurie Shannon, *The Accommodated Animal: Cosmopolity in Shakespearean Locales* (Chicago, IL: University of Chicago Press, 2013) and Andreas Hofele, *Stage, Stake, and Scaffold: Humans and Animals in Shakespeare's Theatre* (Oxford: Oxford University Press, 2014).

9 Eugene Thacker, "Networks, Swarms, Multitudes: Part One," *Ctheory.net*, 2004. www.ctheory.net/articles.aspx?id=422.

10 All references (to act, scene, line or to title and line) are to William Shakespeare, *The New Oxford Shakespeare: Modern Critical Edition*, eds. Gary Taylor et al. (Oxford: Oxford University Press, 2016).

11 Edward Topsell, *History of Four Footed Beasts and Serpents and Insects* (London, 1658), 466.

12 Topsell, *History of Four Footed Beasts and Serpents and Insects*, 466.

13 Ibid., 473.

14 All references (to letter and number) of proverbs are to Morris Palmer Tilley, *Dictionary of the Proverbs in England in the Sixteenth and Seventeenth Centuries: A Collection of the Proverbs Found in English Literature and the Dictionaries of the Period* (Ann Arbor: University of Michigan Press, 1950).

15 *The Birds Harmony* (London, 1680).

16 Anon., *Parlament of Byrdes* (London, 1520).

17 Anon., *The Pleasant History of Cawwood the Rook, or the Assembly of Birds* (London, 1683).

18 John Ray, *The Ornithology of Franics Willoughby* (London, 1678).

19 William Trotter, *Instincts of the Herd in Peace and War* (London: T. Fisher Unwin, 1916), 22.

20 Trotter, *Instincts of the Herd in Peace and War*, 29.

21 Joseph Campana, "The Bee and the Sovereign (II): Segments, Swarms, and the Shakespearean Multitude," in *The Return of Theory in Early Modern English Studies*, eds. Bryan Reynolds, Paul Cefalu, and Gary Kuchar, vol. II (London: Palgrave Macmillan, 2014), 59–80.

22 Moses Rusden, *A Further Discovery of Bees* (London, 1679), A5r–A6v.

23 These lines appear in the Q3 but not the Folio. See William Shakespeare, *The vvhole contention betvveene the tvvo famous houses, Lancaster and Yorke* (London, 1619).

24 On the intertwining of plague and population see Joseph Campana, "Introduction," in "After Sovereignty," Special Issue *Studies in English Literature, 1500–1900* 58, no. 1 (Winter, 2018): 1–21.

25 On this evocative phrase see particularly Holly Dugan, "Coriolanus and 'the Rank-Scented Meinie': Smelling Rank in Early Modern London," in *Masculinity and the Metropolis of Vice, 1550–1650*, eds. Amanda Bailey and Roze Hentschell (New York: Palgrave Macmillan, 2010), 139–59.

26 Samuel Fanous, *A Barrel of Monkeys: A Compendium of Collective Nouns for Animals* (Oxford: Bodleian Library, 2015).

PART 3

Animal Worlds/Animal Language

In Part 2, questions about animal populations culminated in questions about language: the very terms we use to describe animal worlds influence human interaction with them. The chapters in this part explore that claim in greater detail, examining the potential and limits for discursive engagements with animals. As Laurie Shannon emphasized in her work *The Accommodated Animal*, Shakespeare rarely uses the word animal: it appears only eight times in his oeuvre, and when it does it usually applies to humans. His other terms—beast and creature—signal differently, teeming with different kinds of potential. Here, those ideas are explored in greater detail. The first two chapters focus on the way insects raise questions about singularity and collectivity through syntax and temporality.

Keith Botelho explores how words are used to describe insects present in premodern literary sources. Since insects are rarely thought of as anything other than part of a collective, a singular insect presents certain syntactical challenges, which then align with the affective responses insects often engender in humans. Botelho connects the early modern naturalist Thomas Moffet's *Theater of Insects*, famously appended to the 1665 edition of Topsell's *History of Four-Footed Beasts and Serpents*, with Shakespeare's insect theater, reminding us (just as Cole's essay did) that bugs were everywhere in the early modern world. For naturalists like Moffet, the singularity of the insect was perceivable in their magnified anatomy under the microscope, reflecting the majesty of nature in an almost inconceivably miniscule form. Yet insects also unsettled human-oriented modes of understanding: they literally teemed in massive, if microscopic numbers. Shakespeare's language of insect multitudes sorts them in different ways: the "scores," "broods," "assemblies," and "wilderness" of bodies described in Shakespeare's plays are not valued in the same ways as are human or animal bodies. Yet when we return to the singular insect such disparate valuation erodes. The treatment of early modernity's "Little beasts," Botelho shows, highlights the species preferences and omissions that currently drive critical animal studies.

Insects, Nicole Jacobs shows, also challenge narrative temporality. Bees, she points out, keep time. In "Bernardian Ecology and Topsell's Redemptive Bee in *The Tempest*," Jacobs excavates how apian temporality was understood in early modern religious and naturalist discourses. Emphasizing Edward Topsell's religious writings as well as his bestiaries, Jacobs uncovers how Topsell used "bee time" to structure hierarchies of labor, especially those that rewarded working to death with religious redemption. Bee time offers a model both of egalitarian and of redemptive worth, at least within Christian world views; both Protestant and Catholic writers revered St. Bernard, the mellifluous saint, and his use of honey as a metaphor for persuasive speech. But bee time is also a cycle of non-stop labor. Bringing this analysis to bear on Shakespeare's *The Tempest*, Jacobs shows how and why Caliban is stung by Prospero and, more troublingly, denied access to the religious salvation that follows such stinging.

The next two chapters explore animal language from a different perspective, exploring how literary tropes point towards a more expansive linguistic world. In "What does the wolf say: animal language and political noise," Kathryn Vomero Santos and Liza Blake argue for Coriolanus's "wolvish" tongue, a reference that editors routinely gloss as a wolvish togue (a garment, presumably a toga or *toge* in middle French). The play's famously inscrutable politics may be linked to our critical unwillingness to listen to animal sounds. Blake and Santos query: "If we allowed Coriolanus to speak in a wolvish tongue, what would we hear?" Wolves, they remind us, routinely speak in literary fables of the period; in these fabulous accounts, speaking animals critique sovereign power in important ways. Silencing Coriolanus's "wolvish" tongue, they argue, decouples "language from politics, animality from noise." Coriolanus's "wolvish tongue" asks questions about animal language and its ability to articulate political power, ultimately asking "just how human is the body politic in this play?" Allowing Coriolanus's "wolvish tongue" to stand in the text hints that "the problem of the play is not translating martial force to political rule, but translating animal noise and voices into political language."

In "Shrewd Shakespeare," Bruce Boehrer mines linguistic traces of animal behavior embedded within one of Shakespeare's most famous—and most troubling—depictions of domesticity: *The Taming of the Shrew*. The shrew at the heart of play's depiction of "shrewishness," Boehrer argues, is "so deeply buried as to be superficially invisible." Shrews, small mammals often associated with house mice, were known for their poisonous bites; as Boehrer argues, the animal becomes associated with gendered behavior in the early modern period, linking the venom of the bite with demonic power and women's speech. When Petruchio "tames" the shrew, he invokes these misogynist tropes even as the play naturalizes them. Katherina, after all, is no witch; Boehrer shows how the play mobilizes misogynistic tropes of animality against Katherina, and more disturbing, how Petruchio's "shrewd behavior" mirrors shrewishness back to her, in order to fully evacuate any feminized version of power. That the term now signals "astuteness, reason, and intellect" is no irony: it reflects the precise ways in which Petruchio's domestic strategies invoke and flip taming narratives, so that Katherina is positioned as both animal and woman, shrew and wife.

10

SWARM LIFE
Shakespeare's School of Insects

Keith Botelho

> From the School of Insects we may learn vertue, and may lift up our eyes to the power of God.
> —*Thomas Moffett, The Theater of Insects (1634, 1658)*

In his Preface to *The Theater of Insects, or, Lesser living Creatures* (1634, 1658), Thomas Moffett asks, "Where is nature more to be seen than in the smallest matters, where she is entirely all?"[1] John Rowland's 1657 translation of Johannes Jonstonus's *A History of the Wonderful Things of Nature Set Forth* notes that although "bloodless creatures" are contemptible (a sentiment echoed by Moffett when he notes man does not regard small creatures because they are "but the pastimes of lascivious and shrunken Nature"), there is

> no where a more remarkable piece of Nature's Workmanship; and Nature is no where total, more than in the least Creatures … in these that are so small, and almost as nothing, what reason, what force, what unspeakable perfection is there?[2]

He continues, noting that the mind of man ought to be "roused up to contemplate their worth, by the majesty of the internal nature of them, and to verse it self therein"[3] And John Ray, the Royal Society member and noted naturalist, in his 1692 *The Wisdom of God Manifested in the Works of the Creation*, contemplates the remarkable observations of his learned countryman and Royal Society Fellow Robert Hooke, who testified to seeing tens of thousands of "little living Creatures in a quantity of Water no bigger than a grain of Millet," and that Hooke

> magnified those he had discovered to a very great bigness, but discovered many other sorts very much smaller than them he first saw, and some of them so exceeding small, that Millions of Millions might be contained in one drop of Water.[4]

Ray recalls that Pliny was moved to cry out over insects that were just visible to the naked eye, and so he wonders what he would have done "if he had seen Animals of so stupendious smallness … How would he have been rapt into an Extasie of Astonishment and Admiration," at "those incredibly small living Creatures" and the "immense subtilty of their Parts."[5]

Together, these texts display not only esteem for the smallest of Nature's creatures, but also an understanding that we can comprehend all of Nature through the seeming flawlessness of the insect. Perfection, majesty, ecstasy—insects arouse in humans not only awe but also a growing awareness of the gulfs between human and nonhuman. Naturalists, poets, and theologians alike during the period wondered and marveled at the tiniest of earth's creatures in relation to both four-footed beasts and to man. In fact, many of these writers and thinkers seem to assert that we need to consider the smallest creatures first, since in their complexity we can see the whole of Nature, as the epigraph from Moffett above makes clear. In other words, consideration of the smallest (but most populous) beasts actually magnifies humanity, a fact that often proved to elicit anxiety in recognition of how man often falls short in relation to the insect. The diminutive is enlarged through poetry and prose, and what was once small is now scaled, made manifest for man's contemplation.

Size *matters* in the Renaissance, particularly when discussing scale and magnitude as is relates to the nonhuman. For nonhuman animals, difference most often is represented in the period in terms of scale, and literary accounts of the smallest beasts, particularly insects, demand upon us an ethical consideration of mankind's relationship to miniature life in the early modern world. Joseph Campana asks if it is fair to say that, "in certain scholarly treatments, insects—and perhaps many other forms of life—are mere fragments of the so-called animal no less the so-called human?"[6] Yet insects have traditionally been marked, according to Eric Brown, as "humanity's Other," "imaginatively as well as apparently (spatially, temporally) different," often viewed as adversaries to man as they elicit unease.[7] What is so peculiar is that, according to Todd Borlik, "the teeming realm of six-legged creatures has, for the most part, scurried and flitted beneath the ken of animal studies."[8] One of the reasons seems to be a recent scholarly affinity for birds, livestock, and four-footed beasts. We might at first view this as neglect, but in the past decade, scholars including myself, Joseph Campana, Eric Brown, Janice Neri, Mary Baine Campbell, Jonathan Woolfson, and Jessica Wolfe have helped draw attention to the multiplicity of lesser creatures and their place in early modernity. Yet even in this volume in "The New Shakespeare Bestiary" section, we have entire chapters devoted to charismatic individual animals—fish, birds, apes, horses, dogs, bears—but insects, so varied and so many to choose from, are lumped together in one chapter. Is this because of the sheer multiplicity of insects, or do we unknowingly privilege charismatic megafauna and devote our scholarly attention to them instead?

How does Shakespeare articulate and imagine these multitudes? There is often crossover in the terminology used to discuss assemblies of human and nonhuman, megafauna and microfauna. Often in Shakespeare, we see single animals discussed, but the many are given numerous different names to capture multitudes. A sampling helps us to understand Shakespeare's shifting strategies and how he considers multiplicities:

<u>Used in Shakespeare to refer to both humans and nonhuman animals</u>

> Score—from the OE *scorum*, meaning "twenty." In *2 Henry IV*, Silence tells Shallow "A score of good ewes may be ten pounds" (3.2.46), and Gremio in *The Taming of the Shrew* remarking on "six score fat oxen" (2.1.350). But this word also can reference humans, as when in *Timon of Athens* Timon says to the Lords, "Let no assembly of / twenty be without a score of villains" (3.7.70–71).[9]
>
> Assembly—while most of the uses in Shakespeare refer to a gathering of humans (as in *Timon of Athens* example quoted above), we do see one instance where, in *As You Like It*, Touchstone, speaking of the forest, notes, "for here we have no temple but the / wood, no assembly but horn-beasts" (3.3.40–41). The beasts he refers to, however, seem to be the forest's bevy of four-footed beasts, not insects.

Herd—from OE *heordum* meaning "company of domestic animals," although Coriolanus calls retreating Roman soldiers a herd (1.5.2) and Casca in *Julius Caesar* speaks of the people as a "common herd" (1.2.261). More commonly in the plays, herd is used to identify deer and lions.

Flock—the OE *flocc* meant "a group of persons" but came to also mean a group of animals, particularly ones that traveled together. Falstaff in *1 Henry IV* speaks of a "flock of wild geese" (2.5.125) while Iago in *Othello* espies "this flock of drunkards" (2.3.52).

Nest—defined as "a group of birds, insects, or other animals occupying the same habitation" (3a). Usually used to refer to birds, although Queen Margaret in *2 Henry VI* references a "scorpion's nest" (3.2.86); other times it is spoken metaphorically to apply to humans.

Used in Shakespeare to refer only to humans

Band—meaning "an organized company" (1a) but also "a company of persons or animals in movement" (3a). *Band* does not apply to animals in Shakespeare, but only to humans; for instance, Tamora says that Lucius leads "a band of warlike Goths" (5.2.113) and King Harry in *Henry V* rallies his "band of brothers" (4.3.60).

Pack—defined as "a company or set of people" (4a) or "any number of animals kept; a group of wild animals" (4b). The word does not apply to animals in the plays, but is only used to discuss humans, as when Malvolio in *Twelfth Night* sneers, "I'll be revenged on the whole pack of you" (5.1.365).

Tribe—the word can mean "a group of people forming a community" (1a) or "loosely, any group or series of animals" (5a). Again, this word does not apply to animals in Shakespeare, but only to humans, as when Edmund in *King Lear* speaks of "a whole tribe of fops" (1.2.14) and Shylock in *The Merchant of Venice*, speaking of his Jewish ancestors, says, "sufferance is the badge of all our tribe" (1.3.104).

Bevy—the *OED* notes that the word can mean a company of maidens, quails, or larks (1), although its two uses in the plays only refer to humans.

Brood—meaning "offspring, esp. of animals that lay eggs" (1) or "a race, a kind; a species of men, animals, or things" (3). Volumnia in *Coriolanus* speaks of herself as "poor hen, fond of no second brood" (5.2.163).

Troop—meaning "a number of persons; a party, company, or band" (1b) and also "Of animals: a herd, flock, or swarm; esp. a group of apes or monkeys" (1c). Never used for animals in the plays, but rather used to describe everything from strangers to soldiers to fairies.

Parcel—with meaning applicable to both human and nonhuman: "a small party, collection or assembly (of people, animals, or things)" (6a). In the plays, it is not applied to animals, but rather humans, as when Portia speaks of "this parcel of wooers" (1.3.93) in *The Merchant of Venice* and Moth in *Love's Labour's Lost* discusses a "holy parcel of the fairest dames" (5.2.158).

Used in Shakespeare to refer only to nonhuman animals

Bed—meaning "a layer of small animals, especially reptiles, congregated thickly in some particular spot" (14a), it is specifically used for animals in Shakespeare, as when Boult in *Pericles* talks of "beds of eels" (16.126).

Team—defined as "a family of young animals or birds" (3) or "the stock of horses (or other animals) belonging to one owner" (4d). Lance in *The Two Gentlemen of Verona* speaks of "a team of horse" (3.1.263) and, most interestingly of the six uses of the word in the canon, Mercutio in *Romeo and Juliet* speaks of Queen Mab being drawn by a "team of little atomi" (1.4.58). *Atomi*, from the Latin for "diminutive beings," are here dust motes or mites. In fact, her wagon is an insect collective, made of spiders' legs, wings of grasshoppers, cricket's bone, gnats, and grubs.

Litter—defined as "offspring of an animal at birth" (5a). Falstaff uses the term twice, once in *2 Henry IV* (referencing a sow) and another in *The Merry Wives of Windsor* (referencing puppies).

Wilderness—defined as "a mingled, confused, or vast assemblage or collection of persons or things" (4). Shylock, speaking of Leah's ring, tells Tubal, "I would not have given it for a wilderness of monkeys" (3.1.102) while Titus in *Titus Andronicus* remarks that "Rome is but a wilderness of tigers" (3.1.53).

Game—defined as wild animals pursued for sport or hunting (16a, 18). Titus notes in *Titus Andronicus*, "An I have horse will follow where the game / Makes way, and run like swallows o'er the plain" (2.1.23–24).

The prompt for the essays in this section asked us to write on a single animal. However, to speak of a single insect is difficult—they are the stuff of swarms and colonies, of the many, not the individual. One cannot, after all, swarm in the singular. The proposed title for this chapter was "theater of insects," apt phrasing that does have its source in the Renaissance, as others have detailed the theatricality of the flea circus in the period.[10] Although Hamlet speaks of "a whole theatre of others" (3.2.25), *theater* is not a categorization used to define animals in Shakespeare. *Swarm* denotes multitude, and the *OED* attests that the word can mean a large body or multitude of persons, insects, or other small creatures (2a,b). In its limited use in Shakespeare, we see Lord Clifford in *3 Henry VI* note that the "common people swarm like summer flies" (2.6.8) and the First Man in *Richard II* remarks that the garden's herbs are "swarming with caterpillars" (3.4.48). *School* doesn't even quite capture the multitude of the earth's smallest life forms, and the words *colony*, *mob*, and *gang* do not appear in Shakespeare, while words like *bevy*, *congregation*, and *rout* all apply to humans only in the plays.

What, then, is the most appropriate way to classify the insect in Shakespeare's day? Laurie Shannon has usefully shown the mere eight appearances of the word *animal* in Shakespeare's works. In *The Accommodated Animal*, Shannon notes that "together the words 'beast' and 'creature' occur 268 times" while 'animal' appears only 8 times, 3 in *As You Like It*.[11] She writes in "The Eight Animals in Shakespeare" that "animals represented no single, philosophically invested category in early modernity; they instead suggested populations. English speakers almost never grouped together all the creatures we call (nonhuman) animals under the name."[12] Two points here are germane for my discussion. First, as I will later discuss, the word *insect* does not appear in Shakespeare. Its absence from his work shouldn't alarm us that there are no insects in Shakespeare. Rather, it allows us to see that the term in Shakespeare's day was not yet a catch-all for the some of the earth's tiniest inhabitants as it is today. The *OED* confirms that *insect* first appears in English in a 1601 translation of Pliny; it was Aristotle who first categorized them as "entoma" (entomology), pointing to their bodies "cut" or "in sections" or "notched."

The terms *beast* and *creature* refer as much to insects as to birds or four-footed animals in the period. We see this shifting use of terms in Sir Thomas Elyot's 1531 *The Book Named the Governor*, where he calls the bee a "little beast," while in John Worlidge's 1676 *Apiarium*, he calls bees "insects" on the title page but in his "To the Reader" he calls them "resolute Animals" (A2v). Insects often are lumped together with other animals when the terms *beast* and *creature* are used. They are catch-all terms, which resonate with their uses in the Bible, as we see in, for instance, *Timon of Athens* ("beasts and birds and fishes"—4.3.416) or *The Comedy of Errors* ("There's nothing situate under heaven's eye / But hath his bound, in earth, in sea, in sky: / The beasts, the fishes, and the winged fowls"—2.1.18).

Beast can also signal wild and brutish, meaning the opposite of human (as we might today use the term animal); as Duke Senior in *As You Like It* says, "I think he be transform'd into a beast; / For I can nowhere find him like a man" (2.7.1–2). *Beast* often referred to animals, as when we see it referred to a lion in *Henry V* or carrion in *King John* or, in a particularly vivid example in *The Taming of the Shrew*, when Grumio remarks that "winter tames man, woman, and beast" (4.1.19). Yet *beast* can also refer to a human, as when Isabella calls Claudio a beast (3.1) in *Measure for Measure* and as Theseus notes in *A Midsummer Night's Dream*, "Here comes two noble beasts in: a man and a lion" (5.1.212–13). *Creature* can also border on both the human and nonhuman—Lavatch in *All's Well That Ends Well* notes that he has been a "wicked creature" (1.3.30), while Falstaff in *1 Henry IV* interestingly calls himself a "two-legged creature" (2.5.172–73) and King Henry calls Lord Scroop in *Henry V* a "savage and inhuman creature" (2.2.92). The vast majority of usages, in fact, refer to humans, particularly women—Iago refers to Bianca as a "creature that dotes upon Cassio" (4.1.93–94) while *Othello* says of Desdemona, "the world hath not a sweeter creature" (4.1.176), and Lavinia in *Titus Andronicus* calls Tamora a "beastly creature" (2.3.182) and Miranda in *The Tempest* stands amazed at the many people she sees as "goodly creatures" (5.1.185). Less often *creature* can refer to animals: a horse in *Julius Caesar* (4.1.31), honeybees in *Henry V* (1.2), mastiffs in *Henry V* (3.7), and other "creatures of prey" in *The Winter's Tale* (3.3).[13] Even *bug* is used sparingly, a total of five times, not really in usage to mean insect or bedbug until after Shakespeare's death. Most of Shakespeare's bugs were in fact bugbears (from ME *bugge*, meaning "something frightening" or "something that causes dread or terror"). It is interesting to note, however, that built in to the language is revulsion for that thing—the insect; as Jeffrey A. Lockwood writes, insects can invade, evade, harm, and defy humans, thus causing what we might now call entomophobia.[14] As Todd Borlik succinctly notes,

> To be sure, there are ample biological reasons for entomophobia: insects often dwell amid slime and filth; many species bite, sting, or compete with humans for biomass resources; they reproduce at staggering rates; to human eyes they appear emotionless and implacable; social insects act like superorganisms in ways that undercut the growing sense in early modern Europe of the sanctity of the individual, etc.[15]

Such biological realities all contribute to the dread many humans feel when encountering bugs, but the imagination often plays a greater role, and since humans can't control or domesticate most insects, they are thus marked as humanity's creepy crawly other.

The closest thing we get to an all-encompassing term in Shakespeare (like the term *insect* we use today) is the word *fly*. In OE, the word *fleoge* meant "winged insect" and in Renaissance England a fly could mean any winged or flying insect. By the 1590s, the word was being used to mean large numbers of anything. However, Shakespeare also uses it to mean the specific insect, to which I will later return. Thus, when we go looking for insects in Shakespeare, it is indeed hard to see them, if not only because the nomenclature is not used but also for the fact that their size sometimes prohibits our seeing them. Despite advances in the period with the perspective glass and the microscope, allowing early moderns to see the smallest creatures up close, insects remained out of sight. Insects, in other words, are usually implied on the early modern stage, existing in language to denote their presence. Any insect theater is an imagined theater. Audiences encountering insects in rhetorical displays on the stage couldn't hear these lines without some visceral acknowledgment, an association of the insect with the feeling experienced in contact with this little beast.

As Laurie Shannon remarks, Renaissance Europe was well populated with nonhuman beasts, and humans and animals "rubbed shoulders as 'Fellow-commoners' in public spaces."[16] The plethora of creatures that inhabited early modern environs, not to mention early modern imaginations, makes it necessary to consider them individually in order to not fall into deliberate patterns of classification that occlude certain animals like insects. Yet, can and should we talk of the individual insect? How might we move past the perception of insects merely as a collective and discuss them as individual entities? As Gabriel Egan asks,

> Does an entire ant or bee colony constitute an individual or is it composed of individuals working together? This is an important question for ecocritics, since the Gaia hypothesis requires the existence of a worldwide biological interconnectedness that runs counter to how we have hitherto thought of life.[17]

Furthermore, how does the individual insect (or for that matter the swarm) and its encounter with humans affect early modern ideas of collective action or individual sovereignty? Insects are often implied creatures on the early modern stage, not visible but certainly omnipresent, and Shakespeare's plays often magnify the diminutive. I want to use some representative examples in what follows to examine how we should read "real" insects in the plays in relation to imagined insects or those used as rhetorical devices or character names, exploring the actual and imagined spaces that the smallest of earth's creatures occupy on Shakespeare's stage.

There are insects discussed in Shakespeare that only register in terms of language, not meant to be "on stage" as part of the theatrical environment. Bees and ants, noted as eusocial organisms, are often used in Shakespeare as examples for humanity, a didactic tool for his characters to employ. Canterbury in *Henry V* remarks, "For so work the honey-bees, / Creatures that by a rule in nature teach / The act of order to a peopled kingdom" (1.2.187–89). And the Fool in *King Lear* tells Kent, "We'll set thee to school to an ant, to teach thee there's no / laboring i' the winter" (2.4.63–64). Proverbially, bees and ants were seen as orderly and prudent, and they are used here to signal to audiences that by looking to nature's beasts, humans can learn to better themselves. And while *Coriolanus* has two intriguing references to butterflies, they do not open a space for the insect to become an actor on stage.[18] Valeria tells Virgilia and Volumnia that she saw Young Martius "run after a gilded butterfly" and catch it repeatedly before he "did so set his teeth and tear it" (1.3.57,60). The only insect access we have here is through Valeria's narrative. Later, Menenius speaks of Martius in insect terms: "There is differency between a grub and a butterfly, and your butterfly was a grub. This Martius is grown from man to dragon. He has wings, he's more than a creeping thing" (5.4.9–11). The implication here is that Coriolanus has metamorphosed like the grub to become something else, here a threatening creature who treads upon Rome. Is it also supposed that a creeping thing is thus harmless? And what might this say about young Martius, himself a grub who follows in his father's footsteps? A youth is, in fact, sometimes aligned with the smallest of earth's beasts, as is Moth (as he is called in the Quarto, Mote in Folio), Armado's diminutive and pestering boy page in *Love's Labour's Lost*, whose size is often referenced (1.2.20).[19] As Todd Borlik has written regarding the "insectoid fairies" in *A Midsummer Night's Dream* (two of whom are called Mote and Cobweb) "that intone a spell to ward off creepy-crawlies from

Titania's bower," "Shakespeare's insect poetics tinkers not only with the audience's sense of scale but also with anthropocentric notions of who, or rather what, counts as an actor."[20]

The insect inventories in Shakespeare often gesture to real insects lurking behind the metaphor or analogy. Are insects, Eric Brown asks, animals that are always onstage?[21] Are the anxieties they elicit—fear, revulsion, disease—a way to signal something about humanity, or are they meant to draw the species farther apart? Shakespeare's audiences, of course, were no strangers to insect life themselves, and it is worth considering how these depictions might have resonated with audiences in his day. While domestic pets and other charismatic megafauna in urban and rural settings would have been familiar sights and sounds to those living in and around Shakespeare's London, the average individual in the Renaissance might have had the most intimate contact with two insects in particular: fleas and lice. In *1 Henry IV*, the Second Carrier remarks, "I think this be the most villainous house in all London road for fleas; I am stung like a tench" (2.1.13–14). This moment seems ripe for audience identification, as the actor might very well use this line as a cue to scratch an itch. Similarly, one might expect such a visceral reaction to the flea, capable as it was of burrowing into the bodily recesses and acting as a vector of disease. And in *The Merry Wives of Windsor*, it is Sir Hugh Evans who notes, "The dozen white louses do become an old coad well. It / agrees well, passant; it is a familiar beast to man, and signifies / love" (1.1.16–18). We should mark this notion of multiplicity here (a dozen), again pointing to the fact that insects are encountered in multiples; furthermore, Evans's choice of the word *beast* to classify this insect is significant. The intimacy here—the familiarity and love—is a product of the ways in which the louse is on and potentially in the human body. An audience familiar with such intimacy—a perverted sense of human contact—might in fact identify with the inescapability of the flea or the louse. And even though a spectator would not see this pest, the tacit acknowledgement is there—fleas and lice are omnipresent in home, in clothing, and on the body. These little beasts threaten the human body in unseen ways.

As mentioned earlier, *fly* in early modern England often connoted any flying insect. Shakespeare, however, has the specific insect in mind (*Musca domestica*) in a number of uses. Many characters speak of the insect, although usually not in terms of engaging with one as we saw with the flea. Marina in *Pericles* comments that she would not kill earth's creatures: "I never kill'd a mouse, nor hurt a fly. / I trod upon a worm against my will" (4.1). People are said to "swarm like summer flies" in *3 Henry VI* (2.6.17), Cominius in *Coriolanus* mentions "butchers killing flies" (4.6.98), and Romeo speaks of "carrion-flies" (3.3.35). The omnipresent insect registers with the audience through language. Perhaps the most (in)famous scene which "stars" a fly is found in *Titus Andronicus*. Rome, the Andronicii, and Tamora's son Alarbus have all been dismembered in some fashion when Titus, Marcus, Young Lucius, and Lavinia sit together to eat at Titus's home.[22] Seemingly out of nowhere, and disrupting the conversation about all that has befallen the family, Marcus strikes a dish with his knife, killing a fly. Titus's reaction—that his brother is a murderer of the innocent—contrasts sharply to Marcus: "Alas, my lord, I have but killed a fly" (3.2.59). Titus welcomes all creatures, human and nonhuman, into his worldview of woe. Marcus's "but" here seems to minimize the insect, marking it one of the lesser creatures, not an equal to man. Titus picks up on this and responds,

'But'? How if that fly had a father, brother?
How would he hang his slender gilded wings
And buzz lamenting dirges in the air!
Poor harmless fly,
That with his pretty buzzing melody
Came here to make us merry—and thou hast killed him!

(3.2.60–65)

Titus sees species sharing grief. As Perry Guevara notes, "In a moment of cross-species identification … Titus witnesses his family's tragedy in the theater of the insect."[23] However, when Marcus notes that "it was a black ill-favoured fly / Like to the Empress' Moor" (3.2.66–67), Titus's goodwill towards the insect ends, as he then takes the knife and strikes the fly, noting "Yet I think we are not brought so low / But that between us we can kill a fly / That comes in likeness of a coal-black Moor" (3.2.75–77). The fly is no longer innocent in Titus's eyes, and it becomes one of many species in the play whose life is cut short by human actions.

I want to conclude by asking how we might imagine staging such a scene. In another venue, I have argued that it makes sense according to the logic of animal reference in *The Merchant of Venice* that the monkey appears on the stage in the fifth act, as Jessica, who has sold the ring she had stolen to purchase this domestic pet, resides in Belmont with the Christians and this real monkey is her only lifeline to her past.[24] And we should not forget that dogs and bears could have been paraded across the stage or become actors in the play (think *The Two Gentlemen of Verona* or *The Winter's Tale*). However, it is difficult to imagine this possibility with most insects that are used in Shakespeare. Shakespeare's insect imagery allows the audience to picture these creatures but, because of their size, and their inability to be exhibited on the stage and be seen, Shakespeare resorts to metaphor. Shakespeare's insect theater is an imagined theater. Eric Brown, speaking of the fly scene in *Titus Andronicus*, asks, "ought a performance to maintain a stable of expendable Drosophilia understudies? Or should such representations be emptily mimed, time after time, with the buzz of *Musca domestica* artificially contrived or imagined?"[25] Certainly, this hypothetical is intriguing, although we don't even see dead insects as stage properties. Yet considering these performance possibilities highlights that with the art and magic of the early modern theater, one does not need, say, to *see* the flea of *hear* the buzz of the fly. Rather, we must "Suppose," as the Chorus in *Henry V* asks of the audience, and let the insects "on your imaginary forces work" (18–19).

Notes

1 Thomas Moffett, *The Theater of Insects, or, Lesser Living Creatures* (London, 1658), Ffff5-r.
2 Ibid., 241, Hhr1.
3 Ibid., 244, Hhv3.
4 John Ray, *The Wisdom of God Manifested in the Works of the Creation* (London, 1692), 159–60.
5 Ibid., 161.
6 Joseph Campana, "The Bee and the Sovereign (II): Segments, Swarms, and the Shakespearean Multitude," in *The Return of Theory in Early Modern English Studies*, eds. Paul Cefalu, Gary Kuchar, and Bryan Reynolds, vol. II (New York: Palgrave Macmillan, 2014), 59–78, 63.
7 Eric C. Brown, ed., *Insect Poetics* (Minneapolis: University of Minnesota Press, 2006), xi–xv.
8 Todd Andrew Borlik, "Shakespeare's Insect Theater: Fairy Lore as Elizabethan Folk Entomology," in *Performing Animals: History, Agency, Theater*, eds. Karen Raber and Monica Mattfield (University Park: Pennsylvania State University Press, 2017), 123–40, 123.
9 All Shakespearean citations are taken from *The Norton Shakespeare* and are cited parenthetically in the text, as are definitions from *Oxford English Dictionary*, Second Edition.
10 For one notable instance, see Jessica Wolfe, "*Circus Minimus*: The Early Modern Theater of Insects," in *Performing Animals: History, Agency, Theater*, eds. Karen Raber and Monica Mattfield (University Park: Pennsylvania State University Press, 2017), 111–22.
11 Laurie Shannon, *The Accommodated Animal: Cosmopolity in Shakespearean Locales* (Chicago, IL: University of Chicago Press, 2013), 80.
12 Laurie Shannon, "The Eight Animals in Shakespeare; or, before the Human," *PMLA* 124, no. 2 (2009): 477.
13 Hamlet, noting the interconnectedness between human and nonhuman beasts, says that "we fat all creatures else to fat us, and we fat ourselves for maggots" (4.3.22–23).

14 Jeffrey A. Lockwood, *The Infested Mind: Why Humans Fear, Loathe, and Love Insects* (Oxford: Oxford University Press, 2013), 37.

15 Todd Andrew Borlik, "Shakespeare's Insect Theater: Fairy Lore as Elizabethan Folk Entomology," in *Performing Animals: History, Agency, Theater*, eds. Karen Raber and Monica Mattfield (University Park: Pennsylvania State University Press, 2017), 123–40, 123–24.

16 Shannon, *The Accommodated Animal*, 8.

17 Gabriel Egan, *Shakespeare and Ecocritical Theory* (London: Bloomsbury Arden Shakespeare, 2015), 96. The often-controversial Gaia hypothesis, popularized by James Lovelock in the 1970s, asserts that the biosphere is a complex living organism that self-regulates, thereby maintaining life on earth.

18 See Chris Barrett, "Shakespeare's Butterflies," *New Orleans Review* 42 (2016): 286–310, as well as her forthcoming "Butterflies and Moths," in *Lesser Living Creatures: Insect Life in the Renaissance*, eds. Keith Botelho and Joseph Campana (University Park: Pennsylvania State University Press, 2021); and Christopher Givan, "Shakespeare's *Coriolanus*: The Premature Epitaph and the Butterfly," *Shakespeare Studies* 12 (1979): 143–58.

19 As Eric Brown notes in "Performing Insects in Shakespeare's *Coriolanus*," Shakespeare's Moth in *Love's Labour's Lost* "seems an analogue to Jonson's parasites, even if 'Moth' is taken to indicate a tiny 'mote' rather than the insect itself." *Insect Poetics*, ed. Eric C. Brown (Minneapolis: University of Minnesota Press, 2006), 35.

20 Borlik, "Shakespeare's Insect Theater," 124, 136. He goes on to argue that "the fairies are not merely personifications of insects; they also perform human dominion over the world of microfauna."

21 Brown, "Performing Insects," 37.

22 Flies at tables would have been common, as food would draw flies. Interestingly, the murdered fly becomes another beast dead at the table for human consumption or, in the case of the fly, human revenge.

23 Perry D. Guevara, "Of Flyes," in *Lesser Living Creatures: Insect Life in the Renaissance*, eds. Keith Botelho and Joseph Campana. In manuscript.

24 Keith Botelho, "The Beasts of Belmont and Venice," in *Ecological Approaches to Early Modern English Texts: A Field Guide to Reading and Teaching*, eds. Lynne Bruckner, Jennifer Munroe, and Edward J. Geisweidt (Aldershot: Ashgate, 2015), 71–80.

25 Brown, "Performing Insects," 36.

11

BERNARDIAN ECOLOGY AND TOPSELL'S REDEMPTIVE BEE IN *THE TEMPEST*

Nicole A. Jacobs

Bees keep time. It is not necessarily in the human measures of seconds, hours, and years, but their timekeeping goes far beyond instincts of diurnal activity and nocturnal rest. From the hive's perspective, bee time is both cyclical and generational, a concept that applies across many animal and insect species (including humans). An individual worker bee's labor is determined by and shifts with her age, as she graduates from feeding pupae the day she hatches to gathering nectar by one month old. Overall, the beehive structures its architecture, its labor, and its consumption and use of energy on the future. Bees are also keenly attuned to the seasons: spring and summer are times of collection and building food stores; fall brings the killing off of male drones that would drain the hive's resources; all so that in winter, the female workers and queen can make use of the shelter and sustenance their past labor has afforded them. One essential aspect of bee temporality relies upon communication, as the hive consults on time-sensitive issues like when to raise a new queen. Timing is one critical component of what biologist Thomas D. Seeley calls "honeybee democracy."[1] Indeed, modern entomological research tells us that beehives engage in complex negotiations, demonstrating collective intelligence over decisions such as where to swarm. The ultimate goal of this communication is communal survival. And yet, a tension exists between the temporality of the individual worker bee and that of the collective hive.

I would contend that measures of nonhuman time, such as bee time, offer an important consideration in the study of animal and human cultures and how they interact across centuries and circumstances. Some modern critics have denied that insects or animals, more generally, experience time—at least in any way that is recognizable to humans—investing instead in a form of anthropomorphic romanticization of the nonhuman being that lives simply "in the moment." Nietzsche, for one, views livestock as inextricably linked, for better or for worse, to the present, noting that cows "do not know what is meant by yesterday or today ... fettered to the moment and its pleasure or displeasure."[2] He thus generalizes all creatures' relationship to time: "the animal lives unhistorically: for it is contained in the present."[3] On the topic of bees, Michael Pollan similarly muses, "presumably insects can look at a blossom without entertaining thoughts of the past and the future."[4] However, animals' experiences undoubtedly shift across histories, cultures, and technologies of domestication or policies of eradication. I would suggest that consideration of animal time need not be subsumed by arguments about consciousness and its relationship to human timepieces or calendars. Indeed, animal time holds the potential to open up larger considerations of the interdependence between animals and humans, the effects of human displacement of animals (like those shipped to the New World colonies), and animal architecture and aesthetics (where and how they structure their lives). From an early modern perspective, bees and other animals share a complex set of temporalities that factor in not only their labor and suffering, but also their drives, inclinations, and pleasures.[5] Though animal time has broad implications, this chapter will focus specifically on the ways in which Shakespeare's exploration of bee time reveals the toll of exploitation and servitude on living beings. In *The Tempest*, particularly in Ariel's song of present labor and future longing, Shakespeare ultimately reflects upon what it means to look to a future beyond service and struggle.

Sixteenth- and seventeenth-century beekeepers observed with admiration the hive's seemingly inscrutable and precise communication about timekeeping.[6] They perceived the enigmatic yet crucial interface between the temporality of the individual worker bee and that of her collective swarm. For instance, Charles Richardson's *The Repentance of Peter and Judas* (1612) takes from Aristotle the notion that an individual bee is responsible for hive waking and sleeping schedules:

> Early in the morning they are silent, until one bee arouses them by humming two or three times, when they all fly to their work; when they return again there is some disturbance at first, which gradually becomes less and less until one of them flies around with a humming noise, as if warning them to sleep, when on a sudden they become silent.[7]

Richardson's observation of the striking nature of beehive behavior "on a sudden" is also echoed in John Milton's famous bee simile in Book I of *Paradise Lost*. Milton's epic describes the inhabitants of Pandemonium "[a]s Bees / In spring time, when the Sun with Taurus rides" and notes the amazement of the demon hive's simultaneous transformation: "Till the signal given, / Behold a wonder!"[8] This signal is responsible for synchronizing the sudden shrinking of Satan's minions to minute size in preparation for "the great consult."[9] Milton's use of the signal is indicative of the knowledge that the bee communicates orders to the hive instantaneously. Yet the passive construction of "the signal given" begs the question: who gave the signal? And how did the rest of the hive receive it? Although we now understand a great deal more about this process, the early moderns could neither conceptualize nor replicate this means of instant communication and compliance among their own human laborers.

The hive is an excellent subject for exploring connections in the early modern period between time, labor, and the animal. Karen Raber has observed that critics "do not credit animals … with generating a consciously weighted cultural act. They find instead in animal labor a 'natural' sculpting of bodily material that sidesteps issues of a stratified and exploitative labor system."[10] Current research accepts that honeybees are eusocial, or live in a complex social structure, with discrete individuals performing the various functions and tasks of a larger superorganism.[11] Moreover, within this framework, the individual bee is capable of displaying emotional responses, such as pessimism.[12] However, in the early modern period, understandings of bee culture ultimately served human metaphors and perceptions of apian work and socialization. Indeed, beekeepers justified their reliance on essential bee labor by interpreting human expectations of yield as less exacting than the hive's own. In particular, they highlighted a conviction that among bees any individual drive is necessarily subsumed by that of the collective. Elizabeth I's beekeeper Charles Butler, for instance, speaks to the work ethic of elder bees in *The Feminine Monarchie* (1609): "they will never give over, while their wings can bear them: & then when they cease to worke, they will cease also to eate: such enemies are they to idleness."[13] According to this logic, to the worker bee, her past labor is irrelevant to present service. What is so exemplary to Butler—the lesson to be gleaned for human consumption—is the bee's sacrifice. Although a worker bee born in spring will not survive until the winter, she nevertheless prepares for a future in which she will never share.

The natural and moral positionality of the bee also offers a unique contribution to our understanding of what animal studies critics have termed human exceptionalism or negative human exceptionalism, where the human constitutes a distinct category among living beings, for better or for worse.[14] The challenge to this paradigm posed by the status of the bee stems from the fact that it is regarded as at once superior and inferior to the human. In metaphorical terms, the beehive was, from Virgil onward, promoted as an exemplum for human society: all members of a kingdom should be as obedient, self-sacrificing, and industrious as the bee.[15] And yet in actuality, the hive was placed in service of human husbandry and economy, as its honey, wax, and pollinating labor were viewed as commodities for the benefit of humankind. These competing ideas of the hive speak to the larger representations of nonhuman life in the period. For instance, Ayesha Ramachandran and Melissa E. Sanchez have demonstrated the ways in which the human as a category stands as "productively ambiguous and malleable," considering that "animals ... ghosts, angels, subjects of conquest and colonization, and corporations could be both distinguished from and assimilated into the category of the human for polemical, economic, or experimental purposes."[16] Nonetheless, even within this framework of creaturely ambiguity, it is difficult to escape the specter of human dominance within animal studies. Indeed, as Joseph Campana has importantly argued, "to focus on capacity and capabilities" in nonhuman animals "even when invoking shared capacities, shared environments, or shared corporealities—may not be to dislodge the human from a position of centrality and privilege."[17] In Shakespeare's apian metaphor, the dominant status of the human is inescapable, as his worker bee also reflects the struggles of the individual laborer in society. In *The Tempest*, Shakespeare reveals a conflict between, on the one hand, human valorization of the hive's work ethic, and on the other, the worker's desire to follow her own inclinations.

In this chapter, I will first follow the beeline forged through theorizations of the animal from Saint Bernard of Clairvaux (patron saint of beekeepers) to Protestant cleric Edward Topsell to contemporary ecocritics in order to examine the competing scales of servitude and authority in Shakespeare's work. Second, I will examine the ways in which nonhuman flying creatures—especially Ariel and the bee   claim solidarity with suffering laborers. What is at stake in Shakespeare's interventions into popular conceptions of the hive is the matter of whether bees' value is instrumental—contingent upon their usefulness to human agriculture and diet—or intrinsic—based on their own merit within nature. I argue that Shakespeare explores the boundaries between time and labor in the human and the animal in order to question what is lost and who gains when the collective is compelled to spend its time in the service of the few.

I Bernardian Ecology

Shifts in the human metaphor of the hive in response to emergent political and theological debates speak to larger understandings of what it means to live in a hierarchical society. Traditionally, popes and monarchs deployed the apian metaphor as an image of nature meant to authorize a worldview in which the desires of the few supersede the needs of all others, thereby enforcing subservience among the disempowered masses. Following the

Reformation, however, Protestants and resistance theorists sought to dismantle the notion of the Catholic and monarchical hive—a top-down hierarchy, where power and influence flow from one centralized source. As animal studies scholar Paul Waldau indicates, "the dominant views of nonhuman animals changed again and again—ancient views were supplanted in Western Europe during the medieval period by heavily symbolic approaches, which in turn gave way to modern views that were much more representational."[18] In the case of bees, in particular, ongoing questions about the use and value of God's creatures set the conditions for their exceptional and yet shifting status among humans, animals, and insects. In this instance, changes in the perception of the hive are part of a conscious divergence from the Catholic faith and the reverence for bees in Catholic writing and iconography that stretched back over four centuries.

A honeybee cannot survive independently without a hive, and the Catholic Church encouraged the faithful to adopt an apian posture of communal responsibility. Evidence of this agenda can be found in medieval texts like the Aberdeen Bestiary of the twelfth century, which describes bees as an industrious society of workers that shared in the task of promoting the common good without inflicting harm on others:

> see how the bees all compete with each other in carrying out their duties: some keeping watch over those who are seeking food; some keeping a careful guard on the fort, that is the hive; ... you can see too, however, that no bees lie in wait for other creatures, to take advantage of their toil; and none take a life by force.[19]

Also in the twelfth century, St. Anthony of Padua takes the comparison between bees and parishioners even further by saying, "the small bees are penitents, who are little in their own eyes, and are always employed about some work, lest the devil should come and find their house empty and idle."[20]

Perhaps the most influential and resounding connection between Catholicism and bees is forged in the writings and iconography of Saint Bernard of Clairvaux. This twelfth-century French Cistercian abbot is still popularly depicted with a beehive since he was known as the "mellifluous doctor" for his beautifully written or honey-tongued devotions and commentaries on scripture. In his writings, Bernard frequently used references to bees and honey as symbols of consolation and God's grace. For instance, in a translation of his work by Cambridge fellow W.P., *His Meditations, or Sighes, Sobbes, and Tears Upon Our Saviors Passion* (1611), Bernard speaks to Christ's death and passion with a honey comparison:

> So let it be joyfull unto thee, to heare him take his farewell with *Consummatum est*, it is finished. Oh let the Meditation of this word, be more sweet unto mee, then the honie which Samson found in the carkasse of the Lyon, when he was hungry.[21]

This moment refers to Judges when Samson discovers the heaven-sent honey that stands as a symbol of God's approbation of his mission to undercut the Philistines' rule over Israel.

To Bernard, honey is also a potent symbol of Christianity and Christ himself. In *The Sentences*, he demonstrates the significance of honey to the resurrected Christ: "Honey still in the wax ... represents charity in one's observances of the New Testament. Lest anyone think that these should be ignored, after his resurrection Christ is said to have eaten honey with wax, that is the honeycomb."[22] Christians should read Christ's consumption of the honey and its comb as a metaphor for pursuing a more charitable life, not in surface-level deeds, but rather through a desire issued from the conscience:

Honey is separated from the wax in order to bring it to the peak of its strength and sweetness. So too charity is set apart from the observances of the law in the precious and pure vessel of the conscience, in order to be offered to the Lord to taste. Freed from the rote observances as the honey is from the wax, charity naturally develops into a more precious thing of spiritual brilliance. It becomes the candle which, when placed on the lampstand which is Christ, shines equally on all who are in the house of God.[23]

To Bernard, the honey and wax of bees are not merely the stuff of physical or spiritual sustenance. Rather, they represent one of the foundations of faith itself: conscience. "If my minde bee confounded, with great shamefulness of my guiltie conscience, that it cannot pray & crave for mercie," Bernard contends, "it is meete that it should bee overwhelmed with the tempest of exceeding sorrow and doleful sadness."[24]

Bernard's frequent use of the apian metaphor is not surprising given his reverence for the natural world and nonhuman beings. He was quoted as having said to a pupil,

You will find something far greater in the woods than you will in books. Stones and trees will teach you that which you will never learn from masters. Think you not you can suck honey from the rock ...? Do not the mountains drop sweetness, the hills run with milk and honey, and the valleys stand thick with corn?[25]

Beyond this view of the value of nature's instructional bounty, Bernard also believes that animals possess a similarly intrinsic worth. Indeed, he addresses critiques that some animals are dangerous or seemingly do not have a use to human society by making a contention about their divine significance:

Although they be hurtful, although they be pernicious to human safety in this world, still [animals'] bodies do not lack that which worketh together for good to those who, according to the purpose are called saints. For although they be not killed for food, nor apt to render service, yet verily they exercise the wit, agreeably to that benefit of the common discipline which presides over all methods of putting things in use, by which "the invisible things of God are clearly seen, being understood by the things that are made."[26]

This passage provides one illustrative example of what I term Bernardian ecology, an assertion of the inherent and God-given worth of all creatures regardless of whether or not they display an immediate utility to humankind. To Bernard, the faithful are compelled to show an appreciation for the "invisible" divine intentions that created life and nature in the first place. Implicitly, the unknowable intentionality of God's design also serves a future-oriented agenda: to preserve God's plan on earth, whatever that may be, humankind must protect the divine creation in the present. Bernardian ecology provides a foundational idea that, with some revision, would centuries later be promoted by ecocritics.[27]

Bernardian ecology has continued to maintain greater currency than has been acknowledged, particularly in its opposition to the notion of instrumentalism that has dominated so much of humanist discourse. Even in the modern world, Pope Francis's encyclical, *On Care for Our Common Home* (2015), is framed by this paradigm, as it laments the mass extinction of nonhuman life on earth due to human activity: "Because of us, thousands of species will no longer give glory to God by their very existence, nor convey their message to us. We have no such right."[28] Looking back to the early modern period,

Robert N. Watson's analysis of the impact of the Reformation on views of the natural world suggests that such values arise largely from a distinction between the Catholic focus on the sensual experience of the body vs. the Protestant emphasis on the word of Christ.[29] Despite some of the doctrinal differences in views on the environment, evidence throughout early modern religious discourse also reveals that in the case of Bernard, there were notable continuities among some Catholics and Protestants in their approach towards and understanding of creaturely life. Martin Luther himself referenced Bernard's life, legacy, and writing over 500 times not only for the saint's critiques of corruption within the papal regime, but also for the fervency of his faith.[30] An adherent of Luther, Philips van Marnix van Saint Aldegonde, underscores the connection between Bernard, bees, and Protestantism in *The Beehive of the Romish Church* (1569). This popular treatise, translated into English in 1579, initiates the Protestant contempt for the beehive as a symbol of Catholic hierarchy while also seeking to reclaim the work of Bernard for the Calvinist cause, arguing that the saint "did very stoutly strive against the Priestes and Prelates, calling them the servants of Antichrist."[31]

In England, John Panke claimed that Bernard was an ahead-of-his-time Protestant while Antonie Batt, a Benedictine monk, insisted on reclaiming the saint for Catholicism.[32] More than merely a debate over religion, Bernard's legacy confronted the notion of worth. Although Bernard did not grant that animals had rational souls, he did assert that they had lives and bodies worthy of pursuing pleasures and taking rest. Just as significant, he also believed that it was a matter of conscience for humans to protect God's creatures.

II Time, Labor, and the Bee

Worker bees' lives are subsumed by labor. To the ruling class, the worker bee offers the ideal metaphor for the toiling masses because she rejects the laziness of the male drone and spends all of her waking hours at her occupation.[33] In Shakespeare's *The Tempest*, however, Ariel's song, "Where the bee sucks," imagines a different life for the laboring bee, one in which she laments her current servitude and longs for future freedom. Ariel, as a flying creature (albeit a magical rather than organic one), addresses the question of intrinsic worth from the perspective of the unceasing laborer herself. The song frees the insect from her use-value to humans by considering a potential space and time for her leisure. More significantly, as I will demonstrate, Shakespeare's depiction of nonhuman beings in the play also reflects upon the concept of futurity, or the anticipation of the future and the notion of an existence after mortal struggle.

The context of Ariel's song, which has not received much scholarly attention, can best be understood alongside the seventeenth-century discourse of ecology and value. One of the greatest adherents of Bernardian ecology in the time of Shakespeare also happens to be one of the most influential writers for scholars of early modern animal studies. Edward Topsell is most often cited for his *Historie of Four-Footed Beasts* and *Historie of Serpents* (1608); nevertheless, in his own time, he was most well known as a respected Protestant cleric, who also published his own and others' sermons and meditations. Most notably, his *Times Lamentation: Or an Exposition on the Prophet Joel* (1599) frequently references Bernard, even containing an epigraph from *The Sentences* on the title page. The guiding principle of Topsell's meditation is that "Time is the measure of all things" because it quantifies the period before the individual reaches heaven and collective humanity faces its final judgment for "the salvation of their soules."[34] Unsurprisingly given his larger body of work, Topsell's reflections on scripture invoke the role of the animal, particularly the insect. He warns against neglecting the smallest and least powerful members of a society, speaking of the biblical famines wrought by palmer worms, grasshoppers, and other insects:

> small creatures com[e] with great force to invade this country ... [so] that a flocke of little worms should overthrow a whole nation: and these beasts should come successively the one after the other, that whosoever escape the first, should be taken by the last.[35]

Topsell also notes the suffering of animals caused by human iniquity:

> the beastes are punished for mans cause which is the doctrine of this verse even for our sakes are they pined, and fatted, beaten and bruised, because of the sinnes we have committed: All the men in the world could not beare their own plague; but the innocent and harmlesse beastes must helpe out with the matter.[36]

His sympathetic portrayal of animals' suffering demonstrates their intrinsic worth even as their utility to humans makes them subject to anguish. In Topsell's religious prose, creatures serve as a reminder of the injustice wrought by humans' sin and greed, particularly that of the wealthiest and most powerful.

Indeed, it is unmerited creaturely suffering at the mercy of humankind that drives Topsell to exceed the bounds of Bernardian ecology in his model of conservationism. In *The Historie of Adam, or the Foure-fold State of Man* (1606), Topsell revises and edits the rough papers of the late preacher Henry Holland as a tribute to his friend. Topsell and Holland provide a glimpse of the world after the final judgment:

> Wherefore those words being understood of the Elect after the resurrection, like as is afterward, the new city, her foure gates, her pavement with the twelve precious stones, her water, her fruites, her trees, her leaves, her garments all allegoricall. I conclude, that the first division which God made of waters shall stand, both above and beneath the firmament, and that the sea shall not worke nor bee tossed with windes, nor destroy any of the creatures renewed upon the face of the earth, but unto the Saints, they shall no more looke upon sea or land.[37]

In other words, at the end of days, the entirety of redeemed humanity will retreat to heaven (and the damned to hell) while the animals remain free to roam the earth without the interference of humanity or the attendant suffering they faced for the sins of mankind. This passage imagines redemption—a heaven on earth—for animals that need no longer serve humans with their labor. During a period when many sought to justify humans' superiority over animals either through biblical justification or Cartesian logic, Topsell and Holland landed firmly on the side of the suffering creature.

Although Topsell outdoes Bernard in his view of the intrinsic worth and future peace of animals, he also simultaneously promotes a utilitarian perspective on creatures in their capacity to promote human reform. For Topsell, creatures in the present provide a future-oriented labor model that can act as a guide for human action. Accordingly, these nonhuman beings must continue to serve their function until human redemption eventually leads to freedom for all beings. In fact, among all creatures, Topsell insists that God crafted the beehive as an exemplum for human culture:

> Whereas the Almightie hath created all things for the use and service of man, so especially among the rest hath he made the Bees, not onely that they should be unto us

patternes and presidents of politicall and oeconomicall vertues ... but even Teachers and Schoolmaisters instructing us in certaine divine knowledge, and like extraordinary prophets, premonstrating the successe & events of things to come.[38]

What is unique about Topsell's perspective is the notion that the example of the beehive, if heeded, could herald the salvation of humanity. More significantly, Topsell in *The Reward of Religion Delivered in Sundrie Lectures Upon the Booke of Ruth* (1596) links the bee to God's elect, "the poore Saintes of God," who "are the bees for whose sake you enjoy the hony for your delight, and the hony combe for the pleasure of your meat."[39] He continues by emphasizing how interconnected human beings are, so that the wealthiest and most powerful people all rely upon the virtue of the faithful:

> there is not a usurer, but he hath his money for their sake; there is not a Gentleman, but hee hath his landes for their sake; there is not a Prince but hee hath his Crowne for their sake; ... there shoulde bee no peace, prosperitie or plentye, if it were not for them, for the Angels are their servaunts, the earth is their mayntenaunce, and heaven is their inheritance.[40]

To Topsell, the faithful, then, are God's worker bees, promoting the common good without inflicting harm on others. Though the prophetic hive of the faithful suffers mortal trials, they do so in order to earn their promised spiritual deliverance.

As in Topsell's meditations, futurity is the organizing principle of Ariel's song in *The Tempest*. In it, Ariel also demonstrates that the concept of salvation is not exclusive to human beings. Scholars have noted the centrality of this play to Shakespeare's boundaries between the human and the animal, and yet these insights could also benefit by considering the role of temporality in relation to the nonhuman in the play.[41] Tiffany Jo Werth, for instance, points to Prospero's unique position as "sometimes more than, sometimes less than, human. He slips into, out of, below, and above a human register."[42] Steven Mentz makes a case for Ariel as the instrument for restoring human order in the play, noting, "Ariel captures an alien ambivalence at the heart of the human relationship to our nonhuman environment."[43] A crucial distinction between Prospero as master and Ariel as servant lies in Prospero's status as a mortal being. When Ariel tells Prospero of Lord Gonzalo's tears and the repentance of Alonso, Antonio, and Sebastian, Prospero asks if his affections belie some tenderness towards their suffering. The magical sprite responds, "Mine would, sir, were I human" (5.1.19), causing Prospero to chastise himself for not feeling mercy towards "one of [his] kind" (5.1.23).[44] Ariel steps in as the reminder of Prospero's conscience and his responsibility to those under his care. Like Topsell's bee, however, as Ariel leads the path to human redemption, he continues to suffer his master's threats and commands.

Ariel's song, which he sings to Prospero while helping to dress him in preparation for his final revelation of truth, showcases the simultaneous disappointment and hope of the nonhuman laborer awaiting a future reward. Directly following one of Prospero's frequent promises to free Ariel (one of seven such assurances), the winged being reflects upon the single worker bee:

> Where the bee sucks, there suck I,
> In a cowslip's bell I lie;
> There I couch, when owls do cry.
> On the bat's back I do fly
> After summer merrily.
> Merrily, merrily, shall I live now,
> Under the blossom that hangs on the bough.

(5.1.88–94)

Ariel likens himself in his work for Prospero to the laboring bee collecting nectar. Like the bee, Ariel goes about his work in a way that preserves the integrity of nature, not harming the flower upon which he "couch[es]." Cowslip (*Primula veris*) blooms in spring, a busy time for bees, and yet the song anticipates future rest, "after summer merrily. / Merrily, merrily, shall I live," a time after his service has ended. Moreover, Ariel toys with the notion of a defiance of duty; if he hides "under the blossom" at night "when owls do cry," he is neither where he is supposed to be, nor engaging in any work. In Ariel's imagination, he steals time away from his expected duties to Prospero by catching a surreptitious ride on the back of a bat. In addition to the lyrics, recorded in the First Folio, the music, written by Shakespeare's frequent collaborator Robert Johnson, shifts as the season changes, "after summer."[45] According to Jennifer Linhart Wood, "an audible metrical shift between duple and triple time is apparent," hastening the meter of these last lines of the song.[46] In it, Ariel eagerly awaits his imagined life after instrumentality; one in which he has the time to pursue his own pleasures.

However, Ariel's song also reveals important distinctions between the worker bee on a human-dominated earth and the magical being on an island controlled by Prospero. In reality, the worker bee returns to the hive to sleep under the watch of the sentinel bee. Ariel, by contrast, forgoes his nightly shelter in order to practice for his future, a time when he might be free of Prospero's demands, even though as the bee metaphor implies, this moment may never arrive. Ariel embraces an apian model of efficiency. On his next errand, he far exceeds Prospero's orders by restoring the ship to working order while performing the designated minor task of fetching the boatswain. Prospero applauds Ariel's ingenuity and forward thinking, "my tricksy spirit!" (5.1.226). Nevertheless, Ariel anticipates Prospero's future needs and accomplishes the tasks ahead of schedule in order to hasten his own liberation. Ariel's immortality would offer him a unique relationship to time. Prospero's human life is finite, and thus, Ariel's obligations would die with him, and yet Ariel endures his present labor by looking forward to the pleasures of following his own inclinations, of living on his island home after the humans who hold him in durance have left. Ariel's circumstances as a magical being freed from service to humanity, in other words, bear striking similarities to Topsell's conception of the animal-occupied world after revelation.

Shakespeare's winged beings—both magical and apian—also reflect on the service of humans. There is a distinct hierarchy on the island, as royal characters vie for supremacy of Naples and Milan, enslaved and lower status characters like Caliban and the boatswain serve greater physical utility in doing all of the practical work. The only task performed by a royal person is when Ferdinand moves logs for Prospero while flirting with Miranda. During the tempest when Gonzalo chides the boatswain for insubordination, the mariner reveals his frustration with the worldly hierarchy that subordinates him to officials who lack the skills required to save them from the storm, directly accusing Gonzalo, "You mar our labor," and complaining of the councilor's interference, "A plague upon this howling. They are louder than the weather or our office" (1.1.13 and 1.1.35–36). Within this moment of peril, Gonzalo stands upon ceremony and status, "remember whom thou hast aboard" (1.1.19). The boatswain's retort serves as a reminder of his own intrinsic human worth, "None that I love more than myself" (1.1.20).

While there is a difference in degree, the time and labor of human and nonhuman beings helps to frame their mutual suffering as well as their relationship to futurity. Topsell, for instance, connects the subordination of animals with that of human servants. He again refers to Bernard in criticizing those who compel service on the Sabbath "as if there were none that had any soule but those that are called the rulers of families," imploring these people to "search ... in the harts of your servants, that you may bring soules into the kingdom of heaven.[47] In framing the responsibility of the patriarch as saving the souls of his inferiors, Topsell also provides a means of justification for their servitude. When applied to the paradigm of apian labor, those in power over less than human beings squeeze greater productivity out of their workers with the promise of the immortality of the soul. As Marx puts it when he criticizes how the Christian reward of heaven incentivizes relentless service,

> Do you not claim your reasonable right in this world, do you not complain at the smallest increase in taxes, are you not beside yourself at the slightest infringement of your personal liberty? But you have been told that present suffering is nothing compared with future glory, that suffering in patience and bliss in hope are the cardinal virtues.[48]

When Ariel steals away leisure time, it is an act of resistance against the expectations of the patriarch. Yet leisure time is not a practice that would be encouraged for human laborers, as it was considered a luxury exclusively intended for the elite.[49] Prospero calls the sprite's song of transgression "dainty," presumably because the stolen time is at night when the master does not demand productivity from his worker. Ariel's magical exceptionalism signals his privileged status in the economy of beings. When Prospero finally frees Ariel in his last words before the epilogue—"Be free and fare thou well!"—he offers a way out that neither the bee nor those non-magical beings who serve (Caliban, the boatswain, Stephano, or Trinculo) would be granted (5.1.319).

What if there is no future reward, but only the option—like that of the bee—to work until death? When Caliban curses Prospero and Miranda, Prospero threatens him with apian pain: "thou shalt be pinched / As thick as honeycomb, each pinch more stinging / Than bees that made 'em." (1.2.329–31). One act later, Caliban is still contemplating this threat, reflecting on the ways that Prospero's magical spirits are beholden to his will, "they'll nor pinch me ... unless he bid 'em," (2.2.4–7). Indeed, he recognizes some kinship with these spirits, including Ariel, telling Stephano, "They all do hate [Prospero] as rootedly as I" (3.2.94–95). Unlike these spirits, however, Caliban has no true hope of leisure, and thus no distinct promise of futurity. He often reverts, instead, to memories about the island before Prospero's arrival: "This island's mine by Sycorax, my mother, which thou tak'st from me" (1.2.332–33). His role in the play provides an interesting case in relation to the boundary between the human and the nonhuman. As Werth suggests, Caliban's status defies stable categorization: "Prospero's language grudgingly acknowledges ... Caliban to be of 'human shape.' Yet his word choice retracts that human honor even as it concedes it: calling Caliban a 'whelp' from a 'litter' animalizes him."[50]

Caliban's own words offer some insight into his experience as a suffering worker deprived of potential salvation. His speech about pursuing pleasure comes when Stephano promises to kill Prospero: "I am full of pleasure. Let us be jocund. Will you troll the catch you taught me?" (3.2.116–18). Like Ariel, Caliban turns to a song as an escape from his current servitude and suffering. Perhaps part of his relish in the ballad is in the liberating theme of the lyrics, "Flout 'em and scout 'em. / ... Thought is free" (3.2.121–23). Nevertheless, Caliban soon awaits punishment for the plot against Prospero's life, worrying, "I shall be pinched to death" (5.1.276). Certainly, Caliban's ultimate fate following the play is much more ambiguous than Ariel's, as Prospero admits, "this thing of darkness I / acknowledge mine" without offering a final judgment upon him (5.1.275–76).[51] Bee time, for the less-than-human Caliban does not signal a Topsellian immortal salvation; rather bees themselves and the pinch of their stings remain an ever-present threat of physical suffering at the hands of his human master. Ariel's song of time and labor underscores the intrinsic worth of animate life while foreclosing the possibility of human and privileged status for workers. It is not enough to serve a utility, for the promised time for leisure and pursuing pleasures may never come.

Notes

1 See Thomas D. Seeley, *Honeybee Democracy* (Princeton, NJ: Princeton University Press, 2010).
2 Friedrich Nietzsche, *Untimely Meditations*, ed. Daniel Breazeale, trans. R.J. Hollingdale (Cambridge: Cambridge University Press, 1997, rpt. 2004), 60.
3 Nietzsche, *Untimely Meditations*, 61.
4 Michael Pollan, *The Botany of Desire: A Plant's-Eye View of the World* (New York: Random House, 2001), 69.
5 See Jonathan Gil Harris's study time and material culture, *Untimely Matter in the Time of Shakespeare* (Philadelphia: University of Pennsylvania Press, 2008).
6 For a discussion of how timekeeping and timepieces are related to labor, secularism, and the economy, see Michael J. Sauter, "Clockwatchers and Stargazers: Time Discipline in Early Modern Berlin," *The American Historical Review* 112, no. 3 (2007): 685–709.
7 Charles Richardson, *The Repentance of Peter and Judas Together with the Frailtie of the Faithfull, and the Fearfull Ende of Wicked Hypocrites* (London, 1612), 267.
8 John Milton, *Complete Poems and Major Prose*, ed. Merritt Y. Hughes (Indianapolis, IN: Hackett Publishing, rpt. 2003), 776–80.
9 For a discussion of this simile, see Nicole A. Jacobs, "John Milton's Beehive, from Polemic to Epic," *Studies in Philology* 112, no. 4 (2015): 798–816.
10 Karen Raber, *Animal Bodies, Renaissance Culture* (Philadelphia: University Pennsylvania Press, 2013), 131. See also Margo DeMello, *Animals and Society: An Introduction to Human-Animal Studies* (New York: Columbia University Press, 2012), especially 256–80.
11 See Thomas D. Seeley, "The Honeybee Colony as a Superorganism," *American Scientist* 77, no. 6 (November, 1989): 546–53.
12 See Melissa Bateson et al., "Agitated Honeybees Exhibit Pessimistic Cognitive Biases," *Current Biology* 12 (June, 2011): 1070–73.
13 Charles Butler, *The Feminine Monarchie* (London, 1609), B6v.
14 See Laurie Shannon, *The Accommodated Animal: Cosmopolity in Shakespearean Locales* (Chicago, IL: University of Chicago Press, 2013). See also Shannon, "'Poore Wretch, Laid All Naked upon the Bare Earth': Human Negative Exceptionalism among the Humanists," Afterword to *Shakespearean International Yearbook 15: Shakespeare and the Human*, ed. Tiffany Werth (Farnham: Ashgate Publishing, 2015), 205–10.
15 See Cristopher Hollingsworth, *Poetics of the Hive: The Insect Metaphor in Literature* (Iowa City: University of Iowa Press, 2001).
16 Ayesha Ramachandran and Melissa E. Sanchez, "Introduction to *Spenser and the Human*," *Spenser Studies: A Renaissance Poetry Annual* 30 (2015): ix.
17 Joseph Campana, "Humans: Exceptional Humans, Human Exceptionalism, and the Shape of Things to Come," in *Shakespearean International Yearbook 15: Shakespeare and the Human*, ed. Tiffany Jo Werth (Farnham: Ashgate Publishing, 2015), 50.
18 Paul Waldau, *Animal Studies: An Introduction* (Oxford: Oxford University Press, 2013), 214.
19 *The Aberdeen Bestiary*, Special Collections, University of Aberdeen, 64r. www.abdn.ac.uk/bestiary/ (accessed October 10, 2017).
20 St. Anthony of Padua, *Medieval Preachers and Medieval Preaching*, ed. and trans. J.M. Neale (London: J & C Mozley, 1856), 244.
21 Bernard of Clairvaux, *Saint Bernard, His Meditations, or Sighes, Sobbes, and Teares upon Our Saviors Passion*, trans. W.P. (London, 1611), 386.
22 Bernard of Clairvaux, *The Sentences*, trans. Francis R. Swietek (Kalamazoo, MI: Cistercian Publications, 2000), 209–10.
23 Bernard, *The Sentences*, 210.
24 Bernard, *Saint Bernard, His Meditations*, 143.
25 James Cotter Morison, *The Life and Times of Saint Bernard, Abbot of Clairvaux* (New York: Macmillan, 1889), 20.

26 Qtd. in Morison, *The Life and Times of Saint Bernard*, 181.

27 Deep ecologists take a biocentric view that all life, including nonhuman, has a value to the overall system. The idea of "radical ecology" emphasizes "a new consciousness of our responsibilities to the rest of nature and to other humans"; Carolyn Merchant, *Radical Ecology: The Search for a Livable World* (New York: Routledge, 1992), 1.

28 Pope Francis, *Laudato Si': On Care for Our Common Home* (Huntington, IN: Our Sunday Visitor, 2015), 22.

29 Robert N. Watson, *The Green and the Real in the Late Renaissance* (Philadelphia: University Pennsylvania Press, 2006), see especially 36.

30 See Franz Posset, "Bernard of Clairvaux as Luther's Source," *Concordia Theological Quarterly* 54 (1990): 281–304.

31 Philips van Marnix van Saint Aldegonde, *The Beehive of the Romish Church*, trans. George Gilpin (London, 1579), 20.

32 See John Panke, *Collectanea, Out of St. Gregory the Great, and St Bernard the Devout against the Papists Who Adhere to the Doctrine of the Present Church of Rome* (Oxford, 1618) and Antonie Batt, *A Hive of Sacred Honiecombes Containing Most Sweet and Heavenly Counsel* (Oxford, 1631).

33 Although we now understand the male drone is responsible for mating with the queen and thus ensuring the future survival of the hive, early modern theorists tended to view him as a lazy degenerate who sought to exploit the labor of others.

34 Edward Topsell, *Times Lamentation: Or an Exposition on the Prophet Joel* (London, 1599), A2, 308.

35 Topsell, *Times Lamentation*, 66.

36 Ibid., 194.

37 Henry Holland and Edward Topsell, *The Historie of Adam, or the Foure-fold State of Man* (London, 1606), 167v.

38 Edward Topsell, *Historie of Serpents* (London, 1608), 73.

39 Edward Topsell, *The Reward of Religion Delivered in Sundrie Lectures upon the Booke of Ruth* (London, 1596), 298.

40 Topsell, *The Reward of Religion*, 299.

41 For a discussion of Shakespeare's use of honey in relation to human virtue, see Nicole A. Jacobs, "Bees: The Shakespearean Hive and the Virtues of Honey," in *Shakespearean International Yearbook 15: Shakespeare and the Human*, ed. Tiffany Jo Werth (Farnham: Ashgate Publishing, 2015),101–21.

42 Tiffany Jo Werth, introduction to *Shakespeare and the Human*, 2.

43 Steven Mentz, "Airy Spirits: Winds, Bodies, and Ecological Force in Early Modern England," in *Shakespearean International Yearbook 15: Shakespeare and the Human*, Tiffany Jo Werth (Farnham: Ashgate Publishing, 2015), 34.

44 Quotations from *The Tempest* will be cited in-text from William Shakespeare, *The Tempest*, eds. Virginia Mason Vaughan and Alden T. Vaughan (London: Arden, 1999).

45 The music for this song can be found in Folger MS V.a.411 11v.

46 Jennifer Linhart Wood, personal communication, July 27, 2018. For a discussion of some of Ariel's other songs in *The Tempest*, see Jennifer Linhart Wood's "Sounding Spaces: *The Tempest's* Uncanny Near-East Echoes," *Shakespeare Studies* 44 (2016): 173–79.

47 Topsell, *Times Lamentation*, 38.

48 Karl Marx, "Religion, Free Press, and Philosophy," *Writings of the Young Karl Marx on Philosophy and Society*, trans. Loyd D. Easton and Kurt H. Guddat (New York: Doubleday, 1967), 126.

49 As William James Booth notes, "Free time was the precondition of friendship, of citizenship in the better polities, and of the pursuit of the good life, and it was one of the philosophical boundary lines separating the free from the unfree"; William James Booth, "Economies of Time: On the Idea of Time in Marx's Political Economy," *Political Theory* 19 (1991): 7–8.

50 Werth, *Shakespeare and the Human*, 2.

51 See Kim F. Hall, *Things of Darkness: Economies of Race and Gender in Early Modern England* (Ithaca, NY: Cornell University Press, 1995). See also Ania Loomba, *Shakespeare, Race, and Colonialism* (Oxford: Oxford University Press, 2002).

12

WHAT DOES THE WOLF SAY?

Animal Language and Political Noise in *Coriolanus*

Liza Blake and Kathryn Vomero Santos

I Wolvish Tongues and Fabulous Wolves

As Coriolanus stands in the marketplace displaying his wounds and asking for the votes of the citizens, he asks, in most modern editions: "Why in this *wolvish toge* should I stand here / To beg of Hob and Dick that does appear / Their needless vouches?" (2.3.113–15; emphasis added).[1] In the 1623 Folio, however, the question reads rather differently: "Why in this *Wooluish tongue* should I stand heere, / To begge of Hob and Dicke, that does appeere / Their needlesse Vouches" (emphasis added).[2] This chapter will scrutinize the editorial tradition of emending Coriolanus's wolvish tongue (wolvish or deceptive speech) to a wolvish toge (a wolvish garment or outfit) as a means of thinking through the larger questions about animals and animal language in the play. Why are editors so resistant to the idea that Coriolanus might speak in a "wolvish tongue"—to the idea of speaking animals—in a play that so frequently draws on the rich and various fable tradition of the early modern period? What might it mean to hear Coriolanus speak in the tongue of a wolf?

Many editors take their cue to emend Coriolanus's wolvish tongue from the 1632 Second Folio, which reads "gowne" instead of "tongue";[3] they argue that the First Folio's "tongue" must be a compositor's misreading of "toge," a Roman garment.[4] In most cases, these editors further justify "gown" or "toge" by drawing on multiple references to Coriolanus's "gown of humility" (2.3.39), "humble weed" (2.3.218), and "garments" (2.3.144) throughout the scene. However, changing the phrase to "wolvish toge" then raises questions about what exactly a "wolvish" gown might be, prompting several editors to think of the fable of the wolf in sheep's clothing (in which a wolf puts on a sheep's skin to fool the shepherds). The problem then becomes that the wolf in the fable is not wearing a wolvish garment, but a sheepish one, and so pre-twentieth-century editors who read the phrase as a reference to the fable also tended to change "Wooluish" to "woolen," "woolish," or "woolyish."[5] Once Coriolanus is imagined to be in a woolen (sheepish) gown, he is also imagined as weak, and so on the extreme end of this emending tradition is the *Oxford Shakespeare*'s "womanish toge," which the editors attribute to the "manly" Coriolanus contemplating and then denouncing his own submissiveness.[6] The most recent *New Oxford Shakespeare* (2016) emends the phrase to "woolish toge," returning to the nineteenth-century version of the phrase, but still glossing it as a "meek outfit."[7] Almost no editors allow "wolvish tongue" to stand.[8]

This chain of associations—where an emendation to a wolvish garment leads to a fable, which leads to another emendation to better cite that fable, which in one case leads to a gendering of submissive clothing—all hinges on a fundamental misreading of the fable of the wolf in sheep's clothing. This fable is about the distinction between wolvish interior and sheepish exterior; as one 1585 fable collection puts it, "[t]his fable sheweth, that men are not to be judged by their apparel, but by their works. For many under sheep's clothings do wolfish works."[9] For Coriolanus to be in wolvish toge makes no sense here: the wolvishness is not in the clothing, but in the deeds. The manufacture of this crux—the refusal to recognize even the possibility of Coriolanus's wolvish language—removes the connections to ideas of animal language and animal voice that permeate the play, as well as the more explicit connections to the larger world of fables (and the animals who speak in them). If we allowed Coriolanus to speak in wolvish tongue, what would we hear?

This line, we wish to argue, gestures to fables not because of wolvish or sheepish clothing, but precisely because of Coriolanus's wolvish tongue or language. Both the play and the early modern animal fables on which it draws use speaking animals as a way of thinking about sovereign forms of power, and non-sovereign forces that may exist alongside, or in contradistinction to, that power. It conceptualizes that power by thinking about the role of *voice* in the concept of the body politic that governs the play. Is the voice that issues from this body politic a human voice speaking language, or is it reducible to mere (animal) noise? Does noise have power? Just how human is the body politic in Shakespeare's play? Our essay's subtitle follows *Coriolanus* in decoupling language from politics, animality from noise—something the play accomplishes by engaging the robust tradition of speaking animals in Aesopian fables.

There is little doubt that Shakespeare would have been familiar with animal fables, either as a collection of stories to be read or as a set of ideas circulating throughout early modern literary culture. However, locating an exact source of any given Aesopian fable that Shakespeare might be referencing is a difficult task. Aesop is unique among classical authors in that his corpus is distributed and uncertain; there were many families of fables, all going loosely under his name, circulating during Shakespeare's lifetime.[10] If Shakespeare encountered Aesop's fables in English, he almost certainly would have read them in William Caxton's translation, a set of 161 fables with Aesop's biography, which was first published in 1484 and reprinted seven times by six different printers before the end of the sixteenth century. Other fables published in English before Shakespeare's death include Robert Henryson's Middle Scots expanded poetic translations of 13 fables (printed in Scotland in 1570 and 1571, and in London in 1577 in an English "translation" by Richard Smith); William Bullokar's orthographic translations printed in 1585; and Simon Sturtevant's 1602 translation of the 45 short Latin fables typically taught in schoolrooms.[11] Fables circulated in other texts as well; for instance, Peter Holland speculates that a possible source for Menenius's famous fable of the belly and members may be Thomas North's 1570 translation of Indian fables.[12]

If Coriolanus's wolvish tongue is indeed a reference to the speaking wolves of early modern animal fables, what is it meant to communicate? The wolf is a common character in early modern fables, serving a variety of purposes. The wolf sometimes sets himself above or outside the law, a claim made about Coriolanus by Sicinius in 3.1.269–70: "He hath resisted law, / And therefore law shall scorn him further trial." The wolf is often depicted as a less subtle fox, with all the malice and violence but none of the cleverness.[13] The wolf is also frequently the subject of many fables whose moral is that "no one ought to avaunt him to do a thing which he cannot do," "that everyone [should] exercise that art that he knoweth."[14] Fabulous wolves are especially known for lying. In the fable of the wolf and crane, for instance, the wolf asks the crane to help remove a bone from his throat, promising a reward for doing so; afterward the wolf reneges on the reward, saying the crane is lucky not to have been eaten while helping him. "And thus it appiereth by the fable," Caxton's translation moralizes, "how no prouffite cometh of ony good whiche is done to the euyls."[15] The wolf, in the world of the fables, is one who is known to be "customed to doo ony frawde or falshede," and who therefore "shall euer lyue ryght heuyly [heavily] and in suspycion."[16] The wolvish tongue lies, and lies out of malice, breaking legally binding agreements.

Take, for example, Caxton's fable of the sheep, the wolf, and the dogs. In this fable, the sheep, overcome by the wolves, recruit the dogs to help defend them. The dogs turn the wolves away, so the wolves send an ambassador, asking as a sign of peace that the sheep send the dogs to live with them. The sheep assent, and the wolves slaughter the dogs, and then the sheep. Caxton's translation, as with all his fables, gives the clear moral: "Whanne men haue a good hede / and a good defensour ... men oughte not to leue hym."[17] Even the prospect of peace with the wolves should not have persuaded the sheep to give up the one thing keeping the wolves from the door. Coriolanus perhaps references this precise fable when he taunts the plebeians and tribunes following his exile: "Have the power still," he sneers at them, "To banish your defenders" (3.3.126–27).

This fable also appears with different framing and a slightly different moral in the vita or biography of Aesop, a long story of his life with several embedded fables, which appears at the start of Caxton's collection (and its later reprints). In this episode, a king (Croesus) has declared war on the "Samyens" (Samians, inhabitants of the Greek island Samos), among whom Aesop is living. The king, advised that Aesop's counsel will help the Samians win, offers peace on the condition that they send Aesop to him. Having heard the request, Aesop says to the Samians, "my lordes It pleaseth me wel to go toward the kyng But er I go thyder I wyl telle you a fable."[18] His fable begins as follows: "In a tyme whan the bestes coude speke the wolues made werre ageynst the shepe."[19] Having heard the fable, the Samians correctly infer the moral: "Whanne Esope hadde reherced this fable / the Samyens determyned in them self that Esope shold not go toward the kyng."[20]

In the context of the vita, this fable does more than advise people to trust in their protectors, and beware against liars—it is also a commentary on the political efficacy of fables themselves. Aesop could have advised the Samians not to send him away, but instead the fable gets it done by communicating the political and strategic message via animal action. Embedding this and other fables in the vita gestures to their efficacy, to the fact that, as Annabel Patterson argues in her *Fables of Power*, the early modern fable was "a medium of political analysis and communication."[21] That much is fairly uncontroversial, as far as animal fables go.

But what difference does it make that the fable begins with an imagination of a historical time when animals had language: "In a tyme whan the bestes coude speke"? The claim potentially punctures the quasi-allegory of the fable as a genre: the animals, this beginning suggests, are not invented figures standing in for people, or types of people (wolves equal lying men), but instead exist in a historical past.[22] What was the event, the animal equivalent of the Tower of Babel hinted at in this opening, that removed speech from beasts? Language, in this case, also elevates and politicizes the violence of the fable. The wolves killing the sheep is not mere hunting, or slaughter, but *war*, politically motivated and manipulatable; the wolves triumph not by raw violence but by persuasion. It is not power (the ability of the wolves to violently overwhelm the sheep) but language (the power to persuade the sheep to give up the dogs in the name of peace) that is at stake in the action of this fable. In the time when beasts could speak, physical violence was translated into political war.

152

What Does the Wolf Say?

II Animal Languages and Political Voices

When Young Cuddy Banks discovers Tommy the Dog's ability to speak English in *The Witch of Edmonton* (1621), he quickly concludes that the dog has read tales from a time when beasts could speak:

YOUNG BANKS: How now! Who's that speaks? I hope you have not your reading tongue about you.

DOG: Yes, I can speak.

YOUNG BANKS: The devil you can! You have read Aesop's fables, then. I have played one of your parts then, the dog that catched at the shadow in the water.[23]

(3.1.107–12)

Finding a dog capable of speech, Cuddie assumes that the dog has used his "reading tongue" to read stories about fellow canines found in Aesop's fables, specifically the tale of the dog who loses the meat he was already carrying in his mouth as he attempts to steal the meat from the "other" dog he sees reflected in the water. More importantly for our purposes, though, Cuddie also connects the dog's ability to talk to one of the defining features of fables: animal speech. Has the dog read Aesop's fables because he has language, or have Aesop's fables— fables in which animals speak to one another and to humans—given him the ability to speak?

Language is the thing that, according to most modern scientists, divides human from nonhuman animals,[24] and this belief circulated in the early modern period as well. Edward Topsell's *The History of Four-footed Beasts* (1607) describes an experiment in which a group of people catch a satyr and tame him. This taming includes teaching the satyr "to speake some wordes, but with a voice like a Goat, and without all reason."[25] Even though the satyr can parrot human sounds, his words, without reason, do not qualify as language. The story reinforces a generally accepted truth: that animals may be able to replicate sounds, but are unable to genuinely have (a) language.

However, several things complicate the simplicity of this seemingly certain truth. For instance, Topsell notes elsewhere that while cats may not be able to speak, they are certainly able to communicate with humans. This is so obvious, writes Topsell, that it is hardly worth detailing

> how she [the cat] whurleth with her voyce, hauing as many tunes as turnes, for she hath one voice to beg and to complain, another to testifie her delight & pleasure, another among hir own kind by flattring, by hissing, by puffing, by spitting, insomuch as some haue thought that they haue a particular intelligible language among themselues.[26]

The speculation that nonhuman animals may have their own languages, not accessible by humans, appears in multiple early modern texts, from William Baldwin's *Beware the Cat* (1584), where the protagonist mixes a magical potion that lets him understand feline language, to Michel de Montaigne's essay "Apology for Raymond Sebond" (French publication 1580, English translation 1603), in which he says,

> It is a matter of divination to guesse in whom the fault is, that we [human and nonhuman animals] vnderstand not one another. For, we understand them no more then they vs. By the same reason, may they as well esteeme vs beasts, as we them.[27]

Such recurring speculations on animal language find their most concentrated expression in the early modern beast fable, a genre in which animals use language to have conversations, attack one another, and even take one another to court. And yet the fable has been surprisingly neglected in thinking about animal language in the early modern period, perhaps because the animals in animal fables are often read allegorically: a fox is not really a fox, but a representation of a clever person.[28] But fabulists often puncture or complicate that simple allegorical equation, representing their fabulous animals not merely as humans in animal clothing, but as animals, potentially possessing animal language.

Consider, for example, John Ogilby's version of the Aesopian fable "Of the Dog and the Thief," first published in his *Fables of Aesop* in 1651. In the fable, a thief attempts to bribe a dog with bread, but the dog refuses the bribe and scares the thief off by barking—in Ogilby's version, after giving the thief a long speech about his reputation for loyalty. Although man and dog speak to one another, it is not clear if they are speaking the same language. The fable begins:

> '*Bow-wow*, Who's there? *Bow-wow*, Who's that dares break
> Into my master's house? First stand, then speak,
> Or else I'll have you by the throat—ne'er start!—
> You sir, I'll know your business ere we part.'
> Thus in the Cynic language, loud and brief,
> A true dog barked, discov'ring a false thief.[29]

In some editions of Ogilby's text, the whole first line is in blackletter; in others, only the "*Bow-wow*" is in blackletter, a typeface rarely used in Ogilby's collection of 81 Aesopian fables.[30]

The shift in typography corresponds to an equally rare instance of Ogilby recording animal speech in its animal form—as animal sounds—rather than as something already translated into English. The play of this opening is in the uncertainty of the status of animal language in the first line: is the dog alternating between barking and speaking, or is the English "Who's there?" a translation of the animal sound "*Bow-wow*"? Does the animal sound hide an animal language, untranslatable except in fables? Is there a claim here, that most fables may be dubbed, with animals speaking in their own languages, but translated for the ease of human readers?

Lines 5–6 only complicate the question; the "true dog," we are told, addresses the thief "in the Cynic language, loud and brief." The adjectives "loud and brief" are indeed qualities that would describe a dog's bark, which he uses to discover, or reveal, the presence of the thief to the rest of the house. This barking makes him a "true dog," who in true dog fashion barks and is thereby true, or faithful, to his master. However, we are also told that, in addition to barking, he speaks in "Cynic language." The dog is indeed a cynic in the fable, someone who is "disposed to rail or find fault, or one who shows a disposition to disbelieve in the sincerity or goodness of human motives ... a sneering fault-finder,"[31] but calling his language "Cynic" also activates the canine pun latent in the ancient Greek philosophical

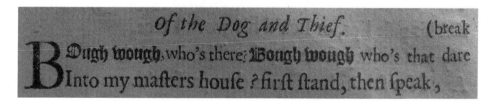

Figure 12.1 John Ogilby, *The Fables of Aesop* (London, 1651), sig. I3r. Call #: 168-220q. Photograph by Liza Blake, from the collections of the Folger Shakespeare Library

system of Cynicism, named because Diogenes the Cynic, in his sneering scorn, was like a κύνικος [*kynikos*] or little dog. Is the dog's language sneering, or is he speaking in doggish tongue? The joke of the dog's Cynic language, told with typography and Ancient Greek puns, is also partly about the inability to distinguish, in this fable, among animal sounds, animal voice, and animal language.[32] The fable suggests, then, that perhaps all animal fables are indeed dubbed, giving silent human translations for animal voices. In the process, it also thinks about the status of the human voice: is a human voice the same as human language, or is it mere sound?

Coriolanus also worries the boundary between animal sounds and human language, but in Shakespeare's play, the stakes are political:

CORIOLANUS: Here come more voices.
        Your voices? For your voices I have fought;
        Watched for your voices; for your voices bear
        Of wounds two dozen odd; battles thrice six
        I have seen and heard of; for your voices
        Have done many things, some less, some more.
        Your voices? Indeed I would be consul.

(2.3.123–29)

In this speech, ten lines after his remark about his wolvish tongue, Coriolanus begs for the voices of the plebeians, whom he has up to this point called rats (1.1.244), hares (1.1.166), geese (1.1.167; 1.4.35), curs or dogs (1.1.163; 1.1.201), and less than apes (1.4.36–37).[33] In wolvish tongue, he begs for animal voices "to voice him consul" (2.3.231). While most readers quite rightly interpret Coriolanus's animal references as insults directed at the plebeians, it is also worth considering what they suggest about the relationship between multiple and singular voices, between the voice of the military leader turned politician and the voices of the people who have the power to confirm or deny his appointment. Coriolanus compares the plebeians to beasts who often travel in packs (rats and dogs) and flocks (geese), and those who reproduce rapidly (hares). The play reinforces the idea that the plebeians are an animal collective by comparing them several times to a herd, a metaphor that makes the tribunes, by extension, the "herdsmen of the beastly plebeians" (2.1.92).

The collective nature of the "beastly plebeians" is perhaps the reason why the play puts so much emphasis not on their language but on their voices. Coriolanus notes that the plebeians give away their *language* in lending their *voices* to the tribunes: "Are these your herd? / Must these have voices, that can yield them now / And straight disclaim their tongues?" (3.1.34–36). The potential for the herd to speak causes Coriolanus to fret nervously about the power of these voices to overpower human language. When Brutus and Sicinius begin to persuade the plebeians to have second thoughts about giving their "[m]ost sweet voices" (2.3.110) to Coriolanus, the proliferating potential of the masses becomes even more apparent:

3 CITIZEN: He's not confirmed; we may deny him yet.
2 CITIZEN: And will deny him!
        I'll have five hundred voices of that sound.
1 CITIZEN: I twice five hundred, and their friends to piece 'em.
BRUTUS: Get you hence instantly, and tell those friends
        They have chose a consul that will from them take
        Their liberties, make them of no more voice

Than dogs that are as often beat for barking
As therefore kept to do so.

(2.3.206–14)

As the citizens promise to gather and exponentially expand their network of voices, they emphasize the shared "sound" of the voices (rather than any linguistic content) as the marker of power and influence. Brutus's encouraging advice, even as it warns against Coriolanus's lack of respect for them, also reduces their voices to mere sound.[34] His response seems to recall the fable of the dog and the thief, but imagines a version in which the very same master who keeps the dog so that it will bark when it is convenient to him (i.e., in the presence of an intruder) also beats the dog for sounding its voice in scenarios that might not match the desires or comforts of the human. The sounds of the plebeians, Brutus would like to suggest, require his translation.

The plebeians' collectivity and their reduction to mere non-linguistic voices becomes crystallized in one of the play's most common terms for them: "rabble." The word "rabble," used to describe the plebeian mob five times, serves not just to label "a disorderly, disorganized, or unruly crowd" or "boistrous throng of people."[35] It also draws an explicit connection between their status as a "group, pack or swarm (of animals)" and producers of "rambling, disjointed discourse or speech."[36] Coriolanus indulges in this connection between the uncontrollable proliferation of the animal mob and its unintelligible sounds when he calls them "barbarians" who reproduce like pigs and cows:

CORIOLANUS: I would they were barbarians, as they are,
        Though in Rome littered; not Romans, as they are not,
        Though calved i'th' porch o'th' Capitol.

(3.1.239–41)

His choice of words casts these Roman citizens as outsiders despite their having been born in Rome, linking the potentially meaningless sounds of their voices (as "barbarians," they would be associated only with unintelligible sounds) and their apparent lack of humanity. He sees them not just as non-Roman but also as nonhuman, and pre-linguistic.

Surprisingly, the reduction of the plebeians to mere noisy, meaningless rabble connects them most closely not to the tribunes, but to Coriolanus. A famous exchange between the tribunes and Menenius draws on the language and lessons of animal fables in order to translate both Coriolanus and the plebeians into mere animals:

MENENIUS: ... [T]he people ... love not Martius.
SICINIUS: Nature teaches beasts to know their friends.
MENENIUS: Pray you, who does the wolf love?
SICINIUS: The lamb.
MENENIUS: Ay, to devour him, as the hungry plebeians would the noble Martius.
BRUTUS: He's a lamb indeed that baas like a bear.
MENENIUS: He's a bear indeed that lives like a lamb.

(2.1.4–12)

Menenius and the tribunes fight a war of words to wrest control over the fable that Menenius is implicitly beginning with his rhetorical question, "Who does the wolf love?" Sicinius emphasizes the wolf's violence (his love of the lamb), and Menenius accepts the violence but changes the allegory, casting Coriolanus as the lamb.[37] Here the debate is about which of the two animal forces, the plebeians or Coriolanus, is more destructive. But the form of the debate redraws the political lines. The play starts out with, and this exchange is a further example of, an attempt to divide Rome into two positions on who should hold sovereign power: on the one hand, the tribunes and people, who think that sovereignty should reside, at least in part, in the people; and on the other hand, Menenius and the patricians, who believe in a more tightly controlled, consolidated sovereignty. But the wordplay, the linguistic manipulation on display in this exchange, also sets Menenius and the tribunes apart both from the rabble and from Coriolanus himself. This passage distinguishes the tribunes from the "voices" they represent. While the rabble can offer up its voices, the tribunes are shrewd political and linguistic manipulators, "The tongues o'th' common mouth," as Coriolanus calls them (3.1.22). "You being their mouths," Coriolanus asks the tribunes, "why rule you not their teeth?" (3.1.37). The rabble have the voice—they have the bark and the bite—but the tribunes control how and whether that voice can become political speech.[38]

The central dividing line of the play, in fact, is not between two understandings of sovereignty (people-power, or patrician-power), but between sovereignty (political manipulation), and non-sovereign, nonhuman, collective animal forces. The plebeians are not the only animals in the play: Coriolanus is also imagined as a kind of stateless animal of prey. While in exile Coriolanus speaks of himself as a "lonely dragon" (4.1.30), and earlier Sicinius calls him a "viper, / That would depopulate the city, and / Be every man himself" (3.1.265–67), a vicious animal that could destroy the life of an entire city. Though Coriolanus is more frequently compared to individual animals than he is to swarms and herds (as are the plebeians), Sicinius's insult reads a kind of parallel collectivity into Coriolanus: his force is such that he would "[b]e every man himself," transforming his body into an entire body politic.[39] But James Kuzner has pointed out that the image of Coriolanus as a lonely dragon is not so lonely after all: "The play figures both Coriolanus and the Roman people as wingless and as winged, and it confuses the meaning that Romans would like to attach to those categories."[40] The collapse of both Coriolanus and the plebeians into animals, in Kuzner's reading, shows the danger of a nascent sovereignty: "There is no telling between friend and foe, human and inhuman, in a state of exception."[41] The play, he argues, "displays no investment in the state of law."[42]

We agree that the play is not invested in defining ideal modes of sovereignty; in fact, we wish to argue that the political thought experiment of the play resides in the exploration of how Coriolanus and the plebeians—who stand in for or embody raw, nonhuman animal force—undermine ideas of sovereign power (whether republican or oligarchical). The problem of the play, the wheels that grind the tragic plot, is that it establishes Coriolanus as a non-sovereign force but then forces him to attempt to integrate into sovereign modes of power. As long as Coriolanus is the instrument of the body politic, his martial prowess keeps enemies at bay. He is the sword of the state, a function he openly acknowledges when he asks, "Make you a sword of me?" (1.6.76). However, the play does not allow him to function only as the sword of state. As a political thought experiment, the play as a whole investigates what the relation of this almost nonhuman animal force, this raw violence, is to sovereignty and the protection of the nation state.

Everyone in the play recognizes that Coriolanus is unable to translate from force to power; as Aufidius puts it, "[It is his] nature, / Not to be other than one thing" (4.7.41–42), and his mother Volumnia complains to him, "You are too absolute" (3.2.40). Volumnia's attempt to get Coriolanus elected involves coaching him in integrating force and political power: "Honour and policy, like unsevered friends, / I'th' war do grow together" (3.2.43–44).

Given his excellent abilities in warcraft, Volumnia argues, Coriolanus should have no problems in politics: just as a thoughtful general must "adopt [his] policy" to the battlefield, so Coriolanus should be able to transfer his abilities at managing war to the political realm (3.2.49). Following this pep talk, Coriolanus imagines politics as force: his soothing flattery will be like the pipes and drums of war, and he promises his mother that smiles will "tent" (encamp) in his cheeks (3.2.117). Coriolanus's encamped smiles do not succeed, however, because the play stages a frequent misalignment between war and politics—force and sovereign rule—in Roman culture. In the ideal version of this culture, there would be no disjunction between these two spheres; military and political prowess *should* line up, which is part of what causes everyone's confusion with Coriolanus's utter failure in the political sphere. Though Coriolanus's rival and later ally Aufidius seems to think he can easily move from one sphere to another (1.10.13–16), the play never allows Coriolanus to do so.

For the plebeians, the problem of the play is not translating martial force into political rule, but translating animal noise and voices into political language. Just as Coriolanus is "not to be other than one thing," the plebeians, though a noisy herd, are imagined as essentially wordless for much of the play. As their volume increases and begins to have an effect on the power structure of Rome, however, Coriolanus imagines a nightmarish scenario in which their unintelligible, barbarian rabble could be recognized as language:

CORIOLANUS: Let deeds express
What's like to be their words: 'We did request it,
We are the greater poll, and in true fear
They gave us our demands.' Thus we debase
The nature of our seats, and make the rabble
Call our cares fears, which will in time
Break ope the locks o'th' Senate and bring in
The crows to peck the eagles.

(3.1.133–40)

Coriolanus worries that by not just acknowledging their sounds, but actually listening to the linguistic content of their demands, the tribunes and senators are allowing the "sweet voices" they courted to erode and even invert the political hierarchy—the pecking order—of Rome. More disturbingly, these lines might suggest not that the plebeians have acquired language, but that even their inarticulate screams can communicate. As a collective, screaming en masse, their cries, even if only inarticulate screams, communicate to anyone listening: "We are the greater poll!"—i.e., We exist, and there are many of us! The tribunes use precisely this noisy power to banish Coriolanus. Plotting before Coriolanus's appearance in the marketplace, Sicinius tells his followers to repeat whatever punishment he decides; Brutus adds, "And when such time they have begun to cry, / Let them not cease but with a din confused / Enforce the present execution" (3.3.19–21). In the marketplace, Coriolanus must beg for the voices or spoken approval of the plebeians; here, Brutus and Sicinius seem to require only the *sound* of their voices—the "din confused" will serve as the means of enforcing their sovereign command. Noisy confusion, devoid of language, is sufficient to effect political change.

Coriolanus famously begins with Menenius's telling of the fable of the belly and the limbs, in which the limbs, upset that the stomach does nothing but eat, stop feeding it, resulting in the death of the whole body. This scene is usually taken as an example of the political effectiveness of fables: reminding the plebeians that they are part of a larger whole, Menenius's fable, his "pretty tale" (1.1.85), calms the riots. However, the fable is powerful not because he reminds them that they are part of a collective, but because he breaks up their collective, and in particular their collective speaking. At the start of the play, the plebeians speak as the "beast / With many heads" (4.1.1–2), in a "multitudinous tongue" (3.1.157).[43] From the very first lines, the plebeians speak in unison, as a collective voice:

1 CITIZEN: Before we proceed any further, hear me speak.
ALL: Speak, speak.

(1.1.1–2)

The speech prefix in the 1623 Folio, "*All*," introduces the plebeians as a group, from which one citizen emerges to speak on their behalf. The rest of the crowd lends their voices in support, either all repeating "speak" individually, or chanting in unison, "speak, speak." As the citizens' rally continues, the crowd's responses become more complex: "All" move from saying things like "We know't. We know't" (1.1.8) to saying, "No more talking on't. Let it be done. Away, away" (1.1.11), and "Against him first. He's a very dog to the commonalty" (1.1.26). Are these fragmented lines, these short sentences, spoken in unison by the crowd, or do different members of the crowd pick one sentence to shout, creating a rabble of sounds? In either case, the group that will later be envisaged as a swarm, or herd, or flock organizes and maintains themselves as a "commonality." But the first scene also shows how difficult it is to maintain a collective: even before Menenius enters the group is already beginning to splinter, the "we" and "us" of the first speeches separating into "I" and "you" pronouns. Menenius's fable of the belly and the members does not bring the masses into one body, but dismembers them, splits off one citizen to turn him into "the great toe of this assembly" (1.1.150). By the end, Menenius can rightly dismiss the crowd with, "Go get you home, you fragments" (1.1.217). The crowd of potentially powerful animal voices has been split up and turned into domesticated, individuated political subjects.[44]

What, then, does it mean to allow Coriolanus to stand in the marketplace, begging the herd of plebeians for their voices "in wolvish tongue"? As we have argued in this chapter, acknowledging and preserving Coriolanus's wolvish tongue allows for a new reading of the politics of *Coriolanus*. As Stanley Cavell has argued, "A political reading is apt to become fairly predictable once you know whose side the reader is taking, that of the patricians or that of the plebeians."[45] However, if the battle lines are redrawn according to the play's discourses of animality and animal language, inherited largely from the tradition of fables and their political contexts, one begins to perceive the two "sides" of the play in different terms. The great factions in this play become not the patricians and the plebeians, but inarticulate animal force and sovereign power.

The ever-increasing "rabble" of plebeians represent the herd that threatens to outnumber and forcibly subsume the holders of sovereign power. Though singular, Coriolanus's natural sovereignty, as defined by Aufidius, similarly threatens to destroy political sovereignty and replace it with raw force: "I think he'll be to Rome / As is the osprey to the fish, who takes it / By sovereignty of nature" (4.7.33–35). As he stands in the marketplace, Coriolanus is not worried about looking weak or womanish; he is worried about *articulation*, and about what it means for him to attempt to become and speak as though he could be something else. Coriolanus recognizes very early in the play that to speak "in wolvish tongue" is to speak as a strong, greedy, hungry animal whose inarticulate voice may not be capable of political language. By admitting that he "cannot bring / [his] tongue to such a pace," Coriolanus perhaps warns his audiences that animal force, and animal voices, cannot ever be fully subsumed into sovereign power (2.3.49–50).

Notes

1 Unless otherwise noted, all references to the play are to William Shakespeare, *Coriolanus*, ed. Peter Holland (London: Bloomsbury Arden Shakespeare, 2013). We give in-text citations to this edition of the play throughout this chapter.

2 William Shakespeare, *The Tragedy of Coriolanus* (London, 1623), 12–13, accessed in *The Bodleian First Folio: Digital Facsimile of the First Folio of Shakespeare's Plays*, Bodleian Arch. G c.7. http://first-folio.bodleian.ox.ac.uk/.

3 William Shakespeare, *The Tragedy of Coriolanus* (London, 1632), 41–42, accessed in *Internet Shakespeare Editions*, University of Victoria, last updated February 3, 2011. http://internetshakespeare.uvic.ca/Library/facsimile/book/SLNSW_F2/.

4 See, e.g., G.B. Harrison, ed., *The Tragedy of Coriolanus* (Harmondsworth: Penguin Books, 1955), 153: "The Folio prints 'tongue', the printer having taken 'toge' in the copy for 'tōge'." Unless otherwise noted, for all variants described in this paragraph see *A New Variorum Edition of Shakespeare: The Tragedy of Coriolanus*, ed. Horace Howard Furness, Jr. (Philadelphia, PA: J.B. Lippincott Company, 1928), 256–64 (hereafter *New Variorum*), and Peter Holland's textual notes in his Arden edition, 2.3.113n (258, 425).

5 The long note on "Wooluish tongue" in the *Coriolanus* variorum (*New Variorum*, 256–64) is an extended debate about whether a "wolvish toge" is a reference to the fable of the wolf in sheep's clothing.

6 *The Oxford Shakespeare: The Complete Works*, eds. Stanley Wells et al., 2nd ed. (Oxford: Oxford University Press, 2005). The textual companion explains, "As well as symbolizing 'Womanish' submission, the toge presumably reminds the manly Coriolanus of a woman's gown" (Stanley Wells and Gary Taylor with John Jowett and William Montgomery, *William Shakespeare: A Textual Companion* [New York: Norton, 1997], 596).

7 *The New Oxford Shakespeare*, eds. Gary Taylor et al. (Oxford: Oxford University Press, 2016), 2.3.95n.

8 The one modern exception is Jonathan Bate and Eric Rasmussen, eds., *Coriolanus* (Basingstoke: Macmillan, 2011); see also Steevens (1773), in *New Variorum*, 256.

9 *Aesops fabl'z in tru ort'ography with grammar-nóts*, trans. William Bullokar (London: Edmund Bollifant, 1585), 187. Because Bullokar's orthography is especially unusual, we have modernized all quotations from his work.

10 For more on fable families circulating during the Renaissance, see Liza Blake and Kathryn Vomero Santos, "Introduction," in *Arthur Golding's A Moral Fabletalk and Other Renaissance Fable Translations*, eds. Liza Blake and Kathryn Vomero Santos (Cambridge: MHRA, 2017), 10–12. See also Liza Blake, "What is an Aesopian Fable? The Case of the Renaissance Catwoman." The Collation. November 8, 2018. https://collation.folger.edu/2018/11/aesopian-fable-catwoman.

11 Both Sturtevant and later John Brinsley indicate that this set of 45 fables was typically taught in grammar schools. For more on Brinsley and fables in grammar schools, see Blake and Santos, "Introduction," 18–22.

12 *The Moral Philosophy of Doni*, trans. Thomas North (London, 1570); see Holland, ed., *Coriolanus*, 1.1.85n. The fable also appears in the life of Coriolanus in North's translation of Plutarch's *Lives* (London, 1579), 240.

13 David Schalkwyk also suggests that Coriolanus represents a powerful animal (a lion rather than a wolf) who fails in his attempt to act and speak like the crafty fox. See David Schalkwyk, "*Coriolanus*: A Tragedy of Language," in *The Oxford Handbook of Shakespearean Tragedy*, eds. Michael Neill and David Schalkwyk (Oxford: Oxford University Press, 2016), 468–86.

14 Caxton, in Blake and Santos, eds., *Fable Translations*, 335; *Aesops fabl'z*, trans. Bullokar, 289. Shakespeare additionally seems to associate the wolf with greed: *King Lear*'s Edgar describes himself as a "hog in sloth, fox in stealth, wolf in greediness" (3.4.85); *Troilus and Cressida* discusses "appetite, an universal wolf" (1.3.120); and the eponymous *Timon of Athens* tells a character, "if thou wert the wolf, thy greediness would afflict thee" (4.3.332–33). References are from *The Norton Shakespeare*, eds. Stephen Greenblatt et al., 3rd ed. (New York: W.W. Norton and Company, 2016).

15 William Caxton, trans., *Here begynneth the book of the subtyl historyes and Fables of Esope* (Westminster: William Caxton, 1484), sig. e3r (hereafter *Fables*). We transcribe Caxton's virgules (a comma-like punctuation) with forward slashes and have silently expanded his yoghs.

16 Caxton, *Fables*, sig. g4r.

17 Ibid., sig. h5v.

18 Ibid., sig. c5r.

19 Ibid., sig. c5v.

20 Ibid., sig. c5v.

21 Annabel Patterson, *Fables of Power: Aesopian Writing and Political History* (Durham, NC: Duke University Press, 1991), 2.

22 See also Philip Sidney's Ister Bank episode, set in a time when the world was populated only by nonhuman animals, and when "their language was a perfect speech" (*The Countesse of Pembrokes Arcadia* [London, 1590], sig. N3r).

23 William Rowley, Thomas Dekker, and John Ford, *The Witch of Edmonton*, ed. Arthur F. Kinney (London: A & C Black, 1998).

24 For just a small sample, see Stephen R. Anderson, *Doctor Dolittle's Delusion: Animals and the Uniqueness of Human Language* (New Haven, CT: Yale University Press, 2004) and Fernand Méry, *Animal Languages*, trans. Michael Ross (Westmead: Saxon House, 1975). Stephen Pinker defines language as "the preeminent trait" of "the human species" in *The Language Instinct: How the Mind Creates Language* (New York: Harper Perennial, 1995), 16.

25 Edward Topsell, *The Historie of Foure-Footed Beastes* (London, 1607), 15. We are grateful to Mary Learner for this reference.

26 Topsell, *Historie*, 105.

27 William Baldwin, *Beware the Cat* (London, 1584); Michel de Montaigne, "An Apologie of Raymond Sebond," in *The essayes or morall, politike and millitarie discourses of Lo: Michaell de Montaigne*, trans. John Florio (London, 1603), 260. See also Miguel de Cervantes's *Coloquio de los perros* (in *Novelas ejemplares* [Madrid, 1613]), a comic dialogue between two dogs overheard by a delirious man. For a survey of early modern natural historical arguments about animal language, see Brian Cummings, "Pliny's Literate Elephant and the Idea of Animal Language in Renaissance Thought," in *Renaissance Beasts: Of Animals, Humans, and Other Wonderful Creatures*, ed. Erica Fudge (Champaign: University of Illinois Press, 2004), 164–85; see also Alison Langdon, ed., *Animal Languages in the Middle Ages: Representations of Interspecies Communication* (New York: Palgrave, 2018).

28 A noteworthy exception is Kathryn Perry, "Unpicking the Seam: Talking Animals and Reader Pleasure in Early Modern Satire," in *Renaissance Beasts: Of Animals, Humans, and Other Wonderful Creatures*, ed. Erica Fudge (Champaign: University of Illinois Press, 2004), 19–36 (especially 33–34).

29 John Ogilby, "Of the Dog and the Thief," in Blake and Santos, eds., *Fable Translations*, 443–45, ll. 1–6. Hereafter cited parenthetically by line numbers.

30 Of the 18 copies of Ogilby's 1651 *Fables* that we collated, in five the line is entirely in blackletter, and in 13 it alternates blackletter with Roman typeface. See John Ogilby, *The Fables of Aesop* (London, 1651), sig. I3r.

31 *The Oxford English Dictionary Online*, second ed., ed. John Simpson et al. (Oxford University Press, 2020), https://www.oed.com (hereafter *OED*), s.v. "cynic, adj. and n.," B.2.

32 Line 47 presents another typographically ambiguous presentation of animal language: "*Erre, erre, bow-wow*, thieves, thieves, with speed awake!" In the 1651 edition (sig. I3v), Ogilby gives this line with the sounds (*Erre, erre, bow-wow*) in blackletter, the phrase or translation (thieves, thieves) in italic, and the rest of the sentence (with speed awake!) in Roman typography, perhaps distinguishing between animal sounds and animal speech, though later editions obscure this typographical separation.

33 For a full list of animal references, see J.C. Maxwell, "Animal Imagery in 'Coriolanus,'" *The Modern Language Review* 42, no. 4 (1947): 417–21. For a reading that links Coriolanus's wolfishness to the story of Romulus and Remus, the founders of Rome suckled by a wolf, see Janet Adelman, "Shakespeare's Romulus and Remus: Who Does the Wolf Love?" in *Identity, Otherness, and Empire in Shakespeare's Rome*, ed. Maria Del Sapio Garbero (London: Routledge, 2009), 1–34.

34 On the plebeians' language as "merely noises or breath," see James Calderwood, "Wordless Meanings and Meaningless Words," *Studies in English Literature, 1500–1900* 6, no. 2 (Spring, 1966), 213.

35 *OED*, s.v. "rabble, n.1 and adj.," A.3.a.

36 *OED*, s.v. "rabble, n.1 and adj.," A.2, A.1.b.

37 Stanley Cavell reads this exchange as an index of the "paradox and reciprocity of hungering" and "the circle of cannibalism" in the play more generally; see Stanley Cavell, "'Who Does the Wolf

Love?' Reading *Coriolanus*," *Representations* 3 (1983): 1–20, 6. See also Adelman, "Shakespeare's Romulus," 29, where she argues that the play's real wolf is Volumnia.

38 For an account of sound, crowds, and revolt in Renaissance urban spaces, see Niall Atkinson, *The Noisy Renaissance: Sound, Architecture, and Florentine Urban Life* (University Park: Pennsylvania State University Press, 2016), 182–200.

39 Stanley Fish argues that when Coriolanus enters into exile, "[t]he world elsewhere he seeks is not another state"; among the Volsces he can become "exactly what he always wanted to be, a natural force whose movement through the world is independent of all supports" (Stanley Fish, *Is There a Text in This Class?: The Authority of Interpretive Communities* [Cambridge, MA: Harvard University Press, 1990], 217).

40 James Kuzner, "Unbuilding the City: *Coriolanus* and the Birth of Republican Rome," *Shakespeare Quarterly* 58, no. 2 (2007): 174–99, 187.

41 Ibid., 187.

42 Ibid., 188.

43 Both quotations are Coriolanus's later insults of the plebeians.

44 Cavell likewise argues for Menenius's fable as domesticating: it is "about what it is that makes a rational animal fit for conversation, for civility" (Cavell, "Who Does the Wolf Love?," 16). We differ, however, in our focus not on the fable itself, but on the plebeians. While for Cavell, the potential opposite of human language—and so domesticating political power—is silence (18), we have argued throughout that it is animal voice.

45 Ibid., 2.

13

SHREWD SHAKESPEARE

Bruce Boehrer

If death admitted of degree, no metaphor in all of Shakespeare would be more dead than the one that describes quarrelsome women as shrews and that constructs adjectival formulations of "shrewd" behavior deriving etymologically from the noun. In such usage, the connection between tenor and vehicle lies so deeply buried as to present a challenge to scholars of animal studies: why (and how) so buried? And given the burial's depth, why resurrect the connection at all? Hasn't it, too, gone defunct?

For Shakespeare's usage, *The Taming of the Shrew* (c. 1593) provides the central evidence. Outside of the play's title, the noun "shrew" and its adjectival variant "shrewd" appear in the comedy some dozen times, never in a context that admits any application, direct or indirect, to nonhuman animals. Hortensio, for example, describes Katherina as "a shrewd ill-favor'd wife."[1] Baptista complains that Petruchio's wedding-day tardiness would "vex a very saint, / Much more a shrew of [Katherina's] impatient humor" (3.2.28–29). Tranio describes Petruchio as knowing how "To tame a shrew and charm her chattering tongue" (4.2.58). And so forth.

With one notable exception (taken up at the end of this chapter), this pattern conforms to Shakespeare's usage in other works as well. Of particular interest in this respect is a series of similes, beginning with Petruchio's insistence that no scolding woman can daunt him, "Be she . . ./ . . . as curst and shrewd/ As Socrates' Xantippe, or a worse" (1.2.70–71). As it happens, similar figures of speech appear elsewhere in Shakespeare, too: in *The Comedy of Errors* (c. 1590–94), where Ephesian Antipholus accuses the goldsmith Angelo of "brawling" in manner "like a shrew" when he demands payment for a chain delivered to the other Antipholus (4.1.51), and in *The Merchant of Venice* (c. 1597), where Lorenzo teasingly declares that "pretty Jessica (like a little shrow), / Slander[ed] her love" by accusing him of inconstancy (5.1.21–22). When—as in these cases—a metaphor repeatedly appears as the vehicle of another figurative construction, we have strong evidence that the author no longer regards the initial metaphor as itself a figure of speech but instinctively treats it instead as a literal expression.

By contrast, consider another, equally common and equally gendered Shakespearian animal-metaphor: the cuckoo in cuckoldry. In *Love's Labor's Lost* (c. 1594) Don Armado sings of how "The cuckoo . . . on every tree/ Mocks married men" (5.2.907–8). The Clown in *All's Well That Ends Well* (c. 1601) sings that "marriage comes by destiny, / Your cuckoo

163

sings by kind" (1.3.62–63). Elsewhere Shakespearian cuckoldry involves itself in different animal metaphors, but the cuckoo nonetheless remains in Shakespeare's work an embodiment of the trans-generational identity theft that made wifely infidelity a unique object of early modern concern. Thus Shakespeare even employs the cuckoo to represent such theft in cases not involving adultery. In *Antony and Cleopatra* (c. 1607), Pompey charges Antony with swindling him of his family estate, remarking that "the cuckoo builds not for himself" (2.6.28). And the Fool remarks to King Lear, "The hedge-sparrow fed the cuckoo so long/ That it had it head bit off by it young" (*King Lear* [c. 1606], 1.4.736–37). Here and elsewhere, animal behavior remains distinctly visible in Shakespeare's language on feminine infidelity and generational displacement.

In what follows, I explore the traces of animal behavior that remain in Shakespeare's references to shrews and shrewishness—traces so deeply buried as to be superficially invisible. As for the word "trace," I use it here self-consciously in the Derridean sense, to refer to the silent excluded term that underpins any effort to generate meaning through difference.[2] Among its resonances, Derrida's *trace* retains, in its French form, the sense of "animal-tracks." As a result, the logic of the trace connects with what Derrida calls "the problem of the animal": the paradox of the nonhuman animal world as simultaneously denied language and subjected to it, standing in the place of the aboriginal colonized.[3] In the case at hand, the trace of the animal lies deeply buried indeed, but may nonetheless be followed through a pattern of gendered appropriations that extends all the way to the dominant device of Shakespeare's main plot in *The Taming of the Shrew*: Petruchio's method of disciplining his unruly wife. To begin, however, we must review what science now understands—and what pre-scientific natural philosophy and folklore understood—about the shrew itself.

★★★

As in Shakespeare's day, the common shrew, *Sorex araneus*, remains one of the most familiar of European mammals. Despite its similarity to the house mouse, modern biological taxonomy groups it not with the rodents but—depending on the taxonomist—in its own family or order, with moles and other shrew species as its closest relatives.[4] (Among the differences between shrews and rodents, the former lack the latter's ever-growing incisors.) By contrast, early natural history confounded mice and shrews, seeing the two species as closely related and thus confusing their names in various languages. For instance, the Latin noun for shrew, *sorex*, provides the root for the French word for mouse, *souris*, whereas the Latin word for mouse, *mus*, lies behind the first element of the French noun for shrew, *musaraigne*.[5] This French word, in turn, is shadowed by the English "shrewmouse," which appears in the sixteenth and seventeenth centuries as an alternative term for the animal the Anglo-Saxons simply called a *screawa*. Thus, Sir Thomas Elyot's *Dictionary* (1559) already refers to the "*Mus Araneus*" as "a kynde of myce called a shrew," while Samuel Johnson's *Dictionary* (1755) defines the "shrewmouse" as "A mouse of which the bite is generally supposed venomous, and to which vulgar tradition assigns such malignity, that she is said to lame the foot over which she runs."[6]

Elyot's "*Mus Araneus*" provides the full Latin counterpart for the French *musaraigne*, as well as the latter half of the Linnaean *S. araneus*. This latter term, the Latin for "spider," attaches to the shrew in consequence of its reputation as described by Johnson, spiders and shrews being equally notorious for their venom. Indeed, the shrew's poisonous bite and generally malign influence have comprised the most distinctive features of the beast's reputation throughout its recorded existence, so much so that by the time Johnson compiled his dictionary, he could draw on numerous sources attesting to these qualities. Aristotle's *Historia Animalium* (c. 350 BCE) declares that "Shrew's bites are dangerous, as also to other beasts of burden; blisters develop. The bite is more severe if the shrew is pregnant when it bites; for then the blisters burst."[7] Pliny the Elder (77–79 CE), too, states that "The bite of the shrew-mouse is venomous" and enumerates a wide range of remedies.[8] Among more recent authorities, Elyot continues his remarks about the "*Mus Araneus*" by claiming that "yf it goo ouer a beastes backe, he shall be lame in the chyne," while Edward Topsell (1607) avers that "the biting of a Shrew is accounted for a very strong poison" and adds, "Shrewes are truly so venomous and full of poyson, that being slaine or killed by Cats, . . . they will not offer to touch or eate the least part of them."[9]

Indeed, Topsell continues, the shrew is not only poisonous but malignant, "a rauening beast [which] beareth a cruell minde, desiring to hurt any thing, neither is there any creature that it loueth, or it loueth him, because it is feared of al."[10] Incidentally, modern biology bears out the tradition that many shrews are poisonous; species such as the Eurasian water shrew (*Neomys fodiens*) and Mediterranean water shrew (*N. anomalus*), which are easily confused with the common shrew, do bear venom.[11] Likewise, the tradition about cats refusing to eat shrews also has a biological basis, there being glands on the shrew's skin that emit a bitter secretion abhorrent to predators.[12] But for our purposes the paramount feature of Topsell's remarks is their elision of physiology and psychology—what we might call character. Not only does the shrew poison her victims with her bite; she bears them (and indeed all creatures) a settled ill-will of which the poisonous bite itself stands as the physiological referent. Here we find ourselves in the presence of metonymy (the bite represents a broader malevolence), which in turn enables metaphor, for this malevolence underlies the traditional lexical connection between shrews and women. As Doctor Johnson explains in his dictionary entry on the shrewmouse, "Our ancestors . . . looked on her with such terror, that they are supposed to have given her name to a scolding woman, whom for her venom they call a *shrew*."[13]

This etymology seems not to have been favored by Johnson, who records it in his dictionary entry for the shrewmouse yet incorrectly traces the derivation of the noun "shrew" itself to the German "*schreyen*, . . . to clamour."[14] But the traditional tie between shrews and vexatious women reappears in the *OED* as its preferred source for the noun "shrew" in its misogynist application.[15] Initially, the *OED* notes, this connection seems to have applied to men and to women equally, with "shrew" in the sense of "[a] wicked, evil-disposed, or malignant man" ("Shrew" sb.[2] 1) predominant in the thirteenth and fourteenth centuries and gradually replaced, from the fifteenth century forward, by the specifically feminine sense of the word. Thus as late as 1587, William Harrison can refer to England's highwaymen as "shrews or close, booted gentlemen as lie in wait for fat booties by the highways."[16] In addition, a less-common medieval sense of the noun "shrew" associates it—presumably again via the animal's reputation for malignancy—with Satan. Thus, Chaucer's Canon's Yeoman (c. 1386) can exclaim of the chaos in an alchemist's laboratory, "Though that the feend nought in oure sighte hym shewe, / I trowe he with us be, that ilke shrewe!"[17]

In sum, Shakespeare's figure of the shrew inherits and obscures a lengthy process of association, undergone in language and natural history and folklore, that transfers symbolic energy between the figures of animal and woman. This transference occurs under the sign of the demonic, and it represents the first point of contact between Shakespeare and the body of animal lore under consideration here. As previous scholarship has shown, the rubric of shrewdness encompassed an impressive range of qualities and behaviors, from "foreignness and criminality" through "spiritual wickedness" and "hypocrisy" to "disorderly abuse" and "lack of masculine control."[18] It has grown popular in recent years to regard these attributes as various aspects of "an imbalance in personal temperament," deriving in turn from a putative imbalance in the bodily humors of Galenic medical theory.[19] Unobjectionable as this view may be from the perspective of animal studies, it requires expansion beyond questions of human anatomy and comportment. The buried metaphorical connection to other forms of life, by contrast, suggests that something more than human character is at stake in constructions of shrewish behavior. To get a better sense of how these constructions work in the Shakespearean context, we need to focus first upon *The Taming of the Shrew*.

★★★

To begin, then, *The Taming of the Shrew* draws indirectly upon a set of conventional misogynist associations to be found also in witch-literature, as, for instance, when the *Malleus Maleficarum* (1484) declares that witches often assume the form of a cat, "an animal which is, in the Scriptures, an appropriate symbol of the perfidious . . .; for cats are always setting snares for each other."[20] Here again, in the continental context, we see animal psychology manifesting itself in baneful feminine symbolic associations. If anything, insular traditions of witch-lore lent additional depth to these associations via the peculiarly English figure of the witch's familiar.[21] Irrespective of who wrote them, the witch-scenes in *Macbeth* (c. 1604) offer a classic instance of how the Shakespearean theater exploited such figures—classic but by no means unique, being paralleled as they are by similar scenes in plays like Thomas Middleton's *The Witch* (c. 1615) and John Ford, Thomas Dekker, and William Rowley's *The Witch of Edmonton* (1623).[22]

So one may be unsurprised to see demonic associations surface in *The Taming of the Shrew*, where Shakespeare's favored adjective accompanying the noun "shrew" is "curst," an archaic variant of "cursed" that the *OED* applies equally to "men or beasts" in the sense of "fierce, savage, vicious" (s.v. "Cursed, curst," ppl. a. 4.b). Thus, Tranio describes Katherina as "curst and shrewd" (1.1.180), Petruchio wonders whether she might be "as curst and shrowd/ As Socrates' Xantippe" (1.2.70–71), and Hortensio affirms her to be "intolerable curst, / And shrowd, and froward" (1.2.88–89)—all before Katherina has uttered a dozen lines of dialogue. As the play's action progresses, the adjective then pairs alliteratively with Katherina's name, turning her into a kind of walking malediction: "Katherine the curst" (1.2.129), "curst Katherine" (1.2.183), "Kate the curst" (2.1.186). When it is first proposed to find her a husband, Gremio erupts, "A husband? A devil. . . . Think'st thou . . . any man is so very a fool as to be married to hell?" (1.1.121–25). Elsewhere, she attracts similar epithets, being variously styled a "fiend of hell" (1.1.88), a "hilding of a devilish spirit" (2.1.26), and "a devil, a devil, the devil's dam" (3.2.156). Like the shrew's bite, Katherina's sharp tongue represents a broader malevolence of character which participates in the energies of anathema and abomination.

All this is to be expected. Slightly more remarkable, however, is Petruchio's occasional association with the same vocabulary. "Why he's a devil, a devil, a very fiend" (3.2.155), exclaims Gremio, right before Tranio says the same thing of Katherina. "Curster than she? Why, 'tis impossible" (3.2.154), marvels Tranio of Petruchio's behavior. Cursing and drinking and cuffing the priest in church on his wedding-day, Petruchio famously holds the mirror up to his wife, so much so that he can boast, in the process, of his ability to out-roar her: "I am as peremptory as she proud-minded" (2.1.131); "I am rough, and woo not like a babe" (2.1.137). "By this reck'ning," Petruchio's servant Curtis observes, "he is more shrew than she" (4.1.85–86). But for the most part, this is not the reckoning the play itself uses. The words "shrew" and "shrewd" appear in it twelve times, with seven specific applications to Katherina and only the one to Petruchio. The words "devil" and "devilish" appear nine times, with four specific applications to Katherina and only the one to Petruchio. The word

Shrewd Shakespeare

"curst" appears eleven times, with nine specific applications to Katherina and only the one to Petruchio. It is as if the play sought to associate Petruchio with Katherina's behavior, but—*pace* Curtis' claim that "he is more shrew than she"—in a milder, less stigmatized way that is also paradoxically understood to be stronger and superior ("more shrew").

Shakespeare accomplishes this feat mainly by directing Petruchio's abusive behavior towards characters other than Katherina, while having Petruchio treat Katherina herself with ironic courtliness. Thus, his claims to roughness and bellicosity ("Have I not heard great ordnance in the field?" [2.1.203]) coexist with competing pretensions to gentleness and civility:

> She eat no meat to-day, nor none shall eat;
> Last night she slept not, nor to-night she shall not;
> . . .
> Ay, and amid this hurly I intend
> That all is done in reverent care of her. . . .
> . . .
> This is a way to kill a wife with kindness.
>
> (4.1.197–98, 203, 208)

So here appears a second point of contact between Shakespeare's comedy and what we might call the cultural life of shrews: not only does Katherina participate in the process of anathematization to which the shrew itself is subject as a beast of evil omen in natural philosophy and folklore; the play exempts Petruchio from this same process, much as the category of the masculine is historically redeemed from traditions of shrewish diabolism. Composed at a moment of etymological history when shrewish behavior is being re-constituted as a gender-specific thing, applicable only to women, Shakespeare's comedy seems to participate in this reconstitution, presenting Petruchio as only vaguely connected to the "curst" behavior he deliberately copies from Katherina. Of course, this parallelism itself need not be deliberate, but, deliberate or not, it speaks to Lisa Jardine's observation that "[i]n literature, from folk-tale to romance, shrews are always women, though philologically they may properly be male."[23] The tension between these alternatives—the consistently feminine character of shrewd behavior in literary representation as opposed to the linguistic potential for it to apply to both sexes—can only be reconciled through some kind of category cleansing. That is what Shakespeare's play gives us in its treatment of Petruchio.

In effect, Petruchio's appropriation of shrewd behavior activates the resources of metaphor against metaphor itself. If Katherina's own identity as shrew draws on figuration by placing identity under erasure—for metaphorical purposes, Katherina simultaneously is and is not a shrew—Petruchio's adoption of Katherina's identity—both "more shrew" and not shrew—redoubles this relation, mapping it onto the vehicle of the original metaphorical identification. Petruchio's shrewdness thus takes form as second-order figuration, a metaphor of a metaphor. In a play rich with Derridean gestures, this one seems particularly noteworthy, fashioning human identity as nature denatured: a chain of association in which Petruchio is/is not Katherina, who is/is not a shrew, which is/is not an embodied fiend or devil.

This chain of association may be understood as an effort to resolve ambiguity by fixing the meaning of terms, establishing Petruchio as gentle and Katherina as curst and shrewd, irrespective of any incidental resemblances between the two and their behavior. But the ambiguity in need of resolution may itself be traced to the source of the original metaphor, the common shrew itself, which enters the folkloric imaginary not only as a beast of ill omen, bearer of an aboriginal curse, but also as a paradigm of Plato's and Derrida's *pharmakon*, the poison that serves as its own homeopathic antidote.[24] This feature of shrew-lore becomes

167

prominent early on. Thus, Pliny declares that "The shrew-mouse itself, torn asunder and applied, is a remedy for its own bite," and that boils may be cured by "a shrew mouse, killed and hung up so that it does not touch the earth after death, and passed three times round the boil."[25] Topsell agrees and carries the idea further, noting that

> The Shrew being cut and applied in the manner of a plaister, doth effectually cure her owne bites. The Shrew being killed and annointed all ouer with Oyle, and durt, or mire, applyed vnto the Vlcers or red swellings which come by her venemous teeth, will very speedily procure them to breake. The Shrew being cut or beaten into small pieces, dryed into powder, mixed with Vineger, and fashioned into the form of a plaister, will very speedily and effectually cure the bites of a Shrew, whether she be great with young or not, so that they be well applied thereunto.[26]

Indeed, Topsell continues,

> [T]here are some which do thinke it nothing conuenient to mingle the Shrew with any other thing whatsoeuer, but that it is onely after this manner to be applied by it selfe as to take it burned or drie it, and then to pound it in powder, and so to sprinkle it in the wound or sore, which in very short time will easily heale it.[27]

And as Thomas Lupton observed in 1579, the shrew was assigned not only curative but also prophylactic powers: "To keepe Beastes safe that the blynde mowse, called a Shrew, do not byte them. Enclose the same mowse quicke in chalke, which when it is hard, hang the same about the neck of the Beast."[27]

Famously, Shakespeare depicts Petruchio's treatment of Katherina as a similar course of homeopathic therapy. "He kills her in her own humour" (4.1.180), Peter declares. "More shrew than she," Petruchio transforms his wife's offensive behavior into an instrument of her social reformation; "curster than she," he models a distinction without a difference and presents this distinction as the necessary precondition for patriarchal civility. Her sister remarks that "Being mad herself, she's madly mated" (3.2.244), and as the references to humors and madness suggest, the entire wife-taming exercise frames itself as a curative and indeed a medical undertaking, a manipulation of the elements of creation itself, all managed according to the dictates of Galenic physiology.

Incidentally, this feature of Shakespeare's *The Taming of the Shrew* helps distinguish it from the anonymous comedy *The Taming of a Shrew*, first printed in quarto in 1594, whose relationship to Shakespeare's play has occasioned much debate.[28] Within the Shakespearean comedy, matters of humoral physiology loom large, as when Petruchio denies Katherina mutton, "For it engenders choler, planteth anger, / And better 'twere that both of us did fast" (4.1.172–73), or when Grumio employs this same pretext to deny her other meats as well: "a neat's foot" ("too choleric" [4.3.17, 19]), "a fat tripe finely broil'd" ("choleric" [4.3.20, 22]), and "a piece of beef and mustard" ("the mustard is too hot a little" [4.3.23, 25]). Moreover, these matters connect the Shakespearean plot to its framing induction scenes, where the tinker Christopher Sly, persuaded he is a lord suffering from mental illness, is offered as entertainment "a pleasant comedy" (the main body of *The Shrew* itself), "For so your doctors hold it very meet, / Seeing too much sadness hath congeal'd your blood, / And melancholy is the nurse of frenzy" (Induction.2.129–31). Almost none of this appears in *The Taming of a Shrew*: no therapeutic connection between the induction and the main play; no reference to choler when Ferando (the play's Petruchio-figure) withholds his wife's supper; only one reference to the "collerick" character of beef and mustard from Saunders (the play's counterpart to Grumio), who denies Kate other foods on other grounds.[29] Whoever wrote *The Taming of a Shrew* (even if it was Shakespeare himself) produced a work less interested than *The Shrew* in modifying character by manipulating the base elements of nature.

The philosophical *locus classicus* for the concept of the *pharmakon*, Plato's *Phaedrus* (c. 370 BCE), remained unavailable in English during Shakespeare's lifetime, and there is no evidence that he studied this dialogue.[30] But he was clearly familiar with the practice of homeopathic medicine, which entered early modern English culture through folk traditions of the sort collected by Topsell and preserved by medieval bestiarists and herbalists following Pliny. These are the authors Shakespeare echoes only a year or two after the composition of *The Taming of the Shrew*, in *Romeo and Juliet* (c. 1595), when Friar Laurence expounds on the properties of the herbs he collects:

> Within the infant rind of this weak flower
> Poison hath residence and medicine power;
> . . .
> Two such opposed kings encamp them still
> In man as well as herbs, grace and rude will.
>
> (2.3.23–24, 27–28)

These lines could serve as commentary upon *The Taming of the Shrew*, whose preoccupation with subduing Katherina's "rude will" thus anticipates the humors comedy of the late 1590s. More to the present purpose, these same lines suggest the instability of homeopathic procedures that seek to establish equilibrium of body and mind through substances and practices that are themselves irreducibly ambiguous in their quality and effects.

★★★

To this point I have argued that Shakespeare's *The Taming of the Shrew* enacts the same gender-specific shift in meaning that the linguistic category of shrewishness undergoes during the medieval and early modern period, and that this enactment also relies upon the medical logic of homeopathy associated with poisonous animals and plants in pre-modern folklore and natural history. On the one hand, the elision of animality and femininity (woman as shrew) rehearses a standard—perhaps *the* standard—ecofeminist *aperçu*: the feminization of nature enables the concomitant masculinization of culture, which emerges as an instrument of virtue in its root sense of masculine strength and potency.[31] On the other hand, these elisions occur in and through language, the phallogocentric order of Derridean theory, which assimilates both animality and femininity to a system of representation that functions equally as a system of repression. Thus, it makes sense that much of Petruchio's struggle with Katherina (whom he insists on calling Kate) centers upon control of language and access to the means of expression. As Katherina puts it on one particularly vexed occasion,

> Why, sir, I trust I may have leave to speak,
> And speak I will. I am no child, no babe;
> Your betters have endur'd me say my mind,
> And if you cannot, best you stop your ears.
>
> (4.3.73–76)

Herein lies one of *The Shrew*'s signal ironies, analogous to the paradoxical resemblance-in-difference that relates Katherina and Petruchio. On the one hand, the play is endlessly amused by Katherina's inability to control language, to use it to compel assent or obedience or even attention; on the other hand, it gives the words of the reformed Kate a kind of *prima facie* authority and compulsive power, apparently grounded in the indisputable facts of anatomy:

> Why are our bodies soft, and weak, and smooth,
> Unapt to toil and trouble in the world,
> But that our soft conditions, and our hearts,
> Should well agree with our external parts?

(5.2.165–68)

It is perhaps the most outrageous rhetorical question ever uttered by a boy in drag, the circumstances of its delivery consigning anatomy and language to separate registers altogether, even as the lines themselves insist on seamless continuity between the two.

The core problem, here as elsewhere in Shakespeare's play, can be formulated as one of presence: when is a being (Katherina or Petruchio; male, female, or other; human, animal, or plant) or quality (virtue or vice; sense or nonsense; strength or weakness) really there? How can we know it when we see it? This same question looms large at the end of the *Phaedrus*, where Socrates dismisses writing as inferior to speech, "the living and breathing word of him who knows, of which the written word may justly be called the image."[32] For Plato's Socrates, writing becomes an ambivalent thing, "an elixir not of memory, but of reminding" (*oukoun mnēmēs all' hupomnēseōs pharmakon*), encouraging in a cycle of dependence the very mental weakness it aims to remedy.[33] It is a typical Platonic move, valuing speech over writing and ideas over their representation by marking the latter terms as secondary, unoriginal, imitative. By contrast, Derrida's critique of Plato challenges this distinction, noting the degree to which Socrates' own words rely upon writing and stage writing as their enabling condition, and noting how those same words ground themselves in myth and hearsay, so that "what writing will be accused of—repeating without knowing—here defines the very approach that leads to the statement and determination of its status."[34] As with Petruchio's treatment of Katherina, we find ourselves here confronting a distinction without a difference, a nexus of indeterminable qualities for which Derrida cites Plato's repeated use of the word *pharmakon*, in its various and contradictory senses, as paradigmatic.

For Derrida, the *pharmakon* serves as a site of "citational play," an instance of "anagrammatic writing" that defies translation by its very nature, signaling the interdependence of the opposed concepts (medicine, poison) encompassed by its meaning.[35] But as Derrida himself acknowledges, these binary terms entail a further extension of meaning as well, from *pharmakon* to *pharmakos*: the living figure of the scapegoat—whether animal, as in the defining case of Leviticus 16, or human, as in the parallel instance of the Athenian Thargelia—raised within a community for the specific purpose of purifying ritual expulsion.[36] Thus behind Socrates' discourse in the *Phaedrus* there lie traditions of lore and ritual broadly similar to those that inform Shakespeare's *The Taming of the Shrew*, and Katherina's scapegoat-like function—as the "curst" creature bred in her family's bosom apparently for the express purpose of reformation—returns us to the distinctive concerns of animal studies.

Not that we have ever strayed far from them: if books are *pharmaka*, after all, they participate in the animal nature of other such preparations just as surely as do the remedies described by Topsell. Shakespeare wrote with a goose-quill pen and with ink whose pigment could be compounded of bone-black. The paper he wrote on was sized with gelatin obtained from animal skins and hooves. And while by Shakespeare's day paper had replaced vellum as the default surface for most writing, any manuscript or printed work marked for preservation would still have been bound in some kind of vellum or leather, the binding secured with animal glue. If Plato and Derrida are right that writing offers only the illusion of an author's presence, one must add that this illusion is constructed out of the real presence of animal bodies, flayed and boiled and burned and reduced until we recognize in them only the contours of our own exorbitant egos.

★★★

One may draw inspiration for this line of conjecture not only from Derrida, but also from that other herald of the postmodern, Walter Benjamin, specifically his oracular pronouncement in the "Theses on the Philosophy of History" that "There is no document of civilization which is not at the same time a document of barbarism."[37] *The Taming of the Shrew* casts itself, in one sense, as a contribution to literature on the civilizing process: as the story of how one unruly woman is successfully assimilated to polite society, and, more broadly, as a model of how such assimilation may be effected with minimal bloodshed. Yet the play's critical history has been dogged with charges of brutality and misogyny, with no less a figure than E.K. Chambers insisting that "[a]n age which flatters itself . . . that it has rounded Cape Turk, must needs make it a point of honour to take offence at the theme and temper of *The Taming of the Shrew*."[38]

We may note Chambers' own anti-Turkish bigotry here in passing: the distinction between barbarism and civility that underlies Shakespeare's opposition between Katharina and Petruchio reappears in Chambers' distinction between Turk and non-Turk now reconfigured in terms of race rather than gender. But lest we view the play as courting barbarism in its subject-matter alone, we should also consider the less-quoted continuation of Benjamin's remark: "And just as such a document is not free of barbarism, barbarism taints also the manner in which it was transmitted from one owner to another." In the case of document transmission, evidence of barbarism may be found in the very ink and paper of the documents themselves, which, as noted above, constitute what Erica Fudge has called "dead animal products."[39] Beyond this, however, the Derridean critique of Plato suggests that barbarism inheres in all the functions of language, especially so if we recall that barbarism itself remains at heart a linguistic formulation, the Greek *barbaros* in its root sense meaning "simply people who make noises like 'bar bar' instead of talking Greek."[40] To this extent, one cannot separate regimes of knowledge from regimes of repression, these latter having historically promoted male at the expense of female, culture at the expense of nature.

This chapter has explored one instance of the linguistic appropriation of animal resources, an appropriation managed for the benefit of certain individuals (Petruchio, his male companions, Shakespeare, his colleagues) and the conceptual structures (language, culture, patriarchy) that subtend them. As to whether *The Taming of the Shrew* should be considered the "coarse" and brutal" play it is sometimes claimed to be, we might respond that its brutality goes hand in hand with its sophistication.[41] In fact, *The Taming of the Shrew* offers its audience a signal refinement of cruelty: a play that reaffirms patriarchy by upholding it primarily through linguistic rather than corporal discipline. To this extent a document of civilization, it maintains its civilizing tendencies in close and ambiguous relation to its barbarism.

In my opening paragraphs I examined Shakespeare's references to shrews and concluded that, with one exception, these all tend to bury as deeply as possible the animal metaphor upon which notions of shrewishness depend for their meaning. Now that we approach the essay's end, it is time to consider the exception, which involves the semantic history of the adjective "shrewd." As the *OED* notes, the "chief current sense" of this word is "favourable," as in *OED* "shrewd" adj. 13: "Clever or keen-witted in practical affairs; astute or sagacious in action or speech." But this sense has only just begun to emerge in the sixteenth century and does not come to the fore until the 1800s (whence the *OED* draws most of its examples). Shakespeare's usage, by contrast, conforms to the earlier standard, as reflected in the *OED*'s preceding 12 entries for the word, which uniformly refer to people, animals, and objects as "depraved, wicked; evil-disposed, malignant" ("shrewd" adj. 1.), "naughty" ("shrewd" adj. 1. b.), "bad-tempered; vicious, fierce" ("shrewd" adj. 1. c.), "[o]f evil nature, character, or influence ("shrewd" adj. 3.), and "of ill omen, ominous" ("shrewd" adj. 10.). These are the meanings consistently foregrounded in Shakespeare's 37 uses of the adjective "shrewd" and its corresponding adverb, as, for instance, when Achilles complains in *Troilus and Cressida* (c. 1601) that his "fame is shrewdly gor'd" (3.3.228), or when *A Midsummer Night's Dream* (c. 1596) describes Puck as a "shrewd and knavish sprite" (2.1.33), or when Lewis laments the "foul shrewd news" of Melune's death in *King John* (c. 1595; 5.5.14).

Among all this, one may perhaps still recognize *S. araneus* itself in the poet's emphasis on the ominous character of shrewdness, where associations with a malignant, ill-starred nature seem to reach back to the shrew's unfortunate reputation among natural philosophers and purveyors of folklore. This is not only the case for the "curst and shrewd" Katherina of *The Taming of the Shrew* but also for the "shrewd and knavish" Puck (who is, after all, a sort of nature spirit), and also for the air that "bites shrewdly" around Hamlet on the battlements of Elsinore (*Hamlet* 1.4.1) and which, in alluding to the shrew's envenomed bite, provides one more instance of the language of poison and putrefaction distinctive of Shakespeare's most famous play. Finally, though, the very concept of shrewdness turns positive in English etymological history, standing the term's root meaning on its head, in effect, by reconstituting it in the image of traditionally masculine attributes: astuteness, reason, and intellect. For his part, Shakespeare does not participate in this reconstitution, at least not on the etymological level, although we may get just a glimpse of it in *Antony and Cleopatra* (c. 1606), ironically enough when Antony complains of his wife Fulvia's "shrowdness of policy" in waging war against Octavius (2.2.69). But Shakespeare's real contribution to this shift in meaning appears in the character of Petruchio, who adopts and purifies his wife's shrewish behavior, re-presenting it as his own distinctively masculine "shrowdness of policy."

Notes

1 William Shakespeare, *The Taming of the Shrew*, 1.2.60, in *The Riverside Shakespeare*, eds. G. Blakemore Evans et al. (Boston, MA: Houghton Mifflin, 1997). All references to Shakespeare will be to this edition.
2 For an introduction to the Derridean trace, see Jacques Derrida, *Of Grammatology*, trans. Gayatri Chakravorty Spivak (Baltimore, MD: Johns Hopkins University Press, 1976), 1–73.
3 For Derrida's formulation of the problem of the animal, see *The Animal that Therefore I Am*, trans. David Wills (New York: Fordham University Press, 2008), 1–51. For an account of Derrida's thought on animals that relates this to his larger *oeuvre*, see Matthew Calarco, *Zoographies: The Question of the Animal from Heidegger to Derrida* (New York: Columbia University Press, 2008), 102–49.
4 Ronald M. Nowak, *Walker's Mammals of the World*, 2 vols. (Baltimore, MD: Johns Hopkins University Press, 1991), 1:114.
5 See John Wright, *The Naming of the Shrew: A Curious History of Latin Names* (London: Bloomsbury, 2014), 17–20.
6 Sir Thomas Elyot, *Biblioteca Eliotae. Eliotes Dictionary* (London, 1559), s.v. "Mus"; Samuel Johnson, *A Dictionary of the English Language* (London, 1755), s.v. "Shrewmouse."
7 Aristotle, *History of Animals: Books 7–10*, trans. D.M. Balme (Cambridge, MA: Harvard University Press, 1991), 7(8).23 [604b19–23; 186–87].
8 Pliny the Elder, *Natural History*, trans. H. Rackham, 10 vols (Cambridge, MA: Harvard University Press, 1983), 8.83.227 [vol. 3, 158–59]; for remedies, see e.g. 20.23, 20.34, 29.27.

Shrewd Shakespeare

9 Edward Topsell, *The Historie of Foure-Footed Beasts* (London, 1607), 537.

10 Topsell, *The Historie of Foure-Footed Beasts*, 536.

11 Wright, *The Naming of the Shrew*, 16279.

12 See Paul Sterry, *Collins Complete Guide to British Wildlife: A Photographic Guide to Every Common Species* (London: HarperCollins, 2008), 402.

13 Johnson s.v. "Shrewmouse."

14 Johnson s.v. "Shrew."

15 *Oxford English Dictionary*, 2nd ed., 20 vols (Oxford: Oxford University Press, 1989), s.v. "Shrew" sb.². Further references are to this edition.

16 William Harrison, *The Description of England: The Classic Account of Tudor Social Life*, ed. George Edelen (Washington, DC: Folger Shakespeare Library 1994), 239.

17 Geoffrey Chaucer, "*The Canterbury Tales*, Canon's Yeoman's Tale, 915–16," in *The Riverside Chaucer*, ed. Larry D. Benson (Boston, MA: Houghton Mifflin, 1987), 275.

18 Holly A. Crocker, "Engendering Shrews: Medieval to Early Modern," in *Gender and Power in Shrew-Taming Narratives, 1500–1700* (New York: Palgrave Macmillan, 2010), 50–52. Also see Lisa Jardine, *Still Harping on Daughters: Women and Drama in the Age of Shakespeare* (New York: Columbia University Press, 1989), 103–40; Pamela Allen Brown, *Better a Shrew than a Sheep: Women. Drama, and the Culture of Jest in Early Modern England* (Ithaca, NY: Cornell University Press, 2003), 1–32; Frances Dolan, "Introduction," William Shakespeare, *The Taming of the Shrew*, ed. Frances Dolan (Boston, MA: St. Martin's P, 1996), 8–14.

19 Crocker, "Engendering Shrews," 50. For early modern drama and Galenic medicine, see particularly Gail Kern Paster, *The Body Embarrassed: Drama and the Disciplines of Shame in Early Modern England* (Ithaca, NY: Cornell University Press, 1993), 1–22.

20 Heinrich Kramer and James Sprenger, *The Malleus Maleficarum*, trans. Montague Summers (1928; rpt. New York: Dover, 1971), 2.1.9 [128].

21 For the familiar as an English tradition, see Molly Hand, "Animals, the Devil, and the Sacred: Animal Familiars in Early Modern Culture," in *Animals and Animality in the Literary Field*, eds. Bruce Boehrer, Molly Hand, and Brian Massumi (Cambridge: Cambridge University Press, 2018), 105–20.

22 See Thomas Middleton, *The Witch*, passim, in *Thomas Middleton: The Collected Works*, eds. Gary Taylor and John Lavagnino (Oxford: Oxford University Press, 2006), passim; John Ford, Thomas Dekker, and William Rowley, *The Witch of Edmonton*, ed. Arthur F. Kinney (London: A & C Black, 2005), passim. For discussion see Hand passim.

23 Lisa Jardine, *Still Harping on Daughters: Women and Drama in the Age of Shakespeare* (Totowa, NJ: Barnes and Noble, 1983), 103.

24 See Plato, *Phaedrus*, in *Plato: Euthyphro, Apology, Crito, Phaedo, Phaedrus*, trans. Harold North Fowler (Cambridge, MA: Harvard University Press, 1914), passim; Jacques Derrida, *Dissemination*, trans. Barbara Johnson (Chicago, IL: University of Chicago Press, 1981), 63–171.

25 Pliny 29.27.89 [vol. 8, 240–41]; 30.34.108 [vol. 8, 346–47].

26 Topsell, *The Historie of Foure-Footed Beasts*, 539.

27 Thomas Lupton, *A Thousand Notable Things, of Sundry Sortes* (London, 1579), 175–76.

28 For the relationship between these two plays, see Brian Morris, "Introduction," 12–50, in William Shakespeare, *The Taming of the Shrew*, ed. Brian Morris (London: Methuen, 1981).

29 *The Taming of a Shrew*, prep. Stephen Roy Miller (1594 facs.; Oxford: Oxford University Press, 1998), 950.

30 No English translations of Plato's dialogues appeared in print prior to 1675. Henri Estienne and Jean de Serres' monumental edition of Plato's works in Greek with Latin translation appeared in 1578, bearing a dedication to Queen Elizabeth (*Platonis opera quae extant omnia*, 3 vols [Geneva, 1578]). But Shakespeare does not appear to have worked closely with this or any other text.

31 For the ecofeminist association of patriarchy with exploitation of the natural world in early modernity, see Carolyn Merchant, *The Death of Nature: Women, Ecology, and the Scientific Revolution* (New York: HarperCollins, 1980); for the feminist association masculinity with the repression of nature, see Sherry B. Ortner, "Is Female to Male as Nature Is to Culture?," *Feminist Studies* 1, no. 2 (Autumn, 1972): 5–31.

32 Plato 276a8–10, [566–67].

33 Plato 275a6–7, [562–63].

34 Derrida, *Dissemination*, 74–75.

35 Ibid., 98.
36 For Derrida's discussion of the *pharmakos*, see *Dissemination* 128–34. For the scapegoat of early Judaism, see Leviticus 16.3–10. For the Athenian Thargelia, see Sir James George Frazer, *The Golden Bough* (New York: Macmillan, 1967), 58.2, [670–75].
37 Walter Benjamin, *Illuminations*, trans. Harry Zohn (New York: Schocken, 1968), 256.
38 E.K. Chambers, *Shakespeare: A Survey* (London: Sidgwick and Jackson, 1925), 40.
39 Erica Fudge, "Renaissance Animal Things," *New Formations* 76 (2012): 86–100, 87.
40 H.D.F. Kitto, *The Greeks* (Harmondsworth: Penguin, 1973), 7.
41 George Bernard Shaw, "The Taming of the Shrew," in *Shaw on Shakespeare*, ed. Edwin Wilson (1961; rpt. New York: Applause Theatre and Cinema Books, 2002), 178.

PART 4

Training, Performance, and Living with Animals

The line between taming and training is a thin one. Not all animals can be trained; yet for those that were, training, as a set of practices and as a discipline, centered upon a paradox: training recognizes intelligence in a fellow creature, even as the training relationship seeks to harness that power for human benefit, often in unequal and unevenly distributed ways. Taking this paradox as her starting point, Elspeth Graham examines how early modern training manuals deal with it. Assembling a surprising array of "semi-trained" creatures in Shakespeare's plays (including Jack Cade, Richard II's horse Barbary, Katherina in *The Taming of the Shrew*, the bear of *The Winter's Tale*, and Crab the dog), Graham excavates how early modern theories of training rest on contradictory sets of claims, thwarting what we tend to assume was the "natural order" of things in the past by imbuing a wider array of human and animal bodies with performance skills.

Nowhere is this more obvious than in the baiting arenas: at once a violent spectacle of blood sport and a highly lucrative and staged spectacle, these "entertainments" were also performances. The dogs, monkeys, and bears pitted against one another were semi-trained in precisely the ways Graham outlines. Todd Borlik takes up the question of the role of performing bears in Elizabethan theaters, reanimating them through new materialist engagements with bear skins while raising ecocritical questions about environmental devastation. Taking Shakespeare's famous stage direction in *The Winter's Tale*, "exit, pursued by a bear," as a starting point, Borlik maneuvers through an expansive archive of early modern furry spectacles, cataloging the overwhelming number of bear skins involved in staging early modern performances. Connecting these spectacles with the industry shifts that transformed England and Europe in the premodern period, Borlik shows how bear carcasses document the de-wilding of Europe. Expanding fur markets, along with sheep-farming and deforestation, is a key cause. The result was that fur-bearing animals, including brown bears, were already endangered in Europe in the sixteenth century. The wearing of animal fur, particularly bear skins, signaled human power. Playing with Agamben's political theory of "bare" life, Borlik's account of "bear" life shows us how bear skin animates human political agency in different ways, through tremendous pain and suffering on the part of the animal. In his account, fur is not just another "insentient" thing that stitches together animal studies with new materialisms.

Julian Yates takes a different approach, tracking animal matter within pastoral literary traditions: beginning with William Empson's argument about the Wakefield *Second Shepherd's Play*, that its doubled plot is key to creating an illusion of "more life," Yates foregrounds the necessary presence of actual as well as metaphorical sheep within pastoral traditions. Sheep, Yates argues, infuse these texts with "liveliness," even as they are consumed as byproducts within literary and wool industries of the early modern period. Tracing the afterlife of this effect in Shakespeare's plays, Yates focuses on three characters who, like the Wakefield play's Coll, Daw, and Mak, spend their time on stage counting sheep: Jack Cade, Shylock, and Autolycus. These characters, Yates argues, demonstrate that even our most human-inflected modes of meaning, including our literary tropes, are activated through animetaphors and retain a trace of those previous human/animal connections.

In the final essay of this segment, Laurie Shannon brings these questions of literary history and the pastoral to bear on performance. Analyzing Missouri Williams' 2014/15 play *King Lear with Sheep*, Shannon explores how the play's core conceit changings the themes of Shakespeare's play. Whereas Shakespeare's *King Lear* explored the boundaries of the human in terms of sovereignty, Williams's postmodern and posthuman counterpart revisits such boundaries in the face of "animal indifference." While the title may, at first blush, seem "silly," *King Lear with Sheep* stages humans as ridiculous; in this way it connects to a much longer literary history about "seely" and "silly" creatures, defined as frail, foolish, and precarious. Estranging us from everything we think we know about Shakespeare's play (and about sheep), *King Lear with Sheep* troubles the category of the human through its investment in animal performers.

14

THE TRAINING RELATIONSHIP
Horses, Hawks, Dogs, Bears, and Humans

Elspeth Graham

I Introduction: Humans and Nonhumans; Nature and Culture

In 1658, 42 years after the death of William Shakespeare, William Cavendish, then marquis of Newcastle, published *La méthode nouvelle et invention extraordinaire de dresser les chevaux*.[1] This horsemanship manual aims to train men—to train horses—in the high equine arts of the manège. Early in the treatise, Cavendish addresses different ways that humans and horses can be taught. While humans, word-centered beings, can learn from a written treatise such as his own, "horses do not form their reasonings from ABC," he points out, but "draw their reasonings from things themselves."[2] Yet in spite of establishing this difference, Cavendish continues throughout *La méthode nouvelle* to identify similarities between humans and horses as students: in their methods of understanding and remembering, in the nature of their knowledge, and in their characters and dispositions. Horses and humans, in Cavendish's articulation, more often than not share common characteristics.

Cavendish's method of argument and his style are equally significant parts of his message. In his first chapter, he uses reference to an extensive list of different human aptitudes to argue that the abilities of horses are equally varied. Referring to "all those ... who make learning their profession," he enumerates the specialist skills, or "sciences," of poets, preachers, lawyers, physicians, mathematicians, astronomers and astrologers, churchmen, and artists, concluding, "[i]t is just the same with horses." And having described how "[a]ll those who go to a ballroom, don't dance equally well: some dance high, others low ..." he states, "[i]n a like manner, horses perform according to their different geniuses"(*General System* 16–17). Cavendish's use of analogy between the familiarly human and horses serves primarily to argue for the diversity of equine talents and the individuality of all horses. But through this, he also implicitly reminds us of what constitutes the human. And his use of analogy itself as a prime mode of argument—since analogy works through setting up apparently separate things only to reveal that they share likenesses—suggests that Cavendish's manual can be read as an exploration of ways in which humans and horses are both similar and dissimilar. Since all of his examples of comparability refer to both inborn qualities and abilities ("geniuses"), and to skills ("sciences"), acquired through training, this opening chapter of *La méthode nouvelle* further works to suggest that nature and culture are differentiable—but also, paradoxically, inseparable. Humans and horses, alike, are subject to both.

That such a simultaneous blurring and separation of nature and culture is not simply a product of Cavendish's own particular writing, but instances a much broader early modern habit of conceptualization, is epitomized in the commonplace, but important, early modern phrase "birth and breeding." This, as Karen Raber has pointed out, appears simultaneously to distinguish the biological from the cultural, while at the same time obscuring such a differentiation through the ambiguities of the word "breeding," which tautologically again "refers to birth (inborn qualities)," but also to "education (superimposed qualities)."[3] Humans, like other forms of creation, are subject to the effects of both their inborn and embodied natures *and* their bio-socio-cultural breeding. For early modern people, the realm of the socio-cultural is perceived as being an aspect of nature at the same time as it, conversely, allows humans to stand above or apart from nature.[4] Although not absolutely congruent, nature and nurture, social order and natural order, are much more entwined in the early modern mind than in the Enlightenment thought of the eighteenth and following centuries.

Nowhere, perhaps, is this more forcefully expressed than in the famous lines from *Macbeth*, describing effects in the wider environment of the murder of Scotland's king, Duncan:

OLD MAN.: 'Tis unnatural,
        Even like the deed that's done. On Tuesday last,
        A falcon, towering in her pride of place,
        Was by a mousing owl haw'd at and kill'd.
ROSSE.:   And Duncan's horses (a thing most strange and certain)
        Beauteous and swift, the minions of their race,
        Turn'd wild in nature, broke their stalls, flung out,
        Contending 'gainst obedience, as they would make war with mankind.
OLD MAN.: 'Tis said, they eat each other.
ROSSE.:   They did so …

(*MACBETH* II.I.10–20)

Here, in a play where almost every scene refers to the natural order and its breaching, the extreme violation of order represented by the murder of a king is not described through *metaphoric* allusion to unnatural behavior in the nonhuman world, or through use of analogy, as in Cavendish's writing. Rather, Duncan's murder actually destroys the whole order of things: human, animal, and even, as suggested in earlier lines, cosmographical. That the animals —falcons and horses—referenced here by the choric Old Man should be those who are trained by humans for hunting and other purposes (and that each represents an elite in the hierarchy of their own kind) are also depicted as owing natural obedience to humankind, demonstrates precisely how, in this traditional understanding of a hierarchical world order, the cultural is intrinsically part of nature, is itself natural. Yet this passage from *Macbeth* also reveals an early modern notion of the specifically domesticated animal—taken from nature into human culture through its training, housing, breeding, feeding, and use—as occupying a separate domain from that of the fully wild. Duncan's fine horses, cared for in their stables, turn wild and break out; a falcon, trained by humans for hunting purposes, is killed by an owl, a non-domesticated animal which sometimes, in the wild, is the prey of falcons. But this episode does not simply depend on demarcation of the boundaries between the domesticated and the wild. The horses here, naturally herbivorous animals, turn cannibalistically carnivorous. The wild itself is rendered unnatural. In *Macbeth*, the order of things is violated on several levels that involve different exchanges between wildness and domestication and between natural and unnatural forms of the wild itself.

The Training Relationship

The training relationship between human and nonhuman animals inevitably focuses on domesticated animals who occupy a threshold domain between the wild and the tame, nature and acculturation, the purely human and the purely animal. But as these opening references to *La méthode nouvelle* and *Macbeth* reveal, for people in early modern England, those very categories of nature and culture, human and animal are more multi-layered and ambiguous than they might seem to us today, or in our recent history. Indeed, as Laurie Shannon observes, although many different species are mentioned in Shakespeare's texts, the collective, categorizing noun "animal" is used only eight times. From this, she argues,

> animals represented no single, philosophically invested category in early modernity ... English speakers almost never grouped together all the creatures we call (nonhuman) animals under that name, preferring a more articulated list influenced by the cadences of Scripture and cognizant of plants and minerals as well.[5]

The beginnings of a transition from this Elizabethan and Jacobean world view to the Enlightenment's full separation of the categories of human and animal can be associated with a range of epistemological, ontological, and socio-cultural shifts that occur throughout the sixteenth and seventeenth centuries.

Significantly, Cavendish's comment that horses "do not form their reasonings from ABC ... [but] ... from things themselves" marks his disagreement with the Cavendish family's client that "most excellent philosopher master Hobbes."[6] The writings of the natural-political philosopher Thomas Hobbes are usually recognized as being among those that provide the keystone for the Enlightenment's emphasis on human rationality and an essential separation from other living beings and components of the natural world.[7] For Hobbes, there is a "mind common to humans and animals – the natural mind – [which] is located in matter" and a second "distinctly human mind – marked by its capacity for general and active thought – [which] emerges from the natural mind through the addition of language."[8] This issue of language, along with the Cartesian emphasis on human rationality and a mind-body split, becomes part of a series of scientific and Enlightenment tenets whereby human agency becomes essentially different from that of both nonhuman animals and vegetables or minerals. It is only recently, in our own historical moment, that a revisioning of forms of human agency in relation to the different but equally significant forms of agency enacted by all material forms, sensible and non-sensible, has begun to be articulated through the philosophy and politics of vital materialism, in the work of, for instance, Bruno Latour, Jane Bennett, Graham Harman, Stacy Alaimo, or with a slightly different emphasis, Hans Ulrich Gumbrecht.[9] Although each of these writers takes a distinct philosophical stance, the overall idea that, in Jeffrey Jerome Cohen's summarizing words, "things matter in a double sense: the study of animals, plants, stones, tracks, stools, and other objects can lead us to important new insights about the past and present; and that they possess integrity, power, independence and vibrancy" is leading to increasing recognition that "the human is not the world's sole meaning-maker, and never has been."[10] And it is such thought, giving us evaluative distance from some Enlightenment assumptions, that perhaps can make us newly alert to ways in which early modern people articulated a sense of the order of things.

II Horses, Bodies, Words, and Power

This phrase, "the order of things," derives originally from the English-language title of Michel Foucault's early work, *The Order of Things*, identifying the epistemic changes that produced the Classical age and then modernity.[11] The original French title, *Les Mots et les Choses*, suggests even more strongly how alterations in habits of language-related category formation shape such transitions. An early modern transition from a medieval world view to that of modernity might also be recognized as a shift from what Hans Ulrich Gumbrecht has called a "culture of presence" and "presence effects" to a "culture of representation" or "meaning effects."[12] Certainly Shakespeare is constantly preoccupied by the relationship between bodies (presence) and words (representation) throughout his plays.

This is instanced in an early play, *2 Henry VI*, which, set at the beginning of the Wars of the Roses, is all about the legitimacy of power.[13] Among the many contests of power that the play depicts, it is the rebellion of the "men of Kent" led by Jack Cade that brings issues of language and bodiliness most emphatically to the fore. In the encounter between the hapless lawyer, Lord Saye, Henry VI's Lord Treasurer, and the Kentish rebels, Jack Cade's indictment of Saye, moves from specific political accusations ("giving up Normandy unto … the Dauphin of France") to more generalized attacks on Saye as a representative of that social class who, in Cavendish's words, "make learning their profession" and seek to provide training in the workings of language to others (*General Method* 16). Cade rants:

> … Thou hast most traitorously corrupted the youth of the realm in erecting a grammar-school; and whereas, before, our forefathers had no other books but the score and tally, thou hast caus'd printing to be used; and … thou hast built a paper-mill. It will be prov'd to thy face that thou hast men about thee that usually talk of a noun, and a verb, and such abominable words as no Christian ear can endure …
>
> *(2 HENRY VI IV.vii.30–38)*

From here, as Saye defends himself, eloquently arguing for his life, this confrontation between rebels and lawyer develops into a series of subtle exchanges between the natural and the unnatural, the physical and the verbal that pivot on a reference to "bridl[ing]":

BUT.: Why dost thou quiver, man?
SAYE.: The palsy, and not fear, provokes me.
CADE. Nay, he nods at us; as who should say, "I'll be even with you": I'll see if his head will stand steadier on a pole or no. Take him away and behead him.
SAYE.: Tell me: wherein have I offended most?
    Have I offended wealth or honour? speak.
        …
CADE.: [Aside] I feel remorse in myself with his words; but I'll bridle it: he shall die, and be it but for pleading so well for his life. Away with him! he has a familiar under his tongue … Go, take him away, I say, and strike off his head presently …

(2 HENRY VI IV.VII.87–104)

Lord Saye, the man of words (his historically accurate name fully exploited by Shakespeare), is reduced to pure bodiliness: his palsy; his eloquence attributed to a physical, diabolic aid, "a familiar under his tongue"; and his end as a "head on a pole." But the resolutely corporeal Cade, who has derided Saye's verbal skills and life in the world of words, and criticized him for letting his "horse wear a cloak, when honester men … go in their hose and doublets," has himself become temporarily susceptible to the effect of words, before "bridl[ing] it."[14] He, through this embedded metaphor, likens himself to a horse whose (natural) impulse must be restrained. A contest between the power of the bodily and the power of words is enacted here. That a fundamental tool of human power used to train and control horses—the bridle—should be invoked in such a scene is subtly telling. Cade in restoring himself to his core self-identity as corporeal man has to reflexively manage his own recoil from seduction by the verbal through metaphoric reference to a primary aid used by riders to guide their mounts.[15] But this splits Cade's being: he becomes aligned with both rider and horse. He is corporeal like the horse, yet he has the agency and awareness of the human rider who directs the horse. Since language, through the bridle metaphor, becomes—ironically, given his earlier resentment of high verbality—aligned with the natural, Cade's oscillating values also enact a chiasmic cross-over between the natural and the human.

The underpinnings, then, of Cade's anger—the class-related issues of training in language skills and the dressing of horses in better "clothing" than that worn by the poor—coalesce through the use of a pivotal word, in a pivotal scene in Act Four of *2 Henry VI*. It opens up the entire play's analysis of values relating to corporeality and identity, human and animal, words and material being—and from these its interrogation of the warrior cultures of the Middle Ages, issues of noble and royal bloodlines, and more broadly those of power, legitimacy, physical violence, social or political organization, human values, natural order and chaos.

If the subtle allusions to horse management in *2 Henry VI* allow us to recognize such issues, more sustained and prolific reference to horses and horse training serves as a form of shorthand description of the nature of men and nation states throughout the history plays. Each manual in the series of horse training treatises produced in England in the early modern period has a different intended audience and purpose: from the address to an equestrian and social elite by William Cavendish to the popularizing works of Gervase Markham, addressed to all landowners from the gentry to yeoman famers. Nevertheless, the title to Thomas Blundeville's sixteenth-century *The fower chiefyst offices belonging to horsemanshippe, that is to saye, the office of the Breeder, of the Rider, of the Keper, and of the Ferrer* (partly a translation of the writings of the Italian horse-master, Federico Grisone) clearly demonstrates four areas of "science" that all treatises share as concerns: breeding and the qualities of different horse breeds, riding, horse care (including feed and treatment of diseases), and matters of farriery and tack. And it is through "dressing"—grooming, tacking up, schooling, or preparing—a horse that the horse–human training relationship is effected. These areas of "science," in turn, represent the forms of knowledge that were generally culturally available to both Shakespeare and his audiences. Such a knowledge enables the numerous references to horses in the *Henriad* to "provide a code of reference ... giving the audience a means by which to understand individual and national identities" as Jennifer Flaherty has suggested.[16] In *Henry V*, for instance, through comparison between the English army's possession of "poor jades" and the French palfrey to whom the Dauphin writes a sonnet, French sensibility is shown to center on the feminine culture of courtly love and fine appearances (the beauty of horses, ornate armor) while the English are defined by manly pragmatism and doggedness. Valor, focus, and fully embodied presence, however physically weakened that embodied condition may be, will triumph over a culture of ornate representational forms in this play.

Horses here have a metonymic function, but at two moments in the *Henriad* horses are depicted as having their own agency. In *Richard II*, the decision of Barbary, originally Richard's horse, to accept Bolingbroke as his new liege, marks the success of Bolingbrook's challenge to Richard's kingship. Barbary's possession of a proper name immediately transports him into the realm of human culture: it signifies his individuality as both a narrative actant and a historical actor.[17] And it is from the figure who has the most intimate relationship with Barbary, his Groom who has "so often dress'd" him, that Richard learns that on the day that Bolingbroke was crowned as Henry IV, he rode on "roan Barbary," the horse that Richard himself "ha[d] st so often bestrid" (*Richard II* V.5.77–80). Barbary, as Flaherty remarks, "takes an active role in accepting the new king" by going well for him.[18] And it is through the mediating figure of his Groom that the emotional impact of Richard II's deposition and Henry IV's crowning is encapsulated. As Steven Mullaney remarks, the Groom "is a divided subject embodied for us on stage, but the lines of his multivalence—pity for Richard, delight in Barbary, grudging admiration for Bolingbroke—are distinct, clear and certain."[19] What is revealed here is the commonplace early modern understanding that horse knowledge and horsemanship are intrinsically linked to the quality and degree of human power as "a moral practice and a political practice," embodying "ideals of physical harmony and social concord" that symbolizes "the proper relationship between subject and sovereign."[20] In *Richard II*, however, it is a full reciprocity of the horse–rider relationship that is suggested by Barbary's agency and the emotional, political, and cultural meanings that are produced by his inclusion in the play as an actant.

The meanings of Barbary's role are also produced by his naming for his breed which signifies his aristocratic nature, and the authority by which he confers sovereignty on his riders. Breeding, a socio-economic negotiation of biology aligned with the double meanings already noted, is a crucial concern of all horsemanship treatises. Barbaries are identified variously as excelling through "their good shape and swiftness in running" (Blundeville); as being, "beyond all horses whatsoever for delicacie of shape and proportion" (Markham); and as "next to the *Spanish* Horse for *Wisdom*, but not neer so *Wise*, [making him] much Easier to be Drest: Besides, he is of a Gentle Nature, Docile, Nervous, and Leight" and "as Fine a *Horse* as can be, but somewhat Slender, and a little Lady-like ..." (Cavendish).[21] It is, perhaps, such a delicacy of physical conformation and the compliant but highly strung nature recognized as typical of the Barb that allows Shakespeare's Barbary to embody Richard's own poetic and irresolute nature, while his docility enables him to transfer his symbolic acceptance of Richard's sovereignty to Bolingbroke as he is crowned as Henry IV. The role of the Groom as mediator and translator of horse meanings, along with audience recognition of breed types, produces the possibility of Barbary's narrative agency.

In contrast, the other named horse in the *Henriad*, Cut in *1 Henry IV*, is a common horse of the common people: Cut, as editorial notes to almost all modern editions of the play explain, is a shortened form of "curtal," a term describing a horse with a docked tail—or a horse used to draw a cart whose tail hair has been cut off short so as not to become entangled in its harness.[22] But again, it is the relationship between the Carrier and Cut, his "[p]oor jade [who] is wrung in the withers," that is revealing. Cut both represents and embodies the hard-working life of ordinary people and the role of animals who work alongside tradesmen in partnership. It is in the care that the Carrier has for Cut in demanding that his saddle be made more comfortable (for both rider and horse, perhaps) that the interdependence of workers, both horse and human, is indicated. Although Cut's role as an equine commoner does not give him agency in terms of major constitutional events in human history as Barbary's more highly bred role does, his participation in the lives of ordinary men and the everyday intimacy between horses and humans implied in the scene in which he is invoked provides a further insight into this world of connected human and animal presences and its material conditions. And it is the mediating function of those who care for, ride, and have the most intimate relationship with horses that amplifies the emotional meanings articulated through the "inter" of these interspecies relationships.

III Training and Nobility: Horses, Hawks, and Humans

The horsemanship and horse management manuals I have been referring to constitute one among many sub-genres of the broader genre of training, and conduct manuals that proliferate in the early modern period. If this is a period of intense transition, need for knowledge of how to negotiate changes in social, religious, and cultural mores in combination with a new print market exploiting an appetite for such information leads to the production of works on familial, household, or inter-human relationships; on medical remedies and culinary recipes to cure or amend bodily disorders, diseases, and distempers; and on the acquisition of skills or "sciences." Those treatises on the physical sciences of dancing, swordsmanship, archery, swimming, hunting (on horseback, on foot, and with falcons), in particular, integrate implicit or explicit rank-appropriate social codes and values with teaching on how to acquire the embodied forms and expertise through which these are manifested and lived.

The notoriously ambivalent values of *The Taming of the Shrew*, and the pervasive referencing of this play's language and plot to the terminology and dynamics of horse management and falconry manuals, might serve as a specific example of how intertextual relationship between dramatic texts and training manuals functions. Differing critical views on the extent to which patriarchal values might be seen to be ultimately endorsed or critiqued by *The Taming of the Shrew* regularly culminates in analyses of Kate's capitulating speech in the final act which articulates central tenets of patriarchal values with textbook clarity:

> Thy husband is thy lord, thy life, thy keeper,
> Thy head, thy sovereign; …
>
> *(THE TAMING OF THE SHREW* V.2.152–53)

Is this speech to be taken at face value? Or is it ironic? Among the many critical evaluations of the play's representation of how Kate, the shrew-like woman, is trained into submission by her husband, Petruchio, a number have focused on the unusually extensive range of animal references in the play. In the abstract of her 1983 article on *The Shrew*, Jeanne Addison Roberts comments that the play "is usually excluded from the number of romantic comedies in which the relationship between, to use Northrop Frye's influential terms, the 'normal world' and the 'green world of romance' [is explored]."[23] She, however, proposes to attend to links between human ("normal") and natural worlds produced through the influence of Ovid's *Metamorphoses*. She writes:

> Kate and Petruchio move through a whole zoo of animal metaphors before they achieve the dignity of human marriage. Each tries insistently and repeatedly to demote the other to bestial status. And while their refusal to respect the gap between the animal and the human in the Great Chain of being is the stuff of low comedy, it is also a violation of humane interrelation.[24]

This perception is worth quoting here for its assumption of "normally" separated human and natural domains, in which the nonhuman animal unquestionably belongs to the natural side of this binary divide. But what if, seen not with the common values of 35 years ago, but through the lens of recent thought that seeks to blur this divide, Shakespearean metamorphoses are understood not as traverses between fully separated categories of human and animal, but as explorations of the much more blurred or indeterminate boundaries between the human and the natural that I have been suggesting is characteristic of the early modern period's everyday thought. In this context, the training or animal management manuals, so frequently referenced in *The Taming of the Shrew*, might then be perceived as comprising a textual genre that offers teaching on how to bring animals and humans alike into a naturally acculturated self-propriety, or self-possession, and social usefulness. Humans, like hawks, falcons, and horses, are domesticated animals who need to be trained or educated into their proper mode of being.

Peter Heaney perhaps comes closest to such a reading in his analysis of the cross-over between horse management terms and the play's events and descriptions.[25] Quoting the speech describing Petruchio's late arrival at his wedding to Kate, Heaney suggests, "attention to metaphor ... (or, more accurately, perhaps, suggestion by analogy) in *The Shrew* must lead the reader to Petruchio's horse. No Shakespearean horse, not even the Dauphin's, is given a fraction of the space devoted to this extraordinary creature."[26] Petruchio's haphazard and disordered dress is replicated in the horse's physical disorder or disease (coterminous words in the period) and poor dressing:

> ... his horse hipped – with an old mothy saddle and stirrups of no kindred – beside, possessed with the glanders and like to mose in the chine; troubled with the lampass, infected with the fashions, full of windgalls, sped with spavins ..., and with a half-cheeked bit and a head-stall of sheep's leather ...
>
> (*The Taming of the Shrew* III.2.48–56)

Everything about this horse is awry. From the list of diseases, commonly identified in all horse management and husbandry manuals, to the faulty, hotch-potched assembly of items of tack that the horse wears, this all points to equine mismanagement on "an epic scale," as Heaney puts it. Certainly, the whole speech comes over as a summarizing parody of manuals such as Gervase Markham's *Cheap and Good Husbandry* where the first part of the book is devoted to different aspects of horse breeding, riding, management, and the treatment of "*all general inward Sickness in Horses, which trouble the whole Body; of Fevers of all sortes, Plagues, Infections, and such like.*"[27] Such intertextual allusion leads Heaney to argue that there is an equivalence between Petruchio and his horse. Glossing the diseases described in the horse, he suggests that Petruchio, too, "exhibit[s] a disease of the mouth," a swollenness, in his excessive volubility. Analysis of such analogies between horse and man leads Heaney to caution, "[t]his 'condition' of Petruchio's should at the very least make one hesitate before endorsing the view that the *Shrew* is foursquare behind Petruchio's manic misogyny."[28] In this, Heaney differs from those who have seen the horse management references throughout *The Shrew*, as uncompromisingly demeaning to Kate. And he differs, too from, Linda Woodbridge who had earlier downplayed the apparently disparaging references to horse management as applied to a woman, through suggesting:

> Rather than comparing a woman to a recalcitrant horse ... Shakespeare softens [the comparison] ... by creating the metaphor of a falcon, an animal which although sub-human is a primate among birds and is allowed a certain amount of autonomy and aggressiveness.[29]

Although the training of hawks (including falcons) is "a most Princely and serious delight," achieved through gentleness in handling the birds, and as Markham states, "their infirmities, for the most part proceede from the indirection of their governors," this hardly seems a plausible defense against misogyny.[30] Falcons are, after all, used for hunting because of their predatory instincts. And, horses, as the manuals regularly insist, should also be "cherished."[31] So, rather than adjudicate between types of training used for different species as comparators to the training of Kate, it might be more useful to recognize that all such readings are predicated on questionable oppositions: between the human and the animal, between Shakespearean texts and more functional forms of writing.

Animal training manuals, with their double aim of training men to train beasts or birds, are not simply transparent texts that supply information about early modern culture that can be used to unlock Shakespearean meanings. They have their own conventions and formal attributes. In an essay on the major falconry manuals of the sixteenth and seventeenth centuries—those of George Turberville, Simon Latham, Edmund Bert, and Richard Blome—John Battalio examines ways in which the manuals' writers exploit "classical rhetoric."[32] This recognition leads us to perceive how, through their application of rhetorical techniques, falconry manuals themselves become intertextually related to the number of popular books on rhetoric (such as Henry Peacham's *The Garden of Eloquence*) that proliferated alongside other forms of instruction manual in the period, and to institutionalized practices of training in rhetoric.[33] In other words, they can be seen to be informed by modes of learning that are typical of the period's grammar schools where, in the horrified words of Jack Cade quoted earlier, one could find "men ... that usually talk of a noun, and a verb, and such abominable words," and where the rhetorical styles appropriate to writers' needs to "teach, please and move their audience" were taught.[34] Recognition of this further layer of educational reference suggests that, rather than seeing *The Shrew*'s references to horse management or falconry manuals as metaphors, or as coded clues to interpreting the extent of the play's misogynist position, the play might be seen to scrutinize the culture of training manuals *per se*. In so doing, it asks questions about the ways in which all domesticated beings—men, women, horses, or falcons—must be subject to training and education so that they may properly fit into the humanly socio-natural order of things. Whether the play parodies, even ridicules, such notions of training in their entirety through its comedy, or how *The Shrew* functions as a commentary on the implications of the early modern notion of "birth and breeding" as determinants of how we become who we are and take up our places in the world are the problems it presents.

IV Bears, Dogs, Materiality, and Performance

The question of the relationship of comedy to animal and human training raised here leads now from issues of print intertextuality to questions of the materiality of performance produced through the embodied practice of players and in the material environment of early playhouses. Immediately, reference to the idea of "play" itself, a word with multiple meanings, reminds us of the proximity of drama to sport and a whole range of other performative forms from which it is only beginning to separate itself in the period. As Louis Montrose has put it:

> The professional drama of Shakespeare's London had its roots in the late medieval civic religious drama ... and in the hodge-podge of popular entertainments – juggling and clowning, singing and miming, dancing and fencing, cockfighting and bearbaiting – from which it was still in the process of separating itself ...[35]

Modern excavation of London's early theaters demonstrates this clearly, providing physical evidence of the contiguous, even overlapping or interchangeable, sites of animal and human play forms, suggesting corresponding conceptual intersections. The archaeological report of the 1999–2000 excavation in the area containing the Hope playhouse on the Thames' south bank describes discoveries of a large number of horse and dog bones and of "a single brown bear fragment, a tibia, belonging to an adult animal ... [with] a small bony growth close to the distal end which may be the result of a knock or fall."[36] Such remains corroborate the textual descriptions of early modern witnesses of animal baiting performances—such as that of the disapproving Puritan, John Field, who described the collapse of Southwark Bear Garden in 1583, under the weight of so "great [a] company of people … the number [of which] had never beene seene there a long time before"[37]—and of modern scholars who point to the overlapping uses of early theaters as both bear baiting arenas and playhouses.[38] Andreas Höfele, most significantly, begins his *Stage, Stake and Scaffold* with a similar reference to archaeological work in the "early modern London theatre district," stating that finds include "the skulls and bones of mastiff dogs, or occasionally, the skull of a bear."[39] From this, he argues that "[p]lay-acting and bear-baiting were joined in active collusion," sharing audiences as well as the same, or adjacent, sites so that there is "a vital spill-over (semantic, but also performative, emotive, visceral) from the bear-garden [into the playhouse.]" This, he argues, "substantially affects the way Shakespeare models his human characters."[40]

Bear baiting, of course, involves semi-trained or semi-domesticated animals. If it is the predatory nature of falcons in combination with their openness to being trained that makes them suitable hunting partners for humans, the nature of mastiffs that is exploited in bear baiting represents a different negotiation of wildness and tameness. Bear baiting dogs enter human culture in a rather different, and less intimate, way than horses and falcons. Their ferocious aggression is exploited as they are set by humans to attack bears chained to a pole and who respond with correspondingly ferocity. It is the pure corporeality of animal, and correspondingly human, life that is focalised in such spectacles. The articulation of sameness and difference that I have argued is central to the period's concepts and practices of human–nonhuman relationships is performed *in extremis* here. Although certain bears, both fighting bears and those trained to perform "tricks," or to "dance," became named celebrities in Elizabethan culture—Harry Hunks is the most famous fighting bear—it is the uncertain extent of their trainability that signifies. The deaths of audience members, including that of a child, at animal baitings at London's Bankside Bear Garden in 1655, late in its history, make manifest the dangerous nature of these animals, the tense dialogue between trainability and wildness, and perhaps their ultimate impossibility of fully taming the wild in any domain of life.[41] Spectators, as witnesses to animal—and occasionally human—deaths experience the thrill and terror of seeing what occurs at the far boundary of that intermediate realm of the domesticated animal. Shakespeare's scattered allusions to bears throughout his plays (most famously the stage direction: "Exit, pursued by a bear," in *The Winter's Tale*) serve not just as knowing references to the culture of spectatorship that brings performing bears and human actors into some sort of collusion, but brings into stage presence the bodily dangers of all animal, including human, being.

The mastiffs and bears used in baiting spectacles represent the precariously acculturated world of the animal—and human—and relate most directly, perhaps, to tragic perspectives on the materiality of life. But the performative nature of animals used in such spectacle may also be perceived as comic. So, it is to the comedic aspects of performativity and the horse Cut in *1 Henry IV* that I will return now. The name Cut, as I remarked earlier, is usually understood to refer to a curtal. It is tempting, however, to think it might also refer to early modern theater practice. As Tiffany Stern's archival research reveals, a play in the Shakespearean period was not produced as a complete written text that was then performed.[42] Rather, play-texts were produced through process: they were simultaneously written and created through performance and audience feedback. Plot was constructed separately from, and before, the "language" of the plays which were both then "tested in first performance" and subject to alteration.[43] This first trial performance is described in the words of one of Middleon's characters in *The Ant and the Nightingale*, as "the first cut," implying, as Stern remarks, "that a second cut, or reshaping of the play" will follow. In modern productions, the scene containing Cut in *1 Henry IV* is invariably "cut" as it has no function in progressing the plot. Since the early modern process of altering, editing, and shortening plays in response to audience reaction is similarly referred to as producing "cuts," it is possible to speculate that the Cut scene might also have edited out in some performances, creating Cut's name as actorly joke. The possibility of such a verbal and theatrical joke of this sort in association with reference to a horse in a comically scatological, but incidental, scene, also leads us to acknowledgment of the always-embodied nature of performance. How performance method and comedic process may be tied to a partnership between human and animal actors, is suggested by Crab in *Two Gentlemen of Verona*.

While it has been remarked that Shakespeare rarely refers to dogs in his plays,[44] the dog Crab stands out as one of the most significant animal actants in all Shakespearean drama. This is not in the way of Barbary who embodies both emotional presence and plot-related meaning. Crab's agency lies in his own performative power—and through that, the power of theatrical performance more generally. Crab is, of course, an onstage actor. In an extensive discussion of Crab in his essay, "Crab's Pedigree," Richard Beadle writes:

> The pedigree of any given Crab may not necessarily be distinguished, but of the theatrical ancestry of his kind there is much to be said, for it is longer than that of any other figure who appears in the play, excepting his master, the clown, whose companion in performance he has been through more than one millennium.[45]

Beadle's essay traces the history of clowning and the influence of the famous Elizabethan clown, Richard Tarlton who had died in 1588. He points out how the partnership between Lance and Crab in Act II, Scene 2 of *The Two Gentlemen of Verona*, must produce some degree of improvisation: both the traditional clown's role and the dog's presence on stage necessitate improvised rather than fully, or partially, scripted performance.[46] Not only does this anchor Crab in a long theatrical tradition, but it presents us with a spectacle—and with spontaneous laughter arising from it, perhaps—that is essentially actorly. It is the animal presence on stage that creates the function of the human actor as improviser—an actor with a directly responsive relationship with the audience. Crab the dog is not simply a comic animal figure but is an actant who generates a pure form of theatricality and an immediacy of relationship between performer and audience.

For modern audiences, the Shakespearean representation of characters from the lower social orders as comic—Dogberry in *Much Ado About Nothing* might be a prime example—can be troubling. Experience of community productions where, for example, all characters from monarchs to mechanicals may speak with a regional accent can profoundly change audience reaction, however. The leveling effects of such performances not only produce new interpretations of a play, but also create a transformed level of rapport between actors and audience. To see Titania played with the exuberantly racy manners and local accent of my own home region, Merseyside in the UK, for instance, produces a re-invigorated understanding of her relationship with the faux-animal, Bottom, as well as of the play overall. In a similar fashion, the performative and pleasurable possibilities offered by Crab (for instance, urinating on stage) create a theatrical experience—perhaps closer than many modern performances to those of Shakespeare's first productions—that mitigates the potential disparagement of ordinary men and women. It is not that humans are reduced to the animal, but rather that boundaries between nature and culture, human and animal become blurred in the ways that I have been suggesting are intrinsic to early modern thought. Gleeful recognition of the unpredictable trainability of both humans and animals as actors, as improvisers, and as audience members provides pure theatrical pleasure.

Notes

1 William Cavendish, Earl (1628), Marquis (1643), and Duke (1665) of Newcastle's first book on horsemanship and the manège, *La méthode nouvelle et invention extraordinaire de dresser les chevaux* (Antwerp: Jacques van Meurs, 1658), was rewritten in a second, slightly different, English version, *A New Method, and Extraordinary Invention, to Dress Horses, and Work Them According to Nature as Also, to Perfect Nature by the Subtility of Art, Which Was Never Found Out, but by … William Cavendishe …* , (London : Printed by Tho. Milbourn, 1667). The 1658 text was republished in 1743 in English. My references are to a facsimile version of this 1743 edition: *A General System of Horsemanship*, intro William C. Steinkraus (North Pomfret, VT: J.A.Allen, 2000).

2 Cavendish, *General System*, 12.

3 Karen Raber, "William Cavendish's Horsemanship Treatises and Cultural Capital," in *Authority, Authorship and Aristocratic Identity in Seventeenth-Century England. William Cavendish, 1st Duke of Newcastle, and His Political, Social and Cultural Connections*', eds. Peter Edwards and Elspeth Graham (Leiden and Boston, MA: Brill, 2017), 331–52, 336.

4 Separation and dominance are central to Platonic and Aristotelian schemes of the Great Chain of Being passed down through medieval Neo-Platonism, and to the whole Western Judeo-Christian tradition with its predication on the biblical statement from *Genesis*, 1.1.26, giving man dominion over all living things.

5 Laurie Shannon, "The Eight Animals in Shakespeare; or before the Human," *PMLA* 124, no. 2 (March, 2009): 477.

6 Cavendish, *General System*, 12.

7 See John Henry, *The Scientific Revolution and the Origins of Modern Science* (Basingstoke: Palgrave Macmillan, 1997, 2008 edn.), 1–5, for a succinct summary of historiographical debates on dating, defining, and delineating the scientific revolution and Enlightenment.

8 Philip Pettit, *Made with Words: Hobbes on Language, Mind, and Politics* (Princeton, NJ: Princeton University Press, 2008), Chapters I and II; Alan Nelson and Matthew Priselac, "Made with Words: Hobbes on Language, Mind, and Politics," *Notre Dame Philosophical Reviews*, January 27 2009. https://ndpr.nd.edu/news/made-with-words-hobbes-on-language-mind-and-politics/ (accessed June 5, 2018).

9 Jane Bennett, *Vibrant Matter: A Political Ecology of Things* (Durham, NC and London: Duke University Press, 2010); Bruno Latour, *Reassembling the Social: An Introduction to Actor-Network-Theory* (Oxford: Oxford University Press, 2007); Graham Harman, *Object-Oriented Ontology. A New Theory of Everything* (London: Pelican Books, 2018); Stacy Alaimo, *Bodily Natures. Science, Environment, and the Material Self* (Bloomington: Indiana University Press, 2010); Hans Ulrich Gumbrecht, *Production of Presence. What Meaning Cannot Convey* (Stanford, CA: Stanford University Press, 2004) and *Atmosphere, Mood, Stimmung. On a Hidden Potential of Literature*, trans. Erik Butler (Stanford, CA: Stanford University Press, 2012).

10 Jeffrey Jerome Cohen, ed., *Animal, Vegetable, Mineral. Ethics and Objects* (Washington, DC: Oliphaunt Books, 2012), 7.

11 Michel Foucault, *The Order of Things: An Archaeology of the Human Sciences* (London: Tavistock Publications, 1970); originally *Les Mots et les Choses: Une archéologie des sciences humaines* (Paris: Éditions Gallimard, 1966).

12 Gumbrecht, *Production of Presence*, 2.

13 For the purposes of this essay, I simply name Shakespeare as author of all plays traditionally included in the Shakespearean canon. There are debates about the attribution of many of the plays. For a summary of issues relating to the attribution of the *Henriad*, see, amongst many articles, Santiago Segarra et al., "Attributing the Authorship of the *Henry VI* Plays by Word Adjacency," *Shakespeare Quarterly* 67, no. 2 (2016).

14 Cade's 'bridle' reference here may also connote the scold's bridle used to restrain the unruly verbosity of women.

15 On the bridle as the primary 'help' in the art of riding see Gervase Markham, *Cauelarice, or the English Horseman Contayning All the Arte of Horse-Manship…*, (London: Printed [by Edward Allde and W. Jaggard] for Edward White, 1607), Book 2, Chapter 2, 12–13.

16 Jennifer Flaherty, "'Know Us by Our Horses': Equine Imagery in Shakespeare's *Henriad*," in *The Horse as Cultural Icon* (Leiden and Boston, MA: Brill, 2017), 307–25, 307, 308.

17 Actant: used in literary studies and semiology to signify a person or thing that has an active role in a written or spoken narrative. Bruno Latour incorporated the term into actor-network theory to signify something that mediates or translates, or operates as the 'inter,' or what is between things.

18 Flaherty, "'Know Us by Our Horses'," 315.

19 Steven Mullaney, *The Reformation of Emotions in the Age of Shakespeare* (Chicago, IL and London: The University of Chicago Press, 2015), 39.

20 Kate van Orden, "From Gens d'Armes to Gentilhommes: Dressage, Civility, and the Ballet à Cheval," in *The Culture of the Horse. Status, Discipline, and Identity in the Early Modern World*, eds. Karen Raber and Treva J. Tucker (New York, Houndmills and Hampshire: Palgrave Macmillan, 2005), 197–222, 199, 207.

21 Thomas Blundeville, *The foure chiefest Offices Belonging to Horsemanship* (London: Imprinted...by Henrie Denham, 1580), 1–2; Markham, *Cauelarice*, 13; Cavendish, *New Method*, 53.

22 Docking horses' tails, unlike dogs' tails, did not involve amputation or cutting the tail bone.

23 Jeanne Addison Roberts, "Horses and Hermaphrodites: Metamorphoses in the Taming of the Shrew," *Shakespeare Quarterly* 34, no. 2 (Summer, 1983): 159.

24 Roberts, "Horses and Hermaphrodites," 160.

25 Peter F. Heaney, "Petruchio's Horse: Equine and Household Mismanagement in *The Taming of the Shrew*," *Early Modern Literary Studies* 2, no. 1–12 (May, 1998), https://extra.shu.ac.uk/emls/04-1/heanshak.html (accessed June 29, 2018).

26 Heaney, "Petruchio's Horse," para 2.

27 Gervase Markham, *Cheap and Good Husbandry, for the Well-Ordering of All Beasts and Fowls, and for the General Cure of Their Diseases* (London: Printed by T.S. for Roger Jackson, 1614), 11.

28 Heaney, "Petruchio's Horse," 4.

29 Linda Woodbridge, *Women and the English Renaissance: Literature and the Nature of Womankind, 1540–1620* (Brighton: Harvester Press, 1984), 206.

30 Markham, *Countrey Contentments*, 87; *Cheap and Good Husbandry*, 135.

31 On cherishing horses, see Elaine Walker, "The Author of Their Skill: Human and Equine Understanding in the Duke of Newcastle's 'New Method'," in *The Horse as Cultural Icon. The Real and the Symbolic Horse in the Early Modern World*, eds. Peter Edwards, Karl A.E. Enenkel and Elspeth Graham (Leiden and Boston, MA: Brill, 2012), 333.

32 John T. Battalio, "Sixteenth- and Seventeenth-Century Falconry Manuals: Technical Writing with a Classical Rhetorical Influence," *Technical Writing and Communication* 43, no. 2 (2013).

33 Henry Peacham, *The Garden of Eloquence Conteyning the Figures of Grammer and Rhetorick* (London: Printed by H. Jackson in Fleetestrete, 1577).

34 Battalio, "Falconry Manuals," 157.

35 Louis Montrose, *The Purpose of Playing: Shakespeare and the Cultural Politics of the Elizabethan Theatre* (Chicago, IL: University of Chicago Press, 1996), 19.

36 Anthony Mackinder et al., *The Hope Playhouse, Animal Baiting and Later Industrial Activity at Bear Gardens on Bankside. Excavations at Riverside House and New Globe Walk, Southwark, 1999–2000* (London: Museum of London Archaeology, 2013), 15.

37 John Field, *A Godly Exhortation, by Occasion of the Late Judgement of God, Shewed at Parris-Garden, the Thirteenth Day of Januarie* (London: Printed by H. Carre, 1583), B vii verso.

38 See, for example, Herbert Berry, "Folger MS V.b.275 and the Deaths of Shakespearean Playhouses," ed. J. Pilcher. *Medieval and Renaissance Drama in England* 10, 1998, 262–93.

39 Andreas Höfele, *Stage, Stake and Scaffold. Humans and Animals in Shakespeare's Theatre* (Oxford: Oxford University Press, 2011), 1.

40 Höfele, *Stage, Stake and Scaffold*, 3.

41 Terence Hawkes sees an implicit opposition between the realm of the law (representing human control) and wildness enacted in the spectacle of bear baiting. Terence Hawkes, *Shakespeare in the Present* (London and New York: Routledge, 2002), 83–106.

42 Tiffany Stern, *Documents of Performance in Early Modern England* (Cambridge: Cambridge University Press, 2009), 81–117.

43 Stern, *Documents of Performance*, 88.

44 Stephen Greenblatt, "A Great Dane Goes to the Dogs," *The New York Review of Books*, March 26, 2009. www.nybooks.com/articles/2009/03/26/a-great-dane-goes-to-the-dogs/ (accessed June 1, 2018).

45 Richard Beadle, "Crab's Pedigree," in *English Comedy*, eds. Michael Cordner, Peter Holland, and John Kerrigan (Cambridge: Cambridge University Press, 1994), 12–35, 12.

46 Many thanks to Stephen Longstaffe for his stimulating ideas about Shakespearean improvisation (personal correspondence.)

15

PERFORMING *THE WINTER'S TALE* IN THE "OPEN"

Bear Plays, Skinners' Pageants, and the Early Modern Fur Trade

Todd A. Borlik

Surely no stage direction in Shakespeare has exercised the ingenuity of scholars and the-ater directors more than "exit pursued by a bear." Among the myriad ways in which it has been staged over the centuries—with actors in bear-suits, taxidermic specimens on wheels, furry puppets, video projections, bear-shaped shadows, offstage growls, and oversize teddy bears—one in particular seems to neatly illustrate the purview of this chapter. In a 1986 Royal Shakespeare Company production of *The Winter's Tale* directed by Terry Hands, a large polar bear skin rug that had adorned Leontes' palace suddenly sprung up from the floor to chase Antigonus.[1] While the moment elicited laughs from the audience, its humor results from its abrupt collapse of the distinction between inanimate object and animate creature, between the domestic and the wild. The undoing of such tidy dichotomies has become one of the chief tasks of animal studies and the new materialism over the past decade. To date, however, little attention has been paid to the importance of fur in the theatrical culture of Renaissance England, as a performing object with a disturbing provenance—one that po-tentially troubles the alliance between these critical approaches.

In the narrative of his 1609 voyage to the Arctic, Jonas Poole recounts killing and skin-ning seven polar bears. Among his victims was a she-bear accompanied by two cubs, whom Poole brought back to London, where they were deposited in Paris Garden.[2] Whereas King Henry III had kept a polar bear (a gift from the King of Norway) in the Tower of London in the 1250s, King James entrusted the cubs to the custody of the actor Edward Alleyn and Alleyn's father-in-law Philip Henslowe, who were not only the Masters of the Royal Game but also two of the most influential figures in Jacobean show business. Theater historians have long speculated about the presence of performing bears on the Renaissance stage. Ar-thur Quiller-Couch proposed that Shakespeare's company could have availed themselves of the stable of trained bears in Southwark when staging *The Winter's Tale*, and J.H.P. Pafford concurred that this was a possibility in the second Arden edition of the play. In an influen-tial article, however, Nevill Coghill insisted that bears were simply too unpredictable and dangerous to let them run amok on stage, and this verdict more or less prevailed during the second half of the twentieth century.[3] The case was reopened in 2001 when Teresa Grant uncovered new evidence of the polar bear cubs among Henslowe and Alleyn's accounts, and she and Barbara Ravelhofer have argued that they were featured in several Renaissance plays.[4] They were likely hitched to a chariot in Ben Jonson's *Oberon*, may have had a cameo in the King's Men revival of *Mucedorus* in 1610 or 1611, or possibly even scampered across the boards in Shakespeare's *The Winter's Tale*.[5] Without Poole's slaughter of the cubs' mother, then, it is conceivable that Shakespeare may never have written the most famous stage direction in English literature.

Today, the polar bear has become an environmental martyr, a symbol of the threat climate change poses to the planet and its biodiversity. In 2009, the 400th anniversary of Poole's voyage, a 16-foot tall polar bear statue was floated down the Thames right past Shakespeare's Globe to raise public awareness of global warming.[6] Needless to say, seventeenth-century audiences would have perceived the cubs very differently. More than just exotic creatures from the frozen north, they would have been regarded as living advertisements of the fortunes to be gained in the early modern fur trade. After all, Poole's voyage was sponsored by the Muscovy Company, which was heavily invested in importing fur from Russia. When Shakespeare's *The Winter's Tale* was performed at court in November 1611, the future Russian ambassador John Meyrick had just returned from a trip to Moscow, and factors from the Muscovy Company were in Pustozersk to negotiate a deal to boost fur imports.[7] Shakespeare's decision to write a play around this time featuring a Russian princess and a bear—which does not appear in his source, Robert Greene's *Pandosto*—may be something more than mere coincidence.[8]

In a witty and theory-savvy essay, Lowell Duckert examines Shakespeare's bear "[as] a transspecies being whose animacy queers ideas of the autonomous human species."[9] This chapter pursues a similar line of argument, but focuses on the animistic power of animal skin as a performing actant in the networks of both Renaissance drama and the global economy. Interestingly, the same Alleyn and Henslowe who took charge of the polar bear cubs were, respectively, the chief actor and financier of the Admiral's company, whose 1598 property inventory includes a "beares skyne" and a "lyone skin" (HD 319). While these entries lend credence to the belief that Elizabethan theater companies (at least prior to 1610) had human actors don fur suits rather than rely on actual bears, this debate has now reached the point of diminishing returns. Worse, it perpetuates the assumption that the species boundary must be clearly drawn. For too long, theater historians have approached the equivocal evidence for ursine performance as a problem in need of solution. In contrast, proponents of animal studies might exercise the Shakespearean virtue of negative capability and argue that the historian's inability to determine conclusively who or what played the bear reflects the ontological confusion that prevailed in the Renaissance before the "invention of the human."[10] By tolerating uncertainty rather than policing boundaries, critics might instead hail the Renaissance playhouse as dramatizing what philosopher Giorgio Agamben refers to as the "Open"—a conceptual space where humans and other species become suspended in indistinction.[11]

Whether or not the cubs participated in Jacobean theatrical spectacles, evidence overwhelmingly indicates that skin and fur—the reason their mother was slaughtered and flayed—did have a conspicuous supporting role in many Renaissance plays. In addition to the bear and lion skin, Henslowe's inventory lists several costumes adorned with fur: "i short clocke of black vellet, with sleves faced with white fore," "i mannes gown faced with whitte fore," and a "blak velvett gowne w[t] wight fure" (HD 322, 291). There is even ocular proof that the leading man of the Admiral's company, Edward Alleyn, wore fur offstage. While most Shakespeareans are familiar with the life-sized painting of Alleyn at the Dulwich Portrait Gallery, few realize that the thick craquelure over his black gown conceals the presence of large bristling furs.[12] Apropos of Renaissance portraiture, Erica Fudge remarks how animals and animal objects are all too often "absented from the picture, made to seem unnecessary and inconsequential, with the result that the human emerges as the only necessary and consequential being in the frame."[13] The painting over of Alleyn's fur perfectly captures this erasure. In contrast, W.B. Morris's copy of the portrait (see Figure 15.1), which portrays the furs clearly, might serve as a visual corollary for this chapter's attempted restoration. The documented presence of fur in the wardrobe of a major Elizabethan acting troupe and upon the body of the era's most celebrated actor should remind us that the entertainment industry in Shakespeare's day was implicated not only in animal baiting but also in the commercial fur trade. Indeed, two of the most popular playwrights in Jacobean London, Thomas Middleton and Thomas Dekker, wrote civic pageants for the "Worshipful Company of Skinners," trumpeting—in Dekker's phrase—the "glory of furs."[14] By pitting some Renaissance bear plays against these pageants, this chapter spotlights the performative power of fur in therianthropic species-crossings while considering how such crossings might threaten the speciesist logic that entitles humans to kill and flay other animals. At the same time, it also aims to demonstrate the limitations of new materialist or object-oriented theory for animal studies, in that erasing the subject/object divide risks colluding with the Skinners' pageant in its refusal to discriminate between an animal and its fur.

Figure 15.1 W.B. Morris. Portrait of Edward Alleyn (c. 1900). DPG 551. Dulwich Portrait Gallery

I Wearing Fur in the Early Anthropocene

Evolutionary biologists now speculate that early hominids lost their fur as far back as a million years ago, perhaps to improve their ability to regulate body temperature or to reduce infestation by disease-bearing parasites.[15] Prior to Darwin, however, some naturalists and skeptics pointed to our lack of fur as evidence that humans had been created under-provisioned or maladapted for survival in the wild. In a piercing study of *King Lear*, Laurie Shannon aligns Shakespeare's deliberate stripping away of the "robes and furred gowns" to expose man as a "poor, bare, forked animal" (3.4.101) with this anti-humanist discourse she labels "negative exceptionalism."[16] Shannon's thesis is thoroughly convincing, yet ecocriticism should also attend to the implications and ecological consequences of humanity's desire to compensate for its furlessness. Along with deforestation and sheep-farming, the market for furs was one of the biggest forces behind de-wilding during the medieval and early modern eras.[17] Brown bears still prowled the woods of Roman Britannia, and were probably killed off in the Anglo-Saxon era (c. 1000)—both for their fur and to protect livestock. The wolf was also exterminated in southern Britain around this time, partially as a result of a tribute of wolf-pelts the English King Edgar I had imposed on the Welsh, though small populations survived until the thirteenth century. The beaver vanished from English and Welsh rivers during the late Middle Ages, and the last record of any in Scotland dates from the Tudor period.[18] The pine marten, the native species most valued for its fur, proved more tenacious, but overhunting severally depleted its numbers. In the late seventeenth century John Aubrey reports that they were "utterly destroyed in North Wiltshire."[19] Badgers, foxes, hare, rabbit, and squirrel would also have been routinely trapped and skinned in large numbers. Sadly, Britain was not the only country to experience a stark decline in furbearers during the Renaissance. In the early seventeenth century, the brown bear was already an endangered species in Bohemia, the site of the notorious bear encounter in *The Winter's Tale*, and the nation's last surviving bear was shot in 1856.[20] While Shakespeare's romance is set in antiquity, the devouring of Antigonus is a mystification of the contemporary environmental reality that inverts the roles of predator and prey. Accounts of fur traders and travel narratives like Poole's reveal that bears had far more reason to fear humans than humans to fear bears. Furthermore, the dwindling or, in some cases, disappearance of native furbearers in Britain and Europe due to habitat loss and overhunting encouraged colonial expansion in North America and the development of global trading networks that fueled the Muscovy Company voyages to Bear Island, and the Russian incursions into the wilds of Siberia. In a particularly vicious circle, the growing scarcity of fur is partially what gave it such allure as a fashion accessory, affordable only to the rich, so some species may have been more highly sought after as their numbers declined.

On the Renaissance stage, the mere wearing of animal fur constituted a dramatic spectacle in and of itself. Beyond signifying wintry weather or a scene in a cold climate, furs would convey detailed information to Elizabethan spectators about the status or profession of the characters, as sumptuary laws strictly dictated which social ranks could wear which variety of fur. A 1574 proclamation restricts the wearing of furs "whereof the kind groweth not in the Queen's dominions" to those with annual incomes in excess of £100, with exceptions made for the pelts of beech marten, grey jennets, and budge or lambskin. The fur of black jennets (civet cats) and "lucerns" (lynxes) was reserved for the monarch, nobles, Knights of the Garter, and members of the Privy Council. Only a king or queen could wear the coveted white fur of the ermine, and the "wight fure" listed in the Admiral's costumes—whatever species it was stripped from—was likely tailored to resemble ermine.[21] Do the high prices ermine fetched explain why Poole and his companions were so eager to kill and flay white-furred polar bears?

A survey of the royal wardrobe expenses from the late medieval and early modern periods offers a shocking glimpse of the mass carnage subsidized by the English monarchy. Between 1392 and 94, the clothes-hound Richard II purchased the fur of 1,634 ermines, 308 pine martens, 18 beavers, and over 200,000 squirrels. Henry IV owned a single robe made from 12,000 squirrels and 80 ermines. In a five-year span between 1413 and 18, Henry V purchased 625 imported pelts of sable and 20,000 martens—that is three times the number of Frenchmen slain at Agincourt! 250 pine martens were killed to line a velvet gown of Henry VI, while Henry VIII possessed a satin gown adorned with the fur of 350 sables.[22] The famed Coronation Portrait of Elizabeth I depicts her in an ermine-lined robe, and each black dot represents the tail of a single dead animal (see Figure 15.2).

As the son of a glover—"you fur your gloves with reason," quips Troilus (2.2.37)—and alderman, Shakespeare would have grown up around both leather and fur, and been personally acquainted with both its ornamental use and its ceremonial power. While no costume inventory survives for Chamberlain's or King's Men, it is a virtual certainty that Shakespeare's acting companies also owned fur-lined robes for the roles of the monarchs

Figure 15.2 Queen Elizabeth (c. 1600). The Coronation Portrait. © National Portrait Gallery, London

listed above. Curiously, in the 1603 quarto of *Hamlet*, the Prince refers to his mourning garb not as an "inky cloak," but a "sable suit" (2.33). This variant may not seem particularly noteworthy, since sable can be glossed as black, as the play itself attests: the ghost's beard is "sable-silvered" (1.2.241), and Pyrrhus sports "sable arms, black as his purpose" (2.2.455). From an ecomaterialist perspective, however, this use of sable as an elegant synonym for black by Renaissance poets risks obfuscating the violence of the fur trade, transforming an animal into an adjective. So it is significant that Shakespeare seems to give the same word a different meaning prior to the Mousetrap when Hamlet, jeering at the brevity of Gertrude's mourning, exclaims, "Nay then let the devil wear black, for I'll have a suit of sables" (3.2.124). This confusing passage only makes sense if Hamlet is talking about the literal fur of the sable, which can be dark brown rather than midnight black. This outburst might also hint that Claudius and Gertrude are wearing furs, which would signify their exalted status as royalty and the play's northern setting. On stage, as at court, furs helped to generate the aura of kingship, with of the dominion of the human hunter over the animal world replicating the monarch's dominion over the realm.

Oddly, however, fur not only was a status symbol for the wealthy elite but also could be a marker of sub-human savagery. Just as the use of leather as a dermal prosthesis in the performance of racial otherness might signify a greater proximity to the animal condition, fur costumes would help radiate the wildness of the "wild men" in medieval and early modern romance. Bremio wears fur in *Mucedorus*; in the prose tale of *Valentine and Orson* (the basis of a lost play), Orson's skin is said to become hirsute like that of the she-bear who suckles him; and the earliest record of Caliban's costume states he was traditionally clad "in a large bearskin or the skin of some other animal."[23] Thanks to the vogue for fine silk and velvet, large fur gowns had declined in popularity in the sixteenth century, and would thus have been perceived as a throwback from an earlier or more primitive era.[24] To some Elizabethans, however, that would have been its appeal. On stage, fur would have helped actors like Alleyn to channel a primal energy, creating spectacles to rival the baiting pit by simulating the charisma and ferocity of an apex predator. Similarly, the furs worn by a hunter would be a badge of his prowess and courage. The "lyone skin" in the Admiral's property inventory, for example, was probably worn by Alleyn in his role as Hercules—"a part to tear a cat in"—as a spoil or trophy of his slaying the Nemean lion. In Shakespeare's *King John*, the Duke of Austria likewise appears in a lion's skin, but the enraged Constance impugns his courage by heckling him instead to "hang a calfskin on those recreant limbs" (3.1.55), a taunt gleefully echoed by Philip the Bastard. Furred gowns and animal skins, then, were more than merely passive objects: even after its original owner was dead and flayed, fur could continue to radiate a bestializing influence, in accordance with the sixteenth-century Swedish writer Olaus Magnus's observation that people who sleep under wolverine-fur blankets "have dreams that agree with the nature of that creature, and have an insatiable stomach ... and seem never to be satisfied."[25] Strangely, a commodity responsible for de-wilding a large swathe of the planet's remaining wilderness might function on stage as an instrument of psychological re-wilding. To defend this claim, the next section turns from the furred gowns of the monarch-hunter to the species-blurring power of fur in the Renaissance bear play.

II Playing the Bear

Bears were even more common in Renaissance drama than many theater historians realize. Besides its scattered references to animal skins and fur, *Henslowe's Diary* mentions a number of now lost plays that almost certainly featured ursine actors. In the absence of extant texts, any claims about the contents of these plays are perforce speculative. However, an examination of the likely sources for their plots combined with an understanding of repertorial practices does permit some responsible conjectures: in this case, that audiences at the Rose in the late 1590s would have been repeatedly treated to the spectacle of humanoid bears, and that fur functioned in these productions as a vehicle for trans-speciesism, which in some ways is as important for animal studies as transvestism is for gender studies. If cross-dressing in Renaissance drama signals the performative nature of gender, animal impersonation might enable a fleeting perception of what Erica Fudge calls "dressing up as human."[26]

Based on a popular medieval French romance first translated around 1510 and reprinted three times during the sixteenth century, *Valentine and Orson* had been the subject of a play staged by the Queen's Men (entered in the Stationers' Register in 1595), which the Admiral's Men may have acquired in 1598. However, the large payment of £5 (the usual fee for a new play was £6) to Hathaway and Munday recorded by Henslowe indicates that revisions must have been substantial (HD 93), if it were not a new adaptation altogether. It seems a reasonable supposition that the lost play would have included the dramatic episode of the birth of the twin brothers in the woods, and Orson's abduction by a she-bear. Given the bearskin listed in the Admiral's inventory, such a scene would not have been beyond their technical means. It is even possible that the actor playing Orson (whose name means bear in French) would have worn some kind of fur suit since the prose romance declares that the abandoned child was naked and, "by reason of the nutriment it received from the beare, became rough all over like a beast."[27]

A bear may also have lumbered across the Rose stage in *Chinon of England*, performed as a new play by the Admiral's Men on January 3, 1596, and staged 14 times during that year (HD 33–54). Although the text is lost, Christopher Middleton published an Arthurian romance with that title, the earliest surviving copy of which dates from 1597. In this prose version, a sorceress transforms a character named Bessarian into a bear, and hangs a parchment around his neck promising to grant the wishes of whoever slays the beast. Despite losing his ability to speak, Bessarian retains the capacity to reason and think. If this episode figured in the lost play, it would have confronted audiences with another ursine-human hybrid.

The sight of a person trapped in a bear's body may also have featured in *The Arcadian Virgin*, for which Henry Chettle and William Haughton were paid an advance of 15 shillings by Henslowe in December 1599 (HD 128).[28] W.W. Greg speculated that it was based on the tale of Atalanta, who was abandoned as an infant (like Perdita) and suckled by a she-bear (like Orson). However, the eponymous virgin could just as plausibly have been Callisto, whose tale (which reveals the shared etymological derivation of Arcadia and Arctic from the Greek for bear) would have been well known from Ovid's *Metamorphoses*.[29] A maiden devotee of the goddess Phoebe, Callisto is raped by Jove and then transformed by jealous Juno into a bear. Ovid makes it clear that Callisto retains her human consciousness, and even her fear of other wild beasts: "for though she were a Bear, / Yet when she spied other Beares she quooke for verie paine" (2.611–12). This play may never have been staged—as Henslowe does not record any additional payments to the two authors—but the advance nevertheless suggests that the Admiral's Men thought ursine impersonation would still make good box office in 1599. Having invested rehearsal time and money in orchestrating bear scenes for *Valentine and Orson*, the company would have been eager both to duplicate the success and to redeploy expensive stage properties such as animal skins rather than use them once and discard them.

Whether or not *The Arcadian Virgin* was ever performed, a bear of some sort certainly did traipse across the Rose stage in another lost play entitled *Cox of Collumpton*. The

Performing The Winter's Tale *in the "Open"*

astrologer-physician Simon Forman attended a performance of it on March 9, 1600, and jotted down a memorandum of how Cox's two wicked sons Peter and John were driven to suicide:

> For peter being *fronted wth the sight of a bear viz a sprite* apering to Jhon & him when they sate vpon deuisio^n of the land^es in *likenes* of a bere & ther wth peter fell out of his wites and way lyed in a darke house & beat out his braines against a post & Jhon stabed him self.[30]

Forman's notation implies that the performance somehow telegraphed that the bear was not merely a bear. Does "likenes" mean animal skin and "sprite" a human actor? While Forman's record of *The Winter's Tale* (which he saw at the Globe in May 1610) curiously fails to mention a bear, other evidence proves that Shakespeare's troupe sought to capitalize on this crowd-pleasing spectacle. To the befuddlement of many literary historians, the most popular play in early modern England was not by Shakespeare or Marlowe. It was the anonymous *Mucedorus*, first performed around 1590 and reprinted 17 times between 1598 and 1668. Significantly, the 1598 publication of this play—described on its title page as "newly set forth"—coincides with the production of *Valentine and Orson* at the Rose, and the spate of bear plays in the Admiral's repertoire. In the 1598 text, however, the play opens with the killing of the bear offstage; only its severed head appears. When the King's Men revived the play in 1610, the bear scene was expanded, perhaps—if Grant and Ravelhofer are correct—to incorporate the polar bear cubs brought back by Poole. In the 1610 quarto, the bear trots on stage and startles a buffoon named Mouse, whose comic monologue seems to offer tantalizing clues as to how the scene may have been performed:

> Was ever poor gentlemen so scared out of his seven senses? A bear? Nay, sure it cannot be a bear, but some devil in a bear's doublet: for a bear could never have had that agility to have frighted me.[31]

Taken literally, this reference to the "bear's doublet" seems a retrospective hint that the staging involved an actor in a bearskin. As a clown character, however, Mouse must be regarded as an unreliable narrator, and the comedy or dramatic irony would be enhanced if the audience saw an actual bear. The phrase might even conceivably refer to a human garment worn by a performing bear and then fitted over a bearskin concealing a human. In other words, there are no clear-cut answers, and the revisions to *Mucedorus* indicate that Renaissance theater companies may have staged the same scene a number of different ways, depending on the venue, audience, and properties or animal performers available. Mouse's confusion may be comic, but it also encapsulates the predicament of critics, unable to strip away the fur to determine what lies beneath.

Even when the play-text survives, the performance of the bear is in some ways "lost"— and this is not necessarily a cause for regret. Theater historians attempting to establish with certainty how bear scenes must have been staged do so in violation of the moral embedded in Renaissance romance about the inextricable entanglement of Nature and Art. As Andrew Gurr shrewdly observes, even "real" trained bears are not the same thing as wild bears, or the King's Men might need a new Antigonus for every performance.[32] Although some of the evidence is circumstantial, this survey of the Renaissance bear play indicates that the theater of Shakespeare's day frequently sought to revel in confusion by presenting ursine-human hybrids. With this in mind, modern productions of *The Winter's Tale* in which the actor playing the horn-mad and lion-like Leontes doubles as the bear are faithful to the Renaissance sense of the precariousness of the animal-human boundary.[33] The point is not that there is one "right way" to stage the bear scene. Rather hybridity and the blending of illusion with reality should be seen as inbuilt features of Shakespeare's tragicomedy, and performances in which it is unclear if one is "supposed" to recognize the actor underneath the animal skin (or perceive a trained bear as a wild bear) can generate a salutary wonder by suspending audiences in Agamben's "Open."

In a passage from *The Open* of particular interest to early modernists, Agamben cites the fascination with the *homo ferus* as an example of how the "anthropological machine" of previous eras sought to produce a "non-man" through the humanization of an animal.[34] Antigonus invokes this motif of the feral child when he wishes for a wild animal to adopt Perdita:

> Some powerful spirit instructs the kites and raves
> To be thy nurses. Wolves and bears, they say,
> Casting their savageness aside have done
> Like offices of pity.
>
> (2.3.186–89)

Adhering its source, *The Winter's Tale* dramatizes the nature/nurture conflict in terms of social class rather than species. Nevertheless, Shakespeare's introduction of the bear, the shepherd's pronunciation of "bairn," and the wrapping of Perdita in a "*bearing cloth*" make her an honorary cub, creating a strange parallel between her and the orphaned polar bears.[35] Cross-species nurture, however, is central to the *Valentine and Orson* tale staged by the Queen's Men and Admiral's Men. Significantly, the courtly knight Valentine and wild man Orson do not realize they are brothers. Only after they save one another's life is it revealed that they were separated at birth, and the recognition scene effectively enacts what Donna Haraway calls "making kin" across species.[36] One might counter that the entire story is premised on the human–animal binary: Orson is not really a bear but an abandoned human, just as the stage bear who abducts him may be a human dressed in bear skin. The virtue of Agamben's "Open" is that it demands we suspend such distinctions, and in this regard it resembles the recovery in early modern romance of an epistemological innocence or poetic faith in which the audience suspends disbelief in the separation of human culture and nonhuman nature. To better appreciate how the fascination with furries in romance might capture a rapport across species, the final section of this chapter draws a contrast not with the familiar spectacle of the baiting pit but with the Skinners' pageant—an "anthropological machine" in which the animal/human distinction is forged with a vengeance.

III The Skinners' Pageant: The Triumph as Anthropological Machine

Established in 1327, the Skinners were recognized as one of the original 12 livery companies of London. The election of a member of any company to Lord Mayor was always a cause for celebration, but the Skinners may have especially relished the occasion since luxurious furs conspicuously adorn the ceremonial gown of office. While the Lord Mayor's show is one of the best-known examples of civic theater in the English Renaissance, there has been little inquiry into the role of fur in these processions or to the distinctive characteristics of the Skinners' pageant in particular. One of the most interesting specimens of this neglected sub-genre is Thomas Middleton's grotesquely mistitled *The Triumphs of Love and Antiquity*, composed to celebrate the installation of the Skinner Sir William Cockayne as Lord Mayor in 1619. After disembarking from their boat on the Thames, the procession marched to the yard around St Paul's Cathedral, where they encountered

> a Wildernesse, most gracefully and artfully furnish't with diuerse kindes of Beasts bearing Furre, proper to the Fraternity; the Presenter, the Musical Orpheus, Great Maister, both in Poesy and Harmony, who by his excellent Musicke, drew after him wild Beasts, Woods and Mountaines.[37]

Curiously, Agamben's theory of the "Open" is derived (via Heidegger) from the poet Rilke, for whom Orpheus symbolizes the possibility of recapturing a "pure relation" with nature. In contrast, Middleton's Orpheus represents human mastery over the environment. While Middleton likens the Greek musician to a "wise magistrate" and the wilderness to an unruly commonwealth, it is the fur merchant's dominion over animals that the performance brandishes as a qualification or exemplum for his rule as Lord Mayor. In a visual pun, Cockayne is represented in the pageant as an "artificial cock," who, unlike the fur-bearing beasts over whom he perches, has the power to speak and command. Of course Middleton, too, possesses this Orphic power. Orpheus's ability to move plants and beasts allies the poet-playwright and set designer with the forces of global commerce, and this conjuring of wilderness to London duplicates the magic of the early modern fur trade to transport the animals' pelts.

A similar scenario unfolds in Thomas Dekker's *Britannia's Honor*, which celebrates the inauguration of the new Lord Mayor of London, Richard Deane, who was both a member of the Skinners' company and an investor in the Muscovy Company.[38] The Muscovy Company's import privileges had just been renewed in 1628 when Dekker composed this puff-piece advertising to a Russian embassy the robust demand for fur in England. A Russian prince and princess actually appear in the pageant, followed by an English Lord, Lady, Judge, University Doctor, Frau, and Skipper, all clad in various animal pelts to illustrate "the necessary, ancient, and general use of Furs, from the highest to the lowest" (B3^v). Instead of Orpheus, Dekker's master of ceremonies is a personification of Fame, who salutes the Russian royalty and proclaims, "Russia now envies London, seeing here spent / Her richest Furs, in graceful ornament" (B3^v). Imitating Middleton's pageant, *Britannia's Honor* concludes with the tableau, like a portable diorama from a natural history museum, of a "wilderness in which are many sorts of such beasts, whose rich skins serve for furs": the lynx, wolf, leopard, fox, rabbits, ferrets, squirrels, represented in "lively, natural postures" (C2^r).

Today, when Lord Mayors' offices throughout England have renounced the use of real fur in ceremonial dress, it is hard to image a fur-themed fashion show including an exhibition of its victims. What made such a spectacle acceptable to a seventeenth-century audience? One possible explanation is that while modern fur companies might publicize that they have raised the animals humanely, the aim of the Skinners' pageant is to dramatize that the animals are inhuman, and thus ineligible for moral concern. Dekker speaks of the usefulness of various furs in "distinguishings" (B4^r) of rank, but the primary distinguishing here is between human and beast. While it would be tempting to compare these furrier pageants to Renaissance fashion shows, both Middleton and Dekker explicitly model them on a far more vicious form of street theater: the Roman triumph. Middleton includes the word Triumph in the title, while Dekker's fur-clad Russian dignitaries sit like military conquerors in "a Chariot Triumphant ... drawn by two Lucernes" or lynxes, a species that features (along with the sable and ermine) on the Skinners' coat of arms (see Figure 15.3). In Roman victory processions, prisoners of war and spoils of conquest would be paraded through the streets, and this is precisely the degraded condition of the furbearers and fur in the Skinners' pageant, whose

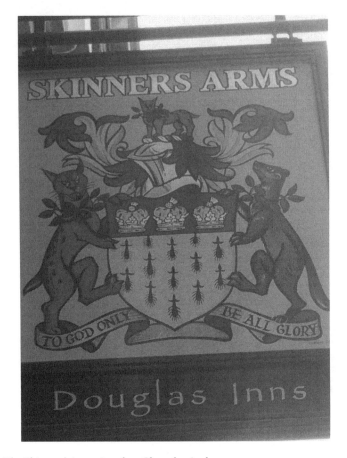

Figure 15.3 The Skinners' Arms, London. Photo by Author

abjection recalls that of the Goths in *Titus Andronicus*, or the defeated kings hitched to the chariot of Marlowe's Tamburlaine.

This casts the spectacle of the orphaned polar bear cubs towing the chariot in Jonson's *Oberon* in a much more sinister light. Musing on the presence of live polar bears in Jonson's play, Ravelhofer views them as proof that "Stuart princes and monarchs are demonstrably capable of conjuring up flesh-and-blood fabulous animals and controlling them" (308), and the Skinners' pageant invests this same power in global commerce, while representing non-human animals as objects, mere stage "property." These two civic processions may feature the most ambitious attempts to represent actual wilderness in Renaissance drama, but it is a wilderness already under human jurisdiction. As political theater, these triumphs annex the wilds of Canada and Siberia into the transnational empire of the global fur trade, which would gradually decimate the very ecosystems here surreally carted down the streets of London in a bizarre spectacle that prefigures the subjugation of the Arctic in the Anthropocene.

If the Skinners' pageant only endows animals with what Agamben calls "bare life"—an existence that has no political or legal status—Renaissance romance revels in the "Open" and (pardon the irresistible pun) "bear life." In contrast to the captive bears in *Oberon* or the furbearers tamed by Middleton's Orpheus, the bear in *The Winter's Tale* roams free across the stage and devours a human whose name, Antigonus, connotes the principle of binary opposition. While implicating Shakespearean drama in the early modern fur trade, this chapter has delineated how fur might perform differently upon the bodies of bears, wild men, mayors, and royalty, and in ways that could work at cross-purposes. Paradoxically, it may have required a human actor in a dead bear skin to dramatize what contemporary ecocritics would term the "animacy" or "openness" of the bear better than a "real" tame bear could.

While this chapter has encouraged critics to stop trying to peek beneath the fur, there is an important caveat with this argument in that it would obscure animal suffering if orphaned polar bears were compelled to perform. That said, even disembodied fur must also be seen as a signifier of animal suffering and cannot be viewed as just another insentient object. This points to a methodological problem with appropriating Agamben's political ontology and Latourian materialism for animal studies. If the Renaissance playhouse could function as a "zone of indeterminancy," Agamben makes it clear that such indeterminancy does not automatically entail an ethical concern. Recalling that werewolf (or "wolf's head") was slang for outlaw, he explains how the bestialized human or "non-man" could become a pariah without any legal rights, and a similar vulnerability applies to nonhuman animals whose slaughter was not classified as murder.[39] If collapsing the animal/human split runs the risk of downplaying the harsh consequences for some minority communities (not to mention the titanic agency homo sapiens possess in the Anthropocene), materialist critics must also be wary of effacing the distinction between objects and animal objects, since treating animal skin as simply another material denies the sentience of the creature from which it came, threatening to duplicate the objectification of the living furbearer as fur in the Skinners' pageant. Only by carefully stitching together animal studies and new materialism in ways that expose and resist the reification of other animals can we do justice to the range of options for staging them in Shakespeare's day, while pursuing more ethical relations with them in our own time.

Notes

1 Judith Dunbar, ed., *The Winter's Tale: Shakespeare in Performance* (Manchester: Manchester University Press, 2010), 49–50, 78, 98, 122, 165, 231.
2 Samuel Purchas, *Purchas His Pilgrims* (1625), 3:559–64, 66.
3 Arthur Quiller-Couch, ed., *The Winter's Tale* (Cambridge: Cambridge University Press, 1931); J.H.P. Pafford, ed., *The Winter's Tale* (Arden, 1963); Nevill Coghill, "Six Points of Stage-Craft in *The Winter's Tale*," *Shakespeare Survey* 11 (1958): 31–41; Dennis Biggins, "Exit Pursued by a Bear: A Problem in *The Winter's Tale*," *Shakespeare Quarterly* 13, no. 1 (1962): 3–13; Ernst Schanzer, ed., *The Winter's Tale* (Harmondsworth: Penguin, 1966); Stephen Orgel, ed., *The Winter's Tale* (Oxford: Oxford University Press, 1996), 155–56n; John Pitcher, ed., *The Winter's Tale* (London: Arden, 2010), 43.
4 Tereasa Grant, "White Bears in *Mucedorus, The Winter's Tale*, and *Oberon*," *Notes and Queries* 246 (2001): 311–13; Barbara Ravelhofer, "Beasts of Recreacion: Henslowe's White Bears," *English Literary Renaissance* 32 (2002): 287–323.
5 Taken from the wild at a young age, the cubs would have been accustomed to humans and could have been trained to obey basic commands; the Clown in *The Winter's Tale* alludes to such practices when he compares authority to "a stubborn bear ... oft led by the nose with gold" (4.4.807).
6 Adam Vaughan, "Polar Bears Sail Down Thames," *Guardian. Environmental Blog*, January 26, 2009. Web.
7 J.T. Kotilaine, *Russia's Foreign Trade and Economic Expansion in the Seventeenth Century* (Leiden: Brill, 2005), 98–99. Fur imports to England declined after 1581, possibly due to overhunting, but seem to have climbed in the seventeenth century as Russian wrested much of Western Siberia from the Tatar khanate. R.H. Fisher, *The Russian Fur Trade 1550–1700* (Berkeley: University of California Press, 1943), 200–201, and John F. Richards, *Unending Frontier: An Environmental History of the Early Modern World* (Berkeley: University of California Press, 2003), 517–25.

8 On the play's interest in Russian politics, see Daryl Palmer, "Jacobean Muscovites: Winter, Tyranny, and Knowledge in *The Winter's Tale*," *Shakespeare Quarterly* 46, no. 3 (1995): 323–39.

9 Lowell Duckert, "'Exit Pursued by a Bear': More to Follow," *Upstart: A Journal of English Renaissance Studies*. 2013. Web.

10 Holly Dugan similarly remarks on the "stunning slippage between human and animal actors" in references to performing apes in "'To Bark with Judgment': Playing Baboon in Early Modern London," *Shakespeare Studies* 41 (2013): 77–93.

11 Giorgio Agamben, *The Open: Man and Animal*, trans. Kevin Attell (Stanford, CA: Stanford University Press, 2004); Paolo Bartolini, "Indistinction," *The Agamben Dictionary*, eds. Alex Murray et al. (Edinburgh: Edinburgh University Press, 2011), 104.

12 John Ingamells, *Dulwich Picture Gallery Collections* (London: Unicorn, 2008), 20.

13 Erica Fudge, "Renaissance Animal Things," *New Formations* 76 (2012): 86–100, 88. Also see Nicole Mennel, "Zibellini as Animal- Made Objects," Sussex Centre for Early Modern and Medieval Studies. March 7, 2017. Web.

14 Thomas Dekker, *Britannia's Honour* (1628), B3[r].

15 Nicholas Wade, "Why Humans and Their Fur Parted Ways," *New York Times*, August 19, 2003. Web.

16 Laurie Shannon, "'Poor, Bare, Forked': Animal Sovereignty, Human Negative Exceptionalism, and the Natural History of *King Lear*," *Shakespeare Quarterly* 60, no. 2 (2009): 168–96.

17 The best-known screed against sheep-farming and its negative impact on bio-diversity is George Monbiot's *Feral: Searching for Enchantment on the Frontiers of Re-Wilding* (London: Penguin, 2013). On the global fur trade, see Richards, *Unending Frontier*, 463–546. Not all animals were hunted for their fur; many were killed because they were deemed threats to livestock or the harvest, as documented in Roger Lovegrove's *Silent Fields: The Long Decline of a Nation's Wildlife* (Oxford: Oxford University Press, 2007).

18 Lee Raye, "The Early Extinction Date of the Beaver (Castor Fiber) in Britain," *Historical Biology* 27 (2014): 1029–41. The beaver's disappearance from England propelled the North American fur trade; in 1637, Thomas Morton reports that a Captain Kirk sent 25,000 beaver skins from Canada back to England (*New English Canaan* 97).

19 John Aubrey, *Natural History of Wiltshire*. Bodleian Aubrey MS 1 f.131. See Lovegrove, *Silent Fields*, 203–8.

20 Christopher Servheen, *Bears: Status Survey and Conservation Action Plan* (Cambridge: IUCN, 1999), 96.

21 In his 1591 book *Of the Russian Commonwealth*, Giles Fletcher reports that the best "white & dun [fox]" were exported from Pechora (in the present-day Komi Republic), "whence also come the white wolfe, and white Beare skin" (7[v]). Since fur imports from the Muscovy Company were still rather modest in the 1590s, the chances it came from a fox or polar bear would seem remote. It is far more likely to have come from white rabbits or even lambshanks, though it may have been somehow doctored to resemble ermine.

22 Elspeth Veale, *The English Fur Trade in the Later Middle Ages* (Oxford: Oxford University Press, 1966), 133–55; Roger Lovegrove, *Silent Fields: The Long Decline of a Nation's Wildlife* (Oxford: Oxford University Press, 2007), 24.

23 Alden and Virginia Vaughan, *Shakespeare's Caliban: A Cultural History* (Cambridge: Cambridge University Press, 1991), 70.

24 Veale, *The English Fur Trade in the Later Middle Ages*.

25 Olaus Magnus, *A Compendious History of the Goths, Swedes, Vandals, and Other Northern Nations 1555* (London, 1658), 180.

26 Erica Fudge, *Animal* (London: Reaktion, 2004), 61.

27 Henry Watson, trans., *The History of the Two Valiant Brethren Valentine and Orson* (London, 1555), L3[r].

28 Henry Chettle and William Haughton, "Arcadian Virgin," *Lost Plays Database*, eds. Roslyn L. Knutson, David McInnis, and Matthew Steggle (Melbourne: University of Melbourne, 2009), Web.

29 Arcadia was named after Callisto's son, Arcas, which derives from the Greek for bear, and when Callisto was stellified as the northern constellation of the Great Bear she would became the etymological origin of the word Arctic.

30 Bodleian Library, MS Ashmole 236, f. 77[v] italics added.

31 Jonathan Bate and Eric Rasmussen, eds., *William Shakespeare and Others: Collaborative Plays* (London: Palgrave MacMillan, 2013), 2.2–3.

32 Andrew Gurr, "The Bear, the Statue, and Hysteria in *The Winter's Tale*," *Shakespeare Quarterly* 34, no. 4 (1983): 420–25.

33 On Leontes as the bear, see Michael Bristol, "In Search of the Bear," *Shakespeare Quarterly* 42 (1991): 145–67.

34 Agamben, *The Open*, 37–38.

35 For the play's recurrent puns on "bear," see Maurice Hunt, "Bearing Hence: Shakespeare's *The Winter's Tale*," *Studies in English Literature* 44, no. 2 (2004): 333–46.

36 Donna Harraway, *Staying with the Trouble: Making Kin in the Cthulucene* (Durham, NC: Duke University Press, 2016). The recognition scene in *Valentine and Orson* was almost certainly part of the lost play, as the brothers' kinship is revealed by an oracular brazen head, a property the Admiral's Men already owned.

37 *The Triumphs of Love and Antiquity* (1619), B2r. See Lawrence Manley's introduction to the pageant in *The Oxford Middleton*, eds. Gary Taylor and John Lavagnino (Oxford: Clarendon, 2007), 1397–99.

38 Deane is listed as a creditor of the company in a petition dated 23 May 1626. HL/PO/JO/10/1/32.

39 It is worth recalling that cultures that have historically practiced animal shamanism often perform the ritual prior to a hunt, and the mimicry of animal behavior often functions to convey the knowledge and harness the courage required to track and kill it.

16

COUNTING SHAKESPEARE'S SHEEP WITH *THE SECOND SHEPHERD'S PLAY*

Julian Yates

Early on in *Some Versions of Pastoral*, William Empson offers the Wakefield *Second Shepherd's Play* as the establishing example for the function of the "double plot" as one enduring pastoral technique. "The mode of action of a double plot," he writes, "is the sort of thing critics are liable to neglect" but, when it works, it has the "obvious effect ... of making you feel the play deals with life as a whole."[1] One plot doesn't quite do it. But synchronizing a second sub-plot to the first orchestrates the two so that between them they reflect or refract one another's terms, and the play feels somehow fuller, more inclusive, more full of life. For Empson, the essence of pastoral derives from this manufactured sense of fullness or richness. Sometimes in the manner of a "trick" (11), a "myth," a "process" (22–23), a "machine" (30), an "organism" (144–45), or a "tap root" (261), pastoral works by what sounds a lot like taxidermy, "putting the complex into the simple" (22–23) so as to "imply a beautiful relation between rich and poor" (11), and so "giv[ing] the impression of dealing with life completely" (29). "In pastoral," he observes, "you take a limited life and pretend it is the full and normal one" (115). What we call pastoral works by a refolding or coordination of surfaces that creates the appearance of depth, of "life," or of "liveliness" from what is in fact a reduced sense of the possible.

It may seem strange to begin an essay about sheep with what may seem like a fairly old-fashioned formalist account of a poetic mode. There seems, on the face of it, something antithetical about the metaphorical sheep and shepherds of pastoral to a consideration of sheep as a material and particular presence in the historical past. It is true that pastoral's origins are said to lie with the rustic songs sung by shepherds whose docile flocks give them an inordinate amount of free time or, in the lexicon of early modern English, "*otium*."[2] "No Shepherds, no pastoral" is how one critic sums up the genre.[3] But the same critic has little to say about sheep, the difficulties of shepherding, or the "material existence" of sheep themselves as historical actors.[4] Sheep serve largely as well-mannered bystanders to pastoral, beings whose status as live/living "stock" or capital pastoral takes as a given.

In this chapter, I aim to disclose the way the assumed presence of sheep serves as a ground or foundation and, in fact, has a constitutive shaping function to pastoral plots and to the "double plots" of early modern and Shakespearean drama. It is this doubleness, the co-articulation of two differently scaled and differently animated multiplicities (the animals we name "human" and the animals we name "sheep") that proves key. "Sheep" and not-sheep "humans"

204

Counting Shakespeare's Sheep with The Second Shepherd's Play

exchange properties, share in the labor of crafting particular modes of life, particular environments, and so, accordingly, shepherding provides the grounding mode and metaphor for the care of the flock, human and otherwise. Yes, the so-called human shepherds, according to one set of metaphors, turn out to be capital fellows. Enter the human subject leading a parade of abjectly sheepish sheep. But this scene belies both the labor of shepherding itself and the fact that these same shepherding metaphors write the forms of care, government, and so association which characterize the management of "human" flocks.

It is no coincidence, in this regard, that the founding scene of biopolitics, as conceived by Michel Foucault in his lecture course on *Security, Territory, Population* (1977–78), derives from the archetypal activity of shepherds counting their sheep. For Foucault, this scene of enumeration in which the shepherd takes stock of his or her flock calves a sheepy metaphorics that writes the story of Christian pastoral care and the more evolved forms of "government" we inherit today. The scene of counting sheep both individualizes and pluralizes. In order to articulate the group, each individual must be articulated one by one, but so altogether, or as Foucault's refrain has it, "*omnes et singulatim.*" "Pastoral power," he writes,

> is an individualizing power. That is to say, it is true that the shepherd directs the whole flock, but he can only really direct it insofar as not a single sheep escapes him. The shepherd counts the sheep; he counts them in the morning when he leads them to pasture, and he counts them in the evening to see that they are all there, and he looks after each of them individually. He does everything for the totality of the flock, but he does everything also for each sheep of the flock ... he must keep his eye on all and on each, *omnes et singulatim.*[5]

Such is the essence of a pastoral power "exercised on a multiplicity rather than on a territory" (129)—a relation defined by the articulation of the animals we name "sheep" and "human" as coeval multiplicities. "Sheep" and not sheep "humans" become each other's measure and mirror. Accordingly, from time to time, the animals we name "human" morph into "sheep" and, likewise, "sheep" find themselves emphatically singularized and individualized. The mechanism at work is not a simple form of anthropomorphism or even a reciprocal zoomorphism, but, instead, a set of figural possibilities generated by the mutual constitution of "sheep" and not-sheep "humans." Such instances stand as one semiotic fine edge of the multispecies basis to our lives, the way in which, in this case, what it means for us to labor comes routed through a set of concerns to do with live or living "stock," variously articulated "pools" of labor power as they were produced in different historical moments. In the figural passages between "sheep" and their not-sheep "humans," in the turning of the tropes by which the two are co-produced, we begin to access the procedures by which the general flesh of being is parceled out to create differently animated forms of being. Biopolitics "writes" the world, and "makes up" people and other animals by and through the management of this collective flesh.

Here it seems important to recall the way for Foucault the articulation of this flesh upon and with which biopower "writes" becomes a way to eventuate a biological continuum and so to "introduce[e] . . . a break into the domain of life that is under power's control: the break between what must live and what must die."[6] Famously, he goes on to remark the way race, "the distinction between races," serves to establish "a biological-type caesura within a population" that allows "power to treat that population as a mixture of races, or to be more accurate, to treat the species, to subdivide the species it controls, into the subspecies known precisely as races." These breaks come rooted through our figural correlations to sheep and cows, to all those animals corralled under the name of "cattle" (as capital) and so articulated, at base, as some fungible biomass. Crucially, then, one of the things critical animal studies may contribute to the study of biopolitics is an increased awareness of the way ostensibly human forms of bio-power are co-imbricated with other forms of species being. As Nicole Shukin puts it, with customary precision,

> sheep are metaphorically omnipresent yet materially missing from the study of a technology of power that, according to Foucault, enfolds *human* individual populations who become subject to forms of pastoral care first institutionalized by the Christian Church and subsequently secularized by the modern state.[7]

As I argue, beyond even the brute, physical fact that so many of our records are backed by animal skin, by parchment, the archives of biopolitics are littered with ovine figures that thematize this co-making of beings and its foreclosure within the discourses of pastoral and pastoral care.[8] No shepherds, no pastoral, then, for sure. But so also, we may add sheep, emending the remark so that it reads: "No sheep, no shepherds, no pastoral." Or, perhaps, we could even radicalize the statement yet further: "No sheep, no parchment, no archive"—let alone no pastoral.[9]

It could not be more significant in this regard that Empson chooses the Wakefield Master's *Second Shepherds' Play* (c. 1500) to illustrate the function of the "double plot" in pastoral. The play tells the story of three humdrum, disgruntled shepherds—Coll, Gib, and Daw—who have one of their flocks stolen from them by the down on his luck, sheep-stealing Mak and Gill, his long-suffering and compellingly outspoken wife. Gill and Mak famously hide the stolen sheep in a cradle, passing it off as their newly born child. In the event, Mak and Gill get caught, Mak is tossed about in a blanket, Gill is scolded, and the shepherds find themselves rewarded by being transformed into "Englished" versions of the Magi, arriving in Bethlehem to praise the baby Jesus. They also learn to sing in the process—which, in the musical register of the play, is tantamount to auditory proof of divine efficacy given the shepherds' inability to carry a tune at the start of the play. As Empson remarks, Mak and Gill's sheep-stealing interlude on the shepherds' way to the true manger scene in the nativity story constitutes "a very detailed parallel to the Paschal Lamb, hidden in the appearance of a newborn child" (28). The interlude serves to literalize and make manifest the metaphorical content of the overarching nativity plot to which the shepherds are bystanders. The structural parallel, as Empson elaborates briefly, derives from a key set of reversals of reciprocities:

> the *Logos* enters humanity from above as this sheep does from below, or takes on the animal nature of man which is like a man becoming a sheep, or sustains all nature and its laws so that in one sense it is truly present in the sheep as the man.
>
> *(28)*

The effect, Empson concludes, is powerful, but at the same time "hard to tape down." This mobility or instability, I argue, derives from the fact that the play is much more than an exercise in sacramental pedagogy. Submerged within the signifying patterns of the Eucharistic gift and the Incarnation are two scenes of enumeration, two moments in which the shepherds explicitly count their sheep. The play generalizes the scene of counting to become, in effect, a general condition of the shepherds' existence and thereby renders palpable the ovine or sheepy quotient to the structures of pastoral care that undergird the play's literal and metaphorical shepherding of wayward and stolen "sheep"—human and not.

In what follows, I join Coll, Gib, and Daw as they count their sheep with the aim of teasing out the way in which sheep-being funds the play. I then go on to trace out some scenes from the afterlife to their sheep-stealing "double plot" in William Shakespeare's *Henry VI, Part II*, *The Merchant of Venice*, and *The Winter's Tale*, focusing in particular on a triad of Shakespearean characters who in different ways find themselves caught up in counting sheep: Jack Cade, Shylock, and Autolycus.

I Wakefield / Bethlehem (c. 1500 / Year Zero)

Winter has come to Wakefield. Two shepherds shiver and stand together for warmth. Neither wishes to be out this night. And neither wishes to have to count their sheep. The two rehearse a litany of their troubles: labor issues, social dislocation caused by land enclosures that convert arable land to pasture, their general sense of dissatisfaction with their conditions. They have to be up early and stay out all night. The weather is bad. If only they were still farmers, they would work shorter hours. Right now, they would be home and in bed. And their labors would be collective not serial. They would work together and not be at one another's throats. Where is young Daw? Why is he late again? Does he really expect that he should get to eat just after he arrives while they have been here for hours?[10] Relations are strained. Coll and Gib pick on him:

> 2 PASTOR: Peasse, boy, I bad.
> No more ianglyng,
> Or I shall make the full rad,
> By the heuens kyng!
> With thy gawdys –
> Where ar oure shepe, boy? – we skorne.
> 3 PASTOR: Sir, this same day at morne
> I thaym left in the corne,
> When thay rang lawdys.
> They haue pasture good,
> Thay can not go wrong.[11]

What's key here is that Daw presents as the stereotypical lazy shepherd or farm worker. Coll and Gib quiz him on the whereabouts and integrity of their flock. But the flock is intact and well-fed. Daw has left them in a harvested corn field as is good shepherding practice.[12] No one has to go and count the sheep because they have already been counted. Daw has done his job and done it well: *Omnes et singulatim* (all together and one by one). For all their grumbling, and for all the bleakness of its beginning, the play goes out of its way to establish that Coll, Gib, and Daw are competent, even good shepherds with the welfare of their flock close to heart. The sheep have been counted. They have been provided for. The labor is hard. It takes a toll on the shepherds—as the play seems to wish its audience to recognize. But all goes well for the sheep.

Enter the differently accented Mak, as the proverbial black sheep or even a wolf in sheep's clothing—an image that haunts Daw's dreams that night when he has a vision of Mak "lapt / In a wolfe-skyn" (532). The next morning the shepherds wake and uneasy at having spent the night with Mak in their midst, they embark on an emergency counting of their sheep in order to assuage their fears and allay their suspicions:

3 PASTOR: Go furth, yll myght thou chefe!
            Now wold I we soght,
            This morne,
            That we had all oure store.
1 PASTOR: Bot I will go before;
            Let vs mete.
2 PASTOR: Whore?
3 PASTOR: At the crokyd thorne.

(575–83)

When the counting is complete, the three meet as planned and share the news that they have lost "a fat wedir" (651)—whose singularity seems emphatically to localize the security of the flock itself. After some wrangling over whether it is fair to accuse Mak, the three follow him home with the intent to search it and brace him with their suspicions. Here the counting assumes a different function: the missing sheep indicates the presence and predation of a fellow Christian, metaphorized in Daw's dream not as the proverbial wolf in sheep's clothing but as a human who puts on the skin of a wolf. The integrity of the flock now requires the shepherds to converge on Mak's home and confront him.

Arriving at the cottage, the shepherds are greeted by great moans coming from Gill as she plays up the fiction of a recent childbirth, allowing her to pretend that the stolen sheep is her newborn baby, placing him in a cradle. Critics since Empson have elaborated on the sacramental pedagogy the *Second Shepherd's Play* unfolds. The nested structure of the double plot (Mak and Gill figure and reverse Joseph and Mary) inscribes the accidental function of the Communion wafer and the Real Presence of the transubstantiated bread and wine in and as the structure of the play itself.[13] Mak and Gill, the bread and the wine, the world, secular time, "host" the theological deep time of the Bible story—a point which sheep-concealing Gill reveals in what Empson describes as a "powerful joke on the eating of Christ in the Sacrament" (28). When the shepherds ask to see inside the cradle, Gill responds with this vow:

UXOR: A, my medyll!
        I pray to God so mylde,
        If euer I you begyld,
        That I ete this chylde
        That lygys in this credyll.

(773–77)

Communicating Christians do, of course, in some sense, "eat" the *agnus dei* (Lamb of God) when they consume the host, but not with the inspired and shocking comic literalism that Gill deploys. Indeed, Gill's oath essentially reverses or collapses the symbolic structure that the priestly consecration and elevation of the host enact. Her words lie but tell a double truth: she shall eat the contents of the cradle in some putative future, either as the sheep becomes her family's dinner or she takes Communion.

The joke broadens as the three shepherds remark the strangeness of this baby but find no evidence of their missing sheep. Empty handed in their accusations, the three leave Mak and Gill's cottage feeling rather low. They have to face up to the fact that they have barged

Counting Shakespeare's Sheep with The Second Shepherd's Play

in on a newborn and his mother, and falsely accused his father of stealing their sheep. What is more their erstwhile righteous invasion now plays back as callous breach of hospitality—especially so given Mak's earlier complaints about the difficulties of his home life, and his inability to feed his own swelling "flock" of children. The three linger guiltily outside the cottage. "Gaf ye the chyld, any thing," asks 1 Pastor? "I trow not oone farthing," responds 3 Pastor (825–26). He tells the other two to wait there while he goes back in to give the baby a present.

All apologies now, Daw asks Mak's permission to "gyf youre barne / Bot sex pence" (836–37), and it is this making amends for their earlier lack of charity that leads him to discover the truth:

3 PASTOR: Gyf me lefe hym to kys
And lyft vp the clowtt.
What the dewill is this?
He has a long snowte!
1 PASTOR: He is markyd amys.
We wate ill abowte.
2 PASTOR: Ill-spon weft, iwys,
Ay commys foull owte.
Ay, so!
He is lyke to oure shepe!

(845–52)

It is no coincidence that the act of charity, the return to the cottage to make amends to Mak and Gill and their newborn "daystarne" (834), serves as the mechanism for the revelation of the child as sheep and so also for the shepherds' discovery of the *agnus dei* when they wake to find themselves in the nativity story. Or, rather, it is precisely a co-incidence in Foucault's sense of pastoral power as a dual technique that articulates the integrity of the flock and through an individualizing power that may, as necessary, assume a corrective function. Here we encounter "the paradoxically distributive side of the Christian pastorate" that, even as it attends to the salvation of each and every sheep, accepts "the sacrifice of a sheep that could compromise the whole." "The sheep that is the cause of scandal," Foucault explains, "or whose corruption is in danger of corrupting the whole flock, must be abandoned, possibly excluded, chased away, and so forth."[14] This individualizing power that singularizes each sheep for care and attention might just as easily be used to "cut" certain individuals from the flock. And the violence with which this power then operates merely realizes a different application of the same differentiating ethic of care and concern offered to each and every member of flock for the general health of the flock. "The salvation of a single sheep," writes Foucault, "calls for as much care from the pastor as does the whole flock; there is no sheep for which he must not suspend all his other responsibilities and occupations, abandon the flock, and try to bring it back." Individualized expulsion and violence unfolds from the same imperative that directs the care, cure, or caress that another individual may receive.

So it is that the shepherds' charity, their inquiry with and by and through a gesture of care and concern, stands as a more effective technique for discovery than their accusations and sniping at Mak. Coll, Gib, and Daw count their sheep. They remark and recover their lost sheep in the process, and discover and discipline the wayward corrupt Mak by and through the same process of counting and taking account. Their act of *caritas*, of Christian charity, towards the newborn leads the shepherds to look more closely and so to apprehend

209

this particular child and so this particular sheep and this reparative act of attention leads quasi-automatically to the revelation of a double truth. It leads the three to discover Mak's sheep stealing ways and the three to be rewarded by a vision or translation into the nativity story—their epiphany—where they witness firsthand the incarnation of the divine. *The Second Shepherd's Play* stands as a self-aware, pastoral, and pastoralizing moment in the long history of the co-making or co-articulation of the animals we name "sheep" and those we name "human." Its ovine-rich pedagogy and emphasis on charity as ultimately a forensic tool in differentiating the "good sheep" from the "bad" who must be "cut" from the flock for the good of the flock offers the distributive and so differentiating function of pastoral care both as an end in itself (the essence of care) and as a dramaturgical technique. Mak and Gill are punished; the three shepherds learn to sing and by the theological-theatrical function of the play enter the nativity story itself. All its characters serve as differently configured exemplars of Christian, which is to say not sheep "human" being. The play takes the scene of shepherds counting their sheep as its foundation. It offers this scene as the essence of Christian sociality.

The structures *The Second Shepherd's Play* deploy governed a medieval and early modern imaginary in which sheep and Christians exchanged properties as part of a material-semiotic chain that created a field of metaphorical possibilities. Given that the only copy of the play dates from a manuscript compiled in the 1570s, the texture it offers stands as a fascinating trading ground between medieval and early modern traditions, both religious and dramatic—especially so given the suppression of cycle drama and mystery plays in the mid-sixteenth century, their archiving, and the rise of public theater in London. Moreover, as Laura Kiser has remarked, the play itself seems especially marked by the social dislocation generated by the enclosure movement, at its height in the first decades of the sixteenth century and still very much at issue in the 1570s. The value the play sets by its shepherds' labor resonates with other invocations of sheep in the period which sought to make the depredations of enclosure knowable. Raphael Hythlodaeus' figure of the homicidal sheep who "devour human beings" from Thomas More's *Utopia* (1516) comes to mind—a figure which condenses the shepherds' complaints into a predatory oveme that travels through the period and beyond.[15] In *A Discourse of the Common Weal of this Realm of England* (1549), when the knight complains that he can only make ends meet by keeping sheep, the husbandman moans "sheep, sheep, sheep."[16] Aphorisms such as "The more sheep, the fewer eggs a penny" and "We want foxes to consume our shepe" circulated throughout the 1540s. And Thomas Becon's dialogue, *The Jewell of Joy* (c. 1550), discloses the real scandal to the figure, explaining that "those beastes which were created of god for the nourishment of man doe nowe devoure man."[17] Enclosure inverts the divine subordination of sheep to humans making shepherds their thrall.

By the end of the sixteenth century, however, when land enclosures fell off, these sheepy invocations lost much of their bite and became a necessary item of ovine lore to be replayed, as it is by Edward Topsell in his *Historie of Four-Footed Beastes* (1607), a curiosity, referring to depredations that now no longer mattered quite so much as they once did, given the collapse of wool exports mid-century, and the down turn of cloth prices.[18] In practice, this meant that the language of sheep and shepherding offered itself as a larger set of metaphors for government in an emerging biopolitical imaginary. Here, then, in what remains of this essay, are three vignettes from this elaborated field of ovine metaphors, three double plots that help fill their plays out, to produce the sense of fullness to which Empson alerts us. I tune into the way these plots' ovine moorings make explicit the biopolitical quotient to each play. Let's fast forward to the 1590s.

II Becoming Sheep (Kent / London c. 1450 / 1592)

A garden in Kent by way of a public stage in London. Rebel leader and self-proclaimed "parliament" of the Commons Jack Cade, summoned to life from chronicles past, has climbed over a wall in search of a meal. Jack shall die in this garden, dispatched by its *otium* seeking owner who just happens to be out for a stroll. But as he dies Jack proclaims that it is not Alexander Iden that kills him but hunger. "O I am slain!" he pronounces, "Famine and no other hath slain me"—the cause of popular complaint and protest still on his lips, he finds himself reduced to eating grass, transforming into a literal, errant, sheep. This is what it feels like to be counted and cut from the flock.[19]

Depending on who we believe, Jack enters the play either as the Duke of York's factor, out to cause "commotion" (3.1.374) among the common people so that York can save the day or as the animated residue of actual insurgent writing practices in Tudor England's recent past. By turns, Jack summons phrases attributed to John Ball, Jack Straw, and Wat Tyler's uprising of 1381; Cade's Kentish uprising of 1450; the 1517 uprising by xenophobic apprentices; the Hackett rebellion in July 1591; and the felt makers revolt of June 1592.[20] He vocalizes an archive of captured speech. He voices that language of protest.

When we first meet Jack in Act 4, just as Dick the Butcher speaks the line that everyone remembers—"The first thing we do, let's kill all the lawyers"—Jack adds these more open-ended lines that momentarily retard the proceedings:

> Is not this a lamentable thing, that of the skin of an innocent lamb should be made parchment; that parchment, being scribbled o'er, should undo a man? Some say the bee stings, but I say, `tis the bee's wax; for I did but seal once to a thing, and I was never mine own man since.

> *(4.2.72–76)*

It's not clear what happens on stage at this moment. Does Jack hold the "this" to which he refers aloft, calling all eyes to a parchment? What exactly does he see, touch, feel, or hear, as he remarks the "lamentable" gathering of resources (the lambs and labor) necessary for the production of legal documents in the period? Uncannily, earnestly, half-jokingly Jack rewrites the truths of common experience: bees don't sting but wax that bears the imprint of a seal does. But the joke's on him. For, once upon a time, as he says, he took upon himself the singular act of putting his name to a legal document and has "never [been his] own man since." Later, we learn that he probably did not sign but made his mark, "like an honest plain-dealing man" (4.2.94–95).

In Jack's hands, parchment becomes mobile, plastic, knowable precisely as a point of convergence between matter and metaphor, and so as a field of affective intensity that momentarily takes hold of him. Jack reverses the mode of production so that the (dead-alive) animal, plant, and mineral remainders a legal document collates become animate once more. He transforms the indexical and so unremarkable remains of the sheep and bees and mineral ores into partial beings. Speaking as if from touch, the parchment speaking through him, it is not clear that Jack understands the depth of the references he sets in motion, just how deep this sheepy archive runs. The biblical coding to the lamb's "innocence" (*agnus dei*) signals that, for his listeners, the parchment manifests both as an historically particular animal, tooled here into a writing surface, and also as a sign of a particular order of Christian charity that the carving up of the world by parchment-backed property rights violates, pitting Christian against Christian. The putative universalism of one theological settlement finds itself deployed here in order to object to its particularizing exclusions. Thereafter, Jack and those who flock to him seek to recut the flesh that constitutes their being, opening this infrastructure to other contracts (sacral, natural, pastoral, legal, economic, ecological) and polities than those to which he has had to "seal" his name. We watch as they marshal their hastily weaponized tools into the instruments of an insurgent writing machine that attempts to rewrite or overwrite the world backed and maintained by parchment.[21]

He speaks from within the process by which enclosure transformed labor, altering the human persons caught up in its recoding of land use. Part Coll, Gib, and Daw, but also part Mak, Jack speaks for a differently animate Commons who has sloughed off its "sheepy" coats as it re-clothes or recoats itself with the skin of its predatory betters.

Come the end of the interlude, however, this same sheepy lexicon bites back at the rebels. Vanquished by "the name of Henry the Fifth" (4.8.56), Jack takes to his heels. We meet him soon after, on the run and "ready to famish" (4.10.2), as an uncertainly ovine or bovine Jack has climbed "o'er a brick wall ... into this garden to see if [he] can eat grass or pick a sallet" (4.10.7–8). He is quickly discovered and dispatched by its owner. Jack dies with famine on his lips—"O I am slain! Famine and no other hath slain me" (4.10.59) and "I, that never feared any, am vanquished by famine" (4.10.74)—a being that must eat. By the end of the scene, we will, in effect, have been watching the retraining of Jack's mouth: no longer the self-predicating "parliament" of the land, the mouth of this sheep turned wolf is denied flesh as he is forced to eat grass. Jack gets to narrate his transformation, his becoming "cattel" (or herd animal) on the way to a becoming "soile" or dirt, the figural process by which he and his fellows are rendered or processed as if sheep.

Some double plot this. In the world of "civil butchery," of failing, predatory shepherds in *Henry VI, Part II*, like Mak, the Commons turns wolfish. Come the end of the sequence or "interlude" the play eats its own sub-plot, the fullness or liveliness that results derives from this dis-animating ingestion of the likes of Jack, transforming them back into nameless historical actors, the docile human "sheep" they should properly be.

III Ewes and Jews (Venice / London c. 1600)

A house in Venice by way of a theater in London. Bassanio visits Shylock at home to seek a loan. He promises that friend Antonio shall be his surety. Bassanio suggests Shylock eat with them. Shylock declines. Antonio enters, and he and Shylock debate the subject of interest, of moneylending, and usury or "lend[ing] and borrow[ing / Upon advantage," to which Antonio replies "I do never use it."[22] Enter the sheep—the literal sheep of biblical precedent by way of the pun on "use" and "ewes":

SHYLOCK: When Jacob graz'd his uncle Laban's sheep—
           This Jacob from our holy Abram was,
           As his wise mother wrought in his behalf,
           The third possessor; ay, he was the third—
ANTONIO: And what of him? did he take interest?
SHYLOCK: No, not take interest, not, as you would say, Directly interest: mark what Jacob did.
           When Laban and himself were compromis'd
           That all the eanlings which were streak'd and pied
           Should fall as Jacob's hire, the ewes, being rank,
           In the end of autumn turned to the rams,
           And, when the work of generation was
           Between these woolly breeders in the act,

The skilful shepherd pill'd me certain wands,
And, in the doing of the deed of kind,
He stuck them up before the fulsome ewes,
Who then conceiving did in eaning time
Fall parti-colour'd lambs, and those were Jacob's.
This was a way to thrive, and he was blest:
And thrift is blessing, if men steal it not.

(1.3.66–85)

But Antonio seems unimpressed; claims that this is a "thing not in his [Jacob's] power to bring to pass," unless, of course, Shylock projects an equivalence between animals and money: "is your gold and silver ewes and rams?" (1.3.86–91). He rejects the analogy between money and animal husbandry that would naturalize and so normalize interest as a legitimate and thrifty derivative. As numerous scholars have observed the word pecuniary derives from the Latin *pecu* or "flock." As Marc Shell explains, "'ewes' and 'rams' … are like monetary principals, and 'lambs' are like monetary 'interest'."[23] But gold and silver are not sheep. The deeper issue to Antonio and Shylock's disagreement over the species of analogy appropriate to explaining interest or "use" goes to the heart of the relations between Venetian privilege and its non-Christian citizen others. Shylock's pun on "use" and "ewes" intrudes the question of species difference, of animal difference, into the conversation by way of an arbitrary linguistic pun that, in effect, discloses the way questions of race, species, and matter are never simply questions of relations between theoretically interchangeable human persons but come rooted through relations to animals otherwise than human.

In effect, Shylock and Antonio disagree on how to count and take account of these biblical sheep. They disagree on what it means to count and on what ultimately counts. This disagreement comes rooted through a story about shepherding that makes the question of species difference explicit as a negotiable difference or a difference to be negotiated and enforced. Shylock's pun correlates to an ovine substrate that might interrupt or hold open to view the "biological-type caesura within a population," in Foucault's terms, that produces the effects of racial difference as a category to be thought and lived.[24] Indeed, Shylock's pun seems proactively to speak back to Antonio's naming him a dog—cursing him when he "spet upon my Jewish gabardine" (1.3.107) treating him as he would a "stranger cur" (1.3.113)— though now he comes calling to ask for a loan as if they were both uncontested members of a universal category. As Shell notes, "Shylock … treat[s] Antonio as if he were from a group of human beings other than his own Jewish one, but Antonio treats Shylock as if he were from a species of animal other than the human one."[25] 'No, no, no. Not so fast,' Shylock seems to say. Though, by play's end, Venice shall have symbolically eaten its others, seeing off the arbitrariness of Shylock's pun that discloses the constitutive relation between species and person and voiding his bond that makes explicit the hold of abstract categories on animal flesh, human, and otherwise. Jessica converts with no apparent Jewish remainder via the miracle of the sacrament of marriage. And Shylock finds himself both dispossessed of his fortune and subject to forced conversion, retained as an included other, marked still by the physical mark of circumcision even as his capital is liquefied and made available for "use" if not "ewes."

IV Bohemia (London c. 1611)

Spring and summer have come to Bohemia. A sheep-shearing festival has been announced. And it is to be hoped that this change of season and so mood shall thaw the tyrannical chill to this seemingly perpetual *Winter's Tale*. Perhaps this double plot's turn to pastoral and to communal celebration shall restore the bonds of family, generation, and sociality interrupted at the end of Act 3. No Coll, Gib, and Daw exactly here to complain of poor labor relations and the appropriation of farming land for pasturage. No, the scales have shifted in this world of romance towards the enclosure of all forms of life by the monarch, whose ailing mind and paranoia lead to the sentencing of Hermione to execution and of their newborn child to death as well as to the death of their son who pines away for lack of his mother. Leontes of Sicilia is no shepherd. On the contrary, he plays, as Hermione and Paulina both aver, as tyrant. But this tyranny is more than a matter of mercurial whim or even fantasy. Leontes' paranoia proves bodily as he aims to purge the realm of bad blood and so cleanse what he perceives to be his threatened genealogy, the integrity of his communal flesh. His fantasies inaugurate a tyranny that rends the general flesh of his realm via a series of biopolitical interventions: "I am glad you did not nurse him," he says to Hermione when he demands their son Mamillus from her. "Though he does bear some signs of me," he observes, "yet you / Have too much blood in him."[26] It is good then that Hermione has apparently not nursed him—for who knows what corruption her blood become milk might impart to the boy.

Leontes leaves Hermione to "sport herself / With that she's big with, for 'tis Polixenes / Has made thee swell thus" (2.1.60–62). Perdita shall take her name from this sense of loss and interruption, this outpouring of generative material. Leontes' horror extends to Hermione's pregnant body and so also to Perdita herself whom he decrees be "instantly consumed with fire" (2.3.133). All distributive justice, Leontes attempts to recut the flesh of his household to purge the "unclean," the physical embodiments of "scandal." Even when Cleomenes and Dion return from Delphos with the "sealed up oracle" that proclaims "Hermione is chaste. Polixenes blameless, Camillo a true subject, Leontes a jealous tyrant, his innocent babe truly begotten'" (3.2.130–33) in what amounts to some celestial auto-correct function, he will have none of it. "There is no truth at all I'th'oracle," he insists, "this is mere falsehood" (3.2.136–37). It takes the death of Mamillus and the apparent death of Hermione to bring Leontes to his senses, by which time all seems lost for as the last part of the oracle reads: "the King shall live without an heir" that is "if that which is lost be not found" (3.2.132–33). All that is left to do, so it seems, is to memorialize Hermione and Mamillus and shed his tears as Bohemia becomes the haunt of "our shame perpetual" (3.2.235).

Enter the sheep. Enter the shepherd (a real one this time). Enter Perdita as shepherdess but all "pranked up" (4.4.10) like a goddess, like Flora, as Florizel has it, in anticipation of the sheep-shearing feast that her foster family hosts. The weather is lovely. It is good to be outside. "Daffodils ... [are] ... peer[ing] / With heigh, the doxy over the dale" (4.3.1–2) or Autolycus' songs shall make you feel as if they are. And so a feast is in order. Though, Perdita, it must be said, needs some encouragement and coaching on her role at such an event. Florizel has to remind her to "address yourself to entertain" the arriving guests "sprightly" (4.4.53). And as her father counsels, she needs to understand what it means to step into the role of his "old wife" who on such occasions "was both pantler [pantry attendant], butler, cook, / Both dame and servant" as she "welcomed all, served all" (4.4.55–57). Perdita rises to the occasion, more than makes up for her initial reserve, ensures that everyone feels as if they are having the celebration that was anticipated—an occasion to celebrate the kinds of labor depicted in this exemplary scene for the month of June in epigrammist Thomas Fella's 1585–88 manuscript *Commonplace Book* (Figure 16.1). The human figures to the left seem entirely absorbed in their labors. They attend to and wait upon their sheep. Given their diligence, it would be good to have a little leisure and reward them for all their virtuous labors. Indeed, the motto to the scene reads as follows:

Counting Shakespeare's Sheep with The Second Shepherd's Play

This hurtlesse beast with meeke moods yelds wool
And skin to cloth our naked clotte of claye.
He gives his flesh to feede our bellies full.
Nought for him selfe he brings but for our staye.

Naturalizing the usefulness of the animals we name sheep as if they existed as some sort of virtuous, self-sacrificing (or, more properly, always already self-sacrificed) anti-narcissism, the motto assimilates sheep to the existence of the "human" "clottes of claye" it depicts and who gaze upon it. This, the image and the motto seem to say, is how relations between animals and "clottes of claye" should be. And this reality serves as a model also for the ideal relation between human "sheep" and their divine shepherd. For it is such abject ovine obedience that marks the ideal form of subjugation to the divine.

The sheep have been counted. The flock is intact (*omnes et singulatim*)—which is of course what happens in *The Winter's Tale*, or rather looks as if it might. Fingers crossed. "Let me see, every 'leven wether tods, every tod yields pound and odd shilling; fifteen hundred shorn" (4.3.31–32) ventures the Clown in Act 4, Scene 3, our introduction to the upcoming feast. But the math proves too hard—"I cannot do't without counters" (4.3.35). The scene of counting has become a scene of accounting. The clown counts the sheep in order to add up the money their shorn fleeces will bring. And as one commentator observes, it brings a tidy sum: "the wool of eleven castrated sheep ('wether') would weigh a tod or 28lbs, so that, at £1 and 1s for each "tod," 1500 sheep shorn would produce £143 and 30s."[27] All that remains to do now is convert this money into supplies for the feast: "three pound of sugar, five pound of currants, rice" not to mention "saffron to colour the warden pies; mace; dates … nutmegs, seven; a race of two of ginger … four pounds of prunes, and as many raisins o'th'sun" (4.3.36–45). It shall be quite a party. Though as the clown's need for "counters" to get his

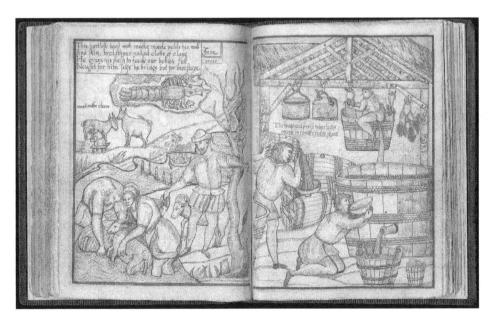

Figure 16.1 "June." Manuscript illustration from Thomas Fella's *Booke of Divers Devises* (Folger Shakespeare Library, V. a. 311), showing the labors of the season. By permission of the Folger Shakespeare Library, Washington, DC

math right, to aid in the conversion from counting sheep, to counting fleeces, and converting them into monetary units, indicates, this pastoral feast is also good business—something that Perdita's shepherd father also knows only too well when he explains to her that the feast is a way "to make us better friends" (4.4.66). The act of hospitality stands surety with the future wealth of the family—so Perdita must "bid us welcome to your sheep-shearing, / As your good flock shall prosper" (4.4.69), which of course she does.

Problem is, as Fella's drawing shows us, the image of "hurtlesse" beasts and perfect meekness is accompanied always by the contrasting "image of idellness." Up in the rafters of the wine house to the right of the sheep-shearing scene, an uncertainly sexed person straddles the troughs below, a stream of urine and feces descending, either into the container holding the wine or behind it. Likewise, the Clown's mental arithmetic is overheard by the itinerant Autolycus, who is only too happy to set a "syringe" (trap) for this "cock" and take his purse. Not quite Mak, who seeks to derive sustenance if not capital from his stolen sheep, still, Autolycus lives off those who labor, returning his songs and stories as recompense, even if a good recompense they are. "Communities of consumption," like the sheep-shearing feast, the play seems to say, are all well and good but they are quite different from "communities of production," from communities that take their identity and mode of being from a broad, inclusive notion of labor that might even, one day, take account of sheep, in addition to all the attendant "clottes of claye."[28] The differential markers of social rank, backed up by biopolitical fantasies of differences of blood, strike hard, voiding the celebration as though this double plot is haunted by its governing first movement. Perdita and Florizel, Prince of Bohemia, find this out to their cost when King Polixenes, his father, arrives disguised as a shepherd and objects to his son's choice of bride. "I'll have they beauty scratched with briars," he torments "and made / More homely than thy state" (4.4.405–6). Perdita shall be disfigured; Forizel disinherited. The only way forward lies, so it seems, in completing the oracle's prophecy and returning to Sicilia. They shall all have to trust to luck which means, in effect, trusting to Paulina's lost and found department. In order to reach closure, the two plots must close upon one another.

Stealing home, returning what it lost and forgiving what has occurred takes time. It also runs the risk of misdirection, as threatens to occur when, rather taken with the newly found but yet to be identified Perdita, Leontes "beg[s Florizel's] ... precious mistress, / Which he counts but a trifle," which leads Paulina to interrupt him to see off the threat of incest as the two plots collide. "Sir, my liege, / Your eye hath too much youth in't," she interjects, "Not a month / Fore your queen died, she was more worth such gazes / Than what you look on now" (5.2.222–27). It will take more than simply arriving to set these plots straight and re-establish tenor and vehicle so that we "feel the play deals with life as a whole."[29] It will take Paulina's statue, her art, her gallery of leisurely devices—*otium* become an end in itself, a zero degree, that reboots the affective feelings of the sovereign.

If it seems that the sheep have simply disappeared or are now taken, as the Clown's accounting seems to indicate, as a given, then that is true. But to accept this truth is to admit merely that the human "clottes of claye" who walk and talk and act as faithful subjects of their kings and fathers, hoping that they shall once again play shepherd and not tyrant, have been constituted by and through their co-articulation with "sheep." As *The Winter's Tale* thaws, and the for-given-ness of its biopolitical "fix" and sculptural technology takes hold, we look on as our sheepy correlations, the transversal relations between the animals we name "sheep" and those "humans" that they, along with Gib, and Coll, and Daw, named "clottes of claye," recede from view.

V Fleeced (an Animetaphor)

Throughout this chapter I have modeled the theater of medieval and early modern England as the semiotic fine edge of discourses of pastoral care from which what we call biopolitics emerge. As I have tried to show, while we tend to take these discourses as exclusively anthropocentric, they assume and indeed function by and through their articulation of the great number of animals that we come into being with. In this chapter, I have privileged sheep, as was my brief, along with the way the co-articulation of "sheep" and "humans" constitutes a founding "double plot" for our pastoral imaginings. Similar stories could be told, and of course are, in this volume, of cows and dogs; of wolves and pigs, and of ducks, and chickens, as well as porcupines and all manner of animals. Shakespeare's plays tune into the metaphorical possibilities that this extended bestiary of animal becomings inscribes. They elaborate these animetaphors, inhabit them, and invite us to consider the ways in which what we take to be "human," in any given historical moment, comes routed through the differently animating relations we presume and have with other animals.[30]

Notes

1 William Empson, *Some Versions of Pastoral* (1935; repr., New York: A New Directions Paper Book, 1974), 27. Unless otherwise indicated, subsequent references appear parenthetically in the text.

2 For a now classic treatment of the emplotting of literary history and human development in Tudor ideology—especially the valorizing the ease of shepherds' labors—see Louis A. Montrose objects "Of Gentlemen and Shepherds: The Politics of Elizabethan Pastoral Form," *English Literary History* 50, no. 3 (Autumn, 1983): 427.

3 Leo Marx, "Pastoralism in America," in *Ideology and Classic American Literature*, eds. Sacvan Bercovitch and Myra Jehlen (Cambridge: Cambridge University Press, 1986), 45.

4 For a compelling call to attend to the material existence of particular animals as they mark our texts, see Karen Raber, *Animal Bodies, Renaissance Culture* (Philadelphia: University of Pennsylvania Press, 2013) and also, in different ways, Andreas Hofele, *Stage, Stake, and Scaffold: Humans and Animals in Shakespeare's Theatre* (Oxford: Oxford University Press, 2011); Bruce Boehrer, *Animal Characters: Nonhuman Beings in Early Modern Literature* (Philadelphia: University of Pennsylvania Press, 2010); and Erica Fudge in *Perceiving Animals: Humans and Beasts in Early Modern English Culture* (Basingstoke: Macmillan, 2000) and *Brutal Reasoning: Animals, Rationality, and Humanity in Early Modern England* (Ithaca, NY: Cornell University Press, 2006).

5 Michel Foucault, *Security, Territory, Population: Lectures at the Collège de France, 1977–1978*, trans. Graham Burchell (New York: Picador: 2007), 128. Unless otherwise indicated, subsequent references appear parenthetically in the text.

6 Michel Foucault, *"Society Must Be Defended": Lectures at the Collège de France, 1975–76*, trans. David Macey (New York: Picador, 2003), 254–55.

7 Nicole Shukin, "Tense Animals: On Other Species of Pastoral Power," *The New Centennial Review* 11, no. 2 (Fall, 2011): 145.

8 For a brilliant speculation into the potential origins of pastoral power that posits the co-management of human and sheepy flocks in such practices as "grazing," see Anand Pandian, "Pastoral Power in the Postcolony: On the Biopolitics of the Criminal Animal in South India," *Cultural Anthropology* 23, no. 1 (2008): 85–117.

9 My thanks go to Holly Dugan for this insight and phrasing.

10 My sense of the local ecology and historical particulars of the shepherds' complaints as deriving from the recoding of labor by changes in land use, enclosure specifically, is indebted to Lisa J. Kiser's excellent "'Mak's Heirs:' Sheep and Humans in the Pastoral Ecology of the Towneley *First* and *Second Shepherds' Plays*," *JEGP* 108, no. 3 (2009): 336–59.

11 Martin Stevens and A.C. Cawley, eds., *The Towneley Plays*, vol. 1 E.E.T.S. s. s. 13 (Oxford: Oxford University Press, 1994), 257–63. Unless otherwise indicated, subsequent references appear parenthetically in the text.

12 On this practice, see Kiser, "Mak's Heirs," 347–48.

13 It is not possible to provide an exhaustive review of this conversation here, but Leah Sinanoglou's "The Christ Child as Sacrifice: A Medieval Tradition and the Corpus Christi," *Speculum* 48, no. 3 (1973): 491–503 remains a signal marshalling of evidence. See also, Kiser, "Mak's Heirs."

14 Foucault, *Security, Territory, Population*, 169.

15 Edward Surtz S.J. and J.H. Hexter, eds., *The Yale Edition of the Complete Works of St. Thomas More* (New Haven, CT and London: Yale University Press, 15), vol. 4, 65/66.

16 *A Discourse of the Commonweal of This Realm of England* (attrib. to Sir Thomas Smith), ed. Mary Dewer (Charlottesville: University of Virginia Press, 1969), 21.

17 For similar proverbial statements see 'The Decay of Tudor England Only by the Great Multitude of Sheep', cited in R.H. Tawney and Eileen Power, eds., *Tudor Economic Documents* (London, 1953), III, 52. See also, Thomas Becon, The Jewell of Joy (1550), f.16b.

18 Edward Topsell, *The Historie of Four-Footed Beastes* (London, 1607), 626.

19 William Shakespeare, *Henry VI, Part 2*, ed. Roger Warren (Oxford: Oxford University Press, 2002), 4.10.59. Unless otherwise indicated, subsequent references appear parenthetically in the text.

20 The list of possible source rebellions derives from Annabel Patterson's *Shakespeare and the Popular Voice* (Oxford: Blackwell, 1989).

21 On "insurgent writing" as a carefully orchestrated and so tactically significant set of attacks on specific forms of legal documents as opposed to on writing *per se*, see Steven Justice, *Writing and Rebellion: England in 1381* (Berkeley and Los Angeles: University of California Press, 1994), 41 and more generally, 13–60.

22 William Shakespeare, *The Merchant of Venice*, ed. John Russell Brown (London: Arden, 1988), 1.3.63–65. Unless otherwise indicated, subsequent references appear parenthetically in the text.

23 Marc Shell, *Money, Language, and Thought* (Baltimore, MD: Johns Hopkins University Press, 1982), 50. See also Laurie Shannon, *The Accommodated Animal: Cosmopolity in Shakespearean Locales* (Chicago, IL: University of Chicago Press, 2013), 270–72.

    Although no source for Shylock's use of Genesis has been found, Thomas Wilson's *A Discourse upon Vsurye* (1572) includes an entire bestiary of parasites summoned to explain predatory economic practices. Wilson trades also on the visual pun that derives "Jews" from "iewes" in early modern orthography.

24 Foucault, *"Society Must Be Defended,"* 254–55.

25 Shell, *Money, Language, and Thought*, 53.

26 William Shakespeare, *The Winter's Tale*, eds. Susan Snyder and Deborah t. Curren-Aquino (Cambridge: Cambridge University Press, 2007), 2.1.56–58. Unless otherwise indicated, subsequent references appear parenthetically in the text.

27 Ibid., 169, note to lines 31–33.

28 Raymond Williams, *The Country and the City* (Oxford: Oxford University Press, 1975), 30–31.

29 Empson, *Some Versions of Pastoral*, 27.

30 The phrase "animetaphor" was coined by Akira Mizuta Lippit in *Electric Animal* (Minneapolis: University of Minnesota Press, 2000).

17

SILLY CREATURES

King Lear (with Sheep)

Laurie Shannon

Silly sports a long pedigree as "a conventional epithet of sheep."[1] Rich etymological crossings mark this genealogy, and most of it precedes the sense that contemporary readers bring to the apparently familiar adjective: "of a person: lacking in judgement or common sense; foolish, thoughtless, empty-headed; characterized by ridiculous or frivolous behaviour" (silly, OED A.6.a). Indeed, a look into *silly*'s history reveals capacities rangy enough to encompass the opposite conditions of being fortunate and being wretched. It derives from the older term, *seely*, and the two operate fairly interchangeably in English usage around Shakespeare's time. Following the OED, a relay of meanings within *seely* moves from happy, blissful, and fortunate, to spiritually blessed, and even to holy, all on the way to a further sense, where *seely* takes on a political or legal valence at the same time as it takes an animal turn: "Innocent, harmless. Often as an expression of compassion for persons or animals suffering undeservedly" (seely, OED 5). From its origins describing a form of happiness, *seely* then extends to reach the opposite state and even to encode a certain ethical imperative of response: "Deserving of pity or sympathy; pitiable, miserable, 'poor'; helpless, defenceless" (seely, OED 6). *Silly*'s sheepy affiliations, on the whole, proceed from these last inflections.

For, moving from *seely* back to *silly* now, we see the very same range of meanings, but a somewhat more acute calibration with respect to species. While the *OED*'s historical note describes the "dominant modern adjectival sense" of *silly* as the foolish empty-headedness cited above (regarding persons), it stresses by contrast that, in the sixteenth and seventeenth centuries, *silly* was "very extensively" used in senses associated with "weakness, vulnerability, or physical incapacity" instead. In the range of meanings between worthy or holy (A.1) and the foolishness specified as human (A.6), species markers and definitional "especiallies" proliferate, co-articulated with breakdowns inside the category of human being. Again we find "Helpless, defenceless, powerless; frequently with the suggestion of innocence or undeserved suffering" (A.2), now sub-specified with "a. Of an animal; esp. as a conventional epithet of sheep" and "b. Of a person, esp. a woman or a child." A.3.b. further indexes *silly* as "Of a person or (esp.) an animal: weak, feeble, frail; lacking strength, size, or endurance." Finally, A.4. indicates that which "provokes sympathy or compassion; that is to be pitied; unfortunate, wretched," while A.5.a., though speaking of persons again, points back to pastoral contexts by giving us "rustic" as a gloss. Across this evolving definition and bearing

219

genetic traces from each step in its earlier development, *silly* thus manages to weave together heavily freighted questions of human status, creaturely (in)capacity, and the glimmer of a duty of care across kinds.

I have begun with this bit of etymological delving to point us to what can, fairly, be said to be "silly" about sheep. The association clearly does not intend, or did not originally intend, frivolity or a lack of Cartesian judgment. Indeed, the silliness of sheep, by these lights, suggests more an exposure to harsh necessity than it does frivolity. It implies, too, at the very least, a cast shadow of some kind of "judgment"—and more profound considerations too—by naming their vulnerability and suggesting their suffering is undeserved. "Silly" turns out to be serious. As Julian Yates puts the point in a consideration of Thomas More's 1516 *Utopia* (regarding those sheep alleged to be "man-eaters" as the human practice of enclosing pastures displaced other humans from the land),

> our understanding of sheep may be determined not by their actual behaviors but by the questions we ask of them ... if it turns out that sheep are, for example, *rhetorically capable*, then a whole new set of pastoral metaphors becomes thinkable.[2]

Karen Raber details this particular opportunity, giving an account of how our critical responses to More's framework have tended to incorporate unthinking commonplaces about sheep (especially their harmlessness). Insisting we attend to the historical and material terms for animal agency, she asks instead that we avoid "defanging" More's sheep.[3] If these grassland grazers can cogently be said to eat people, how many other directions might language: let us go to grasp the possibilities for sheepy signification and "performance"? Where, in turn, might that lead us in construing significant agency for *silly* (that is, *serious*) sheep?

Perhaps no thought experiment has gone further in the service of such an inquiry than Missouri Williams's extraordinary 2014/2015 play and production, *King Lear with Sheep*. The drama starred one bearded human and—in a nice, double reversal of Shakespearean traditions of playing—nine female sheep (of several breeds). First staged in 2014 in a warehouse at Surrey Docks and then in a Sussex barn, *King Lear with Sheep* was revived and produced for two runs at Hoxton's Courtyard Theatre in London in 2015, the first in August and then the second a re-revival in October (with that autumn run also extended, due to popular demand).[4] As a practical matter, that Williams and her producer, Lucy Elven, overcame the patent improbability of this undertaking, with all its unpredictably "moving parts," staggers the imagination. As an achieved multidisciplinary phenomenon, *King Lear with Sheep* raises bracing existential and philosophical questions about species, not least in dramatizing an almost scientific estrangement of that creature known as humankind. It also poses block-buster metatheatrical puzzles about the meaning of playing; for starters, consider the Pandora's box of a query Raber and Monica Mattfield have recently posed, opening their collection, *Performing Animals*, by asking "What does it mean to say an animal performs?"[5] With the formidable assemblage of *King Lear with Sheep* as evidence, this chapter will argue for the arresting seriousness of "silly sheep"—in what might well be English pastoral's most vivid turn yet. If, as William Empson memorably argued, pastoral may be "about" and "by" "the people," but not necessarily "for" them, perhaps Williams's most sheep-ward "version of pastoral" might be said to be "for" people—without being fully or exclusively "about" or "by" them.[6] In addition to its commentary on Shakespeare's *King Lear*, Williams's *King Lear with Sheep* also suggests how we might add a species-crossing "with" to our analyses of humanity and performance.

I Serious Sheep

The constituencies of pastoral have traditionally afforded fruitfully vague ground for rumination, whether a given instance mystifies or exposes our political orthodoxies about nature, order, safety, rapacity, and power. If shepherds, flocks, and wolves usually (or generically) signify as kings/magistrates, the people, and whatever endangers them, the prescriptive implications of pastoral scenes and the roles staged in its habitat still remain surprisingly flexible. Pastoral navigates the theoretical whirlpools inherent in a strictly oppositional or binary conception of humanity *vs.* Nature by conjuring a world that properly belongs to neither domain. A shepherd is a rustic human and not a monarch; the notion of wild sheep, meanwhile, approaches oxymoron. The imperfection of these comparisons blurs their potential political application—and gives it open space in which to flourish.

Sheep humor, of course, familiarly abounds in Shakespeare. In *The Two Gentlemen of Verona*, for example, Valentine's servant Speed jokes that he has "played the sheep" in missing his master's shipping time; Proteus tosses back the sheep-loric (and allegorically political) truism, "indeed, a sheep doth very often stray, /An if the shepherd be awhile away."[7] But a witty thrust and parry ensues, with comedy's temporizing proofs and counter-proofs on the point of whether Speed is or is not "a sheep," "astray," or "a lost mutton." Of special importance here, their exchange "proves" one thing for certain: the figure of the sheep equivocates. In Speed's formulation, "The shepherd seeks the sheep, and not the sheep the shepherd; but I seek my master, and my master seeks not me: therefore I am no sheep." From this foundational question of who attends on whom, Proteus pivots to a different strand of analogical reasoning that reverses the conclusion, arguing that as sheep follow the shepherd for fodder, so Speed follows his master for wages: "therefore thou art a sheep." The volley concludes by stressing Speed's sheep-like return to "a pinfold" (1.1.78–108). But whether or not this comic exchange itself is silly (that is, ridiculous, frivolous, esp. of persons), the silliness (exposure or vulnerability) of the sheep's part implicates mottled questions of custody, authority, and the politics of protection. Having cannily given its master the slip, a defenseless stray might face a wolf alone; the "pinfold" (whether a pound or a polity) to which the sheep returns then operates in the ambivalent senses of being brought into the happy safety of the fold, but also being penned in an enclosure without consenting to it.

In more directly political applications (and far from comedy), we find "silly sheep" in Shakespeare's *The Third Part of King Henry VI* (c. 1591/2). In a long soliloquy, Henry compares the contending forces of the offstage war to the relentless schedule of reversing tides. A king's exposure of his people to the figurative wolf of war was a notorious moral risk for the ruler and the ruled alike, a risk contemplated with concern across the sixteenth century from Erasmus's *Education of a Christian Prince* (1516) to Shakespeare's own *Henry V* (1600).[8] But *Henry VI* is less reflective than *Henry V* on this particular point of royal ethical attention; he thinks only of his own stress and suffering. To figure this, he engages in a counterfactual fantasy about what it would be like to be a swain instead of a king: "Oh god! Methinks it were a happy life, /To be no better than a homely swain" and calmly to count out the passing of time, "So minutes, hours, days, months, and years, /… /Would bring white hairs unto a quiet grave." These lines of pastoral longing instance a commonplace in the representation of royal interiority, and when Lear first cedes his political authority and then further removes himself to the heath, we can see the dystopic reality of any attempt to actualize the fantasy.

Coming to the rhetorical point of his pastoral alternative vision in *Henry VI*, King Henry then asks: "Gives not the hawthorne-bush a sweeter shade /To shepherds looking on their *silly sheep*, /Than doth a rich embroider'd canopy /To kings that fear their subjects' treachery?" (2.5.21–45, emphasis added). On the one hand, silly (innocent) sheep figure for him the sure impossibility of treason; the swain, by comparison to a king, need not be on guard for his own sake, since the sheep's nature guarantees his safety from them. On the other hand, the sovereign himself is constitutionally under-defended and subject to fear, and so he takes on the attributes of exposure and vulnerability that sheep more usually represent, as the "treacherous" flock he protects turns deadly. As natural as they suggest themselves to be, of course, pastoral role assignments readily reverse, and this kind of equivocal potential may be the most intriguing capacity of the pastoral repertoire. Sheep might have fangs. They might even take charge.

On our way to another king likewise beset by unruly sheep, serious sheep who (also) happen to be literal sheep, a retrospective question for *King Lear* presents itself. For Missouri Williams's *King Lear with Sheep* certainly gives a reading "of" Shakespeare's *King Lear*, but it also makes rich use of Lear's fundamental situation (itself a form of siege out on the heath) to deliver new questions—for Shakespeare's play and beyond it. One last preliminary then will set the stage for Williams's flock here and connect it to the perennial questions associated with this most canonical of Shakespeare's plays. That is, what relation might we suppose between the serious forms of *silliness* I have excavated above and Folly itself, that ancient but privileged philosophical gloss on what it might mean to be human?

Elsewhere I have suggested natural history, with its close attention to animal coverings and bodily provision for the challenges of weather and survival, as the period discursive frame within which we might best understand Lear's insight when he observes the naked Edgar ("Poor Tom"), at the height of his exposure to the storm. Lear memorably exclaims, "Thou art the thing itself; unaccommodated man is no more but such as *poor, bare, forked animal* as thou art" (3.4.106–8). Unaccommodated man *is man*, or man as such; by contrast, *accommodated* man would be that poor beast when he has accrued the compensatory benefits of coverage by clothes and a collective (or flock) alike.[9] Here, given his embodiment of the *senex* role to which we all must come, if we live long enough, we can see another way that the old king also plays the part of human being itself in the drama. By that logic, Lear's repeating failure to be wise signals that the shortfall is less a personal tragic flaw than a general or genetic inheritance.

The elevated "wise fool" tradition—a discourse of intellectual penetration that is both Christian and philosophical—appears, of course, in Lear's companion Fool in the play. But Lear's "head /So old and white" suggests a radically different kind of folly, in contrast, as a universal or a quality of human being *as such* (3.2.23–24). The Fool, in this sense, narrates Lear's more generic form of folly correctly, alleging "thou hadst little wit in thy bald crown when thou gav'st thy golden one away." Comparing Lear's head to a broken egg, he observes, "Thou hast pared thy wit o' both sides and left nothing i' th' middle" (1.4.160–61; 184–85). In *Madness and Civilization*, Foucault argues that the passage from late medieval to early modern thought saw themes of madness substitute for a theme of death, in what he calls a "torsion within the same anxiety" about the ultimate nature of human being. As he indelibly puts it, "the head that will become a skull is already empty."[10] To recast that thought in terms of cross-creaturely embodiment and natural history, as woollen-wits and wool-gatherers, we seem to sprout our fleece backward, on the inside of our so-celebrated heads, where it works against us.

If woolly-wittedness offers a rather homespun trope, it nevertheless belongs to the *vanitas* tradition and its durable sense that those avowedly human superpowers of mind lead us, inevitably, to a fall due to our prideful self-reliance. Michel de Montaigne's magisterially cross-species argument about the vanity of human knowledge, his essay entitled "The

Silly Creatures: King Lear *(with Sheep)*

Apologie for Raymond Sebond" contributes ferocious language on this point, and it directly resonates with the etymologies of "silly" traced above. Montaigne demands,

> Is it possible to imagine any thing so *ridiculous*, as this *miserable* and *wreched* [sic] creature, which is not so much as master of himself, exposed and subject to offences of all things, and yet dareth call himself Master and Emperour of this Universe?

The question answers itself, of course; the self-reliance of a seely creature spells disaster. Montaigne (categorizing humans using a third person "they" to emphasize his own aversion to the form of being he critiques) proposes to

> crush, and trample this humane pride … under foot, to make them feele the emptinesse, vacuitie, and no worth of man: and violently to pull out of their hands, the *silly* weapons of their reason; to make them stoope, and bite and snarle at the ground, under the authority and reverence of God's majesty.[11]

Imagining a humanity trampled underfoot and made to bite and snarl at the ground in this multispecies image, Montaigne conjures faith as the supplement to human weakness. The Tudor English translator's phrasing for humanity's own resources, comparing the "silly weapons of our reason" to God's grace, makes clear the ways that "silly" encompasses not only folly but weakness and an extreme helplessness. Shakespeare's *King Lear* notoriously gives no evidence of the faith Montaigne so comfortably invokes. *King Lear with Sheep*, in turn, spectacularly stages this implosive collapse of human being—as we watch its representative "bite and snarl at the ground"—and it makes nine real sheep the relatively calm and intelligent witnesses of the catastrophic scene, with extraordinary (and serious) effects.

II Seely Humans

As I anticipated the performance of *King Lear with Sheep*, my main preoccupation was whether a sheep-cast play would remain a "tragedy"; that was the wrong question. After I had seen it, it seemed the question presented was wider than a puzzle about the terms of tragedy. *King Lear with Sheep* asks, mobilizing Shakespeare's text, whether we have had the fullest understanding of what a play is, *if sheep can perform one so effectively.* For, among the host of plausible yet contradictory critical readings one might have of the theatrical and embodied event, as a member of the audience I never caught myself wondering at a philosophical level whether or not this was "a play." As Williams herself puts the point, "the sheep [do] their job better than I ever could have imagined."[12] Holly Dugan, in her *Shakespeare Quarterly* review essay about the performance, spiritedly concurs that "the sheep hit all their cues."[13] Writing in the ArtsBeat blog of *The New York Times*, Christopher Shea summarizes the dramatic action as follows:

> The production, which lasts under an hour, centers on a director character who decides to stage a production of *King Lear* starring sheep. In the face of the animals' indifference, he breaks down and begins to perform the tale himself.[14]

But Shea's sleeping proposition of animal "indifference" begs the question the entire event seems built to ask.

Shakespeare's original text is perhaps as full of animal references as any play in English.[15] Williams's apt innovation on and with it masterfully delivers the text's implicit drama of kinds to the embodied stage, making drama in this instance a *multispecies* collision of perspectives. A human audience watches human being (personated by one man), but we watch him (and by implication ourselves) "with," and so partly through, the wondering eyes of nine actual sheep. The theatrical functions of the traditional chorus come sharply into play in this respect: although we are watching the sheep, we are invited to see their conjoined perspectives as the potentially correct moral frame for the play's action. Though speechless (if not exactly silent), these sheep surround, attend, and—as we shall see—"comment" on the man. Their sober eyes estrange for us the *seely* human creature—the "poor, infirm, weak, and despised old man" (*King Lear* 3.2.20)—they scrutinize.

The plot of *King Lear with Sheep* concerns a human theater director ("Director") who has taken it upon himself to produce *King Lear* and has engaged a company of sheep to perform all the parts. He does not explain why.[16] Act 1 begins with the Director alone. He is manned with plastic water bottle. There is a chair. Things proceed wordlessly as he evinces increasing anxiety, pacing the stage, checking his watch, and gazing back and forth from the audience to the stage entrance: the flock is unaccountably late for their performance. They are "usually so ... punctual," he frets, and the stage direction indicates, "*Head in hands*."[17] But then he shrilly promises "they're on their way," addressing the audience directly to reassure us that "they really are great. They really know how to *act* .... They really know how to put on a *show*." To play for time, he quotes reviews of the tour so far: "'A playful play' (Pause; smiles) *The New York Times* ... 'Functional' (Pause) *The Guardian* ... 'Apt.' (Smiles again, as if delighted) *The Independent*." Painful pause. He temporizes, insisting "it really is a playful play ... It *plays*." After about ten long minutes of sporadic and almost contagiously nervous talk to the audience, and after some over-compensatory scoffing ("Actors! Who'd have them?"), the director tries to assure himself and us: "I trust them. They're professionals." With that, on cue, as the stage direction puts it, nine "Sheep pour onto the stage." They are of several breeds; some wear cardboard crowns tied with string under their chins, they sport capes, and one cape in particular is duly edged in ermine.

The Director's vivid relief that the troupe of sheep has arrived quickly dissipates in Act 2, displaced by a rising new panic that they are refusing to perform their lines. The stage direction, perhaps needlessly, affirms, "Silence from the sheep behind him." Of course, the business of a hesitation or refusal to speak a desired script represents a canny pivot on Cordelia's refusal to voice hyperbole in Shakespeare's plot. The idea achieves superb additional resonance in this new setting, highlighting the old chestnut that animals cannot "act" (because, as it is said, they cannot lie). Despite that presumptive bias, here they are occupying the stage and interacting with the Director and each other—while we audience members eagerly, tractably, and silently attend their every move. After a series of spiraling, hysterical questions to the flock ("Why aren't you talking to me?" "Oh, so what, the silence game?"), he queries the horned and ermine-collared Lear ("Lear, man, what's the matter?") and then Gloucester ("me old mucker?"), until he darkly concludes, "It's Cordelia, isn't it?" He infers that they are all colluding against him and taking their cue for silence from her. He turns directly to Cordelia. "You *bitch*" (italics in original!); "Silence, huh? Why do you have to be so infuriating? There's no love in you." Here Williams begins actively to interlineate Shakespearean material, and the Director intones, "How now, Cordelia! *Mend your speech a little*, /Lest it may mar your fortunes. /So young, and so untender?" (my italics). When Goneril likewise fails to respond to him, he curses her with Shakespeare's Lear's incendiary "Dry up in her the organs of increase" speech. Picking out the Regan sheep, he's shocked to find her "Quiet too."

Silly Creatures: King Lear (with Sheep)

Figure 17.1 *King Lear with Sheep*, image courtesy of Heather Williams

I have not described any sheep speeches yet, and the reader may be wondering how they conduct themselves onstage. But as the Director promised, the sheep—two Suffolk crosses, two Whitefaced Woodlands (a now-designated Rare Breed, originally from Yorkshire, in which both sexes sport horns), and five Shetlands (a "primitive" sheep not significantly altered by human breeding practices and one that browses gently on grass instead of uprooting it)—*really are professional*. An arm's-length of "filmography" and other credits for Clover, Bluebell, Snowdrop, Hazel, Laurel, Honey, Jamie, Willow, and Anise appear in the October 2015 program.[18] They enter on cue, they calmly eat the kibble strewn onstage just as they had done in their rehearsals, they walk around, they relieve themselves, they interact (especially by their noses) with each other and the Director too. Sometimes one or another of the troupe rests her chin on the iron farm fence that makes a literal fourth wall and openly considers the audience with interest. The sheep have had lots of practice with the loud stage noises that will mark the storm to come.

Most dramatically, however, they (especially the two blackest Shetlands, one of whom is Cordelia) also *watch* the Director off and on as he delivers his lines; they follow him a little;

they nuzzle and butt his legs; one investigates his water bottle and tips it over. If they are nervous about anything, they do seem a little concerned, or watchful, at the signals of an alarming over-excitability coming from the agitated Director-human. In advance, being human, I of course imagined the play would dramatize the absurdity and folly of the Director-human character for casting sheep as actors in the first place. Indeed, *The Telegraph*'s review refers to the sheep as an "impassive flock, whose presence render(s) everything tragic and wholly ridiculous."[19] But *King Lear with Sheep*, I argue, might more plausibly be said to render *humans* tragic and ridiculous—or at least to beg the question of humanity every bit as much as it does of animals. For the sheep's perfectly able performance—both as individuals and in their choreographic demonstration of just the flocking practice that we know so catastrophically collapses among humans in Shakespeare's play—yields instead a powerfully chorus-like wisdom, a kind of species-gloss on humanity. Their apparent reasonableness onstage makes the Director, the human character, responsible for any and all non-sense (see Figure 17.1).

Act 3 begins with the Director nervously repeating the line "It's nearly time for the heath scene"—first declaratively, then screaming at the top of his voice. Telling us then that one sheep seeks his attention, they have a private whisper, and the Director relays shocking news that the sheep now want to cancel the tour. He accuses them of "Mutiny," quoting lines from the forged letter Edmund gives his father, with sarcastic disbelief: "'an idle and fond bondage--! The oppression of aged tyranny!'" "You want to overthrow me?" The political terms of his incredulous reaction cast the emerging relation of humans and sheep, notably, as a sovereignty spurned, just as Henry VI had imagined that revolt. From this point on, the human actor (Alasdair Saksena, who performs with a deeply resourceful brio) delivers a *tour-de-force*, taking the Shakespeare play's many voices upon himself to cobble together some semblance of *King Lear* (the original to have been performed by the now-mutinous sheep). Having represented species diversity on the stage before us, playwright Williams threads Shakespeare's most brilliantly natural-historical speeches into a seamless, multispecies through-line. From the opening "fall ... from the bias of nature" to "blow, winds, and crack your cheeks" to Lear's penultimate "Howl, howl, howl, howl," Shakespearean passages slowly overcome the Director's snarky barbs to the sheep-actors (who are now *also* playing the audience of a play-within-a-play) and nervous apologies to the "real" audience of humans. We humans in the audience are going to be given the *King Lear*, or some version of it, that we "have paid good money to see."

When the human Lear in *King Lear with Sheep* dis-accommodates himself, stripping down to his natural inheritance of naked skin with "Off, off, you lendings!," his heavy, pale, glistening body stands out sharply from the scrum of quite dusty, woolly backs surrounding him. He certainly "ow[es] ... the sheep no wool" (3.4.102–3). As the sweaty human actor leaps back and forth from role to role, occasionally annoying some of the sheep, he suggests Foucault's claim that "madness ... is a ... rapport that man maintains with[in] himself" (26). But *King Lear with Sheep* highlights humanity's mad, skipping babble, our biting and snarling, against a multispecies *dramatis animalia* that plays out in a landscape depicted as unforgiving to the human. The sheep cannot be taken either as mere props or imagined figments in our little earthly epic; here, the sheepy chorus around the raving human shows us just how a flock might have served as some defense against the solitary collapse of this instance of humankind. The juxtaposition of kinds trips up our imperial tendencies with a vision of human being as, instead, lost on earth: a "lost mutton," he has gone *astray*.

Much has been made of Shakespeare's *King Lear* being reduced, in Act 5, to a repetition of terms that suggests a loss or collapse of speech, one of the singular powers most often used to justify claims for humanity's exceptional status in the cosmos. The idiolectic ranter of

Silly Creatures: King Lear *(with Sheep)*

Act 3 now speaks some gibberish, as beasts were said to do. But "Howl, howl, howl, howl," the plaintive emission from Lear as he absorbs the death of his spurned daughter Cordelia, sounds differently when cried out amid a gently milling throng of sheep; the juxtaposition confuses our ordinary categories concerning language, fluency, and comprehensibility and our sense of tragedy too. As the kneeling Saksena holds Snowdrop, a small, paper-crowned, black Shetland sheep, in his arms and asks the universe "Why should a dog, a horse, a rat, have life, /And thou no breath at all?" we experience again a kind of cognitive dissonance at the heart of our presumptions about kind. With such a tableau before us, we can only wonder why should anything have life? Or the reverse: why shouldn't everything have its life? At that moment, in one of the performances I saw, Snowdrop turned her face towards him and seemed to nuzzle him. No audience member, of course, expects her to be or even to play dead, but perhaps too no one was expecting her to investigate or to "care."

Williams's *King Lear with Sheep*, like its great predecessor, stunningly puts the human failure to navigate this world on trial (not sheep). Putting sheep onstage in so effectively choral a form, Williams enables them to be proxy eyes for the viewing audience, or to shepherd our eyes for us. This effect portrays humanity as a little less solitary than our tragic figures tend to make themselves when left to the "silly weapons" of their own reason. In the special kind of dramatic irony achieved by this theater of species-diverse bodies, the production shows us one seely creature in a calamity of exposure, but there is also a choreographic and embodied way in which the sheep circle and enclose the man. Nine woolly actors strip humanity down, as they tip over our water bottles, butt their tender heads against our legs, and completely fail to be overwhelmed by an authority their eyes teach us to see as incoherent. But their encircling bodies and their careful ongoing attention to the bellowing mad human at the center of the stage also put King Lear himself once more inside *some version* of the comic, or cosmic, circle of inclusion. These silly sheep gently surround the silly man; they sometimes gaze at him, and we follow their gazes. Who "plays the sheep" for whom? A heady mix of comedy, tragedy, farmyard, and heath, Williams's *King Lear with Sheep* delivers a brilliant and table-turning version of pastoral.

Notes

1 "Silly," (A.2.a), from *The Oxford English Dictionary* (online edition), consulted August 1, 2019. Subsequent references appear in the text.

2 Julian Yates, "Humanist Habitats; or, 'Eating Well' with Thomas More's *Utopia*," in *Environment and Embodiment in Early Modern England*, eds., Mary Floyd-Wilson and Garrett Sullivan (Basingstoke: Palgrave Macmillan, 2007), 187–209, 206 (emphasis mine). See also Julian Yates, *Of Sheep, Oranges, and Yeast: A Multispecies Impression* (Minneapolis: University of Minnesota Press, 2017).

3 Karen Raber, *Animal Bodies, Renaissance Culture* (Philadelphia: University of Pennsylvania Press, 2013), 161–78, 164.

4 I attended two of the October 2015 performances with Margreta de Grazia. Her welcome and characteristically spirited conversation on those occasions has vitalized my thinking about the entire event; any silliness (*OED* A.6.a) or other mishaps of thought are my own.

5 Karen Raber and Monica Mattfeld, *Performing Animals: History, Agency, Theater* (State College: Pennsylvania State University Press, 2017), 1.

6 William Empson, *Some Versions of Pastoral* (New York: New Directions, 1974), 6.

7 William Shakespeare, *The Two Gentlemen of Verona*, in *The Complete Works of Shakespeare, Fifth Edition*, ed. David Bevington (New York: Pearson Longman, 2004), (1.1.74-76); subsequent references to Shakespeare's works are to this edition.

8 Indeed, the sequence of Erasmus's chapters in *The Education of a Christian Prince* reflects the radical difference he makes between peacetime and war. Erasmus presses all the arguments against the

prince's exposing his or her people to the depredations of war, which he separates categorically from the political arts, seeing war as a terrible contradiction of the prince's fiduciary role of care for the "flock."

9 Laurie Shannon, *The Accommodated Animal: Cosmopolity in Shakespearean Locales* (Chicago, IL: University of Chicago Press, 2013), Chapter 3 ("Poor, Bare, Forked: Animal Happiness and the Zoographic Critique of Humanity"), 127–73.

10 Michel Foucault, *Madness and Civilization: A History of Insanity in the Age of Reason* (New York: Vintage, 1965 [1961]), 16.

11 Michel de Montaigne, "The Apologie for Raymond Sebond," in *The Essayes of Montaigne: John Florio's Translation*, ed. J.I.M. Stewart (New York: Modern Library, 1933 [French, 1580, 1588, and 1595; English translation, 1603]), 395 and 397 (emphases mine). For the French, see "Apologie de Raimond Sebond," in *Les Essais*, ed. Pierre Villey (Lausanne: Guilde du Livre, 1965), 448 ('*les chetives armes de leu raison*") and 450 (diminishing man, simply, as "*pauvret*" – a poor little [thing]). Montaigne's "Apologie" was begun in 1576 and first published as Chapter 12 of Book II in the first edition of the *Essais* and remained its longest chapter. It nominally defends a text from the 1420s or 1430s, Raymond Sebond's *Theologia naturalis; sive liber creaturarum magistri Raimondi de Sebonda* (*Natural Theology; or the Book of Creatures*). Montaigne had previously translated this important but doctrinally risky work in the history of creatures at his father's request.

12 Heather Williams, "How My Production of *King Lear with Sheep* Ended up Generating More Publicity than I Ever Imagined," *The Independent*, September 8, 2015. www.independent.co.uk/voices/how-my-production-of-king-lear-with-sheep-ended-up-generating-more-publicity-than-i-ever-imagined-10491410.html. (Williams used the pen name "Missouri Williams" for the play).

13 Holly Dugan, "Shakespeare Performed: Courtyard Theatre's *King Lear with Sheep*," *Shakespeare Quarterly*, June 2017. https://shakespearequarterly.folger.edu/web_exclusive/shakespeare-performed-courtyard-theatres-king-lear-with-sheep/ (accessed December 7, 2017).

14 Christopher Shea, "'King Lear with Sheep.' Yes, Sheep," *Arts Beat, New York Times Blog*, August 11, 2015. https://artsbeat.blogs.nytimes.com/2015/08/11/king-lear-with-sheep-yes-sheep/.

15 It takes a half page to list the animal references in *The Accommodated Animal*, and that is not counting foul fiends, demons, incubi, or spirits, to whatever order they belong (165).

16 The playwright herself explains: "I wanted to do something extreme that would challenge our ideas about both Shakespeare and the theatre as a whole - to re-establish this sense of presence, a violent, unpredictable animal presence (sheep), that people might feel uneasy, scared or embarrassed by. Expose the performance as a performance, if you will." *The Independent* (September 8, 2015).

17 Missouri Williams, "Sheep King Lear Formal Script," (unpublished manuscript), Act 1 (unpaginated). I'm very, very grateful to the author for access to and permission to quote the play text. All italics are as they appear in the original.

18 Courtyard Theatre program, *King Lear with Sheep, verso*. The entire cast of the sheep persuasion hailed from Vauxhall City Farm, in the London Borough of Lambeth, which also supplied the breed information and detailed film credits for the play's non-human stars.

19 Chris Bennion, "*King Lear with Sheep*, The Courtyard, Review: 'Odd and Wondrous'," *The Telegraph*, August 14, 2015. www.telegraph.co.uk/theatre/what-to-see/king-lear-with-sheep-the-courtyard-review/.

PART 5

Animal Boundaries and Identities

Shakespeare's animals are often humans: his plays invoke misogynistic, racist, anti-Jewish, and class-based insults as characters describe and denigrate others using animal comparisons. These analogies always define animals as lower than humans within hierarchical systems of nature, and thus, by association, position some humans as lower, less worthy, or less valued than others. In this part, essayists focus on human–animal analogical thinking directly, drawing a picture of animal intersectionality—that is, the ways in which animals are used in the generation of an array of identities, including the foreign, feminine, black, queer, poor, mad, or enslaved, but also the noble, regal, beautiful, and desirable. Shakespeare's metaphors create networks of positive and negative associations that implicate certain animals in complex reciprocal relationships to marginalized or devalued humans.

The part, perhaps counterintuitively, begins with a discussion of royal bodies and their animal resonances. In "The Lion King: Shakespeare's Beastly Sovereigns," Nicole Mennell takes up the most iconic image of sovereignty and governance, the lion, examining its majestic and tyrannical power in the period's literary and artistic imagination. As Mennell makes clear, Shakespeare's depictions of rulers invoke the lion as a symbol for the legitimate use of force, usually posed against a wolf predator. Yet force alone was not enough: kings (and queens) also needed to show mercy. Shakespeare's metaphoric lion kings thus embody both kinds of sovereign power, the ability to deal "forcefully with opponents while showing mercy to innocents and suppliants." Mennell argues that reading the imagery of lions in Shakespeare's history and Roman plays reveals how it allowed Shakespeare to depict the "realities and pitfalls" of governance.

Shakespeare's hunt is the subject of "'Wearing the Horn': Class and Community in the Shakespearean Hunt," in which Jennifer Reid analyzes hunt scenes in *As You Like It*, connecting its metaphors of sacrifice to the violence of hunting rituals in the period. Hunting, Reid argues, was an aristocratic technology used to establish class divisions: its carefully scripted rules and etiquette, along with its sanctioned forms of bloodshed, were designed to foster bonds between the most privileged members of society, at incredible cost, labor, and sacrifice, with those who were the least privileged. Shakespeare's comedies, with their parodic invocation of hunting rituals, examine the paradox of hunting practices, arguing that they both create and resolve problems of social division. Though it is unlikely that any live deer appeared on stage, their horns were likely worn by actors, thereby also raising questions about what it meant to play the part of the hunter vs. that of the prey in early modern theaters.

Questions about ritual, violence, and human status are salient in Shakespeare's more troubling animal metaphors. Steven Swarbrick, in "On Eating, the Animal That Therefore I Am: Race and Animal Rites in *Titus Andronicus*," addresses Derrida's "deceptively simple" question, "what is eating?" Tracing the racialized logic of sacrifice embedded within Shakespeare's *Titus Andronicus*, Swarbrick argues that the play allows us to explore the limits of Donna Haraway's posthuman theory of conviviality and companionship outlined in *When Species Meet*. The play upends social divisions through its cannibalistic logic, even as it draws upon violent racist and misogynist tropes to do so. Swarbrick's analysis shows us how "race and animality do not so much interact in Shakespeare's play but rather crosshatch in the making and unmaking of human and nonhuman bodies."

Robert Wakeman's analysis of *Measure for Measure* switches habitats, exploring how and why stockfish and piscine culture provided a rhetoric for non-normative sexual aggression in the play. In "'What's this? what's this?': Fish and Sexuality in *Measure for Measure*," Wakeman argues that the play's sexual politics are both queer and violent; Angelo, he notes, is repeatedly defined in piscine metaphors: characters joke about his cold nature, his "crabbed" demeanor, and opine that he was born of two stockfish. Such jokes, Wakeman argues, position Angelo's embodied cold-blooded sexuality both as non-normative and as destructive. Shakespeare's piscine masculinities thus provide one way of responding to feminist calls for more expansive approaches to the history of rape.

Karen Raber argues that the critical treatment of the Dauphin's adoration of his palfrey in *Henry V* risks cooperating with the reaction of his interlocutors, the Constable and Orleans, in rejecting his apparently infantile, even bestial sexual self-positioning, and thereby affirming the play's enforcement of masculinist heterosexuality. Instead in "My Palfrey, Myself: Toward a Queer Phenomenology of the Horse-Human bond in *Henry V* and Beyond," Raber invites us to recognize the Dauphin's horse love as a thoroughly queer challenge to the play's interwoven threads of human exceptionalism, misogyny, and heteronormativity. The speech inspires Raber's explorative effort to establish a queer phenomenology of the human-equine encounter in early modern England and Europe. The Dauphin's desire for his beautiful palfrey is contextualized alongside horsemanship manuals and other literary texts, where the erotic appeal of a horse's particular physical shape and motion emerge as triggers for embodied erotic communion between human and nonhuman partners.

For Erica Fudge, whose essay rounds out this volume, Shakespeare's *Richard II* opens the door to a different posture in response to the historical transition away from an "enchanted" nature invested with its own agency and human qualities. In "'Forgiveness, horse': The Barbaric World of *Richard II*," Fudge not only examines Richard's conversation about his favorite horse from the perspective of other critical analyses but also questions the absolute nature of their conclusions. In the history of skepticism to which Richard's speech can be linked, Fudge finds not only that Richard's reaction registers the advent of Cartesian modernity; it may, she argues, also offer a subtle counter-current to that pressure in Richard's last words, "forgiveness horse," which invite a kind of "standing down," even "a call for tranquility, for a pause over what is considered to be true and unquestionable." Richard's final assault on his assassins clarifies that this moment can also be understood as part of a humble yet determined resistance to what might seem like the triumph of what is over what ought to be, that is also resistance to the triumph of a purely Cartesian world.

18

THE LION KING

Shakespeare's Beastly Sovereigns

Nicole Mennell

As the unchallenged king of beasts and England's primary heraldic animal, it is unsurprising that Shakespeare often invoked the lion when exploring sovereignty and governance in his plays. However, as the topmost carnivorous predator, the lion was not only an enduring symbol of majesty in the early modern period, it was also an apt metaphor for tyrannical rule. Drawing on the lion's ferocity, in Chapter 18 of *The Prince*, Niccolò Machiavelli infamously suggested that a ruler should imitate the force of the lion and the cunning of the fox, "for the lion is liable to be trapped, whereas the fox cannot ward off wolves."[1] Rebecca Bushnell has shown that Machiavelli's hybridized prince undermined the central precepts of contemporary political treatises, which "oppose the king to tyrant as man against beast."[2] Even so, Hugh Grady argues that many plays written in the 1590s used Machiavelli's political concepts to explore "the necessity of deception, immorality, and violence in politics in a world in which men are not good and he who would be good invites defeat."[3] In such discourses the lion's regal associations temper the use of force by sovereigns, creating an uneasy balance between justified violence and savage brutality.

This chapter argues that Shakespeare employs leonine imagery in a number of plays written in the 1590s to endorse legitimate monarchs emulating the force of the lion when they are required to protect themselves and their subjects from the wolves that encircle the throne.[4] While Shakespeare's more calculating rulers can be said to have fox-like natures they are not directly referred to as such, probably because vulpines were viewed as verminous and deceitful creatures in the early modern period.[5] Shakespeare was perhaps less hesitant to use lion imagery when depicting monarchs because it was said to resemble "in al things a Princely maiesty," and was therefore regarded as an ideal animal for rulers to emulate.[6] This view not only pertained to the lion's crown-like mane but also its perceived capacity to deal forcefully with opponents while showing mercy to innocents and supplicants.[7] For example, Edward Topsell praises lions for their "clemencie in that fierce and angry nature," and claims "if one prostrate himselfe vnto them as it were in petition for his life, they often spare except in extremitie of famine; and likewise they seldome destroy women or children."[8] Shakespeare draws on the lion's duality to suggest that a sovereign needs to know when to be violent and when to be merciful.[9] Although the unjustified imitation of the lion's ferocious nature can lead to tyrannical rule, failing to emulate the force of the lion when necessary is equally damning.

In the early modern period, the line separating sovereign from tyrant was often aligned with the boundary that was perceived to separate human from animal. The belief that humans exclusively possessed a rational soul was integral to the maintenance of this boundary and the notion of human supremacy over all other earthly beings. Keith Thomas argues that the concept of human rationality, which stemmed from Aristotle's *De Anima*, was "taken over by the medieval scholastics and fused with the Judeo-Christian teaching that man was made in the image of God"; effectively, "[i]nstead of representing man as merely a superior animal it elevated him to a wholly different status, halfway between the beasts and the angels."[10] However, there was an anxiety in the early modern period that because humans shared a sensitive soul with animals they could degenerate into animality if their passions were not controlled.[11] The need for sovereigns to govern the sensitive soul was even greater since the supreme ruler had made them, in King James I's words, "a little God to sit on his Throne, & rule ouer other men."[12] While it was acknowledged that sovereigns were susceptible to the same passions as ordinary humans, they could not allow the body politic to be subjected to the imperfections of the body natural. When sovereigns abused their power to indulge their affections, they not only compromised their status as humans but also their position as divinely appointed rulers, which is why the distinction drawn between tyrants and monarchs was often figured through the juxtaposition between beast and man, and in some instances between beast and divinity.

In *The Education of a Christian Prince*, Erasmus describes the difference between a true king and a tyrant as analogous to the difference between a divine being and a beast. For a good ruler, Erasmus suggests the teacher should "depict a sort of celestial creature." For a tyrant, the teacher should portray "a terrible, loathsome beast: formed of a dragon, wolf, lion, viper, bear, and similar monsters; [...] having a hunger that is never satisfied, fattened on human entrails and intoxicated with human blood."[13] Erasmus's figuration of the monstrous tyrant is characteristic of humanist treatises which connected the abuse of power with the unbridled appetites of rulers. Here the lion is listed alongside predatory animals more commonly associated with tyranny, most notably the wolf.[14]

Machiavelli derived the associations of lions with tyrannical rule from Cicero's *De Officiis*, which states, "there are two ways in which injustice may be done, either through force or through deceit; and deceit seems to belong to a little fox, force to a lion. Both of them seem most alien to a human being."[15] Machiavelli reverses the original intention of Cicero's figuration of the lion and the fox to argue that, while a ruler "should not deviate from right conduct if possible," "in order to maintain his power, he is often forced to act treacherously, ruthlessly or inhumanely."[16] Montaigne takes a similar stance to Machiavelli when discussing whether trickery should be used in warfare, concluding: "we say that when the lion's skin does not suffice we must sew on a patch from the fox's."[17] Although the metaphor of wearing a lion skin, which is strengthened by a patch from the fox, suggests more of a superficial and temporary transformation than that advised by Machiavelli, Montaigne also acknowledges that a ruler must emulate the beast when *necessary* to defeat adversaries.[18]

Erica Fudge argues that when humans rely on animals in this way to enforce their superiority, "they reveal the frailty of the supremacy which is being asserted. Paradoxically, humans need animals in order to be human."[19] The specific political corollary of this view is that the sovereign needs the beast to assert their complete supremacy over animals and humans alike. As a ubiquitous symbol of majesty in early modern Europe, no other animal was drawn upon more than the lion to convey the absolute power of rulers. In accordance with Fudge's argument, by relying on the lion as a monarchical emblem, sovereigns inadvertently reveal the human weaknesses that they seek to counterbalance by claiming leonine qualities.

The lion has been the heraldic animal of the English monarch from at least King Henry II's reign and its metaphoric associations with kingship were deeply engrained in the early modern imagination.[20] Due to their symbolic importance, lions occupied a special status in the Royal Menagerie, which was housed at the Tower of London from the twelfth century onwards, with many of the big cats named after English sovereigns, including Elizabeth I and James I.[21] As discussed, the lion was a suitable animal for rulers to compare themselves to because of its supposed ability to be wrathful or merciful in the appropriate circumstances. For example, in July 1574 the French Ambassador, Bertrand de Salignac de La Mothe Fénélon, reported a conversation with Elizabeth I in which the Queen claimed:

> although she was not a lioness, she was nevertheless the offspring of the lion and had inherited much of its constitution. Inasmuch as the King of France would treat her gently, he would find her as gentle and tractable as he might desire; and if he was harsh towards her, she would strive to be as harsh and harmful to him as she could.[22]

Elizabeth made a clear distinction between being a lioness herself and being the descendant of the leonine King Henry VIII, arguably to avoid less flattering comparisons being made to her father and his rapacious appetites. However, by identifying herself as the progeny of the lion-like king, Elizabeth emphasized her political legitimacy—a highly sensitive issue for much of her reign—and cautioned the ambassador that she too was capable of being amenable or malevolent, depending on how she was treated. This account also suggests that while the lion's monarchical associations were typically gendered male, female rulers were attributed with leonine characteristics.[23] In this instance, Elizabeth embraced the lion's duality to assert her authority as the Queen of England.

The lion's symbolic importance also explains why challenges to its regality were taken seriously. For example, in John Caius's *Of Englishe Dogges* there is an account that after being informed four mastiffs could defeat a lion in combat, King Henry VII "commaunded all such dogges […] should be hanged, beyng deeply displeased, and conceauing great disdaine, that an yll fauoured rascall curre should with such violent villany, assault the valiaunt Lyon King of all beastes."[24] The King used this as an "example for all subiectes worthy remembraunce, to admonishe them that it is no aduantage to them to rebell against ye regiment of their ruler, but to keepe them within the limits of Loyaltie."[25] For Henry VII, who had a precarious claim to the English throne, the lion's defeat by supposedly inferior dogs could in turn undermine his sovereignty; the account therefore suggests that the King slaughtered the mastiffs to reassert his power. While the story is probably apocryphal, it illustrates the symbolic potency of the lion as an emblem of monarchy in the early modern period.[26]

James I seemed determined to test the lion's emblematic associations through a series of staged animal combats in the Tower of London. Fudge argues that these contests

> do not so much reveal the animals' natural behavior as the preconceived ideas about animals held by spectators. […] There are, at work in the Tower, narratives about ideal animals, and there are real animals; and the two are not always compatible.[27]

The lion's idealized image would have been of great importance to James, who in *Basilicon Doron* cited the biblical proverb "the wrath of a King is like to the roaring of a Lyon," when outlining the circumstances in which monarchs should be magnanimous and when they should take revenge.[28] However, as Fudge indicates, the combats did not consistently uphold the lion's status as a majestic creature. According to John Stow and Edmond Howes's

Annales, or Generall Chronicle of England, James I first encountered the royal lions in March 1604 during his stay at the Tower before his official entry into London. After being informed that the English mastiff was "of as great courage, as the Lion," the King requested Edward Alleyn (in his role as Joint Master of the Royal Game of Bears, Bulls and Mastiff Dogs with Philip Henslowe), "to fetch secretly 3. of the fellest dogs" from the Bear Garden to bait the "lustiest Lion." The mastiffs, which were set on the lion one at a time, were defeated but at the first opportunity, "and contrary to the kings expectation, the lyon fled into an inward den" to escape the dogs. The lion failed to prove its mettle, causing James to conclude that it "exceede[d] the Dog in strength, but nothing in noble heart and courage."[29]

James I had more success in 1605 when he turned his attention to the lion's mythical and religious associations. He first arranged for two live cockerels to be lowered into an enclosure in the Tower, one after the other, with a lion and lioness. After the cockerels were promptly killed by the lions, "the kinge caused a liue Lambe to be easily let down" into the enclosure. It is recorded that "the Lyons stoode in their former places, and only beheld the Lamb but presently the Lambe rose vp, and went unto the Lyons, who very gently looked vppon him, and smelled on him, without signe of any further hurt."[30] In these combats, the lion's more positive attributes were upheld in several ways. First, the killing of the cockerels undermined the belief, found in medieval bestiaries and natural histories, that the "cocke also both seene and heard for his voice and combe, is a terror to the lion [...] and the lyon runneth from him when he seeth him."[31] In his *Palladis Tamia*, Francis Meres connected such stories to rulers when he observed that "The lyon is feared of all other beastes, and yet feareth the crowing and combe of a cocke: so great princes are compelled sometimes to feare the slanders and re-proches of inferiour people."[32] By killing the cockerels, the lions challenged any implications of cowardice suggested by this myth, reconfirmed their ability to defeat opponents, and dis-regarded the monarch's need to fear their subjects' criticism. In contrast, the gentle treatment of the lamb supported the belief that lions could control their bestial appetites and refrain from harming innocents. As the lamb was a symbol of Christ, the encounter also reinforced the Christian iconography of the lion as an agent of God, which recalls the prophet Daniel's survival in the lion's den: "my God hath sent his angel, and hath shut the lions' mouths, that they have not hurt me: forasmuch as before him innocency was found in me" (Daniel 6:22). James I would no doubt have been pleased that on this occasion his heraldic animal upheld its title as the king of beasts.

The animal combats staged by James I demonstrate that when humans encountered lions their figurative associations were often conflated with the nature of the real animal, just as is the case today. It is impossible to know for certain if Shakespeare had the opportunity to see a lion, especially as the two viewing galleries James I had constructed in the Tower were intended "for the king and great Lords, and [...] speciall personages."[33] He may have seen one at the Paris Garden after 1611 as Philip Henslowe and Edward Alleyn were paid for the keeping of a young lion and two white bears.[34] Even if Shakespeare had never encountered a lion we can assume that he was aware of the animal's notorious ferocity and fabled clemency. Take for example, the Mechanicals' comical concern that Snug's performance as a lion in *A Midsummer Night's Dream*, the only known "lion" Shakespeare represented on stage in his career, would "fright the Duchess and the ladies" (1.2.72).[35] Although their apprehension is ridiculed because the lion in their farcical play-within-a-play is openly portrayed by a human actor, the care Snug takes in his explanatory prologue to reassure the ladies that he is not "a lion-fell" also gestures towards the more allegorical belief that, despite their predatory natures, lions would not harm women, children, or innocents (5.1.221). Snug's lion is both the roaring beast that frightens Thisbe and a "gentle beast [...] of good conscience" (5.1.224).

He thus (albeit in a humorous manner) simultaneously embodies the lion's perceived capacity for both savagery and compassion, the combination of which makes the lion an idealized, but sometimes troubling, emblem of regal authority.[36]

While Shakespeare employs the lion's dual nature for comic effect in *A Midsummer Night's Dream*, the more serious need for a ruler to strike a balance between the animal's ability to be both wrathful and merciful dominates the playwright's appropriation of leonine imagery in *2* and *3 Henry VI*, *Richard II*, and *Henry V*. In these plays, Shakespeare endorses legitimate sovereigns emulating the force of the lion when they are under attack and leniency when their thrones are secure. In contrast, the lion imagery in *Julius Caesar* represents the eponymous character's aspirations to monarchical rule over the Roman Republic and therefore his potential for tyranny. As the following section will show, Shakespeare uses the lion's regal associations to signify contradictory aspects of political power.

At the center of *2* and *3 Henry VI* is a weak and ineffectual ruler who ultimately loses his throne. It is therefore appropriate that it is not King Henry VI but Humphrey, Duke of Gloucester and Lord Protector, who is ascribed leonine qualities. In *2 Henry VI*, Queen Margaret describes Gloucester through an analogy with the king of the beasts to warn her husband: "Small curs are not regarded when they grin, / But great men tremble when the lion roars; / And Humphrey is no little man in England" (3.1.18–20). By comparing him to a roaring lion, Margaret acknowledges Gloucester's royal blood and the power that he holds, thereby emphasizing the threat he poses to Henry VI's sovereignty. She furthers this by contrasting Gloucester's authority with the powerlessness of "small curs," which represents the King as a diminutive, subservient, and inferior breed of dog, who bares his teeth but poses no real danger to his enemies. The hierarchies of the natural world are here mapped onto the human to highlight the unstable power relations between Henry VI and his Lord Protector.

The real "curs," of course, are the self-serving individuals who remove Gloucester from his position of power, leaving the King vulnerable to their predation. To bring about Gloucester's ruin, he is falsely presented to Henry by Queen Margaret and Suffolk as both a "fox" and a "ravenous wol[f]" (3.1.50, 78). Gloucester acknowledges the irony of this false depiction when he informs the King, "Thus is the shepherd beaten from thy side, / And the wolves are gnarling who shall gnarl thee first" (3.1.191–92). The Huguenot tract *Vindiciae Contra Tyrannos* compares the depictions of sovereigns and tyrants in the Bible, with the former traditionally represented as a "shepherd" and the latter as "roaring lion."[37] Gloucester is therefore presented in his role as Lord Protector as a virtuous leader who also possesses the lion's formidable might.

In contrast, Henry is portrayed as a defenseless sheep that requires Gloucester's protection. Bruce Boehrer argues that "[a]mong metaphors, none attaches itself more insistently to the sheep of early modern Europe than the cluster of tropes that depict Christ as sacrificial lamb and/or shepherd to the flock of his believers"; however, Henry can also be attributed with the "pathetic helplessness," with which ovines were commonly associated in the period.[38] While the description of Henry as sheep-like presents him as a sympathetic figure, it also denotes his weaknesses as a sovereign; he does not fulfill the role of shepherd and fails to protect his flock. Indeed, the King allows his Lord Protector to be arrested for treason despite his awareness that Gloucester is "innocent" (3.1.69). Without Gloucester's protection, Henry is consequently left exposed to the Duke of York's political machinations, which culminate in Henry signing away his son's inheritance in *3 Henry VI*. In response to Henry appointing York as Protector of the Realm, Queen Margaret asks: "And yet shalt thou be safe? Such safety finds / The trembling lamb environed with wolves" (1.1.248–49). As Henry lacks both the force of the lion and the cunning of the fox, he is likened to a powerless lamb completely at the mercy of York and his pack of "wolves."

Henry VI's inability to match the cruelty of the Yorkist wolves is powerfully conveyed in *3 Henry VI* when Queen Margaret presents York's head to him and he responds: "To see this sight, it irks my very soul" (2.2.6). The King's reaction causes Clifford to urge:

> My gracious liege, this too much lenity
> And harmful pity must be laid aside.
> To whom do lions cast their gentle looks?
> Not to the beast that would usurp their den.

> (2.2.9–12)

To embolden the King to defend his throne against his enemies, Clifford urges Henry to emulate the lion. However, as Audrey Yoder notes, "[e]ven when Clifford speaks of Henry as a kingly lion, he qualifies the word with 'gentle'."[39] The lion's "gentle looks" refers to the animal's reputed clemency but Clifford advises Henry that in his current situation such qualities are "harmful" and so encourages the King to abandon mercy in favor of violence.

Henry VI allows his "den" to be usurped because he emulates the wrong leonine character-istics. Directly before he is taken prisoner by the soon-to-be King Edward IV, Henry defends his use of "pity," "mildness," and "mercy," claiming that "when the lion fawns upon the lamb, / The lamb will never cease to follow him" (4.8.41, 42, 43, 49–50). Although Henry depicts himself as a lion here, the Edenic image he presents of his relationship with his subjects proves a fantasy. By failing to use violence against his enemies when necessary, Henry VI remains a "harmless sheep" and falls victim to the most bloodthirsty wolf of all, Richard III (5.6.8).

In *2* and *3 Henry VI*, lion imagery highlights the King's limitations rather than his strengths. The lion is used in a similar fashion in *Richard II* to represent the rule of a weak king. In the opening scene of the play, Richard II attempts to resolve a dispute between Thomas Mowbray and Henry Bolingbroke. When Mowbray throws down his gauntlet and refuses to retrieve it, Richard states: "Rage must be withstood: / Give me his gage; li-ons make leopards tame" (1.1.173–74). Richard's attempt to enforce his authority by char-acterizing himself as a lion is undermined when he fails to make peace between Mowbray and Bolingbroke. Mowbray's reply, "Yea, but not change his spots," through its evocation of the proverb "a leopard [...] cannot change his spots," challenges the King's ability to "tame" his subjects and command their loyalty (1.1.175).[40] Mowbray's response also alludes to the lion léopardé found on his family arms, which was an alternative heraldic term for the lion.[41] Through the heraldic symbolism of the lion léopardé, Mowbray asserts his no-bility and provides a subtle reminder that all nobles might become kingly lions. The play thus challenges the lion's symbolic associations with the absolute power of the monarch.

Richard II's failure to embody the lion's might in the opening act of the play foreshadows his deposition in Act 4, Scene 1. When he is deposed, Queen Isabel states:

> The lion dying thrusteth forth his paw
> And wounds the earth, if nothing else, with rage
> To be o'erpow'r'd, and wilt thou, pupil-like,
> Take the correction mildly, kiss the rod
> And fawn on rage with base humility,
> Which art a lion and the king of beasts?

> (5.1.29–34)

Queen Isabel, like Clifford in *3 Henry VI*, draws on the lion's refusal to accept defeat to casti-gate Richard for "mildly" accepting his deposition. Although the Queen identifies Richard as a lion here, the King's reply complicates the regal connotations of this depiction: "A king of beasts, indeed – if aught but beasts, / I had been still a happy king of men" (5.1.35–36). Richard suggests that if it were not for those within his realm who act like "beasts" and rebel against his rule, as Bolingbroke and his followers do, he would still be King. However, as Machiavelli argues, the prince must match his enemies with the lion's force to survive. Richard II, like Henry VI, is not versed in the art of government and so cannot regain his throne. Again, we see the larger elements of the plot figured in the minutiae of the animal imagery. An audience or reader with knowledge of the lion's cultural significance would be aware of the implications of a sovereign who cannot emulate this majestic beast when necessary, effectively failing to defend their throne and the interests of their subjects.

In contrast to Henry VI and Richard II, Henry V is the epitome of the lion king because he knows when it is appropriate to use force and when to be merciful.[42] When facing war with France, Exeter informs Henry V, "Your brother kings and monarchs of the earth / Do all expect that you should rouse yourself / As did the former lions of your blood" (*Henry V* 1.2.122–24). The use of "rouse" suggests bringing forth the beast within rather than ruling constantly in a leonine manner. Furthermore, these lines indicate that Henry is descended from a line of lions, strengthening his legitimacy to rule and use force when required. Indeed, Henry V only takes on the nature of the beast when he has enemies to defeat, which is most powerfully illustrated by his famous rallying cry to his soldiers before Harfleur: "In peace there's nothing so becomes a man / As modest stillness and humility; / But when blast of war blows in our ears, / Then imitate the action of the tiger" (3.1.3–6). Henry's speech echoes York's description of Edward the Black Prince in *Richard II*: "In war was never lion rag'd more fierce, / In peace was never gentle lamb more mild" (2.1.173–74). Here the violent nature of the lion is juxtaposed with the lamb's peacefulness to portray Edward's suitability for governance. Henry V goes further than his great-uncle by imitating the tiger, which was believed to have been "engendred from Lyons" but to be "twice so big" and especially "cruell."[43] The play therefore suggests that in combat the king must go beyond the nature of the noble lion and take on the cruelty of its vicious cousin the tiger.

Henry V specifically invokes the lion to assert his power when Montjoy, the French herald, informs the English King that he should set the amount for his ransom as he faces an "assured otherthrow" (4.3.81). In response, Henry warns, "The man that once did sell the lion's skin / While the beast lived, was killed with hunting him" (4.3.93–94). Shakespeare alludes here to the fable of the hunter who promised a bearskin before he had killed the animal but substitutes the bear for the regal lion to emphasize Henry V's sovereignty.[44] Shakespeare makes a second alteration to this fable as the hunter is not killed but only feigns death after recalling that bears would not touch dead bodies, thus highlighting Henry V's ability to use deadly force when necessary.[45] Nonetheless, the King enacts a "soft mercy" when his enemies are defeated at Harfleur, and establishes peace with France after the English victory at Agincourt (3.3.48). Shakespeare's kingly hero therefore possesses the lion's most idealized attributes: strength, courage, and clemency.

In the plays discussed above, the lion represents the sovereign's need to use violence or mercy when appropriate to maintain their power and protect their subjects. The lion takes on markedly different connotations in *Julius Caesar*, which was probably written in the same year as *Henry V*. The Chorus of *Henry V* connects the two plays through its description of Henry as "conquering Caesar" on his arrival home from France (5.0.28). Unlike Henry V, however, Caesar is not regarded as a legitimate sovereign but a military commander and senator of the Roman republic who aspires above his allotted place and risks becoming a dictatorial monarch.[46] In the opening act of the play Brutus states, "I do fear the people / Choose Caesar for their king" (1.2.78–79). Brutus's fear aligns with Plutarch's suggestion that "the chiefest cause that made [Caesar] mortally hated was the covetous desire he had to be called king."[47] This condemnation arose from the principle that no one individual should rule the Roman republic; in this context, as Bushnell argues, "the term *rex* was virtually interchangeable with *tyrannus*."[48] In the play, the lion signifies monarchical rule as much as the "crown" offered to Caesar and, by extension, his perceived aspirations for absolute power (1.2.220). The lion's conflicting associations with both royalty and bestiality therefore blur the permeable boundaries between sovereign and tyrant.

The lion is more explicitly associated with tyranny in the play when Cassius declares: "And why should Caesar be a tyrant then? / Poor man, I know he would not be a wolf / But that he sees the Romans are but sheep. / He were no lion, were not Romans hinds" (1.3.103–6). Here, the lion becomes synonymous with the wolf, the natural enemy of the flock and the archetypal tyrannical beast. Caesar is aligned with the lion and the wolf but only because Cassius believes the Romans have allowed themselves to become his prey. Cassius, who is laying the foundations at this point in the play for Caesar's assassination, refuses to be devoured.

The association of lions with tyranny in *Julius Caesar* also explains their role as cryptic omens. In Act 1, Scene 3, Caska states that he "met a lion / Who glazed upon me and went surly by" and shortly before Caesar's death Calpurnia recounts how "A lioness hath whelped in the streets" (1.3.20–21, 2.2.17). These lions are not included in Plutarch's account of the storm and portents that precede Caesar's assassination. David Daniell suggests that they are drawn from Plutarch's *Life of Marcus Brutus*, in which it is recounted that Caesar took Cassius's "Lyons from him," and "this was the cause, as some do report, that made Cassius conspire against Caesar."[49] In the source text, the seizure of Cassius's lions is evidence of Caesar's abuse of power; Shakespeare arguably adapts this material to represent the threat Caesar's ambitions posed to the Republic. Describing the storm that precedes the assassination, Cassius informs Caska:

> Now could I, Caska, name to thee a man
> Most like this dreadful night
> That thunders, lightens, opens graves, and roars
> As doth the lion in the Capitol:
> A man no mightier than thyself, or me,
> In personal action, yet prodigious grown
> And fearful, as these strange eruptions are.

(1.3.72–78)

Perhaps alluding to those royal lions which inhabited the Tower of London, Cassius suggests that while Caesar may "roar" like a lion he is "no mightier" than any other man. Nevertheless, Cassius draws upon the lion's status as both the king of beasts and ruthless tyrant to suggest that because Caesar seeks to become a monarch he endangers the republican ideal of equality.[50]

Caesar identifies himself as a threat when, despite the warnings that he should not go to the Senate, he declares:

> Danger knows full well
> That Caesar is more dangerous than he.
> We are two lions littered in one day,
> And I the elder and more terrible.

(2.2.44–47)

Caesar draws on the lion's ferociousness to convey his power over his enemies but, as an individual who allegedly aspires to be king of the Roman republic, Caesar's self-characterization as a "lion" also suggests his potential for tyrannical rule. This potential is never realized as, although he claims to possess the lion's might, Caesar fails to imitate the fox and detect the conspirators' trap. In the following act, Caesar is reduced to a "brave hart [...] strucken by many princes," thus transforming him from predatory lion into royal prey (3.1.204, 209).[51]

In the selection of plays analyzed in this chapter, Shakespeare appropriates the lion as an idealized emblem of monarchical rule to represent the realities and pitfalls of human governance. In line with Machiavelli's political philosophy, he shows that legitimate rulers should emulate leonine attributes when necessary to preserve their power and defend their subjects. Henry V is the embodiment of the mighty and just lion king in this respect as he uses violence to protect the interests of his country and leniency to establish peace when required. However, comparable to the manner in which King James I's animal combats trialed the lion's strength and symbolic associations, Shakespeare challenges the lion's connections with regal authority. Richard II and Henry VI both claim the title of lion king but fail to emulate the animal's ferocity when their authority is threatened and consequently lose their thrones; they are lions in name but not in action. Moreover, in *Julius Caesar*, due to the fundamental principles of republicanism, the lion is transmuted into an emblem of tyranny as it represents Caesar's monarchical aspirations. Although the lion may be universally recognized as the king of beasts, for Shakespeare this majestic animal is a mutable symbol of sovereignty.[52]

Notes

1 Niccolò Machiavelli, *The Prince*, eds. Quentin Skinner and Russell Price (Cambridge: Cambridge University Press, 1988), 61.

2 Rebecca W. Bushnell, *Tragedies of Tyrants: Political Thought and Theater in the English Renaissance* (London: Cornell University Press, 1990), 55.

3 Hugh Grady, *Shakespeare, Machiavelli, and Montaigne: Power and Subjectivity from Richard II to Hamlet* (Oxford: Oxford University press, 2002), 21.

4 All Shakespearean references are from *The Arden Shakespeare*, eds. Richard Proudfoot, Ann Thompson, and David Scott Kastan (London: Arden Shakespeare, 2011).

5 Mary Fissell, "Imagining Vermin in Early Modern England," *The History Workshop Journal* 47, no. 1 (1999): 4. Comparing individuals to foxes could also be hazardous for authors, as is arguably evidenced by the suppression of Edmund Spenser's beast fable *Prosopopoia, or Mother Hubberds Tale* in 1591, due to its satirical representation of William Cecil as the cunning Fox who aids the Ape in stealing the Lion's crown, scepter, and skin. For further discussion, see Richard Peterson, "Laurel Crown and Ape's Tail: New Light on Spenser's Career from Sir Thomas Tresham," *Spenser Studies* 12 (1998): 1–35.

6 Edward Topsell, *The Historie of Foure-Footed Beastes* (London: William Jaggard, 1607), sig.[Rr4ʳ].

7 Margaret Haist argues that in bestiaries from the late twelfth century there was an emphasis on the lion's capacity for mercy, which mirrored changing perspectives of kingship and the importance of the just ruler in political treatises: Margaret Haist, "The Lion, Bloodline, and Kingship," in *The Mark of the Beast: The Medieval Bestiary in Art, Life and Literature*, ed. Debra Hassig (London: Garland Publishing, 1999), 6–10.

8 Topsell, *Beastes*, sig.[Rr6ʳ].

9 Alternatively, Wyndham Lewis suggests that Shakespeare's leonine imagery is influenced by the foolish Aesopian lion: Wyndham Lewis, *The Lion and the Fox: The Role of the Hero in the Plays of Shakespeare* (London: Harper and Brothers, 1927). Audrey Yoder counters Lewis's argument and suggests Shakespeare was influenced by the Aesopian fables that represent the lion's ingenuity and capacity for mercy, as well as the animal's traditional depiction as the king of beasts: Audrey Yoder, *Animal Analogy in Shakespeare's Character Portrayal* (New York: AMS, 1975), 9–16, 19.

10 Aristole, *Aristotle's De Anima: Books II and III*, trans. D.W. Hamlyn (Oxford: Clarendon Press, 1968), 14–17; Keith Thomas, *Man and the Natural World: Changing Attitudes in England 1500–1800* (London: Allen Lane, 1983), 30–31.

11 Erica Fudge, *Brutal Reasoning: Animals, Humanity, and Rationality in Early Modern England* (New York: Cornell University Press, 2006), 60.

12 James I, King of England, *Basilicon Doron 1599: A Scolar Press Facsimile* (Menston: Scolar Press, 1969), sig.[B2ᵛ].

13 Desiderius Erasmus, *The Education of a Christian Prince*, ed. Lisa Jardine and trans. Neil. M. Cheshire and Michael J. Heath (Cambridge: Cambridge University Press, 1997), 26. For an alternative discussion of the connections between monarchs and animals in humanist texts, see Katie Chenoweth, "The Beast, the Sovereign, and the Letter: Vernacular Posthumanism," *Symploke* 23, no. 1–2 (2015): 41–56.

14 In Book Eight of Plato's *Republic* the tyrant is envisaged as one who turns "from man into wolf": Plato, *The Republic*, ed. G.R.F. Ferrari and trans. Tom Griffith (Cambridge: Cambridge University Press, 2001), 280.

15 Marcus Tullius Cicero, *On Duties*, eds. M.T. Griffin and E.M. Atkins (Cambridge: Cambridge University Press, 1991), 19.

16 Machiavelli, *The Prince*, 62. Karen Raber notes that the successful prince requires the instruction of the centaur to master "the nuances of his requisite hybrid nature": Karen Raber, *Animal Bodies, Renaissance Culture* (Philadelphia: University of Pennsylvania Press, 2013), 71.

17 Michel de Montaigne, "Where the Governor of a Besieged Fortress Should Go out and Parley," in *Michel de Montaigne: The Complete Essays of Montaigne*, ed. and trans. M.A. Screech (London: Penguin Classics, 2003), 23.

18 On the Montaigne-Machiavelli connection, see Grady, *Shakespeare, Machiavelli and Montaigne*, 109–15.

19 Erica Fudge, *Perceiving Animals: Humans and Beasts in Early Modern English Culture* (Basingstoke: Macmillan Press, 2000), 4.

20 Michael Pastoureau, *Heraldry: Its Origins and Meaning*, trans. Francisca Garvie (London: Thames and Hudson, 1997), 58.

21 Andreas Höfele, *Stage, Stake and Scaffold: Humans and Animals in Shakespeare's Theatre* (Oxford: Oxford University Press, 2011), 83; Daniel Hahn, *The Tower Menagerie* (London: Simon and Schuster, 2004), 93–106.

22 Bertrand de Salignac de La Mothe Fénélon, *Correspondance diplomatique de Bertrand de Salignac de la Mothe Fénélon ambassadeur de France en Angleterre de 1568 à 1575, Tome Sixieme* (London: Panckoucke, 1840), 190–91:

> qu'lle ne soit lyonne, elle ne layssoit d'estre yssue et tenir beaucoup de la complexion du lyon, et que, sellon que le Roy la traictera doulcement, il la trouvera doucle et traictable, aultant qu'il le scauroit desirer; et s'il luy est rude, elle mettra peyne de luy ester le plus rude et nuysible qu'elle pourra.

I am grateful to Professor Adrian Armstrong for assisting with the translation of this text.

23 In a letter to William Cecil on October 7, 1561, the secretary to Mary Queen of Scots, William Maitland, defended her hereditary right to the English crown in similar terms:

> The Quene my Maistress is descended of the Blood off *England*, and so off the Race off the Lyon on both Sydes. I fear she could be content to haserd all (soche is her Couraige) then receave that dishonour to forgo her Ryght.

Cited in Samuel Haynes, *A Collection of States Papers, Relating to Affairs in the Reigns of King Henry VIII, King Edward VI, Queen Mary, and Queen Elizabeth, From the Year 1542 to 1570* (London: William Bowyer, 1740), 374. In line with this gendering, Shakespeare tends to focus his lion imagery on male characters, however, Samantha Snively has argued that the lioness in *As You Like It* represents the aging and barren Elizabeth I: Samantha N. Snively, "*As You Like It*'s Political, Critical Animal Allusions," *Studies in English Literature 1500–1900* 58, no. 2 (2018): 331–52.

24 John Caius, *Of Englishe Dogges*, trans. Abraham Fleming (London: John Charlewood for Richard Jones, 1576), sig.[Eᵛ].

25 Ibid.

26 The validity of this account is in doubt as it is followed by a remarkably similar story in which Henry VI is said to have ordered that a falcon be killed for attacking an eagle: Caius, *Of Englishe Dogges*, sig.[Eᵛ].

27 Fudge, *Brutal Reasoning*, 114. See also Erica Fudge, "Two Ethics: Killing Animals in the Past and the Present," in *Killing Animals*, ed. The Animal Studies Group (Champaign: Illinois University Press, 2006), 110.

28 James I, *Basilicon*, sig.[Qᵛ]. Proverbs 20:2.

The Lion King: Shakespeare's Beastly Sovereigns

29 John Stow and Edmund Howes, *The Annales, or Generall Chronicle of England* (London: Thomas Dawson, 1615), sig.[Aaaa3ᵛ–Aaaa4ʳ]. James I was also left disappointed when he attempted to use a lion to dispense justice. It is recorded that on June 23, 1609, "[t]he King, Queene, and Prince […] came to the Tower to see a trial of the Lyons single valor against a great fierce Beare, which had kild a child, that was negligently left in the Beare-house." The trial did not go to plan as the lion "gazed a while, but neuer offered to assault or approach the Beare": Stow and Howes, *The Annales*, sig.[Ffff3ᵛ].

30 Stow and Howes, *The Annales*, sig.[Cccc6ᵛ].

31 Topsell, *Beastes*, sig.[Rr4ᵛ–Rr5ʳ].

32 Francis Meres, *Palladis Tamia. Wits Treasury, Being the Second Part of Wits Commonwealth* (London: Peter Short for Cuthbert Burby, 1598), sig.Ff4ʳ.

33 Stow and Howes, *The Annales*, sig.[Cccc6ᵛ].

34 "James 1 – volume 62: March 1611," in *Calendar of State Papers Domestic: James I, 1611–18*, ed. Mary A.E. Green (London: HM Stationery Office, 1858), 17. British History Online. www.british-history.ac.uk/cal-state-papers/domestic/jas1/1611-18/pp14-20 (accessed August 31, 2017). For discussion of the two white bears mentioned in this document, see: Teresa Grant, "White Bears in *Mucedorus, The Winter's Tale* and *Oberon, The Fairy Prince*," *Notes and Queries* 48, no. 3 (2001): 311–13; Barbara Ravelhofer, "'Beasts of Recreacion': Henslowe's White Bears," *English Literary Renaissance* 32, no. 2 (2002): 287–323.

35 The mechanicals' apprehension may allude to Prince Henry's baptismal celebrations in 1594, during which a chariot that "should have bene drawne in by a *Lyon*, (but because his presence might have brought some feare, to the nearest, or that the sight of the lights and torches might have commoved his tameness)," a "*Black-Moore*" was used instead. See William Fowler, *A True Report of the Most Tryumphant, and Royall Accomplishment of the Baptisme of the Most Excellent, Right High, and Mightie Prince, Henry Fredericke* (London: Thomas Creede, 1603), sig.D1ʳ, C4ʳ.

36 For further discussion of Snug's performance as a lion, see Rebecca Ann Bach, "The Animal Continuum in *A Midsummer Night's Dream*," *Textual Practice* 24, no. 1 (2010): 124–28, http://dx.doi.org/10.1080/09502360903471714.

37 Junius Brutus, *A Defence of Liberty Against Tyrants: A Translation of the Vindiciae Contra Tyrannos*, ed. Harold J. Laski (London: G. Bell and Sons, 1924), 188.

38 Bruce Boehrer, *Animal Characters: Nonhuman Beings in Early Modern Literature* (Philadelphia: University of Pennsylvania Press, 2010), 164, 182.

39 Yoder, *Animal Analogy*, 50.

40 R.W. Dent, *Shakespeare's Proverbial Language* (Berkley: University of California Press, 1981), 152.

41 Pastoureau, *Heraldry*, 58.

42 On Henry V as a Machiavellian Prince, see John Roe, *Shakespeare and Machiavelli* (Cambridge: D. S. Brewer, 2002), 67.

43 Topsell, *Beastes*, sig.[Rrᵛ], [Rrᵛ], [Rrr6ᵛ].

44 See Yoder, *Animal Analogy*, 14–15.

45 Topsell, *Beastes*, sig.E3ʳ.

46 For an in-depth study of Shakespeare's engagement with republican ideas, see Andrew Hadfield, *Shakespeare and Republicanism* (Cambridge: Cambridge University Press, 2005).

47 Plutarch, "*The Life of Julius Caesar*," in *The Narrative and Dramatic Sources of Shakespeare, Volume V: The Roman Plays*, ed. Geoffrey Bullough and trans. Thomas North (London: Routledge and Kegan Paul, 1966), 80.

48 Bushnell, *Tragedies of Tyrants*, 145.

49 David Daniell, "Introduction," in *Julius Caesar*, ed. David Daniell (London: Arden Shakespeare, 2002 [1998]), 88; Plutarch, "*The Life of Marcus Brutus*," in *The Narrative and Dramatic Sources of Shakespeare, Volume V: The Roman Plays*, ed. Geoffrey Bullough and trans. Thomas North (London: Routledge and Kegan Paul, 1966), 94.

50 For a discussion of "republican equality" in *Julius Caesar*, see Coppélia Khan, *Roman Shakespeare: Warriors, Wounds and Women* (London: Routledge, 1997), 81–83.

51 A stag was "not to be called a harte unlesse he be hunted or killed by a Prince": George Gascoigne, *The Noble Art of Venerie or Hunting* (London: Printed by Henry Bynneman, 1575), sig.[P6ᵛ]. For further analysis of Caesar's depiction as a "brave hart," see Edward Berry, *Shakespeare and the Hunt: A Cultural and Social Study* (Cambridge: Cambridge University Press, 2001), 89.

52 I am grateful to Andrew Hadfield, Amy Lidster, Emily Bartlett, Louise Logan, Kristina Mennell-January and Vikki-Marie Mennell for their helpful comments on earlier drafts of this chapter.

19

"WEARING THE HORN"

Class and Community in the Shakespearean Hunt

Jennifer Allport Reid

References to and images of the deer hunt recur in two of William Shakespeare's so-called "forest comedies," *As You Like It* and *The Merry Wives of Windsor*, both written in the last few years of the sixteenth century.[1] This chapter will ask why Shakespeare chooses in these plays to draw, not only upon the language and imagery of early modern hunting ceremonies, but also upon contemporary calendrical customs which performed a stylized, parodic version of the hunt. It will further ask how we should understand the relationship between these two related yet virtually opposed activities, and what meanings the animal itself accrues from the interactions and divergences between discourses, which, though dissimilar, nevertheless both centered upon the body of the deer.

Sixteenth-century aristocratic hunting rituals enacted an elaborate dissection and distribution of the corpse of the slain quarry, transforming the animal body into a concrete metaphor for the narratives of power, prestige, and prowess which the noble sport was seen to encapsulate. At the same time, elite readings of the hunt sit alongside an altogether more popular festive performance of hunting, in contemporary calendar customs such as the Abbots Bromley Horn Dance, which saw the processing of a buck's head around the local parish accompanied by costumed participants, dancing, and music. These folk customs demonstrate that a pervasive cultural interest in hunting existed at all levels of early modern society, not solely within its higher echelons.

Building upon the substantial social historical scholarship on hunting and poaching, and in particular upon Roger Manning's influential book on *Hunters and Poachers*, literary scholars such as Edward Berry and Catherine Bates have drawn attention to this ubiquitous preoccupation with hunting in the early modern period, its imaginative draw for playwrights, poets, and songsters, and the ongoing controversies over customary rights and land use which it generated.[2] Following Manning's famous formulation of hunting as a form of symbolic warfare, scholars have tended to view the sport in terms of social division and conflict, a reading certainly supported by the prohibitive expense it incurred, the discourses of entitlement and elitism which surrounded it, and its importance in the construction of noble male identity. Nevertheless, this position can serve to rehearse a polarizing distinction between "high" and "low" culture by characterizing hunting as the domain merely of the former, "a repressive social custom," and by presenting as self-evident the conclusion that, while "the views of commoners on the hunt are rarely recorded, [...] the most important was probably popular rage."[3] This chapter will demonstrate that it is not quite the case that no 'commoner' approaches to hunting exist. While acknowledging my debt to scholarship like Berry's, I suggest that investigating the presence of references to hunting in popular calendrical customs qualifies the assumption that hunting was viewed as the cultural property only of the highest ranks. Further, the explicitly exclusionary nature of the hunt can even be seen to serve an ameliorating social purpose, providing an outlet, as Manning argues, for the feuding and rivalries with which the aristocracy and gentry were beset.[4] In this context it is informative to consider René Girard's discussion of sacrifice as symbolic action intended "to deflect upon a [...] 'sacrificeable' victim, the violence that would otherwise be vented on its own members, the people it most desires to protect":

> Once we have focused attention on the sacrificial victim, the object originally singled out for violence fades from view. Sacrificial substitution implies a degree of misunderstanding. Its vitality as an institution depends on its ability to conceal the displacement upon which the rite is based.[5]

The butchering of the deer works as "a reminder of the common sacrificial element which made hunting and warfare 'symbolically interchangeable'."[6] The dead deer in a quite literal sense comes to replace "the object originally singled out for violence," while the ceremonies which take place after the kill retrospectively work to contain and control unruly and savage behaviors in a ritualistic displacement which redefines the foregoing dramatic action in terms of elite ritual. In her discussion of the ceremonial butchering of the deer, Suzanne Walker identifies a particular anxiety to distinguish self from other behind the hunters' meticulous ceremonies: "the return of that animal's body to a fragmentary state [which] truly concludes the chase" is thus a process whereby "the spectacle of the fragmentation of the other positively reinforce[s] the wholeness of the privileged subject."[7] The hunt's delineation as the preserve only of the nobility could even suggest that on some level for the hunters it might be non-elite members of their own society who represent the true victims that "fad[e] from view" behind "the displacement" onto the animal "upon which the rite is based."[8]

Given the sacrificial resonance of the hunting rituals, perhaps the strangest aspect of customary entertainments featuring the hunt is that they suppress the sport's focus on violence even as they employ the deer's body parts as props or costume. Rather than dwelling on the kill itself, these customs emphasize the chase, or the ceremonial presentation of venison to the lord of the feast. Girard's view of sacrifice as an act which is protective of social harmony, through its substitution of a safer victim than one's own peers or its deflection of violence to an external rather than internal target, seems relevant to these popular imaginings of hunting as well as to the ritualized behaviors which were incorporated into the hunt itself. Thus in the two plays under discussion, the slaughtered deer becomes a useful metaphor for Shakespeare in his exploration and interrogation of communal conflict and division. Reflecting the strange commixture of violence and its effacement, of sacrificial displacement, and of conviviality, in these comedies the hunt emerges not only as aggressively divisive but also as a festive expression of harmony and cohesion.

I The Hunt as Symbolic Event; the Hunt in Symbolic Events

The status, power, and virtue signaled by aristocratic hunting, on the one hand, and its visual emphasis on savagery and sacrifice, on the other, lent it an emblematic charge in contemporary popular culture. As a sport, the hunt delineated and showcased masculine aristocratic identity: the *par force* chase in particular, on horseback and accompanied by a pack of hounds, supplied an impressive visual spectacle at the same time as requiring vast financial outlay and therefore enshrining the sport as a signifier of wealth and status.[9] Its association with rank was mirrored by its importance as a means of rehearsing masculinity. This was explicitly noted by commentators, as, for example, in *The Boke Named the Gouernour* (1531), in which Thomas Elyot praises hunting as "the very imitation of battaile," a claim that was often made by its proponents.[10] Hunting for food was explicitly opposed to the masculine behaviors inculcated by hunting for sport: Elyot goes on to warn against forms of hunting which "serueth well for the pot" and therefore carry distasteful suggestions of "necessitie." As such, "[k]ylling of dere with bowes [...] conteynethe therin no commendable solace or exercise" for specifically "noble men."[11] This imagining of the hunt rests upon and perpetuates its social divisiveness, its inaccessibility, determined impracticality, and aggressive self-definition against the less "commendable" motivations for lower-status hunting. Indeed, the further the sport gets from necessity, the more prestigious it becomes; in a uniquely circular logic, in order to be an efficient marker of social class, it therefore had to be overtly stylized and spectacular, a clear assertion of enacted prowess and lavish pageantry, rather than a means of providing sustenance or even necessarily the excitement of the kill itself.[12]

This deliberate emphasis on ceremonialism rather than practicality is evident in the correct method of dressing the deer, which was "variously called breaking, unmaking or undoing the carcass," and the feeding of the hounds (the *curée*).[13] With their ritualistic patterning and similarity to the symbolic act of sacrifice, these rituals can be seen as part of this attempt to distinguish aristocratic from other forms of hunting.[14] The proper means of carrying out these procedures were detailed in hunting treatises such as Edward of Norwich's *The Master of Game* (c.1406–13), which focuses in particular on the removal of the deer's head:

> ... turn his horns earthwards and the throat upwards, and slit the skin of the throat all along the neck, and cut labelles (small flaps) on either side of the skin, the which shall hang still upon the head, for this belongeth to an hart slain with strength, and else not [...] and this done, every man stand abroad and blow the death.[15]

Edward of Norwich stresses the importance of the beast's characteristics and the specific type of hunt conducted (this treatment serves only for a male red deer of at least six years, and then only if the hunt was *par force*, "with strength").[16] The grisly details of the removal of the head render the dead animal as a bizarre object, an artifact in a choreographed ceremony, rather than a source of butchered meat now fit to be enjoyed. Although the treatise then goes on to outline what type of refreshment (wine, rather than ale) is fitting at the hunters' feast afterward, the venison procured by all this strenuous activity is not mentioned. The ostentatious manner in which the dead deer is dressed magnifies the relationship between hunter and hunted and reformulates their encounter in agonistic terms as a worthy contest, a war-like meeting of equals; at the same time, it therefore implicitly rejects arguments against hunting as violent sport and wasteful, socially divisive land use, instead iterating its importance as a defining feature of aristocratic culture. Formulating the hunted beast as warrior rather than meat worked towards allaying an inherent anxiety that the chase was uncomfortably close to the disreputable killing of animals "for the pot," an anxiety also betrayed by the elaborate spectacle and financial outlay designed to highlight the participants' distance from any more functional forms of hunting.

Given the hunt's deliberate enactment of social exclusion, along with the peculiar mixture of gruesome practicality and ritualism and the simultaneous presence and absence of the deer as animal, we might be surprised to find performances of hunting in the non-elite, celebratory, aristocratically authorized context of popular processions, dances, and ritual animal disguises. As discussed above, the noble hunt was closely tied up with a construction of aristocratic identity that emphasized exclusion along financial and occupational lines, and yet was worryingly precarious and open to destabilization. It is therefore surprising that this is an activity which lower-status communities would wish to incorporate into popular customs, or that this would be approved by the wealthier members of society who, as will be shown, went out of their way to patronize such pastimes. A custom from Staffordshire stands out in particular, namely the Abbots Bromley Horn Dance which is described in Robert Plot's *Natural History of Stafford-shire* in 1686, although fragmentary evidence suggests that the custom might already have been well-established in 1532:

> At *Abbots*, or now rather *Pagets Bromley*, they had also within memory, a sort of sport which they celebrated at *Christmas* (on *New-year*, and *Twelft-day*) call'd the *Hobby-horse dance*, from a person that carried the image of a *horse* between his leggs, [...] and in his hand a *bow* and *arrow* [...]: with this *Man* danced 6 others, carrying on their shoulders as many *Rain deers heads*.[17]

The Horn Dance shares several features of other calendar customs that involved dances and disguisings, including a processional dance broken up by occasional pauses for mock skirmishes.[18] It is, however, distinctive for its inclusion of the antlers, which survive today and still appear annually in the Horn Dance. These visually striking props, in combination with the presence among the dancers not only of the six 'stags,' but also of a hobby horse and its 'rider' carrying a bow, make the dance uniquely evocative of the stag hunt, offering a highly stylized simulation of the chase. It nevertheless contrasts emphatically with the choreographed ceremonies of the aristocratic hunt since, despite the patronage of local gentry, it is clearly demarcated as a tradition belonging to the villagers of Abbots Bromley and its surrounding area. In Plot's description, the Horn Dance is an event which circles the local area, administering "*Cakes and Ale*," and collecting money from "all people who had any kindness [...] with which Mony [...] they not only repaired their *Church* but kept their *poore* too."[19] In further contrast to the hunt which it mimics, this custom noticeably did not require the killing of deer every year, perhaps due to the potential illegality of procuring new antlers annually.

Thus in the Horn Dance the exclusionary symbolism of the hunt itself is negated, transformed into a folk dance that enacts communal inclusion and participation. This is not necessarily to argue that popular festivity is a certain indicator of those expressions of community feeling which it attempts to exhibit; indeed, the presence of the body of the hunted deer in the custom discussed makes evident the possibility for such dances and processions to be as reminiscent of violence as of cohesion. The symbolic similarities outlined in the introduction between sacrifice and the hunt can perhaps explain the latter's rehearsal in this local custom, for despite being an overt statement of community cohesion and co-operation, the dance drew its symbolic charge from the inherent violence of the hunt and the sacrificial prominence of the dead animal's physical dismemberment. On the face of it, the Horn Dance promoted and foregrounded the cordial relationship between villagers and local gentry: Plot emphasizes that the dancers would carry "the *Armes* of the cheif families (viz. of *Paget*, *Bagot*, and *Wells*)," and in its current incarnation the dance still detours to the Bagot family residence at Blithfield Hall.[20] A complicated, and far from transparent, social negotiation is here taking place, with the dancers' costuming as stags (not, noticeably, as hunters) suggesting recognition of the "sacrificial substitution" of the aristocratic hunt and enacting perhaps supplication, perhaps defiance in response to that recognition.

Festal events such as the Horn Dance can therefore reveal ways that early modern communities thought about, displayed, performed, and aspired towards community-building, and as such, it is particularly interesting to see how Shakespeare draws upon these ideas in two comedies concerned with communities in conflict. I will first examine the festive hunt in *As You Like It*, which almost appears to stage a processional version of the Horn Dance or of the celebratory rituals of the kill. The air of festivity thereby evoked is explicitly commented upon by the forest exiles as one built upon tensions between the communities of the pastoral world of Arden and the outside world. I will then turn to the related intertexts of poaching and customary entertainments in *The Merry Wives of Windsor*, in which the political charge of the former crime is mediated, and to an extent resolved, by the context of festive pastime in which it is framed.

II Hunting in Exile: *As You Like It* and "The Old Robin Hood of England"

As You Like It contains one of the most explicit descriptions of a hunted deer in Shakespeare's oeuvre, and one which presents hunting as symbolically connected to exile and to the violent conflicts of the court. This has led some critics to interpret *As You Like It* as a humanist critique of hunting, while the comedy's thematic interest in cross-dressing, disguise, and misrule suggests to new historicist critic Richard Wilson an exposure of the impact of enclosure upon early modern rural communities: "it is a mocking game or "rough music" which authorizes the forest trespass and felony of poaching."[21] Certainly, the hunt does surface in the apparent forest idyll as a reminder both of mortality and inescapable death, and of the violent results of the aristocratic privilege which has led to the ducal usurpation and exile of one brother, and the unjust oppression and attempted murder of another. The hunt as a metaphor for the breakdown of communities appears in Duke Senior's sympathy for the deer whose death is already rendered inevitable by their labeling as "venison":

> Come, shall we go and kill us venison?
> And yet it irks me the poor dappled fools,
> Being native burghers of this desert city,
> Should in their own confines with forked heads
> Have their round haunches gored.[22]

Interestingly, "venison" is a word which only appears in two other of Shakespeare's plays, namely *The Merry Wives of Windsor*, in which, as I will discuss below, a gift of this highly prized meat forms part of a (failed) discourse on social bonding and reconciliation, and *Cymbeline* (c. 1611), in which the stag hunt is also portrayed as a ritualistic occasion for the exiled forest lords, with "he that strikes/The venison first" becoming "the lord o' th' feast."[23] Through the depiction of deer as "native burghers," and the opposition thereby established between the exiled courtiers and the civic citizens of the forest, *As You Like It* portrays a number of distinct worlds, seemingly self-sufficient and certainly not quite capable of comprehending each other: the pastoral community of the shepherds, the machinations of the court, the haven of the forest, and here, by implication, a civic society also subtly preyed upon by the court.

"Wearing the Horn": Class and Community

The First Lord's account of Jaques's sorrow for the wounded deer continues the sense that the courtiers have brought with them the violence of their world: with his hunting, he claims, the Duke "do[es] more usurp/Than doth [his] brother that hath banished [him]" (ll.27–28). Hunting is depicted as a seizure of power: repeating the deer's "native" rights, Jaques claims that the outlaw courtiers

> Are mere usurpers, tyrants and what's worse,
> To fright the animals and to kill them up
> In their assigned and native dwelling-place.

> (ll.61–63)

In this figuration, as in the Duke's earlier speech, the forest is depicted as a settlement in its own right, peopled with "fat and greasy citizens" (l.55), "native burghers" (l.23), suggesting that the court and the forest are in some ways equivalent. Ousted by his brother, Duke Senior has merely replicated this in his seizure of the animals' land; in turn, Jaques's satire reverses the courtiers' hunting as he directs the arrows of his wit towards his compatriots and "pierceth through/The body of country, city, court" (ll.58–59). The impression of civil conflict has already been introduced through the Duke's concern at the deer being gored by the "forked heads" (l.24) of the courtiers' arrows. The ambiguity of the expression, recalling the stag's own antlers, suggests violence within the animals' own community as well as violence from without, lending support to critical assertions of the play's preoccupation with tensions over customary rights and forest law. Wilson's statement that "customary culture is disintegrating in *As You Like It* under the stress of social mobility and competition" is particularly interesting considering the implications here that the forest does have its own strange mixture of violence and festivity.[24] Thus, the First Lord explains that he saw Jaques lying

> Under an oak, whose antic root peeps out
> Upon the brook that brawls along this wood.

> (ll.31–32)

The "antic" oak suggests grotesqueness and age, but also the clowning performance of a theatrical antic. Even more interestingly, the brook's "brawls" could imply either fighting or dancing:

> A brawl was […] a 'noisy, turbulent quarrel.' But it was also a dance, a different kind of dance – boisterous where the round was serene […]. [M]anual labor was central to this dance.[25]

The complication of the play's agonistic political world is implied by Duke Senior's description of exile as a "woeful pageant" (II.vii.139). A number of critics have discussed the holiday atmosphere which pervades *As You Like It*, in particular noting its depiction of the forest of Arden as a place of escape and license set in contrast to the corrupt court, a pastoral haven in which the exiled Duke and his "many merry men […] live like the old Robin Hood of England" (I.i.110–11). Indeed, the words "merry" and "merrily" appear 11 times in the play and "sport(s)" 9 times.[26] Jaques's pity for "the sobbing deer" (II.i.66) is qualified by the equally significant association of the courtiers' hunt with customs such as the Horn Dance, evoked by the hunting ceremony in which the forester outlaws sing a song celebrating their quarry:

> What shall he have that killed the deer?
> His leather skin and horns to wear.
> Then sing him home; the rest shall bear this burden.
> Take thou no scorn to wear the horn –

It was a crest ere thou wast born.
Thy father's father wore it
And thy father bore it.
The horn, the horn, the lusty horn
Is not a thing to laugh to scorn!

(IV.ii.10–19)

The song shares the same cluster of associations around "wearing the horn" as Falstaff's appearance as Herne the Hunter in *Merry Wives*, to which we will return below—the bawdy suggestion that "[t]hy father's father" and "thy father" were both cuckolds need not work against the reference to festive customs and to triumphant hunters' processions wearing the skin and antlers of the slaughtered animal. A similar celebration is suggested in Anthony Munday's *The Death of Robert, Earl of Huntington* (1601), which stages a courtly hunt: after the death of the deer, Friar Tuck enters "*carrying a Stags head, dauncing.*"[27] Alongside the reference to "old Robin Hood of England," this echo is significant. Munday's two-part adaptation of the Robin Hood legend, *The Downfall of Robert, Earl of Huntington* and *The Death of Robert, Earl of Huntington*, depicts the famous outlaw as an exiled courtier, forced to seek refuge from a court full of avarice and intrigue. As a lord of the greenwood, he presides over (but does not participate in) his company's hunting expeditions and merry pastimes. It is plausible to posit that *As You Like It* was written as a direct and competitive rejoinder to the Huntington plays. Certainly, in both Munday's and Shakespeare's texts, the politics of pastoral are played out within a context of festivity, pastime, and hunting custom. I have argued elsewhere that Munday deliberately engaged with customary drama in his reworking of popular material.[28] This example of a Shakespearean comic scene featuring ritualistic animal disguise reminiscent of the Horn Dance suggests a similar impulse at work in *As You Like It*, albeit here deliberately both qualified by and qualifying the play's wider admission that the oppositions between court and country, or court and city, might be to a degree insuperable, an intrinsic part of the very nature of communal identity building.

III Bribed Bucks, Mad Dogs, and Civic Festivity in *The Merry Wives of Windsor*

In *The Merry Wives of Windsor*, written around 1597, references to hunting, to poaching, and to butchered deer similarly work throughout the play to demonstrate the tensions and aggressions being enacted between the townsfolk of Windsor and the representative of the court, Sir John Falstaff.[29] Falstaff's characterization as the unruly poacher and as a threat to social harmony is balanced by a series of humiliations which cast him as butchered deer. At the same time, however, the play's often overlooked intertext of popular festivity enables the comic resolution of the ending, bringing the community together and maneuvering Master and Mistress Page into accepting their daughter's marriage to Fenton.

Conflict between social groups is central to *The Merry Wives of Windsor*: as its very title indicates, this is a play concerned with localism and societal bonds, with the formation and operation of the social identities and community politics which are so potently represented by the festive hunt. Moreover, it is a text throughout which hunting and festivity evoke yet run counter to each other, and are closely bound up in a preoccupation with local conflict. Commentators have noted the persistent association between Falstaff and images of hunting and poaching, through which Shakespeare exploits the symbolic charge of these activities in order to offer "a comic meditation on some of the forces that drive Elizabethan communal life, forces for which poaching becomes a central metaphor."[30] The image of the "bribed" (stolen) deer becomes an important image of the tensions and conflicts of Windsor: between husbands and wives, parents and children, town and court.[31] The significance of the hunted deer is established from the very beginning of the play, which opens with Justice Shallow's outrage that Falstaff has poached his deer and his determination to "make a Star Chamber matter of it" (I.i.1–2). As the reference to legal recourse suggests, Shallow's furious accusation of Falstaff having "beaten my men, killed my deer and broke open my lodge" (ll.104–5) interprets these actions not just as theft but as a form of public disorder. Fittingly enough, for a representative of legal and governmental authority, Shallow chooses to interpret the poaching as "a riot" (l.31). Just as deer-hunting in the Forest of Arden suggested a backdrop of conflict between court, town, and country, at the opening of *The Merry Wives of Windsor* we see that the traditional methods by which communities attempted to reconcile internal conflicts do not appear to be working.[32] Shallow ignores Evans' offer to mediate: "I am of the Church, and will be glad to do my benevolence, to make atonements and compremises between you" (ll.28–30). The intervention of a clergyman loses its force when one party in the dispute is an outsider who has no particular stake in the continuing harmony of the town.

A second attempt at reconciliation is made by the end of the scene, which concludes with Master Page inviting the group to dine at his home: "Come, we have a hot venison pasty to dinner. Come, gentlemen, I hope we shall drink down all unkindness" (ll.180–82). Page's suggestion that they eat venison together is reminiscent not only of the traditional feast after a successful hunt, but also of the reconciliatory meals held as informal attempts to settle local disputes, "at the end of which the disputants would make public resolutions of peace sealed by a familiar toast: 'I drincke to you and all the malice or hatred I beare to you I putt into this glasse'."[33] However, despite Page's formulaic suggestion that they "drink down all unkindness," here the fissures running through Windsor's community, and the complexity of the social negotiations at work, are suggested by the probable provenance of this venison pasty. Although Shallow has gifted it to Page as an overture of friendship to his new acquaintance, his regret that it was "ill killed" (l.77) suggests that it is the very deer that Falstaff poached. Shallow's compliment to Page is rather opportunistic then, taking advantage of an already-slaughtered animal to make a gift which, as a citizen rather than a member of the nobility, Master Page would not necessarily usually warrant.[34] Moreover, as Berry points out, the choice of dish reiterates rather than buries the resentments simmering between the various members of Windsor's community: "the very food itself symbolizes the conflict it is meant to resolve," making it unsurprising that the harmonious social relations supposedly achieved by gift-giving and ceremonial feasting do not manifest themselves in the ensuing action of the play.[35]

The genuine social tensions that we have seen to be evoked by both hunting and poaching in the period appear in this scene as symbolic shorthand for the conflict simmering below the surface in Windsor. Furthermore, the slaughtered deer appears not only as literal poached animal and consumed pasty, but also in the figure of the poacher himself, the "damned Epicurean rascal" Falstaff.[36] Through the three tricks played upon him by the merry wives, the would-be sexual predator emerges as the hunted beast: his pursuer, meanwhile, is the needlessly jealous Master Ford who appears not as aristocratic hunter, but as crazed hunting hound. Their alignment as beasts of the hunt (albeit one hunter and the other hunted) makes evident the ways in which the play forces Falstaff to take on, and be punished for, not only his own crimes but also those of Ford, whose irrational jealousy threatens the social harmony of Windsor as much as does Falstaff's mercenary adulterousness. Here Falstaff's transformation into quarry becomes a necessary act of scapegoating, enacting the "[s]acrificial substitution" suggested by Girard, and even casting the internal cause of social conflict, Ford himself, as beastly agent in the hunt-as-sacrifice.[37] The explicitly domestic punishments which Mistress

Page and Mistress Ford devise for their victim contrast with and yet complement the field sports which, by keeping their husbands out of the house, enable their traps to be laid.[38] The punning "buck-basket" within which Falstaff is hidden is highlighted by the spitting repetition of Ford's plosive invective, the twisted logic of which moves naturally from washing basket to rutting stag ("of the season" to mate) to hunted vermin:

> Buck? I would I could wash myself of the buck! Buck, buck, buck! Ay, buck! I warrant you, buck – and of the season too, it shall appear. [...] I'll warrant we'll unkennel the fox.
>
> *(III.iii.144–50)*

It is moreover significant, given the centrality of the corpse itself to both hunting custom and festive hunt, that the tricks played upon Falstaff more than once reduce him to physically dismembered prey. In response to the humiliation of his dowsing in the Thames, Falstaff figures himself as animal-as-meat, like the ritualistically dissected deer, fit to be fed to the hounds:

> Have I lived to be carried in a basket like a barrow of butcher's offal, and to be thrown in the Thames? Well, if I be served such another trick, I'll have my brains ta'en out and buttered, and give them to a dog for a New Year's gift.
>
> *(III.v.4–8)*

The evocation of New Year interestingly feeds into a discourse of holiday custom to which I will return below, although it is perhaps stretching the point to remember that the Horn Dance took place at New Year. However, the image of the *curée*, the hounds' reward, is echoed in the next punishment, in which it is Ford who is portrayed as a beast of the hunt, the dog to whom Falstaff fears he will be fed. Evans responds with shock to Ford's increasingly frantic jealousy, exclaiming "why, this is lunatics, this is mad as a mad dog" (IV.ii.118), and Ford himself once again figures himself as hunting beast finding the scent:

> Will you follow, gentlemen? [...] If I cry out thus upon no trail, never trust me when I open again.
>
> *(ll.185–87)[39]*

Falstaff's second humiliation, moreover—his disguise as the old woman of Brentford—is necessitated by the genuine peril in which he would be, should he attempt instead to hide in the house. As he casts about for somewhere to hide from her husband who has suddenly arrived home, Falstaff runs to the chimney but is stopped by Mistress Ford, who warns him that hiding there he is likely to meet the genuine fate of the hunted beast: "There they always use to discharge their birding-pieces" (l.52).

In the final punishment, Falstaff's dual identity as socially disruptive poacher and pursued deer unites, in his appearance as Herne the Hunter, the legendary antlered Keeper of Windsor Forest. Despite his swaggering confidence that he is "a Windsor stag, and the fattest [...] i'the forest" (V.v.12–13), the fantasy of sexual promiscuity which he expresses in his invitation to Mistress Page and Mistress Ford figures himself once again as the butchered deer, the spoils of the hunt:

> Divide me like a bribed buck, each a haunch. I will keep my sides to myself, my shoulders for the fellow of this walk, – and my horns I bequeath your husbands.
>
> *(ll.24–27)[40]*

"Wearing the Horn": Class and Community

In his disguise as Herne the Hunter, Falstaff becomes a comical Actaeon, an ambiguous figure representing both cuckolder and cuckolded. Frequently moralized in the period as a hunter brought low by his own desires, an image of the bestiality of unbridled lust, in his human to animal transformation he was also often visually represented with antlers erupting from his forehead, strikingly suggesting the iconography of cuckoldry.[41] The persistent association between Falstaff and hunting, both as illegal poacher and as dissected deer, typifies the conflicts which form the backdrop of the comedy, and necessitates Falstaff being broken "apart like a poached deer as a communal sacrifice that brings the community together again," a triumph of local and unofficial social action over official or governmental action.[42]

Nevertheless, the importance of calendrical traditions to this reading of the hunt run counter to its depiction as symbolic of social conflict. Just as in *As You Like It* the exiled aristocrats' hunting offers a discourse of power and political struggle which is modified by the play's festive intertexts, so in *Merry Wives*, allusions to folk customs complicate the symbolisms of licit and illicit hunting. While Falstaff's costume casts him as both hunter and hunted stag and aligns him with the iconography of cuckoldry, it recalls not only the dancers in the Abbots Bromley Horn Dance, but also the near relative of traditional pastimes, the ritual folk justice of the 'rough riding' or skimmington, which similarly drew upon the rich and varied associations of the hunted deer. Such ridings were usually undertaken in order to punish socially unacceptable sexual relations (usually, although not exclusively, a wife's over-dominance or cuckolding of her husband). These ritual events could involve quite elaborate disguises, often animalistic or involving cross-dressing. A skimmington in Aveton Gifford in 1737 involved men with "black and Disgused Faces carrying a large pair of Rams Horns tipt like Gold," "winding [...] Hunting Horns and [...] making loud Huzzahs Hallows." It is worth noting that these participants employed a form of disguise which, in itself, evoked both the "colourid visages" common in customary drama and, on the other hand, a form of concealment which was to become so closely associated with unlawful hunting that it was referenced in the infamous Black Act of 1723 which made hunting in disguise a felony.[43] In an example of animal disguise more reminiscent of the Horn Dance, another skimmington in Quemerford in 1618 featured "a man riding upon a horse, haveing [...] two shininge hornes hanging by his eares, & counterfayte beard upon his chine made of a deares tayle."[44] Such rough ridings were simultaneously the violent rejection of unwanted social behaviors, and an expression of shared communal values and folk justice: occasionally the target of the skimmington would be subjected to literal punishments such as being ducked. As Leah Marcus and Edward Berry have pointed out, then, Falstaff's ducking in the Thames, his disguise as an old woman, and his ritual disgrace in antlers are strongly reminiscent of the skimmington: "As a man, in disguise as Herne the Hunter, Falstaff is subjected to the raucous humiliation of the charivari. As a deer, he is poached."[45]

However, it is also worth noting that the costumed participants in the above-quoted skimmingtons, like the hunted 'deer' in the Horn Dance, were not the true victims of the shaming ritual, but rather surrogates, participants in a display of communally sanctioned behaviors. Although Falstaff is no willing volunteer (except inadvertently through his adulterous actions), the comedic ending reminds us that in a sense the true source of the community's anxiety centers on the proposed marriage plans for Anne Page. Falstaff might be a scapegoat for the tensions permeating Windsor town, and his shaming a triumph of civic festivity, but this very display of community self-assertion can be seen as the diffusion of conflict necessary for Master and Mistress Page to accept Anne's marriage to Fenton. After all, it is their very absorption in punishing Falstaff that enabled the marriage to take place. The subtexts of the festive hunt and of poaching finally unite, as Falstaff's comment makes clear: "I am glad, though you have ta'en a special stand to strike at me, that your arrow hath glanced. [...] When night-dogs run, all sorts of deer are chased" (ll.228–32). We have come full circle to Falstaff's own illicit hunting at the opening of the play when, to Shallow's accusation that he had killed Shallow's deer, he had responded with a snatch of song: "But not kissed your keeper's daughter!" (I.i.106). In a slippage customary of the play, Page is now associated both with the poacher's "night-dogs" and with the keeper, but Fenton's poaching will not be punished. Instead, both Master and Mistress Page propose a return to the traditional merrymaking which had been in crisis at the beginning of the play: they will all go home to "eat a posset" (V.v.168) and to "laugh this sport o'er by a country fire;/Sir John and all" (ll.236–37).

IV Conclusion: Collaboration and Conflict

In this chapter I have argued that these two late sixteenth-century comedies deliberately exploit the strange cultural resonance of the early modern hunt, a symbolic charge which appears both in the fetishistic value with which the dead animal was imbued by hunting rituals, and in the popular festal entertainments which parodied the kill and transformed it into processions and dances. As we have seen, the hunt is an activity which, even in its most basic form, combines contradictory meanings—a sport providing enjoyable competition and exercise, and a prolonged performative display culminating in the quarry's highly staged death. Less self-evidently, the hunt was also an arena which enabled wealthy and powerful men to enact and displace their impulse to social violence onto the substituted victim of the deer. It has been argued that the hunt operates symbolically in *The Merry Wives of Windsor* and *As You Like It* as a metaphor for social divisions and conflicts within and between communities, and that Shakespeare exploits the uneasy tension found in the festive pastimes which, in order to enact a statement of local and social identity, turn to a violent, exclusionary, and destructive sport. In the process, this chapter has offered some qualification to Berry's statement that Shakespeare "maintains the social hierarchy in the use of hunting language and allusions to the hunt."[46] In a modification of the critical consensus which sees early modern hunting chiefly in terms of the operation of institutional power, Shakespeare's references to merry pastime allow another interpretation of early modern hunting as both socially divisive *and* as a means to bridge division.

Two final questions remain to be asked, namely how all of this worked onstage in the professional theaters, and what early modern audiences might have made of it? It is important to note that, regardless of whether the nobles in these comedies "assume their rightfulness as hunters," they are in fact not appropriate hunters at all, with Falstaff deliberately engaging in riotous poaching, and the exiled lords hunting, not for sport, but "for the pot."[47] In these onstage depictions of the hunt, one of the chief protagonists has disappeared, and, perhaps surprisingly, this is not the stag, but the aristocratic hunter himself. This absence ensures that focus remains on the deer, an emphasis that would be particularly reinforced by the visual impression created by performers wearing antlers. A stage direction in the First Quarto of *Merry Wives* states that in the final forest scene, Falstaff enters "*with a Bucks head vpon him,*" and it is quite clear from his own reference to horns that in his disguise as Herne the Hunter he sports antlers not unlike those worn at Abbots Bromley.[48] When the Chamberlain's Men came to stage *As You Like It*, written perhaps at the same time or within only a few years of *Merry Wives*, one could posit that this particular prop in their inventory would also have suggested itself for the scene of the lords' hunting procession, although no explicit note exists in the text to support the song's implicit stage direction that he "that killed the deer" should have "his leather skin and horns to wear" (IV.ii.10–11). If such a prop was indeed available, however, the headgear would have served as a striking synecdoche both for the animal and for the festive culture in which such costumes contemporaneously appeared. While we have seen that the tensions between the aristocratic and popular hunt characterized the deer as a contested creature, the appearance onstage of the hunter-as-stag adds yet another dimension to the animal's cultural meaning, inviting audience identification with the festal figure. The antlered, illicit hunter-performer visually unites the roles of human hunter and animal hunted, recalling the dynamics of social inclusion and exclusion, hierarchy, status, and local identity which were so bound up in folk customs incorporating the hunt. Staging synecdochally the body of the deer, evoking both the spectacle of the hunt and the festivity of the folk dance, Shakespeare employs the festive hunt as a form of exorcism of communal conflict through which, eventually, reconciliation can be staged.

Notes

1 Jeanne Addison Roberts, *Shakespeare's English Comedy: The Merry Wives of Windsor in Context* (Lincoln and London: University of Nebraska Press, 1979), 120.

2 Roger B. Manning, *Hunters and Poachers: A Social and Cultural History of Unlawful Hunting in England 1485–1640* (Oxford: Clarendon, 1993); Edward Berry, *Shakespeare and the Hunt: A Cultural and Social Study* (Cambridge: Cambridge University Press, 2001); Catherine Bates, *Masculinity and the Hunt: Wyatt to Spenser* (Oxford: Oxford University Press, 2013). Also cf. Richard Wilson, *Will Power: Essays on Shakespearean Authority* (Detroit, MI: Wayne State University Press, 1993); Jeffrey Theis, "The 'Ill Kill'd' Deer: Poaching and Social Order in *The Merry Wives of Windsor*," *Texas Studies in Literature and Language* 43 (2001): *passim*.

3 Berry, *Shakespeare and the Hunt*, 29.

4 For the hunt as preparation for, and as interchangeable with, warfare cf. Manning, *Hunters and Poachers*, especially 1–17, 39.

5 René Girard, *Violence and the Sacred*, trans. Patrick Gregory (London and New York: Continuum, 2005), 4–5.

6 Manning, *Hunters and Poachers*, 39.

7 Suzanne Walker, "Making and Breaking the Stag: The Construction of the Animal in the Early Modern Hunting Treatise," in *Early Modern Zoology: The Construction of Animals in Science, Literature, and the Visual Arts*, eds. Karl A.E. Enenkel and Paul J. Smith (Leiden and Boston, MA: Brill, 2007), 336.

8 Girard, *Violence*, 5.

9 For *par force* hunting, cf. Richard Almond, *Medieval Hunting* (Stroud: The History Press, 2003), 73.

10 Thomas Elyot, *The Boke Named the Gouernour* (London, 1531), sig. I2. Also cf. Thomas Cockayne, *A Short Treatise of Hunting: Compyled for the Delight of Noble Men and Gentlemen* (London, 1591), sig. A3.

11 Elyot, *The Gouernour*, sig. I3.

12 For the argument that hunting should "be understood primarily as a symbolic activity," cf. Catherine Bates, *Masculinity and the Hunt: Wyatt to Spenser* (Oxford: Oxford University Press, 2013), 5 and *passim*.

13 Almond, *Medieval Hunting*, 77–78. Also cf. Manning, *Hunters and Poachers*, 39–40.

14 For the significance of the ritualism of the hunt cf. Jennifer Allport Reid, "'The Hunt is Up': Death, Dismemberment, and Feasting in Shakespeare's Roman Tragedies," *Actes des congrès de la Société française Shakespeare* 38 (forthcoming 2020).

15 Edward of Norwich, *The Master of Game*, eds. William A. Baillie-Grohman and F.N. Baillie-Grohman (Philadelphia: University of Pennsylvania Press, 2005), 174–75.

16 Almond, *Medieval Hunting*, 63.

17 Robert Plot, *The Natural History of Stafford-Shire* (Oxford, 1686), sig. 3I1ᵛ. For dating the tradition, cf. Michael Heaney, "New Evidence for the Abbots Bromley Hobby-Horse," *Folk Music Journal* 5 (1987): *passim*.

18 John Forrest, *The History of Morris Dancing, 1458–1750* (Cambridge: James Clarke & Co., 1999), 102, 116. For a detailed discussion of folk dances involving hobby horses and ritual animal disguises, cf. E.C. Cawte, *Ritual Animal Disguise: A Historical and Geographical Study of Animal Disguise in the British Isles* (Cambridge: D. S. Brewer, 1978).

19 Plot, *The Natural History of Stafford-Shire*, sig. 3I1^v.

20 Ibid.

21 Wilson, *Will Power*, 74; also cf. *As You like It*, ed. Dusinberre, 194n.; Berry, *Shakespeare and the Hunt*, especially 187–89; Claus Uhlig, "'The Sobbing Deer': *As You like It*, II.i.21–66 and the Historical Context," *Renaissance Drama* 3 (1970). For an alternative view, cf. A. Stuart Daley, "The Idea of Hunting in *As You like It*," *Shakespeare Studies* 21 (1993).

22 William Shakespeare, *As You like It*, ed. Juliet Dusinberre, The Arden Shakespeare (London: Thomson Learning, 2006), II.i.21–25. All subsequent references are taken from this edition and embedded in the text. Cf. A.H. Thorndike, "The Relation of *As You like It* to Robin Hood Plays," *The Journal of Germanic Philology* 4, no. 1 (1902).

23 William Shakespeare, *Cymbeline*, ed. Valerie Wayne, The Arden Shakespeare (London: Bloomsbury, 2017), III.iii.74–75.

24 Wilson, *Will Power*, 66.

25 Skiles Howard, "Hands, Feet, and Bottoms: Decentering the Cosmic Dance in *A Midsummer Night's Dream*," *Shakespeare Quarterly* 44 (1993): 331–32. For meanings of antic, cf. "antic, adj. and n.". OED Online. June 2017. Oxford University Press. www.oed.com/view/Entry/8519 (accessed December 1, 2017).

26 Cf. Cesar Lombardi Barber, *Shakespeare's Festive Comedy: A Study of Dramatic Form and Its Relation to Social Custom* (Princeton, NJ: Princeton University Press, 1959), 252–71; "Introduction" in Shakespeare, *As You like It*, ed. Michael Hattaway (Cambridge: Cambridge University Press, 2009).

27 Anthony Munday, *The Death of Robert, Earle of Hvntington* (London, 1601), sig. B2^v.

28 cf. Jennifer Reid, "The 'Heavie Writ of Outlawry': Community and the Transformation of Popular Culture from Early Modern Customary Drama to Anthony Munday's Robin Hood Plays," *The Wenshan Review of Literature and Culture* 10 (2017).

29 On dating the play, cf. Roberts, *Shakespeare's English Comedy*, 42–43.

30 Berry, *Shakespeare and the Hunt*, 139; also cf. Theis, "The 'Ill Kill'd' Deer."

31 William Shakespeare, *The Merry Wives of Windsor*, ed. Giorgio Melchiori, The Arden Shakespeare (London: Thomson Learning, 2000), V.v.24. All subsequent references embedded in the text.

32 Cf. Keith Wrightson, *English Society 1580–1680* (New Brunswick: NJ: Rutgers University Press, 1982), especially 165.

33 Laura Gowing, *Domestic Dangers: Women, Words, and Sex in Early Modern London* (Oxford: Clarendon Press, 1998), 136, citing Anne Haynes *c.* Rachel Cheereseley (1622), DL/C 228, fo. 140.

34 Cf. Dan Beaver, "The Great Deer Massacre: Animals, Honor, and Communication in Early Modern England," *Journal of British Studies* 38 (1999): 195; although on the developing custom towards the end of the period of giving venison as an expression of patronage within civic circles, cf. Susan Whyman, *Sociability and Power in Late-Stuart England: The Cultural World of the Verneys, 1660–1720* (Oxford: Oxford University Press, 1999), 23–33.

35 Berry, *Shakespeare and the Hunt*, 145.

36 II.ii.225; as well as a general insult, "rascal" also meant a young male deer. Cf. Berry, *Shakespeare and the Hunt*, 134.

37 René Girard, *Violence and the Sacred*, trans. Patrick Gregory (London and New York: Continuum, 2005), 5.

38 That Master Ford and Master Page go "a-birding" together is reiterated five times: cf. III.iii.216; III.v.43, 119; IV.ii.6, 44. For domesticity in the play, cf. Richard Helgerson, "The Buck Basket, the Witch, and the Queen of Fairies: The Women's World of Shakespeare's Windsor," in *Renaissance Culture and the Everyday*, eds. Patricia Fumerton and Simon Hunt (Philadelphia: University of Pennsylvania Press, 1999).

39 "cry out is the barking of the hounds, trail the scent of the quarry, open the first barking of the hounds when they think they have found the scent," *Merry Wives*, ed. Melchiori, 253n.

40 Cf. *Merry Wives*, ed. Melchiori, 277n.

41 Cf. Claire McEachern, "Why Do Cuckolds Have Horns?," *Huntington Library Quarterly* 71 (2008).

42 Theis, "'The Ill Kill'd Deer'," 64; for related arguments, cf. Helgerson, "The Buck Basket, the Witch, and the Queen of Fairies," 175; Roberts, *Shakespeare's English Comedy*, 78–82, 110–11, 118; Leah Marcus, *Unediting the Renaissance: Shakespeare, Marlowe, Milton* (London and New York: Routledge, 1996), 88–97.

43 Forrest, *The History of Morris Dancing*, 64; Manning, *Hunters and Poachers*, 15; E.P. Thompson, *Whigs and Hunters: The Origin of the Black Act* (London: Allen Lane, 1975).

44 M.G. Dickinson, "A 'Skimmington Ride' at Aveton Gifford," *Devon and Cornwall Notes and Queries* 34 (1981): 290–92; B. Howard Cunnington, "'A Skimmington'" in 1618," *Folklore* 41 (1930): 287–90; Cf. Martin Ingram, "Ridings, Rough Music and the 'Reform of Popular Culture' in Early Modern England," *Past and Present* 105 (1984): *passim*.

45 Berry, *Shakespeare and the Hunt*, 153; also cf. Marcus, *Unediting the Renaissance*, 89–90.

46 Berry, *Shakespeare and the Hunt*, 12.

47 Ibid.

48 William Shakespeare, *A most pleasaunt and excellent conceited comedie, of Syr Iohn Falstaffe, and the merrie wiues of Windsor* (London, 1602), sig. G1ᵛ.

20

ON EATING, THE ANIMAL THAT THEREFORE I AM

Race and Animal Rites in *Titus Andronicus*

Steven Swarbrick

> Generally speaking, one does not eat one's companion animals (nor get eaten by them).
> —*Donna Haraway*[1]

I would like to begin by setting the table for an investigation into a widely held myth: the myth known as "companion species."

In an interview entitled "'Eating Well,' or the Calculation of the Subject," Jacques Derrida states:

> I am trying ... to underscore the sacrificial structure of the discourses to which I am referring .... [I]t is a matter of discerning a place left open, in the very structure of these discourses (which are also "cultures") for a noncriminal putting to death. Such are the executions of ingestion, incorporation, or introjection of the corpse. An operation as real as it is symbolic when the corpse is "animal[,]" ... a symbolic operation when the corpse is "human." But the "symbolic" is very difficult, truly impossible to delimit.[2]

As an operation that is "impossible to delimit," the act of sacrifice takes on a truly wide-ranging set of real and symbolic actions in Derrida's analysis:

> it suffices to take seriously the idealizing interiorization of the phallus and the necessity of its passage through the mouth, whether it's a matter of words or of things, of sentences, of daily bread or wine, of the tongue, the lips, or the breast of the other.[3]

Derrida calls this sacrificial structure that inheres "at the edge of the orifices" the "scheme of the *dominant*," and places this "scheme" "at the heart of the most pressing concerns of modern societies."[4] For

> the question is no longer [the traditional moral] one of knowing if its "good" to eat the other or if the other is "good" to eat, nor of knowing which other. One eats him regardless and lets oneself be eaten by him.[5]

The question is not, nor has it ever been:

> should one eat or not eat, eat this and not that, the living or the nonliving, man or animal, but since *one must* eat in any case and since it is and tastes good to eat, and since there's no other definition of the good [*du bien*], how for goodness' sake should one eat well [*bien manger*]? And what does this imply? What is eating?[6]

Anticipating in dramatic form and by several centuries Derrida's interrogation of the carnivorous "scheme" at the heart of ethical life, Shakespeare's *Titus Andronicus* stages the many senses of "eating" and "eating well," stretching readers' comprehension of Derrida's deceptively simple question, "What is eating?"[7] In the play's compact opening, Titus's burial of his sons in the family tomb marks the first symbolic incorporation, while the sacrifice of Tamora's son, Alarbus (he is "clean consumed" by flame), marks the second. "Eating" is from the start connected to mourning, burial, racial otherness, the animal, and the earth as tomb. In this chapter, I propose to follow after figures of "eating" in Shakespeare's *Titus Andronicus* in the same way that Derrida follows after the animal in "The Animal that Therefore I Am," by tracing the ontogenetic development of rites of ingestion—the supposed preserve of human exceptionalism when the "thing" eaten is of symbolic value—to its ecological "prehistory" in figures of the nonhuman. For Derrida, we are not only what we eat; "we" are also the outcome of so many inhuman processes of eating/being eaten.

Unlike Derrida, however, whose analysis hovers around the orifices of the body—eyes, mouth, and ears—to show how every act of symbolic incorporation is invested by the cannibalistic violence of eating, maiming, and swallowing, Shakespeare travels in the opposite (and perhaps more radical) direction, from the surface of the lips to the depths of the belly, to show how, in his play, even the substratum of the earth is phantasmatically charged. The geography of *Titus Andronicus* literalizes the problem of "eating well." For, not only is the major feature of its landscape a deep pit, variously described as a "bloodstained hole" or "mouth" (the symmetrical obverse of the Andronicus family tomb [2.2.210, 199]), but also its major event is the rape and silencing of Lavinia, whose "lopped" limbs double the play's opening sacrificial scene ("Alarbus' limbs are lopped" [1.1.146]).[8] Plotting in both senses, as revenge plot and plot of land, combines with figures of eating to produce killable bodies or biopolitical bodies for whom relations of human/animal and racial-norm/other have come undone. Lavinia's becoming-animal[9] has her tracing "signs" in the earth (a "sandy plot" [4.1.69]), raising the question of the relation of human speech to animal markings; Aaron and Tamora's frequent rhetorical animalization puts race (Tamora's "hue," Aaron's Moorishness) at the center of decisions over funeral rite and death. Throughout the play, however, there is a persistent problematizing of this sacrificial "plot," which places animal life and its biopolitical kin (racial otherness) on the side of killability. "Eating well" as it is figured in Shakespeare's play enables a reading of the priority of "animal rites"—rites of burial, language, mourning, and sexual intimacy.[10] In other words, Shakespeare's *Titus Andronicus* reverses the order of things by figuring nature itself as animate. Nature, that is, ruminates (from the Latin *ruminari*, "to revolve, turn over repeatedly in the mind; to meditate deeply upon," *and* "[o]f an animal: to chew again food that has been partially digested") on loss.[11]

Recall that at the start of the play, Titus, upon returning to Rome, proceeds immediately to inter his son in the family tomb and does so by first sacrificing Tamora's son: "Albarus's limbs are lopped / [a]nd entrails feed the sacrificing fire" (1.1.146–47). Interment itself raises the question of incorporation, as when Quintus and Martius refer to the pit wherein Bassianus's corpse is found as a "blood-drinking pit" with a "mouth" and "entrails," a "devouring receptacle, / as hateful as Cocytus' misty mouth" (2.3.235–36). Such imagery continues in Titus's lament: "Let my tears staunch the earth's dry appetite; / … O earth, I will befriend thee more with rain / … [a]nd keep eternal springtime on thy face, / [s]o thou refuse to drink my dear sons' blood" (3.1.14, 21–22). And of course, the play draws to a close with a banquet scene, in which Tamora—disguised as Revenge—eats her flesh and blood. We should also keep in mind the curious form of punishment dealt to Aaron, which follows the themes of interment and incorporation: "Set him breast-deep in earth, and famish him. / There let him stand and rave and cry for food" (5.3.179–80). The play ends, finally, by returning to a scene of burial, in which the agents are beasts of prey: "No mournful bell shall ring her [Tamora's] burial; / [b]ut throw her forth to beasts and birds to prey" (5.3.197–98).

Both Shakespeare and psychoanalysis have much to say about the relationship between eating and thinking. Well before Derrida, it was Melanie Klein who queried the limits of the "symbolic" by suggesting that "mind" itself emerges from the infant's phantasmatic relationships to objects (prototypically the mother's breast). In "Weaning," Klein describes a scene of phantasmatic entombment whereby the infant, in order to save the "good" object (the nourishing object), incorporates that object through the mouth.[12] That this process of psychic incorporation entails the same masticatory violence used to dismember and destroy the "bad" object means that, for the Kleinan infant, symbolic meaning ("good" vs. "bad," "saving" vs. "killing") will always be linked etiologically to the originally undifferentiated landscape of the belly, where, in order to save, one must eat, and where "living on" is, in Derrida's sense of the phrase, already an act of mourning.[13] By reading "incorporation" in this way, as the entanglement of matter and meaning, my goal is not simply to read psychoanalysis back into Shakespeare; rather, my goal is to show that Shakespeare's landscape is already psychically invested, and that we can just as well read the etiology of mourning in "the earth's dry appetite."

Such a reading, I propose, radically suspends what is "proper" to the human by tracing what is before, beyond, and after the human.[14] Whereas the ethical thrust of much ecological scholarship today inclines towards relationships of care, companionship, and symbiosis with the natural world, the present chapter will consider a landscape that is not only enterically inclined—that is, shaped by experiences of hunger and thirst—but also ambivalent to the conciliatory rhetoric of our times. Nature, I will argue, is alive to the worst appetitive tendencies of Shakespeare's *Titus Andronicus*. As a play about the psychic violence of loss and melancholic incorporation ("incorporation" defined here in the psychoanalytic sense of intra-psychic attachment), it unfolds scene after scene of alimentary destruction while enfolding bodies in the very belly of the earth. My goal is to show that these scenes of incorporation enact a theory of mind in which nature is not just the vehicle of symbolic incorporation (eating as a sign of mourning). More precisely, nature, I will argue, is minded. The peristaltic repetitions of the play enact a theory of mind in which, to follow Gilles Deleuze's language of the folding and unfolding of subjectivity, the inside (of thought, consciousness, human being) is merely the inside of the outside, or matter folded inward.[15] Consequently, this chapter will ask the most fundamental questions: can the earth hunger? Do animals mourn? What, finally, is the relationship between nonhuman repetition and human rites and customs? At bottom, is there a nonhuman being-towards-death?[16] But reader—beware—the animism I propose here does not yield the celebrated "companionship" of all things. The environmentalism of *Titus Andronicus* is decidedly non-conciliatory; it traffics in hunger, bile, rape, racism, and revenge. For this reason, Shakespearean animism cannot be restricted to

On Eating, the Animal that Therefore I Am

the higher orders of cognition, nor can it be couched in the palliating language of symbiosis; thinking *with* Shakespeare involves ruminating from the ground up.[17]

I From Companion Species to the Phantasmatic Corpse

In her monumentally influential *entrée* into the world of critical animal studies, *When Species Meet*, Donna J. Haraway invites the reader to dine on a concept that makes a mess of the anthropological distinctions between the "raw" and the "cooked," or the primitive (food) and the cultured (cuisine). In Haraway's evolutionary retelling of the biblical last supper, all species break bread together:

> *Companion* comes from the Latin *cum panis*, "with bread." Messmates at table are companions …. The basic story [of companion species] is simple: ever more complex life forms are the continual result of ever more intricate and multidirectional acts of association of and with other life forms. Trying to make a living together, critters eat critters but can only partly digest one another. Quite a lot of indigestion, not to mention excretion, is the natural result, some of which is the vehicle for new sorts of complex patternings of ones and manys in entangled association …. These are the cobblings together that give meaning to the "becoming with" of companion species in naturecultures. *Cum panis*, messmates, … those are the names of my game.[18]

The emphasis of Haraway's multispecies "game" is on interconnection ("cobblings"), life as collaborative network ("patternings of ones and manys"), mutual redefinition ("becoming with"), and genesis ("ever more complex life"). There is apparently no limit to the feeding frenzy called "life," which curves in the direction of the biblical injunction: to be fruitful and multiply. Yet there is something about the notion of "companion species," with its singular focus on the production of "new sorts of complex patternings," that always seems to stick in the throat. That "something" is, for lack of a better word, the absolute refusal of *lack* or negativity in Haraway's description of "companion species."

Consider by way of comparison Lee Edelman's language of the *sinthome* as negative obverse of Haraway's "companion species." For Edelman, "*sinthome*osexuality" names the action of

> grafting, at an awkward join, the sounds of French and English, to the benefit of neither …. It would assert itself against futurity, against its propagation, insofar as it would designate an impasse in the passage to the future and, by doing so, would pass beyond, pass through, the saving fantasy futurity denotes.[19]

Here, the emphasis is on grafting two foreign bodies or species, "to the benefit of neither." Neither consilience nor interconnectedness but rather dehiscence and bifurcation: the "awkward join" remains, despite their coming together. This remainder suggests two things: first, the coming together, the synthesis of this word, can only happen because of a violent impropriety of the letter, every letter, to "proper" meaning or function; second, the word itself has no proper origin (either in English or in French), but is instead a machine without a proper past (a point of origin or birth place) or future. The word is afutural, a combination of life and nonlife. In this sense, if it "seeks a hearing," it's not to continue a trajectory of living, nor to delay a future that would be its "proper" end. The word is *beyond* the life and

259

death of the organism, in Freud's sense of the beyond of pleasure, because its mode of life is not "propagation" but rather bifurcation and disjunction.

To be clear, my point is not to deny "companion species" their due: new beginnings, new reproductive patternings, new futures. My point, rather, is that what is most vitalizing about our relations with others (human and nonhuman) is the thing that is symptomatically absent from Haraway's theory of "companion species": namely, the violent and disruptive negativity around which relationality curves. The *sinthome*, in short, is what does not break bread at Haraway's table. Not because there is no mention of negativity in "companion species"; after all, Haraway calls "indigestion" and "excretion" the "acidic reminders of mortality made vivid." But these "reminders" are always afterthoughts, whereas life's main purpose remains the same: to eat, to meet, and to multiply. There is, in other words, in Haraway's notion of "companion species," a reproductive logic centered on life's futurity, one that is eerily reminiscent of the capitalist logic of money breeding money (specie). But this logic of "life" begs the question: isn't the join at the heart of every encounter (the "awkward join" that Edelman, after Lacan, calls *sinthome*), is it not also a grave? Why do we assume that meetings and couplings are inherently life affirming?

If, according to Haraway, eating is a way of "getting on" with others, then Act 1 of *Titus Andronicus* should be counted as a radical declination of the principle of pleasure guiding psychic life. Written as if to give the lie to "companion species," Shakespeare's play begins with a scene of incorporation gone horribly awry. At his return to Rome, Titus exclaims:

> Hail, Rome, victorious in thy mourning weed!
> Lo, as the bark that hath discharged his freight
> Returns with precious lading to the bay
> From whence at first she weighed her anchorage,
> Cometh Andronicus, bound with laurel boughs,
> To resalute his country with his tears,
> Tears of true joy for his return to Rome.

> (1.1.73–79)

Titus's "return" turns in two directions at once. On the one hand, "Rome" is imagined as a site of homecoming ("Cometh Andronicus"), and the apostrophized address, "Hail, Rome," animates the site of "return" as a compensation for "the poor remains" of Titus's "five-and-twenty valiant sons," who died in battle with the Goths. Just "as the bark that hath discharged his freight / Returns with precious lading to the bay," so Titus discharges his pains by binding the traumas of war in victory dress, "bound with laurel." We are at an apparent distance from the animal who, according to Derrida's tongue-in-cheek retelling of the Western philosophical tradition, is unable to dress (either in words or in "mourning weed") and therefore does not partake of the "rites" accorded to humans.[20] As Derrida explains, this tradition "assumes, for animal language, a system of signs without response: *reactions* but no *response* .... They distinguish *reactions* from *response*, with everything that depends on this distinction, which is almost limitless."[21] The animal does not convert pain into symbolic pleasure, but merely *reacts* as in a chemical process.

By contrast, Titus hastens to "the rites" intended and buries his sons in the family tomb. He states:

> Behold the poor remains, alive and dead:
> These that survive, let Rome reward with love;
> These that I bring unto their latest home,
> With burial among their ancestors.

> (1.1.84–87)

260

As an entry into the economy of "mourning," the repetition figured as homecoming would, on the surface, appear to bind the psychic "freight" of loss, allowing the wounded to exact compensation in the form of burial. The burial performed in the lines above not only completes the circle of "return" ("their latest home"), but also inducts "the dead" into a time immemorial, the time, that is, of memory and ritual:

> There greet in silence, as the dead are wont,
> And sleep in peace, slain in your country's wars.
> O sacred receptacle of my joys,
> Sweet cell of virtue and nobility,
> How many sons hast thou of mine in store
> That thou wilt never render to me more!

(1.1.93–98)

Even if the "O" of "O sacred receptacle" speaks in cipher, of losses in-articulable, it nonetheless encrypts its loss in a symbolic order that returns the famished mouth to the signifying "joys" of a proper burial. Such is, according to Freud, the *work* of mourning. We ritualize acts of incorporation (the family tomb, breaking bread) as the cultural equivalent of our earliest experiences of deprivation, i.e., an empty belly. In doing so, we—symbolic animals— get our fill.

Were this the end to mourning, however, there'd be little left to dramatize, much less psychoanalyze. The pleasure principle would govern all life. But, as Freud says, there is a beyond of pleasure: the death-drive. The death-drive does not contradict the pleasure principle, but rather extends it by repeating a satisfaction other than and beyond the pleasure of the object. In the famous example from Lacan, the object "food" is of no importance to the mouth, "*it is a matter of total indifference.*"[22] Rather, the mouth eats because it enjoys a fundamental absence. This is why, "[e]ven when you stuff the mouth," Lacan writes, "the mouth that opens in the register of the drive—it is not the food that satisfies it, it is, as one says, the pleasure of the mouth."[23] The mouth has no "proper" object, which is to say that the only true "object" of the mouth is an impossible one— what Lacan famously calls *objet a*.[24]

There is, then, an excessiveness to being that cannot be explained (away) by pleasure or the celebrated multitude of companion species. Since, if we are to take Haraway's etymology seriously and read "company" (*cum panis*) as a form of eating, what this eating neglects in its celebration of the multiplicity of meeting/eating/becoming is precisely the gap or negativity that repeats with every instance of so-called "pleasure." For Freud, no less the realist in these matters, the repetition of loss begins at the very inauguration of life from inanimate matter, as in his speculative example of the tiny "vesicle" which, in order to become, must first divide itself, between organic life on the one hand and inorganic life on the other.[25]

The central problem that *Titus Andronicus* poses, then, is not the conservative question, how to make nice or make "good" through sustainable eating practices, but rather how to "eat well" in an economy *without* reserve, that is, in an economy in which excess and waste are not only inevitable factors of eating but also pleasurable, too, since they foreground the negativity at the heart of life. It is this second, more difficult question, what to do with one's inevitable and not just accidental excess, that emerges in the second part of Titus's "return," which goes beyond the suturing of losses towards a more fundamental (and far less sustainable) repetition of eating qua cutting.

If, in the first instance of "return," burial signifies a symbolic incorporation, whereby the earthly elements house the living dead as in a "receptacle" or *chora*, the *chora* being that catachrestic "site" that, according to Luce Irigaray, philosophers have appropriated and misnamed so as to fix the meaning of the feminine[26] (hence Titus's abortive apostrophe, "[t]hat wilt never render to me more!," which figures the earthly tomb as a mother pregnant with loss), then the second instance of incorporation takes this symbolic meaning to its radical by introducing the language of "sacrifice."

At the site of the Andronicus family tomb, Lucius announces the sacrificial scheme. He commands:

> Give us the proudest prisoner of the Goths,
> That we may hew his limbs and on a pile
> *Ad manes fratrum* sacrifice his flesh
> Before this earthly prison of their bones,
> That so the shadows be not unappeased,
> Nor we disturbed with prodigies on earth.

(1.1.99–104)

Notice the surreptitious change in locale, from "sacred receptacle" and "[s]weet cell" in the previous lines to the "earthly prison" above. Whereas before, the earth as "receptacle" was unable to "render" much of anything, but only receive the dead, here the "earthly prison" is less the object of a wish fulfillment (everlasting life) than the specter of something shadowy, "unappeased," and disturbingly prodigious. The tomb as prison houses an inhuman hunger. Although it would be conventional to assume that the earth hungers only under the yoke of metaphor, it is the contention of this chapter that metaphor itself needs to be rethought: rather than dismiss a hungering earth as a mere metaphor for symbolic practices of inhumation (i.e., culture), we need to think the metaphoricity of nature itself. What happens to our familiar tropes and figures when they are no longer "ours" but (re)turn (as they do in the case of Titus's "return" to Rome) in the direction of the literal, the material, the inhuman? In short, what if the repertoire of acts and symbols that we call culture, the culture of mourning to be exact, was nature all along?

It is at this point in Shakespeare's play, at the very disturbance of "place," that Derrida's inquiry into "a place left open … for a noncriminal putting to death" reasserts its relevance to our reading. Where, after all, to delimit the symbolic from the real in the case of a masticating and prodigious earth? The trauma that the work of mourning was meant to cover over in the first burial returns in the image of a ruminating earth, as it now seems that all of nature is invested in a monstrous reversal of the "rites" of incorporation. Furthermore, if there is "a place left open … for a noncriminal putting to death" in matters of incorporation, that "place" is already divided by Shakespeare along the axes of "species" and "race" (two terms that could be used interchangeably in early modern England[27]). The cut that kills Alarbus enacts the ontological separation not only between animal (meat) and human (murder), but also black/white—where "blackness" connotes bare life, *zoe*, and "whiteness" connotes political life or the "rites" proper to the human (though as we shall see, these relations of domination are equally open to deconstruction). Let us hew closely, then, to the language of sacrifice as it both separates and connects seemingly disparate agencies.

II Dark Shadows

Lucius's Latin phrase "*[a]d manes fratrum*" ("to our brothers' shadows") quoted above does more than just incense the flesh of an otherwise prosaic kill. It appears as a perverse parody of the idea that eating together makes "companions" together. For the message of brotherhood ("*fratrum*") on display in Lucius's speech, though it does combine different species, even ontologies ("*manes*," shadows), centers on the figure of *homo sacer*, a being from Roman law deemed killable and therefore sacred to the fortifying rites of men.[28] (I will note in passing, too, the implicit gendering of this "brotherhood" of the human). It is this logic of "inclusive exclusion," that is, of a brotherhood of man defined in and by abjection, that Tamora, Queen of the Goths, runs up against as she begs her "Roman brethren" for mercy for her son, reasoning that to be "brought to Rome" and "return / Captive" is satisfaction enough for a vengeful appetite. Unmoved by Tamora's pleas, Titus invokes "brethren slain," remarking: "Religiously they ask a sacrifice. / To this your son is marked, and die he must, / T'appease their groaning shadows that are gone" (1.1.126, 127–29).

The brotherhood of "shadows" is an ingenious sleight of hand on the part of Shakespeare, since not only were actors of the early modern stage called "shadows," as in Theseus's remarks in *A Midsummer Night's Dream*, "[t]he best in this kind are but shadows," but also the main villain and threat to the Roman yoke in *Titus Andronicus* is Aaron, whose dark skin marks him both as a literal "shadow," a figure of metaphysical reversal insofar as the "shadows" are supposed to exist elsewhere than *here*, below ground and *not* among the living, and as a figure of racial performance, since to "be" a "shadow" is perforce to adopt a mask.[29] From the start, then, the brotherhood of "shadows" extends beyond the grave to encompass the "living," and the performance of identity (Roman, Goth, Moor) is (un)done via racial counterfeit.

I will have more to say about racial identity and performance momentarily. For now, I would like to call attention to the radical ontological instability of the categories I've been exploring: living/nonliving, human/animal, brother/enemy, symbol/food, animate/inanimate, rite/repetition, species companion/racial outsider. These categories do not just confront each other as independent "units"; rather, they shade and diffract "one" into the "other," without interruption. What marks their (temporary) dislocation is the de-*cision* of "sacrifice," a decision that resolves their entanglements and makes bodies that are literally and not just metaphorically *hewn* into "place" through the action of cutting/being cut.[30] Far from insisting that these categories break bread together in a kind of harmonious admixture of species, Shakespeare represents eating as the event that cuts together and apart each "unit" of being: friend and foe, vital life and viand. Eating, in this sense, is both pre-individual and pre-human; we are not only what "we" eat but also the historical outcome of so many inhuman processes of eating/being eaten. We see this dynamic at the start of Shakespeare's play, as Titus and his kin insist on the "rite" to "feed" a "sacrificing fire." After imploring to his brothers,

> Away with him [Alarbus], and make a fire straight,
> And with our swords upon a pile of wood
> Let's hew his limbs till they be clean consumed,
>
> (1.1.130–32)

Lucius follows the sacrificial speech act with the following observation:

> See, lord and father, how we have performed
> Our Roman rites: Alarbus' limbs are lopped
> And entrails feed the sacrificing fire,
> Whose smoke like incense doth perfume the sky.
> Remaineth nought but to inter our brethren
> And with loud 'larums welcome them to Rome.
>
> (1.1.145–50)

From speech act to constative, the cut that binds the Andronicii to their interred "brethren" also enacts a material-ontological division—with *real* consequences—between human and animal and the enemy Goths, who are treated as food for "the sacrificing fire." At the moment of being hewn, the sacrificed body is neither human nor animal (the play tends to devour such metaphysical niceties) but is rather the animalized (and racialized) outcome of the action of cutting/being cut. Alarbus becomes meat not only because he is cut down but also because cutting marks the provenance of the "human," a word that repeats (mechanically) each time it is used the de-cision between rite and repetition, and human capacity and nonhuman killability.[31]

That this decision is also racialized is manifest in the slippage between "hew" and "hue." After stating his preference for Tamora's "fair" "hue," Saturninus repeats the action of cutting by cleaving "fair" skin from a "cloudy countenance" in the following:

> Clear up, fair queen, that cloudy countenance:
> Though chance of war hath wrought this change of cheer.
>
> (1.1.267–68)

Tamora's skin color becomes an object of carnal intrigue in the play as Saturninus encourages her to "clear" a darkening "countenance." The phrase "cloudy countenance" of course refers to Tamora's emotional and humoral interior. A cloudy disposition in this case becomes analogous to a change in weather—or rather, *more* than analogous, given that the humoral body was thought of less as an enclosed environment than as a porous membrane, open to the passions of the elements.[32] But the expression "cloudy countenance" does not just reside beneath the skin, at the level of Tamora's emotional interior. It also hews in the direction of Tamora's skin color, at the surface where light and dark become as changeable as the movement of light and shadow. On the one hand, this climatological reference enables us to read "race" in *Titus Andronicus* deconstructively, that is, as a diffraction pattern of myriad overlapping differences, including animal, mineral, climatological, and meteorological differences.[33] On the other hand, Saturninus's imperative, "[c]lear up, fair queen," attests to the fact that sedimented differences of race still exert a violent force in the play, and that some can "clear up" more easily than others. To "[c]lear up" a "cloudy countenance" thus means to distance oneself from a racialized and racializing weather pattern—something akin to what critical race scholar Alexander G. Weheliye calls "racial assemblage," which puts the racialization of the flesh at the center of biopolitical definitions of the "human" and of myriad intersectional forces, including bodies, technologies, affects, and, as in Shakespeare's play, the elements.[34]

From dark "shadows" to "cloudy" countenances, then, race and animality do not so much interact in Shakespeare's play but rather crosshatch in the making and unmaking of human ("fair") and nonhuman ("cloudy") bodies. For example, Tamora's animality changes dramatically as she moves from a "fair" countenance to one that changes in direct proximity to Aaron's "cloudy melancholy" (2.2.33). As Bassianus relates in the context of a hunt for animal bodies: "Believe me, queen, your swart Cimmerian / [d]oth make your honour of his body's hue, / [s]potted, detested and abominable" (2.2.72–74). Likewise, Lavinia: "No grace? No womanhood? Ah, beastly creature, / [t]he blot and enemy to our general name" (2.2.182–83). "Blot" signifies not only a moral stain but also an error common to writing and printing. As an instrument of reading and writing, the ink "blot" acts as a kind of racial *techne*: it individuates black/white and animal/human, on the one hand; yet it also stains (puts under erasure) the paper of Tamora's otherwise "fair" skin by exceeding the bounds of the proper. By blotting the edges of "the human" (defined as white, morally transparent, and properly female), Tamora metamorphizes (to follow the Ovidian language of the play) into a "beastly creature," who, the story goes, can neither read nor write (properly). Although it is not her intention, Lavinia's "blot" puts under erasure the very purity she seeks to protect by making "race" qua "species" a matter of writing, blotting, and concealing—akin to an animal covering its tracks.

Finally, this "blot" that interrupts the smooth creation and delineation of racially segregated bodies also bleeds through to the end of the play, where Aaron, "[c]hief architect and plotter," appears em-plot-ed, "[s]et ... breast-deep in earth," with the injunction to "famish him" (5.3.121, 178). That Aaron (the chief "blot" and signifier of darkness in the play) is last rendered as food to the earth, a food that neither we nor the soil swallow in full, but ruminate on (perhaps even savor), suggests that what the play gives us to eat in the end is neither resolution nor the wholesomeness of "companion species" but the lasting condition of "species melancholia"—the idea that non-white and animal bodies are the (enforced) lost objects of psychic and material processes of assimilation to the "human."[35]

III And Say the Earth Responded?

Although I began this chapter by criticizing the optimism of "companion species" and, alas, still cannot see a way to break bread with a concept that would break ties with the negativity that *Titus Andronicus* feeds on, I would like to end with an image of "becoming" that, if it does not offer hope, offers an example of "eating well" as *digestif* to our meal.

Lavinia in Act 4 proves the exception to a play that is (despite its body count) bent on survival. She is the material embodiment of "companion species," a moving assemblage of human, animal (she is compared to Philomel), plant, and earth. What's more, the sexual violence she endures transforms her body into the "awkward join" that, in Edelman's vocabulary, grafts part-objects "to the benefit of neither." As a figure without future, Lavinia's monstrous comportment is manifestly against survival. Not a figure of symbiosis; she is the embodiment rather of sym-thanatosis. Nor is this to deny Lavinia her agency. As she writes the names of her assailants in the earth, Marcus states: "Heaven guide thy pen to print thy sorrows plain, / [t]hat we may know the traitors and the truth" (4.1.75–76). As is often the case in *Titus Andronicus*, reading rushes headlong to a metaphysical "truth" that, though it stands revealed in the written word, misreads the act of writing as a presence to be had. But if we follow Lavinia's embodied signs, we see more than just the names "*Chiron—Demetrius*." We see an animal blotting and unblotting her "sorrows" in the dirt, creating path marks ("path" derives from the Greek word for pathos). Who's to say where this path or pathos begins and ends? For it connects "pen," "print," the racial *techne* of the "blot," "heaven," and earth in a scene of animal writing and en-*crypt*-ion (yet another burial) that is anything but "plain" or plainly "human." Agency here needs to be rethought. In Lavinia's (or is it the earth's?) "dumb show," agency is un-moored from fixed (racialized) bodies and becomes an agency of the multiple—what Derrida playfully calls, in a word (*mot*), *animot*.[36] Instead of exhuming this word, this tomb that will not sustain the future, Lavinia's one "truth" is this: to urge us to become students of the illegible, to learn how to read the animal in our statements.

Notes

1 Donna Haraway, *The Companion Species Manifesto: Dogs, People, and Significant Otherness* (Chicago, IL: Prickly Paradigm Press, 2003), 14.

2 Jacques Derrida, "'Eating Well,' or the Calculation of the Subject," in *Points…Interviews, 1974–1994*, trans. Peter Connor and Avital Ronell and ed. Elisabeth Weber (Stanford, CA: Stanford University Press, 1995), 278.

3 Derrida, "'Eating Well,'" 280.
4 Ibid., 283.
5 Ibid., 282.
6 Ibid.
7 For a related discussion of early modern eating practices in *Titus Andronicus*, see David Goldstein's chapter, "The Cook and the Cannibal: *Titus Andronicus* and New World Eating," in *Eating and Ethics in Shakespeare's England* (Cambridge: Cambridge University Press, 2013), 32–66.
8 All quotations are taken from *The Riverside Shakespeare*, 2nd ed., eds. G. Blakemore Evans and J.J.M. Tobin. Citations refer to line numbers of the play and appear parenthetically in the body of the essay.
9 I derive the language of "becoming-animal" from Gilles Deleuze and Félix Guattari. "Becoming-animal" is never a "filiative" movement, they argue. "Becoming is certainly not imitating, or identifying with something," since this would leave the identity of the original (the "animal") intact (239). Rather, "the animal is defined … by populations that vary from milieu to milieu" (239). Not a metaphor, then, which would suggest an end-point to "becoming," but rather a metonymic process of endless substitution within a multiplicity. "A becoming-animal always involves a pack, a band, a population, a peopling, in short, a multiplicity" (239). See their chapter, "1730: Becoming-Intense, Becoming-Animal, Becoming-Imperceptible …," in *A Thousand Plateaus: Capitalism and Schizophrenia*, trans. Brian Massumi (Minneapolis: University of Minnesota Press, 1987). I return to Lavinia's becoming-animal at the end of this essay, in my discussion of the *animot*, which links human-animal-plant-earth in a non-filiative and futureless assemblage.
10 My reading of "animal rites" in Shakespeare's play draws on the work of Cary Wolfe's *Animal Rites: American Culture, the Discourse of Species, and Posthuman Theory* (Chicago, IL: University of Chicago Press, 2003). See as well Wolfe's essay, "Condors at the End of the World," in *After Extinction*, ed. Richard Grusin (Minneapolis: University of Minnesota Press, 2018). For a related account of early modern burial practices (though one with a strictly human focus), see Thomas W. Laqueur, *The Work of the Dead: A Cultural History of Mortal Remains* (Princeton, NJ: Princeton University Press, 2015).
11 "Ruminate, v." *OED Online*. June 2017. Oxford University Press (accessed January 7, 2018). I also direct the reader's attention to Elizabeth A. Wilson's trenchant work on the animacy of the gut in *Gut Feminism* (Durham, NC: Duke University Press, 2015). See in particular the chapter entitled "Underbelly." For a concise introduction to the propinquity of the stomach to psychological events in early modern discourse, see Michael Schoenfeldt, "Fables of the Belly in Early Modern England," in *The Body in Parts: Fantasies of Corporeality in Early Modern Europe*, eds. David Hillman and Carla Mazzio (New York: Routledge, 1997). Schoenfeldt claims it is because the belly serves as an interface for self and world that it "occupies a central site of ethical discrimination and devotional interiority in early modern culture" (244). The belly "assumed a position of particular importance in early modern regimes of mental and physical health," mediating "inwardness and materialism, soul and stomach," in a period in which "the Galenic regime of the humoral self demanded the invasion of social and psychological realms by biological and environmental processes" (244). See also Caroline Walker Bynum's classic, *Holy Feast and Holy Fast: The Religious Significance of Food to Medieval Women* (Berkeley: University of California Press, 1987), for a related account of the importance of eating to medieval spiritual practices.
12 Melanie Klein, "Weaning," in *Love, Guilt, and Reparation, and Other Works, 1921–1945* (New York: Free Press, 1975).
13 For an extended discussion of the formulation "living on," see Derrida's last interview, *Learning to Live Finally*, trans. Pascale-Anne Brault and Michael Nass (Hoboken, NJ: Melville House, 2007). In it, Derrida states: "I have always been interested in this theme of survival, the meaning of which is *not to be added on* to living and dying. It is originary: life *is* living on, life *is* survival [la vie *est* survie]" (26).
14 Here I reanimate Derrida's well-known theory of the supplement, which puts the integrity or the self-presence of the original under erasure, with an eye towards Derrida's later formulation regarding the animal in "The Animal that Therefore I Am," where the act of following shatters logocentric unities such as "the human" and "the animal" along multiple lines of difference.
15 In his *Foucault* book, Deleuze writes: "The outside is not a fixed limit but a moving matter animated by peristaltic movements, folds and foldings that together make up an inside" (96–97).

Here, the baroque fold becomes a figure for the peristalsis of the digestive tract, and vice versa. All of material life, so figured, becomes a peristaltic wave of contraction and release. See Deleuze, *Foucault*, trans. Seán Hand (Minneapolis: University of Minnesota Press, 1988), 96–97."

16   Of Derrida's many inquiries on the topic of "the animal," this question is perhaps the one that guides the rest, since it goes to the heart of human self-definition as beings who, unlike the rest of the animal kingdom, are aware of their finitude and so have a more "authentic" relationship to time as "being-towards-death" (as in Heidegger's philosophy). To this philosophical and collo-quial way of thinking about the animal's relationship to time, Derrida's response is devastating:

> instead of stopping with a mere confirmation of the Heideggerian diagnosis, which indeed sees in the whole tradition, from Aristotle to Hegel, a hegemony of the vulgar conception of time …, I oriented this very confirmation toward another suggestion…. What if there was no other concept of time than the one that Heidegger calls 'vulgar'? What if, consequently, opposing another concept to the 'vulgar' concept were itself impracticable, nonviable, and impossible? What if it was the same for death, for a vulgar concept of death?
>
> (14)

In short, what if there was no concept of time other than a "vulgar" concept of time? The wall separating "our" relationship to death from the animal would come crashing down. See Derrida, *Aporias*, trans. Thomas Dutoit (Stanford, CA: Stanford University Press, 1993), 14.

17   There has been a spate of recent work on Shakespeare and cognition. Representative examples include Mary Thomas Crane's *Shakespeare's Brain: Reading with Cognitive Theory* (Princeton, NJ: Princeton University Press, 2001); and Raphael Lyne's *Shakespeare, Rhetoric and Cognition* (Cambridge: Cambridge University Press, 2011). More recent work pushes for a theory of the *embodied* mind in Shakespeare, including Laurie Johnson et al.'s collection, *Embodied Cognition and Shakespeare's Theatre: The Early Modern Body-Mind* (New York: Routledge, 2014). Although the "cognitive turn" in Shakespeare studies is not my direct focus, I am cutting against the grain of that work by arguing for a theory of mind that is posthuman. That is, "mind" in my argument is not merely supported by the body, as in the embodied mind argument. More radi-cally, my claim is that Shakespeare's material landscape is already minded (without the supple-ment of the human mind-body). Shakespeare's earth *thinks*, it ruminates. To this end, I'm also thinking with Julia Reinhard Lupton's book, *Thinking with Shakespeare: Essays on Politics and Life* (Chicago, IL: Chicago University Press, 2011), which invites us to rethink Shakespearean politics from the ground up, as a way of life in the Arendtian sense. Although Lupton is not a posthumanist, her book provides useful entryways into thinking "politics" and "life" otherwise in Shakespeare.

18   Donna J. Haraway, *When Species Meet* (Minneapolis: University of Minnesota Press, 2008), 17, 31–32.

19   Lee Edelman, *No Future: Queer Theory and the Death Drive* (Durham, NC: Duke University Press, 2004), 33.

20   See Jacques Derrida, *The Animal that Therefore I Am*, trans. David Wills (New York: Fordham University Press, 2008). "In principle," Derrida writes,

> with the exception of man, no animal has ever thought to dress itself. Clothing would be proper to man, one of the 'properties' of man. 'Dressing oneself' would be inseparable from all the other figures of what is 'proper to man,' even if one talks about it less than speech or reason, the *logos*, history, laughing, mourning, burial, the gift, etc.
>
> (5)

21   Jacques Derrida, interview by Elisabeth Roudinesco, "Violence against Animals," in *For What Tomorrow … A Dialogue*, trans. Jeff Fort (Stanford, CA: Stanford University Press, 2004), 65.

22   Jacques Lacan, *The Seminar of Jacques Lacan, Book XI: The Four Fundamental Concepts of Psychoanal-ysis*, trans. Alan Sheridan (New York: Norton, 1977), 168.

23   Lacan, *The Four Fundamental Concepts of Psychoanalysis*, 167.

24   Ibid., 168. Notably, Lacan sees the drive as a force of unconscious repetition, and so upends the distinction between (mechanical, animal) repetition and (human) response, as defined by Derrida (Derrida, "Violence against Animals," 65). The human organism becomes both more machinic in Lacan's theory and less programmed as the animal-machine takes on the open-ended characteris-tics of the drive.

25 Sigmund Freud, *Beyond the Pleasure Principle*, trans. James Strachey (New York: Norton, 1961), 28–30.

26 See Luce Irigaray, "Plato's Hysteria," in *Speculum of the Other Woman*, trans. Gillian C. Gill (Ithaca, NY: Cornell University Press, 1985). For a "new materialist" reading of the *chora*, see Rebekah Sheldon, "Form/Matter/Chora: Object-Oriented Ontology and Feminist New Materialism," in *The Nonhuman Turn*, ed. Richard Grusin (Minneapolis: University of Minnesota Press, 2015).

27 On the language of "species" and "race" in early modern England, see Ania Loomba and Jonathan Burton's "Introduction," in *Race in Early Modern England: A Documentary Companion*, eds. Ania Loomba and Jonathan Burton (New York: Palgrave Macmillan, 2007); and Steven Swarbrick, "Shakespeare's Blush, or 'the Animal' in *Othello*," *Exemplaria* 28, no. 1 (2016): 70–85.

28 See Giorgio Agamben, *Homo Sacer: Sovereign Power and Bare Life*, trans. Daniel Heller-Roazen (Stanford, CA: Stanford University Press, 1998).

29 The language of "shadows" and shadowing should also be read in connection with the history of racial performance on the early modern stage. As Ian Smith argues, "in the theater of racial cross-dressing, claiming that the materials of staging confer meaning takes on a radically perverse sense," since the "materials" for staging blackness confer an absent or ghostly presence (4). "The prosthetic black cloth" used by actors to simulate black skin "covers and masks the body beneath; its primary function is to materialize the imagined and absent real black subject and to give *it* [the cloth] meaning" (4). Shadows, then, as I employ the word in its dramatic sense, double also for the spectralized appearance that blackness makes on the early modern stage. See Ian Smith, "Othello's Black Handkerchief," *Shakespeare Quarterly* 64, no. 1 (2013): 1–25.

30 Throughout this essay, I draw on Karen Barad's language of "agential realism," which foregrounds the primacy of the cut in material relations. For Barad,

> the primary ontological unit is not independent objects with inherent boundaries and properties but rather *phenomena*. In my agential realist elaboration, phenomena do not merely mark the epistemological inseparability of observer and observed, or the results of measurements; rather, *phenomena are the ontological inseparability/entanglement of intra-acting 'agencies.'* That is, phenomena are ontologically primitive relations—relations without preexisting relata.
>
> (139)

The relata in question (human/animal, black/white, self/other) are not self-contained units; they are constituted in and by agential cuts, and these cuts are radically contingent—that is, open to revision and re-cutting. See Barad, *Meeting the Universe Halfway: Quantum Physics and the Entanglement of Matter and Meaning* (Durham, NC: Duke University Press, 2007).

31 For an illuminating analysis of the material agency of "meat" in the early modern period, one that builds on the performative materialism of Karen Barad and Jane Bennett and sheds important light on the animal's incipient relation to food, see Karen Raber, "Animals at the Table: Performing Meat in Early Modern England and Europe," in *Performing Animals: History, Agency, Theater*, eds. Karen Raber and Monica Mattfeld (University Park: Penn State University Press, 2017), 14–27.

32 See Gail Kern Paster, *Humoring the Body: Emotions and the Shakespearean Stage* (Chicago, IL: University of Chicago Press, 2004).

33 One could fruitfully read this moment of the play in conjunction with Mary Floyd-Wilson's account of "geohumoralism" in early modern England. See Floyd-Wilson, *English Ethnicity and Race in Early Modern Drama* (Cambridge: Cambridge University Press, 2003).

34 See Alexander G. Weheliye, *Habeas Viscus: Racializing Assemblage, Biopolitics, and Black Feminist Theories of the Human* (Durham, NC: Duke University Press, 2014). Weheliye's stated goal in *Habeas Viscus* is to reorient the field of biopolitics by challenging Michel Foucault's and Giorgio Agamben's theorizations of population management and bare life, which tend to leave out racialization as a biopolitical determinate. Through the lens of black studies and, in particular, the black feminist writings of Hortense Spillers and Sylvia Wynter, Weheliye foregrounds the racialized specificity of biopolitical definitions of the human. Here I would add that although Weheliye does not directly consider the weather or climate as assemblages, they undoubtedly play an important role in the racializing assemblages he describes. See, for example, Foucault's early formulation of biopower as it displaces sovereign power within a broader climatic "milieu" of elemental forces:

> [T]he sovereign is no longer someone who exercises his power over a territory on the basis of a geographical localization of his political sovereignty. The sovereign deals with a nature, or rather with the perpetual conjunction, the perpetual intrication of a geographical, climatic,

and physical milieu with the human species insofar as it has a body and a soul, a physical and a moral existence; and the sovereign will be someone who will have to exercise power at that point of connection where nature, in the sense of physical elements, interferes with nature in the sense of the nature of the human species, at that point of articulation where the milieu becomes the determining factor of nature.

(*Security, Territory, Population: Lectures at the College de France*, 1977–1978, trans. Graham Burchell [New York: Picador, 2007], 23)

35 My coinage "species melancholia" is a direct adaptation of the better-known phrase "racial melancholia," which David L. Eng and Shinhee Han have popularized in their essay, "A Dialogue on Racial Melancholia," *Psychoanalytic Dialogues* 10, no. 4 (2000): 667–700. See also Anne Anlin Cheng, *The Melancholy of Race: Psychoanalysis, Assimilation, and Hidden Grief* (New York: Oxford University Press, 2001); David L. Eng's work on race and psychoanalysis in *Racial Castration: Managing Masculinity in Asian America* (Durham, NC: Duke University Press, 2001); Frantz Fanon's early account of racial melancholia in *Black Skin, White Masks* (New York: Grove Press, 2008); and José Esteban Muñoz, *Disidentifications: Queers of Color and the Performance of Politics* (Minneapolis: University of Minnesota Press, 1999). By "species melancholia," I mean to highlight the cross-hatched relations among species differences and racial differences in Shakespeare's play.

36 The word *animot*, when spoken aloud, can be heard in both the plural (*animaux*) and the singular. "Neither a species nor a gender nor an individual," Derrida writes, "[the *animot*] is an irreducible living multiplicity of mortals, and rather than a double clone or a portmanteau word, a sort of monstrous hybrid, a chimera" (*The Animal that Therefore I Am*, 41).

21

"WHAT'S THIS? WHAT'S THIS?"

Fish and Sexuality in *Measure for Measure*

Robert Wakeman

The nameless Amphibian Man in Guillermo del Toro's *The Shape of Water* just may have been the most inevitable sex symbol of 2017. Played by Doug Jones as a strong, silent type tinged with exogamous fetishism, the Amphibian Man's costume was designed to emphasize the creature's wide shoulders and broad chest; his doting puppy dog eyes and soft lips; and, of course, his spectacular butt. At the same time, as one pop culture writer notes, this creature also appears to be "as smooth as a Ken doll."[1] The beautifully statuesque Amphibian Man is thus presented as sexually desirable without initially appearing to be a sexual creature himself. But that smooth exterior belies his desire for his human lover Elisa (Sally Hawkins). When her confidant Zelda (Octavia Spencer) inquires about the mechanics of their sexual relationship, Elisa mimes penile eversion. Zelda shakes her head: "Never trust a man, even if he looks flat down there."

This asexual facade obscuring rampant desire recalls the Lenten setting of Shakespeare's *Measure for Measure*. In a sexually repressed Catholic Vienna, many of the characters struggle to come to terms with erotic feelings amid the tyrannical regime. In this politically conservative setting, where "strict statutes and most biting laws" (1.3.19) discourage sexual self-knowledge, characters use fish and fishing metaphors to connote practices that both adhere to and deviate from what the morality codes command. Where carnality is met with disapproval, attending to fish imagery allows us to investigate how Shakespeare negotiates between the lurid and the chaste, between virtuous sexuality—even abstinent asexuality— and reprobate sexualities.

The complexity of fish imagery becomes especially apparent in Act 3 when the libertine Lucio tells us that the puritanical magistrate Angelo "was not made by man and woman after this downright way of creation." Angelo's "too crabbed" inhumanity must be, so Lucio believes, the result of some other procreative process: "Some report a sea-maid spawned him; some that he was begot between two stockfishes" (3.1.350–54). *Stockfish* is the term for dried and salted gadiforms, the family of piscivorous groundfish including cod, haddock, pollock, and whiting which once dominated the fishing banks of the North Atlantic and which were the bedrock of the Lenten diet in Shakespeare's England. Leaner than salmon, herring, or mackerel, gadiforms are also prized for their white color, which signified a relative bloodlessness to Renaissance dieticians. By suggesting Angelo's nature results from something other than hot-blooded heterosexual reproduction, Lucio insinuates an absence of potency

Fish and Sexuality in Measure for Measure

in the magistrate's body. Instead of "urine" and, presumably, semen, Angelo only excretes "congealed ice" (3.1.345–56).[2] This should make him the perfect deputy to impose severity on Vienna's "headstrong jades" because he is not a beast of the land. Angelo's fishified body, cold and shriveled, stiff and bloodless, is supposed to be depleted of desire and devoid of the drive to create life.

Does Angelo's behavior contradict Shakespeare's other representations of fishy impotence and Shakespeare's figuration of fish as feminized sexual objects ripe for assault? Or does sexual aggression not depend on the passions of warm-blooded beasts? Angelo's similarity to stockfish links him to a host of Shakespeare characters teased or taunted for their "sexual aridity."[3] If his fishlike qualities already suggest a lack of masculinity, then being called a dried fish further implies Angelo's impotence. When Lucio further assures the disguised Duke Vincentio that Angelo is an "ungenitur'd agent [who] will unpeople the province with continency" (3.1.409–10), he recalls Falstaff's bawdy insults directed towards young Prince Hal in *Henry IV, Part 1*: "you starveling, you [eel-]skin, you dried neat's tongue, you bull's pizzle, you stock-fish!" (2.4.224–25). This litany of emaciated flesh alleges that Hal is bloodless, limp, and impotent. Likewise, in *Romeo and Juliet*, Mercutio puns on the Montague scion's impotence:

BENVOLIO: Here comes Romeo! Here comes Romeo!
MERCUTIO: Without his roe, like a dried herring. O flesh, flesh, how art thou fishified!
(2.3.34–36)

According to Gayle Whittier, this passage, like all of Mercutio's bawdy, implies that Romeo's romantic pursuits have "forgotten the flesh." With his head stuck in the clouds of Petrarchan idealism, Romeo is chastised for lacking the red-blooded bravado valued by the other young men of Verona.[4] As Dan Brayton puts it, "A dead fish is a limp thing, and Romeo's lovesickness has, in Mercutio's view, weakened and feminized him, rendering him a poor substitute for the piece of man-flesh he once was."[5] *Romeo and Juliet*'s boastful male wits invoke poor-john for their sexual heckling. Poor-john is cod, or another gadiform that is not dried before it is salted. This makes poor-john equally as emaciated as stockfish, but not as stiff. When, in the opening scene, Samson boasts of his sexual exploits, Gregory badgers him with the unflattering comparison:

SAMSON: Me they shall feel while I am able to stand, and 'tis known I am a pretty piece of flesh.
GREGORY: 'Tis well thou art not fish; if thou hadst, thou hadst been Poor John.
(1.1.26–29)

In these plays, fish imagery is used to describe male bodies drained of capacity for heterosexual reproduction. But, at the same time, this imagery is deployed to maintain the potency of patriarchal sexual power that commodifies women and cheapens virtue. Unlike Shakespearean lovers likened to virile animals such as cocks or bulls, these piscine men are portrayed as not living up to their sexual potential. As Gail Kern Paster has shown, Shakespearean men controlled by cold and wet humors are biologically inferior to the hot and dry male ideal.[6] Fishified flesh is insufficiently animal *and* insufficiently male.

Describing Angelo as a stockfish may suggest that while he is still an animal he deprives himself of all animal passions through rituals of mortification. Like Oliver Cob in Jonson's *Every Man in His Humor* who worries Lenten fasting has made him more fish than man, the

Viennese of *Measure for Measure* suppose that you are what you eat: a diet of stockfish will repress natural lust *and* will transform the body into something cold, infertile, and fishlike. The dried eel, ling, and cod that were staples on fast days are phallic creatures that have been emaciated by salting or air drying. Both symbolically and dietetically, heavy consumption of fish should shrivel a consumer and starve him of desire; yet, Angelo still finds himself given to licentiousness.

Beneath heavy habits and the robes of office lurks what Derek Traversi calls *Measure for Measure*'s "preoccupation with the flesh."[7] Despite abstinent Angelo and novitiate Isabella's chaste exteriors, scholars detect passionate intimations in their language which feeds the play's disturbing sexual dynamic. Even when the play suggests that the principal characters desist from all manner of flesh, their fish imagery attains an erotic inflection. The intensity of this language may support the argument that Angelo's dispassionate nature is only "outward-sainted" (3.1.88). Carolyn Brown argues that the play never implies Angelo's sexual desire is absent, only distorted. In her reading, Angelo's piscine body has undertones of erotic flagellation, since curing stockfish meant beating them with rods or clubs:

> Lucio … intimates that Angelo subjects himself to rigorous mortification to kill his desires. Angelo "rebate[s] and blunt[s] his natural edge" [1.4.61], with "rebates" denoting "to beat out" and suggesting self-abusive practices, much like the self-flagellating techniques commonly practiced by religious devotees.[8]

Lucio's role as the play's sexologist continues when he diagnoses Angelo to be a "motion generative" (3.1.356). While this phrase has caused considerable editorial and critical consternation, Brown maintains that Lucio is defining "Angelo as a sexual 'thing,' abnormal though Angelo's sexuality may be."[9] Angelo's sexual desires may be congealed as ice, but Lucio evidently believes "the vice [of lechery] is of a great kindred, it is well allied; but it is impossible to extirp[ate] it quite … till eating and drinking be put down" (3.1.347–49).

According to this logic, a sexual drive is a natural consequence of the necessity of eating; because all animals are motivated by food and drink, an asexual animal would be a contradiction in terms. Apparently, it would simply be impossible to be a living creature and not feel the pull of sexual desire. This explains Brown's diagnosis of a "malignancy" among the Viennese ascetics and an "undercurrent of a tainted sexuality in all of the characters" who abstain from sex: Duke Vincentio, Angelo, and Isabella.[10] Each of these characters, and not just those who participate in the underworld sex economy, partakes in what Brown calls the "ubiquitous imagery of a diseased sexuality" and the "aberrant, dark carnality" of *Measure for Measure*.[11]

In the second act, Isabella pleads for the life of her brother, sentenced to die for transgressing Vienna's morality laws, but Angelo only offers lenience in exchange for sexual favors, demanding that she "Give up [her] body to such sweet uncleanness" (2.4.53). Angelo stresses that his power and position, "My unsoil'd name, the austereness of my life, / My vouch against you, and my place i' the state" (2.4.152–53), will discredit Isabella should she publicize an account of his intimidation. The full details of Angelo's harassment are only disclosed to two other characters, Isabella's brother Claudio and Duke Vincentio who is disguised as Claudio's confessor. Claudio initially denies what Isabella tells him; he exclaims "O heavens, it cannot be" (3.1.98), and questions whether Angelo is even capable of such an act: "Has he affections in him, that thus can make him bite the law by th' nose when he would force it?" (3.1.107–9). But by the next line Claudio not only accepts what he has been told, he dismisses Angelo's action as too general a vice to be considered criminal: "Sure it is no sin, / Or of the deadly seven it is the least" (3.1.109–110). For his part, the Duke readily believes Isabella and describes Angelo's menacing behavior as "assault" (3.1.151).[12]

But rather than reading *Measure for Measure* as a play about procuring illicit flesh, perhaps we should bear in mind the constellation of fish imagery in Shakespeare's works and rethink the sexuality of the "cod" in the play's "rebellion of a codpiece" (3.1.358–59).[13] Although Lucio's description of Angelo as a stockfish denies both his humanity and his bestiality, the magistrate is still as given to rottenness as any of Vienna's warm-blooded creatures. Therein lies the complex signification of fish in Shakespeare's plays: although early modern English diets incorporated large amounts of dried fish as a cheap alternative to meat, they are prone to stinking. Thus, like the codpiece, that peculiar men's fashion that accentuated male sex organs by obscuring them, references to Angelo's piscine chastity only highlight his fishy perversity. In *Measure for Measure*, it is the virtuous body that putrefies the worst, and Angelo smells his "fault":

> What's this, what's this? Is this her fault or mine? / The tempter or the tempted, who sins most, ha? / Not she, nor doth she tempt. But it is I / That, lying by the violet in the sun, / Do as the carrion does, not as the flower, / Corrupt with virtuous season.
>
> *(2.2.165–70)*

As Dan Brayton reminds us, these plays overflow with fish imagery that is rarely straightforward:

> In coded metaphors and allusions that too often go overlooked, Shakespeare transmuted the reeking remains of the herring, pilchard, eels, whiting, cod, and sprat that he knew so well into a dramatic world that owes some of its pungency to its maritime nature.[14]

While some dietary guides praised fresh fish, most maintained that fish were not very nutritious and only served as a cheap substitute for meat. Comparatively cold and wet according to humoral physiology, fish produced a phlegmatic disposition. This zoological understanding of marine life is appropriated by Shakespeare's bawdy men who often associate women with fish to indicate a lack of enthusiasm for sex. For example, in *The Winter's Tale*, Autolycus hawks the ballad of a "woman … turned into a cold fish, for she would not exchange flesh with one that loved her" (4.4.268–69). Given their reputation for dampening passionate urges, dried fish are the perfect dish for fast days. However, as food historian Ken Albala notes, physicians also warned "against the dangers of eating fish, a watery food prone to corruption."[15] Angelo's fishy sexuality may initially seem contradictory, but he turns out to be as prone to aggression as any of Shakespeare's warm-blooded animals. In addition to suppressing sexuality, fish consumption's role in the fast also reminded the faster of the body's degeneracy. Indeed, as Brayton argues, the ever-present smell of the fish trade along the Thames acted as a kind of fetid memento mori: "The presence of fish in the social body is uncanny, evoking a universal plasticity of matter that bears a whiff of death…. All is vendible; all is corruptible; mortality is a theater of fish."[16]

While stockfish and poor-john were fit food for Lent in early modern England, many other sea creatures ambiguously straddle the line between fasting food and aphrodisiac. Drained of blood, of *anima*, dried fish are not beastly, but animals they remain, serving as powerful signifiers for a range of early modern sexual practices. Seafood still does today: just as sashimi and sushi have today, oysters and clams had sex appeal.[17] The sensory experiences of consuming raw fish have connoted coitus for authors from Aristophanes to Herman Melville to Eve Ensler.[18] Even if Angelo's submarine sexuality seems impossibly removed from human experience, the pull of the deep remains tantalizingly alive. Frigid and bloodless as its creatures might be, what is more ravenously, passionately hungry than the ocean?[19]

Oysters, clams, cockles, and mussels are the most obvious examples of early modern aphrodisiac sea food: all were appropriate for fast days, but each came with a sexual charge. Several other examples of erotic fish idioms are found in Eric Partridge's classic book *Shakespeare's Bawdy*, although his examples can often be quite opaque. Take, for example, Iago's advice to avoid "chang[ing] the cod's head for the salmon's tail" (*Othello* 2.1.151). Partridge calls this "a difficult phrase," even if we accept that *cod's head* stands for the penis and *salmon's tail* refers to the vulva. As he works out the algebra of Shakespeare's innuendos, Partridge admits,

> Occasionally it is almost impossible to determine the exact sense of Shakespeare's sexual witticisms: but, the subtlety and highly developed nature of his sexuality being incontrovertible, we should be ignorant – and stupid – to think that there is no sexual witticism [in Iago's gnomic proverb].[20]

As important as it has been for editors of Shakespeare, Partridge's famous glossary has been challenged on a number of fronts. For instance, while Partridge associates eels and cod with the penis, he interprets "ling" to be "indubitably allusive to the female genitals" because, I quote, the "fish is slimy."[21] Partridge's example for "ling" as "pudenda" comes from *All's Well That Ends Well*: "Our old lings and our Isbels o'th' country are nothing like your old ling and your Isbels o'th' court" (3.2.12–14). However, many editors gloss "ling" in this passage as "salt cod," that is, "penis," instead. Valerie Traub is among those who have complicated Partridge's conclusions, noting that when editors attempt to gloss the fishy erotics of early modern literature, they routinely point "to the reputed resemblance between shellfish and female genitals [and] the early modern use of shellfish as an aphrodisiac."[22] But while Traub acknowledges the suggestive possibilities of the figurative language, she maintains that anatomical explanations always require some leaps of imagination, some mixing of metaphors, and embracing spirit over sense. Traub writes of the

> difficulty and obscurity of sex as a rich epistemological resource – as a heuristic with which to think as well as act. The obstacles we face in *making* sexual history can be used to illuminate the difficulty of *knowing* sexuality; and both impediments might be adopted as a guiding principle of historiography and pedagogy. *Sex may be good to think with, not because it permits us access, but because it doesn't.*[23]

Said another way: to a third party, sex, much less sexual assault, is difficult to name. Sexual assault is defined as a reasonable feeling of intimidation, a state of duress. Although no less real, a feeling, a climate, a state cannot be held in the hand. Unlike sexual battery, which is a crime against the body, sexual assault is a crime against the mind.

Again and again, the play imagines sexuality to be an animal force that lurks at a remove from human reason, even consciousness. As Angelo listens to Isabella's plea for mercy on behalf of Claudio, he puns in an aside on the dual meaning of "sense" as both her good reasoning and his sensory stimulation: "She speaks, and 'tis / Such sense, that my sense breeds with it" (2.2.142–43). Turned on by her pathos, or perhaps her vulnerability, Angelo's "breeding" desire sounds almost as much like the symptom of an alien infestation as it does the natural proclivity of an aroused beast. It should be the opposite, thinks Angelo; reason should tame

Fish and Sexuality in Measure for Measure

passion. But despite the tyrannical crackdown on copulation outside the heterosexual confines of marriage, the underworld characters insist that life still finds a way. The patrons and proprietors of the brothel imagine a kind of reproductive biological determinism at odds with the regulatory politics of sexual moralism. When told bawds will not be allowed in Vienna, Pompey questions the efficacy of the law over the sexual behavior of the citizens: "Does your worship mean to geld and splay all the youth of the city?" (2.1.209–10). Later, Lucio doubles down on his complaints against the tyrannical crackdown on lechery, insisting that the ungoverned and ungovernable autonomy of the male sex organs must be excused: "what a ruthless thing is this in [Angelo], for the rebellion of a codpiece to take away the life of a man!" (3.2.114–16). According to this strand of thought, the fault for sexual indiscretion lies beyond human reason. The fault lies with the codpiece, not with the man.

This strand of thought is evident in the criticism as well. R.A. Foakes argues that Isabella and Angelo, "lacking a sense of proportion, or a sense of humor," would be "healthier" if they did not "shrink from the demands of the flesh."[24] And, in Arthur Quiller-Couch's estimation, *Measure for Measure* explores how "unless restrained by law and the decencies of a social code, our most natural impulses wallow in excess, which is flat sin."[25] And, although he acknowledges it is "subtly disturbing," Robert N. Watson detects an essential biological "function" that seems to operate beyond or outside human consciousness in the play. When it comes to the substitution of Mariana for Isabella in the bed trick, or Barnardine for Claudio at the executioners' block, "from the perspective of nature or the state, in the function of biology or politics, indifference makes perfect sense. Any body will do."[26]

Amid this atmosphere of sexuality alienated from self-knowledge, Carolyn Brown understands Angelo's behavior to be that of an individual with a psychological affliction: "Shakespeare portrays him compassionately as a deeply agitated man, similar to living, troubled saints.… That Angelo conflates physical desires with brutality is betrayed by his heightened viciousness once he is sexually aroused."[27] If Angelo's flaws are the result of a view of sexuality distorted by asceticism, then critics view Isabella in much the same way. Referring to Isabella's role in the bed trick, Arthur Quiller-Couch claims she is

> something rancid in her chastity; and, on top of this, not by any means such a saint as she looks. To put it nakedly, she is all for saving her own soul, and she saves it by turning, of a sudden, into a bare procuress.[28]

Because Isabella and Angelo resist self-identification as sexual creatures, *Measure for Measure* raises questions regarding whether cold-blooded animals have a biological compulsion to procreate. Anxious surprise is clearly evident in the moment when the supposedly frigid Angelo feels his blood flow: "Why does my blood thus muster to my heart, / Making both it unable for itself, / And dispossessing all my other parts / Of necessary fitness?" (2.4.20–23). Angelo's self-diagnosis serves as attempted absolution as he suggests that he is not in control of his "parts." This concept has complicated histories of sexual violence: "ravishment" was the term in late medieval and early modern England "that described involuntary, but usually pleasurable, sensory, sexual, or religious epiphanies experienced by humans." As Holly Dugan has shown, the declaration of an involuntary action was a defense against charges of "rape in socio-legal contexts."[29] Following the argument of Frances Dolan, Dugan asks, "What might it mean … to understand sexual violence outside of the legal categories of victim and perpetrator and to engage instead with messier narratives of coercion and compulsion, narratives that remind us of the ways in which we are 'continually expanding and revising our understanding of what rape is and thus what its history might include.'"[30] Legally speaking, it may strictly be true, as David Thatcher argues, that Angelo has not violated any of the Duke's laws because "Angelo has not really slept with Isabella, and unlike Claudio, he has not made a woman pregnant out of wedlock. In fact, Angelo has not sinned sexually at all."[31] This appears to be Isabella's conclusion, emphasized when she asks the Duke to spare Angelo's life in the play's final 100 lines:

> My brother had but justice, / In that he did the thing for which he died, / For Angelo, his act did not o'ertake his bad intent / And must be buried but as an intent / That perished by the way. Thoughts are no subjects, / Intents but merely thoughts.
>
> *(5.1.451–56)*

But as Dugan makes clear, there is, in both the history of literature and the history of criticism, "a seemingly intransigent belief in sex that is knowable and desire that is culpable, regardless of sharp epistemic, historical, and cultural shifts around how we define rape [and sexual assault], its victims, and its history."[32] This makes the "law" and "legality" a poor foundation for baseline sexual morality.

In the murky waters of sexual innuendo, Shakespeare uses fish imagery can be used to figure sexual assault in ways that are too subtle, too slippery for the narrow letter of the law. In particular, *fishing* abounds as a metaphor for sexual misconduct in Shakespeare's plays.

These images frequently imply duplicity, entrapment, and struggling against fate on the hooked line. King Leontes, in *The Winter's Tale*, worries that "his pond [is] fished by his next neighbor" (1.2.194). In Act 2 of *Antony and Cleopatra*, the Queen of Egypt calls for her

> angle. We'll to th' river. There, / My music playing far off, I will betray / Tawny-finned fishes. My bended hook shall pierce / Their slimy jaws, and as I draw them up, / I'll think them every one an Antony / And say, "Aha! You're caught!"

Cleopatra's attendant Charmian responds: "Twas merry when / You wagered on your angling, when your diver / Did hang a salt fish on his hook which he / With fervency drew up" (2.5.10–18). More good-natured is Ursula in *Much Ado About Nothing* who endeavors to trick her kinswoman Beatrice to fall in love with Benedict: "The pleasantest angling is to see the fish / Cut with her golden oars the silver stream / And greedily devour the treacherous bait" (3.1.26–28). Significantly, these are not metaphors about the animal passions, but metaphors for the deceptiveness of sexual politics. The language of angling suggests an imminent betrayal of the hungry fish, as in the case of *Twelfth Night*'s plot to dupe Malvolio; when the spoilsport steward is seen approaching, Maria ushers her coconspirators away: "Lie thou there, for here comes the trout that must be caught with tickling" (2.5.18–19). Catching a wild trout with only one's hands requires a unique level of intimacy between predator and prey followed by sudden treachery. To tickle a trout, the poacher slowly places his or her hands into the water and waits to feel the caress of the fish hidden between the rocks; along the belly and gills, the trout is petted gently into a lull, not sensing the danger as the hands move into position. And then the poacher strikes, grabbing the trout with two hands and wrenching it from the water. *Measure for Measure* is also a play about "Groping for trouts in a peculiar river" (1.2.82), but in this play the image is a much darker shadow of Maria's fish tickler. Pompey uses this metaphor when asked which law against sexual misconduct has been violated by Claudio. Ultimately, however, it is not Claudio but Angelo who emerges as the play's figure of criminal sexual poaching.

Fish and Sexuality in Measure for Measure

Angelo, apparently surprised at his sexual arousal upon meeting Isabella, initially suspects something diabolical at work: "O cunning enemy [i.e., Satan], that to catch a saint / With saints dost bait thy hook" (2.2.182–83). Three scenes later, Isabella seems to reverse the image as she discloses Angelo's advances to Claudio:

> This outward-sainted deputy, / Whose settled visage and deliberate word / Nips youth i'th' head, and follies doth enew / As falcon doth fowl, is yet a devil. / His filth within being cast, he would appear a pond as deep as hell.
>
> *(3.1.88–93)*

While "cast" here means "spewed forth," it seems to me that Shakespeare intentionally conjures again the image of a fishing line: whereas Angelo believes Satan baits him with the pure Isabella, Isabella sees the devilish Angelo luring her with filth. Even as he imagines himself the fishlike victim of his own desires, Angelo lecherously casts his lure, recalling John Donne's extended comparison of fishing to rape in his 1601 poem *The Progresse of the Soule*:

> Is any kinde subject to rape like fish?
> Ill unto man, they neither doe, nor wish:
> Fishers they kill not, nor with noise awake,
> They doe not hunt, nor strive to make a prey
> Of beasts, nor their young sonnes to bear away;
> Foules they pursue not, nor do undertake
> To spoile the nests industrious birds do make;
> Yet them all these unkinde kinds feed upon,
> To kill them is an occupation,
> And lawes make Fasts, and Lents for their destruction.
>
> *(281–90)*[33]

This stanza likens fish to victims of sexual coercion, but the ambiguous grammar of the first sentence also hints at the piscivorous, cannibalistic qualities of some predatory fish such as cod. They may not make prey of the beasts of the land, but they do feed on their fellow sea creatures. While critics tend to read Angelo's Catholic fishiness as likening his chastity to attempted godliness, it also likens him to the monstrous. As Martha Widmayer puts it, "Angelo seeks to be godly – or godlike. So extreme is the deputy's denial of the flesh that, to Lucio, he is not human."[34] However, he is no angel, but an angler.

According to the natural histories of the sixteenth century, several "outward-sainted" fish lurked in the early modern North Atlantic. In his encyclopedic *L'histoire entière des poissons* (1558), the French physician and naturalist Guillaume Rondelet reports on a "monstre marin en habit de Moine" ["*sea monster in a monk's habit*"] that was caught off the Norwegian coast and a "Monstre marine en habit d'Euesque" ["*sea monster in the habit of a bishop*"] taken in Polish waters.[35] Fanciful or satirical pictorial representations of these specimens circulated in the natural histories of sixteenth-century Europe; they were shown to have the faces of men, mitered or tonsured heads, tails, and fins styled like capuchins or cassocks. Stephen Batman seems to have had Rondelet's sea monsters in mind when he lists "the Monke fish, the Frier, and *Hippotamus*" along with mermaids as "diuers fishes [that] pray vpon man."[36] Although impossible to identify definitively, Rondelet's oceanic monk and bishop, if they existed at all, might have actually been angelsharks (*Squatina squatina*) or members of the *Lophiidae* family of anglerfish such as the nightmarish monkfish (*Lophius piscatorius*).[37] Other species of anglerfish [*mari piscatrix*] were well-known to Pliny; they are so named because they lure prey with wormlike filament that grows out of the dorsal fin spine.[38] Similarly, as Izaak Walton

277

explains, the mitered cuttlefish hunts its prey with a specialized tentacle "like as an Angler doth his line…. and for this reason some have called this fish the Sea-Angler."[39] Clearly, ancient and early modern naturalists found many varieties of sea creatures to be as treacherous as the sexual predators stalking ashore.

When the fantastical Lucio invokes the alien sexual practices of fish to describe Angelo, he may mean to imply the magistrate's asexuality, but he may also suggest that, like the monsters of the sea, Angelo's sexuality does not match his idea of the "downright way of creation." According to Pliny's *Natural History*, the sex lives of fish inspire "curiosity and wonder." While Pliny writes that most fish "couple by rubbing their bellies together so quickly as to escape the sight," he also lists sea creatures produced through spontaneous generation in "rotting mud" (oysters and frogfish), fishes that both lay eggs and give birth live young (certain species of ray), and species said to be able to impregnate themselves.[40] Although unknown to Pliny and to Shakespeare, deeper in the ocean there are even more unthinkable sexualities. As Stacy Alaimo has recently described, "The violet-black depths – cold, dark regions under the crushing weight of the water column – were long thought to be 'azoic,' or devoid of life." In the 1840s, the British naturalist Edward Forbes dismissed the bathypelagic, abyssopelagic, and hadal zones (respectively, 1000, 3000, and 5000 meters below the surface), to be "inert and irrelevant" to marine ecology.[41] But by the end of the nineteenth century, a series of deep-sea dredgings had brought to light a host of previously unknown creatures from the alien depths. Even more nightmarish than the monkfish are the peculiar species living at these depths, including 25 species of anglerfish that practice sexual parasitism, the ultimate representation of Lucio's claim that sex will not be extirpated as long as there is a need to eat. Males among these species of anglerfish do not have the jaws, nor the bioluminescent lures that their female counterparts use to hunt. Instead, a male anglerfish must attach itself to the belly of a mate with whom it will exchange blood, nutrients, and semen for the rest of its life.[42] About as far removed from human experience as is possible on this planet, the challenges of reproduction in the icy reaches of the ocean make clear that sexuality is always something that is difficult to know, much less arrest and subdue; for humans as much as for other animals, sexuality is ceaselessly developing in response to the challenges of its environments.

At the same time, however, I want to take seriously the implications that Angelo's possible sexual aridity has for the sexual politics of Vienna. The compulsory heterosexuality of *Measure for Measure* is not the inevitable result of biological needs, as the play's characters Lucio and Pompey claim, and as critics such as Brown, Foakes, and Quiller-Couch maintain. Instead, it develops from the stiffened will to dominate among those invested with power.[43] A male heterosexual reproductive drive is not necessary in order to commit sexual assault, certainly not when the full force of the law can be wielded in place of a phallus. Brown's reading depends on the idea that Isabella's and Angelo's

> sexuality and their cruelty are interrelated, the saints correlating sexual pleasure with mental and physical pain…. Shakespeare suggests that the protagonists' very asceticism, ironically, causes this deviant desire and that they associate their austere religious practices with pleasurable feelings. Their painful self-abnegation compels them to correlate pain with gratification.[44]

Certainly, Brown is *not* implying that in a world without painful self-abnegation there wouldn't be sexual assault, but I believe it is also incumbent upon us to recognize that sexual aggression is not dependent on sexual attraction, nor a desire to procreate.

In the final scene, Duke Vincentio denounces Angelo for possessing a "salt imagination" (5.1.403). "Salt," in this context, is etymologically akin to "salacious," and Elizabethan and Jacobean authors frequently used the word to describe lecherous behavior.[45] But the other sense seems resonant, too; Angelo may expect his salted flesh to cure his salt imagination, but when he plunges into the ocean depths, into a "pond as deep as hell," he only finds darker desires.

Notes

1 Elahe Izadi, "Admit It: You Want to Know the Deal with the 'Shape of Water' Fish Sex," *Washington Post*, March 5, 2018. www.washingtonpost.com/news/arts-and-entertainment/wp/2018/03/05/admit-it-you-want-to-know-the-deal-with-the-shape-of-water-fish-sex/?utm_term=.35d5f-9da70ec. Director and writer Guillermo del Toro seems to have imagined his Amphibian Man as a response to the Gill-Man from Jack Arnold's *Creature from the Black Lagoon* (1954): whereas the Gill-Man stalks and murders Amazonian explorers, the Amphibian Man is chained and tortured by the American military; the Gill-Man is a rapacious voyeur who kidnaps Kay (Julie Adams), while the Amphibian Man and Elisa practice enthusiastic consent using rudimentary sign language during their budding interspecies romance.
2 All citations from Shakespeare are from *The Norton Shakespeare*, 3rd ed., ed. Stephen Greenblatt (New York: W.W. Norton, 2016).
3 Dan Brayton, *Shakespeare's Ocean: An Ecocritical Exploration* (Charlottesville: University of Virginia Press, 2012), 155.
4 Gayle Whittier, "The Sonnet's Body and the Body Sonnetized in 'Romeo and Juliet,'" *Shakespeare Quarterly* 40, no. 1 (Spring, 1989): 27–41, 34.
5 Brayton, *Shakespeare's Ocean*, 145.
6 Gail Kern Paster, "The Unbearable Coldness of Female Being: Women's Imperfection and the Humoral Economy," *English Literary Renaissance* 28, no. 3 (Autumn, 1998): 416–40, 416. In Act 2, Lucio urges Isabella to flirt with Angelo to win Claudio's pardon, twice chastising her for being "too cold" (2.2.46, 56).
7 Derek A. Traversi, *An Approach to Shakespeare*, 3rd ed. (New York: Doubleday, 1969), 364.
8 Carolyn E. Brown, "Erotic Religious Flagellation and Shakespeare's 'Measure for Measure,'" *English Literary Renaissance* 16, no. 1 (Winter, 1986): 139–65, 143.
9 Brown, "Erotic Religious Flagellation," 152.
10 Ibid., 139.
11 Although many critics have explored the similarities between Angelo and Isabella, Brown admits that she sees their sexuality much more "darkly" than other readers. Brown, "Erotic Religious Flagellation," 139–40.
12 Angelo's threat means not that "Angelo attempts a sexual assault," as Daniel Juan Gil puts it, but, rather, that he actually commits assault. Cf. *OED*, "assault, *n.* 3": "An unlawful attack upon the person of another. (In *Law* a menacing word or action is sufficient to constitute an *assault*, the term *battery* being technically added when an actual blow is inflicted.)" The *Oxford English Dictionary* cites *Eirenarcha* (1582), the standard manual for justices of the peace by the Elizabethan lawyer and antiquarian William Lambarde, under this definition. Gil, *Shakespeare's Anti-Politics: Sovereign Power and the Life of the Flesh* (New York: Palgrave, 2013), 61.
13 Marjorie Garber suggests that there is a conceptual connection between codpiece and codfish: "It is no accident, I think, that one of the most overt and outrageous Dame figures of the twentieth-century stage, Captain Hook of Barrie's Peter Pan, is taunted by Peter in a famous scene in which Peter calls him a 'codfish.' Hook is of course the living embodiment of castration and consequent phallic display, his right hand having been severed by Peter in an earlier encounter." Garber, "Fetish Envy," *October* 54 (Autumn, 1990): 45–56, 53fn19. The etymology of "cod-fish" is contested. Derived from the Dutch word for "bag" or "sack," "cod" could refer to the fish's oily bladder, or it could be a reference to their method of catching. Early modern fishers used a bag-shaped net, or "cod," to haul in groundfish from the banks. See, Brayton, *Shakespeare's Ocean*, 155–56.
14 Brayton, *Shakespeare's Ocean*, 137.
15 Ken Albala, *Eating Right in the Renaissance* (Berkeley: University of California Press), 44, 102–3.

16 Brayton, *Shakespeare's Ocean*, 165

17 *Nyotaimori*, translated as "naked sushi" in English-speaking countries, takes the association between raw fish and sex to one extreme. By serving raw fish off of the body of a naked woman, nyotaimori collapses the differences between two kinds of consumption. See, Melanie Berliet, "Confessions of a Naked Sushi Model," *Vanity Fair*, Oct. 2008; J. Patrick Coolican, "Sushi in the Raw," *Seattle Times*, November 11, 2003.

18 See, Henry Hughes, "Fish, Sex, and Cannibalism: Appetites for Conversion in Melville's *Typee*," *Leviathan* 6, no. 2 (October, 2004): 3–16. Eve Ensler's *The Vagina Monologues* explores the ways in which the relationships between fish and vaginas cannot be reduced to one-to-one equations of signs and signifieds. Ensler's imagery is visceral and sensuous, as is Shakespeare's and Melville's, but she does not use fish to denote heterosexual vaginal penetration. Ensler's monologists can be horrified that the vagina might have a fishy smell, as in the case of a girl at camp, or they might be surprised by it as with a woman from Devonshire, or empowered by it. As the monologue titled "My Angry Vagina" puts it, "My vagina doesn't need to be cleaned up. It smells good already.… I don't want my pussy to smell like rain. All cleaned up like washing a fish after you cook it. Want to *taste* the fish. That's why I ordered it." Eve Ensler, *The Vagina Monologues* (New York: Villard, 2008, o.p., 1998), 41, 45, 70–71.

19 On the sea's hunger, see Brayton, *Shakespeare's Ocean*, 162.

20 Another example ties fish to more vicious sexuality: in *Titus Andronicus*, Aaron describes the "codding spirit" of the rapacious Demetrius and Chiron, a phrase glossed by Partridge as a "tendency to jest" and a "tendency to play with a codpiece." Eric Partridge, *Shakespeare's Bawdy* (London and New York: Routledge, 2002, o.p. 1947), 97–98, 101.

21 Partridge, *Shakespeare's Bawdy*, 135. The association between fish and the female sex organs is also found in use of "fishmonger" as a slang for a procurer of prostitutes.

22 Valerie Traub, *Thinking Sex with the Early Moderns* (Philadelphia: University of Pennsylvania Press, 2015), 172.

23 Valerie Traub, "Making Sexual Knowledge," *Early Modern Women* 5 (Fall, 2010): 251–59, 257. For a more sympathetic reading of Partridge's project, see Peter Cummings, "Shakespeare's Bawdy Planet," *The Sewanee Review* 101, no. 4 (Fall, 1993): 521–35. On mussels and cockles and their association with vulvas in medieval art, see Malcolm Jones, "Folklore Motifs in Late Medieval Art III: Erotic Animal Imagery," *Folklore* 102, no. 2 (1991): 192–219, 201–2.

24 R.A. Foakes, *Shakespeare: The Dark Comedies to the Last Plays* (London: Routledge and Kegan Paul, 1971), 21–22.

25 Arthur Quiller-Couch, introduction to William Shakespeare, *Measure for Measure*, ed., Arthur Quiller-Couch (Cambridge: Cambridge University Press, 1965 [1922]), xliii.

26 Robert N. Watson, "False Immortality in *Measure for Measure*: Comic Means, Tragic Ends," *Shakespeare Quarterly* 41, no. 4 (Winter, 1990): 411–32, 429.

27 Brown, "Erotic Religious Flagellation," 158.

28 Quiller-Couch, introduction to *Measure for Measure*, xxx.

29 Holly Dugan, "A Natural History of Ravishment," in *Renaissance Posthumanism*, eds. Joseph Campana and Scott Maisano (New York: Fordham University Press, 2016), 120–43, 130.

30 Dugan, "A Natural History of Ravishment," 137. Dugan cites Frances Dolan, "Re-Reading Rape in *The Changeling*," *Journal for Early Modern Cultural Studies* 11, no. 1 (Spring, 2011): 4–29.

31 David Thatcher, "Mercy and 'Natural Guiltiness' in *Measure for Measure*," *Texas Studies in Literature and Language* 37, no. 3 (Fall, 1995): 264–84, 271.

32 Dugan, "A Natural History of Ravishment," 122.

33 John Donne, *The Complete Poetry and Selected Prose of John Donne*, Charles M. Coffin, ed. (New York: The Modern Library, 1994).

34 Martha Widmayer. "'To Sin in Loving Virtue': Angelo of *Measure for Measure*," *Texas Studies in Literature and Language* 49, no. 2 (Summer, 2007): 155–80, 164. Similarly, it's peculiar that Lucio's report that "some sea maid spawned" him is taken to be evidence of his asexual docility, rather than an indication of a cruel trap. Angelo's dangerousness lies in his seeming placidity. It may be the case that the "mermaid on a dolphin's back / Utter[s] such a dulcet and harmonious breath / That the rude sea grew civil at her song," but, still, Oberon reports, "certain stars shot madly from their spheres, / To hear the sea-maid's music" (*A Midsummer Night's Dream* 2.1.150–54). More insidiously, Richard III pledges to "drown more sailors than the mermaid" (*Henry VI, Part 3* 3.2.186). Of course, to credit Angelo's mother for his misogyny merely inverts the misogyny, shifting the agency back to the maternal ocean.

Fish and Sexuality in Measure for Measure

35 Guillaume Rondelet, *L'histoire entière des poissons* (1558), 361–63.
36 Stephen Batman, *Batman vppon Bartholome* (London: Thomas East, 1582), 380r–380v.
37 In his dictionary of rare English words, the theologian and naturalist John Ray lists "monkfish" as a name used by the "Ancientist and most experienced fishermen" of Cornwall. Ray seems to identify "monkfish" with the angelshark: "*Monk-fish:* which either is or ought to be called *Skate*, if we follow the Etymology of the word; Squatina. The Italians call it Pesce Angelo, The Angel-Fish." Ray, *A Collection of English Vvords Not Generally Used* (London: Printed by H. Bruges for Thomas Burrell, 1674), 97–98.
38 Perhaps providing the basis for John Ray's identification of monkfish with angelsharks, Pliny says that, like anglerfish, angelsharks [*squatina*] hide in sandy bottoms and "put out their fins and wave them about to look like worms." Pliny the Elder, *Natural History*, vol. III, Book IX, trans. Harris Rackham (Cambridge, MA: Harvard University Press, 1983), 143–4.
39 Izaak Walton and Charles Cotton, *The Compleat Angler, or, The Contemplative Man's Recreation* (New York: Modern Library, 2004), 32–33.
40 Pliny the Elder, *Natural History*, 269–77.
41 Stacy Alaimo, "Violet-Black," in *Prismatic Ecology: Ecotheory Beyond Green*, ed. Jeffrey J. Cohen (Minneapolis: University of Minnesota Press, 2013): 233–48, 233.
42 Matt Simon, "Absurd Creature of the Week: The Anglerfish and the Absolute Worst Sex on Earth," *Wired*, November 8, 2013, www.wired.com/2013/11/absurd-creature-of-the-week-anglerfish/.
43 On the importance of "will" in *Measure for Measure*, and Angelo's tyrannical desires to maintain hierarchies, see Kathryn Schwartz, *What You Will: Gender, Contract, and Shakespearean Social Space* (Philadelphia: University of Pennsylvania Press, 2011), 155–80. On the regime of compulsory heterosexuality as a response to the threat of Isabella's virginity poses to the social order, see Mario DiGangi, "Pleasure and Danger: Measuring Female Sexuality in *Measure for Measure*," *ELH* 60, no. 3 (1993): 589–609
44 Brown, "Erotic Religious Flagellation," 141.
45 *OED*, "salt, *adj.2*." The connection between saltiness and salaciousness does not seem to have been lost on Shakespeare. For an excellent analysis of the relationship between salt as a preservative of fish and meat and Cleopatra's sexuality, see Jennifer Park, "Discandying Cleopatra: Preserving Cleopatra's Infinite Variety in Shakespeare's *Antony and Cleopatra*," *Studies in Philology* 113, no. 3 (Summer, 2016): 595–633.

22

MY PALFREY, MYSELF

Toward a Queer Phenomenology of the Horse-Human Bond in *Henry V* and Beyond

Karen Raber

In Act 3 of Shakespeare's *Henry V* the French Dauphin gives a famously foolish speech concerning his relationship to his horse: he will not exchange the animal, he announces, with any that treads but on four pasterns.

> Ca, ha! he bounds from the earth, as if his entrails were hairs; le cheval volant, the Pegasus, chez les narines de feu! When I bestride him, I soar, I am a hawk: he trots the air; the earth sings when he touches it; the basest horn of his hoof is more musical than the pipe of Hermes.[1]

Throughout the rest of this scene, the constable and the Duc d'Orleans try to repress the Dauphin's exuberant idolatry via an escalating war of words, puns, and innuendo, but only manage to spur him to greater absurdities concerning his "prince of palfreys":

DAU: It [his palfrey] is a theme as fluent as the sea. Turn the sands into eloquent tongues and my horse is argument for them all. 'Tis a subject for a sovereign to reason on, and for a sovereign's sovereign to ride on, and for the world, familiar to us and unknown, to lay apart their particular functions and wonder at him. I once writ a sonnet in his praise, and began it thus, "Wonder of nature!"
ORL: I have heard a sonnet begin so to one's mistress.
DAU: Then did they imitate that which I composed to my courser, for my horse is my mistress.
ORL: Your mistress bears well.
DAU: Me well, which is the prescript praise and perfection of a good and particular mistress.
CONS: Nay, for methought yesterday your mistress shrewdly shook your back.
DAU: So perhaps did yours.
CONS: Mine was not bridled.
DAU: Then belike she was old and gentle, and you rode like a kern of Ireland, your French hose off, and in your strait strossers.

(3.7.33–54)

And so on it goes, as the scene descends from the heights of poetry into a testy, bawdy prose exchange. The Dauphin's attachment to his mount is clearly received by his companions as inappropriate, part of his infantile failure as a leader who, instead of engaging the invading English force at Harfleur, sends Henry a mocking "gift" of tennis balls. Enraged at the insult, Henry threatens to turn "his balls to gun-stones" that will make widows and mourning mothers of France's women (1.2.283–87). The friction we have already witnessed in Act 2, between the Constable who warns the French King to take Henry's threat seriously, and the Dauphin who unwisely dismisses the English army altogether, breaks out in 3.7 into offensive allusions to the Dauphin's sexual tastes, and even, on the Constable's part, the charge of incompetence. Orleans defends the Dauphin, "He never did harm that I heard of," which the Constable parlays into "Nor will do none tomorrow [on the battlefield]" (3.7.100–101). Of course, both the Constable and the Dauphin will be defeated at Agincourt, drowned "fetlock-deep in gore" (4.7.78), and the noble French cavalry will be routed by a much smaller, weaker English army whose mounts are "poor jades … drooping the hides and hips" (4.2.46–47).

Such critical attention as this passage has attracted generally confirms Peter Erickson's judgment that the Dauphin is here proven a "travesty of masculinity" that confirms the play's endorsement of muscular English heteronormativity.[2] And indeed, the Dauphin's adoration of his equine partner seems to reflect if not the fully bestializing erotic attachment that his companions hint at, then at least an infantile fixation on an inappropriate love object. Orleans and the Constable quickly move this uncomfortable moment towards what they seem to consider more suitable ground—jokes about prostitutes, the missionary position, and sexual diseases that substitute allusions to human mistresses for the love between a man and his equine partner. In other words, their banter deflects the discussion away from the Dauphin's troublingly intimate and excessive celebration of his palfrey—what Mel Y. Chen might call his "improper affiliation"—only to make it the horse-shaped elephant in the room.[3]

The constable and Orleans react to the Dauphin's orientation towards the animal with their defensive reorienting conversational interventions.[4] For them, the animal must be either merely a conveyance or a metaphor through which heterosexual desire can be discursively invoked. They are moved by discomfort to restore a degree of marginality or transparency, and thus *invisibility* to the lauded horse as a social actor. I use here the language of orientation, visibility, and discourse to gesture towards what I read as an important crux in this scene, and in critical treatments of it: this discussion among men about a horse struggles with the problem of language's connections to bodily investments in erotic and sexual being, and it registers the complicating role of other regimes than language—like the visual or the sonic, both of which the passage touches on—by specifically repressing them. The Dauphin's poetic celebration threatens to confuse human sexuality with animal love, and to make poetic language a vehicle for elevating erotic experiences that do not conform to the traditional patriarchal schemas of (male) human lover and (female) human love object. The Dauphin's encomium hints of the blazon and anaphora as if to demonstrate his animal's inspirational influence in advance of the unspoken sonnet, but is also replete with images of blocking or usurping: the hoof more musical than Hermes' pipe; the wonder that arrests all "functions" of the world; and, of course, the implied silencing of Orleans and the Constable were the sonnet to be declaimed in due course. Little wonder, then, that the Dauphin's audience is unhappy with him.

Criticism that ties the Dauphin and his horse love to issues like masculinity's implication in social and national identity inadvertently repeats the moves of the Constable and Orleans, refusing the scene's invitation to think more carefully and concretely about the Dauphin's attachment to this animal. Sexual orientation, Sarah Ahmed argues, is a matter of how we reside in space, of how, and who or what we inhabit spaces with, and what habitual actions shape our bodies and worlds. To orient oneself is, as she puts it, to turn towards objects that "help us find our way." If we think with and through orientation, Ahmed suggests, "we might allow moments of disorientation to gather … Queer objects might take us to the very limits of social gathering, even when they still gather us around" (1, 24). I think any reading of the palfrey episode in *Henry V* that tries to plot it on a rigid axis of masculine/feminine, hetero/homoerotic, or even bestial/human would only continue to cooperate with Orleans and the Constable in limiting the objects and bodies that the Dauphin prefers to gather or affiliate with. If our critical attention does not resist the process of erotic normalization—that is, if we take the Dauphin lightly, refuse to give his speech any real weight—we risk straightening out this scene and overlooking the more provocative, perhaps disorienting, nature of the Dauphin's relationship with his animal.

In this chapter, I instead intend to take the Dauphin's claims about his horse both seriously and literally, to offer the beginnings of a prospective queer phenomenology of the human–equine encounter in Tudor and Stewart England. I will do so in part by setting this speech in the context of other early modern human–horse encounters. I also build on the recent insights of animal-centered phenomenology, keeping in mind that the queer orientation Ahmed tracks often omits divergences towards the nonhuman. Thus, instead of examining the social, economic, political, or other inscriptions and meanings of the Dauphin's mount, this chapter asks: What specific and distinct coordinates of desire, pleasure, and affiliation are established in the horse-human dyad? How are both the horse and the human body mapped as they connect and disconnect with one another? What aspects of both bodies enable such a queerly eroticized relationship?[5]

In addressing the problem of how gendered bodies are socially inscribed or constructed, Elizabeth Grosz argues that we must first understand "what these bodies are, such that inscription is possible, what it is in the nature of bodies, of biological evolution, that opens them up to cultural transcription, social immersion and production."[6] We might extend Grosz's formulation to nonhuman entities like horses, which are a particular example of such evolution: no other creature is capable of quite the same bodily relationship to a human partner. Dogs and cats, for instance, are predator species; for them, cooperating with a human being is in a sense a peer-to-peer interaction designed to fulfill more efficiently their predatory imperatives. Horses, on the other hand, are prey, and so encounters with human beings in the course of training require overcoming their evolutionary fear-response to a predator species in order to allow a human not merely to approach them, but to mount and direct their instinct to flight in order to move quite differently through the world. A horse's capacity to accomplish this remarkable feat is tied to a number of factors—herd sociability that can be extended to non-equine "friends," for instance, but mainly their highly developed talents for perception that can be harnessed to the training relationship. Vicki Hearne terms this "skin grammar," the finely tuned perceptual grid the horse applies to its rider; the conversation that ensues queers both language and knowledge.[7] Horses and humans share the capacity for interspecies corporeal synchronizing through manipulations of space and movement; further, the process of harmonizing and synchronizing brings pleasure to *both* participants.[8] Even the animal's capacity to flood its system with endorphins, which in wild contexts allows an injured horse to remain functional enough to escape a predator, allows it to be more effectively domesticated by giving humans a means to soothe and calm a frightened animal of such size and power—the horse's physiology thus provides a powerful aphrodisiac that also lends itself to the development of mutual trust. At the same time, the horse's bodily structure also makes these animals compelling objects of human desire: few other animals require the extensive physical connection necessary for the training relationship with equines; fewer still reward that connection with the kind of transcendence that the Dauphin celebrates—bounding from the earth, soaring, becoming animal in defiance of gravity itself.[9] Even the sheer mass of an equine body can itself be a source of sensory trauma or delight, depending on the events negotiated by horse and rider.

In the two sections that follow, I pursue the issue of the marvelous and compelling equine body that the Dauphin so disconcertingly "turns toward" and lovingly anatomizes in his unspoken sonnet. I catalog some of the equine qualities early moderns attended to that make it "natural" for him to do so, accounting for the material aspects of the human–equine encounter that might explain the frequency and extent to which, as in the Dauphin's case, equine bodies colonize or usurp the erotic positions, roles, or imagined subjectivities otherwise ordinarily ascribed to human partners.[10]

I Shape

When the Dauphin names his animal a palfrey, he evokes a very specific image. A palfrey was usually smaller than a destrier, or battle mount, and was generally considered more beautiful, having a rounded, compact, "baroque" figure, and musculature that made it capable of smoother gaits.[11] By the time Shakespeare writes his play, this type of horse was associated with displays of manège riding, the early modern term for the high arts of dressage, the formal training of the horse to the highest levels of muscular discipline and control. The standard for the palfrey's beauty is everywhere confirmed in treatises on riding and breeding: Michael Baret, for instance, describes the ideal "handsome" horse, as one with ribs that "bear out in rotundity like a barrell" and requires it also be "round-backed."[12] Thomas Blundeville prefers the Neapolitan to the Spanish jennet (a small ambling riding horse) because the latter's "buttocks be somewhat slender"; he generally approves animals that are "full of muscles or brawnes of flesh" with short backs and "great round buttocks."[13] In Gervase Markham's advice to horse purchasers, he refers again and again to the many "swellings" that comprise a perfect equine form: "see that [the breast] be broad out-swelling," he advises in that the animal have "out-swelling forethighs."[14] Of the horse's hind end, he recommends the following:

> Then look upon his Buttocks, and see that they be round, plump, full, and in an even level with his body: or if long, that it be well raised behind, and spread forth at the setting on of the tail, for these are comely and beautifull.
>
> *(124)*

Likewise, the hind legs must be "thick, brawny, full and swelling" (123). *Roundness*, then, is the quality that defines an aesthetically pleasing, valuable, and healthy animal. Shakespeare's *Venus and Adonis* registers this standard (and the requirement for a "broad buttock") in its description of Adonis's mount:

> Round-hoof'd, short-jointed, fetlocks shag and long,
> Broad breast, full eye, small head and nostril wide,
> High crest, short ears, straight legs and passing strong,
> Thin mane, thick tail, broad buttock, tender hide:
> Look, what a horse should have he did not lack,
> Save a proud rider on so proud a back.
>
> *(295–300)*[15]

Renaissance sculpture and painting revel in the sensuous fleshy curves of the baroque horse's body, focusing as obsessively on round shapes as do the manual authors. Kenneth Clark claims this feature distinguishes Renaissance from medieval art, observing that

> The splendid curves of energy [in these paintings of horses]—the neck and rump, united by the passive curve of the belly, and capable of infinite variations, from calm to furious strength—are without question the most satisfying piece of formal relationship in nature.[16]

Albrecht Durer's two studies of horses, *Large Horse* and *Small Horse* (both engravings from 1505), emphasize the roundness of the traditional baroque horse; *Large Horse* in particular depicts the animal standing with its haunches presented to the viewer on a small stone or elevated piece of ground, while the rest of the animal's body is angled away from the viewer. *Large Horse* thus reflects a fascination with those "round, plump, full" buttocks, with its massive, muscled hind end thrusting outward from the engraving.[17] Indeed, it is difficult to find a Renaissance representation of a horse that doesn't include gracefully or powerfully rounded musculature, as much a byproduct of artists' obsession with curvaceous bodies as of the prevalence of baroque breeds in the period.

We could read this focus on the beauty of curvaceous posteriors as a manufactured cultural preference, one that grows out of the prior distinction or class associations of the breeds in question. But there is another way to think about all these swellings and roundnesses. Baret in particular insists on the role of geometry in determining the perfection of the horse's physical being, and indeed the curve represented a monumental challenge to early modern mathematicians—only in the seventeenth century did analytic geometry establish the formula to describe one, a humanist achievement in charting God's elemental design of the cosmos.[18] Baret's references to geometry thus situate the curvy equine as the epitome of divine order.

Current work in neuroscience suggests that the attraction, perhaps even the erotic magnetism of curves for the human observer, may in fact be hardwired in the human brain. University of Toronto psychologist Oshin Vartanian conducted a series of experimental brain scans involving variously curved objects, and found that "Our preference for curves cannot be explained entirely in terms of a 'cold' cognitive assessment of the qualities of curved objects. Curvature appears to affect our feelings, which in turn … drive[s] our preference".[19] Such a bias towards curves may have evolutionary origins in our avoidance of sharp objects, which tend to activate the amygdala, the part of the brain that identifies threats; whatever the origin, the bias is linked to affective stimulation. And equine curves present a viewer or a rider with a range of affordances, in this case telegraphing the potential pleasures of human–equine anatomical engagement. The fleshy roundnesses, those fatty and muscular swellings Baret, Blundeville, and Markham dwell on, both mirror and complement a rider's own curving anatomical structures; they invite eyes, hands, and legs to linger, to touch, to assert pressure or to surrender space to another's form. They seduce with their promise of amplified power, driving forward through the rider's legs and seat. Curves, we might say, are thus primordial, visceral sources of relational and erotic gratification.

II Motion

The Dauphin's adulation of his horse extends to its "musical hoof," which, he says, makes the very earth sing in response to its touch. Elisabeth LeGuin has compared the training of horse and rider to Renaissance musical education, noting that the achievement of perfect kinaesthetic harmony between these two distinct bodies requires the same coordination and synchronized rhythm as does playing an instrument.[20] William Cavendish, for instance, uses the analogy of lute-playing to illustrate the "good music" that good horsemanship produces: "he that has not a musical head," concludes Cavendish, "can never be a good horseman."[21] The Neapolitan horseman Federico Grisone writes in his *Rules of Riding*

> you will accompany him [your horse] in a timely manner, conforming to his motion, just as he responds to your every thought and command, so that it is necessary that your body fits his back evenly, and you are always attuned with him and that you govern him with the same harmony as in music.[22]

The several gaits of the horse (walk, trot, canter, gallop) and variations in breed size and shape require a repertoire of riderly adaptations to different cadences: LeGuin points out that in the production of an artistic equine ballet, it is the horse's bodily intelligence that calls the tune, and "if the rider does not listen," that is follow and enhance the motion with his own corporeal discipline, the result will be forced and effortful.[23]

Supplemented movement such as that made possible by an equine partner is, however, a remarkably queer thing. Through riding, relatively slow human bipedal propulsion is swapped for quadripedal speed, which can be suddenly adjusted, its direction and rhythm modified in an instant, allowing huge alterations in the experience of time and distance. One famous early modern literary example of the way equine movement perplexes the usual rational frameworks for recognizing relative speed is Spenser's Red Cross Knight, who in *The Faerie Queene* travels at an irreconcilably disparate speed from his companion, Una: the knight "pricks" or spurs swiftly across a plain, while she rides slowly behind followed by her dwarf—and yet both somehow remain together.[24] The knight, the image affirms, lives in rapid martial bursts determined by his mount's collected or extended speed. Una moves instead at a lithic pace like the "rock" of the Church that she stands for allegorically. Part of the reason this kind of allegorical interpretation, a commonplace in the criticism, makes sense is tied to the horse's material capacity to move at variable velocities, creating a kind of relativity paradox.

To experience breathless speed on horseback involves entering the alien space and time in which an equid naturally dwells and being defined by it. At the core of Hotspur's rash, impatient nature in *1 Henry 4*, for instance, the need for speed inscribed by his character's nickname as his defining quality is his identification with his mount, the roan he imagines riding to battle Prince Hal "hot horse to horse." I've written elsewhere about the desire that gathers prince, nobleman, and both horses into a queer erotic entanglement; here, it is worth noting in addition that for a human rider to be identified as hotly spurring requires a collapse of bodies, a merging of human and equine that dissolves species distinctions, but in so doing shows the potential for riding (and the animal's movement) to reshape a human partner.[25] Maxine Sheets-Johnstone argues that motion is the first behavior that informs any creature of its world: "We come straightaway moving into the world; we are precisely not *stillborn*. In this respect primal movement is like primal sensibility … we *literally discover ourselves in movement*."[26] A rider extends this primal sensibility to the experience of quadripedal motion, absorbing and controlling a degree of speed over terrain only available to the horse-human dyad, discovering an identity that does not resolve to the usual definition of limited and isolated human embodiment.

The Dauphin registers the experience of equestrian movement as oceanic, naming his palfrey "a theme as fluent as the sea." And like the ocean, equestrian motion implicates human bodies in an unfamiliar and even hostile environment. In the same way that sailing and swimming do, riding a horse requires adaptation to the pulse of a foreign medium, navigating the swell and retreat of wind and waves as they are manifested in the complex tempos of equine gaits.[27] The horse generates the power of lifts, surges, and cascades; the skilled equestrian human body determines when and where these occur, and what their rhythm is. Yet what might appear an act of domination is also an act of surrender—the human body must follow for the process to be successful and pleasurable, and must submerge its will in order to do so. Nor should the pleasure of synchronizing motion be understood as purely available to the rider: Gala Argent notes that "intraspecific corporeal synchrony" is tied to the primal mare-foal communion.[28] The foal learns to remain close to its mother's side, to coordinate its steps and motion with its mother, and later with the herd. *Intra*specific becomes *inter*specific through entraining, leading to the same harmonizing with human bipedal motion, but only through the *willing* co-creation of movements. Play with a horse if you have a chance: note its capacity to read bodily twitches, jinks, leaps, and even smiles, and it quickly becomes clear that the animal can distinguish the joy of a game from any other kind of interaction.[29]

Shakespeare is not alone in remarking the oceanic movement of a horse. When Philip Sidney's Pyrocles first appears in *The Arcadia*, for instance, he emerges from the sea where Musidorus believes his ship lost, he rides the mast of his wrecked vessel:

> But a little way off they saw the mast, whose proud height now lay along … upon the mast they saw a young man – at least if he were a man – bearing show of about eighteen years of age, who sat as on a horse back, having nothing upon him but his shirt ….[30]

Sallie Anglin notes that Pyrocles's appearance is striking and erotic for his near-nakedness, his hair "stirred by the wind," and his feet "kissed" by the ocean itself. Pyrocles is, she argues, depicted as having achieved "in extremis, a momentary union with his environment," a union conveyed by the passage's allusion to horsemanship.[31] For Pyrocles, to be as "fluent as the sea" allows him to ride ships as well as steeds.

But if one can indeed ride a horse like one rides the waves, it also true that riding can result in shipwreck. That which elevates can of a sudden descend and dis-integrate; the ecstasy (literally, the effect of standing outside of oneself) of boundary-crossings in the entrained relationship is vulnerable to assaults from without and breakdowns from within. Steve Mentz locates a "marine element" in the Dauphin's title, which is written as "Dolphin" in some versions of the play. The character's protean and playful nature (remember those tennis balls!) gestures, Mentz argues, towards the possibility of a more-than-earthbound future for humanity.[32] That said, playing around with the massive equine who creates the waves the Dauphin rides so well is a precarious activity. The Dauphin does in fact take a kind of tumble in the play—not perhaps from his horse, but from the heights of poetry in which he praises its accomplishments when he is dragged down into the mire of sexual innuendo that marks the Constable's and Orleans' earthbound prose. Like a drowning man, the Dauphin *tries* to ride out the storm, fighting it as he sinks: he parries the Constable's joking reference to a bridled and so presumably more proper female human sexual partner by warning "they that ride so and ride not warily, fall into foul bogs. I had rather have my horse to my mistress" (3.7.59). The conversation's descent into scurrility mimics the sexually corrupt, fallen state of mankind that makes such a descent inevitable—human mistresses, bridled or not, can still pass along sexual diseases in their "foul bogs." But in hinting that the Constable's mistress will give him the clap, the Dauphin too has taken a catastrophic spill, one that has shattered his transcendent union with his beloved mount. Rather than riding the heights of queer affiliation, making his own unique rhythms in his paean to his horse, the Dauphin struggles in broken prose to come out on top of his companions.

A rider can be elevated by his horse; he can be carried above the earth, defying gravity aboard a Pegasus or a Bucephalus, matching the light fall of its hoofbeats with his supple hip and hand. But the unwary or unskilled rider might also plunge earthward, coming "down, down like glistering Phaethon" as Richard II puts it, to end up as "bemoiled" as is Kate in *The Taming of the Shrew*, when she tumbles down a "foul hill" and is pinned under her mount.[33] Early modern authors unhorse any number of characters to demonstrate their internal, often sexual, disorder: examples include Dametas in the *Arcadia*; in the *Faerie Queene* Paridell, Scudamore, Sangliere, and Archimago; and in Shakespeare, both Richard II and Richard III in their respective plays, Talbot in *I Henry VI*, and Falstaff in *Henry IV Part 1*, to name just a few. Falls like these punctuate early modern literature to illustrate human failures of control over the passions, and to such an extent that the horses involved therefore might be read as primarily bearing the added burden of human exceptionalist ideologies.

But again, refusing to account for the embodied experiences on which these ideologies are built risks erasing the phenomenological engagement between equine and human that makes such thinking possible and meaningful in the first place. A fall is always also simply a fall, a sudden physical return to a limited, frail, vulnerable body at the mercy of its mount's footing or behavior. It is rare that horsemanship treatises address the danger of falling off (one wonders at the degree of defensiveness that governs such an omission), but the French equerry Antoine Pluvinel recommends that a rider squeezes his knees to the saddle "with all one's strength so that, should the horse become animated, he does not throw my ass [mon âne], I mean my man, to the ground."[34] The coy joke here, the confusion of ass (the beast, not the body part) and man, reflects the lowering effect of such ignominious events both on altitude and on status. Together and in unison, horse and human are one superior quasi-divine body; divided, the separate parts become equally bestial, the rider returned to something even less stable than slow bipedalism.

Perhaps the most famous fall in early modern literature is Montaigne's, recounted in his essay "On Practice": out riding one day on his "undemanding but not very reliable horse" one of his men mounted on a huge "fresh and vigorous" farm-horse ends up crashing like a "colossus" or a "thunderbolt" into Montaigne, "a small man on a small horse."[35] Horse and rider are upended, and Montaigne nearly killed. The event prompts Montaigne's reflection on the body's independent agency and mobility when it tries to save itself as it falls. He draws a direct line between its flailing, uncontrolled gestures as it heads earthward and the body's capacity for autonomous sexual arousal: "Every man," he remarks, "knows ... that he has a part of his body which often stirs, erects, and lies down again without his leave" (422). Overpowered and unhorsed, struck as if by lightning, and reminded of his "small" stature by a colossus, Montaigne undergoes a kind of life-threatening *coitus interruptus* that imagines *both* horse and human bodies to be alien and hostile environments. Montaigne's experience amounts to a kind of shipwreck, a catastrophe that impresses upon the human experiencing it the body's indifference to subject, object, or context: humans, his example suggests, are not merely adrift in a perplexing world of more or less suitable targets of desire, but disoriented by the recalcitrant microcosms of their own bodies.

So to conclude: literary texts like *Henry V* involve what Ahmed might call a species of social gathering—of readers; of characters; and of described, implied, and present bodies. What we as critics or scholars choose to turn towards or away from them limits the kinds of phenomenological engagements we recognize and value, and by extension the nature of our understanding of the body's full range of communions and affiliations. By refusing to allow the Constable and Orleans to narrow the range of participants at this gathering, by entering and occupying the territory of the Dauphin's erotic delight in his mount, we can instead acknowledge the qualities that make the horse, to slightly misquote the Dauphin, a "Queer Wonder of nature."

Notes

1 William Shakespeare, *King Henry V*, ed. T.W. Craik (Bloomsbury, 1995), (3.7.11–17). All references to this play are by act, scene, and line number to this edition.
2 Peter Erickson, *Patriarchal Structures in Shakespeare's Drama* (Berkeley: University of California Press, 1985), 54.
3 Mel Y. Chen, *Animacies: Biopolitics, Racial Mattering, and Queer Affect* (Durham, NC and London: Duke University Press, 2012), 104:

> I do not imagine queer or queerness to merely indicate embodied sexual contact among subjects identified as gay and lesbian, ... Rather, I think more in terms of the social and cultural formation of "improper affiliation", so that queerness might well describe an array of subjectivities, intimacies, beings, and spaces located outside of the heteronormative.

4 I am borrowing Sarah Ahmed's language in describing queer orientations from *Queer Phenomenology*, especially 1–24.
5 It is worth noting that scholarly attention to the queer nature of male relationships to horses in the Middle Ages and Renaissance post-dates a body of writing on women's queer engagement with equines in subsequent periods: see, for instance, Weil, "Purebreds and Amazons"; Landry, "Horsy and Persistently Queer"; and McHugh, *Animal Stories*. There are many reasons for this belatedness, but it seems linked in part to the problem of centering the animal to which this chapter is a response: women riders of the eighteenth, nineteenth, and twentieth centuries are not only more present in the literature and culture than they are in early modern texts, but are more clearly marked as anomalous, whereas male riders in all periods are (invisibly) "masculine," drawing less critical attention—yet in both cases, the *rider*'s identity, the rider's pleasures and the rider's freedom or constraint is the driver of critical commentary.
6 Elizabeth Grosz, *The Nick of Time: Politics, Evolution and the Untimely* (Durham, NC and London: Duke University Press, 2004), 2.
7 Vicki Hearne, *Adam's Task: Calling Animals by Name* (New York: Skyhorse Publishing, 2007), 110, 108–116.
8 Gala Argent, "Toward a Privileging of the Nonverbal: Communication, Corporeal Synchrony, and Transcendence in Humans and Horses," in *Experiencing Animal Minds: An Anthology of Animal-Human Encounters*, eds. Julie A. Smith and Robert W. Mitchell (New York: Columbia University Press, 2012), 116, 121.
9 On the mutual development of a complex bodily language, see Keri Brandt, "Intelligent Bodies: Embodied Subjectivity in Human-Horse Communication," in *Body/Embodiment: Symbolic Interaction and the Sociology of the Body*, eds. Dennis Waskul and Phillip Vannini (Burlington, VT: Ashgate, 2012).
10 A continuation of this work would address heat and color (the "ginger" vs. "nutmeg" debate that enters the play's debate later on), size (the relative queerness of human connections to large animals vs. small), number (both the union that makes two into one, and the phenomenon of the herd effect in battle, or the dissolution of the one into many), among other dimensions.
11 The baroque horse—the term is a later creation meant to describe a set of animals rather than a breed—is a compact animal often of the Spanish, Italian, or other Iberian breeds. Renaissance horses used by knights generally fell into a few categories, with the destrier functioning as the larger battle mount, but the courser as the swifter, smaller but still highly trained animal. Both might be described as "baroque," depending on breed origin, but the Spanish and Neapolitan horses would have been more typical of the type with smaller refined heads, rounded bodies, and powerful haunches. Whether there is a substantial difference between a palfrey and a courser in Shakespeare's text is questionable: the Dauphin calls his horse by both terms and Adonis's "courser" is clearly a baroque type.
12 Michael Baret, *An Hipponomie, or The Vineyard of Horsemanship* (London, 1618), 110.
13 Thomas Blundeville, *The Four Chiefest Offices Belonging to Horsemanship* (London, 1580), 8–9.
14 Gervase Markham, *The Perfect Horseman Horseman or the Experienced Secrets of Mr. Markham's Fifty Years Practice* (London, 1656), 120, 124.
15 William Shakespeare, *The Complete Works of Shakespeare,* 5th ed., ed. David Bevington (New York: Pearson Longman, 2004).

16 Kenneth Clark, *Animals and Man: Their Relationship as Reflected in Western Art from Prehistory to the Present Day* (New York: William Morrow and Co., Inc., 1977), 36.

17 *Small Horse* is depicted from the side, giving a perfect silhouette of the baroque type (short, rounded, high- and arched-necked); in it, the animal has one knee lifted as if to trot out of the engraving's frame, while the soldier present in both images is, in *Small Horse*, obscured by the animal in motion. In *Large Horse*, the animal is more docile and static, his accompanying human resting a spear vertically on the ground.

18 Representing two-dimensional curves (with straight edge and compass) was commonplace among Greek and other early mathematicians; however, three-dimensional and probable trajectories of curves were a problem only solved in the seventeenth century, beginning with Descartes' 1637 *Géométrie*. Baret includes a chapter on "Proportion" (*An Hipponomie*, 115–19) that makes the case that all creation rests on the conjunction of "Arithmeticke and Geometry" (117); where proportion is achieved, beauty results and is instantly recognizable to humans in the visual shape of the animal (113).

19 Jaffe; see also Oshin Vartanian et al., "Impact of Contour on Aesthetic Judgments and Approach-Avoidance Decisions in Architecture," *Proceedings of the National Academy of Sciences* 110, Suppl 2 (June 18, 2013).

20 Le Guin Elizabeth, "Man and Horse in Harmony," in *The Culture of the Horse: Status, Discipline and Identity in the Early Modern World*, eds. Karen Raber and Treva J. Tucker (New York: Palgrave Macmillan, 2005).

21 William Cavendish, *A General System of Horsemanship*, intro William C. Steinkraus (Vermont: J.A.Allen, 2000), 93.

22 Federico Grisone, *The Rules of Riding*, ed. and trans. Elizabeth MacKenzie Tobey (Tempe, AZ: ACMRS, 2014), 109. Tobey makes the comparison between the noble horse-master's role and that of the dance master: both taught a practice that was meant to be both physical and aesthetic, emotional and even intellectual (31).

23 Le Guin, "Man and Horse in Harmony," 184.

24 Edmund Spenser, *The Faerie Queene* (London: Penguin Books, 1987), begins with Red Cross "pricking on the plaine," his "angry steede" "chid[ing] his foming bitt" (41); the implied speed of both is repeatedly confirmed.

25 See, for example, my essay on equine erotics, "Equeer."

26 Maxine Sheets-Johnstone, *The Primacy of Movement*, 2nd ed. (Philadelphia: John Benjamins Publishing Company, 2011), 117.

27 For an elaboration of the "entraining" that results in this oceanic experience, see Game, "Riding: Embodying the Centaur." As Game writes, "learning to be carried along in the flow, learning to become in tune with or in the train of" requires "get[ting] into these waves" in a horse-human rhythm" (3). See also Argent, "Toward a Privileging of the Nonverbal," 121.

28 Argent, "Toward a Privileging of the Nonverbal," 116.

29 According to recent research, horses are capable of reading expressions on human faces: see Amy Victoria Smith, et al., "Functionally Relevant Responses to Human Facial Expressions of Emotion in the Domestic Horse (Equus caballus)," *Biology Letters* (2016). http://rsbl.royalsocietypublishing. org/content/12/2. Massumi makes a convincing case for animals' capacity for play (both intentional playfulness and play as performance) in *What Animals Teach Us about Politics*, especially 1–17.

30 Philip Sidney, *The Countess of Pembroke's Arcadia* (London: Penguin Books, 1977), 66.

31 Anglin, "Material Romance: Embodiment, Environment and Ecology in Sidney's New Arcadia," *Sidney Journal* 30, no. 2 (2012): especially 89.

32 Steve Mentz, "Half Fish, Half Flesh: Dolphins, Humans, and the Early Modern Ocean," in *The Indistinct Human in Renaissance Literature*, eds. Jean Feerick and Vin Nardizzi (London: Palgrave, 2012).

33 David Bevington, *The Complete Works of Shakespeare*, 5th ed. (New York: Longman, 2003), (3.3.178), (4.1.67).

34 Antoine Pluvinel, *Le maneige royal*, trans. Hilda Nelson (London: J.A. Allen, 1989), 26.

35 Michel de Montaigne, *The Complete Essays*, transl. M.A. Screech (London: Penguin Books, 2003), 418–19.

23

"FORGIVENESS, HORSE"

The Barbaric World of *Richard II*

Erica Fudge

The ecocritic Greg Garrard has figured the difference between animal studies and ecocriticism as being between one approach that places "emphasis on the individual organism," and another which "demands moral consideration for inanimate things such as rivers and mountains, assuming pain and suffering to be a necessary part of nature."[1] Such a distinction would seem to be reflected in recent essays that attend to the representation of nonhuman nature in Shakespeare's *Richard II*.[2] Here, "animal-sensitive" readings take the play's horses as their focus,[3] while ecocritical ones take the representation of the land as theirs. For the former, it seems, the landscape is the blank canvas onto which animal and human worlds are projected, while for the latter, the animals are absent or, as Simon Estok has put it, perhaps considered to be "outside of the environment."[4]

This would seem to present an impasse—an unbridgeable division between the two approaches which might otherwise be expected to share so much common ground. But the essays on *Richard II* actually do more than mark out distinct critical territories; they converge in their interpretation of the play in interesting ways. They read in its transfer of power from divinely ordained monarch to astute politician a parallel shift from an enchanted to a disenchanted conception of nonhuman nature—with the latter manifested in the sense of animals as lacking agency or the land as a resource for use. What emerges at the end of *Richard II*, the different readings suggest, is not only a new conception of royal power but also a new conception of human power: nature is instrumentalized and mankind's authority established (the masculine terminology is used deliberately).

In this chapter I will track the parallels that exist between ecocritical and animal-sensitive readings of *Richard II*, and offer an alternative interpretation that builds on this work but diverges from it by suggesting that at the end of the play, in the imagined conversation Richard has with "roan Barbary," we can also trace something else, something that resists the separation of human from nature, and that reinstates humanity's place alongside rather than above animals. Voiced in defeat, for sure, but present nonetheless, this other perspective is made manifest in Richard's asking "Forgiveness, horse," which strange request suggests, I argue, that the play represents more than just the ascendancy of an instrumentalized conception of nature. But, before getting to Barbary, the chapter needs to journey through gardens, encounter snakes, and ride a few other horses, because it is via the accumulation of engagements with the play's nonhuman natural worlds, and the interpretations of them, that Barbary must be approached.

I Allegory and Materiality

It is well established that 3.4 of *Richard II* is an allegory of the state of the nation using the nonhuman natural world to figure rule and disorder. The garden is, in short, a microcosm of the realm, and in this moment we, with the Queen and her ladies, overhear the Gardener and his men contrasting their great care with the King's failure. One of the men asks:

> Why should we in the compass of a pale
> Keep law and form and due proportion
> Showing, as in a model, our firm estate
> When our sea-walled garden, the whole land,
> Is full of weeds …[5]

This linking of politics and horticulture, of the realm with the garden, is utterly conventional in Renaissance thought[6] and has been taken up by critics of *Richard II* in different ways. In what is now regarded as a foundational reading from 1947, for example, Richard D. Altick argued that in the play Shakespeare uses "iterative symbolism" to construct a "unity of tone," citing sets of images including "*earth-ground-land, blood,* pallor, garden, sun, tears, *tongue-speech-word, snake-venom*" which, when repeated, "perceptibly deepen" meaning. For Altick, the "untended garden" of 3.4 is part of this iterative symbolism and is linked in the play with other crucial ideas: in particular, with the conception of England as a lost paradise, which is voiced most clearly by John of Gaunt in 2.1.[7]

Altick's reading assumes that there is no need to venture beyond *Richard II*'s imagery to gain insight into its dramatic shifts; it supposes, as Cleanth Brooks put it, in a book published in the same year, that the literary work is a "well wrought urn," complete unto itself.[8] Such a perspective is very different from that voiced by current ecocriticism. Indeed, Jennifer Munroe has distinguished ecocritical analyses from the kind of readings Altick and Brooks perform in a helpfully succinct way, arguing that where the interpretations that focus on the words on the page regard the natural world as a source of metaphors, ecocritics concentrate on "discussion of the physical properties of and material interactions between humans and nonhumans."[9] That contrast is exemplified in Lynne Bruckner's 2013 ecocritical reading of *Richard II* which offers a different conception of the literary text, of the garden scene and of the role of the natural imagery more generally from Altick's essay, and suggests that Richard's failure as a monarch is because he fails to maintain his realm (it is over-grown with allegorical weeds, as the Gardener and his men know), and because he treats "the earth as an economic resource, rather than as a resource to be protected."[10]

Bruckner's argument emerges from a close analysis of the play's language, taking, like Altick, John of Gaunt's statement to Richard, "Landlord of England art thou now, not king" (2.1.113), as a key. But she suggests that the king's exploitation of "the earth for immediate cash in hand" was likely to have resonated with the play's original audience—with their concerns about deforestation and the profiteering land management practices of the time, in particular.[11] That is, she does something with Shakespeare's work that Altick did not, and reads *Richard II* by looking outward to the moment in which the play was created and first staged. For her the garden scene is not only allegorical and thematically tied in with other key image clusters in the text, it is, rather, a "nexus of materiality and allegory" in which Shakespeare's symbolism should be linked to the very pressing reality of his time: in particular to "the Little Ice Age" that was causing poor harvests and famine in England in the late sixteenth century.[12] As such, her reading moves from a detailed discussion of imagery, towards a historicist analysis that sees the play as a comment on its own times.

Alongside this, Bruckner also places *Richard II* within a wider intellectual shift. She argues that John of Gaunt's speech in 2.1 presents the nonhuman world as vibrant: nature has "built" a fortress, he claims; the shore "beats back the envious siege / Of wat'ry Neptune" (2.1.43, 62–63). In recognizing this potential for agency in the nonhuman world, Bruckner argues, Gaunt's speech offers "an important pre-Cartesian sensibility: one that understands the earth as living, lively, and nonmechanistic … filled with vitality."[13] This habit of mind persisted in the sixteenth century, she states, but was in decline, "contested (and largely eradicated) by the rise of science."[14] Richard's use of the land as a source of income epitomizes the change that is coming. "In many ways," Bruckner writes, "*Richard II* rests on an epistemological cusp – straddling the notion that the earth is/is not living."[15]

Having situated the play within this economic and intellectual trajectory, at the end of her essay Bruckner does something else again which traces the logical outcome of this move towards the instrumentalization of nature. She turns to read *Richard II* to address our present (her essay is included in a collection called *Shakespeare and the Urgency of Now*). In particular, she uses it to think about the issue of hydraulic fracturing (fracking) in US National Parks. The play, she writes,

> evinces how the living earth too often is held hostage to a combination of financial mandates and politics as usual. In the very way in which *Richard II* may have sparked political concerns about land management and forests for Elizabethans, the play can readily evoke similar concerns in a contemporary audience. Richard's failure to make appropriate use of national land along with his violation of Bolingbroke's property … is analogous in too many ways to current environmental incursions on our federal and state lands.[16]

In undertaking this final analysis Bruckner is following an established pattern in ecocritical readings which use Shakespeare's work as a way of thinking about current environmental issues. So Sharon O'Dair, who gave the answer "no" to her question "Is it Shakespearean Ecocriticism if it isn't Presentist?,"[17] also linked *Richard II* to current debates, but rather differently from Bruckner. Once again taking the garden scene as a prompt, she focused on the Deepwater Horizon oil spill of 2010, writing:

> One would like to think that the figurative descendants of Shakespeare's gardener, we who make up liberal democratic states, carried with us and enhanced the gardener's wisdom. But our record in the Gulf and elsewhere suggests that we have not.[18]

Careful management, rather than profit-driven land-grabs, should be where we begin, and *Richard II* can help to remind us of this.

There is no doubting the significance of such readings which use Shakespeare's work, which has such a high cultural value, to engage with pressing concerns about human uses of and responsibilities towards the non-animal nonhuman natural world and the same impetus propels animal-sensitive readings of the play as well. Indeed, a history of the critical engagement with *Richard II*'s animals reveals a parallel to that which happened in relation to discussions of the garden. We move, once again, from interpreting imagery to contemplating actual relationships in a way that brings Shakespeare's play into conversation with current debates.

II Reading the Kings' Horses

Despite the fact that *Richard II* is not as full of animal imagery as some of Shakespeare's other plays there are creatures in it that are worth addressing. For that reason, it is odd that these are barely touched upon by Altick because, as I will show, just as the close reading of garden imagery offered up significant meanings, so the play's horses can also reveal much. And yet, Altick noted only one animal-related image set in his article—"*snake-venom*"—which he argued links "the idea of the garden on the one hand (for what grossly untended garden would be without its snakes?) and the idea of the tongue on the other."[19] That is, it connects the corruption of the natural world, figured in the serpent's tempting of Eve (the Queen has the Gardener seduced by both [3.4.75–76]), to the corruption of the political world, figured in the representation of the king's flatterers as "vipers" (3.2.129). As such, "*snake-venom*" reveals a correlation that I will argue is central to Shakespeare's use of horses in the play.

Altick, however, paid no attention to these horses, and this may be because he regarded characters' discussions of them to be referring to real but offstage animals rather than to emblematic ones, reinforcing the sense in which his reading was focused on imagery rather than any materially real nature.[20] It is with Robert N. Watson's 1983 article "Horsemanship in Shakespeare's Second Tetralogy" that horses come to be more fully recognized as possessing symbolic meanings in the plays. In that Watson argues that "literal and figurative references to horsemanship serve to connect the failure of self-rule in such figures as Richard II, Hotspur, Falstaff, and the Dolphin with their exclusion from political rule."[21] Such a reading relates Shakespeare's equine imagery to the figures of the horse and the charioteer in Plato's *Phaedrus* in which controlling a horse models, as Watson puts it, "restraint of unruly passions." This is an image, he suggests, that was "alive in the minds of English Renaissance authors," and so established was the idea that

> By the time Shakespeare began writing his second tetralogy, these associations had evidently been extended and transmuted into the conception of the king as a sort of horseman who must restrain and guide an otherwise unruly state, composed largely of beastly rabble and their crude appetites.[22]

As such, when Bolingbroke, in his hour of triumph, is described by the Duke of York as entering London "Mounted upon a hot and fiery steed, / Which his aspiring rider seemed to know" (5.2.8–9), Watson writes of the moment:

> the horse Bolingbroke rides here reflects his burning ambitious appetites; but as he is able to modulate those appetites within himself … so he is able to regulate the actual horse and thus make a usefully impressive equestrian figure on his way to the throne.[23]

This conception of the symbolic value of horsemanship would seem to be repeated at the end of *Richard II* when, in Watson's words, "Bolingbroke completes his political usurpation by yet another usurpation." Sitting in his prison cell, the deposed Richard is told by his former Groom that Barbary, "That horse that thou so often has bestrid," was ridden by the new king on his coronation day (5.5.79). That Bolingbroke is riding Richard's horse emblematizes the transfer of power: for Jennifer Flaherty, "the act of riding Barbary instils kingship in Henry, marking the shift in power as much as the coronation itself."[24]

Karen Raber has reiterated the value of equine imagery for thinking about political rule in an essay on *1 Henry IV*, reading horse riding as "an ideologically charged skill, conveying the authority of the rider to control the bestial passions of the masses as their rightful ruler."[25] But alongside this Platonic vision she also traces how, in exercising the very skills that make manifest the control that is symbolized in horse riding, something else can emerge. She turns, that is, away from the philosophical debate to think about real horses and real riding and traces these encounters back to her analysis of *1 Henry IV*. In a sense, this parallels the shift in focus from allegory to material reality that can be traced in Bruckner's reading of the garden in *Richard II*, and indeed, I am using Raber's essay as an important way of addressing that earlier play.

Raber shows how, in early modern thought, riding could also represent a kind of cross-species collaboration in that "the 'horse' becomes a reciprocal portion of that construct, the 'horse-man', which is always understood in early modern formulations as the temporary and provisional union of one perceiving and embodied creature with another." Or, as Michel Baret wrote in his early seventeenth-century horse training manual *An Hipponomie, or the Vineyard of Horsemanship*: "you shall thinke to bring your Horse, and your selfe to seeme but one body."[26] This union of horse and man (and it is men who are being written of here) has a flip-side, however: "Becoming one with a horse," Raber writes, "can always slide into becoming something too much like a horse."[27] Such a double potential in the early modern understanding allows for an ambiguity to exist in the symbolic meaning of riding: a hierarchical relationship of control can become one of loss of differentiation. And it is in the context of this ambiguity that we should revisit York's description of Bolingbroke's entry into London in 5.2, because it is my argument that *Richard II* is more ambivalent in its representation of his rise to political power, and of human power more generally, than Watson and Flaherty propose.

York, as noted above, describes "great Bolingbroke, / Mounted upon a hot and fiery steed, / Which his aspiring rider seemed to know" (5.2.7–9), and Watson reads this as evidencing Bolingbroke's control—a Platonic reading that is certainly one possible interpretation of this moment. I suggest, however, that just as the man on top of the horse which symbolizes human dominion can become the image of a bestialization of the rider, so another reading of York's description might be available. The line "[w]hich his aspiring rider seemed to know" is ambiguous: the "which" refers to the animal as the subject of the sentence (which horse seemed to know his rider), an image that reiterates Gaunt's sense of the active presence of the nonhuman world. But there is the chance that the "which" in York's description might also be referring to the horse as the passive object of knowledge (which horse the rider seemed to know). As such, Bolingbroke's horse could be read as the embodiment of the "epistemological cusp" that Bruckner wrote of: it is a creature that "is/is not living." But I think we can also link the ambiguity of York's "which" to Raber's reading of horsemanship. In this triumphant entry the animal fits the man to the extent that human and horse, subject and object, cannot be told apart, and this moment of conquest is shadowed by an image of Bolingbroke as less than properly human.

The slippage from human to beast that Raber finds in horse riding, and that I am tracing at this moment in *Richard II*, is made present in another way in 5.2 in a possible echo of a text from less than a decade earlier. In *Tamburlaine* II.4.3, Marlowe's hero, who is, like Bolingbroke, a self-made rather than God-ordained monarch, enters the stage in triumph in a chariot pulled by two kings: he has literally bridled and made-horse those he has defeated. Timothy Francisco states that Tamburlaine's actions push his captives "along the species grid from animalized human, to animalized animal, and finally to object, denied any semblance of agency." In enacting his triumph in this way, however, Francisco argues that it is Tamburlaine's own status that is undermined: "Marlowe's play evokes chivalric masculinity …

296

only to reveal the violent, bestial core of the martial subject position. In so doing, the play ultimately reduces violent masculine subjectivity to brute animalism."[28] Riding, as Raber showed, slides into becoming beast. Now, Bolingbroke, of course, has not literally bridled Richard as he enters London, but York's description of this moment does offer a perspective that has the potential to undermine the new king. In an echo of Francisco's reading of *Tamburlaine* pushing his rivals "along the species grid," York tells how "rude misgoverned hands from windows' tops / Threw dust and rubbish on King Richard's head" (5.2.5–6). In this image it is as if Richard has not only ceased to be regarded as king but has ceased to be regarded as human and has been objectified, made into a cadaver fit only to be interred beneath the ground.[29] But, as in *Tamburlaine*, the moment also signals Bolingbroke's undoing: the "hands" that throw the dust are "misgoverned"; their new king, riding a hot and fiery steed, is not actually in control at all.

York's subsequent description of Bolingbroke in 5.2 reinforces this reading in that it continues to problematize his status. Responding to the popular acclaim—"all tongues cried, 'God save thee, Bolingbroke!'" (5.2.11)—Bolingbroke, York says, "Bare-headed, lower than his proud steed's neck, / Bespake them thus: 'I thank you, countrymen'" (19–20). The image is of social parity, with Bolingbroke leaning over so as to place himself on a level—literally and socially—with the on-lookers. Jeffrey S. Doty has written of this moment: "Just as his courteous gestures efface differences in rank, so too does his language introduce terms of fraternity," but this reading can only work if the presence of the animal is ignored.[30] If we keep the horse in focus, as York's description requires us to do, then Bolingbroke's riding posture becomes central. His strange position—"lower than his proud steed's neck"— suggests that his presentation of equality might also be read as being a contortion of what is correct.

In addition, and bringing the Platonic conception back into view, in performing equivalence and placing his head below his horse's, a link between Bolingbroke's mind and the animal's is surely being made. Indeed, this moment in *Richard II* seems to be staging a diametrically opposite vision of kingship to that which was presented just over 40 years later in a painting of another king on horseback. Raber and Treva J. Tucker have argued that Anthony Van Dyke's 1638 *Equestrian Portrait of Charles I* is "part of a general salute to Charles' rational rule." In the image, they note, "the king's head … is nearly as large as the horse's unusually diminutive noggin … indicating the triumph of royal intellect over bestial power."[31] Bolingbroke's head being "lower" than his animal's at this moment should thus perhaps be read to suggest much about what is to happen under his governance, and as such, it is possible to see that this is not simply, as Watson had it, a play in which representations of horsemanship evidence Bolingbroke's success. The equine imagery reveals an ambiguity in the play's representation of power.

For Raber, this ambiguity is put to rest in *1 Henry IV* where she argues that "Hal's supposed triumph over Hotspur proleptically performs Cartesianism's abstraction of mind from body, and the reduction of equine other to mere machinery."[32] That is, she argues that the moment when Hal kills Hotspur marks a shift in authority in the play, for sure, but that it marks something else as well. Hal is described as riding in his armor, thus separated from his horse by a layer of metal (flesh does not meet flesh), while Hotspur is presented as being embodied in and through his horse. It is this difference which presages not only Hal's emergence as the true heir to his father's throne, but also a new sense of the human. In Raber's reading, Hal's armor-plating is a kind of physical manifestation of the separation of human from animal that was happening in the intellectual sphere, and his victory marks the triumph of that worldview.

Like Bruckner's then, Raber's reading has Shakespeare pointing towards a new conception of the human, and her thinking fits also with Bruce Boehrer's argument in *Animal Characters* where he suggests that René Descartes' ideas resolved the crisis caused by the entanglement of human and nonhuman that classical thought had bequeathed to the Renaissance "by granting humanity exclusive access to consciousness."[33] And Boehrer's discussion of this emerging Cartesian sense of self is illustrated through a reading of *Richard II*, a reading that takes us, finally, to Barbary.

III Barbary and Barbarity

Having been told that Bolingbroke rode Barbary on his coronation day, Richard asks the Groom "How went he under him?" (5.5.82). This question is not only an acknowledgment of the link between horsemanship and kingship that Watson and Flaherty have noted. Rather, Boehrer argues, it also invokes the story of the stallion Baiardo who appears in Ariosto's *Orlando furioso*, a text from 1516 which was first published in English in 1591, just four years before the likely date of *Richard II*. In possession of what Ariosto termed "intelletto umano," Baiardo, in Boehrer's words, "distinguishes between persons, responds to certain ones with loyalty and intimacy, and confronts others with willful resistance."[34] In short, this horse refuses to be ridden by any but his true owner. Following this lead, Boehrer argues that Richard's question about Barbary is invoking Ariosto's story of Baiardo and that, through this connection, Shakespeare presents his deposed monarch holding on to a worldview in which a horse can possess human qualities; in which nature can have agency. Richard discovers that Barbary is no such creature when, in response to his question, the Groom tells him that the horse went under Bolingbroke "So proudly as if he disdained the ground" (5.5.83), and the deposed monarch responds:

> So proud that Bolingbroke was on his back?
> That jade hath eat bread from my royal hand;
> This hand hath made him proud with clapping him.
> Would he not stumble? Would he not fall down,
> Since pride must have a fall, and break the neck
> Of that proud man that did usurp his back?
>
> *(5.5.84–89)*

For Boehrer, this moment signals the beginning of what he calls "a post-Baiardan universe, marked by the absence of equine reason, equine agency, and a sympathetic concord between human and nonhuman animals." "The play performs," he writes, "the loss of an entire world and the language that conjured it into being."[35] What Gaunt had warned of three acts earlier has come to pass.

Boehrer's reading, like Bruckner's ecocritical one and Raber's animal-sensitive one, thus places *Richard II* within its historical context, here reading it alongside *Orlando furioso*. In particular, he links Shakespeare's representation of Barbary to the way Sir John Harington's English translation of Ariosto departs from its original in its downplaying of "the moments … that endow the horse with intelligence and agency." Boehrer argues that Harington's changes seek to

> reaffirm the categorical distinction between human and nonhuman animals[, and] it seems reasonable to read [his] translation as participating in broad cultural anxieties concerning the character of humanity, anxieties which were also coming to the fore in the philosophical discourse of Harington's contemporaries.[36]

As with Raber's reading of Hal, and Bruckner's reading of the rise of science, so Boehrer's reading sees Harington as presaging a dualist view that classical ideas never suggested. In those classical ideas, in Juliana Schiesari's terms, there is "a continuum of life in which humans also partake reciprocally in animal characteristics"[37]; in this new worldview, however, the human is figured as being utterly separate from the nonhuman natural world.

What is clear from the various essays that have underpinned my analysis so far, then, is that a connection exists between the ecocritical and the animal-sensitive readings. Despite their very different foci, all converge on a view that the plays are offering insight into Shakespeare's sense of writing at a moment of profound change in relationships with the natural world, changes which saw a shift from a conception of humans living in a world of lively nature to one in which nature was instrumentalized. And although the explicit presentism of ecocritical readings is more difficult to trace in animal-sensitive ones, there is a clear connection there too. The ecocritical readings use *Richard II* to point beyond the early modern to the present: to oil spills and fracking, while the animal-sensitive ones consider the implications of the changes they trace for conceptions of the human; but it is these humans, of course, who are creating the oil spills, doing the fracking. What emerges from *Richard II* in these readings, in short, is the advent of a dualist conception in which humans are using nature as a resource rather than viewing themselves as embedded within an animated nonhuman world.

There is no question that these readings are right in their tracing of this shift in Shakespeare's second tetralogy, and, my particular focus, *Richard II*.[38] But I wonder if something else might be present at the end of that play as well, something that undercuts their sense of the completeness of the shift from one way of being to another (a completeness proved, you might say, by the appearance of Descartes' ideas 40 years later). I think the play might harbor doubts about the shift, and my reassessment of York's representation of Bolingbroke's entry into London in 5.2 is an attempt to show one place where we might trace them.

Indeed, there is more to say about that scene to reinforce this point, and to link it to Barbary's appearance three scenes later. After he has told of Bolingbroke's entry, York turns once again to describe how Richard, coming in after his conqueror, was regarded with "contempt" by the crowds: "No man cried God save him!" he says, and he repeats the image from earlier in the scene as if to emphasize its import: "But dust was thrown upon his sacred head" (5.2.27, 28, 30). He goes on:

> had not God for some strong purpose steeled
> The hearts of men, they must perforce have melted
> And barbarism itself have pitied him.
>
> *(5.2.34–36)*

The people, it seems, like the horse later, might have acted differently but did not: barbarism could be transformed into pity but wasn't. And York's use of "barbarism" here links this moment linguistically to Barbary through his name which invokes the horse's North African origins.[39] As such, the connection made between these two moments once again reinforces Raber's sense of the potentially double-edged meaning of horse riding: just as Tamburlaine's animalizing of his rivals dehumanized himself, so the dust-throwing crowd's lack of pity reveals their savagery, and their reduction of status is reinforced through their linguistic link to a horse.[40]

The coincidence of barbarity and a victory parade that can be traced here is repeated in a much later text that, while an accidental connection, offers another way of thinking about this moment in *Richard II*. In his 1940 *Theses on the Philosophy of History*, Walter Benjamin wrote:

> Whoever has emerged victorious participates to this day in the triumphal procession in which the present rulers step over those who are lying prostrate. According to traditional practice, the spoils are carried along in the procession. They are called cultural treasures, and a historical materialist views them with cautious detachment. For without exception the cultural treasures he surveys have an origin which he cannot contemplate without horror.[41]

The role of the materialist critic in response to recognizing the horror, Benjamin writes, is to "brush history against the grain"—to read in a way that interrogates the apparently smooth inevitability of the exercise of power.[42] Benjamin is not, of course, writing about *Richard II* but his ideas seem to fit. York's statement that "had not God for some strong purpose steeled / The hearts of men" they would have acted differently implicitly claims a divine mandate for Bolingbroke's usurpation: the fact that the onlookers did not pity Richard is presented as evidence of God's agreement to the transfer of power. Such a reading, of course, makes true, inevitable, and right the change but, in invoking God's purpose at the point at which a divinely ordained monarch has been overthrown, York is also, I suggest, inviting us to doubt its presence, is asking us, you might say, to read against the grain. And what that reading reveals is the brutality of the usurpation: is a vision of power exercised with unvarnished violence in which Richard is dehumanized, becoming simply one of the spoils of war.

Benjamin continues, echoing York's use of "barbarism" (in Benjamin the German term is "Barbarei"):

> There is no document of civilisation which is not at the same time a document of barbarism. And just as the document is not free of barbarism, barbarism taints also the manner in which it was transmitted from one owner to another.[43]

This is not only a fortunate repetition of terms; the ideas presented by Benjamin offer more than a linguistic link to York's description. They offer a way of understanding why the ambiguity that I suggest exists in *Richard II* may not have been attended to in other critical readings. Benjamin's ideas suggest that it is possible that readings that assume links between political rule and human dominion, and which regard *Richard II* as a play that marks the emergence of instrumentalized conception of nature, might be tainted by the very "barbarism" they are holding up for scrutiny. We might view such readings as having been written, you might say, after Cartesianism has triumphed. In what remains of this chapter I want to read *Richard II* "against the grain"; to show that Bolingbroke's rise to power and the parallel shift in attitude to the nonhuman world can be interpreted as presenting, in addition, a glimpse of a very different conception of human status. Such a view is undoubtedly in a marginalized position in the play, but its presence, if quietly, undermines the sense of the completeness of the victory of the oncoming Cartesianism that *Richard II* seems to project.

IV God a Mercy Horse

Having complained that Barbary did not stumble when asked to carry Bolingbroke, Richard states:

> Forgiveness, horse. Why do I rail on thee,
> Since thou, created to be awed by man,
> Wast born to bear? I was not made a horse,
> And yet I bear a burden like an ass,
> Spurred, galled and tired by jaucing Bolingbroke.

(5.5.90–94)

It is possible to hear a double meaning like the one that persists in the "which" in York's description of Bolingbroke's fiery steed here. "I was not made a horse" is obviously a simple claim about species (I was created a human), and yet it could be read as a reference to the kind of transformation that happened to Tamburlaine's rivals who were literally bridled. This did not happen in *Richard II* but perhaps stating "I was not made a horse" raises it as a possibility.

But even if we ignore this potential ambiguity, the slippage of human into animal in Richard's speech is worth contemplating from another perspective. It seems ironic that at the very moment when Barbary has been relegated to the role of mindless tool—"born to bear" weight rather than meaning—the former king directly addresses the absent creature as if he were a fellow being rather than a lesser one. But the fellowship here emerges as a logical outcome of the shift in power in the play. By 5.5, this is Bolingbroke's England and, just as the horse has become an animal incapable of possessing meaning beyond his function for humans, so the former king by this point recognizes himself as being an outdated symbol—like the idea of the loyal horse. Richard comes to see, in short, that he also has no place in Henry IV's kingdom.

His claim to kinship with the horse ("I bear a burden like an ass") thus seems to end almost as soon as it begins, and it seems strangely appropriate that this moment is prologue to Richard's assassination. His role is over; his supernatural, divinely ordained rule is no longer required or relevant in this new world. But there is something else going on here as well, something that might offer a hint that an alternative to the instrumental view of nature might be present as the play ends. This is not a return of the enchanted world in which a kind of reciprocity might exist between human and nonhuman nature, that "This earth shall have a feeling" as Richard had declared before his defeat (3.2.24). Rather, it is to be found in the persistence of the very doubt that Descartes' philosophy was an attempt to overcome.

A prompt for this suggestion comes through a possible connection between Richard's "Forgiveness, horse" and words attributed to the comedian Richard Tarlton (d.1588) in a posthumously recorded story of his encounter with Morocco the Intelligent Horse at the Cross Keys Inn in London.[44] Morocco, who was still performing at the time *Richard II* was first staged, appeared to be able to count, answer questions, and make judgments, and on the day Tarlton went to see the act, so the narrative has it, the comedian was spotted in the crowd by Morocco's owner, Banks, who

> (to maketh the people laugh) saies *Signior* (to his horse) Go fetch me the veryest foole in the company. The Jade comes immediately, and with his mouth drawes *Tarlton* forth: *Tarlton* (with merry words) said nothing, but *God a mercy Horse*.

The story has it that the comedian was "angry inwardly," and took his revenge by requesting, in turn, that the horse should

> bring me the veryest whore-master in this company. He shall (saies *Banks*) *Signior* (saies he) bring Master *Tarlton* here the veryest whore-master in the company. The horse leades his Master to him. Then God a mercy horse indeed, says *Tarlton*.

The anecdote concludes with a claim: "ever after, it was a by-word thorow *London, God a mercy Horse,* and so is to this day."[45]

The assertion that "God a mercy horse" became a familiar part of the city's conversation is difficult to substantiate, of course, but a basic search on the Early English Books Online Text Creation Partnership website for "mercy horse" reveals "God-a-mercy horse," along with "cry you mercy horse" and "gra-mercy horse," in 16 texts from the period, the earliest dating from 1613.[46] The same search on the English Broadside Ballad Archive website reveals another usage, from c. 1619–29. In "Ragged, and Torne and True. / Or, the poore mans Resoltion [sic]" one verse tells how:

> The Hostler, to maintaine
> himselfe with money ins purse,
> Approves the Proverbe true,
> and says Gramercy Horse:
> He robs the travelling beast,
> that cannot divulge his ill,
> He steales a whole handfull at least,
> from every halfe peck he should fill.[47]

This is hardly evidence of common usage, but such repetition does suggest that the phrase had some popular value, and I wonder if Richard II's "Forgiveness, horse" might also be read as another rendition of it.

What would it mean to have the deposed king invoke for his audience the encounter between a recently deceased clown and a performing horse? It is, of course, another way of diminishing Richard's status: the former monarch becomes the "veryest foole in the company," like his namesake the comedian. But I think this possible connection also allows us to see Richard's "Forgiveness, horse" as a glimpse of another way of being in the world. I have suggested elsewhere that Tarlton's response to Morocco is a popular instantiation of the skepticism that was increasingly significant in intellectual debate in the late sixteenth century.[48] In this philosophy human superiority was challenged in part through a consideration of animals' engagement with the world. Their capacities for self-medication, home-building, rearing their young—all done without the aid of books—were represented as contesting the apparently natural superiority of humans: for if human superiority was so natural, why did humans require guidance to do these things? In the story of Tarlton's encounter with him, Morocco's calling Banks a "whore-master" is a mark of something more than obedience; it is a performance of an animal's capacity to think for itself in a way that counters human wishes. At this moment Morocco appears to undo his master's mastery.

The classical foundation for early modern skepticism was Sextus Empiricus' second-century CE *Outlines of Scepticism,* which was first printed in 1562. A partial English translation—*The Sceptick*—was circulating in manuscript in the 1590s,[49] and this translation focused on the importance of the senses to human understanding of the world, recognizing that we need to think, for example, about the nature of eyes in order to properly consider what is seen with them, and the point of reference here is animals' different sensory engagement with the world. This leads the author of *The Sceptick* to ask:

> why should I presume to prefer my conceit and imagination in affirming that a thing is thus or thus in its own nature, because it seemeth to me to be so, before the conceit of other living creatures, who may as well think it to be otherwise in its own nature, because it appeareth otherwise to them than it doth to me?[50]

The aim of asking this question is not to answer it: "The Sceptick doth neither affirm nor deny any position," the author writes.[51] Rather, the point of skeptical inquiry is to pause over the human sense of superiority—the human's triumphal procession of knowing, you might say—in order to undercut it. And the aim of this suspension of judgment is, as Sextus Empiricus put it, "the hope of becoming tranquil," of letting go of the reins, you might say.[52]

David Bevington has written that while "'Sceptic,' 'sceptical,' and 'scepticism' form no part of Shakespeare's vocabulary … he may have pondered what we would call sceptical ideas," and he is not alone in tracing these, in particular, in plays written in the 15 years after *Richard II*.[53] I am suggesting that the link to Tarlton's encounter with Morocco might reveal an earlier engagement with at least a popular conception of skeptical ideas. And if this is so, then it is possible that the appearance of Barbary might be read not only as another rendition of Bolingbroke's usurpation of the throne but as something more disruptive. "Forgiveness, horse" is a version of *The Sceptick*'s refusal to affirm or deny in the face of animal being. It is a moment in which order, and the exercise of power it is based upon, is suspended, in which fellowship rather than dominion is possible.

By 5.5 Richard has thus come to recognize that his earlier claim that "Not all the water in the rough rude sea / Can wash the balm off from an anointed king" (3.2.54–55) is a lie, and that the divine purpose that underpins such an idea is absent. Instead, he comes to realize that a king is, in fact, a human construct: that a monarch can be "kinged" and "unkinged" (5.5.36, 37). As a parallel—and the political and the natural spheres have been constantly paralleled in the play—asking forgiveness of Barbary could be an acknowledgment that humanity's special status might also be a construction made by humans rather than a product of divine fiat. At the end of *Richard II* it is possible, then, that while we are looking at the emergence of a new world of instrumentalized nature, the play also suggests that this world—this barbaric construction—can also be seen, if only briefly, for what it is: not natural, inevitable, unquestionable, but just one possible outcome.

Richard dies, though. He launches himself at his assassins with a cry of impatience which seems completely at odds with the tranquility that skepticism is meant to bring, and is killed in the struggle just 12 lines after asking "Forgiveness, horse." As such, this seems to cancel the possibility of the skepticism he has voiced persisting in the play. It seems to suggest that this is simply Richard's fantasy of another way of being, akin to his imagining himself to be a beggar (5.5.33). But as the scene which follows shows, his murder is far from ending his power.

5.6, *Richard II*'s final scene, begins with reports confirming Bolingbroke's victory which is evidenced by the display of the spoils yet again. The heads of his enemies, we are told, have been sent to London, and the listing of those who have been decapitated—Salisbury, Spencer, Blunt, Kent, Brocas, Sir Bennet Seely (5.6.8, 14)—underlines the very real violence that underpins his rise to power. And it is at this moment that Richard's body is brought onto the stage. Here is another of the spoils that have ensured Henry's ascent; here is another piece of barbarity. But Bolingbroke's response is far from triumphant; it does not reflect a clarity of mind that might be expected of the new ruler of the realm: "Though I did wish him dead, /

I hate the murderer, love him murdered" (5.6.39–40). What we are seeing here is a king whose mind is divided, whose desires (wishes, hates, loves) seem contradictory, seem to exceed what is reasonable and orderly. And so when he states, "I'll make a voyage to the Holy Land / To wash this blood off from my guilty hand" (5.6.49–50) this appears to be a solution to the upheaval. But, just as his feelings of hate and love dispute with one another, so his invocation of Pontius Pilate works against him. The image of hand-washing gives Richard a Christ-like status which, in turn, suggests he has an enduring power. And this is a power that can be traced right through to the very end of the second tetralogy where, in the final speech in *Henry V*, the Chorus takes us right back to the story's beginning and reminds us of Richard's failures by extolling Henry V's great achievement as being the creation of "the world's best garden." But this accomplishment is temporary: the Chorus follows with a brief history of the reign of Henry VI, during which "they lost France and made his England bleed." The world's best garden, like Gaunt's England, was destroyed, "Which oft our stage hath shown."[54] Victories are momentary; triumphal processions performances; new worldviews provisional; alternatives available.

As such, the ecocritical and animal-sensitive readings that see *Richard II* as marking the emergence of modernity through land and equestrian imagery are surely right. But there is also something else possible; something that might challenge the sense of the completeness of the transformation of political and human power that appears to be in place at the end of the play. This other perspective can be a call for tranquility, for a pause over what is considered to be true and unquestionable, and as such "Forgiveness, horse" could be read as an act of standing-down rather than a call to action. But Richard's final fight tells us that from a realization that things are not as they have to be can come a refusal to accept how things are. The skeptical question, how do I know?, is a call to action that can challenge what is, apparently, inevitable and natural. "Forgiveness, horse," as such, is a humbled way forward, not just a regretful recollection of what has been lost.

Notes

1 Greg Garrard, *Ecocriticism*, 2nd ed. (London: Routledge, 2012), 149.
2 Charles R. Forker, the editor of the Arden edition used here, gives the play the title *King Richard II*, but I have opted to call it by its more familiar title *Richard II* throughout.
3 I take the adjectival form "animal-sensitive" from Sandra Swart, "Settler Stock: Animals and Power in Mid-Seventeenth-Century Contact at the Cape, circa 1652–62," in *Animals and Early Modern Identity*, ed. Pia F. Cuneo (Farnham: Ashgate, 2014), 258.
4 Simon Estok, "Theory from the Fringes: Animals, Ecocriticism, Shakespeare," *Mosaic* 40, no. 1 (2007): 69.
5 William Shakespeare, *King Richard II*, ed. Charles R. Forker (London: Arden, 2002), 3.4.40–44. Subsequent references to this edition are included in the text.
6 See Andrew Cunningham, "The Culture of Gardens," in *Cultures of Natural History*, ed. N. Jardine, J.A. Secord and E.C. Spary (Cambridge: Cambridge University Press, 1996), especially 41–47.
7 Richard D. Altick, "Symphonic Imagery in *Richard II*," *PMLA* 62, no. 2 (1947): 339, 359, 340, 351.
8 Cleanth Brooks, *The Well Wrought Urn: Studies in the Structure of Poetry* (London: Dobson Books, 1947).
9 Jennifer Munroe, "Shakespeare and Ecocriticism Reconsidered," *Literature Compass* 12, no. 9 (2015): 462. In another essay, Munroe writing with Rebecca Laroche offers a reading of the garden scene with "a focus on intersecting material practices related to the female body, animals, and plants": Laroche and Munroe, "On a Bank of Rue; or Material Ecofeminist Inquiry and the Garden of *Richard II*," *Shakespeare Studies* 42 (2014): 42–50.
10 Lynne Bruckner, "'Consuming Means, Soon Preys upon Itself': Political Expedience and Environmental Degradation in *Richard II*," in *Shakespeare and the Urgency of Now: Criticism and Theory in the 21st Century*, eds. Cary DiPietro and Hugh Grady (London: Palgrave Macmillan, 2013), 128.
11 Bruckner, "'Consuming Means'," 133, 135–36.

"Forgiveness, Horse"

12 Ibid., 131. The relevance of these contemporary concerns to *Richard II*'s representation of the non-human natural world is also outlined in Amy L. Tigner, *Literature and the Renaissance Garden from Elizabeth I to Charles II England's Paradise* (London: Routledge, 2012), 13.

13 Bruckner, "'Consuming Means'," 133.

14 Ibid., 133. Carolyn Merchant traced the wider shift from a nature recognized as full of life, to an object to be penetrated, categorized, and used in the development of the new science in her classic *The Death of Nature: Women, Ecology and the Scientific Revolution* (London: Harper Row, 1980).

15 Bruckner, "'Consuming Means'," 133.

16 Ibid., 143–44.

17 Sharon O'Dair, "Is It Shakespearean Ecocriticism If It Isn't Presentist?," in *Ecocritical Shakespeare*, eds. Lynne Bruckner and Dan Brayton (London: Routledge, 2016), 71–85.

18 Sharon O'Dair, "'To Fright the Animals and to Kill Them Up': Shakespeare and Ecology," *Shakespeare Studies* 29 (2011): 81. See also Heidi Scott, "Ecological Microcosms Envisioned in Shakespeare's *Richard II*," *The Explicator* 67, no. 4 (2009): 267–71, for another reading that brings *Richard II* into conversation with current ecological issues.

19 Altick, "Symphonic," 351.

20 Indeed, it is as a kind of mid-point between Altick's reading and one that might reflect on the reality of horses that we can read Harry Levin's "Falstaff Uncolted." Here it is the very off-stage-ness of the horses that is the focus – they are used by Shakespeare, he argues, to think about the limits of the theater. Levin, "Falstaff Uncolted," *Modern Language Notes* 61, no. 5 (1946): 305–10.

21 Robert N. Watson, "Horsemanship in Shakespeare's Second Tetralogy," *English Literary Renaissance* 13, no. 3 (1983): 274.

22 Watson, "Horsemanship," 274–75, 276, 278.

23 Ibid., 285.

24 Jennifer Flaherty, "'Know Us by Our Horses': Equine Imagery in Shakespeare's *Henriad*," in *The Horse as Cultural Icon: The Real and the Symbolic Horse in the Early Modern World*, eds. Peter Edwards, Karl A.E. Enenkel, and Elspeth Graham (Leiden: Brill, 2012), 315.

25 Karen Raber, "Equeer: Human-Equine Erotics in *1 Henry IV*," in *The Oxford Handbook of Shakespeare and Embodiment: Gender, Sexuality, and Race* ed. Valerie Traub (Oxford: Oxford University Press, 2016), 348.

26 Raber, "Equeer," 355 and citing Michel Baret, *An Hipponomie, or Vineyard of Horsemanship* (1618), 356.

27 Raber, "Equeer," 356.

28 Timothy Francisco, "Marlowe's War Horses: Cyborgs, Soldiers, and Queer Companions," in *Violent Masculinities: Male Aggression in Early Modern Texts and Culture*, eds. Jennifer Feather and Catherine E. Thomas (New York: Palgrave Macmillan, 2013), 59, 48. Thanks to Holly Dugan for drawing my attention to this essay.

29 This is also an echo of Richard's request to be "buried in the King's highway," uttered as he acknowledged his defeat (3.3.155).

30 Jeffrey S. Doty, "Shakespeare's *Richard II*, 'Popularity,' and the Early Modern Public Sphere," *Shakespeare Quarterly* 61, no. 2 (2010): 195. My analysis here echoes Raber's reading of Jonathan Goldberg's and Matt Bell's readings of *1 Henry IV* which responds to the fact that both "ignore entirely the animals upon whose backs the whole image rides." Raber, "Equeer," 350.

31 Karen Raber and Treva J. Tucker, "Introduction," in *The Culture of the Horse: Status, Discipline, and Identity in the Early Modern World* (Basingstoke: Palgrave Macmillan, 2005), 16.

32 Raber, "Equeer," 360.

33 Bruce Thomas Boehrer, *Animal Characters: Nonhuman Beings in Early Modern Literature* (Philadelphia: University of Pennsylvania Press, 2010), 10. On the relationship between Descartes' ideas and earlier thinking in English culture, much of which was informed by classical ideas, see also Erica Fudge, *Brutal Reasoning: Animals, Rationality, and Humanity in Early Modern England* (Ithaca, NY: Cornell University Press, 2006).

34 Boehrer, *Animal Characters*, 29.

35 Ibid., 50, 54.

36 Ibid., 38, 41.

37 Juliana Schiesari, "Rethinking Humanism: Animals and the Analogic Imagination in the Italian Renaissance," *Shakespeare Studies* 41 (2013): 61.

38 The shift the ecocritical and animal sensitive readings trace mirrors that which Terence Hawkes traced in a different register in 1973. He argued that the "central dramatic concern with opposition [in *Richard II*], embodied in its most extreme form as a civil strife, is quite literally made manifest through the language of the play." Richard, Hawkes suggests, believes that "he can mould reality (and so society) as *he* wishes, simply by the use of 'comfortable' words [ignoring] a reality larger than himself." For Bolingbroke, on the other hand, "reality cannot be changed by language." Hawkes, *Shakespeare's Talking Animals: Language and Drama in Society* (London: Edward Arnold, 1973), 76, 86, 94.

39 See Paul Fatout, "Roan Barbary," *The Shakespeare Association Bulletin* 15, no. 2 (1940): 67–74; and Sandra Swart, "Dark Horses: The Horse in Africa in the Sixteenth and Seventeenth Centuries," in *Horse as Cultural Icon*, 241–60.

40 See Patricia Parker, "Barbers and Barbary: Early Modern Cultural Semantics," *Renaissance Drama* 33 (2004): 201–44.

41 Walter Benjamin, *Theses on the Philosophy of History* (1940), in *Illuminations* ed. Hannah Arendt (London: Fontana, 1992), 248.

42 Benjamin, *Theses,* 248.

43 Ibid.

44 I have written about Morocco at greater length in "A Reasonable Animal?" in Fudge, *Brutal Reasoning*, 123–46.

45 Richard Tarlton, *Tarltons Jests* (London: I.H., 1638), C2r-v.

46 https://quod.lib.umich.edu/e/eebogroup/ (accessed July 3, 2019).

47 "Ragged, and Torne and True. / or, the Poore Mans Resoltion," EBBA 30240 (c. 1619–29), British Library, Roxburgh Ballad. https://ebba.english.ucsb.edu/ballad/30240/xml (accessed July 19, 2019).

48 Fudge, *Brutal Reasoning*, 144.

49 On the dating of this MS see William M. Hamlin, "A Lost Translation Found? An Edition of *The Sceptick* (c.1590) Based on Extant Manuscripts [with Text]," *English Literary Renaissance* 31, no. 1 (2001): 36.

50 Anon, *The Sceptick*, in Hamlin, "Lost Translation," 45.

51 Anon, *The Sceptick*, 42.

52 Sextus Empiricus, *Outlines of Scepticism*, trans. and ed. Julia Annas and Julian Barnes (Cambridge: Cambridge University Press, 2000), 5.

53 David Bevington, *Shakespeare's Ideas: More Things in Heaven and Earth* (Chichester: Wiley Blackwell, 2008), 9 [ebook].

54 William Shakespeare, *Henry V,* in *The Complete Works*, eds. Stanley Wells and Gary Taylor (Oxford: Oxford University Press, 1989), Epilogue 7 and 12–13.

APPENDIX

Cat Tracks: Alternative Ways through the Volume

Themes and Connections

<u>Animal Matter, Animals as Matter</u>
Chapter 1, Rebecca Ann Bach, "Avian Shakespeare"
Chapter 2, Dan Brayton, "Shakespeare's Fish Ponds: Matter, Metaphor, and Market"
Chapter 6, Ian MacInnes, "Cow-Cross Lane and Curriers Row: Animal Networks in Early Modern England"
Chapter 13, Bruce Boehrer, "Shrewd Shakespeare"
Chapter 15, Todd A. Borlik, "Performing *The Winter's Tale* in the 'Open': Bear Plays, Skinners' Pageants, and the Early Modern Fur Trade"
Chapter 19, Jennifer Allport Reid, "'Wearing the Horn': Class and Community in the Shakespearean Hunt"

<u>Animal Language</u>
Chapter 12, Liza Blake and Kathryn Vomero Santos, "What Does the Wolf Say?: Animal Language and Political Noise in *Coriolanus*"
Chapter 13, Bruce Boehrer, "Shrewd Shakespeare"

<u>Etymology</u>
Chapter 1, Rebecca Ann Bach, "Avian Shakespeare"
Chapter 13, Bruce Boehrer, "Shrewd Shakespeare"
Chapter 17, Laurie Shannon, "Silly Creatures: *King Lear* (with Sheep)"

<u>Disease and Death</u>
Chapter 8, Lucinda Cole, "Zoonotic Shakespeare: Animals, Plagues, and the Medical Posthumanities"
Chapter 23, Erica Fudge, "'Forgiveness, Horse': The Barbaric World of *Richard II*"

<u>Domestication</u>
Chapter 3, Bryan Alkemeyer, "'I Am the Dog': Canine Abjection, Species Reversal, and Misanthropic Satire in *The Two Gentlemen of Verona*"
Chapter 4, Crystal Bartolovich, "Learning from Crab: Primitive Accumulation, Migration, Species Being"

Appendix

Chapter 8, Lucinda Cole, "Zoonotic Shakespeare: Animals, Plagues, and the Medical Posthumanities"
Chapter 10, Keith Botelho, "Swarm Life: Shakespeare's School of Insects"

Labor
Chapter 4, Crystal Bartolovich, "Learning from Crab: Primitive Accumulation, Migration, Species Being"
Chapter 11, Nicole Jacobs, "Bernardian Ecology and Topsell's Redemptive Bee in *The Tempest*"
Chapter 14, Elspeth Graham, "The Training Relationship: Horses, Hawks, Dogs, Bears and Humans"
Chapter 16, Julian Yates, "Counting Shakespeare's Sheep with *The Second Shepherd's Play*"
Chapter 19, Jennifer Allport Reid, "'Wearing the Horn': Class and Community in the Shakespearean Hunt"

Material History
Chapter 6, Ian MacInnes, "Cow-Cross Lane and Curriers Row: Animal Networks in Early Modern England"
Chapter 8, Lucinda Cole, "Zoonotic Shakespeare: Animals, Plagues, and the Medical Posthumanities"

Performance:
Chapter 15, Todd A. Borlik, "Performing *The Winter's Tale* in the 'Open': Bear Plays, Skinners' Pageants, and the Early Modern Fur Trade"
Chapter 16, Julian Yates, "Counting Shakespeare's Sheep with the Second Shepherd's Play"
Chapter 17, Laurie Shannon, "Silly Creatures: *King Lear* (with Sheep)"

Race
Chapter 3, Bryan Alkemeyer, "'I Am the Dog': Canine Abjection, Species Reversal, and Misanthropic Satire in *The Two Gentlemen of Verona*"
Chapter 7, Benjamin Bertram: "'Everything Exists by Strife': War and Creaturely Violence in Shakespeare's Late Tragedies"
Chapter 20, Steven Swarbrick, "On Eating, the Animal that Therefore I Am: Race and Animal Rites in *Titus Andronicus*"

Sexuality
Chapter 20, Steven Swarbrick, "On Eating, the Animal that Therefore I Am: Race and Animal Rites in *Titus Andronicus*"
Chapter 21, Robert Wakeman, "'What's This? What's This? Fish and Sexuality in *Measure for Measure*"
Chapter 22, Karen Raber, "My Palfrey, Myself: Toward a Queer Phenomenology of the Horse-Human Bond in *Henry V* and Beyond"

Single Creatures vs. Collectives
Chapter 4, Crystal Bartolovich, "Learning from Crab: Primitive Accumulation, Migration, Species Being"
Chapter 5, Karl Steel, "Beasts, Animals, and Animal Metaphor, in Shakespeare and His Fellow Dramatists"
Chapter 9, Joseph Campana, "Flock, Herd, Swarm: A Shakespearean Lexicon of Creaturely Collectivity"

Appendix

Chapter 10, Keith Botelho, "Swarm Life: Shakespeare's School of Insects"
Chapter 12, Liza Blake and Kathryn Vomero Santos, "What Does the Wolf Say?: Animal Language and Political Noise in *Coriolanus*"

Sound
Chapter 11, Nicole Jacobs, "Bernardian Ecology and Topsell's Redemptive Bee in *The Tempest*"
Chapter 12, Liza Blake and Kathryn Vomero Santos, "What Does the Wolf Say?: Animal Language and Political Noise in *Coriolanus*"

Sovereignty
Chapter 9, Joseph Campana, "Flock, Herd, Swarm: A Shakespearean Lexicon of Creaturely Collectivity"
Chapter 11, Nicole Jacobs, "Bernardian Ecology and Topsell's Redemptive Bee in *The Tempest*"
Chapter 18, Nicole Mennell, "The Lion King: Shakespeare's Beastly Sovereigns"
Chapter 23, Erica Fudge, "'Forgiveness, Horse': The Barbaric World of *Richard II*"

Space and Environment
Chapter 2, Daniel Brayton, "Shakespeare's Fishponds: Matter, Metaphor, and Market"
Chapter 6, Ian MacInnes, "Cow-Cross Lane and Curriers Row: Animal Networks in Early Modern England"
Chapter 8, Lucinda Cole, "Zoonotic Shakespeare: Animals, Plagues, and the Medical Posthumanities"

War and Violence
Chapter 7, Benjamin Bertram, "'Everything Exists by Strife': War and Creaturely Violence in Shakespeare's Late Tragedies"
Chapter 23, Erica Fudge, "'Forgiveness, Horse': The Barbaric World of *Richard II*"

Philosophers and Theorists

Aesop
Chapter 12, Liza Blake and Kathryn Vomero Santos, "What Does the Wolf Say?: Animal Language and Political Noise in *Coriolanus*"

Sarah Ahmed
Chapter 22, Karen Raber, "My Palfrey, Myself: Toward a Queer Phenomenology of the Horse-Human Bond in *Henry V* and Beyond"

Giorgio Agamben
Chapter 15, Todd A. Borlik, "Performing *The Winter's Tale* in the 'Open': Bear Plays, Skinners' Pageants, and the Early Modern Fur Trade"

Karen Barad
Chapter 20, Steven Swarbrick, "On Eating, the Animal that Therefore I Am: Race and Animal Rites in *Titus Andronicus*"

Gilles Deleuze
Chapter 20, Steven Swarbrick, "On Eating, the Animal that Therefore I Am: Race and Animal Rites in *Titus Andronicus*"

Appendix

Jacques Derrida
Chapter 5, Karl Steel, "Beasts, Animals, and Animal Metaphor, in Shakespeare and His Fellow Dramatists"
Chapter 8, Lucinda Cole, "Zoonotic Shakespeare: Animals, Plagues, and the Medical Posthumanities"
Chapter 13, Bruce Boehrer, "Shrewd Shakespeare"
Chapter 20, Steven Swarbrick, "On Eating, the Animal that Therefore I Am: Race and Animal Rites in *Titus Andronicus*"

Michel Foucault
Chapter 9, Joseph Campana, "Flock, Herd, Swarm: A Shakespearean Lexicon of Creaturely Collectivity"
Chapter 16, Julian Yates, "Counting Shakespeare's Sheep with *The Second Shepherd's Play*"

Rene Girard
Chapter 19, Jennifer Allport Reid, "'Wearing the Horn': Class and Community in the Shakespearean Hunt"

Donna Haraway
Chapter 20, Steven Swarbrick, "On Eating, the Animal that Therefore I Am: Race and Animal Rites in *Titus Andronicus*"
Chapter 4, Crystal Bartolovich, "Learning from Crab: Primitive Accumulation, Migration, Species Being"

Graham Harman
Chapter 4, Crystal Bartolovich, "Learning from Crab: Primitive Accumulation, Migration, Species Being"

Melanie Klein
Chapter 20, Steven Swarbrick, "On Eating, the Animal that Therefore I Am: Race and Animal Rites in *Titus Andronicus*"

Bruno Latour
Chapter 1, Rebecca Ann Bach, "Avian Shakespeare"

Karl Marx
Chapter 4, Crystal Bartolovich, "Learning from Crab: Primitive Accumulation, Migration, Species Being"

Freidrich Nietzsche
Chapter 11, Nicole Jacobs, "'Bernardian Ecology and Topsell's Redemptive Bee in *The Tempest*"

Petrarch
Chapter 7, Benjamin Bertram, "'Everything Exists by Strife': War and Creaturely Violence in Shakespeare's Late Tragedies"

Cary Wolfe
Chapter 3, Bryan Alkemeyer, "'I Am the Dog': Canine Abjection, Species Reversal, and Misanthropic Satire in *The Two Gentlemen of Verona*"

Appendix

Shakespeare's Works

All's Well that Ends Well
Chapter 2, Daniel Brayton, "Shakespeare's Fishponds: Matter, Metaphor, and Market"

As You Like It
Chapter 19, Jennifer Allport Reid, "'Wearing the Horn': Class and Community in the Shakespearean Hunt"

Coriolanus
Chapter 7, Benjamin Bertram, "'Everything Exists by Strife': War and Creaturely Violence in Shakespeare's Late Tragedies"
Chapter 8, Lucinda Cole, "Zoonotic Shakespeare: Animals, Plagues, and the Medical Posthumanities"
Chapter 12, Liza Blake and Kathryn Vomero Santos, "What Does the Wolf Say?: Animal Language and Political Noise in *Coriolanus*"
Chapter 9, Joseph Campana, "Flock, Herd, Swarm: A Shakespearean Lexicon of Creaturely Collectivity"

Julius Caesar
Chapter 1, Rebecca Ann Bach, "Avian Shakespeare"

2 Henry IV
Chapter 9, Joseph Campana, "Flock, Herd, Swarm: A Shakespearean Lexicon of Creaturely Collectivity"

Henry V
Chapter 22, Karen Raber, "My Palfrey, Myself: Toward a Queer Phenomenology of the Horse-Human Bond in *Henry V* and Beyond"

2 Henry VI
Chapter 6, Ian MacInnes, "Cow-Cross Lane and Curriers Row: Animal Networks in Early Modern England"
Chapter 18, Nicole Mennell, "The Lion King: Shakespeare's Beastly Sovereigns"

3 Henry VI
Chapter 6, Ian MacInnes, "Cow-Cross Lane and Curriers Row: Animal Networks in Early Modern England"
Chapter 18, Nicole Mennell, "The Lion King: Shakespeare's Beastly Sovereigns"

King Lear
Chapter 17, Laurie Shannon, "Silly Creatures: *King Lear* (with Sheep)"

Macbeth
Chapter 7, Benjamin Bertram, "'Everything Exists by Strife': War and Creaturely Violence in Shakespeare's Late Tragedies"

Measure for Measure
Chapter 21, Robert Wakeman, "'What's This? What's This?': Fish and Sexuality in *Measure for Measure*"

Appendix

Merchant of Venice
Chapter 8, Lucinda Cole, "Zoonotic Shakespeare: Animals, Plagues, and the Medical Posthumanities"

Merry Wives of Windsor
Chapter 19, Jennifer Allport Reid, "'Wearing the Horn': Class and Community in the Shakespearean Hunt"

Othello
Chapter 7, Benjamin Bertram, "'Everything Exists by Strife': War and Creaturely Violence in Shakespeare's Late Tragedies"

Rape of Lucrece
Chapter 9, Joseph Campana, "Flock, Herd, Swarm: A Shakespearean Lexicon of Creaturely Collectivity"

Richard II
Chapter 18, Nicole Mennell, "The Lion King: Shakespeare's Beastly Sovereigns"
Chapter 23, Erica Fudge, "'Forgiveness, Horse': The Barbaric World of *Richard II*"

Taming of the Shrew
Chapter 13, Bruce Boehrer, "Shrewd Shakespeare"

The Tempest
Chapter 11, Nicole Jacobs, "'Bernardian Ecology and Topsell's Redemptive Bee in *The Tempest*"

Timon of Athens
Chapter 5, Karl Steel, "Beasts, Animals, and Animal Metaphor, in Shakespeare and His Fellow Dramatists"

Titus Andronicus
Chapter 20, Steven Swarbrick, "On Eating, the Animal that Therefore I Am: Race and Animal Rites in *Titus Andronicus*"

Troilus and Cressida
Chapter 8, Lucinda Cole, "Zoonotic Shakespeare: Animals, Plagues, and the Medical Posthumanities"

Twelfth Night
Chapter 2, Dan Brayton, "Shakespeare's Fishponds: Matter, Metaphor, and Market"

Two Gentleman of Verona
Chapter 3, Bryan Alkemeyer, "'I Am the Dog': Canine Abjection, Species Reversal, and Misanthropic Satire in *The Two Gentlemen of Verona*"
Chapter 4, Crystal Bartolovich, "Learning from Crab: Primitive Accumulation, Migration, Species Being"

The Winter's Tale
Chapter 15, Todd A. Borlik, "Performing *The Winter's Tale in* the 'Open': Bear Plays, Skinners' Pageants, and the Early Modern Fur Trade"

NOTES ON CONTRIBUTORS

Bryan Alkemeyer is an Associate Professor of English at The College of Wooster. His article "Remembering the Elephant: Animal Reason before the Eighteenth Century" appeared in the October 2017 issue of *PMLA*. In 2019–20, he is an ACLS Burkhardt Fellow at UCLA, where he is completing a book called *Before the Primates: Metamorphoses, Miscegenation, and Speciesism, 1550–1750*.

Rebecca Ann Bach is a Professor of English at the University of Alabama at Birmingham, specializing in Shakespeare and Renaissance Drama. She is the author of *Birds and Other Creatures in Renaissance Literature: Shakespeare, Descartes, and Animal Studies* (Routledge, 2017); *Shakespeare and Renaissance Literature before Heterosexuality* (Palgrave, 2007); and *Colonial Transformations: The Cultural Production of the New Atlantic World 1580–1640* (Palgrave, 2000). With Gwynne Kennedy, she co-edited *Feminisms and Early Modern Texts: Essays for Phyllis Rackin* (Susquehanna University Press, 2010). She has published many articles on Shakespeare, Renaissance Drama, animals, sexuality, masculinity, and race.

Crystal Bartolovich is an Associate Professor of English at Syracuse University. With Jean Howard and David Hillman, she wrote *Marx and Freud: Great Shakespeareans*, and with Neil Lazarus, she edited *Marxism, Modernity and Postcolonial Studies*. Her current project is "A Natural History of the Common," which considers the specificity and importance of dialectical approaches to understanding the "common" in the face of the so-called New Materialism.

Benjamin Bertram is a Professor of English at the University of Southern Maine. His areas of interest include sixteenth- and seventeenth-century English literature and culture, Shakespeare, ecocriticism, animal studies, science fiction, film studies, and critical theory. He is the author of *Bestial Oblivion: War, Humanism, and Ecology in Early Modern England* (Routledge, 2018) and *The Time Is out of Joint: Skepticism in Shakespeare's England* (University of Delaware Press, 2004). Other publications include articles in *Criticism* (Forthcoming), *Modern Philology, English Literature, Exemplaria*, and *boundary 2*.

Notes on Contributors

Liza Blake is an Associate Professor of English at the University of Toronto, working on literature and science, women's writing, and Margaret Cavendish. She has published (with Jacques Lezra) the edited collection *Lucretius and Modernity*, as well as two scholarly editions: *Margaret Cavendish's Poems and Fancies: A Digital Critical Edition* and (with Kathryn Vomero Santos) *Arthur Golding's Moral Fabletalk and Other Renaissance Fable Translations*. She has articles published and forthcoming in the journals *postmedieval, SEL, ELR, Criticism,* and *JEMCS,* and is currently finishing a monograph project entitled *Early Modern Literary Physics*.

Bruce Boehrer is the Bertram H. Davis Professor of early modern literature at Florida State University. His latest books are *Environmental Degradation in Jacobean Drama* (Cambridge, 2013) and *Animals, Animality, and Literature* (Cambridge 2018; co-edited with Molly Hand and Brian Massumi).

Todd A. Borlik is a Senior Lecturer in Renaissance Drama at the University of Huddersfield. His research interests include Shakespeare and the pre-history of environmentalism, magic and science, repertory and performance studies, and Global Shakespeare. He is the author of *Ecocriticism and Early Modern English Literature: Green Pastures* and *Literature and Nature in the English Renaissance: An Ecocritical Anthology*, as well as over a dozen articles in journals such as *Shakespeare, Shakespeare Quarterly, Shakespeare Survey,* and *English Literary Renaissance*. He is currently preparing a monograph on representations of nature at the Rose and Globe.

Keith Botelho is a Professor of English at Kennesaw State University. His book, *Renaissance Earwitnesses: Rumor and Early Modern Masculinity*, was published by Palgrave Macmillan, and he has published articles and essays in journals such as *Studies in English Literature, Early Modern Culture,* and *Comparative Drama*, and in scholarly collections that include *MLA Approaches to Teaching Aphra Behn's Oroonoko, Ecological Approaches to Early Modern English Texts, Object Oriented Environs,* and *Ground-Work: English Renaissance Literature and Soil Science*. He is currently co-editing a two-volume collection of essays on insects in the early modern world entitled *Lesser Living Creatures: Insect Life in the Renaissance*, which will be published by Pennsylvania State University Press in 2021.

Dan Brayton is the Julian W. Abernethy Professor of Literature and the Director of the Environmental Studies Program at Middlebury College. His articles on early modern natural history, blue cultural studies, Shakespeare, and traditional boat building have been published in such venues as ELH, Forum for Modern Language Studies, and WoodenBoat. His book, *Shakespeare's Ocean: An Ecocritical Exploration*, published by the University of Virginia Press in 2012, won the Northeast Modern Language Association Book Prize. In addition to teaching at Middlebury, he has also taught for Sea Education Association; the Williams–Mystic Program in Maritime Studies; and Semester-at-Sea, ashore and at sea.

Joseph Campana is a poet, critic, and scholar of Renaissance literature. He is the author of *The Pain of Reformation: Spenser, Vulnerability, and the Ethics of Masculinity* (Fordham University Press, 2012), the co-editor of *Renaissance Posthumanism*, and the author of three collections of poetry: *The Book of Faces* (2005); *Natural Selections* (2012), which received the Iowa Poetry Prize; and *The Book of Life* (2019). Current projects include a study of children and sovereignty in the works of Shakespeare entitled *The Child's Two Bodies*; a two-volume co-edited collection on insect life in the Renaissance called *Lesser Living Creatures*; and *Living Figures*, a study of literary lives and creaturely forms, from busy bees and bleeding trees to crocodile tears and beyond. He serves as Alan Dugald McKillop Professor of English at Rice University where he is also the Director of the Center for Environmental Studies and Editor for *1500–1659* of *SEL: Studies in English Literature, 1500–1900*.

Lucinda Cole, Research Associate Professor at the University of Illinois, Urbana-Champaign and Affiliate Professor, Institute for Sustainability, Energy, and Environment, is the author of *Imperfect Creatures: Vermin, Literatures, and the Sciences of Life, 1600–1740* (University of Michigan Press, 2016). Her articles have appeared in many collections and in such venues as *ELH, Criticism, JEMCS, Configurations, Journal for Critical Animal Studies*, and *Eighteenth-Century Fiction*. She is now writing a book on zoonosis and literature.

Erica Fudge is a Professor of English Studies at the University of Strathclyde, Glasgow, and is the Director of the British Animal Studies Network. Her books include *Perceiving Animals: Humans and Beasts in Early Modern English Culture* (Macmillan, 2000); *Animal* (Reaktion, 2002); *Brutal Reasoning: Animals, Rationality, and Humanity in Early Modern England* (Cornell, 2006); and most recently *Quick Cattle and Dying Wishes: People and Their Animals in Early Modern England* (Cornell, 2018).

Elspeth Graham is a Professor of Early Modern Literature at Liverpool John Moores University, UK. For many years she has published on seventeenth-century women's writing, religious radicalism and nonconformity. For the past 15 years or so she has also written on relationships between early modern humans and non-human animals (particularly horses and fish). A collection of essays that she co-edited with Peter Edwards, *The Horse as Cultural Icon*, came out in 2011. She is a Director of the Shakespeare North Trust which has been working since 2004 on a project to build a Shakespearean theater in Prescot, Merseyside, to commemorate this small town's Elizabethan and Jacobean theatrical activities and concerns. The Shakespeare North Playhouse, a replica of Inigo Jones'/John Webb's Cockpit-in-Court, will open in 2022. She is currently editing a special edition of *Shakespeare Bulletin* devoted to the theatrical interests of the Earls of Derby in relation to Prescot's playhouse.

Nicole A. Jacobs teaches in English and Women's and Gender Studies at California Polytechnic, San Luis Obispo. Her articles have appeared in *Studies in Philology, Criticism, The Shakespearean International Yearbook*, and *Appositions*. She is completing a monograph on the beehive in seventeenth-century England and America, *Bees in Early Modern Transatlantic Literature: Sovereign Colony*.

Ian F. MacInnes (BA Swarthmore College, PhD University of Virginia) is the Howard L McGregor Jr. Professor of the Humanities at Albion College, Michigan. His scholarship focuses on representations of animals and the environment in Renaissance literature, particularly in Shakespeare. He has published essays on topics such as horse breeding and geohumoralism in *Henry V* and on invertebrate bodies in *Hamlet*. His long-running website, Ian's English Calendar, calculates dates for scholars of English history and Literature.

Nicole Mennell completed her doctorate with the Centre for Early Modern and Medieval Studies at the University of Sussex. Her thesis, "Shakespeare's Sovereign Beasts: Human-Animal Relations and Political Discourse in Early Modern Drama," examines why animals were used to symbolize the power and status of political leaders, both figuratively and literally, in the early modern period and how this reliance conversely undermines human dominion over nature.

Notes on Contributors

Nicole has written on the wider representation of animals in early modern culture and her chapter, "'The Dignity of Mankind': Edward Tyson's *Anatomy of a Pygmie* and the Ape-Man Boundary," was published in the edited collection *Seeing Animals after Derrida* (2018). Before embarking on her PhD, Nicole undertook an internship at the National Portrait Gallery, where she conducted research for a proposed exhibition on "man and beast" in portraiture. During her doctoral studies, she co-organized several academic events, including the London Renaissance Seminar on *Animal Lives in Early Modern Culture* (2016), and was a research assistant on "Hidden Persuaders," a Wellcome Trust funded project at Birkbeck, University of London, which explores the impact of "brainwashing" on conceptions of the human.

Karen Raber is a Distinguished Professor of English at the University of Mississippi. She is the author of *Shakespeare and Posthumanist Theory* (2018) and *Animal Bodies, Renaissance Culture* (2013), and editor with Monica Mattfeld of *Performing Animals: History, Agency, Theater* (2017).

Jennifer Allport Reid is completing a PhD in the Department of English and Humanities at Birkbeck, University of London. She has published on the relationship between early modern customary drama and Anthony Munday's Robin Hood plays (*The Wenshan Review of Literature and Culture*, June 2017), and on the folklore of being pixie-led in *Reading the Road, from Shakespeare's Crossways to Bunyan's Highways*, edited by Lisa Hopkins and Bill Angus (Edinburgh University Press, 2019). She is particularly interested in how customary culture expresses the beliefs and relationships of the early modern community, as well as how it reflects interactions between humans, animals, and the landscape.

Kathryn Vomero Santos is an Assistant Professor of English at Trinity University. Her research focuses on early modern cultural histories of translation as well as the intersections among race, gender, and linguistic identity in contemporary adaptations and appropriations of Shakespeare. Her current book project on early modern interpreters explores the performative practices of translating in real time between speakers of different languages in a wide range of social, cultural, commercial, political, and colonial contexts. Santos co-edited *Arthur Golding's A Moral Fabletalk and Other Renaissance Fable Translations* with Liza Blake for the MHRA Tudor & Stuart Translations Series (2017), and she has published essays in *Philological Quarterly, Shakespeare Studies*, and several edited collections. With Louise Geddes and Geoffrey Way, she is co-editing a collection on Shakespeare at the intersection of performance and appropriation.

Laurie Shannon is the Franklyn Bliss Snyder Professor of Literature at Northwestern University. Her first book, *Sovereign Amity: Figures of Friendship in Shakespearean Contexts* (Chicago, 2002), assessed the impact of classical friendship on the political imaginary of the long sixteenth century. Her second book, *The Accommodated Animal: Cosmopolity in Shakespearean Locales* (Chicago, 2013), analyzed the species concept before Descartes and earned the Elizabeth Dietz Memorial Prize for its contribution to literary studies of the English Renaissance. She is now working on two projects: *Frailty's Name: Shakespeare's Natural History of Human Being* and an inquiry tracing the natural historical thought in Anne Lister's manuscript diaries, tentatively entitled *Anne Lister's Hand*.

Karl Steel is Professor of English at Brooklyn College and the Graduate Center, CUNY. He is the author of many articles and two books: *How to Make a Human: Animals and Violence in the Middle Ages* (Ohio State University Press, 2011) and *How Not to Make a Human: Pets, Feral*

Children, Worms, Sky Burial, Oysters (University of Minnesota Press, 2019), and has co-edited special issues of *Glossator* (with Nicola Masciandaro, on *Pearl*), *Postmedieval* (with Peggy McCracken, on animals), and *Early Modern Culture* (with Holly Dugan, also on animals).

Steven Swarbrick is an Assistant Professor of English at Baruch College, CUNY, specializing in English Renaissance literature, environmental humanities, and queer theory. His work has appeared or is forthcoming in journals such as *Cultural Critique, Postmodern Culture, Journal of Narrative Theory*, and *postmedieval*, as well as in several edited anthologies, including *Queer Milton*. He has also co-edited (with Karen Raber) a special issue of *Criticism* on Renaissance posthumanism. He is currently working on two book projects: *Materialism without Matter: Environmental Poetics from Spenser to Milton* and an inquiry into Shakespeare's critical climate awareness, *Shakespeare's Earth: Life Outside the Human Climate Zone*.

Robert Wakeman is an Assistant Professor of English at Mount St. Mary College. He teaches classes on Shakespeare, medieval and early modern literatures, food writing, and academic writing. His research explores a literary history of four meals that shaped the ecological, economic, and spiritual values of sixteenth-century England: the hunting banquet, the shepherd's repast, takeaway from London cookshops, and the religious holiday feast.

Julian Yates is the H. Fletcher Professor of English and Material Culture Studies at the University of Delaware. His books include *Error, Misuse, Failure: Object Lessons from the English Renaissance* (University of Minnesota Press, 2003), which was a finalist for the Modern Language Association's Best First Book Prize; *What's the Worst Thing You Can Do to Shakespeare?* (Palgrave Macmillan, 2013), co-authored with Richard Burt; *Object-Oriented Environs in Early Modern England* (Punctum Books, 2016), co-edited with Jeffrey Jerome Cohen; and *Of Sheep, Oranges, and Yeast: A Multispecies Impression* (University of Minnesota Press, 2017), winner of the Michelle Kendrick Memorial Book Prize from SLSA (Society for Literature, Science, and the Arts).

BIBLIOGRAPHY

Ackroyd, Peter. *Thames: The Biography*. New York: Anchor, 2008.

Adelman, Janet. "Shakespeare's Romulus and Remus: Who Does the Wolf Love?" In *Identity, Otherness, and Empire in Shakespeare's Rome*, edited by Maria Del Sapio Garbero, 19–34. London: Routledge, 2009.

———. *Suffocating Mothers: Fantasies of Maternal Origin in Shakespeare's Plays, Hamlet to the Tempest*. New York: Routledge, 1992, 2012.

Adorno, Theodor. *Negative Dialectics*. Translated by E.B. Ashton. London: Continuum, 1973.

———. *Mimima Moralia: Reflections from Damaged Life*. Translated by E.F.N. Jephcott. New York: Verso, 1978.

Aesop. *Here Begynneth the Book of the Subtyl Historyes and Fables of Esope*. Translated by William Caxton. Westminster: William Caxton, 1484.

Aesops fabl'z in tru ort'ography with grammar-nóts. Translated by William Bullokar. London: Edmund Bollifant, 1585.

Agamben, Giorgio. *Homo Sacer: Sovereign Power and Bare Life*. Translated by Daniel Heller-Roazen. Stanford, CA: Stanford University Press, 1998.

———. *The Open: Man and Animal*. Translated by Kevin Attell. Stanford, CA: Stanford University Press, 2004.

Ahmed, Sarah. *Queer Phenomenology: Orientations, Objects, Others*. Durham, NC and London: Duke University Press, 2006.

Alaimo, Stacy. *Bodily Natures. Science, Environment, and the Material Self*. Bloomington and Indianapolis: Indiana University Press, 2010.

———. "Violet-Black." In *Prismatic Ecology: Ecotheory beyond Green*, edited by Jeffrey J. Cohen, 233–51. Minneapolis: University of Minnesota Press, 2013.

Albala, Ken. *Eating Right in the Renaissance*. Berkeley: University of California Press, 2002.

Almond, Richard. *Medieval Hunting*. Stroud: The History Press, 2003.

Altick, Richard D. "Symphonic Imagery in *Richard II*." *PMLA* 62, no. 2 (1947): 339–65.

Anderson, John G.T. *Deep Things Out of Darkness: A History of Natural History*. Berkeley: University of California Press, 2013.

Anderson, Stephen. *Doctor Dolittle's Delusion: Animals and the Uniqueness of Human Language*. New Haven, CT: Yale University Press, 2004.

Anglin, Sallie. "Material Romance: Embodiment, Environment and Ecology in Sidney's New Arcadia." *Sidney Journal* 30, no. 2 (2012): 87–107.

Anon. *Parlayment of Byrdes*. London, 1520.

Anon. *A True Report of Certaine Wonderfull Ouerflowings of Waters, Now Lately in Summerset-Shire, Norfolke, and Other Places of England*. London, 1607.

Anon. *The Pleasant History of Cawwood the Rook, or the Assembly of Birds*. London, 1683.

Bibliography

Anon. *The Taming of a Shrew.*, Edited by Stephen Roy Miller. Cambridge: Cambridge University Press, 1998.

Applebaum, Robert. "Aguecheek's Beef." *Textual Practice* 14, no. 2 (2000): 327–41.

Argent, Gala. "Toward a Privileging of the Nonverbal: Communication, Corporeal Synchrony, and Transcendence in Humans and Horses." In *Experiencing Animal Minds: An Anthology of Animal-Human Encounters*, edited by Julie A. Smith and Robert W. Mitchell, 110–28. New York: Columbia University Press, 2012.

Aristole. *Aristotle's De Anima: Books II and III.* Translated by D.W. Hamlyn. Oxford: Clarendon Press, 1968.

———. *History of Animals: Books 7–10.* Translated by D.M. Balme. Cambridge, MA: Harvard University Press, 1991.

Arthur, Charles. "Scientists Discover Why Fungi Have 36,000 Sexes." *The Independent*, September 15, 1999, www.independent.co.uk/news/scientists-discover-why-fungi-have-36000-sexes-1119181.html.

Ash, Eric H. *The Draining of the Fens: Projectors, Popular Politics, and State Building in Early Modern England.* Baltimore, MD: Johns Hopkins University Press, 2017.

Atkinson, Niall. *The Noisy Renaissance: Sound, Architecture, and Florentine Urban Life.* University Park: Pennsylvania State University Press, 2016.

Aubrey, John. *Natural History of Wiltshire.* Bodleian Aubrey MS 1.

Babington, Gervase. *Comfortable Notes upon the Bookes of Exodus and Leviticus, as before upon Genesis Gathered and Laid Downe Still in This Plaine Manner.* London, 1604.

Bach, Rebecca Ann. "Bearbaiting, Dominion and Colonialism." In *Race, Ethnicity and Power in the Renaissance*, edited by Joyce MacDonald, 19–37. Madison, NJ: Fairleigh Dickenson University Press, 1997.

———. "The Animal Continuum in *A Midsummer Night's Dream*." *Textual Practice* 24, no. 1 (2010): 123–47. doi:10.1080/09502360903471714.

———. *Birds and Other Creatures in Renaissance Literature: Shakespeare, Descartes, and Animal Studies.* New York: Routledge, 2017.

Bailey, Amanda. *Of Bondage: Debt, Property, and Personhood in Early Modern England.* Philadelphia: University of Pennsylvania Press, 2013.

Barad, Karen. *Meeting the Universe Halfway: Quantum Physics and the Entanglement of Matter and Meaning.* Durham, NC: Duke University Press, 2007.

Barber, Cesar Lombardi. *Shakespeare's Festive Comedy: A Study of Dramatic Form and Its Relation to Social Custom.* Princeton, NJ: Princeton University Press, 1959.

Baret, Michael. *An Hipponomie, or the Vineyard of Horsemanship.* London, 1618.

Barney, Richard A. and Warren Montag, eds. *Systems of Life: Biopolitics, Economics, and Literature on the Cusp of Modernity.* New York: Fordham University Press, 2019.

Barrett, Chris. "Shakespeare's Butterflies." *New Orleans Review* 42 (2016): 286–310.

———. "Butterflies and Moths." In *Lesser Living Creatures: Insect Life in the Renaissance*, edited by Keith Botelho and Joseph Campana. University Park: Pennsylvania State University Press, forthcoming 2021.

Bartolini, Paolo. "Indistinction." In *The Agamben Dictionary*, edited by Alex Murray et al, 102–5. Edinburgh: Edinburgh University Press, 2011.

Bartolovich, Crystal. "'First as Tragedy, then as…': Gender, Genre, History and *Romeo and Juliet*." In *Rethinking Feminism in Early Modern Studies*, edited by Ania Loomba and Melissa Sanchez, 75–91. New York: Routledge, 2016.

Bate, Jonathan and Eric Rasmussen. *William Shakespeare and Others: Collaborative Plays.* London: Palgrave MacMillan, 2013.

Bates, Catherine. *Masculinity and the Hunt: Wyatt to Spenser.* Oxford: Oxford University Press, 2013.

Bateson, Melissa, Suzanne Desire, Sarah E. Gartside, and Geraldine A. Wright. "Agitated Honeybees Exhibit Pessimistic Cognitive Biases." *Current Biology* 12 (June 2011): 1070–73.

Batman, Stephan. *Batman vppon Bartholome his Booke De proprietatibus rerum.* London, 1582.

Batt, Antonie. *A Hive of Sacred Honiecombes Containing Most Sweet and Heavenly Counsel.* Oxford, 1631.

Battalio, John T. "Sixteenth- and Seventeenth-Century Falconry Manuals: Technical Writing with a Classical Rhetorical Influence." *Technical Writing and Communication* 43, no. 2 (2013): 145–64.

Bibliography

Beadle, Richard. "Crab's Pedigree." In *English Comedy*, edited by Michael Cordner et al., 12–35. Cambridge: Cambridge University Press, 1994.

Beaver, Dan. "The Great Deer Massacre: Animals Honor and Communication in Early Modern England." *Journal of British Studies* 38 (1999): 187–216.

Becon, Thomas. *The Jewell of Joy*. London, 1550.

Beier, A.L. *Masterless Men: The Vagrancy Problem in England 1560–1640*. New York: Methuen, 1985.

Benjamin, Walter. *Illuminations*. Translated by Harry Zohn and edited by Hannah Arendt. New York: Schocken, 1968.

———. *Theses on the Philosophy of History* (1940). In *Illuminations*, translated by Harry Zohn and edited by Hannah Arendt, 253–264. New York: Schocken, 1968.

Bennett, Jane. *Vibrant Matter: A Political Economy of Things*. Durham, NC and London: Duke University Press, 2010.

Berger, John. *Why Look at Animals?* New York: Penguin, 2009.

Bergman, Charles. "A Spectacle of Beasts: Hunting Rituals and Animal Rights in Early Modern England." In *A Cultural History of Animals*, vol. 3, edited by Bruce Boehrer, 53–73. New York: Berg, 2007.

Berliet, Melanie. "Confessions of a Naked Sushi Model." *Vanity Fair*, October 2008.

Berry, Edward. *Shakespeare and the Hunt: A Cultural and Social Study*. Cambridge: Cambridge University Press, 2001.

Berry, Herbert. "Folger MS V.b.275 and the Deaths of Shakespearean Playhouses." *Medieval and Renaissance Drama in England* 10 (1998): 262–93; ed. J. Pitcher.

Bertram, Benjamin. *Bestial Oblivion: War, Humanism, and Ecology in Early Modern England*. New York: Routledge, 2018.

Bevington, David, ed. *The Complete Works of Shakespeare*, 5th ed. New York: Longman, 2003.

———. *Shakespeare's Ideas: More Things in Heaven and Earth*. Chichester: Wiley Blackwell, 2008.

———, ed. *The Complete Works of Shakespeare*, 7th ed. Boston, MA: Pearson, 2014.

Biggins, Dennis. "Exit Pursued by a Bear: A Problem in *The Winter's Tale*." *Shakespeare Quarterly* 13, no. 1 (1962): 3–13.

Blaisdell, John. "Rabies in Shakespeare's England." *Historia Medicinae Veterinariae* 16 (1991): 1–80.

———. "A Frightful, but Not Necessarily Fatal, Madness': Rabies in Eighteenth-Century England and English North America." Retrospective Theses and Dissertations, Iowa State University, 1995.

Blake, Liza and Kathryn Vomero Santos, eds. *Arthur Golding's a Moral Fabletalk and Other Renaissance Fable Translations*. Cambridge: MHRA, 2017.

Blake, Liza and Kathryn Vomero Santos. "Introduction." In *Arthur Golding's a Moral Fabletalk and Other Renaissance Fable Translations*, 10–12. Cambridge: MHRA, 2017.

Blanchard, Ian. "The Continental European Cattle Trades." *The Economic History Review* 39 (1986): 427–60.

Bloom, Harold. *Shakespeare: The Invention of the Human*. New York: Riverhead Books, 1998.

Blundeville, Thomas. *The Foure Chiefest Offices Belonging to Horsemanship*. London, 1580.

Bode, Katherine. "The Equivalence of 'Close' and 'Distant' Reading; or, toward a New Object for Data-Rich Literary History." *Modern Language Quarterly* 78, no. 1 (2017): 77–106.

Boehrer, Bruce. "Shylock and the Rise of the Household Pet." *Shakespeare Quarterly* 50, no. 2 (1999): 152–70.

———. *Shakespeare among the Animals: Nature and Society in the Drama of Early Modern England*. New York: Palgrave, 2002.

———. *Parrot Culture*. Philadelphia: University of Pennsylvania Press, 2004.

———. *Animal Characters: Nonhuman Beings in Early Modern Literature*. Philadelphia: University of Pennsylvania Press, 2010.

Bolster, W. Jeffrey. *The Mortal Sea: Fishing the Atlantic in the Age of Sail*. Cambridge, MA: The Belknap Press of Harvard University Press, 2012.

Boorde, Andrew. *Here Foloweth a Compendyous Regimente or Dyetary of Health Made in Mount Pyllor*. London, 1562.

Booth, William James. "Economies of Time: On the Idea of Time in Marx's Political Economy." *Political Theory* 19 (1991): 7–27.

Borlik, Todd Andrew. "Shakespeare's Insect Theater: Fairy Lore as Elizabethan Folk Entomology." In *Performing Animals: History, Agency, Theater*, edited by Karen Raber and Monica Mattfeld, 123–40. University Park: Pennsylvania State University Press, 2017.

Bibliography

Botelho, Keith. "The Beasts of Belmont and Venice." In *Ecological Approaches to Early Modern English Texts: A Field Guide to Reading and Teaching*, edited by Lynne Bruckner, Jennifer Munroe, and Edward J. Geisweidt, 71–80. Aldershot: Ashgate, 2015.

Botero, Giovanni. *On the Causes of the Greatness and Magnificence of Cities*. Translated by Geoffrey Symcox. Toronto: University of Toronto Press, 2012.

Botkin, Daniel B. *Discordant Harmonies: New Ecologies for the Twenty-first Century*. Oxford: Oxford University Press, 1990.

Bowsher, Julian and Pat Miller. *The Rose and the Globe: Playhouses of Shakespeare's Bankside, Southwark: Excavations 1988–1991*. London: Museum of London Archeology, 2009.

Brandt, Keri. "Intelligent Bodies: Embodied Subjectivity in Human-Horse Communication." In *Body/Embodiment: Symbolic Interaction and the Sociology of the Body*, edited by Dennis Waskul and Phillip Vannini, 141–52. Burlington, VT: Ashgate, 2012.

Brayton, Dan. *Shakespeare's Ocean: An Ecocritical Exploration*. Charlottesville: University of Virginia Press, 2012.

Bristol, Michael. "In Search of the Bear: Spatiotemporal Form and Heterogeneity of Economies in *The Winter's Tale*." *Shakespeare Quarterly* 42 (1991): 145–67.

British Petroleum Statistical Review of World Energy, 67th ed., June 2018, www.bp.com/content/dam/bp/en/corporate/pdf/energy-economics/statistical-review/bp-stats-review-2018-full-report.pdf.

Brooks, Cleanth. *The Well Wrought Urn: Studies in the Structure of Poetry*. London: Dobson Books, 1947.

Brooks, Harold F. "Two Clowns in a Comedy (To Say Nothing of the Dog): Speed, Launce (and Crab) in *The Two Gentlemen of Verona*." *Essays and Studies* 16 (1963): 91–100.

Brooks, Thomas. *A Heavenly Cordial for All Those Servants of the Lord that Have Had the Plague*. London, 1666.

Brown, Carolyn E. "Erotic Religious Flagellation and Shakespeare's 'Measure for Measure'." *English Literary Renaissance* 16, no. 1 (Winter 1986): 139–65.

Brown, Eric C., ed. *Insect Poetics*. Minneapolis: University of Minnesota Press, 2006.

Brown, Laura. *Homeless Dogs and Melancholy Apes: Humans and Other Animals in the Modern Literary Imagination*. Ithaca, NY: Cornell University Press, 2010.

Brown, Pamela Allen. *Better a Shrew than a Sheep: Women. Drama, and the Culture of Jest in Early Modern England*. Ithaca, NY: Cornell University Press, 2003.

Brownstein, Oscar. "The Popularity of Baiting in England before 1600: A Study in Social and Theatrical History." *Educational Theatre Journal* 21 (1969): 237–50.

Bruckner, Lynne. "'Consuming Means, Soon Preys upon Itself': Political Expedience and Environmental Degradation in *Richard II*." In *Shakespeare and the Urgency of Now: Criticism and Theory in the 21st Century*, edited by Cary DiPietro and Hugh Grady, 126–47. London: Palgrave Macmillan, 2013.

Brutus, Junius. *A Defence of Liberty against Tyrants: A Translation of the Vindiciae Contra Tyrannos*. Edited by Harold J. Laski. London: G. Bell and Sons, 1924.

Bucholz, Robert and Newton Key. *Early Modern England, 1485–1714*, 2nd ed. Hoboken, NJ: Wiley-Blackwell, 2008.

Bullein, William. *Bulleins Bulwarke of Defense against All Sicknesse*. London, 1579.

Bullough, Geoffrey, ed. *Narrative and Dramatic Sources of Shakespeare, Volume V: The Roman Plays*. London: Routledge and Kegan Paul, 1964.

Bushnell, Rebecca W. *Tragedies of Tyrants: Political Thought and Theater in the English Renaissance*. London: Cornell University Press, 1990.

Butler, Charles. *The Feminine Monarchie*. London, 1609.

Bynum, Caroline Walker. *Holy Feast and Holy Fast: The Religious Significance of Food to Medieval Women*. Berkeley: University of California Press, 1987.

Caius, John. *Of Englishe Dogges*. Translated by Abraham Fleming. London, 1576.

Calarco, Matthew. *Zoographies: The Question of the Animal from Heidegger to Derrida*. New York: Columbia University Press, 2008.

Calderwood, James. "Wordless Meanings and Meaningless Words." *Studies in English Literature, 1500–1900* 6, no. 2 (Spring 1966): 211–24.

Callaghan, Dympna and Suzanne Gossett, eds. *Shakespeare in Our Time*. New York: Bloomsbury, 2016.

Bibliography

Campana, Joseph. "The Bee and the Sovereign (II): Segments, Swarms, and the Shakespearean Multitude." In *The Return of Theory in Early Modern English Studies*, vol. II, edited by Bryan Reynolds, Paul Cefalu, and Gary Kuchar, 59–80. London: Palgrave Macmillan, 2014.

———. "Humans: Exceptional Humans, Human Exceptionalism, and the Shape of Things to Come." In *Shakespearean International Yearbook 15: Shakespeare and the Human*, edited by Tiffany Werth, 39–63. Farnham: Ashgate Publishing, 2015.

———. "Introduction," in "After Sovereignty." Special Issue, *Studies in English Literature, 1500–1900* 58, no. 1 (Winter 2018): 1–21.

Campana, Joseph, and Scott Maisano. "Introduction." In *Renaissance Posthumanism*, edited by Joseph Campana and Scott Maisano, 1–36. New York: Fordham University Press, 2016.

Campbell, Kathleen. "Shakespeare's Actors as Collaborators: Will Kempe and *The Two Gentlemen of Verona*." In *Two Gentlemen of Verona: Critical Essays*, edited by June Schlueter, 179–87. New York: Routledge, 1996.

Carroll, William C. Introduction to *The Two Gentlemen of Verona*, edited by William Shakespeare, 1–130. London: Bloomsbury, 2004.

Cartmill, Matt. *A View to a Death in the Morning*. Cambridge, MA: Harvard University Press, 1993.

Cavell, Stanley. "'Who Does the Wolf Love?' Reading *Coriolanus*." *Representations* 3 (1983): 1–20.

Cavendish, William. *La méthode nouvelle et invention extraordinaire de dresser les chevaux*. Antwerp: Jacques van Meurs, 1658.

———. *A New Method, and Extraordinary Invention, to Dress Horses, and Work Them According to Nature as Also, to Perfect Nature by the Subtility of Art, Which Was Never Found out, but by… William Cavendishe….* London: Printed by Tho. Milbourn, 1667.

———. *A General System of Horsemanship*. Introduction by William C. Steinkraus. North Pomfret, VT: J.A. Allen, 2000.

———. *A General System of Horsemanship*. London, 1743.

Cawte, E.C. *Ritual Animal Disguise: A Historical and Geographical Study of Animal Disguise in the British Isles*. Cambridge: D. S. Brewer, 1978.

Caxton, William, trans. *Here Begynneth the Book of the Subtyl Historyes and Fables of Esope*. Westminster: William Caxton, 1484.

Cervantes, Miguel de. *Coloquio de los perros*. In *Novelas ejemplares*. Madrid, 1613.

Chakravarty, Urvashi. "More than Kin, Less than Kind: Similitude, Strangeness, and Early Modern English Homonationalisms." *Shakespeare Quarterly* 67, no. 1 (2016): 14–29.

Chambers, E.K. *Shakespeare: A Survey*. London: Sidgwick and Jackson, 1925.

Chapman, George, trans. *Homer's Odysses*. London, n.d.

Chaucer, Geoffrey. *The Riverside Chaucer*. Edited by Larry D. Benson. Boston, MA: Houghton Mifflin, 1987.

Chen, Mel Y. *Animacies: Biopolitics, Racial Mattering, and Queer Affect*. Durham, NC and London: Duke University Press, 2012.

Cheng, Anne Anlin. *The Melancholy of Race: Psychoanalysis, Assimilation, and Hidden Grief*. New York: Oxford University Press, 2001.

Chenoweth, Katie. "The Beast, the Sovereign, and the Letter: Vernacular Posthumanism." *Symploke* 23, no. 1–2 (2015): 41–56.

Chettle, Henry and William Haughton. "Arcadian Virigin." In *Lost Plays Database*, edited by Roslyn L. Knutson, David McInnis, and Matthew Steggle. Melbourne: University of Melbourne, 2009. Web.

Clairvaux, Bernard of. *Saint Bernard, His Meditations, or Sighes, Sobbes, and Teares upon Our Saviors Passion*. Translated by W.P. London, 1611.

———. *The Sentences*. Translated by Francis R. Swietek. Kalamazoo, MI: Cistercian Publications, 2000.

Clark, Kenneth. *Animals and Man: Their Relationship as Reflected in Western Art from Prehistory to the Present Day*. New York: William Morrow and Co., Inc., 1977.

Cockayne, Emily. "Who Did Let the Dogs out?—Nuisance Dogs in Late Medieval and Early Modern England." In *Our Dogs, Ourselves*, edited by Laura Gelfand, 41–67. Leiden: Brill, 2016.

Cockayne, Thomas. *A Short Treatise of Hunting: Compyled for the Delight of Noble Men and Gentlemen*. London, 1591.

Cogan, Thomas. *The Haven of Health*. London, 1612.

Coghill, Neville. "Six Points of Stage-Craft in *The Winter's Tale*." *Shakespeare Survey* 11 (1958): 31–41.

Bibliography

Cohen, Jeffrey Jerome. "Inventing with Animals in the Middle Ages." In *Engaging with Nature: Essays on the Natural World in Medieval and Early Modern Europe*, edited by Barbara A. Hanawalt and Lisa J. Kiser, 39–62. Notre Dame: University of Notre Dame, 2008.

———, ed. *Animal, Vegetable, Mineral. Ethics and Objects*. Washington, DC: Oliphaunt Books, 2012.

Cohen, Jeffrey Jerome and Lowell Duckert, eds. *Elemental Ecocriticism: Thinking with Earth, Air, Water, and Fire*. Minneapolis: University of Minnesota Press, 2015.

Cole, Lucinda. "Out of Africa: Locust Infestation, Universal History, and the Early Modern Theological Imaginary." In *Lesser Living Creatures: Insect Life in the Renaissance*, edited by Keith Botelho and Joseph Campana. University Park: Pennsylvania State University Press, forthcoming 2021.

———. *Imperfect Creatures: Vermin, Literature, and the Science of Life 1600–1740*. London and Ann Arbor: University of Michigan Press, 2016.

Collins, Samuel. *A Systeme of Anatomy, Treating of the Body of Man, Beasts, Birds, Fish, Insects, and Plants*. London, 1685.

Conti, Natale. *Mythologiae*. Translated and edited by John Mulryan and Steven Brown. 2 vols. Tempe: Arizona Center for Medieval and Renaissance Studies, 2006.

Coolican, J. Patrick. "Sushi in the raw." *Seattle Times*, November 11, 2003.

Crane, Mary Thomas. *Shakespeare's Brain: Reading with Cognitive Theory*. Princeton, NJ: Princeton University Press, 2001.

Crocker, Holly A. "Engendering Shrews: Medieval to Early Modern." In *Gender and Power in Shrew-Taming Narratives, 1500–1700*, edited by D. Wooton and G. Holderness, 48–69. New York: Palgrave Macmillan, 2010.

Cummings, Brian. "Pliny's Literate Elephant and the Idea of Animal Language in Renaissance Thought." In *Renaissance Beasts: Of Animals, Humans, and Other Wonderful Creatures*, edited by Erica Fudge, 164–85. Champaign: University of Illinois Press, 2004.

Cummings, Peter. "Shakespeare's Bawdy Planet." *The Sewanee Review* 101, no. 4 (Fall 1993): 521–35.

Cunliffe, Barry. *Facing the Ocean: The Atlantic and Its Peoples, 1000 BC–AD 1500*. Oxford: Oxford University Press, 2001.

———. *Europe between the Oceans: 9000 BC–AD 1000*. New Haven, CT: Yale University Press, 2011.

Cunningham, Andrew. "The Culture of Gardens." In *Cultures of Natural History*, edited by N. Jardine, J.A. Secord, and E.C. Spary, 38–56. Cambridge: Cambridge University Press, 1996.

Cunningham, Andrew and Ole Peter Grell. *The Four Horsemen of the Apocalypse: Religion, War, Famine and Death in Reformation Europe*. Cambridge: Cambridge University Press, 2000.

Cunnington, B. Howard. "'A Skimmington' in 1618." *Folklore* 41 (1930): 287–90.

Currie, Christopher K. "The Early History of Carp and Its Economic Significance in England." *The Agricultural History Review* 39, no. 2 (1991): 97–107.

D'Avenant, William. *Dramatic Works*, edited by James Maidment and W.H. Logan, 5 vols. Edinburgh: William Patterson, 1872. Vol. 1.

Daley, A. Stuart. "The Idea of Hunting in *As You like It*." *Shakespeare Studies* 21 (1993): 72–95.

Daly, Peter. "Of *Macbeth*, Martlets, and Other 'Fowles of Heaven'." *Mosaic* 12, no. 1 (1978): 23–46.

Davidson, Clifford. "*Timon of Athens*: The Iconography of False Friendship." *Huntington Library Quarterly* 43, no. 3 (1980): 181–200.

Davidson, James. *Courtesans and Fishcakes: The Consuming Passions of Classical Athens*. New York: St. Martin's Press, 1997.

Dayan, Colin. *The Law Is a White Dog: How Legal Rituals Make and Unmake Persons*. Princeton, NJ: Princeton University Press, 2011.

de Vries, Jan and Ad van der Voude. *The First Modern Economy: Success, Failure, and Perseverance of the Dutch Economy, 1500–1800*. New York: Cambridge University Press, 1997.

Dekker, Thomas. *Britannia's Honour*. 1628.

DeLanda, Manuel. *New Philosophy of Society*. London: Continuum, 2006.

Deleuze, Gilles. "On the Superiority of Anglo-American Literature." In *Dialogues II*, edited by Gilles Deleuze and Claire Parne, 36–76. New York: Columbia University Press, 1977.

———. *Foucault*. Translated by Seán Hand. Minneapolis: University of Minnesota Press, 1988.

Deleuze, Gilles and Felix Guattari. *A Thousand Plateaus: Capitalism and Schizophrenia*. Translated by Brian Massumi. Minneapolis: University of Minnesota Press, 1987.

DeMello, Margo. *Animals and Society: An Introduction to Human-Animal Studies*. New York: Columbia University Press, 2012.

Dent, R.W. *Shakespeare's Proverbial Language*. Berkley: University of California Press, 1981.

Bibliography

———. *Proverbial Language in English Drama Exclusive of Shakespeare, 1495–1616: An Index*. Berkeley: University of California Press, 1984.

———. "'Eating Well,' or the Calculation of the Subject: An Interview with Jacque Derrida." In *Who Comes after the Subject?* edited by Eduardo Cadava, Peter Conner, and Jean-Luc Nancy, 96–119. London: Routledge, 1991.

Derrida, Jacques. *Of Grammatology*. Translated by Gayatri Chakravorty Spivak. Baltimore, MD: Johns Hopkins University Press, 1976.

———. *Dissemination*. Translated by Barbara Johnson. Chicago, IL: University of Chicago Press, 1981.

———. *Aporias*. Translated by Thomas Dutoit. Stanford, CA: Stanford University Press, 1993.

———. "'Eating Well,' or the Calculation of the Subject." In *Points…Interviews, 1974–1994*, edited by Elisabeth Weber and translated by Peter Connor and Avital Ronell, 255–87. Stanford, CA: Stanford University Press, 1995.

———. "The Animal that Therefore I Am (More to Follow)." Translated by David Willis. *Critical Inquiry* 28 (2002): 369–418.

———. "Hostipitality." In *Acts of Religion*, edited and translated by Gil Andijar, 356–420. New York: Routledge, 2002.

———. *For What Tomorrow … A Dialogue*. Translated by Jeff Fort. Stanford, CA: Stanford University Press, 2004.

———. *Learning to Live Finally*. Translated by Pascale-Anne Brault and Michael Nass. Hoboken, NJ: Melville House, 2007.

———. *The Animal that Therefore I Am*. Translated by David Wills. New York: Fordham University Press, 2008.

———. *The Beast and the Sovereign*. Edited by Marie-Louise Mallet, Ginette Michaud, and Michel Lisse, translated by Geoffrey Bennington, 2 vols. Chicago, IL: University of Chicago Press, 2009. Vol. 2.

Despret, Vinciane. *What Would Animals Say If We Asked the Right Questions?* Translated by Brett Buchanan. Minneapolis: University of Minnesota Press, 2016.

Dibley, Ben. "Nature Is Us: The Anthropocene and Species-Being." *Transformations* 21 (2012): 1–22.

Dickey, Colin. "The Sex Lives of Sea Creatures." *The New Republic*, February 11, 2016, https://newrepublic.com/article/129669/sex-lives-sea-creatures.

Dickinson, M.G. "A "Skimmington Ride" at Aveton Gifford." *Devon and Cornwall Notes and Queries* 34 (1981): 290–92.

Dionne, Craig and Steve Mentz, eds. *Rogues and Early Modern English Culture*. Ann Arbor: University of Michigan press, 2004.

Dobson, Michael. "A Dog at All Things: The Transformation of the Onstage Canine, 1550–1850." *Performance Research* 5, no. 2 (2000): 116–24.

Dolan, Frances. "Introduction." In William Shakespeare, *The Taming of the Shrew*, edited by Frances Dolan, 1–38. Boston, MA: St. Martin's Press, 1996.

Donne, John. *The Complete Poetry and Selected Prose of John Donne*. Edited by Charles M. Coffin. New York: The Modern Library, 1994.

Doty, Jeffrey S. "Shakespeare's *Richard II*, 'Popularity,' and the Early Modern Public Sphere." *Shakespeare Quarterly* 61, no. 2 (2010): 183–205.

Drayton, Michael. *The Tragicall Legend of Robert, Duke of Normandy, Surnamed Short-Thigh, Eldest Sonne to William Conqueror*. London, 1596.

Driscoll, Kári and Eva Hoffmann. "Introduction." In *What Is Zoopoetics?: Texts, Bodies, Entanglement*, edited by Kári Driscoll and Eva Hoffmann, 1–13. Palgrave, Macmillan, 2018.

Duckert, Lowell. "'Exit Pursued by a Bear': More to Follow." *Upstart: A Journal of English Renaissance Studies* (2013). Web.

Dugan, Holly. "*Coriolanus* and the 'Rank-Scented Meinie'." In *Masculinity and the Metropolis of Vice 1550–1650*, edited by Amanda Bailey and Roze Hentschell, 139–59. London: Palgrave, 2010.

———. *The Ephemeral History of Perfume: Scent and Sense in Early Modern England*. Baltimore, MD: The Johns Hopkins University Press, 2011.

———. "'To Bark with Judgment': Playing Baboon in Early Modern London." *Shakespeare Studies* 41 (2013): 77–93.

———. "A Natural History of Ravishment." In *Renaissance Posthumanism*, edited by Joseph Campana and Scott Maisano, 120–43. New York: Fordham University Press, 2016.

Bibliography

———. "Shakespeare Performed: Courtyard Theatre's *King Lear with Sheep*." *Shakespeare Quarterly*, June 2017, accessed December 7, 2017, https://shakespearequarterly.folger.edu/web_exclusive/shakespeare-performed-courtyard-theatres-king-lear-with-sheep/.

Dunbar, Judith, ed. *The Winter's Tale: Shakespeare in Performance*. Manchester: Manchester University Press, 2010.

Duncan-Jones, Katherine. "Did the Boy Shakespeare Kill Calves?" *Review of English Studies*, new series 55 (2004).

Dyer, Christopher. "Poverty and Its Relief in Late Medieval England." *Past and Present* 216 (2012): 41–78.

Edelman, Lee. *No Future: Queer Theory and the Death Drive*. Durham, NC: Duke University Press, 2004.

Edward of Norwich. *The Master of Game*. Edited by William A. Baillie-Grohman and F.N. Baillie-Grohman. Philadelphia: University of Pennsylvania Press, 2005.

Egan, Gabriel. *Shakespeare and Ecocritical Theory*. London: Bloomsbury Arden Shakespeare, 2015.

Egerton, John. "Letter to Sir Peter Legh." *Legh of Lyme Correspondence*, 1615.

Eilidh Kane, Eilidh. "Shakespeare and Middleton's Co-Authorship of *Timon of Athens*." *Journal of Early Modern Studies* 5 (2016): 217–35.

Eliav-Feldon, Miriam, Benjamin Isaac, and Joseph Ziegler, eds. *The Origins of Racism in the West*. New York: Cambridge University Press, 2009.

Elyot, Thomas. *The boke named the Gouernour*. London, 1531.

———. *Biblioteca Eliotae. Eliotes Dictionary*. London, 1559.

Emig, Ranier. "Renaissance Self-Unfashioning: Shakespeare's Late Plays as Exercises in Unravelling the Human." In *Posthumanist Shakespeare*, edited by Stefan Herbrechter and Ivan Callus, 133–59. New York: Palgrave MacMillan, 2012.

Empiricus, Sextus. *Outlines of Scepticism*. Translated and edited by Julia Annas and Julian Barnes. Cambridge: Cambridge University Press, 2000.

Empson, William. *Some Versions of Pastoral*. 1935; reprint New York: A New Directions Paper Book, 1974.

Eng, David L. *Racial Castration: Managing Masculinity in Asian America*. Durham, NC: Duke University Press, 2001.

Eng, David L. and Shinhee Han. "A Dialogue on Racial Melancholia." *Psychoanalytic Dialogues* 10, no. 4 (2000): 667–700.

Engels, Freidrich and Karl Marx. *The Communist Manifesto*. Translated by Samuel Moore. New York: Penguin Classics, 2015.

Ensler, Eve. *The Vagina Monologues*. New York: Villard, 2008; o.p., 1998.

Erasmus, Desiderius. *Opera Omnia Desiderii Erasmi Roterodami*. Amsterdam: Elzevier, 1969.

———. "On the War against the Turks." In *The Erasmus Reader*, edited by Erika Rummel, 315–330. Toronto: University of Toronto Press, 1990.

———. *The Education of a Christian Prince*. Edited by Lisa Jardine and translated by Neil. M. Cheshire and Michael J. Heath. Cambridge: Cambridge University Press, 1997.

Erickson, Peter. *Patriarchal Structures in Shakespeare's Drama*. Berkeley: University of California Press, 1985.

Estok, Simon. "Theory from the Fringes: Animals, Ecocriticism, Shakespeare." *Mosaic* 40, no. 1 (2007): 61–78.

Everitt, A. "The Marketing of Agricultural Produce." In *The Agrarian History of England and Wales*, vol. 4, edited by J. Thirsk, 466–589. Cambridge: Cambridge University press, 1967.

Faber, J.A. *Cattle Plague in the Netherlands during the Eighteenth Century*. Amsterdam: Veenman-Zonen, 1962.

Fagan, Brian. *Fish on Friday: Feasting, Fasting, and the Discovery of the New World*. New York: Basic Books, 2006.

———. *Fishing: How the Sea Fed Civilization*. New Haven, CT: Yale University Press, 2017.

Fanon, Frantz. *Black Skins, White Masks*. New York: Grove Press, 2008.

Fanous, Samuel. *A Barrel of Monkeys: A Compendium of Collective Nouns for Animals*. Oxford: Bodleian Library, 2015.

Fatout, Paul. "Roan Barbary." *The Shakespeare Association Bulletin* 15, no. 2 (1940): 67–74.

Felski, Rita. "Context Stinks!" *New Literary History* 42, no. 4 (2011): 573–91.

Field, John. *A Godly Exhortation, by Occasion of the Late Iudgement of God, Shewed at Parris-Garden, the Thirteenth Day of Januarie*. London, 1583.

Bibliography

Fish, Stanley. *Is There a Text in This Class?: The Authority of Interpretive Communities*. Cambridge, MA: Harvard University Press, 1980.

Fisher, F.J. "The Development of the London Food Market, 1540–1640." *The Economic History Review* a5, no. 2 (1935): 46–64.

Fisher, R.H. *The Russian Fur Trade 1550–1700*. Berkeley: University of California Press, 1943.

Fissell, Mary. "Imagining Vermin in Early Modern England." *The History Workshop Journal* 47, no. 1 (1999): 1–29.

Fitzherbert, John (attributed). *The Boke of Husbandry*. London, 1540.

Flaherty, Jennifer. "'Know Us by Our Horses': Equine Imagery in Shakespeare's *Henriad*." In *The Horse as Cultural Icon*, edited by Peter Edwards, Karl A.E. Enenkel and Elspeth Graham, 307–25. Leiden and Boston, MA: Brill, 2017.

Fletcher, Giles. *Of the Russe Commonwealth*. London, 1591.

Floyd-Wilson, Mary. *English Ethnicity and Race in Early Modern Drama*. Cambridge: Cambridge University Press, 2003.

Fludd, Robert. *Mosaicall Philosophy Grounded upon the Essentiall Truth, or Eternal Sapience*. London, 1659.

Foakes, R.A. *Shakespeare: The Dark Comedies to the Last Plays*. London: Routledge and Kegan Paul, 1971.

Ford, John, Thomas Dekker, and William Rowley. *The Witch of Edmonton*. Edited by Arthur F. Kinney. London: A & C Black, 2005.

Forrest, John. *The History of Morris Dancing, 1458–1750*. Cambridge: James Clarke & Co., 1999.

Fort, Tom. *The Book of Eels: On the Trail of the Thin-Heads*. London: Harper Collins 2003.

Foucault, Michel. *Madness and Civilization: A History of Insanity in the Age of Reason*. New York: Vintage, 1965; 1961.

———. *The Order of Things: An Archaeology of the Human Sciences*. London: Tavistock Publications, 1970.

———. "What Is Enlightenment?" Translated by Catherine Porter. In *The Foucault Reader*, edited by Paul Rabinow, 32–50. New York: Pantheon, 1984.

———. *Society Must Be Defended: Lectures at the Collège de France 1975–1976*. Translated by David Macey. New York: Picador, 1997, 2003.

———. *Security, Territory, Population: Lectures at the Collège de France, 1977–1978*. Translated by Graham Burchell, edited by Michel Senellart. New York: Picador: 2007.

Fowler, William. *A True Report of the Most Tryumphant, and Royall Accomplishment of the Baptisme of the Most Excellent, Right High, and Mightie Prince, Henry Fredericke*. London, 1603.

Fracastoro, Girolamo. *De Contagione et Contagiosis Morbis*. Rome, 1546.

Francis, Pope. *Laudato Si': On Care for Our Common Home*. Huntington, IN: Our Sunday Visitor, 2015.

Francisco, Timothy. "Marlowe's War Horses: Cyborgs, Soldiers, and Queer Companions." In *Violent Masculinities: Male Aggression in Early Modern Texts and Culture*, edited by Jennifer Feather and Catherine E. Thomas, 47–65. New York: Palgrave Macmillan, 2013.

Frazer, James George. *The Golden Bough*. New York: Macmillan, 1967.

Free Butchers of London. *Reasons Tendred by the Free Butchers of London against the Bill in Parliament to Restraine Butchers from Grazing of Cattle*. London, 1624.

Freud, Sigmund. *Beyond the Pleasure Principle*. Translated by James Strachey. New York: Norton, 1961.

———. *Civilization and Its Discontents*. Translated and edited by James Strachey. New York: Norton, 1961.

Fudge, Erica. *Perceiving Animals: Humans and Beasts in Early Modern English Culture*. Basingstoke: Macmillan Press, 2000.

———. *Perceiving Animals: Humans and Beasts in Early Modern Culture*. Urbana: University of Illinois Press, 2002.

———. *Animal*. London: Reaktion, 2004.

———. *Brutal Reasoning: Animals, Humanity, and Rationality in Early Modern England*. New York: Cornell University Press, 2006.

———. "Two Ethics: Killing Animals in the Past and the Present." In *Killing Animals*, edited by The Animal Studies Group, 99–119. Urbana: Illinois University Press, 2006.

———. "'The Dog Is Himself': Humans, Animals, and Self-Control in *The Two Gentlemen of Verona*." In *How To Do Things with Shakespeare: New Approaches, New Essays*, edited by Laurie Maguire 185–209. Malden, MA: Blackwell, 2008.

———. "Renaissance Animal Things." In *Gorgeous Beasts: Animal Bodies in Historical Perspective*, edited by Joan B. Landes, Paula Young Lee, and Paul Youngquist, 41–56. University Park: Pennsylvania State University Press, 2012.

Bibliography

———. "Renaissance Animal Things." *New Formations* 76 (2012): 86–100.

———. *Quick Cattle and Dying Wishes: People and Their Animals in Early Modern England*. Ithaca, NY: Cornell University Press, 2018.

Fudge, Erica, Ruth Gilbert, and Susan Wiseman, eds. *At the Borders of the Human: Beasts, Bodies, and Natural Philosophy in the Early Modern Period*. New York: St. Martin's Press, 1999.

Fumerton, Paricia. *Unsettled*. Chicago, IL: University of Chicago Press, 2006.

Game, Ann. "Riding: Embodying the Centaur." *Body & Society* 7, no. 4 (2001): 1–12.

Garber, Marjorie. "Fetish Envy." *October* 54 (Autumn 1990): 45–56.

———. *Dog Love*. New York: Simon & Schuster, 1996.

———. *Shakespeare after All*. New York: Pantheon, 2004.

Garrard, Greg. *Ecocriticism*, 2nd ed. London: Routledge, 2012.

Gascoigne, George. *The Noble Art of Venerie or Hunting*. London: Printed by Henry Bynneman, 1575.

Gerald of Wales. *The History and Topography of Ireland*. Translated by John Joseph O'Meara, Revised. London: Penguin, 1982.

Gerard, John. *The Herball*. London: John Norton, 1597.

Gessner, Conrad. *Historiae animalium: de quadrupedibus viviparis*, 2nd ed. Frankfurt, 1602.

———. *Historiae Animalium: Liber III, de Avium Natura*. Frankfurt, 1635.

Gil, Daniel Juan. *Shakespeare's Anti-Politics: Sovereign Power and the Life of the Flesh*. New York: Palgrave, 2013.

Girard, René. *Violence and the Sacred*. Translated by Patrick Gregory. London and New York: Continuum, 2005.

Givan, Christopher. "Shakespeare's *Coriolanus*: The Premature Epitaph and the Butterfly." *Shakespeare Studies* 12 (1979): 143–58.

Glimp, David and Michelle Warren, eds. *Arts of Calculation: Numerical Thought in Early Modern Europe*. New York: Palgrave Macmillan, 2004.

Goddard, Emily. "Calais: 'Dogs Are Allowed in Cars Here, but Refugees Are Not'." *Independent*, May 26 2017, www.independent.co.uk/news/long_reads/calais-refugees-france-uk-pakistan-a7742136.html.

Goldstein, David. *Eating and Ethics in Shakespeare's England*. Cambridge: Cambridge University Press, 2013.

Gordon, Rebecca Louise. "Feeding the City: Zooarchaeological Perspectives on Urban Provisioning and Consumption Behaviours in Post-Medieval England (AD1500–AD1900)." University of Leicester, School of Archaeology and Ancient History, 2016.

———. "From Pests to Pets: Social and Cultural Perceptions of Animals in Post-Medieval Centres in England (AD 1500-1900)," Papers from the Institute of Archeology, 27 (2017), https://pia-journal.co.uk/articles/10.5334/pia-478/

Gouwens, Kenneth. "What Posthumanism Isn't: On Humanism and Human Exceptionalism in the Renaissance." In *Renaissance Posthumanism*, edited by Joseph Campana and Scott Maisano, 37–63. New York: Fordham University Press, 2016.

Gowing, Laura. *Domestic Dangers: Women, Words, and Sex in Early Modern London*. Oxford: Clarendon Press, 1998.

Grady, Hugh. *Shakespeare, Machiavelli, and Montaigne: Power and Subjectivity from Richard II to Hamlet*. Oxford: Oxford University Press, 2002.

Grant, Teresa. "White Bears in *Mucedorus, The Winter's Tale* and *Oberon, The Fairy Prince*." *Notes and Queries* 48, no. 3 (2001): 311–13.

Green, Mary A.E., ed. *Calendar of State Papers Domestic: James I, 1611–18*. London: HM Stationery Office, 1858. British History Online, accessed August 31, 2017, www.british-history.ac.uk/cal-state-papers/domestic/jas1/1611-18.

Greenblatt, Stephen. "A Great Dane Goes to the Dogs." *The New York Review of Books*, March 26, 2009, accessed June 1, 2018, www.nybooks.com/articles/2009/03/26/a-great-dane-goes-to-the-dogs/.

Greetham, David. "On Cultural Translation." reprint In *Textual Transgressions: Essays toward the Construction of a Biobibliography*, 496–512. New York: Routledge, 1998.

Grisone, Federigo. *The Rules of Riding*. Edited and translated by Elizabeth MacKenzie Tobey. Tempe, AZ: ACMRS, 2014.

Grosz, Elizabeth. *The Nick of Time: Politics, Evolution and the Untimely*. Durham, NC and London: Duke University Press, 2004.

Guerrini, Anita. "The Pathological Environment." *The Eighteenth Century: Theory and Interpretation* 31 (1990): 173–79.

Bibliography

Guevara, Perry D. "Of Flyes." In *Lesser Living Creatures: Insect Life in the Renaissance*, edited by Keith Botelho and Joseph Campana. University Park: Pennsylvania State University Press, forthcoming 2021.

Gumbrecht, Hans Ulrich. *Production of Presence. What Meaning Cannot Convey.* Stanford, CA: Stanford University Press, 2004.

———. *Atmosphere, Mood, Stimmung. On a Hidden Potential of Literature.* Translated by Erik Butler. Stanford, CA: Stanford University Press, 2012.

Gurr, Andrew. "The Bear, the Statue, and Hysteria in *The Winter's Tale*." *Shakespeare Quarterly* 34, no. 4 (1983): 420–25.

Guy-Bray, Stephen. "Shakespeare and the Invention of the Heterosexual." *EMLS* 13 (2007): 12.1–28.

Hadfield, Andrew. *Shakespeare and Republicanism.* Cambridge: Cambridge University Press, 2005.

Hahn, Daniel. *The Tower Menagerie.* London: Simon and Schuster, 2004.

Haist, Margaret. "The Lion, Bloodline, and Kingship." In *The Mark of the Beast: The Medieval Bestiary in Art, Life and Literature*, edited by Debra Hassig, 3–21. London: Garland Publishing, 1999.

Hall, Kim F. *Things of Darkness: Economies of Race and Gender in Early Modern England.* Ithaca, NY: Cornell University Press, 1995.

Hallett, Charles A. "'Metamorphosing' Proteus: Reversal Strategies in *The Two Gentlemen of Verona*." In *Two Gentlemen of Verona: Critical Essays*, edited by June Schlueter, 153–77. New York: Garland, 1996.

Hamlin, William M. "A Lost Translation Found? An Edition of *The Sceptick* (c.1590) Based on Extant Manuscripts [with Text]." *English Literary Renaissance* 31, no. 1 (2001).

Hand, Molly. "Animals, the Devil, and the Sacred in Early Modern English Culture." In *Animals, Animality, and Literature*, edited by Bruce Boehrer, Molly Hand, and Brian Massumi, 105–20. Cambridge: Cambridge University Press, 2018.

Haraway, Donna. *The Companion Species Manifesto: Dogs, People, and Significant Otherness.* Chicago, IL: Prickly Paradigm Press, 2003.

———. "Conversations with Donna Haraway." In *Donna Haraway: Live Theory*, edited by Joseph Schneider, 114–56. London: Continuum, 2005.

———. *When Species Meet.* Minneapolis: University of Minnesota Press, 2008.

———. "Anthropocene, Capitalocene, Plantationocene, Chthulucene: Making Kin." *Environmental Humanities* 6 (2015): 159–61.

———. *Staying with the Trouble: Making Kin in the Cthulucene.* Durham, NC: Duke University Press, 2016.

Harman, Graham. *Bruno Latour: Assembling the Political.* London: Pluto, 2014.

———. *Object-Oriented Ontology. A New Theory of Everything.* London: Pelican Books, 2018.

Harman, Thomas. *Caveat or Warning for Common Cursitors.* London, 1567.

Harris, Jonathan Gil. "'The Enterprise Is Sick': Pathologies of Value and Transnationality in *Troilus and Cressida*." *Renaissance Drama* 29 (1998): 3–37.

———. *Untimely Matter in the Time of Shakespeare.* Philadelphia: University of Pennsylvania Press, 2008.

Harrison, William. *The Description of England.* Ithaca, NY: Cornell University Press, 1968.

———. *The Description of England: The Classic Account of Tudor Social Life.* Edited by George Edelen. Washington, DC: Folger Shakespeare Library 1994.

Hart, James. *Klinikh or the Diet of the Diseased.* London, 1633.

Harvey, David. *The New Imperialism.* Oxford: Oxford University Press, 2003.

Harward, Michael. *The Herds-Man's Mate, or, A Guide for Herds-Men Teaching How to Cure All Diseases in Bulls, Oxen, Cows and Calves.* Dublin, 1673.Hawkes, Terrance. *Shakespeare's Talking Animals: Language and Drama in Society.* London: Edward Arnold, 1973.

———. *Shakespeare in the Present.* London and New York: Routledge, 2002.

Haynes, Samuel. *A Collection of States Papers, Relating to Affairs in the Reigns of King Henry VIII, King Edward VI, Queen Mary, and Queen Elizabeth, from the Year 1542 to 1570.* London: William Bowyer, 1740.

Haywood, Richard. "Notes and Queries: Which British Town Is Furthest from the Sea?" *The Guardian*, April 25, 2012, https://www.theguardian.com/theguardian/2012/apr/25/british-town-furthest-from-sea.

Heaney, Michael. "New Evidence for the Abbots Bromley Hobby-Horse." *Folk Music Journal* 5 (1987): 359–60.

Bibliography

Heaney, Peter F. "Petruchio's Horse: Equine and Household Management in *The Taming of the Shrew*." *Early Modern Literary Studies* 4, no. 1 (1998): 1–12.

Hearne, Vicki. *Adam's Task: Calling Animals by Name*. New York: Skyhorse Publishing, 2007.

Helgerson, Richard. "The Buck Basket, the Witch, and the Queen of Fairies: The Women's World of Shakespeare's Windsor." In *Renaissance Culture and the Everyday*, edited by Patricia Fumerton and Simon Hunt, 162–82. Philadelphia: University of Pennsylvania Press, 1999.

Henry, John. *The Scientific Revolution and the Origins of Modern Science*. Basingstoke: Palgrave Macmillan, 1997, 2008.

Hershinow, David. "Diogenes the Cynic and Shakespeare's Bitter Fool: The Politics and Aesthetics of Free Speech." *Criticism* 56, no. 5 (2015): 807–35.

Hickling, Alfred. "Two Gentlemen of Verona Review—Shakespeare on a Gap-Year Adventure." *Guardian*, August 14, 2016, www.theguardian.com/stage/2016/aug/04/two-gentlemen-of-verona-review-shakespeare-grosvenor-park-theatre-chester.

Hoeniger, F. David, and J.F.M. Hoeniger. *The Development of Natural History in Tudor England*. Boston, MA: MIT Press, 1979.

Höfele, Andreas. *Stage, Stake, and Scaffold: Humans and Animals in Shakespeare's Theatre*. Oxford: Oxford University Press, 2011.

Holland, Henry. *The Historie of Adam, or the Foure-Fold State of Man*, edited by Edward Topsell. London, 1606.

Hollingsworth, Christopher. *Poetics of the Hive: The Insect Metaphor in Literature*. Iowa City: University of Iowa Press, 2001.

Howard, Skiles. "Hands Feet and Bottoms: Decentering the Cosmic Dance in *A Midsummer Night's Dream*." *Shakespeare Quarterly* 44 (1993): 325–42.

Hughes, Henry. "Fish, Sex, and Cannibalism: Appetites for Conversion in Melville's *Typee*." *Leviathan* 6, no. 2 (October 2004): 3–16.

Hunt, Katherine, and Rebecca Tomlin. "Numbers in Early Modern Writing." Special Issue, *Journal of the Northern Renaissance* 6 (2014), https://www.northernrenaissance.org/editorial-numbers-in-early-modern-writing/.

Hunt, Maurice. "Bearing Hence: Shakespeare's *The Winter's Tale*." *Studies in English Literature* 44, no. 2 (2004): 333–46.

Ingamells, John. *Dulwich Picture Gallery Collections*. London: Unicorn, 2008.

Ingram, Martin. "Ridings Rough Music and the 'Reform of Popular Culture' in Early Modern England." *Past and Present* 105 (1984): 79–113.

Irigaray, Luce. *Speculum of the Other Woman*. Translated by Gillian C. Gill. Ithaca, NY: Cornell University Press, 1985.

Izadi, Elahe. "Admit It: You Want to Know the Deal with the 'Shape of Water' Fish Sex." *Washington Post*, March 5, 2018, https://www.washingtonpost.com/news/arts-and-entertainment/wp/2018/03/05/admit-it-you-want-to-know-the-deal-with-the-shape-of-water-fish-sex/.

Jacobs, Nicole A. "Bees: The Shakespearean Hive and the Virtues of Honey." In *Shakespearean International Yearbook 15: Shakespeare and the Human*, edited by Tiffany Jo Werth, 101–21. Farnham: Ashgate Publishing, 2015

———. "John Milton's Beehive, from Polemic to Epic." *Studies in Philology* 112, no. 4 (2015): 798–816.

Jaffe, Eric. "Why Our Brains Love Curvy Architecture." *Fast Company*, October 17, 2013, www.fastcompany.com/3020075/why-our-brains-love-curvy-architecture.

James I, King of England. *Basilicon Doron 1599: A Scolar Press Facsimile*. Menston: Scolar Press, 1969.

Jardine, Lisa. *Still Harping on Daughters: Women and Drama in the Age of Shakespeare*. New York: Columbia University Press, 1989.

Jenner, Mark. "The Great Dog Massacre." In *Fear in Early Modern Society*, edited by William G. Naphy and Penny Roberts, 44–61. Manchester: St. Martin's Press, 1997.

Jenstad, Jenelle, ed. The Agas Map. *The Map of Early Modern London* (*MoEML*). 2012.

Johnson, Elizabeth. "At the Limits of Species Being." *South Atlantic Quarterly* 116, no. 2 (2017): 275–92.

Johnson, Laurie, John Sutton, and Evelyn Tribble, eds. *Embodied Cognition and Shakespeare's Theatre: The Early Modern Body-Mind*. New York: Routledge, 2014.

Johnson, Samuel. *A Dictionary of the English Language*. London, 1755.

Jones, Malcolm. "Folklore Motifs in Late Medieval Art III: Erotic Animal Imagery." *Folklore* 102, no. 2 (1991): 192–219.

Jones, Reece. *Violent Borders: Refugees and the Right to Move*. New York: Verso, 2016.

Bibliography

Jonson, Ben. *The Devil Is an Ass and Other Plays.* Edited by Margaret Jane Kidnie. New York: Oxford University Press, 2000.

———. *Four Plays.* Edited by Robert N. Watson. London: Methuen, 2014.

Justice, Steven. *Writing and Rebellion: England in 1381.* Berkeley and Los Angeles: University of California Press, 1994.

Kahn, Coppelia. "'Magic of Bounty': Timon of Athens, Jacobean Patronage, and Maternal Power." *Shakespeare Quarterly* 38 (1987): 34–57.

Kahn, Victoria. "Humanism and the Resistance to Theory." In *Rhetoric and Hermeneutics in Our Time: A Reader,* edited by Walter Jost and Michael J. Hyde, 149–70. New Haven, CT: Yale University Press, 1997.

———. "Humanism and the Resistance to Theory." In *Rhetoric and Hermeneutics in Our Time,* edited by Jerrold E. Levy and Stephen J. Kunitz, 149–70. New Haven, CT: Yale University Press, 2017.

Kamuf, Peggy. "'This Were Kindness': Economies of Difference in the *Merchant of Venice.*" *Oxford Literary* Review 34, no. 1 (2012): 71–87.

Kane, Eilidh. "Shakespeare and Middleton's Co-Authorship of *Timon of Athens.*" *Journal of Early Modern Studies* 5 (2016): 217–35.

Karras, Ruth. "Regulation of Brothels in Later Medieval England." *Signs* 14, no. 2 (1989): 399–433.

Keen, Elizabeth. *The Journey of a Book: Bartholomew the Englishman and the Properties of Things.* Canberra: Australian National University E Press, 2007.

Kellaway, Kate. "Claudia Rankine: 'Blackness in White Imagination Has Nothing to Do with Black People." *Guardian,* December 2015, https://www.theguardian.com/books/2015/dec/27/claudia-rankine-poet-citizen-american-lyric-feature.

Khan, Coppélia. *Roman Shakespeare: Warriors, Wounds and Women.* London: Routledge, 1997.

King, Lonnie et al. "One Health Initiative Task Force." *JAVMA* 233, no. 2 (July 15, 2008), https://www.avma.org/resources-tools/one-health.

Kirk G.S. and J.E. Raven, eds. *The Presocratic Philosophers: A Critical History with a Selection of Texts.* Cambridge: Cambridge University Press, 1957.

Kiser, Lisa J. "'Mak's Heirs:' Sheep and Humans in the Pastoral Ecology of the Towneley *First* and *Second Shepherds' Plays.*" *JEGP* 108, no. 3 (2009): 336–59.

Kitto, H.D.F. *The Greeks.* Harmondsworth: Penguin, 1973.

Klein, Melanie. "Weaning." In *Love, Guilt, and Reparation, and Other Works, 1921–1945,* 290–305. New York: Free Press, 1975.

Kolb, Laura. "Debt's Poetry in *Timon of Athens.*" *Studies in English Literature 1500–1900* 58, no. 2 (2018): 399–419.

Kopnina, Helen. "Beyond Multispecies Ethnography: Engaging with Violence and Animal Rights in Anthropology." *Critique of Anthropology* 37, no. 3 (September 2017): 333–57.

Kordecki, Lesley. "True Love and the Nonhuman." *Social Alternatives* 32, no. 4 (2013): 28–33.

Kotilaine, J.T. *Russia's Foreign Trade and Economic Expanion in the Seventeenth Century.* Leiden: Brill, 2005.

Kramer, Heinrich and James Sprenger. *The Malleus Maleficarum.* Translated by Montague Summers, 1928; reprint New York: Dover, 1971.

Kristeva, Julia. *Powers of Horror: An Essay on Abjection.* Translated by Leon S. Roudiez. New York: Columbia University Press, 1982.

Kurlansky, Mark. *Cod: A Biography of the Fish that Changed the World.* New York: Penguin, 1997.

Kuzner, James. "Unbuilding the City: *Coriolanus* and the Birth of Republican Rome." *Shakespeare Quarterly* 58, no. 2 (2007): 174–99.

Lacan, Jacques. *The Seminar of Jacques Lacan, Book XI: The Four Fundamental Concepts of Psychoanalysis.* Translated by Alan Sheridan. New York: Norton, 1977.

Landes, Lee and Youngquist, eds. *Gorgeous Beasts: Animal Bodies in Historical Perspective.* University Park: Pennsylvania State University Press, 2012.

Landry, Donna. "Horsy and Persistently Queer: Imperialism, Feminism and Bestiality." *Textual Practice* 15, no. 3 (Winter 2001): 467–85.

Langdon, Alison, ed. *Animal Languages in the Middle Ages Representations of Interspecies Communication.* New York: Palgrave, 2018.

Laqueur, Thomas W. *The Work of the Dead: A Cultural History of Mortal Remains.* Princeton, NJ: Princeton University Press, 2015.

Laroche, Rebecca and Jennifer Munro. "On a Bank of Rue; or Material Ecofeminist Inquiry and the Garden of *Richard II.*" *Shakespeare Studies* 42 (2014): 42–50.

Bibliography

Latour, Bruno. *We Have Never Been Modern*. Translated by Catherine Porter. Cambridge, MA: Harvard University Press, 1993.

———. *Pandora's Hope: Essays on the Reality of Science Studies*. Cambridge, MA: Harvard University Press, 1999.

———. *Reassembling the Social: An Introduction to Actor-Network-Theory*. Oxford: Oxford University Press, 2005.

Layard, Daniel. *An Essay on the Bite of a Mad Dog*, 2nd ed. London, 1763.

Leech, Clifford. Introduction to *The Two Gentlemen of Verona*, by William Shakespeare, edited by Clifford Leech, xiii–lxxv. London: Methuen, 1969.

Le Guin, Elizabeth. "Man and Horse in Harmony." In *The Culture of the Horse: Status, Discipline and Identity in the Early Modern World*, edited by Karen Raber and Treva J. Tucker, 175–96. New York: Palgrave Macmillan, 2005.

Lenz, Joseph. "Base Trade: Theater as Prostitution." *ELH* 60, no. 4 (Winter 1993): 833–55.

Levin, Harry. "Falstaff Uncolted." *Modern Language Notes* 61, no. 5 (1946): 305–10.

Lewis, Wyndham. *The Lion and the Fox: The Role of the Hero in the Plays of Shakespeare*. London: Harper and Brothers, 1927.

Lippit, Akira Mizuta. *Electric Animal*. Minneapolis: University of Minnesota Press, 2000.

———. "From Wild Technology to Electric Animals." In *Representing Animals*, edited by Nigel Rothfels, 119–36. Bloomington: Indiana University Press, 2002.

Lockwood, Jeffrey A. *The Infested Mind: Why Humans Fear, Loathe, and Love Insects*. Oxford: Oxford University Press, 2013.

Loomba, Ania. *Shakespeare, Race, and Colonialism*. New York: Oxford University Press, 2002.

Loomba, Ania and Jonathan Burton, eds. *Race in Early Modern England: A Documentary Companion*. New York: Palgrave Macmillan, 2007.

Lorenzi, Rosella. "Oysters and Crabs, the Popcorn of Shakespearean Theatergoers." *London Times*, 2010, https://www.seeker.com/oysters-and-crabs-the-popcorn-of-shakespearean-theatergoers-1765021687.html.

Love, Heather. "Small Change: Realism, Immanence, and the Politics of the Micro." *Modern Language Quarterly* 77, no. 3 (2016): 419–45.

Lovegrove, Roger. *Silent Fields: The Long Decline of a Nation's Wildlife*. Oxford: Oxford University Press, 2007.

Lupton, Julia Reinhard. "Othello Circumcised: Shakespeare and the Pauline Discourse of Nations." *Representations* 57 (1997): 73–89.

———. *Thinking with Shakespeare: Essays on Politics and Life*. Chicago, IL: Chicago University Press, 2011.

Lupton, Thomas. *A Thousand Notable Things, of Sundry Sortes*. London, 1579.

Lutz, Cora E. "Bishop Dubravius on Fishponds." *The Yale University Library Gazette* 48, no. 1 (July 1973): 12–16.

Lyly, John. *Galatea; Midas*. Edited by G.K. Hunter. Manchester: Manchester University Press, 2000.

Lyne, Raphael. *Shakespeare, Rhetoric and Cognition*. Cambridge: Cambridge University Press, 2011.

Lymberry, Philip. *Farmageddon*. London: Bloomsbury, 2014.

Maathai, Wangari. *The Green Belt Movement*. Seattle: Lantern Books, 2003.

Machiavelli, Niccolò. *The Prince*. Edited by Quentin Skinner and Russell Price. Cambridge: Cambridge University Press, 1988.

MacInnes, Ian. "Mastiffs and Spaniels: Gender and Nation in the English Dog." *Textual Practice* 17, no. 1 (2003): 21–40.

Mackinder, Anthony, Lyn Blackmore, Julian Bowsher, and Christopher Phillpotts. *The Hope Playhouse, Animal Baiting and Later Industrial Activity at Bear Gardens on Bankside. Excavations at Riverside House and New Globe Walk, Southwark, 1999–2000*. London: Museum of London Archaeology, 2013.

Magnus, Olaus. *A Compendious History of the Goths, Swedes, Vandals, and Other Northern Nations 1555*. London, 1658.

Malm, Andreas. *The Progress of this Storm*. New York: Verso, 2018.

Malthus, Thomas Robert. *An Essay on the Principle of Population*. New York: Norton, 2004.

Mangan, Michael. *A Preface to Shakespeare's Comedies: 1594–1603*. London: Longman, 1996.

Mann, Jenny. "Pygmalion's Wax: 'Fruitful Knowledge' in Bacon and Montaigne." *Journal of Medieval and Early Modern Studies* 45 (2015): 367–93.

Bibliography

Manning, Roger B. *Hunters and Poachers: A Social and Cultural History of Unlawful Hunting in England 1485–1640*. Oxford: Clarendon, 1993.

Marcus, Leah. *Unediting the Renaissance: Shakespeare, Marlowe, Milton*. London and New York: Routledge, 1996.

Markham, Gervase. *Cauelarice, or the English Horseman Contayning All the Arte of Horse-Manship...* London, 1607.

———. *Cheap and Good Husbandry, for the Well-Ordering of All Beasts and Fowls, and for the General Cure of Their Diseases*. London: Printed by T.S. for Roger Jackson, 1614.

———. *Cheape and Good Husbandry. . . . .* London, 1634.

———. *The Perfect Horseman or the Experienced Secrets of Mr. Markham's Fifty Years Practice*. London, 1656.

Marlowe, Christopher. *Tamburlaine Parts One and Two*. Edited by Anthony B. Dawson. New York: WW Norton, 1997.

Marston, John. *Works*. Edited by A.H. Bullen, 3 vols. London: J.C. Nimmo, 1887. Vol. 3, 115.

———. *The Malcontent*. Edited by George K. Hunter. Manchester: Manchester University Press, 2001.

Martin, Randall. *Shakespeare and Ecology*. Oxford: Oxford University Press, 2015.

Marvin, Spevack. *The Harvard Concordance to Shakespeare*. Cambridge, MA: Harvard University Press. 1973.

Marx, Leo. "Pastoralism in America." In *Ideology and Classic American Literature*, edited by Sacvan Bercovitch and Myra Jehlen, 36–69. Cambridge: Cambridge University Press, 1986.

Marx, Karl. "Religion, Free Press, and Philosophy." In *Writings of the Young Karl Marx on Philosophy and Society*, translated by Loyd D. Easton and Kurt H. Guddat, 109–31. New York: Doubleday, 1967.

———. *Early Writings*, trans. Rodney Livingstone,. New York, Vintage Books, 1975.

———. *Capital*, vol. 1. Translated by Ben Fowkes. New York: Penguin, 1990.

Marx, Steve. "Shakespeare's Pacifism." *Renaissance Quarterly* 45:1 (Spring 1992), 49–95.

Mascall, Leonard. *The First Book of Cattel*. London, 1587.

Massumi, Brian. *What Animals Teach Us About Politics*. Durham and London: Duke University Press, 2014.

Masten, Jeffrey. "Two Gentlemen of Verona." In *A Companion to Shakespeare's Works, Vol III: The Comedies*, edited by Richard Dutton and Jean Howard, 266–88, 2003.

———. *Textual Intercourse*. New York: Cambridge University Press, 1997.

Masters, Roger D. *Fortune Is a River: Leonardo da Vinci and Niccolò Machiavelli's Dream to Change the Course of Florentine History*. New York: Free Press, 1998.

Maxwell, J.C. "Animal Imagery in 'Coriolanus,' " *The Modern Language Review* 42:4 (1947): 417–21.

Mayhew, Robert. *The Female in Aristotle's Biology: Reason or Rationalization*. Chicago, IL: University of Chicago Press, 2010.

Mazella, David. *The Making of Modern Cynicism*. Charlottesville: University of Virginia Press, 2007.

McEachern, Claire. "Why Do Cuckolds Have Horns?" *Huntington Library Quarterly* 71 (2008): 607–31.

McHugh, Susan. *Animal Stories: Narrating across Species Lines*. Minneapolis: University of Minnesota Press, 2011.

Melling, John Kennedy. *London's Guilds and Liveries*. London: Bloomsbury Publishing, 2003.

Mennell, Nicole. "Zibellini as Animal- Made Objects." Sussex Centre for Early Modern and Medieval Studies. March 7, 2017, https://sussexcemms.wordpress.com/2017/03/07/zibellini-as-animal-made-objects/.

Mentz, Steve. "Airy Spirits: Winds, Bodies, and Ecological Force in Early Modern England." In *Shakespearean International Yearbook 15: Shakespeare and the Human*, edited by Tiffany Jo Werth, 21–38. Farnham: Ashgate Publishing, 2015.

———. "Shakespeare's Beach House, or The Green and the Blue in *Macbeth*." *Shakespeare Studies* 39 (2011): 84–93.

———. "Half Fish, Half Flesh: Dolphins, Humans, and the Early Modern Ocean." In *The Indistinct Human in Renaissance Literature*, edited by Jean Feerick and Vin Nardizzi, 29–46. London: Palgrave, 2012.

Merchant, Carolyn. *Radical Ecology: The Search for a Livable World*. New York: Routledge, 1992.

Meres, Francis. *Palladis Tamia. Wits Treasury, Being the Second Part of Wits Commonwealth*. London: Peter Short for Cuthbert Burby, 1598.

Méry, Fernand. *Animal Languages*. Translated by Michael Ross. Westmead: Saxon House, 1975.

Middleton, Thomas. *Thomas Middleton: The Collected Works*. Edited by Gary Taylor and John Lavagnino. Oxford: Oxford University Press, 2006.

Bibliography

Miller, John MacNeill. "When Drama Went to the Dogs; or, Staging Otherness in the Animal Melodrama." *PMLA* 132, no. 3 (2017): 526–42.

Milton, John. *Complete Poems and Major Prose*. Edited by Merritt Y. Hughes. Indianapolis, IN: Hackett Publishing, reprint 2003.

Moffett, Thomas. *The Theater of Insects, or, Lesser Living Creatures*. London, 1658.

Monbiot, George. *Feral: Searching for Enchantment on the Frontiers of Re-wilding*. London: Penguin, 2013.

Montaigne, Michel de. "An Apologie of Raymond Sebond." In *The Essayes or Morall, Politike and Millitarie Discourses of Lo: Michaell de Montaigne*, translated by John Florio. London, 1603.

———. "The Apologie for Raymond Sebond." In *The Essayes of Montaigne: John Florio's Translation*, edited by J.I.M. Stewart, 385–547. New York: Modern Library, 1933.

———. *The Complete Essays*. Translated by M.A. Screech. London: Penguin Books, 2003.

———. *Michel de Montaigne: The Complete Essays of Montaigne*. Edited and translated by M.A. Screech. London: Penguin Classics, 2003.

Montrose, Louis A. "Of Gentlemen and Shepherds: The Politics of Elizabethan Pastoral Form." *English Literary History* 50, no. 3 (Autumn 1983): 439–42.

———. *The Purpose of Playing: Shakespeare and the Cultural Politics of the Elizabethan Theatre*. Chicago, IL: University of Chicago Press, 1996.

Moore, Jason. *Capitalism in the Web of Life*. New York: Verso, 2015.

More, Alexander. *A Sermon Preached at the Hague, at the Funeral of the Late Prince of Orange*. Translated by Daniel la Fite. London, 1694.

Morison, James Cotter. *The Life and Times of Saint Bernard, Abbot of Clairvaux*. New York: Macmillan, 1889.

Morris, Brian. "Introduction." In William Shakespeare, *The Taming of the Shrew*, edited by Brian Morris, 12–50. London: Methuen, 1981.

Mortimer, Caroline. "Having Children Is One of the Most Destructive Things You Can Do to the Environment, Says Researchers." *Independent*, July 12, 2017, www.independent.co.uk/environment/children-carbon-footprint-climate-change-damage-having-kids-research-a7837961.html.

Morton, Timothy. *Humankind*. Brooklyn, NY: Verso, 2017.

Mowat, Barbara, Paul Werstine, Michael Poston, and Rebecca Niles, eds. *Henry V.* Washington, DC: Folger Shakespeare Library, n.d. www.folgerdigitaltexts.org.

Mullaney, Steven. *The Place of the Stage: License, Play, and Power in Elizabethan London*. Chicago, IL: University of Chicago Press, 1988.

———. *The Reformation of Emotions in the Age of Shakespeare*. Chicago, IL and London: The University of Chicago Press, 2015.

Mullett, Charles F. "Some Neglected Aspects of Plague Medicine in Sixteenth-Century England." *The Scientific Monthly* 44, no. 4 (1937): 325–37.

Munday, Anthony. *The Death of Robert, Earle of Huntington. OTHERWISE CALLED Robin Hood of merrie Sherwodde: with the lamentable Tragedie of chaste MATILDA, his faire maid MARIAN, poisoned at Dunmowe by King IOHN*. London, 1601.

Muñoz, José Esteban. *Disidentifications: Queers of Color and the Performance of Politics*. Minneapolis: University of Minnesota Press, 1999.

Munroe, Jennifer. "Shakespeare and Ecocriticism Reconsidered." *Literature Compass* 12, no. 9 (2015): 37–50.

Nagy, Kelsi and Phillip David Johnson, eds. *Trash Animals*. Minneapolis: University of Minnesota Press, 2013.

Nancy, Jean-Luc. "L'Intrus." Translated by Susan Hanson. *CR: The New Centennial Review* 2, no. 3 (2002): 1–14.

Nelson, Alan and Matthew Priselac, "Made with Words: Hobbes on Language, Mind, and Politics." *Notre Dame Philosophical Reviews*, January 27, 2009, accessed June 5, 2018, https://ndpr.nd.edu/news/made-with-words-hobbes-on-language-mind-and-politics/.

Nietzsche, Friedrich. *Untimely Meditations*. Edited by Daniel Breazeale and Translated by R.J. Hollingdale. Cambridge: Cambridge University Press, 1997; reprint 2004.

Nowak, Ronald M. *Walker's Mammals of the World*, 2 vols. Baltimore, MD: Johns Hopkins University Press, 1991.

O'Dair, Sharon. "'To Fright the Animals and To Kill Them Up': Shakespeare and Ecology." *Shakespeare Studies* 29 (2011): 11–30.

———. "Is It Shakespearean Ecocriticism If It Isn't Presentist?" In *Ecocritical Shakespeare,* edited by Lynne Bruckner and Dan Brayton, 71–85. London: Routledge, 2016.

Bibliography

Ogden, Laura, A. Billy Hall, and Kimiko Tanita, "Animals, Plants, People, and Things." *Environment and Society* 4, no. 1 (September 1, 2013): 5–24. doi:10.3167/ares.2013.040102

Ogilby, John. *The Fables of Aesop*. London, 1651.

Okin, Gregory. "Environmental Impacts of Food Consumption by Dogs and Cats." *PLoS One* 12, no. 8 (2017), https://doi.org/10.1371/journal.pone.0181301.

Oldenburg, Scott. *Alien Albion*. Toronto: University of Toronto Press, 2014.

Orgel, Stephen, ed. *The Winter's Tale*. Oxford: Oxford University Press, 1996.

Ortner, Sherry B. "Is Female to Male as Nature Is to Culture?" *Feminist Studies* 1, no. 2 (Autumn 1972): 5–31.

Orvis, Davis. "'Which Is the Worthiest Love.'" In *Queer Shakespeare: Desire and Sexuality*, edited by Goran Stanivukovic, 33–49. London: Bloomsbury, 2017.

Overton, Mark. *Agricultural Revolution in England: The Transformation of the Agrarian Economy 1500–1850*. Cambridge: Cambridge University Press, 1996.

The Oxford English Dictionary Online. Second Edition. Edited by John Simpson et al. Oxford University Press, 2020. http://home.comcast.net/~modean52/oeme_dictionaries.htm

Padua, St. Anthony of. *Medieval Preachers and Medieval Preaching*. Edited and translated by J.M. Neale. London: J & C Mozley, 1856.

Pafford, J.H.P., ed. *The Winter's Tale*. Cambridge, MA: Arden, 1963.

Painter, William. *The Palace of Pleasure*. Edited by Joseph Jacobs, vol. 1. London: D. Nutt, 1890.

Palmer, Daryl. "Jacobean Muscovites: Winter, Tyranny, and Knowledge in *The Winter's Tale*." *Shakespeare Quarterly* 46, no. 3 (1995): 323–39.

Palmierei, Frank, ed. *Humans and Other Animals in Eighteenth-Century British Culture: Representation, Hybridity, Ethics*. Burlington, VT: Ashgate, 2006.

Pandian, Anand. "Pastoral Power in the Postcolony: On the Biopolitics of the Criminal Animal in South India." *Cultural Anthropology* 23, no. 1 (2008): 85–117.

Panke, John. *Collectanea, Out of St. Gregory the Great, and St Bernard the Devout against the Papists Who Adhere to the Doctrine of the Present Church of Rome*. Oxford, 1618.

Parker, Patricia. "Barbers and Barbary: Early Modern Cultural Semantics." *Renaissance Drama* 33 (2004): 201–44.

Partridge, Eric. *Shakespeare's Bawdy*. London and New York: Routledge, 2002, o.p. 1947.

Paster, Gail Kern. *The Body Embarrassed: Drama and the Disciplines of Shame in Early Modern England*. Ithaca, NY: Cornell University Press, 1993.

———. "The Unbearable Coldness of Female Being: Women's Imperfection and the Humoral Economy." *English Literary Renaissance* 28, no. 3 (Autumn 1998): 416–40.

———. *Humoring the Body*. Chicago, IL: University of Chicago Press, 2004.

Pastoureau, Michael. *Heraldry: Its Origins and Meaning*. Translated by Francisca Garvie. London: Thames and Hudson, 1997.

Patel, Raj. *Stuffed and Starved*. New York: Melville House, 2012.

Patterson, Annabel. *Fables of Power: Aesopian Writing and Political History*. Durham, NC: Duke University Press, 1991.

Peacham, Henry. *The Garden of Eloquence Conteyning the Figures of Grammer and Rhetorick*. London, 1577.

Peeples, Lynne. "Contagion Connections: How Links among Humans, Animals, and the Environment May Be Spawning Infectious Disease." *Huffington Post*, September 30, 2011, www.huffingtonpost.com/2011/09/30/contagion-infectious-disease-animals-environment-health_n_987455.html.

Pemberton, Neil and Michael Worboys. *Dogs, Diseases and, and Culture, 1830–2000*. Basingstoke: Palgrave Macmillan, 2007.

Perry, Kathryn. "Unpicking the Seam: Talking Animals and Reader Pleasure in Early Modern Satire." In *Renaissance Beasts: Of Animals, Humans, and Other Wonderful Creatures*, edited by Erica Fudge, 19–36. Champaign: University of Illinois Press, 2004.

Peterson, Richard. "Laurel Crown and Ape's Tail: New Light on Spenser's Career from Sir Thomas Tresham." *Spenser Studies* 12 (1998): 1–35.

Petrarch's Remedies for Fortune Fair and Foul, vol. 3. Translated by Conrad H. Rawski. Bloomington: Indiana University Press, 1991.

Pettit, Philip. *Made with Words: Hobbes on Language, Mind, and Politics*. Princeton, NJ: Princeton University Press, 2008.

Philips van Marnix van St. Aldegonde. *The Beehive of the Romish Church*. Translated by George Gilpin. London, 1579.

Bibliography

Phipson, Emma. *The Animal Lore of Shakespeare's Time Including Quadrupeds, Birds, Reptiles, Fish and Insects*. London: Kegan Paul, Trench, and Co., 1883.

Pinker Stephen. *The Language Instinct: How the Mind Creates Language*. New York: Harper Perennial, 1995.

Plato. "Phaedrus." In *Plato: Euthyphro, Apology, Crito, Phaedo, Phaedrus*, trans. Harold North Fowler, 195–405. Cambridge, MA: Harvard University Press, 1914.

———. *The Republic*. Edited by G.R.F. Ferrari and Translated by Tom Griffith. Cambridge: Cambridge University Press, 2001.

Pliny the Elder. *Natural History*. Translated by H. Rackham, 10 vols. Cambridge, MA: Harvard University Press, 1983.

Plot, Robert. *The Natural History of Stafford-Shire*. Oxford: The Theatre, 1686.

Pluvinel, Antoine. *Le maneige royal*. Translated by Hilda Nelson. London: J.A. Allen, 1989.

Pollan, Michael. *The Botany of Desire: A Plant's-Eye View of the World*. New York: Random House, 2001.

———. *Omnivore's Dilemma*. New York: Bloomsbury, 2007.

Pollock, Linda. "The Practice of Kindness in Early Modern Elite Society." *Past and Present* 211 (2011): 121–58.

Poor Robin's Jests, London: 1667.

Pope, Alexander, trans. *The Odyssey of Homer*. 5 vols. London, 1725–26.

Posset, Franz. "Bernard of Clairvaux as Luther's Source." *Concordia Theological Quarterly* 54 (1990): 281–304.

Purchas, Samuel. *Purchas His Pilgrims*, 1625.

Quiller-Couch, Arthur. Introduction to *The Two Gentlemen of Verona*, by William Shakespeare, edited by Arthur Quiller-Couch and John Dover Wilson, vii–xix. Cambridge: Cambridge University Press, 1921.

Quiller-Couch, Arthur, ed. "Introduction." In *Measure for Measure*, edited by Arthur Quiller-Couch, vii–xliii. Cambridge University Press, 1965, o.p. 1922.

———. *The Winter's Tale*. Cambridge: Cambridge University Press, 1931.

Raber, Karen. "A Horse of a Different Color; Nation and Race in Early Modern Horsemanship Treatises." In *The Culture of the Horse: Status, Discipline, and Identity in the Early Modern World*, 225–44. New York: Palgrave, 2005.

———. *Animal Bodies, Renaissance Culture*. Philadelphia: University of Pennsylvania Press, 2013.

———. "Shakespeare and Animal Studies." *Literature Compass* 12, no. 6 (2015): 286–98.

———. "Equeer: Human-Equine Erotics in *1 Henry IV*." In *The Oxford Handbook of Shakespeare and Embodiment: Gender, Sexuality, and Race*, edited by Valerie Traub, 347–269. Oxford: Oxford University Press, 2016.

———. "William Cavendish's Horsemanship Treatises and Cultural Capital." In *Authority, Authorship and Aristocratic Identity in Seventeenth-Century England. William Cavendish*, 1st Duke of Newcastle, and his Political, Social and Cultural Connections, edited by Peter Edwards and Elspeth Graham, 331–52. Leiden and Boston, MA: Brill, 2017.

———. *Shakespeare and Posthumanist Theory*. London: Bloomsbury, 2018.

Raber, Karen and Monica Mattfield. *Performing Animals: History, Agency, Theater*. State College: Penn State University Press, 2017.

Raber, Karen and Treva J. Tucker. "Introduction." In *The Culture of the Horse: Status, Discipline, and Identity in the Early Modern World*, edited by Raber and Tucker, 1–42. Basingstoke: Palgrave Macmillan, 2005.

Ralegh, Walter. "A Discourse of War in General." In *The Works of Sir Walter Ralegh*, edited by William Oldys and Thomas Birch, 253–298. New York: Burt Franklin, 1829.

Ramachandran, Ayesha. *The Worldmakers*. Chicago, IL: University of Chicago Press, 2015.

Ramachandran, Ayesha and Melissa E. Sanchez. "Spenser and 'the Human': An Introduction," *Spenser Studies: A Renaissance Poetry Annual* 30 (2015): vii–v.

Ravelhofer, Barbara. "'Beasts of Recreacion': Henslowe's White Bears." *English Literary Renaissance* 32, no. 2 (2002): 287–323.

Rawlins, Thomas. *The Rebellion*. London, 1640.

Ray, John. *The Ornithology of Franics Willoughby*. London, 1678.

———. *The Wisdom of God Manifested in the Works of the Creation*. London, 1692, 159–60.

Raye, Lee. "The Early Extinction Date of the Beaver (Castor fiber) in Britain." *Historical Biology* 27 (2014): 1029–41.

Bibliography

Reid, Jennifer. "The 'heavie writ of outlawry': Community and the Transformation of Popular Culture from Early Modern Customary Drama to Anthony Munday's Robin Hood Plays." *The Wenshan Review of Literature and Culture* 10 (2017): 69–91.

———. "'The Hunt is Up': Death, Dismemberment, and Feasting in Shakespeare's Roman Tragedies." *Actes des congrès de la Société française Shakespeare* 38 (forthcoming 2020).

Richards, John F. *Unending Frontier: An Environmental History of the Early Modern World*. Berkeley: University of California Press, 2003.

Richardson, Charles. *The Repentance of Peter and Judas Together with the Frailtie of the Faithfull, and the Fearfull Ende of Wicked Hypocrites*. London, 1612.

Rivlin, Elizabeth. "Mimetic Service in Two Gentlemen of Verona." *ELH* 72, no. 1 (2005): 105–28.

———. "Service and Servants in Early Modern English Culture to 1660." *Journal of Early Modern Studies* 4 (2015): 17–41.

Roberts, Callum. *The Unnatural History of the Sea*. Washington, DC: Island Press, 2007.

Roberts, Jeanne Addison. *Shakespeare's English Comedy: The Merry Wives of Windsor in Context*. Lincoln and London: University of Nebraska Press, 1979.

———. "Horses and Hermaphrodites: Metamorphoses in the Taming of the Shrew." *Shakespeare Quarterly* 34, no. 2 (Summer 1983): 159–71.

Roe, John. *Shakespeare and Machiavelli*. Cambridge: D. S. Brewer, 2002.

Roelvink, Gerda. "Rethinking Species-Being for the Anthropocene." *Rethinking Marxism* 25, no. 1 (2013): 52–69.

Rose, Deborah Bird, et al. "Thinking through the Environment, Unsettling the Humanities." *Environmental Humanities* 1 (2012): 1–5, http://environmentalhumanities.org.

Rogers, Ben. *Beef and Liberty*. New York: Vintage, 2004.

Rowley, William, Thomas Dekker, and John Ford. *The Witch of Edmonton*. Edited by Arthur F. Kinney. London: A & C Black, 1998.

"Roxburghe Ballads," *English Broadside Ballads Archive,* University of California, Santa Barbara, accessed June 19, 2019, https://ebba.english.ucsb.edu/ballad/30240/xml.

Rusden, Moses. *A Further Discovery of Bees*. London, 1679.

Ryan, Kiernan. *Shakespeare's Comedies*. New York: Palgrave Macmillan, 2009.

Saint Bernard, His Meditations, or Sighes, Sobbes, and Teares upon Our Saviors Passion, Translated by W.P. London, 1611.

Salignac de La Mothe Fénélon, Bertrand de. *Correspondance diplomatique de Bertrand de Salignac de la Mothe Fénélon ambassadeur de France en Angleterre de 1568 à 1575, Tome Sixieme*. London: Panckoucke, 1840.

Sanchez, Melissa E. "'Use Me But as Your Spaniel': Feminism, Queer Theory, and Early Modern Sexualities." *PMLA* 127, no. 3 (May 2012): 493–511.

Sanders, Julie. *The Cultural Geography of Early Modern Drama, 1620–1650*. New York: Cambridge University Press, 2011.

Sauter, Michael J. "Clockwatchers and Stargazers: Time Discipline in Early Modern Berlin." *The American Historical Review* 112, no. 3 (2007): 685–709.

Schalkwyk, David. "Coriolanus: A Tragedy of Language." In *The Oxford Handbook of Shakespearean Tragedy*, edited by Michael Neill and David Schalkwyk, 468–86. Oxford: Oxford University Press, 2016.

Schanzer, Ernst, ed. *The Winter's Tale*. Hammondsworth: Penguin, 1966.

Schiesari, Juliana. "Rethinking Humanism: Animals and the Analogic Imagination in the Italian Renaissance." *Shakespeare Studies* 41 (2013): 54–63.

Schlueter, June, ed. *"Two Gentlemen of Verona": Critical Essays*. New York: Garland, 1996.

Schneider, Joseph. *Donna Haraway: Live Theory*. London: Continuum, 2005.

Schoenbaum, Samuel. *William Shakespeare: A Documentary Life*. Oxford: Clarendon, 1975.

Schoenfeldt, Michael. "Fables of the Belly in Early Modern England." In *The Body in Parts: Fantasies of Corporeality in Early Modern Europe*, edited by David Hillman and Carla Mazzio, 242–61. New York: Routledge, 1997.

Schrikx, Willem. "Pickleherring and English Actors in Germany." *Shakespeare Survey* 36 (1983): 135–48.

Scott, Heidi. "Ecological Microcosms Envisioned in Shakespeare's *Richard II*." *The Explicator* 67, no. 4 (2009): 267–71.

Bibliography

Seeley, Thomas D. "The Honeybee Colony as a Superorganism." *American Scientist* 77, no. 6 (November 1989): 546–53.

———. *Honeybee Democracy*. Princeton, NJ: Princeton University Press, 2010.

Segarra, Santiago et al. "Attributing the Authorship of the *Henry VI* Plays by Word Adjacency." *Shakespeare Quarterly* 67, no. 2 (2016): 232–56.

Selwood, Jacob. *Diversity and Difference in Early Modern London*. New York: Routledge, 2010, 2016.

Servheen, Christopher. *Bears: Status Survey and Conservation Action Plan*. Cambridge: IUCN, 1999.

Shakespeare William. *A most pleasaunt and excellent conceited comedie, of Syr Iohn Falstaffe, and the merrie wiues of Windsor* Entermixed with sundrie variable and pleasing humors, of Syr Hugh the Welch knight, Iustice Shallow, and his wise cousin M. Slender. With the swaggering vaine of Auncient Pistoll, and Corporall Nym. By William Shakespeare. As it hath bene diuers times acted by the right Honorable my Lord Camberlaines seruants. Both before her Maiestie, and else-where. London, 1602.

———. *Shakes-speares Sonnets*. London, 1609.

———. *The Whole Contention between the Two Famous Houses, Lancaster and York*. London, 1619.

———. *The Tragedy of Coriolanus*. London, 1623. *The Bodleian First Folio: Digital Facsimile of the First Folio of Shakespeare's Plays*. Bodleian Arch. G c.7, http://firstfolio.bodleian.ox.ac.uk/.

———. *The Tragedy of Coriolanus* (London, 1632). *Internet Shakespeare Editions*, University of Victoria, last updated February 3, 2011, http://internetshakespeare.uvic.ca/Library/facsimile/book/SLNSW_F2/.

———. *The Dramatick Writings of William Shakspere*, vol. III. London, 1788.

———. *The Plays and Poems of William Shakespeare*. London: R. C. and J. Rivington, etc, 1821.

———. *A New Variorum Edition of Shakespeare: The Tragedy of Coriolanus*. Edited by Horace Howard Furness, Jr. Philadelphia: J.B. Lippincott Company, 1928.

———. *The Tragedy of Coriolanus*. Edited by G.B. Harrison. Harmondsworth: Penguin Books, 1955.

———. "The Comedy of Errors." In *The Norton Shakespeare*, edited by Stephen Greenblatt et al., 683–89. New York and London: Norton, 1997.

———. *Macbeth*. Edited by Kenneth Muir. London: Methuen, 1984.

———. *The Merchant of Venice*. Edited by John Russell Brown. London: Arden, 1959.

———. *Troilus and Cressida*. Edited by Kenneth Palmer. London: Routledge, 1989.

———. *King Henry V*. Edited by T.W. Craik. London: Bloomsbury, 1995.

———. "The Taming of the Shrew." In *The Riverside Shakespeare*, edited by G. Blakemore Evans et al, 106–42. Boston, MA: Houghton Mifflin, 1997.

———. *The Tempest*. Edited by Virginia Mason Vaughan and Alden T. Vaughan. London: Arden, 1999.

———. *The Merry Wives of Windsor*. Edited by Giorgio Melchiori, The Arden Shakespeare. London: Thomson Learning, 2000.

———. *Henry VI, Part 2*. Edited by Roger Warren. Oxford: Oxford University Press, 2002.

———. *King Richard II*. Edited by Charles R. Forker. London: Arden, 2002.

———. *Julius Caesar*. Edited by David Daniell. London: Arden Shakespeare, 2002 [1998].

———. *The Complete Works of Shakespeare, Fifth Edition*. Edited by David Bevington. New York: Pearson Longman, 2004.

———. *Two Gentlemen of Verona*. Edited by William C. Carroll. London: Arden, 2004.

———. *The Oxford Shakespeare: The Complete Works*. Edited by Stanley Wells, et al., 2nd ed. Oxford: Oxford University Press, 2005.

———. *As You Like It*. Edited by Juliet Dusinberre, The Arden Shakespeare. London: Thomson Learning, 2006.

———. *Othello*. Edited by Kim F. Hall. Boston: Bedford Books, 2007.

———. *The Winter's Tale*. Edited by Susan Snyder and Deborah T. Curren-Aquino. Cambridge: Cambridge University Press, 2007.

———. *As You Like It*. Edited by Michael Hattaway. Cambridge: Cambridge University Press, 2000, 2009.

———. *Henry V*. Edited by T.W. Craik. New York: Bloomsbury, 2009.

———. *The Winter's Tale*. Edited by John Pitcher. London: Arden, 2010.

———. *The Arden Shakespeare*. Edited by Richard Proudfoot, Ann Thompson and David Scott Kastan. London: Arden Shakespeare, 2011.

———. *Coriolanus*. Edited by Jonathan Bate and Eric Rasmussen. Basingstoke: Macmillan, 2011.

———. *Coriolanus*. Edited by Peter Holland. London: Bloomsbury Arden Shakespeare, 2013.

Bibliography

———. *The Complete Works of Shakespeare*. Edited by David Bevington, 7th ed. Boston, MA: Pearson, 2014.

———. *The New Oxford Shakespeare: Modern Critical Edition*. Edited by Gary Taylor, John Jowett, Terri Bourus, and Gabriel Egan. Oxford: Oxford University Press, 2016.

———. *Cymbeline*. Edited by Valerie Wayne, The Arden Shakespeare. London: Bloomsbury, 2017.

———. "*A Midsummer Night's Dream*." In *The Complete Works of Shakespeare*, 152–79. Boston, MA: Pearson, 2014.

———. "*Coriolanus*." In *The Complete Works of Shakespeare*. Edited by David Bevington, 7th ed., 1388–436. Boston, MA: Pearson, 2014.

———. "*Julius Caesar*." In *The Complete Works of Shakespeare*, edited by David Bevington, 7th ed., 1055–90. Boston, MA: Pearson, 2014.

———. "*King Lear*." In *The Complete Works of Shakespeare*, edited by David Bevington, 7th ed., 1207–54. Boston, MA: Pearson, 2014.

———. "*Othello, the Moor of Venice*." In *The Complete Works of Shakespeare*, edited by David Bevington, 7th ed., 1156–200. Boston, MA: Pearson, 2014.

———. "*The First Part of King Henry the Fourth*." In *The Complete Works of Shakespeare*. Edited by David Bevington, 7th ed., 787–825. Boston, MA: Pearson, 2014.

———. "*The Merchant of Venice*." In *The Complete Works of Shakespeare*, edited by David Bevington, 7th ed., 185–218. Boston, MA: Pearson, 2014.

———. *The Riverside Shakespeare*. Edited by G. Blakemore Evans and J.J.M. Tobin, 2nd ed.

———. "*The Tragedy of King Richard the Second*." In *The Complete Works of Shakespeare*, edited by David Bevington, 7th ed.,, 745–83. Boston, MA: Pearson, 2014.

———. "*The Two Gentlemen of Verona*." In *The Complete Works of Shakespeare*, edited by David Bevington, 7th ed., 78–103. Boston, MA: Pearson, 2014.

———. "*Timon of Athens*." In *The Complete Works of Shakespeare*, edited by David Bevington, 7th ed., 1296–330. Boston, MA: Pearson, 2014.

———. "*Titus Andronicus*." In *The Complete Works of Shakespeare*, edited by David Bevington, 7th ed., 970–1004. Boston, MA: Pearson, 2014.

Shakespeare William and Thomas Middleton. *Timon of Athens*. Edited by John Jowett, The Oxford Shakespeare. New York: Oxford University Press, 2009.

Shannon, Laurie. "The Eight Animals in Shakespeare; or, Before the Human." *PMLA* 124, no. 2 (2009): 472–79.

———. "Poor, Bare, Forked: Animal Sovereignty, Human Negative Exceptionalism, and the Natural History of *King Lear*." *Shakespeare Quarterly* 60, no. 2 (Summer 2009): 168–96.

———. *The Accommodated Animal: Cosmopolity in Shakespearean Locales*. Chicago, IL: University of Chicago Press, 2013.

———. "'Poore Wretch, Laid All Naked upon the Bare Earth': Human Negative Exceptionalism among the Humanists." *Shakespearean International Yearbook 15: Shakespeare and the Human*, edited by Tiffany Werth, 205–10. Farnham: Ashgate Publishing, 2015.

———. "Poor Things, Vile Things: Shakespeare's Comedy of Kinds." In *Oxford Handbook of Shakespearean Comedy*, edited by Heather Hirschfield, 358–73. New York: Oxford University Press, 2018.

Shaw, George Bernard. "The Taming of the Shrew." In *Shaw on Shakespeare*, edited by Edwin Wilson. New York: Applause Theatre and Cinema Books, 2002; reprint 1961.

Sheets-Johnstone, Maxine. *The Primacy of Movement*, 2nd ed. Philadelphia, PA: John Benjamins Publishing Company, 2011.

Sheldon, Rebekah. "Form/Matter/Chora: Object-Oriented Ontology and Feminist New Materialism." In *The Nonhuman Turn*, edited by Richard Grusin. Minneapolis: University of Minnesota Press, 2015.

Shell, Marc. *Money, Language, and Thought*. Baltimore, MD: Johns Hopkins University Press, 1982.

Shrewsbury, J.F.D. "The Plague of Athens." *Bulletin of the History of Medicine* 24 (1950): 1–25.

Shukin, Nicole. *Animal Capital: Rendering Life in Biopolitical Times*. Minneapolis: University of Minnesota Press, 2009.

———. "Tense Animals: On Other Species of Pastoral Power." *The New Centennial Review* 11, no. 2 (Fall 2011): 143–67.

Sidney, Philip. *The Countesse of Pembrokes Arcadia*. London, 1590.

———. *The Countess of Pembroke's Arcadia*. London: Penguin Books, 1977.

Bibliography

Simon, Matt. "Absurd Creature of the Week: The Anglerfish and the Absolute Worst Sex on Earth." *Wired*, November 8, 2013, https://www.wired.com/2013/11/absurd-creature-of-the-week-anglerfish/.

Small, S. Asa. "The Ending of *The Two Gentlemen of Verona*." *PMLA* 48, no. 3 (1933): 767–76.

Smith, Amy Victoria, Leanne Proops, Kate Grounds, Jennifer Wathan and Karen McComb. "Functionally Relevant Responses to Human Facial Expressions of Emotion in the Domestic Horse (Equus caballus)." *Biology Letters*, 2016, http://rsbl.royalsocietypublishing.org/content/12/2.

Smith, Ian. "Othello's Black Handkerchief." *Shakespeare Quarterly* 64, no. 1 (2013): 1–25.

Smith, Thomas (attributed). *A Discourse of the Commonweal of this Realm of England*. Edited by Mary Dewer. Charlottesville: University of Virginia Press, 1969.

Smylie, Mike. *The Perilous Catch: A History of Commercial Fishing*. Stroud: History Press, 2015.

Snively, Samantha N. "*As You Like It*'s Political, Critical Animal Allusions." *Studies in English Literature 1500–1900* 58, no. 2 (2018): 331–52.

Speed, John. *The Theatre of the Empire of Great Britaine Presenting an Exact Geography of the Kingdomes of England, Scotland, Ireland, and the Iles Adioyning*. London, 1611.

Spenser, Edmund. *The Faerie Queene*, edited by Thomas Roche, Jr., London: Penguin Books, 1987.

Spevack, Marvin. *A Complete and Systematic Concordance to the Works of Shakespeare*. 9 vols. Hildesheim: Georg Olms, 1968.

Spivak, Gayatri. *A Critique of Postcolonial Reason*. Cambridge, MA: Harvard University Press, 1999.

———. *Death of a Discipline*. New York, Columbia University Press, 2003.

Stanton, Kay. *Shakespeare's 'Whores': Erotics, Politics, and Poetics*. New York: Palgrave MacMillan, 2014.

Steel, Karl. *How to Make a Human*. Columbus: Ohio State University Press, 2011.

Stern, Tiffany. *Documents of Performance in Early Modern England*. Cambridge: Cambridge University Press, 2009.

Sterry, Paul. *Collins Complete Guide to British Wildlife: A Photographic Guide to Every Common Species*. London: HarperCollins, 2008.

Stow, John and Edmund Howes. *The Annales, or Generall Chronicle of England*. London, 1615.

Strode, William. *The Floating Island*. London, 1600.

Swarbrick, Steven. "Shakespeare's Blush, or 'the Animal' in *Othello*." *Exemplaria* 28, no. 1 (2016): 70–85.

Swart, Sandra. "Dark Horses: The Horse in Africa in the Sixteenth and Seventeenth Centuries." In *The Horse as Cultural Icon*, edited by Peter Edwards, Karl A.E. Enenkel and Elspeth Graham, 241–60. Leiden: Brill, 2012.

———. "Settler Stock: Animals and Power in Mid-Seventeenth-Century Contact at the Cape, circa 1652–62." In *Animals and Early Modern Identity*, edited by Pia F. Cuneo, 243–70. Farnham: Ashgate, 2014.

Tarlton, Richard. *Tarltons Jests*. London, 1638.

Taverner, John. *Certaine Experiments Concerning Fish and Fruite: Practiced by John Teverner Gentleman, and by Him Published for the Benefit of Others*. London, 1600.

Tawney, R.H. and Eileen Power, eds. *Tudor Economic Documents*. London: Longmans, 1953.

Taylor, John. *Bull, Beare, and Horse*. London, 1638.

Thacker, Eugene. "Networks, Swarms, Multitudes: Part One." *Ctheory.net*, 2004, https://journals.uvic.ca/index.php/ctheory/article/view/14542.

Thatcher, David. "Mercy and 'Natural Guiltiness' in *Measure for Measure*." *Texas Studies in Literature and Language* 37, no. 3 (Fall 1995): 264–84.

The Aberdeen Bestiary, Special Collections, University of Aberdeen, 64r, accessed October 10, 2017. www.abdn.ac.uk/bestiary/

The Birds Harmony. London, 1680.

The Complete Fables of Jean de la Fontaine, Book VII. Translated by Norman Shapiro. Urbana: University of Illinois Press, 2007.

The History of the Two Valiant Brethern Valentine and Orson. Translated by Henry Watson. London, 1555.

The London and Westminster Guide, Through the Cities and Suburbs. To Which Is Added an Alphabetical List of All the Streets, Etc. London: W. Nicoll, 1768.

The Moral Philosophy of Doni. Translated by Thomas North. London, 1570.

The Towneley Plays. Edited by Martin Stevens and A.C. Cawley, vol. 1 E.E.T.S. s. s. 13. Oxford: Oxford University Press, 1994.

The Triumphs of Love and Antiquity. London, 1619.

Bibliography

The Yale Edition of the Complete Works of St. Thomas More. Edited by S.J. Edward Surtz and J.H. Hexter. New Haven, CT and London: Yale University Press, 1965.

Theis, Jeffrey. "The 'ill kill'd' Deer: Poaching and Social Order in *The Merry Wives of Windsor.*" *Texas Studies in Literature and Language* 43 (2001): 46–73.

Thirsk, Joan, ed. *The Agrarian History of England and Wales*; General editor H.P.R. Finberg, vol. 4. London: Cambridge University Press, 1967.

Thomas, Keith. *Man and the Natural World: Changing Attitudes in England 1500–1800.* London: Allen Lane, 1983.

———. *Man and the Natural World: Changing Attitudes in England 1500–1800.* New York: Oxford University Press, 1983.

———. *Man and the Natural World: Changing Attitudes in England, 1500–1800.* New York: Oxford University Press, 1996.

Thompson, E.P. *Whigs and Hunters: The Origin of the Black Act.* London: Allen Lane, 1975.

Thorndike, A.H. "The Relation of *As You like It* to Robin Hood Plays." *The Journal of Germanic Philology* 4 (1902): 56–69.

Tigner Amy L. *Literature and the Renaissance Garden from Elizabeth I to Charles II England's Paradise.* London: Routledge, 2012.

Tilley, Morris Palmer. *Dictionary of the Proverbs in England in the Sixteenth and Seventeenth Centuries: A Collection of the Proverbs Found in English Literature and the Dictionaries of the Period.* Ann Arbor: University of Michigan Press, 1950.

Tindol, Robert. "The Best Friend of the Murderers: Guard Dogs and the Nazi Holocaust." In *Animals and War*, edited by Ryan Hediger, 105–21. Leiden: Brill, 2012.

Topsell, Edward. *The Reward of Religion Delivered in Sundrie Lectures Upon the Booke of Ruth.* London, 1596.

———. *Times Lamentation: Or an Exposition on the Prophet Joel.* London, 1599.

———. *The Historie of Foure-Footed Beastes.* London, 1607.

———. *Historie of Serpents.* London,1608.

———. *History of Four Footed Beasts and Serpents and Insects.* London, 1658.

Traub, Valerie. "Making Sexual Knowledge." *Early Modern Women* 5 (Fall 2010): 251–59.

———. *Thinking Sex with the Early Moderns.* Philadelphia: University Pennsylvania Press, 2015.

Traversi, Derek A. *An Approach to Shakespeare*, 3rd ed. New York: Doubleday, 1969.

Trotter, William. *Instincts of the Herd in Peace and War.* London: T. Fisher Unwin, 1916.

Turner, Henry. "Nashe's Red Herring: Epistemologies of the Commodity in Lenten Stuffe (1599)." *ELH* 68, no. 3 (2001): 529–61.

Turner, William. *Avium Praecipuarum, Quarum apud Plinium et Aristotelem Mentio Est, Brevis et Succincta Historia.* Cologne, 1544.

Uhlig, Claus. "'The Sobbing Deer': *As You Like It* IIi21–66 and the Historical Context." *Renaissance Drama* 3 (1970): 79–109.

van Orden, Kate. "From Gens d'Armes to Gentilhommes: Dressage, Civility, and the Ballet à Cheval." In *The Culture of the Horse. Status, Discipline, and Identity in the Early Modern World*, edited by Karen Raber and Treva J. Tucker, 175–223. New York and Houndsmill, Hampshire: Palgrave Macmillan, 2005.

Vartanian, Oshin et al. "Impact of Contour on Aesthetic Judgments and Approach-Avoidance Decisions in Architecture." *Proceedings of the National Academy of Sciences* 110, Suppl. 2 (June 18, 2013): 10446–453.

Vaughan, Adam. "Polar Bears Sail Down Thames." *Guardian. Environmental Blog*, January 26, 2009. https://www.theguardian.com/environment/blog/2009/jan/26/conservation-poles.

Vaughan, Alden and Virginia Vaughan. *Shakespeare's Caliban: A Cultural History.* Cambridge: Cambridge University Press, 1991.

Veale, Elspeth. *The English Fur Trade in the Later Middle Ages.* Oxford: Oxford University Press, 1966.

Varnado, Christine. "Queer Nature, or the Weather in *Macbeth.*" In *Queer Shakespeare: Desire and Sexuality*, edited by Goran Stanivukovic, 177–95. New York: Bloomsbury, 2017.

Verney, Lady Frances Parthenope and Lady Margaret Maria Williams-Hay Verney. *Memoirs of the Verney Family during the Seventeenth Century.* New York: Longmans, Green, and Co., 1904.

Vitkus, Daniel. *Turning Turk: English Theater and the Multicultural Mediterranean, 1570–1630.* New York: Palgrave, 2003.

Wade, Nicholas. "Why Humans and Their Fur Parted Ways." *New York Times*, August 19, 2003. Web., https://www.nytimes.com/2003/08/19/science/why-humans-and-their-fur-parted-ways.html.

Bibliography

Waldau, Paul. *Animal Studies: An Introduction*. Oxford: Oxford University Press, 2013.

Wales, Gerald of. *The History and Topography of Ireland*. Translated by John Joseph O'Meara, Revised. London: Penguin, 1982.

Walker, Elaine. "The Author of Their Skill: Human and Equine Understanding in the Duke of Newcastle's 'New Method.'" In *The Horse as Cultural Icon. The Real and the Symbolic Horse in the Early Modern World*, edited by P. Edwards, Karl A.E. Enkenel, and Elspeth Graham, 327–50. Leiden and Boston, MA: Brill, 2012.

Walker, Suzanne. "Making and Breaking the Stag: The Construction of the Animal in the Early Modern Hunting Treatise." In *Early Modern Zoology: The Construction of Animals in Science, Literature, and the Visual Arts*, edited by Karl A.E. Enenkel and Paul J. Smith, 317–37. Leiden and Boston, MA: Brill, 2007.

Wall, Tyler. "'For the Very Existence of Civilization': Police Dogs and Racial Terror." *American Quarterly* 68, no. 4 (2016): 861–82.

Watson, Robert N. "Horsemanship in Shakespeare's Second Tetralogy." *English Literary Renaissance* 13 (1983): 274–300.

———. *Shakespeare and the Hazards of Ambition*. Cambridge, MA: Harvard University Press, 1984.

———. "False Immortality in *Measure for Measure*: Comic Means, Tragic Ends." *Shakespeare Quarterly* 41, no. 4 (Winter 1990): 411–32.

———. *The Green and the Real in the Late Renaissance*. Philadelphia: University Pennsylvania Press, 2006.

Weheliye, Alexander G. *Habeas Viscus: Racializing Assemblage, Biopolitics, and Black Feminist Theories of the Human*. Durham, NC: Duke University Press, 2014.

Weil, Kari. "Purebreds and Amazons: Saying Things with Horses in Nineteenth Century France." *Differences: A Journal of Feminist Cultural Studies* 11, no. 1 (Spring 1999): 1–37.

Weimann, Robert. *Author's Pen and Actor's Voice: Playing and Writing in Shakespeare's Theatre*. Cambridge: Cambridge University Press, 2000.

Wells, Stanley. "The Failure of The Two Gentlemen of Verona." *Shakespeare Jahrbuch* 99 (1963): 161–73.

Wells, Stanley and Gary Taylor with John Jowett and William Montgomery. *William Shakespeare: A Textual Companion*. New York: Norton, 1997.

Werth, Tiffany Jo. "Introduction." In *Shakespearean International Yearbook 15: Shakespeare and the Human*, edited by Tiffany Werth, 1–21. Farnham: Ashgate Publishing, 2015.

White, William. *A New Booke Of good Husbandry, very pleasaunt, and of great profite both for Gentlemen and Yomen: Conteining, The Order and maner of making of Fish-pondes, with the breeding, preserving, and multiplying of the Carpe, Tench, Pike, and Troute, and diverse kindes of other Fresh-fish*. London, 1599.

Whittier, Gayle. "The Sonnet's Body and the Body Sonnetized in 'Romeo and Juliet,'" *Shakespeare Quarterly* 40, no. 1 (Spring 1989): 27–41.

Whyman, Susan. *Sociability and Power in Late-Stuart England: The Cultural World of the Verneys, 1660–1720*. Oxford: Oxford University Press, 1999.

Widmayer, Martha. "'To Sin in Loving Virtue': Angelo of *Measure for Measure*." *Texas Studies in Literature and Language* 49, no. 2 (Summer 2007): 155–80.

Williams, Heather ("Missouri"). "Sheep King Lear Formal Script." unpublished manuscript.

———. "How My Production of *King Lear with Sheep* Ended up Generating More Publicity than I Ever Imagined." *The Independent*, September 8, 2015, https://www.independent.co.uk/voices/how-my-production-of-king-lear-with-sheep-ended-up-generating-more-publicity-than-i-ever-imagined-10491410.html.

———.William, Painter, *The Palace of Pleasure*. Edited by Joseph Jacobs, vol. 1, 112–13. London: D. Nutt, 1890.

Williams, Raymond. *The Country and the City*. Oxford: Oxford University Press, 1975.

———. *Marxism and Literature*. New York: Oxford University Press, 1977.

Wilson, Elizabeth A. *Gut Feminism*. Durham, NC: Duke University Press, 2015.

Wilson, Richard. *Will Power: Essays on Shakespearean Authority*. Detroit: Wayne State University Press, 1993.

Wilson, Thomas. *A Discourse upon Usurye*. London, 1572.

Wolfe, Cary. *Animal Rites: American Culture, the Discourse of Species, and Posthuman Theory*. Chicago, IL: University of Chicago Press, 2003.

———. *What Is Posthumanism?* Minneapolis: University of Minnesota Press, 2010.

Bibliography

———. "Condors at the End of the World." In *After Extinction*, edited by Richard Grusin. Minneapolis: University of Minnesota Press, 2018: 107–22.

Wolfe, Jessica. "*Circus Minimus*: The Early Modern Theater of Insects." In *Performing Animals: History, Agency, Theater*, edited by Karen Raber and Monica Mattfield, 111–22. University Park: Pennsylvania State University Press, 2017.

Wolloch, Nathaniel. *Subjugated Animals: Animals and Anthropocentrism in Early Modern European Culture*. New York: Prometheus Books, 2006.

Wood, Andy. *The Memory of the People*. Cambridge: Cambridge University Press, 2013.

Wood, Jennifer Linhart. "Sounding Spaces: *The Tempest's* Uncanny Near-East Echoes." *Shakespeare Studies* 44 (2016): 173–79.

Woodbridge, Linda. *Women and the English Renaissance: Literature and the Nature of Womankind, 1540–1620*. Brighton: Harvester Press, 1984.

———. "Jestbooks, the Literature of Roguery and the Vagrant Poor." *English Literary Renaissance* 33, no. 2 (2003): 201–10.

———. "The Neglected Soldier as Vagrant, Revenger, Tyrant Slayer." In *Cast Out: Vagrancy and Homelessness in Global and Historical Perspective*, edited by A.L. Beier and Paul Ocobock, 64–87. Columbus: Ohio University Press, 2008.

Woodhouse, A.S.P., ed. *Puritanism and Liberty*. Chicago, IL: University of Chicago Press, 1951.

Woods, Abigail, Michael Bresalier, Angelo Cassidy, and Rachel Mason Dentiger, eds. *Animals and the Shaping of Modern Medicine: One Health and Its Histories*. Basingstoke: Palgrave Macmillan, 2018.

Woodward, D.M. "Cattle Droving in the Seventeenth Century: A Yorkshire Example." In *Trade and Transport: Essays in Economic History in Honour of T. S. Willan*, edited by William Henry Chaloner and Barrie M. Ratcliffe, 35–58. Manchester: Manchester University Press, 1977.

Wright, John. *The Naming of the Shrew: A Curious History of Latin Names*. London: Bloomsbury, 2014.

Wrightson, Keith. *English Society 1580–1680*. New Brunswick, NJ: Rutgers University Press, 1982.

Wrigley, E.A. "A Simple Model of London's Importance in Changing English Society and Economy." *Past and Present* 37 (1967): 44–70.

Yates, Julian. "Humanist Habitats; or, 'Eating Well' with Thomas More's *Utopia*." In *Environment and Embodiment in Early Modern England*, edited by Mary Floyd-Wilson and Garrett Sullivan, 187–209. Basingstoke: Palgrave Macmillan, 2007.

———. *Of Sheep, Oranges, and Yeast: A Multispecies Impression*. Minneapolis: University of Minnesota Press, 2017.

Yeomans, Lisa. "A Zooarchaeological and Historical Study of the Animal Product Based Industries Operating in London during the Post-Medieval Period." Ph.D. Thesis. University College London, 2006.

Yoder, Audrey. *Animal Analogy in Shakespeare's Character Portrayal*. New York: AMS, 1975.

INDEX

Accommodated Animal, The (Shannon) 4, 132
Adorno, Theodor 48, 54
Aesop, fables 150–9
Agamben, Giorgio 9, 63, 191, 198, 199, 200
Agas map 79–80
Ahmed, Sarah 283–4, 289
Alaimo, Stacy 179
Albert the Great 67, 69
Alchemist, The (Jonson) 70
Alleyn, Edward 190, 191, 195, 234; portrait
  of 192
All's Well that Ends Well 16, 274; bird imagery 17;
  and cuckoldry 163–4; fishpond as metaphor
  26–7, 28, 30; image of drone 123; use of term
  "creature" 133
Altick, Richard D. 293, 295
Anglin, Sallie 288
Animal Bodies, Renaissance Culture (Raber) 4
Animal Characters (Boehrer) 298
animals: on Agas map 78–80; animal-made
  objects 84–6; *vs.* beasts, creatures 62, 132–3;
  and body politic 151; bodies, and hunting
  242; butchering 83–4; categorizing, in
  early modern world 130–1; classification
  61; companion species and mistreatment
  of 259–60; Lavinia as 265; comparisons as
  slurs 96; contamination by 106–7; cuckoos
  and cuckoldry 164; and climate change
  191; diseases 104–13; and ecocriticism
  292; in English national economy 78–9;
  exterminated in England 193; fables 111–12,
  150–1; feeding, confined operations (CAFOs)
  112; flocks 118; as food 86; fur 190–201;
  and sumptuary laws 193–4; herds 120–3;
  and hierarchy 178, 180–1; human kinship
  with 301; and humoral theory 271; hunting
  of 242–53; language, possession of 150–9;
  in *King Lear with Sheep* 227; livestock 79;
  as metaphors 65–7, 217, 235–9; for women
  163–72; for human education 184–5; murrain
  110; and objects (cf "objects, animal-made")
  6, 9, 77, 87; as performers 136, 186–7, 190–1,
  220, 223–7; populations, groups 116–24; and
  race 97–9; and religion 107; sovereignty 63;
  species, concepts of 117–18; swarm 123–4;
  terminology for groups of 124, 130–2; trade
  in 78; and diseases 105; in Venice 107–8;
  training 177–87; veterinarians 113; and war
  90–100; and witchcraft 166; wolves, and
  speech acts 150
"Animals Ill with the Plague" (La Fontaine) 111–12
Annales, or General Chronicle of England (Stow and
  Howe) 233–4
Anthony and Cleopatra 1, 66, 172; angling
  imagery 276; cuckold's horns 121; cuckoo 164
Apes 81
Apiarium (Worlidge) 132–3
"Apology for Raymond Sebond" (Montaigne)
  153, 222–3
Arcadia, The (Sidney) 288, 289
Arcadian Virgin, The (Chettle and Haughton) 196
Arcimboldo, Giuseppe 23
Argent, Gala 288
Ariosto, Ludovico 123, 298
Aristotle 63, 139, 165, 232; ideas about
  conception 70
As You Like It 2, 61, 67, 242; and hunting
  246–8; and pastoral 118; distinction
  between beast and human 133; reference
  to herd 121
Aubrey, John 193

Bach, Rebecca Ann 5
Baldwin, William 153

Index

Baret, Michael 285, 286, 296
Barnacle goose 69
Barrel of Monkeys: A Compendium of Collective Nouns for Animals, A (Berwick) 124
Bartholomew the Englishman 67
Basilikon Doron (James I) 233
Bates, Catherine 242
Batman, Stephen 67, 68
Batt, Antonie 143
Beadle, Richard 187
bears: baiting 186; Bear Garden 18; cubs 67–8, 70; in England 193; fur 190, 191; humans performing as 195–6, 201; polar bear 190–1; used in theater 190–1
beast: categorical designation 61; characterological qualities 62; and sovereign 63
Beauvais, Vincent of 67
beavers 68, 70
Becon, Thomas 210
Beehive of the Romish Church, The (Van Saint Aldegonde) 143
bees 138–48; ability to keep time 138–48; drone 122; hives 122–3, 140–1; as metaphors 138–48; in religion 140–3; Shakespeare's characters as 145–6; signaling 139; in *The Tempest* 140, 143–8; as workers 139–48
Beier, A.L. 49
Benjamin, Walter 30, 66, 171
Bennett, Jane 179
Bernard, patron saint of bees *see* Clairvaux, St. Bernard of
Berners, Dame Julian 29
Berry, Edward 242, 243, 251
Berwick, Thomas 124
Bevington, David 303
Beware the Cat (Baldwin) 153
Bible 67, 109, 112
biopolitics 205–6, 216; and animal life 257
birds 13–20; in ballads 120; buzzards 14; chicken 18; cuckoos 163–4; eagles 14, 15; falcons 15; falcon training manuals 185; flocks 118–20; as food 13; fur 191–4; and hierarchy 13–14; kites 14–15, 18; and language 16–17; larks 15–16, 18; in literature 13–19, 93–4, 95; martlets 93; owls 15, 17–18; parrots 16–17; and songs 17; and trapping 19
Birds and Other Creatures in Renaissance Literature (Bach) 5
Birds of Shakespeare, The (Harting) 3
Black Act of 1723 251
Bloom, Harold 40
Blundeville, Thomas 181, 285, 286
Boas, George 6
Boehrer, Bruce 4, 39, 40–1, 106, 108, 235, 298
Boke Named the Governour, The (Elyot) 132, 244
Boke of Husbandry, (Fitzherbert) 104

Boke of Saint Albans (Berners) 29
Book Named the Governor, The (Elyot) 132
Borlik, Todd 130, 133, 134
Botelho, Keith 5
Botero, Giovanni 116
Brayton, Dan 271, 273
Britannia's Honor (Dekker) 199
Brooks, Cleanth 293
Brooks, Thomas 109
Brown, Carolyn 272, 275, 278
Brown, Eric 130, 135, 136
Brown, Laura 34
Bruckner, Lynne 293–4
Bruegel, Pieter the Elder 23
Brutal Reasoning (Fudge) 4
bug, as bugbear not insect 133
Bulkwarke of Defense against Sickness (Bullein) 68
Bull, Beare & Horse (Taylor) 81, 84
bull-baiting 81
Bullein, William 68
Bullokar, William 151
Bushnell, Rebecca 231, 238
Butler, Charles 139

Caius, John 34, 35, 49–51, 52–3, 233
Campana, Joseph 5, 130, 140; and Keith Botehlo 5; and Scott Maisano 41, 42
Campbell, Mary Baine 130
Cantimpré, Thomas of 67
capitalism 45–56
cats, voice of 153
cattle: diseases of 107–8; diseases and human plague 109; murrain 110–11
Cattle Plague, (Spinage) 107
Caveat or Warning for Common Cursitors (Harman) 45, 48–9
Cavell, Stanley 159
Cavendish, William 177–9, 181, 287
Caxton, William 151, 152
Chambers, E.K. 1/1
Chapman, George 36
Charles 1, Equestrian portrait of 297
Chaucer, Geoffrey 120, 165
Cheap and Good Husbandry (Markham) 184
Chen, Mel Y. 283
Chettle, Henry and William Haughton 196
chicken 18
Chinon of England 196
Civitas Londinium see Agas map
Clairvaux, Saint Bernard of 141–3, 144
Clark, Kenneth 286
Climate, Little Ice Age 293
Clody, Michael 7
Cockayne, Sir William, Lord Mayer of London 198–9
Cogan, Thomas 86
Coghill, Nevill 190

Index

Cohen, Jeffrey Jerome 179

Collection of English Words, A (Ray) 120, 129

Comedy of Errors, The 2, 133, 163, 165; reference to rabies 105

Commonplace Book (Fella) 214, 215–16

Communist Manifesto (Marx) 47

Conti, Natalie 40

Coriolanus 18, 66, 110, 111, 155–9; animal passions in 95; cur as insult 37; derogatory animal comparisons 121–2, 123; editorial disputes over "tongue" 150; and human identity 95–6; human voice as animal noise 155; and ideas of sovereignty 157–8; images for multitude 124; and justifications of war 94–5; and plebeians 95, 155–9; references to butterflies 134; and war as strife 94–6

Cox of Collumpton 196

critical animal theory 66

Cronon, William 4

Crosby, Alfred 4

cuckoldry 163–4

Cunningham, Andrew 117

Cymbeline 2, 65, 67, 246; and bird imagery 16

Davenant, William 70

De Anima (Aristotle) 232

De Baptismo (Tertullian) 21

De remediis utriusque fortunae (Petrarch) 90, 94

Deane, Richard, Lord Mayor of London 199

Death of Robert, Earl of Huntington, The (Munday) 248

Deepwater Horizon 294

Dekker, Thomas 199

Del Toro, Guillermo 270

DeLanda, Manuel 48

Deleuze, Gilles 95, 258; and Felix Guattari 66

demographics *see* populations

Dent, Anthony 6

Derrida, Jacques 9, 61–2, 99, 112, 164, 167, 169, 170, 171, 256–2

Descartes, Rene 299

Description of England (Harrison) 29

Desprét, Vinciane 70

Dickey, Colin 70

Dictionary (Elyot) 164

Dictionary (Johnson) 164

Diogenes the Cynic 155

Dionne, Craig 6

Discourse of the Common Weal of this Realm of England, A (Dickey) 210

disease: anthrax 110; miasma theory 105–7, 108–9; plague 105–7; rabies 105; zoonotic 104–13

dog: Argus, in *The Odyssey* (Homer) 36; barking as speech 154; Crab, character in *Two Gentlemen of Verona* (Shakespeare) 39, 51–3, 187; history of 34–5; and love plot in theater 39–40; images of 45; in bull-baiting 81; as insult 106; massacres of 106; mastiffs 49–50, 186; as pet 34, 35; Saint Guinefort 36; as source of disease 105–6; and sycophancy 34–6, 37

Dolan, Frances 275

Donne, John 277

Downfall of Robert, Earl of Huntington, The (Munday) 248

Drayton, Michael 68

Duckert, Lowell 191

Dugan, Holly 25–6, 223, 275–6

Duncan-Jones, Katherine 110

Durer, Albrecht 286

Eastward Ho (Marston) 70

ecocriticism, and animals 292

Economic and Philosophical Manuscripts (Marx) 47

Edelman, Lee 259, 260, 265

Education of a Christian Prince (Erasmus) 221, 222, 232

Egan, Gabriel 134

Elizabeth I, Queen of England 233; Coronation Portrait 194; as lioness 233

Elven, Lucy 220

Elyot, Sir Thomas 164–5, 244

Empiricus, Sextus 302

Empson, William 204, 206, 220

England, growth of industry 28; waterways 28

Ensler, Eve 273

Erasmus 99, 221, 232

Erickson, Peter 283

Estok, Simon 292

Every Man in His Humor (Jonson) 271

Faerie Queene, The (Spenser) 287, 289

fables 151–2

Fables of Aesop (Ogilby) 154

Fagan, Brian 28

falconry manuals 185

falcons, and training 182–4

feathers 13

Fella, Thomas 214, 215–16

Feminine Monarchie, The (Butler) 139

Field, John 186

First Boke of Cattell (Mascall) 104

fish 21–31, 270–9; as aphrodisiac 273; carp 27, 29; cod 24, 272–3; and decay 25; eel 23; fishponds 27–9; fishwife 25; as food 21–4; freshwater 23; habitat for 28; herring 22, 23; and human flesh 24–6; and human sexuality 270–9; mollusks 22, 24; pilchards 22; religious symbolism 21–2; and sexual innuendo 25; shellfish 273–4; and smell 25–6; stockfish 22, 24, 271; and theater 23–30; trade in 22–3; *vs.* warm-blooded animals 270–1

Fisher, F.J. 78

347

Index

fishing, technology 22
fishponds 27–9
Fitzherbert, John 104
Flaherty, Jennifer 181, 295–6, 298
Floating Island, The (Strode) 69–70
flocks, of sheep 118–19; of birds 119–20; as derogatory term 121
Fludd, Robert 112
Foakes, R.A. 275, 278
food: animals as 256–65; global production system 56; Lenten diet 270–2; and rites of eating 256–65; and sex drive 272
fool, tradition of 222
Forman, Simon 197
Forrest, The (Jonson) 30
Foucault, Michel 9, 41, 116–17, 179–80, 205, 209, 222, 226; and animal life 257; and biopower 116; and biopolitics 205–6, 216
Four Chiefest Offices Belonging to Horsemanship (Blundeville) 181
Fracastoro, Girolamo 104
Francis, Pope 142
Francisco, Timothy 296
Freud, Sigmund 34
Fudge, Erica 3, 4, 39, 77, 104, 108, 171, 191, 196, 232; animal-made objects 84–6
fur, and human identity 194–5
Further Discovery of Bees, A (Rusden) 123

Garber, Marjorie 37
Garrard, Greg 292
gender: and animals 163–72; and hunting 250–1; and misogyny 63–4; and race 171
General System of Horsemanship, A (Cavendish) 177
Gerard, John 69
Gessner, Conrad 68
Girard, René 243
Grady, Hugh 231
Grant, Teresa 190
Greene, Robert 191
Greg, W.W. 196
Grell, Ole Peter 117
Grisone, Federico 286
Grosz, Elizabeth 283
Guevara, Perry 136
Gumbrecht, Hans Ulrich 179
Gurr, Andrew 197
Guy-Bray, Stephen 39

Hall, Kim 98
Hamlet 16, 62, 132, 172, 195; image of pelican 70
Happy Beast, The (Boas) 6
Haraway, Donna 9, 47–8, 54–5, 198, 259, 260
Harington, Sir John 298
Harman, Graham 179
Harman, Thomas 45, 48–9

Harris, Jonathan Gil 110
Harrison, William 29, 165
Harting, James 3
Harvard Concordance to Shakespeare (Spevack) 37
Harvey, David 46
Harward, Michael 108–9
Haven of Health (Cogan) 84
Hawks, and training 182–4
Heaney, Peter 184
Hearne, Vicki 284
Henry IV Part 1 17, 65, 133, 271, 287, 289; dogs as sycophants 37; flea 135; and flocks 118; owls 18; role of horse in 186; swarm imagery 123; use of term "creature" 133
Henry IV Part 2 66, 133, 182, 271; bee imagery 123; and flocks 118–19
Henry V 100, 136, 181, 221; bee analogy 134; English as animal-centered 90–1; horses and eroticism in 282–4, 288, 289; imagery of war 90–1; lion analogies in 235, 237; reference to pasture 79; swarm image 123; use of terms "beast", "creature" 133, 134
Henry VI Part 1 289; soldiers as herd 121
Henry VI Part 2 180–1, 207, 211–12, 235–7, 211–12; and ideology of training 180–1; image of butcher taking calf 83, 84
Henry VI Part 3 132, 134; comparison of shepherd to king 118; comparison to bear cub 69; image of hives 122; lion analogies in 235–7; sheep imagery in 235; shepherds 222–3; suffering in war 221; troops as herd 121
Henryson, Robert 151
Henslowe, Philip 190, 191, 234
Herball (Gerard) 69
Herne the Hunter 248, 252
An Hipponomie, or the Vineyard of Horsemanship (Baret) 296
His Meditations, or Sighes, Sobbes, and Tears Upon Our Saviors Passion (W.P.) 141
Histoire entière des poisons (Rondelet) 277
Historie of Adam, or the Foure-fold State of Man (Topsell) 144
History and Topography of Ireland (Gerald of Wales) 68, 69
History of Four-Footed Beasts (Topsell) 34, 35, 67, 119, 139, 143, 153, 165, 168, 210, 231
History of the Peloponnesian War (Thucydides) 110
History of the Wonderful Things of Nature, A (Rowland) 129
hive, as description of human groups 122
Hobbes, Thomas 179
Höfele, Andreas 4
Holland, Peter 151
honey 140–2
Homo Sacer (Agamben) 63
Horn Dance 242, 245–6, 248, 250

Index

horses 66, 177–87, 282–9; allegory of nation
293; in art 286, 297; and barbarism 292–304;
bodies 282–9; bodily power 179–80; breeds
182; and ecocriticism 292–304; Equestrian
portrait of Charles 1, 297; falling off 288–90;
in *Henry V* 282–4, 288, 289; and human
sexuality 282–9; palfrey 285; as prey 284; and
relationships with humans 181–2; in *Richard II*
292–304; shape and human psychology 286;
training 177–87, 284
Horses in Shakespeare's England (Dent) 6
human exceptionalism 15, 140
human language, as animal noise 158
human nature, and dogs 37–40
human, the "invention of" 40
humans: class and power 179–80; collective
as rabble 158–9; humoral theory 166, 168;
as sheep 204–17; training, and hierarchies
179–80
Hunters and Poachers (Manning) 242
hunting 242–3; and animal bodies 242;
butchering of deer 243; and class 242–3; and
cuckoldry 250–1; Herne the Hunter 248, 252;
horn dance 242, 245–6, 248, 250; poaching
248–52; and social codes 242–53; as symbolic
event 242, 243–6; as tyranny 247
husbandry 108; husbandry manuals 29

insects: bees 138–48; depicting on stage
136; fly 133–4; as model for perfection of
creation 129–130; omission of from study
130; as reflection of difference from human
130; revulsion for 133; size 129–36; and
sovereignty 134; swarms 123–4; terminology
in Shakespeare 132
Instincts of the Herd in Peace and War (Trotter) 121

James I, King of England 233–4
Jardine, Lisa 167
Jenner, Mark 106
Jewell of Joy, The (Becon) 210
Johnson, Robert 146
Johnson, Samuel 165
Jones, Reese 55
Jonson, Ben 29, 30, 70, 191, 200, 271
Julius Caesar 14–15, 17, 133; dogs as flatterers
37; eagles *vs.* carrion birds 14–15; herd as
derogatory term 121; lion analogies in 237–9
Just Italian, The (Davenant) 70

Kafka, Franz 66
Kahn, Victoria 42
Karras, Ruth Mazo 28
King John 65, 67, 133, 172; and animal skins 195
King Lear 37, 61, 65, 99, 134, 219–27, 134; bird
imagery 14, 15–16; cuckoo 164; madness in
dogs 105–6; pelican 70

King Lear with Sheep (Williams) 220–7;
reviews of 224
Kiser, Laura 210
Klein, Melanie 258

La Fontaine, Jean de 111–12
language: animal 150–9, 227; bird song as 16–17;
in fables 151; human, as animal noise 158;
human control over 169–70
Latour, Bruno 13, 56, 179
Lent, and dietary restrictions 270–2
Lenten Stuffe (Nashe) 24
Lesser Living Creatures (Campana and Botelho) 5
Life of Marcus Brutus (Plutarch) 238
lion 231–9; and baiting 234; Christian
iconography 234; *vs.* fox, Machiavelli 231–2;
and heraldry 233; In *Julius Caesar* 237–9; as
omens 238; as symbols of political power
235–7; and tyranny 237–9
Lippitz, Akira Mizuzata 66
London: animal rendering 77, 78; as assemblage
77, 87; Bear Garden 186; dog massacre
106; food trade 78; liberties 28; mapping
77; population growth 124; shambles 81;
Smithfield 81; Southwark 27; street names
after animals 81–4; stews 28; urbanization 77
London and Westminster Guide 83
Love's Labor's Lost, cuckoo and cuckoldry
163; Moth (character) 134; use of "animal"
in 62, 67
Lupton, Julia Reinhard 37
Lyly, John 70

Macbeth 65, 66, 86; birds and familial ties 19;
birds and language 17; bird imagery 15;
"natural" order 93–4; owl 18; regicide's effect
on nature 178; swarm imagery 123; war and
the non-human 92–4; witches 93–4, 166
Machiavelli, Niccolò 231, 232
MacInnes, Ian 37
Madden, John, *Shakespeare in Love* 53
Madness and Civilization (Foucault) 222, 226
Malleus Maleficarum 166
Malthus, Thomas 116
Man and the Natural World (Thomas) 4, 6
Manning, Roger 242–3
Marcus, Leah 251
Markham, Gervase 29, 184, 285, 286
Marlowe, Christopher 92, 296
Marston, John 69, 70
Marx, Karl 9, 46–7, 147; and capitalism 46–7;
and Primitive Accumulation 46, 48, 49, 53;
Species Being 46–7
Mascall, Leonard 104, 110–11
Masten, Jeffrey 39
Master of Game, The (Norwich) 244
Mastiffs, baiting lions 234

349

Index

materialism, theory 77, 190

Measure for Measure 61, 133, 270–9; Angelo's cold nature 270–2; fish and sexuality 270–9

meat-eating 54–5, 89, 256–65; and agriculture 56; as cannibalism 257; and capitalism 54–6

Melville, Herman 273

Mentz, Steve 145, 288

Merchant of Venice, The 122; dogs as source of disease 106; and global trade 107; monkey in 136; sheep in 207, 212–13; shrew 163; Shylock as dog 37, 107

Meres, Francis 234

Merry Wives of Windsor, The 242, 246; and hunting; and lice 135; and poaching 248–53

Metamorphoses (Ovid) 183, 196

Méthode nouvelle et invention extraordinaire de dresser les chevaux, La (Cavendish) 177

Meyrick, John 191

Midas (Lyly) 70

Middleton, Thomas 166, 186, 198, 199

Midsummer Night's Dream, A 172; actors as shadows 263; and ecological disaster 118; fairies as insects 134–5; Helena as spaniel 38; lion in 5, 234–5; use of term "beast" 133

Milton, John 139

Mirror of Nature, The (Vincent of Beauvais) 67

Moffett, Thomas 129–30

Montaigne, Michel de 153, 222, 232, 289

Montrose, Louis 185

Moore, Jason 46

More, Thomas 210, 220

Morocco, performing horse 301–2

Morris, W.B. 192

Morton, Timothy 93

Mucedorus 191, 197

Much Ado About Nothing 16, 19, 187, 276; bird imagery 16; birds and courtship 19

Mullaney, Steven 28, 182

Munday, Anthony 248

Muscovy Company 191, 199

Nashe, Thomas 24

National Geographic 1

natural histories 67–70, 277

Natural History (Pliny) 278

Natural History of Stafford-Shire (Plot) 245

nature, and appetite 258

nature-cultures 13, 16, 178–9; *see also* Latour, Bruno

Neri, Janice 130

Nietzsche, Friedrich 138

North, Thomas 151

Norwich, Edward of 244

Oberon (Jonson) 191

Objects, animal-made 84–6

O'Dair, Sharon 294

Of English Dogs (Caius) 49–51, 52–3, 233

Ogilby, John 154

Okin, Gregory 56

On Animals, (Albert the Great) 67

On Care for Our Common Home (Pope Francis) 142

On the Causes of the Greatness and Magnificence of Cities (Machiavelli) 116

On the Nature of Things (Thomas of Cantimpré) 67

On the Properties of Things (Bartholomew the Englishman) 67

Open, The (Agamben) 198–9

Order of Things, The (Foucault) 179–80

Orlando Furioso (Ariosto) 298

Ornithology of Francis Willoughby (Ray) 120

Othello: and dog as insult 37; and human/animal distinction 97–8; Iago as figure of strife 98; and psychological conflict 96–9; and race 98–9; and reason 96; use of term "creature" 133; as war play 96

Outlines of Scepticism (Empiricus) 302

Overton, Mark 78, 79

Ovid 183, 196

Oxford Dictionary of Ancient Idioms 35

Padua, Saint Anthony of 141

Pafford, J.H.P. 190

Painter, William 62, 64

Painting, Dutch and Flemish 23; of horses 286; Equestrian Portrait of Charles I 297

Palace of Pleasure (Painter) 62, 64

Palladis Tamia (Meres) 234

Pandosto (Greene) 191

Panke, John 143

Paradise Lost (Milton) 139

Parliament of Bees (Butler) 139

Parliament of Fowls (Chaucer) 120

Partridge, Eric 274

Paster, Gail Kern 98, 271

Pastoral form 221–2

Patterson, Annabel 152

pelican 70

Perceiving Animals (Fudge) 4

Performing Animals (Raber and Mattfeld) 220

Pericles, fly 135

Petrarch 90, 92, 93

pets, pet passports 54

Phaedrus (Plato) 169

phenomenology 283

Photo Ark (Sartore) 1, 2

Plato 167, 169, 170, 171

Pleasant History of Cawwood the Rook, The 120

Pliny the Elder 165, 168, 278

Plot, Robert 245

Plutarch 238

Pluvinel, Antoine 289

Poetaster, The (Jonson) 70

Pollan, Michael 54, 138

Index

Poole, Jonas 190, 193
Pope, Alexander 37
Pope, Francis 142
populations, counting and representing 116–24; and politics 117–24
Posthuman Lear (Dionne) 6
posthumanism 41; medical posthumanities 104–5, 113
Prince, The (Machiavelli) 231
Principle Birds mentioned by Pliny and Aristotle (Turner) 69
Progress of the Soule, The (Donne) 277

Quick Cattle and Dying Wishes: People and Their Animals in Early Modern England (Fudge) 104
Quiller-Couch, Arthur 190, 275, 278

Raber, Karen 4, 41, 108, 139, 178, 220, 295–7, 299; and Monica Mattfeld 220
race: and animals 97–9; and gender 171; and *Othello* 98–9; and racial identity 263–5; and *Titus Andronicus* 263–5
Ralegh, Walter 92
Ramachandran, Ayesha 140
Ravelhofer, Barbara 190, 200
Rawlins, Thomas 69
Ray, John 120, 129
Reason of State, The (Machiavelli) 116
Rebellion, The (Rawlins) 69
Renaissance Beasts (Fudge) 4
Renaissance Posthumanism (Campana and Maisano) 41
Repentance of Peter and Judas, The (Richardson) 139
Richard II 132; allegory of state 293; ecocritical readings of 293–4; horses in 292–304; lion analogies, in 235, 236–7; pelican 70; role of horse Barbary 181–2, 298–302
Richard III 18, 61; birds and telling time 18; carrion birds 14; flock image 119
Richardson, Charles 139
Roberts, Callum 30
Roberts, Jeanne Addison 183
Romeo and Juliet 18, 168, 271; lark *vs.* nightingale 18
Rondelet, Guillaume 277
Rose Theater 26
Rowland, John 129
Rowley, Thomas, Thomas Dekker and John Ford, authors 153, 166
Royal Menagerie 233
Rules of Riding (Grisone) 287
Rusden, Moses 123
Ryan, Kiernan 38

Saksena, Alasdair 226
Sanchez, Melissa E. 38, 140

Sartore, Joel 1, 2
Schiesari, Juliana 299
Second Shepherd's Play 204, 206–10
Security, Territory, Population (Foucault) 205
Seeley, Thomas, D. 138
Shakespeare Among the Animals (Boehrer) 4
Shakespeare, William (*see individual plays by title*): acting companies 194; father's trade 110, 194; *Rape of Lucrece*, hive imagery 122; Sonnet XII 121
Shakespeare's Bawdy (Partridge) 274
Shakespeare's Imagery and What It Tells Us (Spurgeon) 6
Shannon, Laurie 4, 41, 62, 108, 132, 134, 192
Shape of Water, The (del Toro) 270
Shea, Christopher 223
sheep 51, 204–17; as actors in *King Lear With Sheep* 219–27; as "animetaphor" 217; and capitalism 205–17; counting 208–9; economics of, in England 210; flocks 118; labor 205; mutual constitution with humans 204–17; as parchment 206, 211–12; and pastoral form 204–17, 221–2; as performers 220, 223–7; in proverbs 119–20; rebellious 226; and sacrament 208–10; and shepherding 205–17; as "silly" 219–20; violence of 118; wool, value of 215; Shell, Marc 213
shepherds 205–17; as analogy for sovereign 119
shrew 163–72
Shukin, Nicole 66, 206
Sidney, Philip 288
skepticism 302–4
Skinners' livery company 198–201
Some Versions of Pastoral (Empson) 204
Sovereignty, and early modern kings 232
Speed, John 104
Spenser, Edmund 287
Spevack, Marvin 37
Spinage, C.A. 107
Spivak, Gayatri 54
Spurgeon, Caroline 6
Stage, Stake and Scaffold (Höfele) 4
Steel, Karl 95
Stern, Tiffany 186
Stoicism 90
Strode, William 69–70
Swarm, logic and imagery of 123–4; of insects 129–31

Tamburlaine (Marlowe) 296
Taming of a Shrew, The (Anonymous) 168
Taming of the Shrew, The 18, 19, 108, 133, 163–72, 289; demonic elements in 166–7; gendering of shrewish behavior 167; knowledge of birds 19; training of hawks in 182–4
Tarlton, Richard 187, 301–2

Index

Taverner, John 29
Taylor, John 81, 85
Tempest, The 61, 69, 139, 143; Ariel as bee 145–6; bees in 145–6; bees and time in 146; birds and language 16; herd of lions 121; human labor in 146; and leisure time 147; and miasma theory 106; pleasure *vs.* punishment in 147
Tertullian 21
Thacker, Eugene 118
Thames River 22–3
Thatcher, David 276
Theater of Insects, The (Moffett) 129–30
Theater, London 185
Theses on the Philosophy of History (Benjamin) 300
Thirsk, Joan 4, 78
Thomas, Keith 4, 6, 34, 232
Thucydides 110
Times Lamentation (Topsell) 143
Timon of Athens 37, 38, 133; animal metaphors in 64–7; limitrophy in 61; misogyny in 63; the term "beast" in 61–5
Titus Andronicus 67, 200; Aaron as dog 37; death and funeral rites 257–65; economy of excess 261–2; fly in 135–6; and "the human" 258; human sacrifice 257–8; and race 263–5; social and religious dimensions of eating 260–1; use of "beast" 133
To Penshurst (Jonson) 30
Topsell, Edward 34, 35, 67, 119, 139, 143, 153, 165, 168, 210, 231; religious writings 143–5
training, horses 284
trapping, birds 19
Traub, Valerie 274
Traversi, Derek 272
Trevais, John 67
Triumphs of Love and Antiquity, The (Middleton) 198, 199
Troilus and Cressida 67, 100, 108, 100, 172, 194; birds and courtship 19
Trotter, William 121
Turner, William 69
Twelfth Night, fish imagery 24–6
Two Gentlemen of Verona, The 187; Crab the dog as character 5, 34, 38–41, 51–3; human nature and morality 39; love and faithfulness, compared to dog's 38–40; sheep and shepherds 51; shepherds and sheep 221, 222; and substitution of human for dog 51

Utopia (More) 220

Valentine and Orson 196, 198
Van Dyk, Anthony 297
Van Marnix, Philip van Saint Aldegonde 143
Varnado, Christine 92
Vartanian, Oshin 286
Verney, Edmund 81
Vindiciae Contra Tyrannos 235
Virgil 140
Visscher, Claes 81–3

Waldau, Paul 2, 141
Wales, Gerald of 68, 69
Walker, Suzanne 243
Walton, Izaak 23, 277–8
war 90–100; and animal violence 95–6; and queer nature 92; military manuals 97; and strife 90–100
Watson, Robert N. 143, 295–7, 298
Weheliye, Alexander G. 264
Weimann, Robert 53
Werth, Tiffany Jo 145, 146
What Would Animals Say If We Asked the Right Questions (Déspret) 70
What You Will (Marston) 70
When *Species Meet* (Haraway) 46–8, 54–5, 259
Whittier, Gayle 271
Williams, Missouri, *King Lear with Sheep* 220–7
Wilson, Richard 246, 247
Windsor forest, and hunting 249
Winter's Tale, The 30–1, 133, 186, 197–8, 207, 213–16, 273, 276; bear in 5, 190, 193; enclosure and policing of women 214; and sheep 214–15
Wisdom of God Manifested in the Works of the Creation (Ray) 129
Witch, The (Middleton) 166
Witch of Edmonton (Rowley, Dekker and Ford) 153, 166
Wolfe, Cary 41
Wolfe, Jessica 130
Wolves, and language 151; in *Coriolanus* 150–9
Wolloch, Nathaniel 108
Wood, Jennifer Linhart 146
Woodbridge, Linda 49, 184
wool 215
Woolfson, Jonathan 130
Worlidge, John, *Apiarium* 132–3

Yates, Julian 7, 220
Yeomans, Lisa 78
Yoder, Audrey 236